Civil War in China

Civil War in China

The Political Struggle 1945–1949

Suzanne Pepper

ROWMAN & LITTLEFIELD PUBLISHERS, INC.
Lanham • Boulder • New York • Toronto • Oxford

To V. G.

ROWMAN & LITTLEFIELD PUBLISHERS, INC.

Published in the United States of America
by Rowman & Littlefield Publishers, Inc.
A wholly owned subsidary of The Rowman & Littlefield Publishing Group, Inc.
4501 Forbes Boulevard, Suite 200, Lanham, Maryland 20706
www.rowmanlittlefield.com

PO Box 317
Oxford
OX2 9RU, UK

British Library Cataloguing in Publication Information Available

Library of Congress Cataloging-in-Publication Data

Pepper, Suzanne.
    Civil war in China : the political struggle, 1945–1949 / Suzanne
Pepper.
      p. cm.
    Includes bibliographical references and index.
    ISBN 0-8476-9133-0 (cloth : alk. paper). — ISBN 0-8476-9134-9
(paper : alk. paper)
     1. China—History—Civil War, 1945–1949. I. Title.
DS777.54.P44   1999
951.04′2—DC21   99-10885
                                      CIP

Printed in the United States of America

∞ ™ The paper used in this publication meets the minimum requirements of American
National Standard for Information Sciences—Permanence of Paper for Printed Library
Materials, ANSI Z39.48–1992.

Contents

Acknowledgments

For their diverse contributions to this book, I owe a special debt of gratitude to three people. Professor Chalmers Johnson provided the unfailing support necessary to sustain a project such as this through many years of debate and controversy. John S. Service has been an invaluable source of information and encouragement. For a novice China scholar first drawn to the field by the issues surrounding America's role in Asia, it was a lucky twist of fate that made him initially a fellow-student at Berkeley and later the editor of this book. It might never have materialized, however, but for the interest taken in it by the late Anderson Ch'eng-chih Shih. His guidance was indispensable during the earliest and most difficult stage of this study and I regret that the completed manuscript could not benefit from his criticism.

For their critical commentaries on individual chapters, I would like to thank Jerome Ch'en, C.Y. Soong, Mah Feng-hwa, Sylvia Chan, Gordon Bennett, Marc Blecher, and Bob Marks. They are not to blame if I sometimes put their ideas to work in ways rather different than they intended. This book also owes a greater intellectual debt to Professor Warren Ilchman's seminars on development administration than might be apparent at first glance.

Without the help of far more people than I can name here, the tasks of collecting and translating information would have been impossible. At the Center for Chinese Studies, Berkeley, C.P. Chen and Chi Wen-shun bore the brunt of my seemingly endless pleas for assistance. At the Universities Service Centre in Hong Kong, Lau Yee-fui, Ho Wan-yee, and the staff helped in many ways as did Gerald Berkley, Leslie Chan, John Dolfin, Loren Fessler, Guy Searls, Janet Swislow, and Larry Weiss. The librarians and staff of the Hoover Institution at Stanford University, the Microfilm and Newspaper Reading Rooms at the Library of Congress, the East Asian section of Columbia University Library, and at the University of Hong Kong the Fung Ping Shan Library and the Centre of Asian Studies, all assisted my research work. So too did the many friends and acquaintances who have shared their recollections with me.

The University of California and its Center for Chinese Studies underwrote this project with many years of financial support. For their assistance, I would also like to thank members of the University of California Press. *The China Quarterly* (No. 48) and the University of Washington Press (Chalmers Johnson, ed., *Ideology and Politics in Contemporary China*) have published abbreviated versions of Chapters Three, Five, and Six, and I am grateful for permission to republish this material here.

The map is from William W. Whitson, *The Chinese High Command: A History of Communist Military Politics, 1927-71* (New York: Praeger, 1973), pages 80-81, and is used with the kind permission of the publishers.

Equivalents and Abbreviations

LOCAL ADMINISTRATIVE UNITS IN KMT CHINA, 1945-49

hsien—county
ch'eng-shih—municipality
ch'ü—district
chen—town

hsiang—administrative village
ts'un—village
pao—6 to 15 *chia*
chia—6 to 15 families

WEIGHTS AND MEASURES

liang or tael—ounce, 1/16 of a catty
chin or catty—1-1/3 pounds
sheng or pint—1/10 of a *tou*,
    approx. 1 catty weight
tou or peck—approx. 10 catties
    weight

tan or picul—100 catties weight,
    approx. 133 pounds
mou—1/6 acre
li—1/3 mile

ABBREVIATIONS: GENERAL

CCP—Chinese Communist Party
CLA—Chinese Labor Association
DL—Democratic League
KMT—Kuomintang or Nationalist
    Party

PCC— Political Consultative
    Conference
PLA—People's Liberation Army

ABBREVIATIONS: SOURCES

CFJP—*Chieh-fang jih-pao*
CPR—*Chinese Press Review*, U.S.
    Consular press translation service
CYJP—*Chung-yang jih-pao*
FYI—*For Your Information*, U.S.I.S.
    Yenan radio monitoring service

KC—*Kuan-ch'a*
STPP—*Shih-tai p'i-p'ing*
TKP—*Ta kung pao*
WHP—*Wen hui pao*

Newspapers: Political Affiliations

Political orientations and associations of newspapers
and news agencies cited frequently

Chieh-fang jih-pao—CCP, Yenan, Peiping, Shanghai
Chien-feng jih-pao—KMT
Chin-ch'a-chi jih-pao—CCP, Shansi-Chahar-Hopei Border Region
Chiu kuo jih-pao—anti-Communist
Chung-hua shih-pao—Young China Party
Chung-yang jih-pao—KMT Government
Chungyang News Agency—KMT Government news agency
Ha-erh-pin jih-pao—CCP, Manchuria
Hsin hua jih-pao—CCP, Chungking
Hsinhua News Agency—official CCP news agency
Hsin min pao—liberal
Hsin min wan-pao—liberal
Hsin pao—Youth Army (KMT)
Hsin-wen pao—right-wing CC Clique of the KMT
Ho-p'ing jih-pao—Ministry of Defense (KMT Government)
Lien-ho jih-pao—liberal
Lih pao—KMT Government-sponsored Shanghai General Labor Union
Min-chu pao—Democratic League
Shang-wu jih-pao—Chamber of Commerce
Shih-tai jih-pao—Embassy of the U.S.S.R. in China
Shun pao—KMT-supervised
Ta kang pao—right-wing CC Clique of the KMT
Ta kung pao—liberal, Political Study Clique of the KMT (see Bibliographic
    Notes)
Tung-nan jih-pao—Southeast branch organization of the KMT
Tung-pei chien-feng jih-pao—KMT, Manchuria
Tung-pei jih-pao—CCP, Manchuria
Wen hui pao—leftist
Yi shih pao—the Catholic Church

A Note on Romanization

Romanization of Chinese uses the Wade-Giles system (see C. H. Fenn, *The Five Thousand Dictionary*) except in the following respects:

(1) Place and personal names follow custom and contemporary usage.

(2) The umlaut *(ü)* is used only when necessary to avoid confusion: as in *chu* and *chü, nu* and *nü.* Where no confusion exists, it is omitted: hence *yuan, hsueh,* et cetera.

(3) The non-Communist newspapers cited are taken from the U.S. Consular press translation services, which did not adhere consistently to Wade-Giles. Since these translation services are the most accessible reference source, the *Chinese Press Review* romanization of these newspaper titles has been retained.

(4) New sections in the second edition (that is, the preface, bibliographic essay, and bibliographic update of Chinese-language sources) used the now-standard *pinyin* system. Such eclecticism was deemed necessary after considering the alternatives. Converting to *pinyin* throughout was neither technically nor economically feasible for the second edition which reprints the original text in its entirety. Yet transliterating the new titles into Wade-Giles seemed inappropriate, since most originated in the People's Republic while Wade-Giles remains standard usage only in Taiwan (as well as in many change-resistant library catalogs elsewhere). However unsatisfactory, so great a compromise with the publisher's golden rule of consistency may be seen as symbolic of the real life consequences that continue to follow from the divisions and wars of long ago.

Chronology

The following are the major political and military events
which marked in formal terms the progression of the
Chinese Civil War from 1945 to 1949:

1945

February

Breakdown of negotiations between the KMT Government in Chungking
and the CCP, under way since 1944, concerning a political settlement
between them and the possible formation of a coalition government.

April

Mao Tse-tung outlined the CCP's strength at its Seventh National Congress: 1,210,000 Party members; a regular army of 910,000; a militia of
2,200,000; and base areas with a population of 95.5 million.

August

9   U.S.S.R. entered the war against Japan; Soviet forces began entry into
Manchuria.

10   Japanese indicated willingness to surrender.

11   General Chu Teh, in Yenan, ordered Communist troops to advance on all
fronts to take the Japanese surrender. Generalissimo Chiang Kai-shek, in
Chungking, ordered Communist forces to remain in position and not to
accept the Japanese surrender.

14   Japan surrendered. Treaty of Friendship and Alliance concluded between
the KMT Government and the U.S.S.R.

15   General Order No. 1 from General Douglas MacArthur, Allied Headquarters, ordered the Japanese in China to surrender to Chiang Kai-shek's
forces.

16   Chu Teh and Mao Tse-tung cabled rejection of Chiang's August 11 order.

20-   CCP forces took the city of Kalgan from the Japanese.
28

23   Commander-in-Chief Ho Ying-ch'in, Chinese Army, ordered the Japanese
to hold positions until relieved by KMT forces, and to retake positions lost
to the Communists, in accordance with General Order No. 1.

28   U.S. Ambassador Patrick Hurley escorted Mao from Yenan to Chungking for peace negotiations with Chiang Kai-shek.

September

CCP forces proceeded in accordance with Chu Teh's August 11 order; Japanese and collaborator forces proceeded in accordance with General Ho's of August 23. CCP forces also began moving into Manchuria and organizing locally.

October

U.S. began airlift of KMT troops from south to north China. Clashes occurred between KMT and CCP forces. U.S. Marines landed in north China to take the surrender of the Japanese for the KMT Government prior to the arrival of its forces.

10   Mao and Chiang signed the October 10 Agreement summarizing their negotiations. Agreement was reached on general principles but not on specifics, particularly with regard to control and administration of CCP armies and liberated areas.

11   Mao returned to Yenan leaving Chou En-lai in Chungking to continue negotiations.

November

10   Chiang Kai-shek, still unable to move enough of his forces into Manchuria to occupy the area, requested a delay in the Soviet withdrawal scheduled to begin November 15. Soviets agreed and later reaffirmed their intention to allow KMT troops to enter Manchuria.

15   KMT forces attacked Shanhaikuan and began advancing into Manchuria.

25   Chou En-lai returned to Yenan. Troops disrupted a student anti-civil-war meeting in Kunming, precipitating the December First Movement.

26   Patrick Hurley submitted his resignation as Ambassador to China.

27   President Truman announced the appointment of General George Marshall as Special Representative to China.

December

Delivery of equipment for 39 divisions of the KMT army and 8-1/3 air wings completed by the U.S.

1   Student protest stemming from the November 25 incident culminated in the killing of four young people at Southwest Associated University in Kunming.

15   President Truman announced the Marshall Mission in an effort to mediate the KMT-CCP dispute. Marshall arrived in China on December 23.

1946

January

10   Ceasefire announced between KMT and CCP forces, to go into effect at midnight January 13. Agreement set up an Executive Headquarters in

Peiping to supervise the truce, consisting of three commissioners representing the U.S., the KMT Government, and the CCP.

11- Political Consultative Conference (PCC) met in Chungking, attended by
31 delegates representing the KMT, the CCP, and minor parties; decisions subject to approval of governing bodies of parties represented; agreement reached on virtually all political and military problems outstanding between the KMT and CCP; resolutions never fully implemented.

February

10 A public meeting at Chiao-ch'ang-k'ou in Chungking to celebrate successful ending of PCC violently disrupted, allegedly by right-wing KMT elements opposed to the PCC agreements.

25 KMT-CCP agreement on military reorganization and the integration of CCP forces into the National Army announced; agreement never implemented.

March

After additional delays at Chiang's request, Soviet troops began withdrawal from Manchuria; withdrawal completed on May 3.

17 The KMT Central Executive Committee announced acceptance of the PCC resolutions with certain reservations. The CCP and the Democratic League then refused to participate in the implementation of the resolutions.

April

Numerous violations of the January 13 ceasefire by both sides.

18 CCP troops occupied Changchun as Russians withdrew, in violation of the ceasefire agreement; city retaken a month later by KMT forces.

28 CCP forces occupied Harbin as the Russians withdrew; city remained in CCP hands.

May

5 KMT Government returned to Nanking from wartime capital at Chungking.

June

6 A second truce announced, to last 15 days from June 7, intended specifically to end fighting in Manchuria.

July

Agreement reached on the balance of military forces, but Chiang's demand for the right to appoint officials in north China unacceptable to the CCP; Chiang announced his decision to convene unilaterally a National Constitutional Assembly in November.

Democratic League members Wen-I-to and Li Kung-p'u assassinated in Kunming.

J. L. Stuart, President of Yenching University, named U.S. Ambassador to China.

General Marshall becoming convinced of his inability to bring about a peace agreement.

The Government's general offensive against CCP areas began with an advance into Shantung and Kiangsu, marking the start of the "Third Revolutionary Civil War." Communist historians describe the first year— July 1946 to June 1947—as the defensive stage during which KMT troops took over the major cities in the Northeast, recaptured *hsien* towns, and cleared communications lines north of the Yangtze River. CCP forces followed a policy of mobile warfare and strategic withdrawal from the towns back to the countryside. CCP military forces renamed the People's Liberation Army (PLA).

August
30 U.S. agreed to turn over U.S.$900 million in war surplus supplies to the KMT Government.

September
In August and September, U.S. imposed a partial ban on the shipment of combat materiel to the KMT Government to bolster Marshall's credibility as mediator between the KMT and the CCP.

October
KMT Government announced formal resumption of national conscription halted in August, 1945.

10 KMT troops captured city of Kalgan from CCP.

November
4 U.S. and KMT Governments signed a Treaty of Friendship, Commerce, and Navigation.

15-
December
25 The National Constitutional Assembly met with neither the CCP nor DL participating; Constitution adopted on December 25 and promulgated by the Central Government on January 1, 1947. The Constitution was to go into effect after one year, to establish democracy and end KMT political tutelage.

December
18 President Truman issued a major statement on China policy reaffirming that the U.S. would not become directly involved in the KMT-CCP conflict.

1947
January
Anti-American demonstrations occurred nationwide in early January precipitated by the alleged rape of a Peking University girl student by a U.S. Marine on December 24.

In Manchuria, Lin Piao's forces launched the first of five diversionary offensives to follow in rapid succession until June, giving the CCP the initiative in the Northeast.

6 General Marshall recalled to Washington.

29 U.S. announced the formal termination of its mediation effort.

February

KMT Government notified CCP representatives in Nanking that their presence in Government-controlled territory was no longer desired and that CCP journals and newspapers there must cease publication.

Rebellion broke out in Taiwan against the KMT authorities there.

March

2 CCP delegation left Nanking for Yenan.

19 KMT forces occupied Yenan.

May

Rice riots broke out in many central China cities

Student demonstrations occurred nationwide, protesting economic disruption and the Civil War.

U.S. Government lifted its embargo on the delivery of combat materiel to the KMT Government.

July

4 State Council of the KMT Government ordered general nationwide mobilization for war to suppress the Communist rebellion.

9 President Truman instructed the Wedemeyer fact-finding mission. General Wedemeyer remained in China for one month, arriving in Nanking on July 24.

July-August marked the start of the second stage of the war, with CCP forces commencing a limited counteroffensive directed against overextended KMT troops in central China north of the Yangtze.

August

11- Liu Po-ch'eng's forces crossed the Lunghai Railway to begin the CCP
12 counteroffensive in central China

October

10 CCP promulgated the Outline Agrarian Law formally terminating property rights of rural landlords.

28 KMT Government banned the Democratic League.

November

KMT campaign to recapture Shantung, begun in 1946, ended in defeat; CCP troops captured the city of Shihchiachuang, linking up the Shansi-Chahar-Hopei and Shansi-Hopei-Shantung-Honan Border Regions.

21- Elections held in KMT areas to elect delegates to the National Assembly.
23

December

A major rectification campaign began in the CCP areas to curb "excesses" in the land reform movement and in many aspects of urban policy.

1948

March

Manchurian cities of Szupingkai and Kirin occupied by CCP forces.

29- National Assembly convened in Nanking, electing Chiang Kai-shek and Li
May Tsung-jen President and Vice-president.
1

April

2 U.S. Congress passed the China Aid Act, authorizing U.S.$338 million in economic aid and $125 million in special grants for the KMT Government during the 1948-49 fiscal year.

7 Loyang, Honan, occupied by CCP forces.

May

20 President Truman officially appropriated U.S.$100 million from the 1948-49 budget for the rehabilitation of the Japanese economy.

May-June students protested the new U.S. policy of rebuilding Japan.

June

19 Kaifeng, Honan, occupied by CCP forces.

August

19 Emergency economic reform program inaugurated by the KMT; a new currency issued; and drastic measures undertaken for a few weeks against speculators and profiteers primarily in Shanghai where Chiang's son, Chiang Ching-kuo, was responsible for implementing the program.

September

By Communist reckoning, the start of the third and final stage of the Civil War: the all-out strategic offensive.

12 The Liaohsi-Shenyang Campaign commenced, ending on November 1 with the surrender of Mukden and the final collapse of the KMT army in Manchuria.

24 Tsinan, Shantung, occupied by CCP forces.

October

15 Chinchow occupied by CCP forces.

20 Changchun occupied by CCP forces.

November

1 Mukden surrendered to CCP forces.

5 The decisive Huai-Hai Campaign began for control of the railway center of Hsuchow in northern Kiangsu

December

11   The Peiping-Tientsin Campaign began.

24   Kalgan re-occupied by CCP forces.

1949

January

10   The Huai-Hai Campaign ended in victory for CCP forces, clearing the last obstacle from their march to the Yangtze.

15   CCP forces occupied Tientsin.

21   Chiang Kai-shek announced his retirement; Li Tsung-jen became Acting President.

22   General Fu Tso-i surrendered Peiping; CCP troops entered the city in force on January 31.

February

KMT Government offices moved from Nanking to Canton; a peace delegation sent by Li Tsung-jen arrived in Peiping to negotiate a settlement with the CCP.

March

5   Mao declared that the center of gravity of CCP work had shifted from the village to the city and that the period of "the city leading the village" had begun.

24   Taiyuan, Shansi, occupied by CCP forces.

25   Mao Tse-tung and the Party leadership took up residence in Peiping; Hsinhua radio began broadcasting from that city.

April

20   Li Tsung-jen rejected CCP conditions for peace; CCP forces began the crossing of the Yangtze River.

23   Nanking occupied by CCP forces; Li Tsung-jen fled to Canton; KMT Government formally established in Canton.

May

3   Hangchow, Chekiang, occupied by CCP forces.

16   Hankow occupied by CCP forces.

17   All of Wuhan occupied by CCP forces.

25   Shanghai occupied by CCP forces.

June

Chiang Kai-shek resumed active control of KMT affairs.

August

26   CCP forces occupied Lanchow and soon completed the take-over of the northwest provinces.

September

21-   A new Political Consultative Conference consisting of 662 representatives
28   from the CCP, the Democratic League, regional democratic groups, labor, peasants, business, and industry met in Peiping. Among other things, the Conference adopted the Common Program of the People's Republic of China and designated Peiping the official capital, formally changing its name back to Peking on September 27.

October

1   Mao Tse-tung officially proclaimed the establishment of the People's Republic of China in Peking.

15   Canton occupied by CCP forces; the KMT Government moved to Chungking.

November

25   The KMT Government moved to Chengtu.

30   Chungking occupied by CCP forces.

December

5   Li Tsung-jen left China for the U.S.

9   The KMT Government moved to Taiwan.

16   Mao travelled to Moscow for negotiations with Stalin.

27   All of Szechwan province occupied by CCP forces.

1950

February

14   Sino-Soviet Treaty of Friendship, Alliance, and Mutual Aid announced, the result of Mao's negotiations in Moscow.

April

Hainan Island occupied by CCP forces.

Preface to the Second Edition

Nothing serves better than the new edition of an old book to reaffirm the axiom that historical writing is defined as much by its own present as by the past it seeks to illuminate. So many political and academic generations have passed since *Civil War in China* was first published in 1978, that its reappearance now, within the field of late 20th-century scholarship on China, must begin by identifying the time, place, and circumstances of origin. For readers of a certain age, this recapitulation will naturally be unnecessary, except perhaps to revive memories of times past. History has more than one dimension, however, and the Chinese edition published in 1997 provided reminders of a different sort, namely, that time zones are not the only barriers that books must cross.

In fact, the new Chinese constituency should be introduced at the outset, since it defines the changing nature of interest in the book and thus demonstrates a major reason for its reissue. Among the changes in China following Mao Zedong's death in 1976 has been the opening of state archives and relaxation of, if not complete liberation from, publishing constraints for many kinds of historical scholarship. As a result, enormous amounts of new Chinese primary and secondary sources are now available for further research on many periods of China's recent history including the late 1940s civil war between the government, then led by the Kuomintang (KMT) or Nationalist Party, and its communist challenger.[1] One additional feature of this new era has been the publication in China of many works about China written by non-Chinese scholars. These translations make available the same books that Chinese students find on their reading lists in North American and European universities. In this way, several generations of Chinese readers, both at home and abroad, are simultaneously being introduced to segments of their own history written by authors with perspectives far removed from those of their new audience. Chinese readers then return the favor by putting the books to use in ways their authors never envisaged, a result elaborated at greater length below.

---

1. See the revised bibliography for a selection of the new Chinese-language materials on the 1945–1949 civil war years.

My own research on China's 1945–1949 civil war began in 1969, as part of a Ph.D. dissertation in political science at the University of California, Berkeley. The dissertation was completed three years later. Additional work for publication took place between 1973 and 1975. After remaining "in press" and out of reach for three years, the first edition finally appeared in 1978 and the paperback in 1980. It opened to mixed reviews, meaning some really liked it and some really didn't. Together these sentiments mirrored my own, although not necessarily for all the same reasons. I did not like it because it was not the book I wanted to write. Both subject matter and sources, and then the publication delays, seemed to keep the work always just beyond reach by limiting options and curtailing lines of inquiry short of satisfactory conclusion. Yet to the extent that the book succeeded, it did so because of the compelling nature of that same subject matter and the lines of inquiry it opened. Ironically, the significance of those questions was also extended and enhanced by the decade-long production process. Such a time span may be standard now but seemed calculated then to doom the book to oblivion, given the momentous changes that influenced perspectives between 1969 and 1980.

THE QUESTIONS THEN:
AMERICA'S ASIA, CHINA'S WAR

The essential questions in 1969, when my research began, were fast receding by 1980, when most people were reading the book and the ground was already shifting beneath our feet. In 1969, among the burning issues for students of China's revolutionary history were Vietnam and Chalmers Johnson, and the two were becoming inextricably linked. As my dissertation committee chairman, Johnson's own controversial thesis on peasant nationalism loomed much larger than it would have in any other political science department at any other time.[2] The Vietnam war had by then become the focus of everyone's daily existence, giving immediate relevance to issues no student of politics could escape. The issues concerned United States foreign policy in a post-colonial world, participation in other peoples' wars, the nature of those wars, and especially the communist challenge that gave impetus to the entire range of controversy.

Inevitably, such questions once raised were traced back in a direct line of descent to where they all began in the acrimonious debate over America's responsibility for the "fall" of China to communism in 1949. Following the logic of that debate, considerations that had kept the U.S. from intervening directly in China's 1945–1949 civil war were overridden. Washington accordingly resolved to draw the line against communism in Korea and then reiterated that decision in Vietnam. Yet despite those decisions, or more accurately because of their consequences, the late 1960s were also a transitional time when all such questions returned to the arena of public debate. The consensus that had allowed hard-line

---

2. Chalmers Johnson, *Peasant Nationalism and Communist Power: The Emergence of Revolutionary China, 1937–1945* (Stanford: Stanford University Press, 1962).

anti-communist assumptions to prevail throughout the 1950s cold war era, was broken as its bipolar certainties eroded. That era then receded much as it began, with the search for a new consensus marked by another period of rancorous national debate.

Ultimately, communist forces prevailed in Vietnam as they had in China, and the U.S. moved on to find a new balance with its adversaries somewhere between coexistence and containment. But military and policy decisions reached on battlefields and by heads of state have a chronological finality that the intellectual arguments surrounding them often lack. In this case, peasant nationalism almost immediately took on a complex life of its own and has been defying proclamations of its death ever since. Its mix of scholarly aims and political implications gave it a dual significance that allows it to be acknowledged still—both as a liberal pioneer for the first post-cold war generation of academic research on China, and as a conservative standard bearer in that transitional time when the search for a new policy consensus seemed to go on forever.

Kathleen Hartford and Steve Goldstein have recently summarized the evolution of Western scholarship on China's pre-1949 communist revolutionary history. Their summary is recommended reading in all but one respect: the differences between Johnson and his original detractors were certainly not "more apparent than real."[3] That verdict was based on years of subsequent research and reflects also the less contentious state of our understanding today. Its origins were considerably less serene, and scholarly differences grew more real as the political implications multiplied.

Johnson's thesis, published in 1962, was seen as a clear break with the previous themes of 1950s scholarship on communism's 1949 victory in China. Those themes were all about conspiracy theories, American responsibility, the Soviet Union's responsibility, communist parties as organizational weapons, elite decisions, and policy making at the highest levels. Johnson's focus on World War II and the catalytic role of Japan's occupation for post-war, anti-colonial nationalist movements throughout Asia was not new. His innovation was to apply that theme to the victory of Chinese communism. Even more unusual, he applied it to the rural areas, coined the term "peasant nationalism," and argued that communist success was rooted in the mass support mobilized by the Chinese Communist Party (CCP) as leader of China's anti-Japanese resistance movement in north and east China between 1937 and 1945. The CCP was no longer just a Soviet transplant but had acquired legitimate, indigenous roots along with the mantle of Chinese nationalism and the regional communist-led base areas established during those years.

It was a measure of the shift already underway in American political discourse, however, that virtually all the challenges to Johnson's argument came not from the old conservative right it was supplanting, but from the fast-emerging

---

3. Kathleen Hartford and Steven M. Goldstein, "Introduction: Perspectives on the Chinese Communist Revolution," in *Single Sparks: China's Rural Revolutions,* ed. Hartford and Goldstein (Armonk, N.Y.: M. E. Sharpe, 1989), p. 19.

left. The challenge derived from his forceful insistence on nationalism, resistance war, and the united front policy of class conciliation as chief reasons for communist success in galvanizing a popular movement under its leadership. Johnson derided the "vulgar Marxist" emphasis on socio-economic reform, radical or otherwise. He dug in his heels along a right-of-center line and further infuriated critics by applying his theories to Vietnam and other liberation wars as well. "In terms of revolutionary strategy," he wrote in his 1973 *Autopsy on People's War,* "communism has succeeded only when it has been able to coopt a national liberation struggle. . . . In mobilizing the peasantry for purposes of supporting guerrilla warfare, purely peasant interests, such as land reform, may be catered to, but it is recognized that the ultimate source and only truly effective basis of peasant mobilization will be imperialist depredations, usually as a result of foreign military intervention."[4]

Johnson thus provoked ongoing storms of controversy and helped motivate a whole new genre of regional base-area studies all bent on discovering the socio-economic reasons for Chinese communism's success.[5] By 1969, of course, most everyone had mastered the basic principles of guerrilla warfare. We therefore understood the need to assess contradictions and devise strategies for use against superior forces. In this case, the graduate students knew that, however strong his views, Johnson had a weakness for densely documented, closely woven arguments. After he rejected two other dissertation proposals (first, the Yenan legacy, and then cultural revolutionary reforms in education), we settled on the 1945–1949 civil war. I reasoned that this was just far enough from the 1937–1945 period to avoid a direct confrontation, yet close enough to be able to craft a countervailing argument he could not reject.

Alas, my careful strategy collapsed within months. Initially, it seemed a perfect plan. Preliminary readings all pointed in the same direction. Between 1945 and 1949, the CCP had been able to shift from guerrilla, to mobile, to conventional warfare, and win a decisive victory on the battlefield. But contemporary accounts—whether by communist friends or foes, foreign observers, Chinese participants, ex-military officers, or civilian commentators—invariably reverted to the underlying "political" reasons for communist success. Many went further, characterizing the communist triumph as primarily political rather than military. According to these contemporary arguments, moreover, the KMT's political defeat through corruption, incompetence, and economic mismanagement was as de-

---

4. Chalmers Johnson, *Autopsy on People's War* (Berkeley: University of California Press, 1973), pp. 10, 15–16.

5. In addition to the above-cited Hartford and Goldstein summary of this scholarship, see also Stephen Averill, "More States of the Field, Part Two: The Communist-Led Revolutionary Movement," *Republican China,* vol. 18, no. 1 (November 1992), pp. 225–255. The first book-length alternative to peasant nationalism was Mark Selden's *The Yenan Way in Revolutionary China* (Cambridge: Harvard University Press, 1971). Both Johnson and Selden subsequently published point-by-point answers to their critics—and yielded them little ground, allowing the original formulations to stand more or less unchanged. See Chalmers Johnson, "Peasant Nationalism Revisited: The Biography of a Book," *China Quarterly,* no. 72 (December 1977), pp. 766–785; and Mark Selden, "Epilogue," *China in Revolution: The Yenan Way Revisited* (Armonk, N.Y.: M. E. Sharpe, 1995), pp. 222–258.

cisive as the CCP's victory. And foremost among the political reasons for that victory was said to be the CCP land reform policy, seemingly the perfect foil for a peasant nationalism rebuttal.

Research progressed to the next stage, and primary sources promised more of the same. Hsueh Chun-tu's bibliographic introduction for the land reform materials at Stanford University's Hoover Library reminds us still of the old conventional wisdom. He began with a reassuring note: "One of the most important factors that contributed to the military victory of the CCP was the land reform which had been carried out in Communist regions. It won the active support of the peasants in the war against the KMT. The agrarian policies of the Party were clearly defined by the promulgation of the 'Outline Land Law' in 1947."[6]

"Progress" soon reached a dead end, however, since the sources offered little hope of demonstrating any such causal relationship. A selective reading of those available for the 1945–1949 period were insufficient (given my grasp of the subject then) even to draft a passable chapter on the subject, much less sustain a combative thesis on the socio-economic roots of military victory. As explained below, it was only much later, while pre-publication revisions were underway, that I finally realized the initial trap into which everyone must have fallen by singling out "land reform," interpreting it literally, and accepting the official CCP inauguration date of 1947. That periodization then seems to have been incorporated, with little concrete information as to the actual dynamics of the relationship between political and military victory, into the prevailing conventional wisdom about communist strength and KMT weakness.

In this way a compromise study evolved, as it became clear that the conditions necessary for communist success had undoubtedly been established prior to 1945. The subsequent final 1945–1949 phase of the CCP's rise to power was not a time when necessary sites were selected and essential foundations laid, but when the added structures of military and political power required for final victory were completed. By a further process of elimination, I factored out the foreign policy questions that had dominated American perspectives on China's civil war. These were epitomized for 1960s critics by the old conservative rallying cry about losing China to the communists. The new assumption held that China was not ours to lose and I therefore concentrated on the Chinese principals themselves. I also factored out the important military dimension for several, mostly practical, reasons including the need to limit length plus my own lack of expertise (and inclination), as well as the existence of one general military account and another then in progress.[7]

With the boundaries thus delineated, I could not presume to seek a definitive

6. Hsueh Chun-tu, *The Chinese Communist Movement 1937–1949: An Annotated Bibliography of Selected Materials in the Chinese Collection of the Hoover Institution* (Stanford, Calif.: The Hoover Institution, 1962), Bibliographical Series, no. 11, p. 226.

7. Lionel Max Chassin, *The Communist Conquest of China: A History of the Civil War 1945–1949,* trans. Timothy Osato and Louis Gelas (Cambridge: Harvard University Press, 1965); William Whitson with Huang Chen-hsia, *The Chinese High Command: A History of Communist Military Politics, 1927–1971* (New York: Praeger, 1973).

or theoretical explanation for communist success. Nor did I set out to write a political history of the 1945–1949 civil war. My aims were instead preliminary, seen as laying foundations for future work, and limited to exploring the comparative political performance of the two main rivals. The focus was on practice, policy implementation, and their impact on the general public. I did not extrapolate on deeper reasons for communist strengths and KMT deficiencies partly because it seemed more important to explore and establish their parameters, given the contention surrounding those claims; and partly to avoid being drawn into argument about the inevitability of communist victory, which was then an even more contentious issue. But I did ultimately aim to establish a benchmark for assessing the controversies we had inherited from the 1945–1949 years by demonstrating the nature of comparative political success and failure.

PERSPECTIVES NOW:
CHINESE POLITICS, WESTERN TRENDS

The most striking development since *Civil War in China*'s 1978 publication date is the great disparity that has emerged between current Chinese interests and Western scholarship. For several reasons, the latter has moved off in different directions, leaving the 1945–1949 years still under-researched. By contrast, and for several other reasons, Chinese interest has continued to strengthen producing the flood of publications mentioned above. The Chinese translation of *Civil War* adds but one more title to the voluminous output that as yet shows no sign of diminishing. Ironically, that output has already produced enough primary and secondary source materials to underwrite multiple research projects, at a time when Western scholars are looking just about everywhere else for topics and sources of inspiration.

CIVIL WAR STUDIES AND SHIFTING WESTERN CONCERNS

In its original Western incarnation, *Civil War in China* ran its course along the mainstream of academic interest in communism's rise to power. Then, as concern about communist threats and alternatives faded during the 1980s, the book drifted onto a new side current. In this variation, the civil war period is no longer important for itself, as a crucial episode in China's transition to communism, but becomes instead one of several precedent-setting stages in the 20th-century evolution of China's post-traditional political order.

To summarize *Civil War*'s original place in the arguments over Chinese communism's pre-1949 success, the book is divided into two more or less equal parts. Part one deals with KMT weaknesses and part two with communist strengths. Part one concentrates on urban issues and city people: corruption, inflation, students, and intellectuals. Part two focuses on rural land reform that initially attracted the most attention because the field was then alive to the debate over peasant nationalism and alternative explanations for Chinese communist victory.

Had I understood initially that the starting date for "land reform," or the radical redistribution of rural land, property, and political power was not actually 1947 but much earlier, I might have been able to achieve the original goal of concentrating on that one issue. As it happened, the dissertation chapter on land reform still defied logic in 1974, with inconsistencies too great for publication. The questions that had obstructed progress at the start remained unanswered. Hence, despite all the conventional wisdom and official CCP claims to the contrary, documents associated with the 1947 shift to land reform could not substantiate the conclusion that it mobilized peasant support for the communist war effort. Specifically, two major contradictions needed to be explained. First, how could land reform have mobilized peasant support in the key north China provinces where it was initially implemented, when tenancy rates there were uniformly low and small-holding owner-tillers the norm? Second, if Johnson was right in arguing that the communists had been able to win a substantial rural following only *after* abandoning their divisive 1930s land reform program, then why would CCP leaders risk returning to such a course under conditions of full-scale civil war?

Ultimately, the effort to unravel these contradictions took an extra year of research, added nearly one hundred pages to the manuscript, and finally made it possible to address the questions then motivating mainstream research about communist success. The new effort turned up virtually nothing about peasant nationalism *per se.* But the findings did indicate that, given certain conditions of security, radical socio-economic reform was indeed compatible with successful, CCP-led mobilization of rural populations both before and after Japan's surrender in 1945. The condition of relative local security was essential, however, and what had evidently changed by 1947 was the much greater strength of the communist-led rural-based movement, a strength that allowed it to sustain the widespread shift back to radical economic and political reform.

By tracing the pragmatic process of revolutionary institution-building from below, "step-by-step" and "directive-by-directive," the new findings also paralleled those of the regional base-area studies that continued to be published throughout the 1980s.[8] Almost all these formulations rejected the earlier, single-factor explanations of Chinese communism's rise to power, be they ideology, organization, foreign intervention, impoverishment, or whatever. Everyone rejected as well the idea of spontaneous combustion based on some preordained mix of such factors. The studies ultimately emphasized not absolutes and givens but relativities and human creations, especially strategies, process, and flexibility. These came to be seen as the necessary (even if not sufficient) conditions, learned over time, that allowed the alien doctrine to take root in rural Chinese soil. The CCP thus acquired the ability to adapt as needed to a great variety of local environments and adversaries, the latter both Chinese and foreign, in the process of building a rural-based, revolutionary movement strong enough to support a return to the cities and final victory.

---

8. Elaborations of this research were still appearing in the mid-1990s. See, for example, Tony Saich and Hans van de Ven, eds., *New Perspectives on the Chinese Communist Revolution* (Armonk, N.Y.: M. E. Sharpe, 1995), Part 2, Regional Variations.

If revolutions can be made, of course, they can also be unmade, and the moderation that settled over arguments as research projects matured undoubtedly had as much to do with post-1976 changes in China as with the research findings themselves. China's rejection of Mao's revolutionary vision, with its class-based social aims and rural ideals, destroyed the aura of infallibility that had formed around it. Destroyed as well was the sense of predetermination associated with a Maoist legacy that had self-consciously traced its antecedents to those same agrarian origins we were all so carefully dissecting. The drive to discover the secrets of Chinese communism's rural-based success decelerated accordingly, and mainstream concerns motivating Western research began moving in several different directions.

Meanwhile, among the most immediate changes for post-Mao China was its "return" to the cities. Urban youth returned to town from rural work assignments, intellectuals were welcomed back into the service of socialism, class stigmas were formally erased, and developmental priorities were reordered. Readers of *Civil War* followed these trends, reassessing its chapters within the context of China's evolving political order. As interest in agrarian revolution waned, readers' attention refocused on urban issues and city people. And as Chinese intellectual dissent grew in the 1980s, reader-interest turned more specifically to the intellectuals' dissenting forebears, whose struggle to sustain independent lines of public commentary between the disintegrating KMT and an untested CCP still provide some of the most dramatic insights on China's civil war experience.

For the civil war period itself, however, the new trends seem to have sent everyone off on an extended detour around it. To claim "everyone" moved away is, of course, an exaggeration. In fact, the earlier emphasis on foreign policy, Sino-American relations, and cold war diplomacy has continued in a steady line of evolution from the original 1940s concerns to those of our own post–cold war era.[9] Left to languish, however, have been the main events that, for China, defined the last crucial stage of the CCP's ascent to power. Western scholarship has thus circled around them in almost every way possible, as if to avoid the military and political epicenter that seems somehow to have collapsed under the weight of pressures surrounding it.

As a result, to the best that can be ascertained, that epicenter has inspired just one new book-length research project in the past 20 years, namely, Joseph Yick's *Making Urban Revolution in China.*[10] A second book not directly related to the CCP-KMT conflict but dealing with the February 28, 1947, incident and uprising

---

9. The revised, English-language bibliography contains a selection of this scholarship on the 1940s, and William Kirby provides a useful survey in his "More States of the Field," *Republican China*, vol. 18, no. 1 (November 1992), esp. pp. 211–218. Moving beyond the new Chinese sources, this area of research especially will benefit from the gradual opening of former Soviet bloc archives in Russia and Eastern Europe (see the new bibliographic note; also Mark Kramer, "Archival Research in Moscow: Progress and Pitfalls," *Cold War International History Project Bulletin,* Woodrow Wilson International Center for Scholars, Washington, D.C. [fall 1993], pp. 1, 18–39).

10. Joseph K. S. Yick, *Making Urban Revolution in China: The CCP-GMD Struggle for Beiping-Tianjin, 1945–1949* (Armonk, N.Y.: M. E. Sharpe, 1995).

against the KMT in Taiwan, might also be counted.[11] Steven Levine's *Anvil of Victory,* the only other scholarly work focusing exclusively on late 1940s civil war politics to be published since 1978, actually began life as a research project in the decade preceding, and thus owed its initial inspiration to that earlier time.[12] So, too, did Lloyd Eastman's *Seeds of Destruction,* which in any case straddles the 1945 dividing line between the anti-Japanese and civil wars. Supplementing the list is a new military survey for general reading, which also is not exclusively concerned with the 1945–1949 period.[13] A selection of relevant articles and individual book chapters must similarly be sought on either side of the 1945 chronological boundary.

So brief a list is all the more surprising in a period dominated by full-scale war and its political equivalents, which led to the single greatest change in China's 20th-century history. Reasons for this scholarly void are, however, easy to identify and not entirely new. Generations past and present share responsibility about equally, along with the civil war legacy itself. As for generations past, the adversarial nature of our differences with one another discouraged any further focus on the military dimension. Ideology, organization, and war were all "conservative" themes, and we were searching for the origins of Chinese communism in a deliberate challenge to our conservative predecessors. We looked for explanations elsewhere and not surprisingly found them elsewhere—in social history, economics (Marxist or otherwise), ecological anthropology, and the generalized political process of building a revolutionary movement.

Yet everyone was still motivated by the same objective, namely, to explain how and why Chinese communism emerged victorious in 1949. Hence the most definitive break with the conservative past and its fear of communism occurred not with the liberal-left challenge of the 1960s and 1970s, but somewhat later as the means, in a sense, became the end and the search more meaningful than the original aim. That change occurred gradually in the 1980s, reinforced by the cumulative impact of China's own post-Mao transformation.[14] Then, once all the underlying props and challenges themselves collapsed along with the international communist movement in 1991, the old question was finally overwhelmed in the sudden, massive, political readjustments that followed everywhere. By the mid-1990s, the practical consequences of this change were being registered definitively—and not just for the China field—in the new, "post-modern," apolitical publications lists of trend-setting American university presses. But by then,

11. Lai Tse-han, Ramon H. Myers, and Wei Wou. *A Tragic Beginning: The Taiwan Uprising of February 28, 1947* (Stanford: Stanford University Press, 1991).

12. Steven I. Levine, *Anvil of Victory: The Communist Revolution in Manchuria, 1945–1948* (New York: Columbia University Press, 1987).

13. Lloyd E. Eastman, *Seeds of Destruction: Nationalist China in War and Revolution, 1937–1949* (Stanford: Stanford University Press, 1983); E. R. Hooton, *The Greatest Tumult: The Chinese Civil War, 1936–1949* (London: Brassey's, 1991).

14. Marie-Claire Bergere surveys the new post-revolutionary emphasis on social and cultural history in "Civil Society and Urban Change in Republican China," *China Quarterly,* no. 150 (June 1997), pp. 309–328.

questions about the origins of Chinese communism in general, and civil war studies in particular, had already completed their precipitous slide off the favored-priorities list of topics competing for scarce research funds, editorial interest, and scholarly attention.

CIVIL WAR AND CHINA'S EVOLVING POLITICAL ORDER

Fortunately, every end has a new beginning, and civil war studies are currently experiencing rebirth, not in any Western setting but in China itself, including both the People's Republic and its Taiwan-based Republic of China rival. This development, with its wealth of new publications and newly available archival materials, also underlines one additional reason for the earlier avoidance of this period. Research projects inevitably devolved into a time-consuming search for adequate sources, the lack of which was exacerbated by the civil war's ongoing legacy as a conflict the communists won but did not end. Writing political and military histories of such a period naturally requires equal access to comparable materials from both sides (and indeed all sides), which even now remains an elusive goal. The KMT, although defeated, did not surrender and carried all its secrets to Taiwan, while those of the CCP remained on the mainland. In both cases, the management of these secrets is still monopolized by the guardians of official party orthodoxy.

Hence, even if our inclinations had not pulled us in other directions, the ever-increasing methodological demands of our investigative scholarship would have inhibited more "conservative" lines of inquiry for lack of necessary means. A similar situation exists today, even in the midst of relative plenty. As noted in the bibliographic essay, current scholarly preferences for social history and economics are fortuitous but also reinforced because of the easier access being granted for research in these areas. By contrast, access is still most strictly controlled for materials on military and political history, the very areas most needed for research on the civil war period.

Consequently, as a net result of all the circumstances past and present, there is still no definitive military history of the civil war in English. Indeed, no such history exists for the 1937–1945 Sino-Japanese war either, giving the China theater a unique distinction in this regard among all those of World War II.[15] Having accepted the conventional wisdom of an earlier age about the relative importance of politics over war, both our questions and answers were confined largely within the political realm, and everyone then lost interest before we were able to finish the equation. Yet we still lack definitive political accounts of the combatants, their policies, and the government institutions they led. With so much groundwork left undone, it is hardly surprising that the old arguments are currently recorded nei-

---

15. See James Hsiung's comment on this void, which he blames on continuing enmity between the CCP and KMT, official secrecy, and consequent restricted access to research materials, in "Preface," ed. James C. Hsiung and Steven I. Levine, *China's Bitter Victory: The War with Japan, 1937–1945* (Armonk, N.Y.: M. E. Sharpe, 1992).

ther as having ended nor as continuing, but rather as remaining in a state of "inconclusive" suspension.

Such questions left untended naturally produce anomalies everywhere. For example, without any authoritative record to the contrary, Japan can continue to create its own revisionist interpretations of the China war while leaving its complex legacy for future generations to define. Peasant nationalism may have been well and truly buried. But without the necessary strategic assessments of communist military growth during the Japanese occupation, we cannot reconcile the old academic dispute with Mao's repeated declarations of gratitude to the Japanese! He routinely acknowledged their help in creating the conditions necessary for Chinese socialism's rise to power by teaching revolution to the Chinese people and provoking them to fight.[16] Also unreconciled are the ongoing positive claims for KMT-led state-building in earlier years, and the clear evidence of cumulative KMT decline between 1937 and 1949, a result that KMT leaders themselves have repeatedly acknowledged.

Together, these plus many other empty spaces and half-answered questions suggest the directions that future research might take. They can also help us understand the gulf that has emerged between "East and West" or between Chinese and Western interest in China's recent history, and how new research directions are likely to be influenced by the interaction between them. For the time being, Western scholars are responding as if liberated from the constraints of earlier scholarship. Continuity and sustained interest seem evident only among foreign policy historians. Scholars have otherwise pursued the new opportunities in a multitude of new directions, which do include some research on war, government institutions, and political parties, even amid the predominance of social and cultural themes. There are also occasional partisan thrusts just sufficient to keep alive the memory of old controversies. But these new studies all concentrate on earlier decades and at the current rate of advance, several academic generations may pass before Western scholars—if left to themselves—work their way back to the 1945–1949 civil war period.[17]

In all likelihood, however, Western researchers will not be left to themselves since interaction between the two Chinese and Western constituencies of interest

16. See Mao's comment in "On the Correct Handling of Contradictions among the People (Speaking Notes)," February 27, 1957, *The Secret Speeches of Chairman Mao,* ed. Roderick MacFarquhar, Timothy Cheek, and Eugene Wu (Cambridge: Harvard University Press, 1989), p. 182. Edgar Snow traced this assessment back to a prediction Mao made in 1936 (Snow, *The Other Side of the River: Red China Today* [New York: Random House, 1962], p. 41). After the fact, Mao commented on Japan's role as revolutionary teacher to the Chinese people during interviews with Snow in 1965 and 1970 (Edgar Snow, *The Long Revolution,* [New York: Vintage, 1973], pp. 173, 198–199). See also, Mao Zedong, "Jiejian Riben shehuidang renshi de tanhua" [Discussion with members of Japan's Socialist Party], July 10, 1964, *Mao Zedong sixiang wansui* [Long live the thought of Mao Zedong], N.p.: No pub., 1969), p. 533.

17. For two good representative selections of the new research on pre-1949 Republican China (which are also representative in bypassing the 1945–1949 years), see: "Reappraising Republican China," special issue, *China Quarterly,* no. 150 (June 1997), *passim*; and Hsiung and Levine, *China's Bitter Victory, passim.*

seems unavoidable. And for everyone on the Chinese side, the political concerns surrounding CCP-KMT enmity have acquired much the same degree of immediate relevance that previously motivated Western research on China's pre-1949 history. For us today, communism is over, and all its challenges—including China's civil war—belong to another time. For China, the challenges are real and ongoing since it remains in the final phase of that particular historical cycle, ruled by a Communist Party that is trying to control the conditions of its own transformation much as the KMT has done in Taiwan. Equally significant, the partisan contest between them has once again become a fact of daily political life and the contenders are well-matched, much as they were in 1945, albeit in a complex, reverse order of formation.

Fifty years ago, the communists had honed their political and military skills to build and defend a revolutionary movement against which the ruling KMT could no longer compete. Today, the CCP may remain preeminent nationally, but the balance of world forces has shifted irrevocably in the opposite direction, due to the intervening cumulative record of ruling communist parties everywhere. And 20th-century Chinese of all political persuasions are perhaps more acutely aware than others of shifting "world trends," because China has spent the entire century in a self-conscious, dialectical confrontation with them. The generalized "end" is now clearly written, and the CCP itself has been adjusting incrementally on that basis throughout the past 20 years of economic reform and political relaxation. The question is no longer whether China is moving in the same general direction as everyone else, but only what the specific Chinese destination will look like and how long it will take to get there.

Those questions, for example, sustained the long debate over Hong Kong's future that preceded its 1997 return to Chinese sovereignty, and Deng Xiaoping himself stepped in to finalize China's position. The "one country, two systems" formula entailed capitalist economics and a snail's pace progression toward democratically elected government timed, he suggested, to dovetail with his vision of China's overall 50-year evolution toward that same end.[18] Hong Kong ultimately had little choice but to accept those terms albeit reinforced, after years of lobbying, by additional civil rights guarantees.

Beijing has made similar promises to Taiwan as a means of ending the historic CCP-KMT dispute. For its part, however, Taiwan's own transformation from authoritarian, one-party, KMT rule began in the 1970s and has moved at a much faster pace. Taiwan might also have agreed more readily to the "one country, two systems" solution but for Beijing's suppression of its Tiananmen student protest

18. See, for example, Deng Xiaoping, "Huijian Xianggang tebie xingzhengqu jibenfa qicao weiyuanhui weiyuan shi de jianghua" [Talk to members of the Hong Kong Special Administrative Region Basic Law Drafting Committee], April 16, 1987, and "Yao xishou guoji de jingyan" [The need to absorb international experience], June 3, 1988, in Deng Xiaoping, *Lun Xianggang wenti* [On Hong Kong questions] (Hong Kong: Sanlian, 1993), pp. 30–37, 38–39. For some preliminary insights concerning this grand political reform design and Hong Kong's place within it, see Suzanne Pepper, "Hong Kong Joins the National People's Congress: A First Test for One Country with Two Political Systems," *Journal of Contemporary China* (March 1999).

movement in 1989, the collapse of international communism two years later, and the CCP's absolute determination to avoid a similar fate. Both literally and figuratively, then, the state of "civil war" continues although, except as a matter of principle punctuated by occasional saber-rattling, the conflict has now receded back wholly into the political sphere. The conflict has also acquired added significance, however, since the protracted negotiations over mutual terms of accommodation for ending the CCP-KMT dispute have become, in effect, a campaign for partisan advantage in the debate over China's evolving political order.

The stakes thus remain as high as before and the guardians of party orthodoxy as important, with each side striving to make the most of past and present achievements. The recent quantum leap in volume of research materials has been achieved in this way, partly by the receding need for secrecy as liberalization proceeds, and partly by the competitive urge of the disputants to establish their legacies for once and future use. This explains outsiders' difficulties in gaining direct access to the most important party and military records. Both sides naturally strive to maintain control over their respective histories in order to emphasize strengths and camouflage weaknesses. KMT materials therefore concentrate on the pre-1945 years and even earlier, when the foundations of its administrative governing apparatus were being laid. Institution-building is foremost in this legacy, along with foreign relations triumphs that finally won for China great power status in the world of international diplomacy. This record also highlights continuities between the pre-1949 past and post-1949, KMT-led achievements in Taiwan.

By contrast, the CCP's version of history concentrates heavily on the glorious exploits of a successful rise to power. Civil war battles loom large in this record as do politics, albeit not the class-based, mass-struggle politics of land reform that set precedents for the revolutionary transformation of post-1949 Chinese society. Instead, the CCP now hopes to be remembered for its conciliatory united front stratagems, the dangerous underground work of partisan loyalists in KMT-held cities, and the negotiated surrender of KMT armies recounted in volume after volume of old war stories and veterans' memoirs. Here, the present political implications are also clear: to bolster the CCP's weakened authority with reminders of its own greatest triumphs. The emphasis on defeated adversaries rejoining the fold recalls past efforts, in hopeful anticipation of an eventual CCP-KMT reconciliation under CCP leadership.

In all these ways, both sides are currently revisiting China's recent past, not just for itself but also selectively, to serve present political ends. This time around, however, the political arena is greatly changed. The CCP and KMT remain the chief competitors, to be sure, and at issue still are the bedrock differences created by the old communist challenge to alternate forms of economic and political governance. Those differences have, moreover, been compounded many times over by comparative records accumulated during the past 50 years of success, failure, and confrontation. Additionally, the two main contenders remain in absolute control over the most authoritative documentary evidence of their respective histories. Yet in deference to the intervening 50 years of change, the public domain into which records are being released allows considerable margin for alternate maneuvers. In fact, such records can now be put to all sorts of interesting uses besides those presumably intended by official guardians.

The new book cited above on the February 28, 1947, incident in Taiwan exemplifies this careful power play across historical boundaries. Political events and incidents long banned from public discourse can now take their rightful places in history—and immediately become part of current political agendas as well. Similarly, KMT corruption and economic mismanagement during the late 1940s contain many lessons and implications for present-day China. So, too, does the liberal intellectual community's pre-1949 struggle to keep open an independent channel of political commentary, while the student movement's many causes then against war, the Japanese, poverty, and so on, have parallels extending both backward and forward in time. The CCP and KMT principals are clearly not alone in their search for precedents, continuities, and legacies. This game is one that many can play, as an ancient Chinese political pastime is put to new uses in the current contest for influence over China's future.

Chinese and Western scholarly interest in this retroactive Chinese experience with political history may well remain divergent, and Western research may continue to circumvent the civil war period especially as a result. One or two new books based on the new materials are not enough to signal the onset of a new trend. Nevertheless, the new studies plus other recent and current research on government, politics, and war in earlier periods of China's pre-1949 history suggest the wealth of possibilities lying in store beneath the mountain of new materials. Fulfilling their potential anticipates forays across conventional time zones and divisions of scholarly labor, but that potential also suggests the multiple ways in which the questions we have left untended can ultimately be answered.

Civil War in China is thus being reissued, in its entirety and without revision, on the assumption that sooner or later others will return to the questions and pick up where their elders left off. Further toward that end, the bibliography has been revised to illustrate, by selective example, the new sources now capable of sustaining such inquiries and a host of others as well. Many more debts, both intellectual and personal, have accumulated in pursuing this inter-generational enterprise than can be acknowledged here by name. They include especially those whose continuing interest kept the book alive and in use, thereby providing the rationale for its current "re-commissioning." In this respect, I would also like to express my appreciation to those at Rowman & Littlefield who helped produce this new edition and especially to Susan McEachern who made it possible, as well as to Karen Johnson who guided the production process. But for Jin Guang-yao of Fudan University, I would probably have taken much longer to appreciate the interests of younger Chinese generations in their eclectic search for sources on China's past. Professor Jin also presided over the translation team which made possible the book's 1997 Chinese edition. Friends new and old who offered advice and suggestions while I was familiarizing myself with the new sources are gratefully noted in the introduction to the revised bibliography.

Given the thirty years that have passed since my civil war studies began, however, some acknowledgments must be mixed with sadness for those who contributed in different ways but are no longer present to receive thanks. The recent deaths of John Service and Doak Barnett, in February and March 1999, renewed memories of the many debts this book has accumulated. Although neither of them probably realized it, both provided moral support at different times when it was otherwise hard to come by. More important, they both provided political object lessons by giving our generation a clear sense of th barriers we were surmounting as we picked up where our pre-1949 predecessors had left off. Professor Barnett's *China on the Eve of Communist Takeover* was one of several eyewitness accounts from the 1940s that had remained tucked away in drawers and filing cabinets for almost twenty years. Too controversial to be published in the 1950s, these old reports by journalists, diplomats, and others, quickly resumed their rightful places as part of our own historical record.

Jack Service provided an even more direct link with the pre-1949 past when he suddenly appeared in our midst as a graduate student in the 1960s. The state department's loss was Berkeley's gain, we said. But his story was representative of the costs associated with communism's victory in China and the recriminations that became a major issue in U.S. politics for years thereafter. As a young American Foreign Service officer in China during World War II, he had, like many of his contemporaries, reported on the comparative strengths and weaknesses of the main contenders for power there. Service was the first of the "old China hands" to be purged from the state department for these reports and the most tenacious in seeking to clear his name of disloyalty. After the U.S. Supreme Court ruled in his favor, he was reinstated but then sidelined to an obscure consular post in England between 1956 and 1962. After retiring to Berkeley, he put fellow students to shame with his straight-A average, received a Master's degree, worked for several years in the University of California's Center for Chinese Studies, and lived happily ever after as honorary adviser to successive generations of graduate students. However great the differences among us, we thus shared a common memory of our predecessors. Barnett's and Service's passing serves not just as a reminder of old debts and contributions, but of the multiple transitions across time and space that allow the work of earlier generations to be carried forward by those who follow.

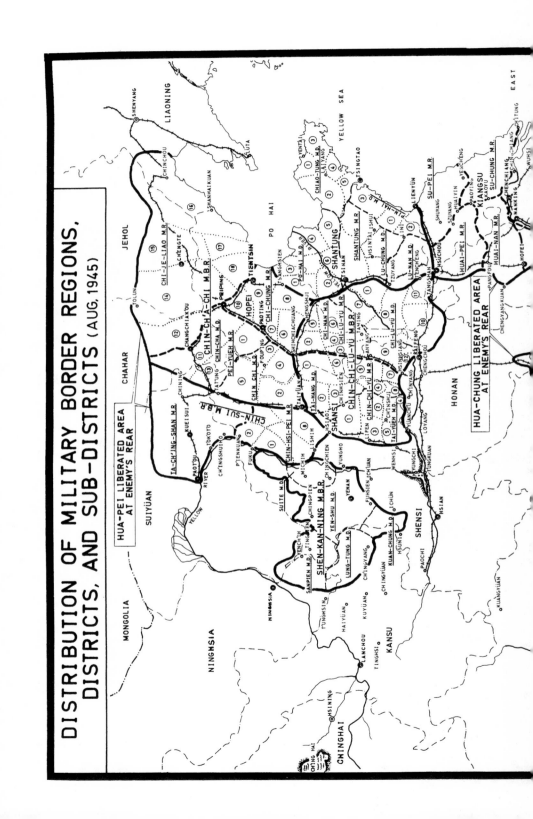

DISTRIBUTION OF MILITARY BORDER REGIONS, DISTRICTS, AND SUB-DISTRICTS (AUG. 1945)

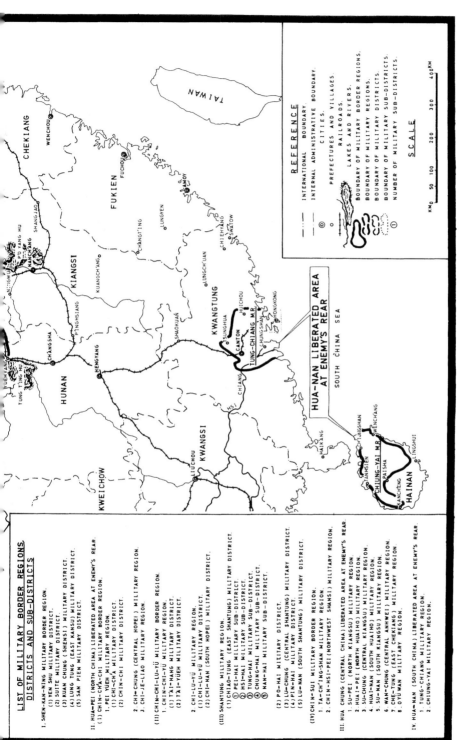

SOURCE: (1) MAP 1, SITUATION OF LIBERATION ZONE DURING SINO-JAPANESE WAR (JEN-MIN CH'U-PAN SHE, NOV, 1953.)
(2) MAP 1, CHINESE CIVIL WAR (1946-1950), HISTORY BUREAU M.N.D., JUNE, 1962. (TAIPEI)

PART ONE

The Last Years of Kuomintang Rule

I
Introduction

In the eyes of the outside world, the years 1945-49 marked the shift of the largest nation in Asia from one international power bloc to another. In the United States, the proclamation of the Chinese People's Republic on October 1, 1949, brought an upsurge of political debate and recrimination that has continued for a quarter of a century. The victory of the Chinese Communists inspired a new resolve to prevent the expansion of communism in Asia that led directly to American involvement in the Korean and Indochina wars.

Reflecting these events, scholars in the West have focused primarily on the military development of the conflict between the Chinese Communist Party (CCP) and the Kuomintang (KMT), and on the American efforts to influence and contain it. Addressing a Western audience, historians have addressed the interests and concerns of that audience. In the U.S., where most of the writing about China since 1949 has been done, the KMT defeat was immediately interpreted as a political loss, and the Communist victory as an illegitimate seizure of power. Interpreted also as an American failure, the most pressing concern in discussing the "fall of China" was either to fix responsibility or deflect it. This preoccupation has inspired scholarly research, government publications, and partisan political debates alike. For the English-speaking reader, the history of the Chinese Civil War during its 1945-49 phase,[1] has remained essentially a record of battles won and lost, of American aid proffered and withheld, and of investigations into the motives of those dispensing it.

Whether this is entirely the result of political interests and ideological bias—reinforced by the intimidating influence of the McCarthy era—need not detain us here. Several contemporary eyewitness accounts by American journalists and others did adopt a wider perspective and this book takes up where they left off.[2]

1. Chinese historians refer to the 1945-49 period as the Chinese People's War of Liberation, or the Third Revolutionary Civil War. The First and Second Revolutionary Civil Wars were the periods 1924-27 and 1927-37.
2. Among the best known: A. Doak Barnett, *China on the Eve of Communist Takeover;* Jack Belden, *China Shakes the World;* Derk Bodde, *Peking Diary: 1948-1949 a Year of*

It is an attempt to expand the historical record of the 1945-49 period to include the political content that gave meaning to the military struggle for those directly concerned.

This book is preliminary and partial in many respects. It is at best an introduction to issues and questions that, for the most part, have remained unexplored. Source materials are not abundant. Documentary gaps are major and in some cases may never be filled. Nor is this a political history in the conventional sense. It does not provide a consistent record of political personages, events, ideologies, or organizations. It is limited instead to the level of policy and practice on the part of the two main contenders for political power. More specifically, it is a comparative analysis of their relationship with the society that each aspired to govern.

The Chinese Civil War was a military struggle for the political power of the nation. War being politics by other means, the political arena must contain the clues as to the nature and outcome of the conflict. The political context of the struggle defines not only who the contenders are but why they fight, the nature of their commitment, and the resources at their disposal. For the purposes of this study, politics is defined as a process of interaction and exchange between the government and the governed. To be more precise, it is an exchange between those who occupy positions of public power and the individuals, groups, sectors, and classes of the population over which that power is exercised. Political resources provide the medium of exchange, and are traded between these elements and the political regime for the purpose of achieving the goals of each.

While the various groupings into which the population is divided can maintain a form of existence separate from the political regime, the reverse is not true. The political regime is sustained by them and cannot exist in isolation from them. Political regimes differ in the nature of their exchange relationships with different groups. But this definition assumes that the individuals and parties that would participate in the political arena can neither seize power nor retain it without engaging in this transaction. It occurs when alliances are made, policies adopted, and programs implemented.

A key element in the contender's bid for power is the withdrawal of resources from the incumbent regime. This can obviously be achieved more easily if the latter has weaknesses to exploit. The weaker its relationship with the various sectors of the population, the more chance the contender has to neutralize their opposition and ultimately to win their support. The relationship may be strengthened in several ways, such as policies pursued, promises made, the personalities involved, and so on. "Support," like "opposition," takes many forms both tangible and otherwise. Political resources are numerous and varied. They include the millet and manpower that were necessary to sustain the armies of the CCP and KMT in their mutual struggle. The conditions surrounding

---

Revolution; William Hinton, *Fanshen: A Documentary of Revolution in a Chinese Village;* and John F. Melby, *The Mandate of Heaven: Record of a Civil War, China, 1945-1949.* For details of publication, and translations of Chinese book titles, see the Selected Bibliography.

the exchange of these and other resources between the Chinese people and the two contending parties constitute the subject matter of our inquiry.

The conceptualization of politics as a process of interaction and exchange has gained some acceptance among social scientists,[3] but is not necessarily current in other circles. For this reason, it may be useful to adopt it in a study, such as this, where the subject is an unfamiliar political system in the midst of revolutionary change. In a cultural milieu with which we are more intimately familiar, such as our own, there is no need to remind anyone of these fundamentals of politics. No American journalist or political analyst would try to evaluate the results of a presidential election without considering the various issues which may have influenced the voting in the South, the farm belt, among blacks, labor, white-collar workers, and so on. That an exchange relationship exists between these sectors of the population and the administration in Washington is too obvious to require comment.

These same assumptions are not necessarily applied, however, when the form and style of politics differ from our own. This is especially true when one of the political contenders is a Communist party actively engaged in the violent overthrow of an existing political regime. Indeed, to attempt a political analysis of such an episode in the history of any society is to place oneself in the very eye of the storm. It is not particularly useful to think of political legitimacy as a derivative of established patterns of organization and procedure and accepted norms of political behavior, when those very patterns and norms are not only being questioned but forcefully challenged. The more important issue surely is the nature of the challenge itself and the conditions that make it possible. Such conditions must have roots in the past. But in the immediate present, they must also derive from the uses to which the organizational and procedural forms have been put by the individuals who occupy and operate within them.

Neither is it sufficient to treat the challenge as deriving primarily from Stalinist methods of organization and control, another common theme running through the Western critique of Communist-led revolutionary movements. One of the clearest examples of the analytical difficulties this assumption can generate is contained within an authoritative study of the National Liberation Front of South Vietnam.[4] The book begins by describing how the regime of Ngo Dinh Diem provided virtually every sector of South Vietnamese society with major grievances between 1954 and 1963, when the "collapse of Diem's authority" culminated in his overthrow. Listing chronologically the progressive alienation of each sector, the author concludes: "One felt that one was witnessing an entire social structure coming apart at the seams."[5] Yet the remainder of the book essentially ignores the implications of the chapter on the Diem environ-

3. See, for example, Warren F. Ilchman and Norman Thomas Uphoff, *The Political Economy of Change,* and the references they cite.

4. Douglas Pike, *Viet Cong: the Organization and Techniques of the National Liberation Front of South Vietnam* (Cambridge: The Massachusetts Institute of Technology Press, 1966).

5. *Ibid.,* p. 73.

ment, while describing the organization and techniques of the National Liberation Front which came into existence during that period. The author suggests that only persons suffering genuine grievances can build genuine revolutionary organizations, and continues: "Exactly the reverse was the case with the NLF. It sprang full-blown into existence and then was fleshed out. The grievances were developed or manufactured almost as a necessary afterthought."[6]

The assumptions that allow such contradictions to pass unnoticed have had repercussions well beyond the realm of academic controversy. Having inspired the preoccupation with America's failure to prevent a Communist victory in China and, by extension, the rationalization for the American adventure in Vietnam, these same assumptions will undoubtedly inspire attempts to explain the American failure there as well. Nevertheless, the political limits of military intervention are now fully apparent. So too are the incentives for exploring more deeply the relationship between political organization and political issues, and between the contenders for political power and those over whom they would exercise it.

Elaborating on Machiavelli's advice to aspirant rulers concerning the art of gaining and maintaining power, one scholar has written:

> Above all, the new Prince must provide more surely for the safety of the State, the great need for which the very fact of his own recent emergence into power makes apparent. He must take stronger and more effective measures than the government he supersedes in order to give people thenceforward a greater sense of security. Such developments, however, rarely occur without previous default of authority. . . . The shift of allegiance can readily occur in such circumstances. Old habits of loyalty are dissolved . . . and the people look to the new authority with better promise of security, peace, and law.[7]

This study seeks to determine if and to what extent there was actually a "default of authority" by the ruling KMT or Nationalist Party during its final years in power. Conversely, the second objective is to determine the extent to which the CCP was successful in gaining the allegiance that comes with public acceptance of those who occupy positions of political power. Did the Chinese Communists win a genuine mandate to rule, or were they primarily the beneficiaries of KMT mistakes and Japanese excesses?

6. *Ibid.,* p. 76.
7. Charles W. Hendel, "An Exploration of the Nature of Authority," in Carl J. Friedrich, ed., *Authority* (Cambridge: Harvard University Press, 1958), pp. 10-11.

II
The Beginning of the End: Take-over from the Japanese

World War II and the Japanese adventure in China affected the political fortunes of the two main contenders for power there in diverse ways. Initially, the Japanese attack evoked a nationalistic response which brought Chiang Kai-shek and the Chinese Communists together in a unified anti-Japanese resistance movement. This movement placed the Generalissimo at its head because he alone possessed sufficient national stature to lead the country in its struggle against the Japanese.[1] Chiang and the Government he headed came to be recognized by friend and foe alike as the symbols of a truly national Chinese determination to resist the invader.

In order to keep the symbol alive as the substance disintegrated, Chiang and the KMT Government were forced to withdraw from north China and the coastal areas into the Southwest before the advancing Japanese troops. The Chinese collaborator government led by Wang Ching-wei took over the positions of authority vacated by the retreating KMT. Meanwhile, the Communists from their base in Yenan were able to take advantage of the Japanese incursion into north China. The Communists were particularly well equipped to do so because they had been forced to develop guerrilla warfare and peasant revolution following the destruction of their urban base in 1927. Applying this experience, they began at once to organize a resistance movement in the countryside behind the lines of the enemy's military penetration. As a result, they emerged from World War II the most dynamic political force in the country. By April, 1945, the CCP could claim control over areas containing some 95.5 million people.

The KMT Government, by contrast, did little to exploit the opportunity that the Japanese invasion had similarly provided to it. The Government may have won national and international recognition as the representative of Free China, but in terms of domestic political strength or popular support it had achieved little by 1945. The Government did sponsor guerrilla and underground operations in Japanese-occupied territory. But these were never expanded into a

1. This point is developed in James M. Bertram, *Crisis in China: the Story of the Sian Mutiny.*

widespread resistance movement. The years of retreat in Chungking were used to no constructive purpose, and the weaknesses inherent in the KMT political system developed accordingly. In mid-1944, one American Foreign Service officer wrote that the KMT was weaker than it had been at any time during the previous ten years. "The Generalissimo," he wrote, "is losing the support of a China which, by unity in the face of violent aggression, found a new and unexpected strength during the first two years of the war with Japan. Internal weaknesses are becoming accentuated and there is taking place a reversal of the process of unification."[2] Popular discontent, political opposition, maladministration, and unprecedented corruption in the governmental and military structure were measures of the KMT's deterioration.

In August, 1945, however, the Japanese defeat presented the KMT with one final opportunity, or so the commentators said. Suddenly, the Government found itself in a position to reestablish its authority over an area which contained, together with the provinces of Free China, more than three-quarters of the nation's population. The *Ta kung pao*, calling it the sort of chance that happens but once in a thousand years, urged the Government to take advantage of the Japanese surrender to renew its political mandate and revive the political morale of the people. "On no account," warned the paper, "should we dissipate the confidence of the people in the recovered areas."[3]

Today, thirty years later, when Chinese of that generation reminisce about the Civil War years or when their children recall the parents' memories of that time, they almost invariably focus on the take-over of the Japanese-occupied territories during the fall and winter of 1945 as the beginning of popular urban disillusionment with KMT rule. The Chinese phrase for "take-over" *(chieh-shou)* is neutral, implying nothing more than to accept or receive. But as public experience grew with KMT application, it became popular to substitute one of several homophonous phrases (with different characters) meaning to plunder, seize openly, or rob poor.[4]

The erosion of popular confidence was most apparent in the urban areas, where the effects of the reconversion period were most keenly felt. Government officials assigned to take over enemy political and administrative units and enemy-owned properties descended on the cities in the greatest numbers. It was in the cities that the greed of these officials found the fattest opportunities, and the reconversion policies they were implementing could wreak the greatest havoc on economic production. Finally, it was in the cities that public awareness of

2. John S. Service, in *The China White Paper*, p. 567.

3. *TKP* (see Abbreviations), Chungking, Sept. 27, 1945 (*CPR*, Chungking, same date). The *Ta kung pao* was then a liberal newspaper associated with the Political Study Clique of the KMT, and the country's most prestigious paper. See Bibliographic Notes.

4. These phrases appeared often in print. For example, Ch'ien Pang-k'ai, "Tung-pei yen-chung-hsing tsen-yang ts'u-ch'eng-te?" [What has precipitated the grave situation in the Northeast?], *Ch'ing-tao shih-pao*, Feb. 19, 1948 (reprinted in *KC*, Mar. 27, 1948, p. 16); and Special Correspondent, "Ch'ung-ch'ing cheng-wen" [Political news from Chungking], *KC*, Dec. 21, 1946, p. 16.

these conditions was greatest, not only because of flagrancy and scale but also because the cities were the base of an only partially controlled press.

The crucial development during these months was the change in the Government's popular image. The Government itself did not change with the move back to the coast. Those who were aware of KMT deficiencies anticipated and cautioned against the problems that could arise when it returned to the occupied territories.[5] But the extent of those deficiencies did not become common knowledge until the immediate post-war period. The sense of public disillusionment was greater because the incompetence and corruption came from a Government that had stood for eight years as the symbol of the nation's will to survive. The discovery came abruptly that the KMT's wartime prestige would be no measure of its post-war behavior.

The public's memory, together with the political significance of the event, would no doubt have faded rapidly had the Government acted in the months that followed to correct the mistakes of the reconversion period. Unfortunately for the KMT, most of the issues that aroused such widespread criticism and protest during the take-over were never satisfactorily resolved. Hence its importance in the politics of the Civil War years as the first turning point in the balance of urban public opinion away from the KMT. At the same time, the take-over period also marked the culmination of the Government's failure to respond to the challenge of the Japanese invasion.

Public criticism and controversy revolved around four major issues. One was the slowness with which the Japanese were disarmed, and the Government's obvious reluctance to punish Chinese collaborators. The second, and most notorious problem, was the venality of the officials sent by the Chungking Government to take over Japanese and puppet properties and organizations. A third general issue was the inadequacy of the economic and financial measures implemented at this time. Finally, more subtle but no less important, was the condescending attitude adopted by returning officials toward the general population that had—in their eyes—remained behind to live under Japanese rule rather than evacuate to the interior with the KMT.

VICTORS AND VANQUISHED

Whatever the moral arguments, there was a widespread public demand that the KMT Government act at once after V-J Day to remove from political and military authority those Chinese who had actively collaborated with the Japanese-sponsored regime, and to mete out due punishment to them. The Government's slowness in doing so resulted primarily from its need to rely on the

5. For example, the lengthy appraisal by the KMT-affiliated economist Wu Ch'i-yuan, trained at the London School of Economics and a professor at Southwest Associated University, in *Shih-chieh jih-pao*, Chungking, Aug. 18, 1945 (*CPR*, Chungking, Aug. 26, 1945); and a similar article in *TKP*, Chungking, Aug. 17, 1945 (*CPR*, Chungking, same date). City and/or date of *CPR* translation will hereafter be shown only when they differ from the place and/or date of the Chinese newspaper publication.

Japanese and their Chinese "puppets"—as the collaborators were called—to maintain "law and order" following Japan's surrender. The Government's main concern was not civil disorder but more specifically the threat posed by the Chinese Communists. The lack of adequate transportation facilities made it impossible for sufficient numbers of KMT troops, peace-keeping authorities, and administrative personnel to return immediately to the extensive areas under Japanese control. Yet the Government found itself engaged at once in a race with the Communists to take over Japanese-occupied territory north of the Yangtze. The Government, based in the Southwest, was at a clear disadvantage since the Communists were already in control of much of the north China countryside.

In addition, however, there were charges that the Government was totally unprepared for the eventuality of Japan's surrender and had made few plans in anticipation of it. There were also rumors that factionalism within the KMT military establishment, and Chiang Kai-shek's reluctance to trust those commanders not personally loyal to him, kept him from deploying his troops to their most effective advantage during the crucial weeks after Japan's surrender. In any event, Chiang's main objective at this time was to reestablish and strengthen his own power by destroying the regional power bases of his rivals wherever possible. Besides the Communists, his rivals included Lung Yun in Yunnan province and the Chang family in the Northeast. Hence Chiang's willingness to ally with whoever would help him in that task, so long as their power did not threaten his own. In the Northeast, for example, the Government was obliged to ally with former collaborators because this was virtually the only group that could be counted on to support neither the Communists nor the sons of the old warlord, Chang Tso-lin.[6]

The KMT's open "alliance" with the Japanese began on August 23, with the order issued by General Ho Ying-ch'in, Commander-in-Chief of the Chinese Army, to General Okamura Yasuji, Commander-in-Chief of Japanese forces in China. The order stated that Japanese troops were to undertake effective defense of their original positions, keep communication lines open, and await the arrival of KMT troops. The Japanese were also held responsible for the recovery of positions recently taken by any "irregular forces," that is, the Communists. Offensive operations were subsequently undertaken by Japanese and puppet troops in accordance with this order.

Despite Chiang Kai-shek's order of August 11, 1945, that Communist forces were to maintain their existing positions pending further instructions, the Communists insisted on their right to accept the surrender of the enemy's troops. In accordance with orders from Yenan on August 10 and 11, Communist forces launched a general offensive against key points and major communication lines controlled by the Japanese in order to compel their surrender. When General Ho issued his order to Okamura on August 23, the Communists were

6. On Chiang's power play in Yunnan, see Chapter Three, "The December First Movement." The political situation in the Northeast is described in Chapters Five and Six.

engaged in taking over the city of Kalgan from the Japanese. From late August to the end of September, over one hundred clashes were reported between Communist troops and those of the Japanese and puppet armies. These forces succeeded in recovering from the Communists some twenty towns and cities in Anhwei, Honan, Hopei, Kiangsu, Shansi, Shantung, and Suiyuan.[7] According to General Ho Ying-ch'in, there were still some 100,000 armed Japanese troops in the three provinces of Shansi, Chahar, and Hopei at the end of November.[8]

The use of enemy troops in this way would have aroused less controversy had the Government been more alert to the political importance of reestablishing its own authority in the recovered areas as soon as possible. Instead, the Government compromised its position by unnecessarily delegating authority to the discredited quisling government. The result was an extended period of time during which the Japanese or their collaborators continued to function in authoritative positions with the explicit sanction of the KMT Government. The *Ta kung pao* attributed this to the highest KMT authorities and referred to it somewhat caustically as the principle of "signing the surrender first and taking over the government later."[9]

The Communist press took advantage of the situation to question specifically why proclamations and decrees were being issued in the recovered areas on the authority of the puppet officials themselves rather than the KMT Government, and why high-ranking collaborators were being rewarded with equally high-ranking positions by the KMT. Why, queried the *Hsin hua jih-pao,* are men such as the puppet Mayor of Shanghai, Chou Fo-hai, and the puppet military commander in Nanking being allowed to publish in their own right proclamations which should come from Chungking?[10]

The first newspaper correspondents to arrive in Nanking, capital of the Wang Ching-wei government, found it odd that except for a few Chinese soldiers in the streets and the occasional arrival of American transport planes, "there is nothing in Nanking that indicates its liberation. . . . Okamura is still enthroned in the Foreign Ministry Building. Japanese gendarmes still occupy the former premises of the Judicial Yuan. Japanese sentries are posted everywhere, with orders to maintain peace and protect their compatriots . . ."[11]. Another correspondent reported the same conditions a week later. He wrote also that until September 4,

7. *Hsin hua jih-pao*, Chungking, Sept. 17 and 20, Oct. 5, 6 and 22, 1945 (*CPR*, same dates except Oct. 23 for last cited).

8. *Shih-shih hsin pao*, Chungking, Nov. 30, 1945 (*CPR*, Dec. 3). In January, 1947, there were still 80,000 Japanese troops in the Northeast being used to fight the Communists (Melby, *Mandate of Heaven*, p. 183). Japanese troops were retained in Shansi until 1949 for the same purpose at the request of Yen Hsi-shan. When Taiyuan fell to the Communists in April, 1949, the Shansi forces were under the command of one General Imamura Hosaku, who committed suicide rather than surrender (Donald G. Gillin, *Warlord: Yen Hsi-shan in Shansi Province, 1911-1949*, pp. 286-88; John Hunter Boyle, *China and Japan at War, 1937-45: the Politics of Collaboration*, pp. 329-31).

9. *TKP*, Chungking, Sept. 9, 1945 (*CPR*, Sept. 12).

10. *Hsin hua jih-pao*, Chungking, Aug. 25 and Oct. 3, 1945 (*CPR*, Aug. 28 and Oct. 3).

11. Report dated Aug. 30 in *TKP*, Chungking, Sept. 9, 1945 (*CPR*, Sept. 12).

Nanking newspapers were still being censored by Japanese agents. Posters and slogans of the puppet government, of which the motto "National Salvation through Peace" was the most prominent, were still to be seen in all parts of the city.[12] Similar conditions were reported from other cities as well.

In addition, Chungking newspapers soon began reporting the ease with which officials in the former puppet government were returning to the KMT fold. The process was said to be no more difficult than putting up a new signboard outside one's office. Demands that puppet officials be subjected to some form of punishment or moral sanction and barred from holding public office were supported by the Government in official statements but often ignored in practice. There were reports that high-ranking Chinese collaborators were being allowed to escape to Japan and that many lesser puppet officials were busy contacting members of the Advance Command Post of the Chinese Army in Nanking, the first official representative of the KMT Government to return to the capital. "In China," wrote the *Ta kung pao* on September 9, "no matter what happens, there is always the same set of career bureaucrats. They are so interrelated that no one of them can go without drawing the whole bunch after him. The more sensitive of the newspaper people turned their coats one after another, and puppet papers are now singing the same tune as their Chungking brothers although their editors had before the Japanese surrender vigorously advocated the 'Greater East Asia' and the 'National Salvation through Peace' policy."

Among the cases that aroused the sharpest comment was that of Chou Fo-hai, Mayor of Shanghai at the end of the war, a former vice-chairman of the puppet Executive Yuan while concurrently Minister of Finance in the Wang Ching-wei government, and the most powerful man in the puppet regime after Wang's demise in 1944. As soon as Japan surrendered, Chou announced the formation of a special action corps with which he promised to ensure public order in Shanghai and thereby demonstrate his loyalty to the KMT and the nation. Commenting on this case, one correspondent wrote that "the common people can only raise infuriated cries as they see how those people who used to bully and oppress them are still assuming and enjoying power."[13]

By the end of September, the issue had grown to major proportions. The press was unanimous in demanding punishment for the collaborators. At stake, it was argued, was the integrity of the nation. If these people were not punished in some way, queried the critics, why should people remain loyal in the event of another national crisis?[14] During the public clamor and in apparent response, a set of regulations for the punishment of collaborators was drafted by the Executive Yuan, revised by the Resident Committee of the People's Political Council, and approved by the Council. Some rushed to praise the regulations, and a number of arrests that followed their publication in late September, as

12. *Shih-chieh jih-pao*, Chungking, Sept. 9, 1945 (*CPR*, Sept. 10).
13. *Ta kung wan-pao*, Chungking, Sept. 12, 1945 (*CPR*, Sept. 14).
14. *Shih-shih hsin pao*, Chungking, Sept. 19, 1945 *(CPR)*; *WHP*, Shanghai, Sept. 29, 1945 *(CPR)*; *TKP*, Chungking, Oct. 3, 1945 *(CPR)*.

having "completely dispelled" the doubts created by the Government's delay in punishing puppets and traitors.[15]

Others looked more closely at the regulations and found much to criticize. The most heated questions arose over article four. This stipulated that puppet officials who had served the war of resistance, or done something beneficial for the people during their tenure in office, could appeal for leniency. Before a week had passed, even those who had initially applauded the regulations acknowledged that some of the most notorious collaborators—who until a few months previously had been the mere mouthpieces of the Japanese—had suddenly turned themselves into patriots. This they did claiming to have aided the anti-Japanese resistance in "underground activities," a claim that could often be substantiated for an appropriate monetary consideration. Public cynicism grew as claims of secret patriotism proliferated.

Another controversial loophole in the regulations allowed special treatment for those who had surrendered prior to August 10, 1945. No one had to wait until that date, the critics claimed, to know that Japan was going to lose the war. Finally, the regulations were criticized for placing too much emphasis on position and rank while neglecting even to level moral sanctions against lower-level puppet officials who had, in the process of carrying out orders, committed crimes against the people. Despite the arrest at this time of several prominent members of the Wang Ching-wei regime, including Chou Fo-hai, there was no systematic effort to bring all of the claims and accusations before an impartial court or official body.[16]

One report in late November noted that, while a number of the most notorious collaborators had finally been arrested in Shanghai, Nanking, and Canton, not even one had yet been taken into custody in the North.[17] A few

15. *Chien-sien jih-pao,* Shanghai, Sept. 29, 1945 *(CPR); Lih pao* and *Lien-ho jih-pao,* Shanghai, Oct. 2, 1945 *(CPR).*

16. *Chien-sien jih-pao,* Shanghai, Oct. 4, 1945 *(CPR); Chung mei jih-pao* and *WHP,* Shanghai, Sept. 29, 1945 *(CPR).*

Chou Fo-hai was taken into custody on October 3, 1945, and flown to Chungking under house arrest. At his trial in 1946, he declared, like many others, that he had been in underground contact with agents of the Chungking Government and specifically with its secret service chief, General Tai Li, during the war. Chou claimed he had been in contact with Tai Li since 1941, and had been placed in command of the special action corps by Chungking on August 14, 1945, to hold Shanghai against the Communists, then rumored to be preparing an attack against the city. KMT troops did not arrive in force in Shanghai for over a month, during which time Chou was responsible for maintaining law and order. But Tai Li's death in a plane crash on March 17, 1946, removed the primary source of knowledge about the claimed underground contacts with Chungking. After Chou was sentenced to death, Chiang Kai-shek commuted the sentence to life imprisonment. Chou died in prison in 1948. Collaborators actually executed by the KMT Government included Ch'en Kung-po, Liang Hung-chih, Wang I-t'ang, Mei Szu-p'ing, Lin Pai-sheng, and Ch'u Min-i. *Hsin sheng pao,* Peiping, July 21, 1946 *(CPR,* Peiping-Tientsin, July 23); *Shih-chieh jih-pao,* Peiping, Jan. 29, 1947 *(CPR,* Peiping-Tientsin); Chu Tzu-chia, *Wang cheng-ch'üan te k'ai-ch'ang yü shou-ch'ang,* 3:77; Boyle, *China and Japan,* pp. 332-33.

17. *TKP,* Shanghai, Nov. 28, 1945 *(CPR);* also *Shih-chieh jih-pao,* Peiping, Apr. 24, 1946 *(CPR,* Peiping-Tientsin).

were arrested there, but many more who had served the Japanese in official capacities were entrusted with equally influential posts by the KMT Government. Ch'en I, accused of collaborating during his tenure as Governor of Fukien province (1934-41), was appointed Governor of Taiwan.[18] Two full years after the Japanese surrender, a non-Communist newspaper in Mukden would express wonder that the Government had still made no move to punish former officials of the puppet Manchukuo government, but was instead allowing them to fill political and administrative posts in the KMT-controlled areas of the Northeast.[19]

Perhaps most resented was the Government's use of high-ranking military collaborators who had been directly engaged in fighting their compatriots on behalf of the Japanese.[20] Among these collaborators was Li Shou-hsin, Minister of War in the puppet Mongolian Autonomous Government. A non-Communist newspaper identified Li as one of the first generals to betray his country and lead a force under the Japanese, even before the Marco Polo Bridge Incident in 1937 which marked the official beginning of the Anti-Japanese War in China.[21] After the war, the KMT Government appointed him commander of its Tenth Route Army. Another puppet military leader, Men Ping-yueh, was made commander of the Government's Ninth Route Army. Yet another was Li Hsien-liang. An officer in the Imperial Cooperation Army in the region of Tsingtao before the Japanese surrender, he was appointed mayor of the city shortly afterwards.

Chao Pao-yuan was a commander in the Manchukuo Army before 1937. After the Marco Polo Bridge Incident, the Japanese transferred him to Shantung where he allegedly participated in the Japanese mopping-up campaigns against the Communist guerrillas and their peasant supporters. In 1944, the Japanese appointed him commander of the Anti-Communist Army of the Chiaotung Peninsula. After their surrender, he fled to Tsingtao but returned to the field shortly thereafter having been recommissioned a divisional commander in the Chinese armed forces. He was killed either during or after a skirmish with the Communists near Tsingtao in June, 1946. Another alleged participant in the notorious mopping-up campaigns was Wang Chi-mei, who was recommissioned by the KMT in January, 1946, and captured in June by the Communists who tried and executed him as a war criminal.

Chiang Peng-fei worked with the Japanese in Dairen and Mukden, organized puppet armies for them in eastern Hopei, and had been sent to Japan for further military studies. After the war, he was placed in command of the KMT's New Twenty-Seventh Army, also in eastern Hopei. In March, 1946, he and his troops were flown to Changchun in the Northeast to take over from the departing forces of the Soviet Union. He was entrusted with the tasks of re-grouping the Manchukuo

18. The accusations against Ch'en I (not to be confused with the Communist general having a similar name) are cited in Boyle, *China and Japan*, p. 334. Concerning the case of Wang K'o-min, who died in a Peiping prison in December, 1945, see p. 333.

19. *Tung-pei chien-feng jih-pao*, Mukden, Sept. 20, 1947 *(CPR)*.

20. *Shih-chieh jih-pao*, Peiping, Apr. 24, 1946 (*CPR*, Peiping-Tientsin).

21. *Yi shih pao*, Peiping, Sept. 21, 1946 (*CPR*, Peiping-Tientsin).

troops and organizing uprisings in the Communist-held areas of the Northeast. He was executed in Harbin on September 10, 1946, together with Li Ming-hsin and Chui Ta-kang, as conspirators to stage an armed uprising there and retake the city from the Chinese Communists. Li Ming-hsin, said to have been a Japanese agent during the war, was military commissioner of the Enemy Rear Area Work Committee under the KMT Central Executive Committee afterward. Chui Ta-kang was said to have moved back and forth between the Japanese and Government sides several times during his career and was an officer in the KMT Sixth Route Army at the time of the ill-fated plot in Harbin. A similar plot in the Communist-occupied city of Kalgan resulted in the execution there of Liu Chieh-hsun. Liu allegedly headed a secret service detachment under the Japanese in Tientsin and had been recruited into the KMT secret police soon after the Japanese surrender.[22]

General Ho Ying-ch'in described the Japanese Commander-in-Chief, Okamura Yasuji, as being engaged in "liaison work" at the end of November, 1945.[23] One Nanking newspaper noted on the occasion of his return to Japan in February, 1947, that the Government obviously felt no concern about this man's responsibility for so many Chinese deaths. "We wonder," concluded the editorial, "if a grand farewell party will be given in his honor to mark this occasion."[24]

The KMT was apparently not alone, however, in its use of enemy forces. At his trial, Chou Fo-hai declared that he had resisted offers made by Communist agents to put him at the head of one of their armies, a claim not easily verified. The case of Hao Peng-chu was more substantial. He had served as a commander in the puppet forces. After 1945, he went over to the Communists who appointed him commander of their Kiangsu-Shantung Democratic Allied Army. Toward the end of 1946 at the height of the Government offensive in the area, he changed his mind again and brought his troops over to the Government side, seriously damaging the Communist position in northern Kiangsu. Nevertheless, the allegations of post-war Communist cooperation with the Japanese and their collaborators were far exceeded by the number of confirmed cases on the Government side. As a result, the Government bore the brunt of public resentment over the issue.

Thus, however necessary the Government may have regarded the assistance of the Japanese and their collaborators in its conflict with the Communists, that help—and the seemingly unconcerned manner in which it was solicited—was not without heavy cost. In a typical comment, one Peiping (the official name of the city until changed back to Peking by the Communists in September, 1949) newspaper declared it "impossible to hide our contempt and anger with regard to such a serious problem." A few thousand puppet rifles, it asserted, could not be decisive in defeating the CCP; but the use of them was a major blow against

22. *Hsin hua jih-pao,* Chungking, Sept. 17 and 27, Oct. 3 and 25, Nov. 7, 1945 (*CPR,* same dates); Hsinhua News Agency, Yenan, June 14 and 20, Sept. 15 and 28, 1946 (*FYI,* Shanghai, June 15 and 21, Sept. 16 and 29).
23. *Shih-shih hsin pao,* Chungking, Nov. 30, 1945 (*CPR,* Dec. 3).
24. *Hsin min pao,* Nanking, Feb. 21, 1947 (*CPR,* Feb. 24).

national discipline and morality.[25] A Chungking newspaper summarized the issue in similar terms:

> One more disappointment of the people is the question of traitors. One batch of traitors has been arrested, but the whole group of traitors and puppets in the Tientsin and Peiping area has scarcely been touched. Most of the traitors in the puppet army have been "reorganized" and "reverted to normal" and are occupying their original posts in security. In Nanking and Shanghai, many traitors have changed their coats and are seeking new posts in the various government offices. These traitors were objects of intense hatred of the people. Now victory is here they have not been summarily brought to punishment. Can there still be any sense of justice in the world?[26]

CORRUPTION

Just as the Government offered no authoritative procedures for resolving fairly the issue of collaboration, so also it failed to provide any equitable and orderly means for disposing of enemy property. The carpetbagging official from Chungking became the hallmark of the reconversion period. According to his popular image, he had five preoccupations: gold bars, automobiles, houses, Japanese women, and face.[27] It was largely over the issue of official corruption that the *Ta kung pao* wrote on September 27: "We have lost the hearts of the people in Nanking and Shanghai within a short span of twenty or more days."

Simply stated, *chieh-shou* (reconversion) referred to the process whereby civilian and military officials representing the KMT Government took control of all political, administrative, and military organs of the puppet government, as well as all properties—both public and private—owned by the Japanese and their collaborators in the former occupied territories of China. In the case of property such as factories, offices, storage facilities, and dwellings, the take-over process involved sealing the asset in question. After investigation, the property was to be either returned to its original owner if it had been taken illegally by the Japanese, or handed over to a new owner in accordance with officially established procedure. Pending disposal in this manner, sealed factories were required to cease production. The movement of stocks in or out of sealed warehouses was officially prohibited. Tenants and occupants of sealed dwellings were required to vacate them.

The success of such an endeavor at such a time depended in large measure on the integrity of the implementing officials, for there were few institutional

---

25. *Shih-chieh jih-pao*, Peiping, Jan. 29, 1947 (*CPR*, Peiping-Tientsin).

26. *Hsin min pao*, Chungking, Nov. 5, 1945 (*CPR*, Nov. 4-5).

27. Wang Chien-min, *Chung-kuo kung-ch'an-tang shih-kao*, 3:544. The five items are *chin-tzu, ch'e-tzu, fang-tzu, jih-pen nü-tzu, mien-tzu*. As well as being descriptive, these five words are puns on the word "tzu," which means son but, as here, is also a common noun ending. During this period, the five items were popularly referred to as *wu tzu teng-k'o*, an old expression meaning "five sons have passed the examinations." The prosperity of such a family was assured—as was the prosperity of the reconversion officials. For a fictionalized account of the period, see the novel by Chang Hen-shui, *Wu tzu teng-k'o*.

safeguards. The path to corruption lay open, uncluttered by any overall plan or coordinated policy delineating what was to be taken over by whom. Instead, there issued in August and September a disconcerting array of orders and decrees by a variety of military and government authorities.

THE FORMALITIES: OFFICIAL DECREES AND ADMINISTRATIVE MACHINERY

On August 28, the Executive Yuan of the Chinese Government issued a decree declaring null and void all land deeds registered with the Japanese and puppet authorities. [28] Almost a month passed, however, before the authorities began announcing specific regulations for the liquidation of enemy-owned land and property. Meanwhile, a diverse assortment of individuals representing various military, political, and administrative bodies had begun arriving from Chungking. These officials converged first on Nanking and Shanghai and then fanned out to reoccupy cities and towns to the north and south. Alleged enemy property was taken over by whoever was able to stake the first claim. A report dated September 7 described how this was being accomplished in Shanghai. Japanese and puppet troops were still being used to maintain law and order in the city and its suburbs. Nevertheless, anyone with a rifle or two could put on the armband of the Shanghai Military Affairs Council. Under the pretext of rounding up traitors and puppets, such people were occupying houses, making arbitrary arrests, requisitioning automobiles, and taking over entire factories. [29]

A decree issued on September 14, by the Commanding Headquarters of the Chinese Armed Forces sought to inject some order into the process. The movement or destruction of furniture, equipment, machinery, documents, or records belonging to the Japanese Army was forbidden. All properties originally belonging to Chinese or allied nationals, which had been occupied by the Japanese Army, were to be handed over to the Chinese military authorities. All Japanese stores, factories, and banks were to compile and present to the Chinese Army detailed records describing the assets, liabilities, and location of the enterprises. [30]

On September 19, the take-over of civilian properties "officially" began in Shanghai. The Ministry of Economic Affairs, on orders from the Commander-in-Chief of the Army, began the take-over of Japanese cotton mills in the city. [31] By September 20, the Ministry of Finance had completed a set of draft regulations for the liquidation of civilian financial and business organs. All commercial and financial establishments registered with the puppet government were to be liquidated and their shareholders required to bear unlimited liability. In the Nanking-Shanghai area, the liquidation of financial organs would be supervised by a Special Representative of the Ministry of Finance. The Special

28. *Ch'ing-nien jih-pao,* Shanghai, Sept. 22, 1945 *(CPR).*
29. *Ta kung wan-pao,* Chungking, Sept. 12, 1945 *(CPR,* Sept. 14).
30. *Ch'ing-nien jih-pao,* Shanghai, Sept. 17, 1945 *(CPR).*
31. *Chien-sien jih-pao,* Shanghai, Sept. 20, 1945 *(CPR).*

Representative immediately announced the transfer of five major Japanese banking institutions to the control of Chinese bankers.[32]

During the next four months, national and local officials issued a succession of *ad hoc* measures inadequate in design and more so in application. On September 21, the headquarters of the Third Army Group (responsible for the defense of the Shanghai area), called a meeting of local military, administrative, and KMT officials. Among the decisions reached was that "no individuals or organs will be allowed to arrest people or seal properties without following legal procedures and, in order to protect lawful rights, those who violate this order will be accorded severe punishment by the Commanding Headquarters if such matters are discovered." It was also decided to set up a joint group of local military, administrative, and Party authorities to coordinate their take-over operations. Such a group was formed as the Surrendered Enemy and Puppet Organs and Properties Acceptance Committee.[33] During the final week of September, offices and properties in Shanghai taken over by this Committee included eighty-three hospitals; ninety-three pharmaceutical companies, dispensaries, and dairies; eighteen cultural enterprises; forty-four motor companies; seven broadcasting stations; ninety-five chemical companies; the Shanghai Urban Transportation Company; the Central China Salt Company and its warehouses; the Income Tax Bureau and its affiliated offices; the Tax Revenue Bureau and its affiliated offices; and the wharves belonging to the Whangpoo Conservancy Bureau.[34]

The Surrendered Enemy and Puppet Organs and Properties Acceptance Committee did not, however, remain in charge of all take-over activities in Shanghai. At the National Day celebrations on October 10, the Mayor of Shanghai announced the formation of two additional organs to handle disputes arising locally over the restoration of surrendered enemy properties to their original owners in cases where such properties had been illegally seized and occupied. These two bodies were the Realty Disposal Committee and the Enemy and Puppet Occupied Civilian Industrial and Commercial Enterprises Disposal Committee. Also on October 10, the *Chung-yang jih-pao* reported that during the preceding few days, over five hundred factory units had been taken over in the name of the Special Representatives of the Wartime Productions Bureau of the Ministry of Economic Affairs for the Nanking-Shanghai area. The Bureau had authorized over a thousand persons to carry out this task. By November, enemy property in Shanghai had been taken over in the name of at least ten different organizations. These included the Third Army Group, the Chief Command

32. *Chien-sien jih-pao,* and *Kuang hua jih-pao,* Shanghai, Sept. 21, 1945 *(CPR).* The Bank of Taiwan was taken over by the Farmers Bank of China; the Yokohama Specie Bank by the Bank of China; the Sumitomo Bank by the Bank of Communications; and the Mitsui and Mitsubishi Banks by the Central Trust.

33. *Chung mei jih-pao,* Shanghai, Sept. 22, 1945 *(CPR); CYJP,* Shanghai, Oct. 4, 1945 *(CPR).*

34. *Cheng yien pao,* Shanghai, Oct. 3, 1945 *(CPR).*

Headquarters of the Chinese Navy, the Shanghai Office of the Ministry of War, the Shanghai Office of the Special Commissioner of the Ministry of Economic Affairs, the Shanghai Office of the Special Representative of the Food Administration, the Shanghai Municipal Government, and the Ministry of Communications.[35]

As a gesture in the direction of national coordination, the Temporary Office of the Executive Yuan issued an order on October 12, requiring all central party, governmental, and military bodies, as well as local Party and governmental administrative units, to submit detailed reports by 6:00 P.M. on October 15, concerning all enemy and puppet organs, factories, warehouses, buildings, real estate, automobiles, trucks, shipping vessels, and other materials taken over as of October 12.[36] Then on October 20, the formation of a National Surrendered Enemy and Puppet Properties Acceptance Commission was announced. This was headed by Dr. Weng Wen-hao, Vice-president of the Executive Yuan and Minister of Economic Affairs. The Commission was to include officials appointed by the Ministries of Finance, Communications, Agriculture, and experts selected from local financial and industrial circles.[37]

In the Shanghai area, two additional bodies were formed in late October to supervise take-over work. These were a Committee for the Supervision of Enemy and Puppet Properties and a Bureau for the Disposal of Enemy and Puppet Properties both under Dr. Weng's National Commission.[38] At the same time, the Shanghai office of the Maritime Customs was assigned the task of investigating, taking over, and guarding all of the stocks in enemy-owned warehouses in Shanghai. This meant that Maritime Customs personnel often had to retake these warehouses, since the majority had already been taken over by officials representing various military units and government departments. Over two hundred men from the Customs embarked upon this task in mid-November. By the first week of January, 1946, they had taken control of some five hundred warehouses.[39]

In addition to all of the above, an Office of the Special Commissioner of the Control Yuan for Kiangsu Province was opened in Shanghai and was largely occupied with the investigation of reported corruption cases. On the basis of its investigations, this office made recommendations for punishment and sent reports of findings to the central authorities.[40] Then, on December 10, two Special Representatives of the Central Government for the Southeast Region arrived in Shanghai to investigate popular complaints arising from the take-over

35. *Shih-shih hsin pao,* Shanghai, Oct. 11, 1945 *(CPR); Cheng yien pao,* Shanghai, Nov. 14, 1945 *(CPR).*

36. *CYJP,* Shanghai, Oct. 13, 1945 *(CPR).*

37. *CYJP,* Shanghai, Oct. 20, 1945 *(CPR).*

38. *Lien-ho jih-pao,* Shanghai, Oct. 30, 1945 *(CPR).*

39. *Cheng yien pao,* Shanghai, Nov. 14, 1945; *Chien-sien jih-pao,* Shanghai, Nov. 27, 1945; *Hsin-wen pao,* Shanghai, Jan. 7, 1946 (*CPR,* same dates).

40. *Shen-chou jih-pao,* Shanghai, Nov. 29 and Dec. 5, 1945; *Chien-sien jih-pao,* Shanghai, Dec. 5, 1945 (*CPR,* same dates).

work.[41] And finally, the "Generalissimo's letterboxes" were set up in a few cities toward the end of December so that Chiang Kai-shek might acquaint himself personally with the grievances of anyone who wished to write an anonymous complaint against corrupt officials.[42]

THE REALITIES

The confused nature of the formal administrative apparatus, outlined above with particular reference to the Shanghai area, provides only a rough indication of the "irregularities" that characterized the take-over operation in practice.[43] On October 26, Chiang Kai-shek sent a telegram to Ch'ien Ta-chun, the new Mayor of Shanghai, reading in part:

> It has been reliably brought to my knowledge that the military, political and party officials in Nanking, Shanghai, Peiping and Tientsin have been leading extravagant lives, indulging in prostitution and gambling, and have forcibly occupied the people's larger buildings as offices under the assumed names of various party, military or political organizations. They have resorted to every perverse act, even including blackmailing. The worst conditions are said to be found in Shanghai and Peiping. I wonder if these officials are aware of what they are doing. Have you heard or seen anything in this connection? To be corrupted to this extent without any self-respect in the recovered areas is a disgrace to the local people, and a sin committed against our heroic martyrs who have been sacrificed in the war. I have been greatly distressed, and have also felt ashamed, on hearing reports of such conditions. . . . Upon receipt of this telegram you may give orders to the various departments to strictly forbid prostitution and gambling, and to close all those offices that have opened under the assumed names of various organizations. Any case of blackmailing or illegal occupation of the people's houses, must be severely dealt with by the municipal authorities on the one hand, and reported to me on the other. No culprit is to be harbored by personal favors.[44]

Yet no concerted actions were taken either by central or local authorities to enforce Chiang's wishes. In any event, by early November when those wishes were made public, most of the damage had already been done. The *Hsin min pao* noted the public gratitude for the President's warning to government officials; but it went on to speculate: if a few words for justice could evoke such gratitude, how great would be the loyal support of the Generalissimo by the people in the recovered areas if his words were put into practice. "Unfortunately," concluded the writer, "his subordinates make a great reduction of his

41. *Hsin-wen pao,* Shanghai, Dec. 13, 1945 (*CPR,* Dec. 14); *Chung mei jih-pao,* Shanghai, Dec. 27, 1945 *(CPR).*

42. *Cheng yien pao,* Shanghai, Dec. 22, 1945 *(CPR).*

43. The most detailed description in English of these irregularities may be the account of the take-over in Taiwan by George H. Kerr, *Formosa Betrayed,* esp. Chapters Five and Six.

44. *Hsin min pao,* Chungking, Nov. 2, 1945 (*CPR,* Nov. 3).

efforts. The affairs of the nation cannot rely entirely on one good Generalissimo and the good people."[45]

The Shanghai-Nanking Area

Orders and admonitions aimed at curbing corrupt practices were issued repeatedly. But the local officials responsible for their implementation were in most cases themselves engaged in the very practices the regulations were intended to control. For example, many of the returning officials brought with them large amounts of Chinese Government currency *(fapi)*, thus taking advantage of a situation in which the Central Government could not immediately supply the necessary amounts of *fapi* to the recovered areas, and at the same time delayed in fixing an exchange rate between *fapi* and puppet currency. The latter declined rapidly in value after V-J Day, but continued to circulate as legal tender for several months. Meanwhile, the commercial activities of the returning officials contributed to the rise in prices. Many persons, finding themselves in financial difficulties due to the inflation of puppet currency, were forced to sell their houses, land, and other property. The buyers were usually these government and military officials returning from the interior with large quantities of *fapi* in their pockets. The kindest evaluation of their conduct was the one suggesting that a number of profiteering merchants must have been "mixed in" with the returning officials.[46]

In late September, after such criticism had been widely aired in the press, the Central Government issued an order to all government organs in Chungking forbidding their take-over officials to carry large amounts of currency with them when returning to the recovered areas. Orders also prohibited reconversion personnel in the Nanking-Shanghai area from engaging in commercial activities, purchasing gold at arbitrarily fixed prices, or buying real estate in the name of government agencies.

Nevertheless, conditions did not improve. By the end of October, the word "Chungking-ite" had become a popular term of derision in Shanghai, where newly arrived personnel were rushing to appropriate for their own use property taken from the Japanese and their collaborators. Officials representing the Ministry of War quarreled with their counterparts in the Ministry of Economic Affairs over a certain flour mill—instead of returning it to the original Chinese owner from whom it had been seized by the Japanese.[47] Another famous case was that of the Twenty-third Regiment of the Central Gendarmerie Corps, ostensibly an elite unit restricted to high school and college graduates. Arriving in late August, 1945, it was one of the first military units to enter Shanghai. Members of the regiment were involved in the illegal arrest of civilians under the pretext of rounding up traitors, the take-over of privately-owned houses and vehicles, and

45. *Hsin min pao*, Chungking, Nov. 7, 1945 *(CPR)*.
46. *Shih-chieh jih-pao*, Chungking, Sept. 23, 1945 *(CPR)*.
47. *TKP*, Shanghai, Nov. 26, 1945 *(CPR)*.

the seizure of large quantities of essential commodities. After an unheeded warning from the Woosung-Shanghai Garrison Headquarters, the regimental commander was finally detained on October 12, and an official investigation announced.[48]

The reprimand to the Twenty-third Regiment, though a move in the right direction, was not sufficient to bring order to the overall situation. One of the most unfortunate consequences was the damage done to the economy. Factory equipment was dismantled and, together with stocks of commodities and raw materials, either sold or hoarded for future profit making. Commenting on the economic disruption, the *Ta kung pao* placed primary blame on the military units which had initially taken over many factories and warehouses in Shanghai. The military often refused to turn these over to the "rightful authorities." Factories could not resume production because army personnel refused to release raw materials sealed in factory warehouses, or to return transport vehicles. When civilian telephone workers began the job of putting communications back into operation, they discovered that a large number of telephones and other equipment had been removed and installed in the offices of army officers. Similarly, railway workers found they could not make necessary repairs because of the quantity of material and equipment removed by army personnel.[49]

Many of these irregularities were not officially "discovered" until the Shanghai Maritime Customs began its work in November. Some of its discoveries were disclosed in a report issued by the Special Commissioner of the Control Yuan for Kiangsu Province. He acknowledged that Customs personnel were encountering a number of difficulties in their investigatory work. For example, when turning over warehouses to the Customs officials, some government departments neglected to submit the names of warehouses located in outlying areas. Two warehouses mysteriously burned down within days after the Customs investigation was launched. Some officials and government units that had taken over warehouses flatly refused to transfer them to the Customs investigators, or even to allow inspection. In one instance, investigators were in the process of checking a warehouse when several unidentified trucks arrived. The goods in the godown were loaded onto the trucks which then drove off, the entire operation having been carried out under the eyes of the inspectors.[50]

A number of newspapers tried to make public in greater detail the cases to which the Commissioner's report referred. The Shanghai *Ta wan pao* reported that thirty drums of oil had disappeared from a warehouse on the evening of

48. *Ta wan pao,* Shanghai, Oct. 2, 1945 (*CPR,* Oct. 3); *Lien-ho jih-pao, Chien-sien jih-pao,* and *Lih pao,* all Shanghai, all Oct. 14, 1945 (all in *CPR,* Oct. 15). At this time, due to disruption caused by the large numbers of irregular troops in the Shanghai-Nanking area, General T'ang En-po, Commander of the Third Army Group, ordered their classification and reorganization into a special garrison army. Funds and salaries were to be officially provided, and their past practice of requisitioning supplies from the people was now officially prohibited.

49. *TKP,* Shanghai, Nov. 26, 1945 *(CPR).*

50. *Shen-chou jih-pao,* Shanghai, Nov. 29, 1945 *(CPR); TKP,* Shanghai, Dec. 4, 1945 *(CPR).*

November 7. On the night of November 11, a group of armed men were known to have broken into another warehouse. Yet the authorities refused to disclose any further details of these and other cases. The two warehouses which had mysteriously burned down were the second warehouse at the North Railway Station on November 20, and the Sakata Warehouse on Kowloon Road on November 26. The fires were allegedly set to destroy evidence against suspected thefts, but no investigations were made by local authorities after either incident.[51]

During the first month of its existence, that is from October 29 to the end of November, the Enemy and Puppet Properties Supervision Committee, on the basis of information supplied by the public, handled over five hundred cases of attempts to conceal enemy property in the Shanghai area. The property in question included four thousand tons of copper and iron, over five hundred pieces of machinery, eighty rolls of newsprint, five factories, and large quantities of cloth, rice, flour, and liquor.

Other cases brought to light at this time included the chief of the Chapei police station in Shanghai, who collaborated with other policemen in the theft of fifty bags of sugar from a sealed warehouse. Another was the Peilin and Shanghai Cold Storage Plant, formerly managed by the Ordnance Bureau of the Japanese Navy. The plant, containing large stores of fish and meat, was taken over by Chinese naval authorities shortly after V-J Day. In late November, it was discovered that these officers had used part of the stock to feed their own men and war prisoners. But they had sold the rest together with stores in a warehouse at the Tunghsuntai Wharf for over $56 million *fapi*.[52]

As for the Enemy and Puppet Properties Disposal Bureau, one Shanghai newspaper acknowledged two months after its formation that the Bureau had entrusted the Customs authorities with the task of checking up and taking over the surrendered warehouses; that there had been a public sale of salt-preserved fish and cotton cloth; and that T. V. Soong, President of the Executive Yuan, had been making inquiries into the work of the Disposal Bureau. But little else was known about its work or that of the Customs inspectors. By this time, commented the paper, they should have submitted a detailed report concerning the exact nature of the commodities stored in the five hundred warehouses they had taken over. This was all the more important given the shortage of materials necessary to maintain the people's livelihood and the city's industrial production. Many months later, the public did learn what had happened to some of the goods. Officials of the Shanghai municipal government were charged with the illegal sale of enemy-owned commodities valued at $4 billion in *fapi*. Information about this sale was given by a former employee of the city government after a smaller case was made public involving the illegal sale of 130 automobiles by city officials.[53]

51. *Ta wan pao,* Shanghai, Dec. 5, 1945 *(CPR,* Dec. 6).

52. *TKP,* Shanghai, Dec. 3 and 4, 1945 *(CPR); Lih pao,* Shanghai, Nov. 29, 1945 *(CPR).*

53. *Hsin-wen pao,* Shanghai, Jan. 7, 1946 *(CPR); WHP,* Shanghai, Sept. 3, 1946 *(CPR).*

In Soochow, commercial establishments reportedly had to pay up to $10 million in Japanese puppet currency to the new authorities before being allowed to reopen their doors for business. Many small towns were ordered to contribute large sums on a monthly basis to irregular pro-Government troops operating in their vicinity.[54] Government officials in nearby rural areas took it upon themselves to search civilian houses on any pretext and occupied many illegally. Local merchants were often compelled to sell commodities to officials at artificially low prices.[55]

In Hsuchow, four waves of take-over officials swept through the city between August, 1945, and March, 1946, when the take-over of enemy properties still had not been completed. The first batch of officials came as part of the Advance Headquarters of the Tenth War Zone. The second came with the return of the local headquarters of the KMT. The third was officials from the Ministry of War; and the fourth, officials from the Ministries of Food and Economic Affairs. These officials seized large quantities of goods including rice, flour, cigarettes, and other daily necessities. In many cases, factory production could not resume—due to the disappearance of raw materials and the dismantling of machinery.[56]

The Hunan Motor Vehicles Case

Since the Shanghai-Nanking area was the first to be reoccupied by Central Government personnel, it might have been expected that the irregularities committed there would not be repeated elsewhere. Such was not the case. At a press conference in mid-April, 1946, responsible officials of the Highway Bureau of Hunan made public the extent of the corruption that had accompanied the take-over of enemy vehicles in the province. Most of these were originally taken over by the Hunan office of the War Transportation Board, an agency supervised by the Ministry of Communications. Approximately 3,500 vehicles were taken over by the Board; 1,000 of these were then turned over to the Highway Bureau.

According to the report of the Highway Bureau, its work was accomplished in three stages. The first lasted from November 3 to early December, 1945. During this time, the Bureau took over 50 trucks from the Fourth Service of Supply Station of the Army. About 20 percent of the parts were missing from these vehicles. During the next phase, which lasted from mid-December to January, 1946, the Bureau took over 250 vehicles from the Hunan Office of the War Transportation Board. The Highway Bureau charged that approximately half the parts of these vehicles were missing at the time of take-over. Finally, between the end of February and mid-April, the Bureau took over another 700 vehicles from the War Transportation Board, but these had been so thoroughly picked over that they "no longer looked like vehicles." Not one of the 1,000 Japanese and puppet vehicles taken over by the Highway Bureau could be used. The

54. *TKP*, Chungking, Nov. 1, 1945 (*CPR*, Nov. 3).
55. *Hsin-wen pao*, Shanghai, Dec. 13, 1945 (*CPR*, Dec. 14).
56. *WHP*, Shanghai, Mar. 18, 1946 (*CPR*, Mar. 27).

dismantled portions gradually made their reappearance as spare parts in the auto repair shops and hardware stores of Hunan. Meanwhile, the Hunan Highway Bureau had only 60 to 70 vehicles with which to maintain government transport for the entire province.

On the day following these disclosures, the Hunan office of the War Transportation Board, conscious that its reputation had been compromised by the Bureau's report, called a press conference of its own. Its representatives declared that of the 3,438 vehicles taken over by the Board, including the 1,000 handed over to the Highway Bureau, none was intact when the Board originally took possession of them.[57] During this period, the Government was experiencing serious communications difficulties. These were regularly blamed for the shortages of raw materials and other commodities, as well as for military logistical problems. Apparently, these difficulties were not all caused by the "military situation," as was usually claimed.

The Northeast

Even more serious, in view of the Government's rapidly deteriorating military position there and the strategic significance of the area, were the conditions created by take-over personnel in Manchuria. In early 1946, the Democratic League newspaper, *Min-chu pao,* quoted Ning Meng-yen, a veteran political figure in the Northeast, as saying that the disregard by reconversion officials for the feelings and demands of the local population was the chief cause underlying the Government's difficulties in Manchuria.[58] Almost two years after the Japanese surrender, a KMT newspaper in Mukden, commenting on the reasons for the loss of popular confidence in the Central Government, expressed regret that the reconversion personnel sent to Manchuria had "behaved so peculiarly." It called for the immediate dismissal of all corrupt officials still holding responsible positions.[59]

Despite the Soviet removal of a large portion of the Northeast's industrial equipment, much still remained. According to the *Ta kung pao,* 80 percent of the machinery in the Fushun coal mines was undamaged, and the equipment remaining in the Showa Iron Works at Anshan was capable of turning out three locomotives and one hundred railway cars per month. Steel refining equipment was left untouched; installations in the industrial districts of Chinhsi remained intact; and part of the equipment in the cotton mills of Liaoyang was also serviceable. Hydroelectric power generating equipment also remained intact, although most thermal power equipment had been removed. Thus the industrial capacity of Manchuria was still considerable after the Soviet departure.[60] But once the Soviet Army moved out, the KMT officials moved in to claim their

57. *Hsin-wen pao,* Shanghai, Apr. 29, 1946 *(CPR,* May 15).

58. *Min-chu pao,* Chungking, Feb. 17, 1946 *(CPR,* Feb. 18).

59. *Tung-pei chien-feng jih-pao,* Mukden, July 31 and Aug. 23, 1947 *(CPR).*

60. *TKP,* Shanghai, May 3, 1946 *(CPR).* On the Soviet removals from Manchuria, see *China White Paper,* pp. 596-604.

share of the spoils. [61] The Mukden edition of the *Ho-p'ing jih-pao,* reporting on the disposal of enemy-owned industry in the Northeast admitted: "There have even been cases where the successful bidders not only have made no attempt to put the factories into operation, but have stripped them and sold the dismantled machinery as scrap iron." [62]

In Manchuria, as elsewhere, properties of the Japanese and of the Manchukuo government were requisitioned for the personal use or profit of the officials who were able to stake the first claim to them. In a story dated March 23, 1946, the correspondent of a Chungking newspaper described what he had seen in Mukden:

> There has been great confusion in the taking over. . . . First there was a scramble for industrial equipment, then for public buildings and real estate, and now government officials are competing for furniture. Buildings which have been empty for the past few months are now guarded by men sent by a certain official. A certain army officer has already taken over several thousand houses. The China Cultural Service, a KMT enterprise, has sent an expedition here and is busy taking over Japanese printing houses and book shops. A certain government agency whose representatives have just arrived here is very much disappointed because there is nothing left to take over. Some agencies, however, merely tore away the *feng t'iao* [paper strips bearing official seals used in sealing up houses, etc.,] of other government agencies and put up their own instead. The local populace was surprised by the fact that "Central Government men" are "no better" than others. [63]

Commenting on the possible consequences, another eyewitness account of these same conditions in Mukden concluded, "I fear that we will lose not only the Northeast, but the goodwill of the people." [64]

Over a year after these reports, the Mukden edition of the official *Chung-yang jih-pao* acknowledged that only a small fraction of the take-over work there had been satisfactorily accomplished. As an example, it cited conditions in one district of Mukden. Nearly all of the buildings had belonged to the Japanese, making them liable for take-over by the Chinese government. But instead of reverting to government custody pending disposal, the buildings soon became the private property of a few individuals. By September, 1947, some of the houses in the district had even been rented out to civilians who were paying rent to the new "owners." [65]

Swatting Flies

A meeting of the People's Political Council on March 29, 1946, strongly criticized the Government for refusing to take action against its take-over

61. Kao Ch'ao, Mukden dispatch, "Lei-yen k'an tung-pei" [Looking at the Northeast with tearful eyes], *KC,* Feb. 28, 1948, p. 17.

62. *Ho-p'ing jih-pao,* Mukden, Sept. 4, 1947 *(CPR).*

63. *Kuo-min kung pao,* Chungking, Mar. 25, 1946 *(CPR).*

64. *Hsin-wen pao,* Shanghai, Apr. 4, 1946 (*CPR,* Apr. 5); also, *TKP,* Shanghai, May 27, 1946 *(CPR).*

65. *CYJP,* Mukden, Sept. 13, 1947 *(CPR).*

officials, and accused it of purposely trying to shield them. One member after another rose to condemn conditions in his province. Han Han-fan, a member from Kwangtung, described the take-over work on Hainan Island as chaotic. Air Force officials took over many agricultural farms, although the Navy at least gained control of the China Merchants' Steam Navigation Company. One group of officials took over all gasoline stores, and another group seized all the automobiles. The result was that "those who have gasoline have no automobiles, while those who have cars have no gas for them." In another report on Kwangtung Province, Chang Liang-hsiu listed four examples to justify his charge that a "world of racketeers" had descended upon Canton: (1) The Governor of Kwangtung and the Commander of the New First Army agreed to allocate a number of buildings taken over from the Japanese for the use of the Provincial Political Council; before the Council could make use of the buildings, however, the troops had removed all the furniture. (2) The Shipping Control Commission of the Army Supply Corps seized for its own use all vessels in good condition. (3) All water and electrical equipment at Chungshan University, and equipment from other schools, was dismantled and removed by military personnel. (4) Persons who had actually worked as KMT underground agents in Japanese-occupied territory were now accepting bribes from Chinese collaborators in return for covering up their wartime activities.

Wang Li-chi reported that take-over personnel in Shantung had falsified the inventories of enemy and puppet properties, and that many such officials had grown wealthy through the sale of the properties in question. Liu Shu-mo disclosed how scores of government officials sent to the city of Hankow had appropriated everything they could lay their hands on. The meeting proposed that an investigation commission be set up by the Central Government to look once again into the events surrounding the take-over and disposal of Japanese properties.[66]

The proposal led to the formation of several Take-over Operations Investigation Teams by the Central Government. They began work the following summer. The teams were empowered to probe allegations of official malfeasance, to fix responsibility in specific cases, and to recommend punishment. Their work resulted only in a final wave of unfavorable publicity for the Government. Investigation teams for the Hopei-Chahar-Jehol-Suiyuan region, the Hunan-Hupei-Kiangsi region, and of course the Shanghai area, all unearthed many additional cases of malfeasance. Some were flamboyant enough to create minor sensations, even among a public now jaded by such disclosures. One of these involved Liu Nai-i, Director of the Naval Commissioner's Office in Peiping, whose three concubines were found to be in possession of over 100 ounces of gold, $10,000 in U.S. currency, 15 catties of pearls, and 150 expensive furs. Another famous disclosure at this time was the bribe of 1,000 ounces of gold reportedly accepted by C. K. Chang, Special Commissioner of the Ministry of

66. *Kuo-min kung pao,* Chungking, Mar. 30, 1946 *(CPR).*

Economic Affairs in Shanghai, in return for overlooking irregularities in the take-over of a textile mill by certain unnamed government officials.[67]

Investigators also learned that the Japanese had not only attached detailed inventories to all the properties they surrendered to Chinese officials, but had in addition kept duplicate copies. Japanese authorities turned over to Chiang Kai-shek five large crates of these duplicates to aid in the investigations after most of the take-over officials refused to submit the original inventories for inspection.[68]

But however incriminating the evidence, the Government failed once more to take decisive action. The teams had no authority to enforce their recommendations. After their investigations had been completed, the cases were often simply turned over to local authorities for prosecution. In some instances, local officials even barred the press from publishing the evidence uncovered by the investigation teams. For the most part, the culprits were subjected only to moral sanctions handed down by the informal court of public opinion. Cynicism as regards the investigation itself was openly expressed. It is difficult for a corrupt organization to cleanse itself, wrote a correspondent in the new Shanghai journal, *Kuan-ch'a*. He warned that the Government would have to expect even sharper barbs in the future if its investigators contented themselves with merely swatting flies.[69]

The leftist *Wen hui pao* was more explicit in its criticism, but concluded that the Government might still regain the confidence of the people if it insisted on a really thorough investigation and setting all accounts straight.[70] Three weeks later, however, the Government announced that the investigation teams would soon be de-activated, and the comments of the *Ta kung pao* indicated that their work had done little to restore public confidence. "From the take-over operations, as well as the investigation work, we can clearly see that in a country governed by bureaucrats, it is too difficult to prevent corruption," wrote the editor. "If we still desire honest administration, we should cultivate the power of the people . . . so that they may exercise their power in politics."[71]

Thus ended what was for the Government the most harmful episode of the take-over period.

THE ECONOMY

The third issue that undermined public confidence in the Government was its failure to implement effective economic and financial measures which the early

67. These and other disclosures were extensively reported in the Shanghai press from late August to the end of September, 1946. For example, *Ho-p'ing jih-pao*, Aug. 28; *Shun pao*, Aug. 30; *TKP*, Sept. 4; *WHP*, Sept. 28 (all in *CPR*, Shanghai, on dates of publication).

68. *Shun pao*, Shanghai, Sept. 18, 1946 *(CPR)*.

69. Tientsin correspondent, "T'an-wu t'ai to, t'uan-yuan t'ai shao; ta-hai lao chen, wu-ts'ung chuo-mo" [Greed is too great, team members are too few; there is no way to extract a needle from the sea], *KC*, Sept. 28, 1946, p. 20. In referring to swatting flies, the writer probably had in mind the old-fashioned horsehair fly whisk, which did little harm to the flies but only encouraged them to move on.

70. *WHP*, Shanghai, Sept. 4, 1946 *(CPR)*.

71. *TKP*, Shanghai, Sept. 25, 1946 *(CPR)*.

months of reconversion demanded. As many writers pointed out, these included measures to stabilize prices, curb speculation, and ease dislocations caused by the transition to a peace-time economy. The conduct of reconversion officials raised serious doubts about the Government's integrity and its actual—as opposed to its avowed—concern for the public welfare. In the economic sphere, the Government's record raised equally grave doubts about its political wisdom, as well as its competence in economic matters. The two issues of integrity and competence were, moreover, closely related. The Government's failure to minimize the economic dislocations caused by the war's end was in many respects the consequence of its failure to control the conduct of its take-over officials.

PROBLEMS IN THE SOUTHWEST

It had been assumed that the government would use the enterprises taken over from the Japanese and collaborators to compensate factory owners and businessmen who would be hurt by the inevitable demise of the now unprofitable wartime industries in the hinterland. In this way, the industrial base in the Japanese-occupied territories would be able to absorb the managerial and productive resources from the depressed areas of the interior. Secondly, the Government would be able to provide a suitable reward for its supporters in business and industrial circles who had followed it to the Southwest. Instead, the Government virtually abandoned them, as officials, profiteers, and bureaucratic capitalists were allowed to take over the industrial wealth of the recovered territories.

The key figures in this controversy were the medium and small industrialists who had left enterprises in Shanghai and elsewhere after the Japanese occupation, and moved to the hinterland. There they developed, with the minimal resources available to them, an industrial base which served the Government-controlled areas throughout the war. Their enterprises were handicapped by a scarcity of raw materials and capital, inferior equipment and techniques, small capacity, and transportation difficulties. Since many had suffered financial loss in the pursuit of what was generally considered to be patriotic duty, these entrepreneurs expected—and, indeed, had been promised—some sort of compensation for their loyalty once the war ended.

Suspicions that the Government might overlook its political and economic debt to them arose soon after the Japanese surrender. Rumors began to circulate in Chungking that certain highly-placed officials were showing unexpected concern for the hardship suffered by industry in the occupied areas during the war. Industrial leaders in the wartime capital, sensing that something was amiss, issued a public statement appealing for the transfer of all Japanese and puppet-owned factories to industrialists who had followed the Government to the Southwest. They also proposed that the Government invite them to participate in the planning and initial take-over of these factories.[72]

For many of these men the question soon became one of economic survival. By mid-September, the industrial economy in the Southwest was verging on collapse. The signs were indisputable: declining demand, a sharp fall in prices, a

---

72. *Shang-wu jih-pao,* Chungking, Aug. 18, 1945 *(CPR).*

shortage of liquid capital, closing factories, an increase in the number of bankruptcy cases, and rising unemployment. Within one month after V-J Day, the price of gold in Chungking fell from CNC (Chinese Nationalist Currency) $200,000 to CNC$48,000 per ounce, the price of wool from CNC$110,000 to CNC$30,000 per *tan,* and the price of tung oil from CNC$70,000 to CNC$17,000 per *tan.* Other prices followed suit.[73] The sharp drop in commodity prices fell heavily on speculator and legitimate entrepreneur alike, since investment in gold and merchandise had become the most common hedge against wartime inflation.

But despite the slump in prices there were few buyers. Many factories in the Southwest had been established to meet wartime needs and were maintained almost entirely by orders from the War Production Board. These were forced to suspend operations after orders were reduced or curtailed in mid-August. One major producer of iron and steel in the Southwest during the war had closed down most of its installations by mid-September. The state-operated Chungking Iron and Steel Works had virtually suspended operations by the end of the month. At the same time, it was also reported that cotton mills in Szechwan would soon have to stop production due to the scarcity of cotton. Despite good harvests in Hupeh and Shensi, transportation difficulties made it impossible to bring the raw cotton to Szechwan. An estimated 100,000 *tan* of enemy-owned cotton was sealed and therefore frozen in the godowns of the recovered areas. The cotton was thus unavailable for use even if it had been feasible to transport it to the interior.[74] Most of the small-scale tobacco factories in Chungking were also forced to close down, as were many commercial firms.

According to statistics compiled by the Yunnan Branch of the China Federation of Industries in November, 1945, thirty-seven of the seventy-seven industrial establishments in the city of Kunming had closed down. The others were operating on a reduced basis. By February, 1946, an estimated 90 percent of Kunming's industries had ceased production.[75]

Seeking to make political capital from the Government's failure to acknowledge the "patriotic contributions" of its capitalist supporters, the Communists issued a statement supporting the appeals of Chungking industrialists and demanding relief for unemployed workers.[76] The Government did announce a five billion dollar appropriation for industrial relief loans, but this figure was insufficient to meet even the needs of industrial and mining concerns in the vicinity of Chungking.

A hastily organized Szechwan Reconversion Association presented a petition to the Central Government requesting immediate substantial relief for agricultural, industrial, commercial, mining, and financial enterprises in the province.[77] It was generally acknowledged, however, that even if these demands were met it

73. *Hsin hua jih-pao,* Chungking, Sept. 13, 1945 *(CPR).*
74. *Hsin min pao,* Chungking, Sept. 22, 1945 *(CPR).*
75. *China Weekly Review,* Feb. 16, 1946, pp. 201-2.
76. *Hsin hua jih-pao,* Chungking, Sept. 11, 13, and 14, 1945 *(CPR,* same dates).
77. *Hsin min pao,* Chungking, Sept. 18, 1945 *(CPR).*

would still represent only a stop-gap effort, since the Government could not continue indefinitely to support the non-competitive enterprises of the Southwest. More fundamental solutions would have to be sought.

With this in mind, the various industrial associations in the Southwest intensified their demand that all factories and mines taken over from the enemy which were not officially reserved for public management, be placed immediately under the control of those concerns that had relocated in the hinterland during the Anti-Japanese War. On September 19, Mr. Wu Yun-cho, Chairman of the All-China Industrial Association, arrived in Shanghai from Chungking to "assist Government authorities in recovering factories and plants in this city, which were formerly seized by the enemy and puppets from their Chinese owners."[78]

Despite these efforts, the claims of original owners and the pleas for special preference from industrialists in the interior were as often as not ignored. In this matter, too, the Government's actions belied its avowed intentions—for it continued to assert that the claims of these two groups would be given top priority. According to official policy statements, the disposal of enemy-owned properties was to be based on the principles laid down in the Outline of Industrial Reconstruction passed by the Sixth Congress of the KMT. The Outline stipulated that large-scale heavy industries and public utilities were to be classified as state enterprises. Smaller-scale and light industries would be owned and operated by private entrepreneurs. Privately-owned enterprises that had been seized by the enemy were to be returned to their original owners after ownership had been verified and approval granted by the Special Commissioner of the Ministry of Economic Affairs. In disposing of privately-owned Japanese and puppet enterprises, the recipients were listed in the following official order of priority: (1) factories or industrialists that had moved to the interior during the war and made a genuine contribution to the war effort; (2) factories or industrialists that did not move to the interior, but did not cooperate with the enemy despite enemy occupation of their concerns; (3) new factories or industrialists, with the necessary capital and experience.[79]

Five days after this official statement was published, the Chamber of Commerce newspaper in Chungking reported that over forty factories in Shanghai had so far been taken over by C. K. Chang, Special Commissioner of the Ministry of Economic Affairs. After their take-over, the factories were sealed and therefore required to suspend operations pending further instructions from the Ministry. The Office of the Commissioner had not at any point requested the "cooperation" of technical or managerial personnel from enterprises in the Southwest.[80]

At a meeting of the All-China Industrial Association on October 25, the Director of the Association's executive committee discussed the take-over of enemy factories in the Shanghai area. He reported that some of them were still

78. *Kuang hua jih-pao,* Shanghai, Sept. 20, 1945 *(CPR).*

79. *CYJP,* Chungking, Oct. 9, 1945, *(CPR).*

80. *Shang-wu jih-pao,* Chungking, Oct. 14, 1945 *(CPR,* Oct. 15).

being held by former collaborators.[81] In late November, the All-China Industrial Association and the United Federation of Industries Removed to Szechwan Province sent a "final" appeal to the Executive Yuan that enemy industries be distributed to those who had contributed to the resistance effort. Appeals were also made to the appropriate officials at the Ministry of Economic Affairs, and the Enemy and Puppet Properties Supervision Committee for the Shanghai area. These pleas were inspired by the news that forty-eight recently surrendered enemy enterprises were to be put up for auction—in obvious disregard of the official order of priorities.[82]

When the Political Consultative Conference met in January, 1946, a group called the Chungking Medium and Small Factories Federation could do no more than lodge a written protest outlining again the plight of industrialists in the Southwest and blaming the Government for it. The Federation charged that the Government had requested medium and small-scale industries in the Southwest to close down and had offered no interim aid to help tide them over the resulting dislocations. In addition, the Government itself was moving to monopolize the operations of light industries, especially textiles, in violation of its previously stated policies. Finally, the Government was allowing the purchase of shoes, cotton, and spinning and weaving equipment from the United States and Brazil, thus forcing domestic producers of those products into bankruptcy.[83]

Any remaining hopes for assistance were finally dashed in April when the Government announced that, with the exception of factories being operated directly by government agencies, all other Japanese and puppet-owned factories were to be auctioned off to the highest bidder. Most of the buyers were allegedly persons who had remained in the occupied areas or who had become rich through profiteering. Few industrialists returning to the coastal areas could afford to purchase the factories despite the relatively low selling prices.[84]

THE RECOVERED TERRITORIES

The relatively low level of physical destruction in the former Japanese-occupied territories should have made it possible for industrial production to continue with little interruption, thus helping to offset the adverse effects of the depression in the interior. Instead, the depression there was accompanied by several months of economic stagnation in the recovered areas, a consequence of the take-over operations described above.

Economic Stagnation

In late September, 1945, the official *Chung-yang jih-pao* reported that the economic disruption in the recovered areas was in no way related to victory and the return of government personnel. Rather, it was "due entirely" to the poisonous remnants of Japanese rule. Continued the paper, "they [the workers]

---

81. *TKP*, Chungking, Oct. 25, 1945 *(CPR)*.
82. *TKP*, Shanghai, Nov. 30, 1945 *(CPR)*.
83. *Hsin hua jih-pao*, Chungking, Jan. 22, 1946 *(CPR)*.
84. *WHP*, Shanghai, Apr. 22, 1946 *(CPR*, Apr. 23).

are now experiencing great distress, causing some of the simpleminded elements to begin doubting about what victory has brought them."[85] A Soviet citizen returning to Chungking in early November from a visit to north and east China, claimed that 90 percent of the factories in Shanghai were closed down.[86] A local Tientsin paper reported that about 90 percent of that city's factories, too, had ceased production.[87]

The Unemployed Workers Relief Commission of the Ministry of Social Affairs drew up plans for relief and subsistance allowances for unemployed and low-paid workers. But the magnitude of the problem was such that it was impossible to extend relief to all of the unemployed. Estimates of their numbers varied from two hundred thousand to half a million in Shanghai alone by the end of September. The take-over created at one stroke a fertile field for labor agitation. After years of suppression, both during the war and before, the labor force was suddenly freed from the bonds of government control. Disputes and demonstrations multiplied as unemployed workers demanded relief and adequate severance pay to tide them over an indefinite period of unemployment. Those who did not lose their jobs agitated for pay increases, owing to the rapid depreciation of the puppet currency in which they were still being paid.

On September 27, the headquarters of the Garrison Command for the Woosung-Shanghai area announced that all instigators of strikes and labor disputes would henceforth be severely punished. Workers were told to follow legal procedures in seeking relief.[88] Strikes and demonstrations nevertheless continued. Finally, in mid-November, martial law was declared in Shanghai and all strikes banned. At the time, the employees of six leading Shanghai department stores, the Shanghai Tram Company, the French Tram Company, the Post Office, and the Shanghai Power Company were all striking for higher pay.

A year later, however, the Ministry of Economic Affairs announced that only 852 of the estimated 2,411 factory units taken over from Japanese and collaborators had resumed production.[89] Official sources no longer claimed that this was due to the poisonous remnants of Japanese rule, but blamed instead a shortage of raw materials, transportation difficulties created by the military situation, and a declining demand for domestic products caused by the import of cheaper foreign goods.

Other sources viewed the problem in a different light. They pointed out that the new owners of Japanese or puppet enterprises were often reluctant to invest in them for productive purposes. Many who purchased the fifty to sixty factory units auctioned off in Shanghai up to April, 1946, dismantled the machinery and sold it.[90] As indicated, this occurred in other places as well, and contributed further to the destruction already resulting from the activities of the take-over

85. *CYJP*, Shanghai, Sept. 27, 1945 *(CPR)*.
86. *Hsin min pao*, Chungking, Nov. 9, 1945 *(CPR)*.
87. *Min-kuo jih-pao*, Tientsin, Nov. 18, 1945 *(CPR, Nov. 20)*.
88. *Ch'ing-nien jih-pao*, Shanghai, Sept. 28, 1945 *(CPR)*.
89. *Ho-p'ing jih-pao*, Shanghai, Nov. 13, 1946 (*CPR*, Dec. 27).
90. *WHP*, Shanghai, Apr. 22, 1946 (*CPR*, Apr. 23).

officials. Speculators were also exploiting the situation by buying up all available commodities. There was heavy buying and selling of such goods in September and October, 1945. The chief culprits were allegedly local merchants seeking to force up the prices of goods in hand, together with the early arrivals among the take-over officials.

Nevertheless, speculators and profiteers could not be blamed for the stagnation of industrial production. They were more a symptom than a cause. The market in the recovered areas soon deteriorated to the point where it was often more profitable to sell factory machinery than to operate it. By mid-1946, there were a number of reasons for this which will be discussed in Chapter Four. In the immediate post-war period, however, the primary cause of the economic stagnation in the recovered areas was the Government's take-over policy itself, which closed all enemy-owned industrial enterprises and banned the movement of raw materials, food, and other commodities from enemy-owned warehouses. The resulting sharp decline in output was accompanied, after an initial post-war slump, by soaring prices and the rapid growth of black market activities. Between September 9 and October 19, commodity prices registered 100 to 200 percent increases.[91]

Exchange Rates

The Government also delayed too long in fixing official exchange rates between *fapi* and puppet notes in the various currency areas of the former occupied territories.[92] The Government waited six weeks before fixing the exchange rate in the central China area, three months in north China, and several months longer in Manchuria. The *Ta kung pao* reported that speculators were rushing with their *fapi* into the chaotic currency markets of the recovered areas, where exchange rates varied from place to place even within one currency area. On September 14, for example, the rate between *fapi* and puppet notes was 1:40 in Hankow, 1:150 in Shanghai, and 1:200 in Nanking.[93] By September 26, the rate had risen to 1:250 in Shanghai. The value of commercial assets and personal savings shrank accordingly. Merchants in Nanking and Shanghai blamed it all on the "invasion of capital from the interior" and responded by raising their prices, hoping to offset through immediate gain at least part of the losses suffered from the depreciation of their puppet currency.

Some also responded by using their capital for speculative purposes. In early November, "a major portion" of official and commercial capital was reportedly being invested in this manner. At that time, the exchange rate between Chinese

91. *Chien-sien jih-pao,* Shanghai, Oct. 19, 1945 *(CPR).*

92. The separate regional governments of the Japanese-sponsored Chinese puppet regime during the war each had its own currency. Manchukuo currency began circulating after 1931, and a separate currency was issued in Inner Mongolia in 1937. Federal Reserve Bank (FRB) notes began circulating in north China in March 1938; another currency was issued for south China in 1940; and Central Reserve Bank (CRB) notes began circulating in the Nanking-Shanghai area in 1941. (Arthur Young, *China's Wartime Finance and Inflation, 1937-1945,* p. 165.)

93. *TKP,* Chungking, Sept. 14, 1945 *(CPR).*

and U.S. currency in Tientsin was 700:1, whereas in Shanghai it was as high as 1,500:1. Speculators were said to move frequently between the two cities, buying U.S. dollars in Tientsin and selling in Shanghai.[94]

An official exchange rate between *fapi* and puppet (Central Reserve Bank) currency in the Chekiang-Kiangsu area was finally announced on September 27. The Government was widely criticized for fixing the rate at what was considered the artificially low level of 1:200. In the North, the official exchange rate between *fapi* and Federal Reserve Bank notes was not announced until November 21. But the rate itself, 1:5, was comparable to the black market rate and therefore reflected the real value of FRB notes.[95]

In the Shanghai area, on the other hand, a crisis situation rapidly developed. The *Ta kung pao* noted that the exchange rate amounted to a direct confiscation of people's property and was helping to destroy the middle class in Kiangsu and Chekiang. The paper suggested that the policies and activities of the KMT authorities had, in less than three months, brought the richest area of the country to the brink of economic collapse.[96]

Retail dealers used the occasion of National Day, October 10, to announce a general rise in prices and reduced business hours. On the same day, the Mayor of Shanghai issued two proclamations: one prohibiting any further rise in commodity prices, and the other demanding that local factories resume production. The proclamations had little effect. Some shops suspended business altogether rather than sell merchandise at fixed prices. On October 17, all the major department stores in Shanghai reduced business hours, opening at noon and closing at 2:00 P.M. The Shanghai Chamber of Commerce lodged a formal request with the municipal authorities that a general rise in prices be sanctioned to compensate businessmen for losses arising from the difference between the official and the real value of CRB notes. There was some question as to whether prices had not already been raised enough to provide such compensation, but the request was granted on October 19.[97] Prices resumed their upward course, while the livelihood of the people "worsened day by day."[98] The only beneficiaries seemed to be the take-over officials themselves and a relatively small group of industrialists with political connections. Both were able to profit not only from the take-over process but also from the increasingly direct government involvement in the economy that grew out of the reconversion period.[99]

94. *Hsin min pao*, Chungking, Nov. 9, 1945 *(CPR)*.
95. *Min-kuo jih-pao*, Tientsin, Nov. 22, 1945 *(CPR)*; *TKP*, Tientsin, Dec. 21, 1945 *(CPR,* Dec. 22); *Hua-pei jih-pao*, Peiping, Jan. 7, 1946 *(CPR,* Peiping-Tientsin).
96. *TKP*, Chungking, Oct. 24, 1945 *(CPR)*.
97. *Lih pao*, Shanghai, Oct. 20, 1945 *(CPR)*.
98. *Chung mei jih-pao*, Shanghai, Dec. 27, 1945 *(CPR)*.
99. Since the early 1930s, the National Resources Commission of the Executive Yuan had operated certain key heavy industries. During the reconversion period the Ministry of Economic Affairs also began to involve itself directly in production. This involvement affected light industries and brought cries of unfair competition from private industrialists, an instance of which has already been cited. In addition, the special supervisory committees created by the Government to regulate various industries were actually directing operations

THE "NEW NOBILITY"

A Tientsin newspaper referred to the take-over personnel and others returning from the Southwest as a "new nobility," interested only in the prices of gold, clothing, houses, and automobiles, and contemptuous of everyone who had remained in the Japanese-occupied areas. At first, noted the editorial, the people of Tientsin did feel themselves small and mean and regretted not having retreated with the Government to the interior. But after witnessing the disorders created by the returning officials, people no longer felt the need of appearing too humble.[100]

The official attitude of condescension was particularly apparent in the Government's take-over of Taiwan and Manchuria. Both regions had long been under Japanese rule and, in the case of Taiwan at least, the population had evolved a certain *modus vivendi* with the alien ruler. [101] Initially, the Taiwanese seem to have given as well as they received. The mutual hostility that developed between them and the take-over personnel from the mainland led by the new governor, General Ch'en I, culminated in the rebellion of February, 1947.[102]

In the Northeast, the irritation that was generally felt towards the new authorities was expressed in a Mukden editorial which declared that some "short-sighted people" had misjudged the Northeast by regarding it as a "special" region. But most of the present inhabitants were natives of Shantung and Hopei; they spoke Chinese, practiced Chinese customs, and loved China; and they had been oppressed by the Japanese for fourteen years. Yet after the Japanese left, another kind of people had arrived who also thought they were superior to the Northeasterners. These people were really not superior at all, concluded the editorial; they were only selfish political opportunists.[103]

Elsewhere, this attitude of superiority was most overtly manifested in the Government's policy of educational reconversion. The opposition that this policy aroused in the recovered territories was a prelude to the mutual antagonism that would develop in the Government's relationship with the entire student community during the coming four years. Public demands for the punishment of "educational traitors," particularly those in responsible positions, were widespread—like the feeling against all collaborators. China's most prestigious universities had chosen to follow the Government into the interior during the war. The hardships suffered by their students and teachers were well known.

---

in many factories, including some which produced or processed cotton, wool, silk, flax, chemicals, paper, and food. It is unclear whether this was a deliberate although unannounced policy, or simply the unintended consequence of the take-over operations. See *Ho-p'ing jih-pao*, Shanghai, Nov. 13, 1946 *(CPR, Dec. 27)*; and *WHP,* Shanghai, Jan. 21 and 24, 1946 *(CPR).* For more on bureaucratic capitalism, see Chapter Four.

100. *Yi shih pao,* Tientsin, Dec. 26, 1945 *(CPR, Dec. 28).*

101. The post-war problems which this would entail for the Taiwanese were anticipated in an article by Nieh Shao, "The Loyalty and Localism of the Formosan People", *The Voice of Formosa Semi-Monthly,* August 1, 1945 *(CPR,* Chungking, Sept. 9).

102. The Taiwanese rebellion is described at length in Kerr, *Formosa Betrayed, passim.* On the Taiwanese ridicule of the first Mainlanders to arrive, see pp. 73-74, 104-5.

103. *Tung-pei chien-feng jih-pao,* Mukden, July 29, 1947 *(CPR).*

Hence the general feeling that these schools should be favored and that some action should be taken against institutions which had remained in the relative comfort and security of occupied China.[104]

The aim of the Government's educational policy in the recovered areas became, therefore, the political "rehabilitation" of teachers and students. There was little quarrel with this objective. But the successful implementation of such a program required more sensitivity than could perhaps be expected under the circumstances. A perceptive article in the Communist *Hsin hua jih-pao* in Chungking requested a Government-sponsored Education Rehabilitation Conference to beware the pitfalls while formulating the reeducation program for those who had been students during the Japanese occupation. Declared the writer, "We must not make them conscious of a sense of difference. They should, as far as possible, be given the normal kind of education in no way different from other children, and brought back gradually to a normal life." He concluded, however, with a plea for the "solemn denouncement of those educational people who collaborated with the enemy and puppets," so that the Government would not extend to the educational sphere its already apparent unwillingness to punish genuine collaborators in other walks of life.[105]

Whether the Conference kept such principles in mind is uncertain. But officials in the Ministry of Education responsible for implementing the reconversion policy did not. In October, the Ministry announced the formation of temporary reeducation centers in the major cities of the recovered areas. University students would be expected to attend courses designed to reacquaint them with the needs of "national reconstruction" and the ideology of the KMT Government. The reorientation courses included the study of Sun Yat-sen's teachings, the public speeches of Chiang Kai-shek, Chinese history and geography, current events, and military training. Some students enrolled at these centers, known in each city as the Temporary (or Provisional) University. Other students attended courses in the Three People's Principles, current events, and so on, offered in colleges and universities by order of the Ministry of Education.

Similar courses were also made mandatory at the middle and primary school levels. Special examinations were to be conducted by the Ministry as students completed the reorientation courses. Only those who received passing marks were to be allowed to continue their schooling. Those who had graduated from colleges, universities, and middle schools during the occupation were required to pass a written examination on the Three People's Principles before their diplomas could be recognized. Teachers, too, were required to take an examina-

104. The following is one of the more forceful expressions of this feeling: "The Government should take emergency measures to reform the youths who have been instilled with 'slave thought' in the once enemy-occupied areas, especially in Formosa and the Northeast. . . . While school teachers in recovered areas who aided the Japanese in carrying out their colonial education policy should be treated and punished with discrimination as traitors, the youths should be given opportunity for reeducation." *Shih-shih hsin pao,* Chungking, Sept. 12, 1945 *(CPR).* Also *CYJP,* Chungking, Sept. 12, 1945, and *TKP,* Chungking, Sept. 11 (both in *CPR,* Sept. 13).

105. *Hsin hua jih-pao,* Chungking, Sept. 22, 1945 *(CPR).*

tion on academic competence, as well as their knowledge of and loyalty to the KMT.

The controversy arose not over the reorientation program *per se,* but rather the stigma officially attached to all who were required to participate in it. Thus, in announcing the program, the Ministry of Education asserted that all students who had attended schools in areas controlled by the puppet government were assumed to have been corrupted by enemy propaganda. Until these students were suitably reeducated and their thoughts purged, they would be deemed unfit for further education.

Government officials reiterated the Ministry's line, referring to the young people as "puppet students" who were being helped to "wash off their ideological stains." [106] In one incident, when a delegation of "puppet college graduates" called upon the Secretary-general of the Generalissimo's Peiping Field Headquarters to protest the compulsory examination, the official responded by telling them they were doubly unfortunate. First, they had remained in Peiping during the Japanese occupation; and second, they had been born into poor families which could not afford to send them to one of the three private universities in Peiping. [107] Private schools in occupied China had been able to maintain a greater degree of independence from government interference than state-supported schools. Because of this, the reeducation program for students of the former institutions was less stringent.

Resentment and opposition arose at once among the students. Parents, educators, and leading citizens also expressed their indignation. The American missionary-educator, John Leighton Stuart, then President of Yenching University (and soon to be appointed U.S. Ambassador), was among them. He said publicly that, if anything, the students had become more anti-Japanese as a result of attending puppet-controlled schools. He also suggested that the Government's attitude was alienating young people, and that many were turning toward the Communists as a result. [108]

Students in Nanking, Shanghai, Peiping, Tientsin, and elsewhere held meetings and demonstrations to express their opposition. Among the first were the above-mentioned puppet college graduates in Peiping. They belonged to the Joint Association of the Alumni of Peking University and Peking Normal University, which issued a statement demanding "rational treatment" for students in the recovered territories. Members of the group took up the issue with officials and called a meeting of recent college graduates. The authorities in Peiping did eventually agree to a revised set of regulations, replacing the written examination with a reading report on the Three People's Principles and a thesis of not less than twenty thousand words on the subject in which each student had majored. Peiping college students accepted the revised regulations; but the graduates did not, claiming that they were still being stigmatized for a situation

106. *Chung mei jih-pao,* Shanghai, Nov. 20, 1945 *(CPR).*
107. *Peiping Chronicle,* Jan. 29, 1946, p. 2.
108. *China Weekly Review,* Nov. 24, 1945, p. 83.

over which they had no control. They organized an association and began publishing a journal to publicize their grievances. [109]

Protest over the reeducation program took a dramatic turn with the killing of a school teacher in Tsingtao in late December. The incident occurred when police opened fire on a group of teachers and students from middle and primary schools previously registered with the puppet government. The group was posting notices explaining their opposition to the compulsory government examinations for students and teachers. The killing precipitated a city-wide students' strike that received much support from the people of Tsingtao and other cities as well. [110]

In Tientsin on December 31, several thousand middle school students staged a two-hour demonstration at the municipal Education Bureau protesting the examination of their political status. The students finally won a six-point concession which included the promise that neither students nor teachers in Tientsin would be required to take the government exams. [111] Similarly in Shanghai, the increasing opposition of students and teachers led educational authorities there to petition the Ministry of Education to allow a more lenient implementation of the retraining program. At the very least, suggested one local paper, they ought to do away with the words "examination of status." The elimination of that term would do much to reduce the level of irritation in schools throughout the recovered areas.

Nevertheless, during the following summer the Central Government was still issuing orders to provincial governments to carry out the registration of graduates from former puppet middle schools for the purpose of examination and "official recognition" of their academic status. By this time, however, the examination itself was merely a formality in many places. The examination for middle school graduates in Hopei province, for example, consisted only of a written report on the Three People's Principles, together with the student's graduation certificate and a recent photograph. Those whose reports and records were deemed satisfactory were issued official diplomas; others had to submit to reeducation; and those who refused to participate in the examination surrendered their status as middle school graduates. [112]

The irritation these measures aroused was summarized by the Tientsin edition of the *Ch'ing-nien jih-pao* shortly after the Tsingtao shooting incident. With the coming of victory, people in the recovered areas had begun to feel a sense of difference between themselves and those who had withdrawn to the interior. This feeling was intensified by the behavior of the take-over officials who were the first to return from the hinterland. They seemed to have a superiority complex; but in their conduct, these men of position and influence had not shown themselves superior to the local population in any way. Yet these were

109. *Peiping Chronicle*, Jan. 29, 1946, p. 2; *News and Views Weekly*, Peiping, Feb. 16, 1946 (*CPR*, Peiping-Tientsin).

110. *TKP*, Shanghai, Jan. 3, 1946 *(CPR)*.

111. *China Weekly Review*, Jan. 12, 1946.

112. *Shih-chieh jih-pao*, Peiping, June 27, 1946 (*CPR*, Peiping-Tientsin).

the same individuals who would sit in judgment over local students and teachers, and place on their records a black mark that would remain with them throughout their professional lives. Under such circumstances, the intellectuals could scarcely be blamed for speaking out in protest. "In view of the lesson of the tragedy in Tsingtao," concluded the editorial, "we hope that the Government will not only examine teachers and students. It also had better consider its public functionaries and other things, so far as the psychology of the people in the liberated areas is concerned."[113]

Perhaps it was no mere coincidence that the most radical edge of student opposition to the Central Government and its civil war policy during the coming four years did not develop in the North, where the leading educational institutions had followed the Government into the interior. Student opposition to the Government was sharpest in the Nanking-Shanghai area, where a larger section of the student community had been stigmatized by the Government's reconversion policy.

Such was the record of the Central Government as the year 1946 began. The reconversion period provided every sector of the population in the nation's major urban centers with specific grievances for which the Government's policies and the behavior of its officials were held directly responsible. The only beneficiaries seemed to be take-over officials, speculators, profiteers, and industrialists with political connections. Hundreds of thousands of workers found themselves without adequate relief to tide them over several months of unemployment caused by the suspension of industrial production in the recovered areas and the depression in the hinterland. Rising prices reduced the incomes of salaried groups. In the Kiangsu-Chekiang area, medium and small industrialists and businessmen suffered considerable losses as a result of the depreciation of puppet currency formalized in the official exchange rate between that currency and *fapi*. Entrepreneurs in the interior were forced into bankruptcy when anticipated compensation did not materialize. Students were antagonized by the Government's reconversion policy in education. And above all else was the damage done to the economy and to the Government's popular image by the venality of the take-over officials.

The words "incompetent" and "corrupt" had already become standard shorthand terms in some circles to describe all that was wrong with KMT administration. During the reconversion period, the meaning of these words with reference to the Government's performance was defined by firsthand experience for virtually everyone in the former Japanese-occupied cities of east, north, and northeast China. The administrative structure set up to implement the take-over from the Japanese was chaotic and incapable of performing the tasks required of it. Lacking adequate institutional constraints, the men who staffed such a structure could hardly be blamed when they failed to rise above it. The take-over policies themselves were either ill-conceived or improperly implemented.

113. *Ch'ing-nien jih-pao*, Tientsin, Dec. 28, 1945 *(CPR)*.

Finally, the clumsy efforts to right the wrongs, as well as the pleas to reform moral conduct, only highlighted the wide gap between officially proclaimed norms and the reality of official behavior. Such efforts did serve one purpose, however. They helped to deflect responsibility from the topmost levels of the Central Government, and from the person of Chiang Kai-shek. The public seemed incapable of believing that the Generalissimo himself willed anything but good for his country. Hence, it was always "subordinates" and lower-level officials who were to blame. This was probably one reason why the widespread disappointment with the Government's performance during the reconversion period did not provide grounds for challenging the KMT's right to rule. It paid for its record during this period with a significant loss of prestige, but there were few demands for a change of government.

Communist publications denounced the performance of the Government and sympathized with each of the aggrieved sectors of the population. Nevertheless, the Communist propaganda effort was relatively weak in the urban areas at this time. Few people seemed to regard the Communists as a real challenge to the Government or as a possible alternative to it. There was, to be sure, a certain feeling of helplessness born of the growing lack of confidence in the Government's ability to cope with the nation's problems. "To whom can we complain?" queried one writer. "We do not have an organ to represent the opinion of the people."[114]

The most common plea, however, was simply for reform. The following comment from the Democratic League newspaper was more representative of the prevailing attitude:

> It is deplorable that the prestige of the National Government has been perceptibly lowered among the people. Why is this so? This question may be answered by answering the following: Why are the government officials who have disturbed the life of the people . . . not punished? Why do commodity prices keep rising with nothing done to stabilize them? Why are the civil liberties of the people repeatedly violated? Let us be frank and direct. It is the government officials themselves who have undermined the credit of the Government with the people. Therefore, it is also they who can best restore it.[115]

Unfortunately for the Government, they did not restore it. Most of the issues that aroused such widespread criticism during the take-over period were never satisfactorily resolved. Thus what might have been dismissed as a temporary interlude of confusion and maladministration immediately following the Japanese surrender, came to be recognized with the passage of time as the beginning of the end of popular urban support for KMT rule in China.

114. *Shih-shih hsin pao,* Shanghai, Jan. 19, 1946 *(CPR).*
115. *Min-chu pao,* Chungking, Apr. 2, 1946 *(CPR).*

III
The Student Anti-war Movement

Student protests became one of the KMT Government's most constant irritations during the 1945-49 period. Essentially an anti-war movement, student actions focused public attention on the KMT-CCP conflict and thus became an issue in the politics of the Civil War itself. Students were involved in scores of individual protests, strikes, and incidents. Some of these developed over political issues, others over academic and school-related matters. In addition to these more or less isolated protests, four major demonstrations, or student tides *(hsueh-ch'ao)*, as they were called, aroused nationwide attention and response. The December First [1945] Movement in Kunming was the smallest of these. It was followed a year later, in late December 1946 and early 1947, by the demonstrations protesting the "violent actions of American military personnel in China." In May and June 1947, the Anti-Hunger Anti-Civil War Movement swept through universities and middle schools in most major cities of the Government-controlled areas. The last big tide was the Anti-Oppression Anti-Hunger Movement, which merged with the Movement to Protest American Support of Japan, between April and June, 1948.

Despite the local issues and personalities that could not but play a part in demonstrations as widespread as these, the basic concerns sustaining the student protests were everywhere the same. The students' primary demands were an immediate end to the Civil War, an end to U.S. backing for the Government in that war, and a shift in public expenditure from military to civilian needs.

Refusing to accept overt opposition to its civil war policy, the Government denounced the student protest movement as a creation of the Communist Party. As the conflict between the Government and the Communists progressed into full-scale war, Government authorities became increasingly ruthless in their efforts to suppress the students. In addition, the Government also tried to divert the movement into other channels. But, as a former KMT youth worker remarked some twenty-five years later, this was an impossible task—so unpopular had the Government become with the students.

There were reports of group pressure, of apolitical students, and students who retained some sympathy for the KMT but went along with the tide rather than risk the censure of their peers. There were also schools where anti-government student demonstrators did not dominate the campus scene, and where the KMT's San-min-chu-i Youth Corps held sway instead. These were not, however, the best schools in the biggest cities with the nation's brightest students. And those who only went along with the tide could not exert much influence on it. Such students were left to taunt the KMT youth cadres with the challenge to their Party to "do something sensible for a change so that we can support you!" Dissatisfaction with the Government and its war policy was so deeply felt by so many that their movement could not be deflected from its course.[1]

At the root of the Government's intransigence *vis-à-vis* the students was the student willingness to recognize the CCP as a legitimate entity within a coalition government. This willingness was inherent in the students' demand for an immediate end to the war short of military victory. Nor was this merely an implied condition. The students openly expressed their desire for a coalition government. They did so to the virtual exclusion of the only alternative solution, namely, some form of national partition. The KMT leaders, committed to the annihilation of the Communists, regarded any willingness to accept the CCP in a coalition government as a direct affront. Their ire was increased by the Communists' own references to their political objectives in terms of a united front and a coalition government.

The students, for their part, were seeking not to overthrow the KMT but merely to limit its power—or perhaps to redefine the limits of its power. As we shall see below, a majority of them apparently did not favor the idea of national rule by the CCP. Yet they were dissatisfied with the insensitivity and corruption of the KMT Government. A civil war, they reasoned, was too high a price to pay in order to keep such a regime in power.

Nevertheless, student opposition to the Government did not simply spring up full-blown as the nation moved toward civil war. Rather, the opposition developed in the course of the demonstrations themselves, and the Government's response to them. Many observers, both Chinese and foreign, commented that the Government's harsh measures were further alienating the students, even driving many into the Communist camp. The full political implications of the students' opposition thus emerged only within the process of interaction be-

1. In addition to the informers and secret agents planted by the authorities in schools where activity was greatest, students sympathetic to the Government (and particularly members of the Youth Corps) were supposed to organize and lead student activities, contest student elections, and the like. In most schools, interest centered around the periodic election of officers for the student self-governing associations in which the entire student body participated. Another informant recalled the plight of the pro-Government students in his middle school in Fukien. The brightest and most energetic student leaders were all critical of the Government and the war, and almost always gained the support of a majority of the students at election time. Rarely were the right-wingers able to take control of the student association. (From interviews conducted during the spring and summer of 1969.) The Chinese middle school was the equivalent of the American high school but typically offered a six-year course, the first three being junior middle school and the last three senior middle school. On the Youth Corps, see below, note 29.

tween the student demonstrators and the authorities. What had begun essentially as a maneuver to publicize the students' demands, developed—as much by default as by conscious design—into a movement that challenged the authority of the KMT Government. Perhaps this was why it was not until May, 1947, that Mao Tse-tung mentioned the student movement as a second front in the Civil War: it had only just become so.[2]

The demonstrations were not well-planned civil disobedience campaigns designed to achieve specific political ends. In some cases the students did seek a definite limited objective, such as compensation to the victims of official violence or the revocation of a local decree. But with the meager political resources at their command, the students were powerless to bring about the basic changes their primary demands would have necessitated. The students themselves did not always seem to be aware of this. Instead, they assumed that if public opinion could be sufficiently aroused, the Government would somehow be pressured into accepting their demands.

Toward this end, the students concentrated on publicity and protest demonstrations. The students publicized their demands at press conferences and on street corners. They distributed pamphlets and newssheets, and posted notices, cartoons, slogans, and wall newspapers. They held lectures, dramatic performances, and exhibitions. Forms of protest included meetings, parades, presentation of petitions, and classroom strikes. These efforts developed into acts of deliberate confrontation when the students carried them out in defiance of Government orders. On occasion, students purposely invited arrest and provoked a violent reaction from the police in order to discredit the Government or its local representatives in the eyes of the public. But, with a few rare exceptions, the students were never armed nor did they engage in destructive activities.

THE DECEMBER FIRST MOVEMENT[3]

On December 1, 1945, Lu Han was installed as the new governor of Yunnan province—although he did not formally take over the duties of the office from Acting Governor Li Tsung-huang for several days. Lu Han was appointed to the post as part of a maneuver by the Central Government to bring the southwestern province under its direct control. This was, in turn, part of the Government's larger strategy of consolidating its position in the wake of the Japanese surrender by attempting to eliminate all semi-autonomous regional power centers.

2. Mao Tse-tung, "The Chiang Kai-shek Government Is Besieged by the Whole People," *Selected Works*, 4:135.

3. This outline of the December First Movement is based on a comparative reading of the following: Hu Lin, *I-er-i te hui-i*, pp. 1-70; Wang Nien-k'un, *Hsueh-sheng yun-tung shih-yao chiang-hua*, pp. 64-73; *Ch'ing-nien sheng-huo*, Vol. 1, No. 1, December, 1948, *passim;* Yang Hsieh, ed., *Chung-kuo hsueh-sheng yun-tung te ku-shih*, pp. 23-33; A Che, *Chung-kuo hsien-tai hsueh-sheng yun-tung chien-shih*, pp. 108-123; Robert Payne, *China Awake*, pp. 200-260; *Chieh-fang jih-pao*, Yenan, November, December 1945, January, 1946; *CPR*, Chungking, November, December, 1945, January, 1946.

Yunnan's long tradition of autonomy had been continued in the KMT era by Lung Yun, who had ruled the province since the late 1920s. He had nevertheless allied with the Central Government during World War II; and Yunnanese forces commanded by his relative, Lu Han, fought alongside KMT armies against the Japanese. At the end of the war, the Central Government immediately dispatched Lu Han and his forces to Indochina to accept the Japanese surrender there. Meanwhile back in Kunming, the Government's Fifth Army under General Tu Yü-ming surrounded the provincial capital on October 3 and 4, and demanded Governor Lung's surrender. This was received after a minor show of resistance, and Yunnan came under the direct control of the Central Government. The chairman of the provincial KMT organization, Li Tsung-huang, was assigned to act as governor until Lu Han could assume his new post.

During the same month of October, 1945, Mao Tse-tung had returned to his capital at Yenan after forty-three days of negotiations with Chiang Kai-shek in Chungking. General principles had been agreed upon, but the details remained to be worked out. Mindful of the widespread aversion to civil war, representatives of the two sides continued to negotiate. But hostilities between their armies continued. In this threatening situation, anti-war sentiment began to grow. In mid-November, an Anti-Civil War Association was formed in Chungking and issued a call to workers, students, merchants, and government employees to go on strike as a means of demonstrating their opposition to the gathering clouds of war.

THE INITIAL INCIDENT

For all practical purposes, the anti-civil war movement among the students began on the evening of November 25, 1945. Students from a number of schools in Kunming gathered to protest the continuing clashes between Government and Communist forces. This was not the first such meeting in the city. Students had already expressed their opposition to civil war at a gathering, held to discuss the problems of victory and peace, while the Chungking negotiations were in progress. That meeting had been held on the Southwest Associated University campus. It was appropriate that students there should have been among the first to join the protest against the new threat to their hopes for peace and a normal life. Many of these students had spent the war years in the Southwest as refugees from the Japanese-occupied areas. The hardships they and their teachers had suffered were still fresh in their memories and they were eagerly anticipating their return to the North.[4] The Democratic League (DL), a federation of minor opposition parties that was involved in the establishment of the Anti-Civil War Association, also had many strong supporters among the refugee academics and intellectuals in Kunming.[5]

4. Southwest Associated University was the wartime union of three northern universities, Peking, Tsinghua, and Nankai, which moved to the Southwest to escape the Japanese occupation. The name was commonly abbreviated as Lienta.

5. Founded in 1941 and reorganized in 1944, the Democratic League was made up of the following groups at the end of WW II: the China Youth Party, the Third Party, the

Despite the peace negotiations still in progress, official sources in Chungking attacked the nascent anti-war effort as the creation of Communist instigators, ambitious politicians, and unsuspecting idealists.[6] Consistent with this line, the local KMT and military authorities in Kunming—now completely in control since the removal of Lung Yun—tried to prevent the students from holding another meeting. This one was scheduled for November 25, to be held on the Yunnan University campus, and was advertised explicitly as an anti-war meeting. Under pressure, the president of the university refused to allow the meeting to be held there. On the 24th, the authorities prohibited all gatherings unless first approved by local security officials. The students ignored this order, calling it a violation of their civil liberties. They held their meeting in front of the library on the Southwest Associated University campus located just outside the city walls. By seven o'clock, several thousand students had gathered to listen to four prominent professors speak against civil war and in favor of a coalition government in which all political parties would be allowed to participate.[7] Their speeches did not proceed entirely as planned.

Shortly after the first speaker rose to address the students, the sound of gunfire could be heard outside the university compound. The meeting continued, since no one realized at first why the guns were being fired. Then the electricity was cut off and the microphone went dead. The firing drew closer until finally it became clear that the shots were being aimed directly over the heads of the audience seated on the ground. A loudspeaker outside ordered the meeting to disperse. The meeting ignored the order. The program continued as the remaining speakers tried to make themselves heard between the bursts of

---

National-Socialist Party (reorganized as the Democratic-Socialist Party in 1946), the National Salvation Association, the Vocational Education Group, the Rural Reconstruction Group founded by Liang Shu-ming, and many individuals belonging to no party. These diverse groups were all critical of the KMT and desirous of reforms albeit moderate and non-revolutionary. The DL's demands for a coalition government and an end to the Civil War aroused the ire of the Government, which finally banned it in October, 1947, for alleged association with the CCP. See, Ch'ien Tuan-sheng, *The Government and Politics of China*, pp. 350-62; and Lyman P. Van Slyke, *Enemies and Friends: the United Front in Chinese Communist History*, pp. 171-81.

6. *Ho-p'ing jih-pao*, Chungking, November 21, 1945 *(CPR)*.

7. The professors who addressed the meeting were Ch'ien Tuan-sheng, the Harvard-trained professor of government with KMT connections (according to some sources he was a member of the KMT, while others state only that he occupied certain low-level positions in the Government), who nevertheless often criticized the Government; the sociologist Fei Hsiao-t'ung then associated with the National-Socialist Party; and P'an Ta-k'uei. The identity of the fourth professor is uncertain. Hu Lin (p. 4) referred to him as the outspoken leftist, Wu Han. But Payne *(China Awake, p. 203)* identified the fourth professor as the more conservative economist, Wu Ch'i-yuan, who, like Prof. Ch'ien, often criticised the KMT despite his connections with it (see Chapter Two, note 5). The *Hsin hua jih-pao* on November 29, 1945, also identified the fourth speaker as Wu Ch'i-yuan in a lengthy report of the meeting sent by air mail from Kunming on November 26. He reportedly spoke on "Relations Between the Financial and Economic Situation, and the Civil War," saying that China could not afford to fight a civil war, because the country's financial and economic structure would be destroyed, and it would lose the opportunity to become a modern industrialized state.

gunfire. An additional interruption came when a Mr. Wang, accompanied by thirty or forty men, pushed his way into the meeting. The gunfire ceased as he shouted out the Government position: the situation in China was not civil war; rather, Communist bandits had instigated a rebellion which the Government was doing its best to quell. The man was later identified, so the students claimed, as an official of the Yunnan provincial branch of the Bureau of Investigation and Statistics.[8]

After the professors had concluded their speeches as best they could, the students resolved to send messages to Chiang Kai-shek and Mao Tse-tung requesting them to settle their differences peacefully. The meeting then adjourned. But as the students began to disperse, they found the way back to the city blocked by the soldiers who had been firing and by the men who had accompanied Mr. Wang. The next day, Kunming newspapers carried a dispatch from the official Chungyang News Agency reporting that there had been a bandit alarm in the suburbs the night before.

ACTION AND REACTION: STUDENTS AND AUTHORITIES

After reading the official news account, officers of the Student Self-governing Associations at Lienta and Yunnan University met and decided on a three-day class boycott to protest the "fascist actions" of the authorities. Other schools responded at once and sent representatives to participate in the meetings of the newly-formed Kunming Student Strike Committee. That evening, the Com-

---

8. There were actually two secret service organizations, both formally established in 1938 although based on formerly-existing groups. The sources are unclear as to which organization the mysterious Mr. Wang belonged to. One was the Bureau of Investigation and Statistics of the National Military Affairs Commission. The other was the Bureau of Investigation and Statistics of the KMT Central Executive Committee, more often referred to simply as the Central Bureau of Investigation and Statistics. Both organizations operated extensive and competing intelligence-gathering networks throughout the country, but were ultimately responsible to Chiang Kai-shek. Their respective spheres of operations were not precisely defined and sometimes overlapped. In theory at least, the former concentrated on military matters, while the latter focused on the civilian administration, both within the KMT and without, and on economic, labor, educational, and cultural matters.

The military Bureau was dominated by the Whampoa Clique and more specifically by the notorious General Tai Li who controlled the Bureau from 1938 until his death in a plane crash in March, 1946. The KMT's Organization Department, controlled by the right-wing CC Clique of the Ch'en brothers (Li-fu and Kuo-fu), dominated the other Bureau. As with most such organizations, the Bureaus did not confine themselves to the passive task of intelligence-gathering. Both engaged in underground cloak and dagger work in the Japanese-occupied territories during WW II. Foreign observers in KMT China regularly referred to the entire secret service operation as "Chiang's Gestapo." This reflected the tasks for which both Bureaus were best known and most feared, namely, their efforts to ferret out, spy upon, intimidate, and if possible silence Communist suspects and domestic critics of the KMT regime. The military Bureau underwent some reorganization after Tai Li's death. But an order issued for the amalgamation of the two services was never implemented, apparently because of the jealous rivalry between the two cliques controlling them. Ch'en Shao-hsiao (Major Ch'en) offers a detailed description of the entire secret service network in volume 5 of his *Chin-ling ts'an-chao chi: hei wang lu, passim.* See also note 31 below. For more on the KMT cliques, see Bibliographic Notes on the history of the *Ta kung pao.*

mittee decided to print a strike announcement and groups of students went out into the city to distribute them. They worked most of the night, trying to leave a notice at every door so that townspeople might know the truth about what had happened and why the students had been provoked to strike.

On November 27, over thirty thousand students from virtually all of Kunming's thirty-some universities and middle schools refused to attend classes. The following day, the Strike Committee met again. Agreeing that the November 25 incident was not an isolated event but a reflection of the general political situation, the meeting drew up four demands and resolved on an indefinite strike in order to realize them. The demands were: (1) an end to the Civil War; (2) the realization of democracy with freedom of assembly, speech, and the press; (3) the establishment of a coalition government; and (4) no foreign intervention in the Civil War.

Meanwhile, the provincial authorities were casting about for some means of coping with the student strike. They called for the formation of anti-strike committees in schools and colleges. The head of the provincial Department of Education called a meeting of middle school principals and university presidents. At the meeting, the President of Yunnan University reportedly remarked that it would have been better had the soldiers not opened fire at the student meeting. General Ch'iu Ch'ing-ch'üan, Commander of the Fifth Army newly arrived in Kunming, was widely quoted as retorting: "Your students have freedom of speech; my soldiers have freedom to fire their guns." Li Tsung-huang nevertheless promised to issue a statement supporting civil liberties.

On November 30, the students went out into the streets of Kunming in small groups to publicize their four new demands. They were obstructed everywhere by plainclothes men and police. At an emergency meeting, the students decided the situation was too dangerous and that they would not venture off campus the next day. Shortly after 10:00 A.M. on December 1, however, a large group of strangers, some in military uniform and others dressed as coolies and ordinary civilians, pushed their way through the main gate of Yunnan University. Students gathered quickly, forcing the intruders to withdraw under a shower of rocks. The men then moved toward Southwest Associated University, smashing doors and breaking windows along the way at the middle school attached to the University. One group went to attack the dormitory and another forced its way into the Teachers Training College. Students at the College were just beginning lunch when the mob rushed into the dining room. A melee ensued and students from the nearby Kunhua Technical School, hearing the commotion, rushed over to help. The trouble-makers were finally forced out the main gate. This time they responded by throwing a hand grenade over the wall. One student was hit and the rest fell back. The mob once again forced its way through the gate and a second grenade was thrown. Many students were injured. A girl rushed forward to help and was stabbed repeatedly.

At the dormitory, students had been warned of the impending attack and had prepared themselves as best they could. But a middle school music teacher had just come out of the university barber shop when a hand grenade fell across his path. He picked it up, apparently intending to throw it back. The grenade exploded before it left his hand. At the Engineering School, equipment was destroyed and a professor beaten. Students from Yunnan University Medical School came to aid the wounded, but the intruders blocked the path back to the hospital and attacked one student being carried on a stretcher. The trouble-makers did not withdraw until after 5:00 P.M. Three students, including the girl, and the music teacher lay dying. One boy lost a leg in the grenade attack, and at least ten other students suffered serious injuries.

Weeks passed before calm returned to the academic community of Kunming. In the interim, the dead assumed the status of martyrs. Their classmates cleared furniture from the university library and placed the sealed coffins there sur-rounded by funeral scrolls and incense. The coffins remained in the library for three and a half months while the students sought permission to conduct the funeral procession through the streets of the city. During those months, half the population of Kunming came, either out of sympathy or curiosity, to pay their respects to the dead.

Within a few days of the incident, Kunming authorities announced that two ex-soldiers had been apprehended, tried, and found guilty. The two men were summarily executed. Officials in Chungking and Kunming subsequently claimed that the men had been paid by the Communists to create trouble among the students, and also that the Kunming students' anti-war activities had been instigated by the CCP.[9] One source associated with the Defense Ministry in Chungking asserted that the Communists had "bribed gangsters with money and high posts, who slipped into the holy academic institution with arms hidden, where they slaughtered the totally unarmed youths thus bringing about the tragedy."[10]

The students dismissed the trial, which was held in secret, and the executions as a whitewash. There was a widespread rumor that the two men had been criminals picked at random from a local prison. The students generally held KMT Provincial Chairman, Li Tsung-huang, and the Garrison Commander of Yunnan Province, General Kuan Lin-cheng, personally responsible for the acts of violence.[11] The students were particularly hostile toward Li because of an incident many years previously. As a young KMT official, he had allegedly been responsible for the death of a student, Liang Yuan-pin, during an education reform campaign in Kunming.

On December 5, the Kunming Student Strike Committee decided on eleven demands, grouped under three basic objectives, as the conditions for returning to class. The three objectives were: the immediate end of the Civil War; a full investigation of the December First incident; and punishment of the culprits including the dismissal and trial of the suspected organizers of the tragedy,

9. *CYJP,* Chungking, Dec. 6, 1945 *(CPR).*

10. *Ho-p'ing jih-pao,* Chungking, Dec. 5, 1945 *(CPR).*

11. Payne, *China Awake,* pp. 221-22; Liang Shu-ming and Chou Hsin-min also indicated that Li and Kuan were in control of affairs in the province at this time: *Li Wen an tiao-ch'a pao-kao-shu,* p. 8.

namely, Li and Kuan. The detailed demands under these three main headings included: formation of a coalition government, the safeguarding of civil liberties, guarantees against indiscriminate arrest, a retraction of the Chungyang News Agency statements slandering Lienta and calling professors and students Communists, and compensation for the dead and wounded.[12]

A statement from Chiang Kai-shek on December 8 urged the students to call off their strike. At Lienta, students did not return to classes until December 26, still insisting that their demands had not been met. Meanwhile, a nationwide wave of sympathy had arisen as the facts of the case gradually became known. By the time the students were allowed to conduct the funeral procession in March, 1946, commemorative meetings for the music teacher and the three students had been held in cities and towns throughout the country.[13]

RESULTS

If the November 25 meeting was really ordered from Yenan to provoke an incident and discredit the KMT authorities, the plan was entirely successful. It is plausible that pro-Communist elements among the students sought to organize the meeting as a means of consolidating sentiment against the impending war. At the time, Yenan was being very forthright in its expressions of support for the anti-war movement developing in the Government-controlled areas. It is also plausible that pro-Communist students sought to exploit the situation created by the intransigence of the local authorities and the initial disruption of the November 25 meeting.[14] But the accusation of Communist responsibility was

12. According to a Dec. 6 airmail report from Kunming in *Hsin hua jih-pao*, Chungking, Dec. 9, 1945 (*CPR*, Dec. 10).

13. Yü Tsai hsien-sheng chi-nien wei-yuan-hui, ed., *I-erh-i min-chu yun-tung chi-nien chi, passim.*

In Chungking, representatives of all the opposition parties attended memorial services, including Tung Pi-wu for the Communists, Liang Shu-ming for the Democratic League, Chang Po-chün for the Third Party, and Shen Chün-ju for the National Salvation Association. Others participating included Kuo Mo-jo, Lo Lung-chi, Liu Ya-tzu, Chang Tung-sun, Chang Nai-ch'i and Li Kung-p'u (who would himself be assassinated in Kunming the following summer).

The December 1 affair also provoked widespread press comment. *CFJP*, Yenan, Dec. 7 and 12, 1945; *TKP*, Shanghai, Dec. 10, 1945 *(CPR);* and the following Chungking papers: *Hsin min pao* and *Shih-shih hsin pao*, Dec. 4, *Shang-wu jih-pao*, Dec. 6, and *TKP*, Dec. 7 (all in *CPR*, Chungking, on same dates). All these sympathized with the students and blamed the local political and military authorities for the violence. One exception was the *Yi shih pao* (Chungking, Dec. 4, 1945), which criticized the students for choosing the wrong road "under instigation of intriguers."

14. Garrison Commander Kuan, in an interview with Robert Payne, maintained that there were such elements at Lienta but could provide no concrete information (*China Awake*, p. 214). An article in *KC* a year later also asserted that there had been Communists at Lienta but gave no details of numbers or identity. "Hsi-nan lien-ta jen-wu wan-ch'eng, hua cheng wei ling" [Its mission completed, Lienta has disbanded], *KC*, Oct. 5, 1946, p. 17. In 1973, a leftist informant in Hong Kong asserted that officers of the Student Self-governing Association at Lienta had included pro-Communist students. On expressions of support in Yenan, see *CFJP*, Nov. 24, 29 and 30, 1945, all p. 1; and Dec. 12, 1945, p. 4.

compromised by the claim that the December 1 murderers were hired by the Communists. This charge was given little credence by anyone, and no one even tried to claim that the Communists were responsible for the gunfire on November 25. Moreover, one fact overweighed all the rumors and accusations that accumulated in the wake of the affair: anti-war sentiment was genuine and widespread among the refugee students and academics in Kunming. Little effort was needed to bring several thousand of them to the November 25 meeting.

The Communists made a telling point—certainly one with which many non-Communists agreed—when they wrote: "We do not believe that a few political intriguers are able to instigate more than ten thousand students and professors to take unanimous action. If they can be so easily deceived, why cannot the universal cry of anti-civil war be suppressed by the special service men . . . who are planted in every school?"[15] Students and professors supported the protest effort, hoping to contribute to the mounting public pressure for a peaceful settlement at a time when negotiations between the Government and the Communists were still in progress. Whether the student protest actually had any such effect is, of course, open to question. But the ceasefire of January 13, 1946, which grew out of those negotiations, must have reflected to some degree the popular aversion to the KMT-CCP conflict.

As for the students' secondary demands, these were only partially achieved. Some gestures were made to compensate the victims of December 1, but the students remained convinced that those responsible for the violence remained unpunished. Both Chairman Li and Commander Kuan soon left Kunming. Because he was responsible for the maintenance of public order in Yunnan, Garrison Commander Kuan publicly accepted general responsibility for the incident. But the details of the plot, including who devised and implemented it, were never revealed. Nor did the departure of Li and Kuan make Kunming any safer for the Government's anti-war critics. The following summer, Wen I-to and Li Kung-p'u, both active supporters of the Democratic League, were assassinated on the streets of the city by "unidentified persons."

The Kunming students' anti-war protest did, however, achieve national recognition—and hence significance—as the first important student declaration against the Civil War. The students could not have anticipated that their efforts would provoke the reaction they did from the local authorities. But that reaction was directly responsible for the development of the movement, and gave larger political meaning to it.

Since the Central Government was just then in the process of establishing its control over Yunnan at the expense of the local warlord, the December 1 affair also became the first such incident during the Civil War years for which the Central Government had to bear ultimate responsibility. A historian, removed from the scene by space and time, might be tempted to suggest that in December, 1945, the center was not yet able to control the behavior of those acting in its name in Yunnan. This was not a popular line of argument at the

15. *Hsin hua jih-pao*, Chungking, Dec. 5, 1945 *(CPR)*.

time. The more common assumption was that the KMT's local agents and supporters had at last been given a free hand to act in the manner to which they were accustomed.[16] As similar incidents continued to occur throughout the country, it would become apparent that the Central Government was not just unable or even unwilling to control the actions of its local representatives. The Government finally gave them clear and specific authority to use these methods to deal with its student critics.

THE MOVEMENT PROTESTING THE BRUTALITY OF AMERICAN MILITARY PERSONNEL IN CHINA[17]

By the end of 1946, the Central Government had returned to Nanking and was engaged in its first major offensive against the Communists.[18] After the Japanese surrender, American troops remained in China to assist the Government in reoccupying key positions in north China and Manchuria. American troops also aided in the repatriation of Japanese forces and personnel in China, and were used as part of the mediation effort of the Marshall Mission to help supervise the January 13, 1946, truce between the Government and Communist armies. By the end of 1946, the truce had ceased to have any meaning, but approximately twelve thousand U.S. troops remained in China.[19]

The conduct of the Americans was a frequent subject of news and comment throughout 1946. Newspapers as politically diverse as the *Ho-p'ing jih-pao* and the leftist *Wen hui pao* reported numerous instances of reckless driving, robbery, drunkenness, rape, and even murder. Complaints were made to the American military authorities, investigations authorized, and punishments often handed down. Still, the incidents continued.

In the autumn of 1946, the Central Government declared that the Communists were behind the complaints. With the KMT offensive against the Communist areas and the failure of the Marshall Mission, Yenan had begun to level increasingly angry attacks against the Americans and to demand the withdrawal of the remaining U.S. troops. The KMT Government was more

16. For example, Liang Shu-ming and Chou Hsin-min, in their report on the Li-Wen assassinations, commented that under Lung Yun "various kinds of secret agents" had not been allowed to operate at will, as they had ever since the Central Government took over. Governor Lung had no great love for the Central Government and had tended to be fairly permissive with its critics (see above, note 11). On the Li-Wen case, see also Chapter Five, note 27.

17. This account is based on: Hua-pei hsueh-sheng yun-tung hsiao-shih pien-chi wei-yuan-hui, ed., *Hua-pei hsueh-sheng yun-tung hsiao-shih*, pp. 12-32; *I-chiu-szu-pa-nien shou-ts'e*, pp. chia 57-58; Hu En-tse, *Hui-i ti-san tz'u kuo-nei ko-ming chan-cheng shih-chi te shang-hai hsueh-sheng yun-tung*, pp. 16-19; Thurston Griggs, *Americans in China: Some Chinese Views*, pp. 7-14; U.S. Department of State, *Foreign Relations of the United States, 1947, the Far East, China*, pp. 1-6; *CFJP*, Yenan; Yenan radio broadcasts (covered by *FYI*); and the Chinese press in general (covered by *CPR* in the principal KMT-held cities).

18. See Chronology, July, 1946.

19. *China White Paper*, 2:694. This figure was down from a peak strength, at the end of 1945, of about 113,000.

inclined to play down the issue of their conduct than to demand a resolution of it—and perhaps risk alienating its major source of aid and support. This relationship between the Americans and the Government was the main underlying cause of the resentment toward the American presence in China by all who opposed the Civil War. The U.S. was not just playing the role of disinterested mediator, as dramatized by the Marshall Mission during 1946. The Americans were actually aiding one of the parties to the conflict in a number of substantive ways.

The Americans had helped the Government in its race with the Communists to take over key points in former Japanese-occupied territories by airlifting and otherwise transporting close to half a million Government troops. Some fifty thousand Marines occupied Peiping, Tientsin, Tsingtao, and their environs for the Government. By the end of 1945, the Americans had turned over to the Government full equipment for thirty-nine army divisions. The Americans contributed U.S.$500 million to the United Nations Relief and Rehabilitation Administration's China aid program, the great bulk of which was delivered to the KMT areas. In June, 1946, the Americans signed a Lend-Lease Credit Agreement extending credit to the Chinese for the purchase of civilian equipment and supplies. In August, 1946, after the KMT offensive against the Communist areas in central China had already begun, the Americans concluded another agreement authorizing the sale on credit of U.S.$900 million worth of war surplus property to the KMT Government for a net sum of $175 million. The property included small ships, vehicles, construction materials, air-force supplies and equipment, and communications equipment.[20]

In the eyes of all who opposed the Civil War, the U.S. was thus helping to perpetuate it. They agreed with the Communists when the latter argued—for reasons of their own to be sure—that such aid and support served only to stiffen Chiang Kai-shek's determination to fight. The problem of discipline among the American troops was but an added aggravation.

The grievances of business and industrial circles also contributed to the growing anti-American climate at this time. On November 4, 1946, the U.S. and Chinese governments signed a Treaty of Friendship, Commerce, and Navigation. The non-official press uniformly criticized the treaty, asserting that it was folly for an economically underdeveloped country to grant such extensive commercial privileges to a partner as formidable as the U.S.[21] Even prior to the signing of the treaty, Chinese businessmen throughout the country had been complaining about unfair competition from American products. Certainly there were domestic causes enough for the disruption of business and industry. Nevertheless, American commodities were clearly visible as the immediate beneficiaries. They had inspired the "Buy Chinese Movement" launched by Chinese businessmen with official approval toward the end of 1946.

20. *Ibid.*, 1:225-29, 311-12, 354; see also U.S. Department of State, *Foreign Relations of the United States, Diplomatic Papers, 1945, the Far East, China*, pp. 527-721.

21. See, for example, *WHP* and *Hsin-wen pao*, Shanghai, Nov. 5, 1946, and *TKP*, Shanghai, Nov. 6, 1946 (*CPR*, same dates); *Hsin min pao*, Nanking, Nov. 5, and *Chung-kuo jih-pao*, Nanking, Nov. 6 (*CPR*, same dates).

THE INITIAL INCIDENT

Such was the immediate context within which two American Marines assaulted a Chinese girl in Peiping on Christmas Eve, 1946. Passersby heard her cries and apparently witnessed at least part of the act. Police apprehended one of the men on the spot and took the girl, Shen Ch'ung, to a police station where she made a statement that she had been raped. The following day, some Peiping newspapers carried a short account of the incident by the Yakuang News Agency. Later in the day, the police issued a brief statement. It appeared little different than most others that had occurred during 1946, except that Shen Ch'ung was not the sort of girl typically involved in such incidents with American Marines. She was a student at Peking University. At least five Peiping newspapers carried the story in their December 26 editions.

OFFICIALS AND STUDENTS REACT

On December 27, the Chungyang News Agency, ever eager to play down such incidents, issued what students close to the girl insisted was a deliberately distorted account. The dispatch reported that she "seemed" to be from a good family; was twenty years old; attended a Peiping middle school; and had been out on the street alone at 10:30 P.M. when she was threatened by the Americans. This argument had its intended effect. The American consular report on the incident noted that it was not customary for Chinese girls "of good breeding" to go unaccompanied to "late evening moving pictures." Shen Ch'ung was leaving a movie theater when the assault occurred.

She was indeed of good breeding, asserted the students. A Peita student could scarcely have been otherwise. Her grandfather had been a provincial viceroy and her father was an official in the Communications Ministry in Nanking. She was nineteen not twenty, and had come to Peiping the previous January when she enrolled in the preparatory class *(hsien hsiu pan)* at Peking University. She had been to see a film and was leaving the theater at about 8:30 P.M. when she was not only threatened but raped. At Peita, the number of angry comments posted on the Democratic Wall began to grow, the Democratic Wall being a sort of central bulletin board designated as the one place on campus where all news, sentiment, and opinion could be freely aired.

Peita had only recently completed the move back to Peiping from its wartime campus in Kunming, and student body elections had not yet been held. Some said this was due to the purposeful obstruction of the university's "reactionary" proctor, Ch'en Hsueh-p'ing, whose relationship with the right-wing CC Clique of the KMT was well-known. Be that as it may, Peita was without the group of student body officers that usually took the lead in organizing activities such as the incident seemed to call for. On the afternoon of December 27, the History Society called a meeting of representatives of various departments and societies at the university. This meeting provided the nucleus of leadership for the protest as it developed in Peiping. When the meeting finally broke up at 11:00 P.M. several resolutions had been agreed upon. December 30 was set as the day for a protest strike, and a Preparatory Committee of Peking University Students

Protesting the Brutality of American Military Personnel was formed. The students' initial demands were: (1) that the men involved in the incident be tried by a joint Sino-American court; (2) that American military authorities issue a public apology and a guarantee against the recurrence of similar incidents; and (3) that all American military personnel be withdrawn from China immediately.

The authorities made clumsy attempts to defuse the issue. Peita's proctor made a statement questioning Shen Ch'ung's status as a student of the University. Rumors began to circulate that she was really a Communist agent, a member of the Eighth Route Army who had purposely set out to seduce the Marines in order to create an incident. There were other rumors that she was a streetwalker, that she had been previously acquainted with the men, that she had accompanied them for a full three hours before the assault occurred, and so forth.

Hu Shih, president of the university, adopted a more moderate tone: that the issue was one for a court of law and should not be made the occasion for anti-American parades and classroom strikes. The Mayor of Peiping, Ho Szu-yuan, fell between two stools, as did a number of government officials throughout the period who felt some sympathy for the students' protest activities. First he sent a letter to U.S. Marine headquarters protesting that the two men had conspired to commit rape. Then he called at the American Consulate to express regret over the mounting public protest. Finally, he announced that the medical examination had proved inconclusive in determining whether or not Miss Shen had in fact been raped. The students saw this as another attempt at official obfuscation.

Meanwhile, students in other schools in Peiping were beginning to react much as had students at Peita. At Tsinghua University, a protest notice appeared on a wall in the dining room on December 26. After a social studies lecture the next evening, the discussion period turned to the topic immediately at hand. The students resolved to start a petition demanding that the Student Self-governing Association take some action. By noon on the twenty-eighth, over one-third of the student body had signed the petition. That evening, the meeting voted to support the demands of Peita students and to strike classes on the thirtieth. Virtually all of the faculty supported the students' action.

At Yenching University, an American-financed institution, support came more slowly. But a meeting of the Student Self-governing Committee on the twenty-ninth agreed to support the main demands. Some Tsinghua students attended this meeting at Yenching and, after a good deal of persuasion, the meeting agreed that Yenching would also participate in the joint protest parade the next day. About five thousand students from eight colleges and universities in Peiping paraded on December 30.[22] They marched along several streets of the

22. The proportion of students active in this and later demonstrations may be indicated by some overall figures. During 1947-48 there were 153,472 students in Peiping, of which 18,332 were in colleges and universities and 39,524 at the secondary level. National Peking University had 3,537 students: *Shun pao*, Shanghai, Jan. 12, 1948 *(CPR)*. One of the largest schools in the country was National Central University in Nanking with 4,500 students at

city, but protest activities were confined largely to shouting anti-American slogans. The parade went off without major incident though machine guns were mounted on the walls of the U.S. Marine barracks.

EXPANSION OF THE MOVEMENT

Unlike the December First Movement, the anti-American demonstrations did not remain confined to one city. In Tientsin on January 1 and 3, several thousand students paraded and presented petitions to the city government. In Shanghai, there was a large protest demonstration on January 1. Shanghai's Mayor, Wu Kuo-chen, had summoned the president of National Chiaotung (Communications) University to the Mayor's office "for a talk." The president would not be dissuaded and reiterated his support for the students' anti-American protest. Earlier he had announced that he would participate personally in the January 1 parade, an action virtually unprecedented for a university president.

The president of Shanghai Law College also supported the students, saying that their protest represented all of Chinese public opinion. Students at Chekiang University not only protested the behavior of American troops, but called for an end to the Civil War as well—suggesting that, were it not for the war, the Americans would have had no cause to remain in China. In Nanking, university students staged a three-day strike. The American Ambassador received a student delegation and expressed regret over the incident. By the end of January, students in over twenty cities and towns as far distant from the scene of the precipitating incident as Canton, Kunming, and Taipei had organized protest parades, rallies, and classroom strikes.

Also, unlike the December First Movement, the authorities generally refrained from using force to suppress student activities. Perhaps one reason for the official restraint was the widespread sympathy that existed for the anti-American theme of the protest. Eleven citizens' associations in Shanghai, including commercial and women's groups, issued a joint statement on December 30 demanding the withdrawal of U.S. troops from China. The Nanking chapter of the China Women's Friendship Association sent a telegram to Peita expressing support for the students' protest activities there.

In Chungking, a meeting of the Chamber of Commerce expressed anger over the incident and suggested that business and industrial circles support the students' demands for a complete withdrawal of U.S. forces from China. If that could be accomplished, the meeting reasoned, it might hasten the end of the Civil War which the American presence was only serving to prolong. Moreover, it would cut down by at least one-third the amount of U.S. goods coming onto the Chinese market. By January 17, the day the court-martial of one of the Marines began, even official and KMT newspapers were cautiously demanding punishment for the accused.

---

the end of 1946. National figures of the Ministry of Education for late 1946 showed 182 college level institutions with 80,646 students and 18,094 teaching staff. Middle schools totalled 3,745 with 1,163,116 students and 90,635 staff: *Shun pao,* Shanghai, Nov. 13, 1946 *(CPR).*

Public protest subsided within a few weeks, but the nationwide student organizing effort continued. On December 31, seventeen schools in Shanghai formed a Shanghai Students Protest American Brutality Association. Similar city-wide associations soon appeared in Peiping and Tientsin, and on January 28, these merged to form a joint association. Its demands, significantly broader than those originally adopted by the Peita students' meeting on December 27, included: the adoption of an independent foreign policy by the Central Government, an immediate end to the Civil War, and the establishment of a coalition government. Representatives of the Protest Associations of Peiping-Tientsin, Nanking, and Hangchow travelled to Shanghai in February to make plans for a national organization, which was established there on March 8.

RESULTS

In terms of its initial objectives, this anti-American movement had minimal success. There was no trial by a Sino-American court. One of the Marines, Corporal William G. Pierson, was court-martialed, found guilty, and sentenced to ten years imprisonment. Five months later, however, the case was reviewed by U.S. naval authorities in Washington, who overturned the conviction on the grounds that it was difficult to verify the charges of rape against him. The review also noted that the original verdict had been handed down while nationwide student demonstrations in China calling for a conviction had created an atmosphere which made it impossible for the accused to receive a fair trial.

As for the broader objectives that all U.S. troops be withdrawn from China and the Civil War ended, these were—like the more ambitious goals of the December First Movement—beyond the power of the students to accomplish. On January 29, 1947, the U.S. announced it had decided to abandon its role as mediator between the Government and the Communists. American personnel involved in that effort would be withdrawn as rapidly as possible. However, a plan for the continuing reduction of U.S. forces in China had already been announced in the United States on December 18, 1946.[23] Hence there is some question as to just how much credit can be given to the students for hastening its implementation in the course of the formal termination of the Marshall Mission. Moreover, an American military presence did remain in China: a contingent of Marines at Tsingtao together with the U.S. Naval Training Group there, and the Military Advisory Group in Nanking.[24]

Yet in terms of its larger significance, this campaign did provide an opportunity to express, openly and on a nationwide scale, anti-American and anti-Government sentiments that had for several months been simmering just beneath the surface of popular opinion. What began as a student protest in Peiping over a relatively minor incident, was able within days to become a vehicle for the articulation of widespread resentment. In the process, the anti-American

23. "Statement by President Truman on U.S. China Policy," *China White Paper*, 2:694.
24. Tang Tsou, *America's Failure in China, 1941-1950*, p. 444; O. Edmund Clubb, *Twentieth Century China*, p. 279.

demonstrations mobilized a popular base strong enough to support the fledgling organization of a national student movement.

As noted, coordinated student activities first developed among schools within individual cities, then expanded on an inter-city level, and were finally attempted on a nationwide basis. This was the first move, since the start of the Anti-Japanese War, in the direction of nationally organized student activity independent of the Government and the KMT. It developed into an All-China Students Association which was established a few months later during the next round of student demonstrations. Thus the Peiping rape case provided the opportunity for the development of a national student movement which marked, in an explicit and formal way, the end of KMT control within the student community.

THE ANTI-HUNGER ANTI-CIVIL WAR MOVEMENT[25]

Student activity subsided briefly in February and March but resumed in April and May, focusing directly on the issues of economic hardship and the Civil War. This time there was no single precipitating incident. Instead, the movement gathered strength from a number of sources, including the momentum built up during the anti-American demonstrations just past.

The first half of 1947 marked a turning point in many respects. The formal withdrawal of the U.S. mediation effort in January indicated the final extinction of all hope for a negotiated peace settlement. Government and Communist armies were now openly engaged in full-scale war. This meant that the post-World War II dream of economic recovery was also finally destroyed. In February, the Government announced an emergency economic reform program, freezing the cost-of-living index to which wages had been pegged. Ceilings were placed on the prices of essential commodities. Yet prices continued to rise. Between February and the end of April, various price indices rose by 50 to 100 percent. During the five-day period from May 5 to 10, the general index of commodity prices rose 15 percent. The rice market was in a state of confusion: the price of rice in Shanghai rose 20 percent between May 4 and 8. Due to transportation difficulties, government requisitions for military purposes, and the dislocations caused by the emergency economic reform program, sufficient rice could not reach the cities from producing areas. Shortages were greatest where the reform measures had been most vigorously enforced—in the Yangtze River cities where the authority of the Central Government was strongest. Rice shops closed and rice riots broke out in many cities. Workers escalated pressure on the Government to unfreeze the cost-of-living index.[26]

25. This account is based on: Ch'en Lei, *Hsiang p'ao-k'ou yao fan ch'ih*, pp. 1-134; Hua-pei hsueh-sheng yun-tung hsiao-shih pien-chi wei-yuan-hui, ed., pp. 33-89; *I-chiu-szu-pa-nien shou-ts'e*, pp. *chia* 58-61; Hu En-tse, pp. 21-41; Wang Nien-k'un, pp. 82-86; *Foreign Relations of the United States, 1947*, pp. 131-190. Also, for the period involved: *KC*, Shanghai; *Shih-tai p'i-p'ing (STPP)*, Hong Kong; and the press of the KMT-controlled cities as covered by the various *CPR* reports.

26. *WHP*, Shanghai, April 29 and 30, 1947 *(CPR)*; *TKP*, Shanghai, April 29 and May 14, 1947 *(CPR)*. On the emergency economic reform program, see below, Chapter Four.

The academic community could not remain unaffected by the economic chaos. Some students had to abandon their studies because they had no way of meeting school expenses; other students lacked sufficient food or clothing. There were numerous reports of malnutrition, of subsistence diets based on millet and cabbage, and of students without enough physical stamina to participate in gymnasium work. Inflation had reduced professors' salaries to a fraction of their pre-World War II value. A few professors had even committed suicide, allegedly because they could no longer bear the burden of poverty. Unemployment was a major problem for middle school and college graduates. The saying: "Unemployment follows graduation" had become a by-word in student circles. Under these circumstances, student and teacher alike saw the Civil War as the chief cause of the country's economic plight, as well as their own. They—and many others—decried the small proportion of the national budget allotted to education, approximately 4 percent, as compared with the overwhelming portion for military expenditure.[27]

Contrary to its attitude during the eight years of the anti-Japanese resistance, the intellectual community now refused to accept without complaint the personal sacrifices the Civil War demanded. This was the climate within which the May, 1947, student demonstrations erupted. They originated in state-supported schools [28] in the Nanking-Shanghai area, where the demand was: "resolve the crisis in education." In Peiping and Tientsin, the key slogan was: "oppose hunger, oppose Civil War."

INITIAL DEVELOPMENT

Ironically, the right-wing CC Clique of the KMT was said to have instigated this student tide. American Embassy reports quoted "competent observers" and Chinese government officials as the source of this information. Details varied, but these informants agreed that student activities and protests soon gained considerable "public backing," whereupon the CC Clique lost "control" and the initiative passed to the leftists. CC Clique leader and ex-Education Minister, Ch'en Li-fu, did still exercise significant control over educational matters and he did not get along with his successor, Chu Chia-hua. The Ministry of Education issued a number of decisions affecting state-supported schools that provoked a hostile student response, as could have been anticipated. Beyond these points of common knowledge, the diplomatic reports were unfortunately as vague concerning the exact nature of CC Clique responsibility as they were about allegations of Communist involvement. The one point on which all sources agreed, however, was the convergence of popular backing and "leftist" goals. This combination turned the "disturbances" into the largest student anti-war protest of the period. The protest developed roughly as follows.

27. See, for example, a *TKP* editorial shortly after the 1947 national budget was announced: *TKP*, Shanghai, Dec. 24, 1946 *(CPR)*.

28. Approximately two-thirds of China's colleges and universities were state-supported. According to a 1947 report there were 122 government-supported institutions (72 supported by the central and 50 by provincial governments); and 58 private institutions. *TKP*, Tientsin, July 10, 1947 *(CPR*, July 11).

On April 26, professors at National Central University in Nanking petitioned the Ministry of Education for an increase in educational appropriations from the current 4.5 to 15 percent of the national budget. In addition, they also requested: (1) an increase in the basic salary of the teaching staff; (2) that salaries be linked to the rise in the cost-of-living index; (3) that the Government allocate foreign exchange to the schools so they themselves could purchase urgently needed books and supplies from abroad; and (4) that expenditures for KMT-sponsored activities and organizations, such as the San-min-chu-i Youth Corps,[29] not be included in the national education budget. A few days later, professors at Shantung University in Tsingtao, Honan University in Kaifeng, and Northeast University in Mukden all went on strike protesting the insufficient expenditure for education and demanding a readjustment of their salaries.

When the professors received no concrete response, the students began to take up the issue. On May 13, students at Central University held a meeting of department representatives and decided not only to support the professors' demands but to bring forward one of their own. They requested an increase in their monthly food allowance. The granting of food allowances to students in state-supported schools had been started during World War II when refugee students in the Southwest were often separated from their families and cut off from private means of support. The students at Central University requested that their monthly stipend be raised to CNC$100,000 per person. They pointed out that since prices had risen four times in Nanking between December, 1946, and May, 1947, their food allowance should now be four times the CNC$24,000 sum granted in December. Actually, they were receiving CNC$60,000 or less per month. Medical students drew up a detailed report showing how, at current prices in Nanking, a monthly food allowance of CNC$60,000 made possible an average diet of only 1,859 calories daily instead of the necessary 2,584. Nevertheless, the students' requests were turned down. The Minister of Education suggested they return quietly to their studies.

Meanwhile, pressures from other issues were building up. For example, the Education Ministry issued a new order, effective immediately, that all graduating middle school students in the country would be required to take a uniform final examination. Middle school students in Nanking and Shanghai launched a protest campaign and gained immediate support in other cities.

Students of the Shanghai Law College became involved in a dispute with police on May 4, over the posting of notices and slogans in public places. Two students and a policeman were injured in the ensuing fracas and the entire

---

29. The San-min-chu-i (Three People's Principles) Youth Corps, or *San ch'ing t'uan* as usually abbreviated, was established in 1938 as the youth organization of the KMT. Originally intended to recruit young people into the Party, the leadership remained in the hands of the older generation. The Youth Corps was used specifically to promote KMT policies in the schools and to attempt to exert control over the student body organizations, which turned many of the country's young intellectuals against it. The Corps ceased to exist as a formally autonomous organization in September, 1947, when it was amalgamated with the KMT in the aftermath of the Anti-Hunger Anti-Civil War Movement. See, Ch'ien Tuan-sheng, *Government and Politics*, pp. 126-28; and note 36 below.

student body went out on strike. Mayor Wu agreed to assume responsibility for the injured students' medical expenses, but refused to take any action against the police pending an investigation. Dissatisfied, the law students then mobilized support from thirty-four colleges and middle schools in the Shanghai area and once again took their demands to the Mayor's office on May 9.

The two most dramatic cases at this stage occurred when students at Yingshih University in Hangchow and National Chiaotung University in Shanghai commandeered trains and attempted to transport themselves to Nanking in order to present petitions to the Government. The issue at Chiaotung University, a technical and engineering school in the forefront of the student movement throughout the Civil War years, involved an order by the Education Ministry abolishing the Departments of Navigation and Marine Engineering. The students regarded this as an attempt by reactionaries in Nanking to wreck their university.

The Ministry rejected a petition to rescind the order, and student representatives who had presented the petition in the capital brought back rumors of more cutbacks in the offing. Chiaota students planned to go to Nanking *en masse* and vowed not to return to Shanghai until the threat to their school had been lifted. On the morning of May 13, 2,800 students, virtually the entire Chiaota student body, gathered at Shanghai's North Station carrying bedrolls and twenty days' supplies. Railway officials would not allow them to use the passenger service, but a number of fourth-year students explored the railway yard and found an old locomotive which they were able to start up. They joined several freight cars to it, the students climbed aboard, and the train pulled out for Nanking. In the meantime, a section of the track two stations up the line was torn up to block the train's progress. Undaunted, the students worked through the night repairing the tracks. Armed guards stood by but did not intervene. Finally, about 7:30 A.M. Mayor Wu announced over a loudspeaker that Minister of Education Chu Chia-hua had flown from Nanking during the night, and agreed to accept the students' demands. This was one of the few clear-cut victories the students won.

ACTION AND REACTION BY GOVERNMENT AND STUDENTS

The following week saw a continuous series of strikes and demonstrations by many colleges and universities over a variety of issues, some general and others limited to problems in individual schools. In Peiping, students at Tsinghua University called a three-day strike, to begin on May 17, protesting the Civil War and the Government's lack of concern for the living conditions of teachers and students. Peita soon followed, as did many other schools with strikes of their own. Students went into the streets to publicize the reasons for the protest strikes. On May 18, groups of students doing propaganda work in the center of the city were attacked and beaten by men of the 208th Division of the Youth Army. [30] Eight students were injured. At an emergency meeting that evening,

30. The plan to form the Youth Army or *Ch'ing-nien chün*, to consist of nine elite divisions of student and graduate volunteers from colleges and middle schools, was announced in 1944. The Army came into being during the closing months of World War II.

students from eleven schools gathered to plan a new round of protest activities in response to the incident. A big parade was to be held on May 20, one of many being scheduled in various cities on that day. In addition, student representatives from Tientsin and Tangshan met in Peiping on or about May 18 and formed the North China Students Anti-Hunger Anti-Civil War Association.

The Government reacted to halt the planned May 20 demonstrations. On May 18, the State Council, meeting in Nanking, promulgated the Provisional Measures for the Maintenance of Public Order. These banned strikes, parades, and petitioning by more than ten persons; local law enforcement authorities were empowered to use all necessary means of enforcement. The next day, seven thousand students holding broken rice bowls marched through the streets of Shanghai. That evening, the Garrison Commander returned from Nanking and declared to the press that there would be no more demonstrations so long as the Provisional Measures remained in force. These instructions, he said, came from Chiang Kai-shek himself. According to the U.S. Embassy's information, Chiang told a group of concerned academics that he had issued the order banning demonstrations, and that he did indeed intend it to be enforced by whatever means necessary. He also told the group that the Communists were leading the student protests. This meant that the kind of tactics initially adopted by its local representatives in Kunming in November and December, 1945, had now been officially sanctioned by the Central Government.

The authorities in Peiping at first refrained from using force to suppress the students' activities. The May 18 attack by Youth Army men was the exception rather than the rule. It indicated the differences that existed among the authorities in Peiping, and between Peiping and the Central Government, over how best to cope with the students. The response in Peiping to the promulgation of the Provisional Measures provided further illustration of this point. In an interview the day after they were promulgated, Peita President, Hu Shih, said that the Provisional Measures were obviously designed to cope with the coercive actions of student petitioners in Nanking and Shanghai. Certainly, he continued, the Government could not have had in mind the simple propaganda activities of Peiping students. The Tientsin *Ta Kung Pao* suggested: "The proclamation made by President Chiang has placed the local authorities in a difficult position by reason of the incompatibility of the contents of the proclamation with realities. . . ." General Li Tsung-jen, Director of Chiang Kai-shek's Field Headquarters in Peiping, called over one hundred professors and university administrators to a conference to discuss the situation. The meeting was uniformly in sympathy with the students.

General Li decided to adopt a policy of non-intervention for the May 20 parade. All soldiers and police on the streets that day were unarmed. They obeyed the order to stand back and allow student monitors to direct the march of several thousand students, but plainclothes men of unknown identity

---

Students in China were exempt from conscription, hence the necessity of making this a volunteer force.

attacked the students, at one point pelting them with rocks from atop a building. Elsewhere, a student was severely beaten and by the end of the day several students were reported "missing."

Nevertheless, General Li continued to maintain a lenient attitude toward the students. A delegation visited his office on May 21 demanding, among other things, punishment of those responsible for the recent acts of violence. According to press accounts, General Li responded positively to all of the students' demands, including that for a guarantee against a future recurrence of such incidents. Assuming that he was acting in good faith, as many students did at the time, it would appear that Li Tsung-jen did not have full control over the various police and military units under his nominal jurisdiction. [31] During the following week the situation deteriorated as incidents continued to occur despite his guarantees. Finally on May 27, the Peiping Headquarters announced that the Provisional Measures would henceforth be fully implemented in Peiping, and that the general strike being planned for June 2 would be dealt with accordingly.

In academic circles, support for the students grew as the position of the authorities hardened. On May 28, a formal statement of support for the student protest movement signed by 585 professors and personnel from universities and colleges in the Peiping-Tientsin area was made public. The statement also demanded an immediate end to the Civil War and the formation of a coalition government. Students and professors nevertheless agreed that there should be no more public demonstrations, since the students' safety on the streets could no longer be guaranteed. On June 2, at a meeting on the Peita campus, President Hu Shih commended the students for their restraint—and expressed disbelief that they were being manipulated by the Communists, as the Central Government was charging. Outside the campus, however, barbed wire had been strung, and soldiers stood with fixed bayonets.

Meanwhile, in Nanking where law enforcement authorities were under the eye of the Generalissimo, there was never any question of a lenient enforcement of the Provisional Measures. Students there refused to cancel their parade after the Provisional Measures were announced, and went ahead with plans to march with a petitioning group from the Nanking-Shanghai-Soochow-Hangchow Association of State-Supported Schools to Resolve the Crisis in Education. Their demands were essentially the same as those originally brought forward by Central University professors in April.

As the parade units prepared to move out on the morning of May 20, they discovered the roads blockaded by soldiers and police. Students from only three

31. Many years later, Li Tsung-jen claimed this had in fact been the case and that he had served only as a figurehead in Peiping. When he took over the post of Director of the Generalissimo's Peiping Headquarters in the autumn of 1945, Li found himself with no means of enforcing his supervisory powers over the take-over personnel flying in from Chungking. He was especially bitter about Tai Li's secret service organization, which Li held responsible for many illegal arrests and for the torture-killing of several Normal College students. According to Li, Tai took orders only from Chiang Kai-shek; and the head of Tai's secret police in Peiping, Ma Han-san, worked under Tai's personal direction. Li Tsung-jen, "The Reminiscences of General Li Tsung-jen," Chapter 43, pp. 1-5, 18-23.

universities were able to leave their campuses and they began the march as planned. As they turned down Pearl River Street along the main parade route, they found it, too, blockaded by some four hundred police. Parade leaders requested permission to pass. When this was refused, they decided—"in order to guarantee the rightful freedom of the people to petition and parade"—to attempt to break through the police lines. Ordered to disperse the crowd, the police turned clubs, leather belts, and fire hoses against the students. Over fifty were injured and some arrested. But, in the confusion, many were able to break through the cordon. About noon, they arrived at National Government Road where the defenses drawn up against them included machine gunners and mounted police. Here the students finally halted and stood facing the soldiers and police for six hours, part of that time in a driving rain. Student leaders temporarily abandoned their original petition and made new demands related to the incident just past. As their condition for dispersing, the students demanded that all those just arrested be released, that the Garrison Command assume responsibility for all medical expenses of the injured, and that the mounted police withdraw. These demands were eventually accepted and the students returned to their campuses claiming victory.

Once again a tide of student activity swept through the universities, colleges, and middle schools around the country. But this time, the Provisional Measures ensured that the student tide interacted with an equally high tide of police activity, intensifying thereby the level of protest. Strikes, parades, and propaganda teams protested against the Civil War, and against oppression and police brutality as well.

In Nanking on May 23 and 27, formal petitions were presented to the Government demanding more funds for education, the abolition of the Provisional Measures, and the restoration of three newspapers banned on May 24 because of their anti-Government stand. Students at Hunan University held an anti-Civil War parade on May 22. Two days later, Chekiang University students marched to protest the Nanking incident; students at National Chungshan (Sun Yat-sen) University in Canton called a three-day strike; students throughout the city of Kunming began a five-day classroom boycott. In Shanghai, thirty-seven schools formed the Support Committee for the May 20 Tragedy and called a classroom strike. Over seventy schools responded to the call. Aside from releasing the students arrested in Nanking, the Government ignored the students' major demands. Meanwhile, the students had proclaimed June 2 as Anti-Civil War Day and were making plans for another series of nationwide demonstrations. The authorities, for their part, set about preventing them.

During the two weeks following May 20, newspapers were filled with reports of "incidents" which included beatings, arbitrary arrests, and the abduction of students by a variety of law-enforcement authorities including police, Youth Army men, garrison troops, and plainclothes men. Martial law was declared in a number of cities including Mukden, Tientsin, Kaifeng, Foochow, and Chungking. In addition to the three papers banned in Shanghai, news censorship was temporarily imposed in Tientsin.[32] Student leaders, particularly officials of the student self-governing associations, were the main targets of the Government counterattack. Many were abducted by plainclothes men and simply disappeared. Blacklists of student leaders, activists, and suspected "Communist elements" were drawn up. These students, if not caught off campus, were sought in night raids on school dormitories. A student informer or secret agent planted within the school would guide the raiding party through rooms and among the bunks while soldiers and police surrounded and cordoned off the school in question.

The most notorious incident of this kind occurred at Wuhan University, where student protesters had not been particularly active. During the early hours of June 1, several students and at least five professors were awakened and marched out to waiting police vans. The entire campus was aroused in the process, and a large group of students surrounded one of the vans to prevent its departure. Several rounds of gunfire were aimed over the heads of the crowd; but as it happened, a dormitory was in the line of fire. Three students were killed, two as they stood on the steps of the dormitory and a third as he was looking out a window. Five others were seriously wounded. Examinations of the injured and the dead revealed that their wounds had been inflicted by dumdum bullets, the use of which is prohibited in international law. The furor this incident aroused prompted Chiang Kai-shek to issue a statement condemning it. He declared that in this case the murdered students were not Communist elements. The head of the detective squad of the Wuhan Garrison Command was

32. The press gave intensive coverage to the students' activities, as well as to the Government's efforts to silence them. One of the most persistent was the Tientsin edition of the *Ta kung pao* which, unlike its sister edition in Shanghai, was outspoken in support of the May, 1947, student demonstrations. Before press censorship was imposed, the paper had published no less than fourteen editorials in support of the students, three special reports, numerous dispatches describing the development of the protest movement in other parts of the country, and full coverage of its progress in the North. The paper's editor-in-chief, Wang Yun-sheng, who presided over the Shanghai edition, was at this time travelling in the North. On May 15, 16, and 17, he gave lectures at Peking, Tsinghua, and Yenching Universities. He also gave at least six public lectures in Tientsin (in addition to two closed meetings with the editorial staff of the Tientsin *Ta kung pao*). At Nankai University he urged the students to expand their movement into industrial and commercial circles. In the opinion of one sympathetic observer, the paper's forthright stand and the attitude of Wang Yun-sheng had considerable influence on intellectural circles, and contributed to the upsurge of the May, 1947, student demonstrations in the Peiping-Tientsin area. See Wang Shui, "Pei-fang hsueh yun te yuan-yuan-pen-pen" [The origins of the student movement in the North], *KC*, June 21, 1947, p. 20.

Wang Yun-sheng's absence was felt in Shanghai, however. His friend, Professor Ch'u An-p'ing, editor of *Kuan-ch'a,* took the Shanghai *Ta kung pao* severely to task for not being more positive in support of the students. He suggested that if Wang had not been out of town and the editorial-writing had not fallen into other more conservative hands, the paper would not have fallen into such error. See his "Lun *Wen hui, Hsin min, Lien-ho wan-pao* pei-feng chi *Ta kung pao* tsai che tz'u hsueh ch'ao chung so piao-shih te t'ai-tu" [On the banning of the *Wen hui pao,* the *Hsin min wan-pao,* and the *Lien-ho wan-pao* and the attitude of the *Ta kung pao* during this student tide], *KC*, May 31, 1947, pp. 5-7.

ultimately held responsible for the "negligence" of his subordinates. He was discharged from his post and soon thereafter his body was found in the Yangtze, allegedly a suicide.

A similar incident occurred in Chungking, also during the early hours of June 1, when close to two hundred students, journalists, and newspaper editors were arrested as Communist suspects. Two students were shot and killed in the process. In Foochow, over thirty students were arrested on the night of May 31. Several professors and students at Chungshan University were similarly taken into custody. In Shanghai, raids were carried out at the dormitories of the Shanghai Law College, Chinan University, Futan University, the Shanghai Business College, the Shanghai Medical College, and Chiaotung University. Student body officials at Tatung University were arrested on campus after plainclothes men disrupted their meeting and beat up many of them.

In addition, the members of propaganda teams, including those from a number of middle schools, were arrested. The propaganda teams actually invited arrest, since they often carried out their activities off campus and therefore in deliberate violation of the Provisional Measures. On one occasion when Chiaota students received word that one of their teams had been arrested, they sent another team to the same spot to continue the work the first had begun. The students reasoned that this would provide yet another opportunity "to let more townspeople see with their own eyes the brutality of the rulers." As anticipated, the police also arrested the second team. Undaunted, its members continued their efforts inside the police station.[33]

The crackdown achieved its immediate purpose. Little activity occurred in the streets on Anti-Civil War Day, June 2. But the number of arrests, and the violence that accompanied them, far from intimidating the students only antagonized them further. Their defiant rejection of the Government's decrees and the orders of its local representatives indicated the confrontation that had developed between the students and the Government. This was what prompted Mao to write on May 30 that a second front had emerged in the struggle against the KMT.

AFTERMATH

Reverberations from the events of May continued through the summer of 1947. Student leaders in Peiping and Shanghai moved quickly to take advantage of the momentum that had built up among the students. The objective was to transform the various *ad hoc* protest associations into a more permanent organization. In the Peiping-Tientsin area, the Anti-Hunger Anti-Civil War Association was reorganized into the North China Students Association in early June. On June 14, representatives arrived in Shanghai to participate with other student leaders in preparations for a national student association. The decision to establish the All-China Students Association was reportedly made at a meeting

33. Ch'en Lei, pp. 25-26.

on or about June 15. The founding date was later given as June 19.[34] On that same date the Ministries of Social Affairs and Education in Nanking ordered it dissolved on grounds that it was not properly registered with the Ministries. Student leaders ignored the order and announced the formal establishment of the Association in July. The Government subsequently declared it to be a Communist front organization. The Association then went underground where it remained until reestablished under Communist auspices in Peiping in March, 1949.[35]

A Shanghai Federation of Arrested Students' Parents was formed in July. About fifty Shanghai students arrested in May continued to be held in jail, although no formal charges had been lodged against them. The parents filed a plea with the Shanghai High Court for writs of *habeas corpus*. The Garrison Commander accused the parents of making unreasonable demands, since the students had been detained under martial law. Martial law, declared in November, 1945, in response to the labor unrest of the reconversion period, had never been formally lifted. Since many of the students had been apprehended on campus or abducted off the city streets, they could not be charged under the Provisional Measures for Maintaining Public Order as these dealt only with public demonstrations.

The parents reaffirmed their demands and issued an angry rebuttal to the Garrison Commander challenging the legality of his use of martial law. Gradually, the students were released. By mid-August, all but five had been turned over to their parents. Although no formal charges were made, the parents had to sign statements admitting their children were guilty of disrupting the peace, and guaranteeing they would not commit similar mistakes of thought and action in the future.

In Kunming, the Association of Students' Parents was still negotiating at the end of November for the release of arrested students and teachers, and clemency for those on the blacklist but not yet apprehended. Only about thirty young people were in jail in Kunming as a result of their protest activities. But Governor Lu Han had published the names of many "pro-Communist elements" alleged still to be hiding in the schools.

Meanwhile, punitive actions against students were intensified. As the release of students arrested in May continued through the summer, so did the blacklisting procedures as the authorities tried to apprehend the "real" Communist

34. U.S. Consulate, Peiping, Hsinhua radio, North Shensi, Feb. 3, 1949.
35. The Association nevertheless did try to function openly for a time despite the Government's immediate dissolution order. The student aid campaign carried out in a number of cities that summer was organized in the name of the Association. Moreover, in Peiping the honorary advisers of the campaign were the presidents of Peking, Tsinghua and Yenching universities. Although municipal officials declared it illegal, no concerted effort was made to stop the aid campaign. Some CNC$500,000,000 was collected in Peiping which was distributed to about 1,500 needy students. The North China Students Association was not banned, although students actively associated with it continued to be harassed by the police.

agents allegedly at the root of the student protests. This became increasingly difficult. Students rallied to protect one another, sometimes helping blacklisted students to escape or confronting the raiding parties *en masse* in order to hinder their search. Students at Chiaota responded this way one night when police converged on the dormitories with a blacklist containing sixteen names. Everyone in the dorms was awakened by the emergency ringing of the school bell, the customary method in all schools of calling an immediate assembly. About two thousand students rushed outside and stood with closely linked arms confronting the police and singing "In Unity There Is Strength," a Chinese student song most often sung to the tune of "The Battle Hymn of the Republic." The sixteen were spared, at least temporarily.

In another move, many Shanghai students received letters advising them as to the instructions of the city government. All undergraduates who had either been arrested, or whose names had appeared on blacklists but had not given themselves up, would not be permitted to remain on the school premises. In mid-July, over eighty students at Tatung University and thirty-one students of the middle school attached to it were dismissed. Similar action was taken in other schools including Chiaotung, Chinan, and Futan Universities. By the end of the summer, close to five hundred students in Shanghai alone had been dismissed. Dismissals were also reported from universities, colleges, and middle schools in Nanking, Canton, Kunming and Peiping. Once again, irate parents rose to their children's defense. Most of the students involved were of high academic calibre and active members in the student associations of their schools.

Punitive action was also taken against faculty members. As indicated, widespread support existed among them for the students' anti-war protests. In early July, the Minister of Education gave instructions to college and university presidents concerning faculty reappointments. Faculty members in state-supported schools were appointed on a yearly basis. The appointments of some thirty professors and assistants at Chinan University were subsequently terminated. An official statement said that they had been unable to "cooperate closely" with the school. Approximately thirty faculty members from Futan University and twenty from Chiaotung University were also dismissed. This treatment was widespread. In some cases, questions of academic competence were raised, but it was generally assumed that the chief reason for the dismissals was to remove "all factors obstructing stability." This was the reason given by the President of Chungshan University when questioned about the termination of several faculty appointments there.

Enrollment was still another means whereby the Government hoped to control the students. While the number of entering freshmen in state-supported schools was kept to a minimum, more than half the new places in some schools were reserved for newly demobilized Youth Army men. In order to prepare them for their return to civilian life, the Government sent them to summer camp, where their training classes included an examination of the recent "May student tide" as well as briefings on methods of work once they returned to school. The intention was that they should counteract the predominantly anti-Government line of the student movement. According to one report, this operation was under the joint supervision of the newly-established Youth Department of the KMT and the Government's Student Movement Leadership Committee.[36]

Finally, in late August, the Education Ministry began making plans to reduce the power and autonomy of the student self-governing associations. The plans were formally announced on December 8, when the Ministry issued revised regulations governing the associations. The new regulations placed them under the direction of the president or the proctor at each college and university; forbade anyone who had been punished or suspended for violating school regulations to hold office in the associations; and severely limited the scope of their activities. The revised regulations caused another long series of disputes between students and local school authorities.[37]

RESULTS

The demand for an end to the Civil War remained, of course, no more than that. In July, the Government ordered a general nationwide mobilization for war. Professors' salaries were revised upwards in August; but, as with previous such readjustments, salaries were not brought into line with the rise in the cost of living. In a letter to President Hu Shih on September 1, professors at Peking University pleaded for a subsistence income—writing that "the recent salary readjustment was indeed a mockery." As for the students' allowances, the National Economic Council issued a new ruling eliminating altogether the system of allowances for students in state-supported schools. Instead, only a limited number of government fellowships were to be made available: the quota of recipients was set at about one-tenth of newly enrolled students. In addition to this blow, tuition was raised in a number of private schools, making it impossible for many students to return to school for the fall semester.

As in the case of the two previous movements, however, the Anti-Hunger Anti-Civil War Movement was significant for reasons not directly related to the achievement of announced goals. Its importance lay, instead, in its contribution to the further development of the student movement and the progressive alienation of the academic community from the KMT Government. The orga-

36. The Youth Department was formed to coordinate youth work when the San-min-chu-i Youth Corps was reorganized and amalgamated with the KMT in September, 1947. This was apparently an attempt to render the KMT's youth work more effective and somewhat less offensive in the wake of the May, 1947, demonstrations and the criticism of the Youth Corps which developed at that time. Chang Tung-sun, "K'ai-ch'u, chieh-p'in, pao-sung" [Expulsions, dismissals, admissions without examinations], *STPP,* Oct. 16, 1947, p. 31.

37. This account of the government's attempts to control the student movement is based on press reports during the latter half of 1947; and Chang Tung-sun, "K'ai-ch'u . . .", *STPP,* Oct. 16, 1947, p. 31, 24; Wen Ch'i, "Chang Tung-sun chiang 'nan hsing chien-wen' " [Chang Tung-sun discussing "what was seen and heard in the South"], *STPP,* Sept. 16, 1947, pp. 23-24; Hao Chia, "Chung-ta hsueh-sheng tzu-chih yun-tung te hsin chieh-tuan" [The new stage of the student self-governing movement at Central University], *KC,* May 1, 1948, pp. 16-17.

nization of a national student association completed a process begun a few months earlier during the anti-American demonstrations. The students' alienation was most clearly manifested in their repeated refusal to respect the orders of the Central Government. The prime example was the students' calculated disregard of the Provisional Measures for the Maintenance of Public Order.

During the December First Movement in 1945, Robert Payne had written emotionally of the students' stubborn determination to defy the locally imposed ban on a public funeral procession for the dead students. He interpreted this as a death wish on the part of the living, a selfish desire to follow their classmates to martyrdom. No one could interpret the student defiance in May, 1947, in that light. Students deliberately provoked police violence on the streets of Nanking and invited arrest in Shanghai so that more people would be able "to see with their own eyes the brutality of their rulers." Something of a desire for martyrdom remained perhaps, but it was now sustained by conscious political motives. The students' protest movement had developed into a technique for discrediting the KMT Government and in this they were successful.[38]

According to a self-conscious appraisal made within the student movement itself, the Anti-Hunger Anti-Civil War protest made possible the organization and unification of the student community on a national level. As a result, student activities were able to overcome their temporary nature, their fragmentation, and local limitations. This protest had also drawn increasing numbers of professors to the side of their students because it was the first to relate the Civil War to issues that directly concerned a majority of the population. This had served to broaden the base of support for the anti-Civil War movement, and in turn the base of dissatisfaction with the Government. The movement, the report concluded, had made people more aware of the futility of demanding peace from the KMT Government.[39]

38. In three sharp editorials, *Kuan-ch'a* editor Ch'u An-p'ing declared support for the students, deplored the violence against them, and blamed the government for causing the demonstrations: *KC*, May 24, 1947, pp. 3-4, and May 31, pp. 3-4 and 5-7.

39. *Hua-pei hsueh-sheng yun-tung hsiao-shih pien-chi wei-yuan-hui, ed.*, pp. 69-74. This interesting, if somewhat rambling, appraisal published in 1948, contained a lengthy criticism of the Movement's shortcomings in the North—while noting that many had already been remedied. There had been too many meetings and they were too long and boring. The leadership was separated from ordinary students, hence many did not understand much that was going on. For example, many did not understand the difference between the Anti-Hunger Anti-Civil War Association and the All-China Students Association. Preparation for the May 18 street propaganda activities in Peiping had been insufficient. Thus when one propaganda team was attacked by Youth Army men, other teams were not informed so they could avoid the area. Also, the Peiping students' attitude toward soldiers and policemen was erroneous, as was that of students in Nanking. Their propaganda was too full of "student spirit" and there was too much talk about how the war made it impossible for civilians to have white rice to eat since it was all going to feed the soldiers. This angered the soldiers and police and provoked unnecessary violence. The proper attitude, admonished the report, should be that students have no quarrel with those who are conscripted and who must work for a living; the real struggle is with the rulers.

THE ANTI-OPPRESSION ANTI-HUNGER MOVEMENT, AND THE MOVEMENT PROTESTING UNITED STATES SUPPORT OF JAPAN[40]

The last nationwide series of student demonstrations prior to Communist victory took place in April, May, and June, 1948. The Anti-Oppression Anti-Hunger Movement was essentially a continuation of the Anti-Hunger Anti-Civil War Movement of the year before. The demonstrations protesting U.S. policy toward Japan derived ultimately from the fear that this policy would prolong the Chinese Civil War by direct American or Japanese intervention.

The schools had been far from quiet during the preceding year. But protests and demonstrations were generally contained within individual schools. Some issues did arouse wider attention, yet these too remained relatively limited both in terms of objectives and student activity. Protests occurred, for example, over: the alleged suicide in jail of Yü Tzu-san, Chairman of the National Chekiang University Student Self-governing Association, in late October, 1947; a confrontation in Hong Kong between the inhabitants of the old walled city of Kowloon and the police; and the dismissal of seven students from Tungchi University in Shanghai for an infraction of university rules relating to student elections in January, 1948.

THE ANTI-OPPRESSION ANTI-HUNGER PROTESTS

Students and teachers had continued their protests against economic hardship and the war. In February, 1948, an estimated ten thousand persons joined a new Shanghai Association of Students' Guardians to promote demands for an increase in teachers' salaries, more public financial support for education, and protection of the right to attend school, since many students had to interrupt their studies due to economic hardship.

Student leaders continued to be dealt with harshly. In early February, six university students in Peiping were arrested on charges of being Communist underground agents. Students, professors, and university officials came to their defense. Four of the arrested students were accused of sponsoring the Socialist Youth Alliance, an alleged front for the CCP. Another student, whose plight aroused the most sympathy, was Teng T'e, a demobilized soldier from the 208th Division of the Youth Army studying at Peita. He was accused of working for the CCP under the direction of the North China Students Association. His specific crime was the publication of a wall newspaper. He had registered the paper with the proctor's office according to university regulations, but the political authorities found it too critical of the Government. Peita President, Hu Shih, and Proctor Ho Lin both spoke in defense of the students and especially of Teng, whose release on bail the university finally secured. From his hospital bed,

---

40. This summary of the anti-American demonstrations and the Anti-Oppression Anti-Hunger Movement which preceded them is based on: Chang Hui, ed., *Shang-hai chin pai nien ko-ming shih hua*, pp. 201-208; Hu En-tse, pp. 41-56; *I-chiu-szu-chiu-nien shou-ts'e*, pp. *chia* 112-18; A Che, pp. 158-73; *China White Paper*, 1:276-77, 387-90 and 2:869-71, 901-19; *KC* for the period; and *CPR* covering the press in the main KMT-controlled cities.

the young man described how he had been beaten and subjected to the two most common forms of police torture at this time: the water treatment and the tiger chair.[41]

New slogans appeared to "oppose oppression, oppose hunger." Students in Peiping, Tientsin, Nanking, and Shanghai tried to organize a joint self-defense movement. In early April, lecturers, assistants, and staff at the Peiping Research Institute went on strike. This action was followed by a joint anti-oppression anti-hunger strike by students at the seven major universities in Peiping and Tientsin: Peking, Tsinghua, Yenching, Normal, Sino-French, Nankai, and Peiyang.

During April, the level of protest accelerated. Students boycotted classes and sponsored protests in cities throughout the country. These included, in addition to the four just mentioned, Hangchow, Wuhan, Chungking, Nanchang, Lanchow, Mukden, Canton, Changsha, and Foochow. As the "eventful month of May" approached, a new wave of student activity had developed. This was known as the Anti-Oppression Anti-Hunger Movement. It was soon overshadowed, however, by a nationwide series of anti-American demonstrations.

AMERICA, JAPAN, AND THE COLD WAR

Government oppression, economic hardship, and the Civil War were the major preoccupations of the intellectual community in 1948. Related to these was the issue of Japan's revival. Concern began to grow as soon as U.S. plans for the rehabilitation of the Japanese economy and defense capabilities became known. Under Secretary of State, Dean Acheson, revealed the intention to rebuild the Japanese and German economies in May, 1947. This sharp break with immediate post-war occupation policy grew out of the developing Cold War and the American desire to build a strong anti-Communist front in Europe and Asia. The Soviet Union was consolidating its hold over Eastern Europe. The U.S. was responding with the Truman Doctrine, aid to Greece and Turkey, and the Marshall Plan for Western Europe. The post-war world had divided itself into two camps. In China the two sides were already at war, and America's ally was not winning.

Wang Yun-sheng, editor-in-chief of the *Ta kung pao,* was among the first to sound the alarm after a two-week trip he made to Japan in 1947. While there he learned that Japanese naval bases and airfields were being repaired rather than dismantled, that the U.S. was training Japanese fliers, and that arms and heavy industries were being restored. The reason for all of this, he declared, was

41. Peiping correspondent, "Pei-p'ing hsueh-sheng yu pei-pu" [Peiping students have again been arrested], *KC,* Feb. 28, 1948, pp. 19, 18. The water treatment involved forcing a hose down the prisoner's throat. After the stomach became bloated, someone would stamp on it until the water was expelled from one end or the other. In the tiger chair interrogation, the victim was seated in one chair with his feet on another. Weights would then be placed on the knees until the joints bent backwards. The Chinese police were said to have learned these methods from the Japanese. (According to informants.)

defense against communism and against the Soviet Union. The implications for China—where American-supported anti-Communist forces already included Japanese troops [42]—seemed clear. Should any incident break out between the U.S. and the U.S.S.R., he wrote: "American warships will carry Japan's 'Kwantung Army' to land again on our Northeast soil fighting Russia on the one hand, and directly undertaking, on behalf of China, the task of 'defense against communism' and 'Chinese Communist suppression' on the other." [43] This apprehension lay at the heart of the opposition to America's new Japan policy.

Resentment against Japan was so great that the protest struck a responsive chord at points all along the political spectrum, and well beyond the student community. Thus, when the U.S. submitted a memorandum on its plans to the Far Eastern Commission and the Chinese Ministry of Foreign Affairs in January, 1948, the Chinese reaction was uniformly suspicious. Only the official *Chung-yang jih-pao* seemed willing to endorse the plan. In two editorials on January 26 and 28, the *Ta kung pao* criticized it sharply, as did other publications associated with the Political Study Clique of the KMT. [44] The *Hsin-wen pao,* on March 9, suggested that it was one thing to take precautionary measures against the Soviet Union and quite another to build up Japan for that purpose. Also on March 9, the *Lih pao* suggested: ". . . while we should be grateful to the U.S. for her aid to China, yet besides feeling sincerely grateful to her, we must not forget to oppose the current U.S. policy of building up Japan." Three major fears pervaded the editorial comment: first, the danger of renewed aggression once Japan's military capability had been restored; second, the threat of economic domination of East Asia by an industrialized Japan; and third, that in the event of war between the Soviet Union and the U.S., Japan would become an American base, and China the battleground.

This editorial activity paralleled the publicity campaign carried out by the Truman Administration, the U.S. Department of the Army, and General MacArthur's Occupation Headquarters in Tokyo during the first half of 1948. The plan drawn up by MacArthur's headquarters estimated the cost of putting the Japanese economy back on a self-supporting basis at U.S.$1 billion over a four-year period. As a first installment, the plan called for Congress to approve U.S.$180 million in economic rehabilitation funds during the fiscal year to begin July 1, 1948. Also publicized was the Army Department's recommendation that only Japan's "primary" war industries be dismantled. "Secondary" defense industries, initially scheduled for removal to neighboring Asian countries as reparations, should be left intact in Japan and turned to peaceful uses.

42. See Chapter Two, note 8.

43. Wang Yun-sheng, "A Stone in MacArthur's Hand", *Kuo hsin chou-k'an* (published by Huang Yen-p'ei, leader of the Vocational Education Group), No. 433, reprinted in *TKP,* Shanghai, Oct. 16, 1947 (*CPR,* Oct. 24).

44. An alternative translation for *Cheng hsueh hsi,* often used during the 1940s, was Political Science Clique. Since this translation implies a group of political scientists (which it was not), I have adopted the more literal translation, Political Study Clique. For more on this group and its association with the *Ta kung pao,* see the Bibliographic Notes.

On March 20, a committee headed by New York banker Percy Johnston and Under Secretary of the Army William Draper arrived in Tokyo on the first leg of a hurried "fact-finding" mission to Japan and Korea. The group returned to the U.S. on April 7. Its members announced their conclusions at once, and repeatedly during the month of April. Their investigation had proved that the views of MacArthur and the Army Department were correct. The rehabilitation of Japan's economy must become the primary objective of the U.S. occupation and this would require large-scale economic aid. The U.S. Government published the committee's report on May 19; the next day, President Truman included U.S.$100 million in the 1948-49 budget for Japanese economic rehabilitation.

The change of U.S. occupation policy in Japan was the subject of widespread comment in the Chinese press. On Chinese campuses, slogans against hunger and oppression gave way almost entirely during May to new ones protesting U.S. policy toward Japan. The U.S. Embassy found the new outburst "puzzling," and concluded that the protest was actually a "sublimated" attack on U.S. aid to the KMT Government. On April 2, the U.S. Congress had passed the China Aid Act of 1948, authorizing U.S.$338 million in economic aid and $125 million in special grants for the Chinese Government during the 1948-49 fiscal year. By now the Americans were well aware that all who opposed the Civil War condemned such aid as an attempt to prop up an unregenerate Chiang Kai-shek and prolong his battle with the Communists.

But if the students did not fully understand what inspired that attempt, by 1948 the older generation of intellectuals did. The Americans supported Chiang, and would continue to do so whatever the weaknesses of his regime, because Chiang was anti-Communist. Yet economic aid alone could not give him a victory over his chief enemy: only active U.S. intervention might do that. KMT stalwarts saw this clearly, and so did Chinese intellectuals, while people everywhere were speculating on the possibility of a third world war. The new U.S. policy toward Japan—so effectively publicized by the Americans themselves— was perceived within the context of the developing Cold War as a greater threat to an eventual peace in China than the mere extension of economic aid to the KMT. With hindsight, this basic fear that in the event of war between the U.S. and the forces of communism, Japan would become an American base and China the battleground, came close to reality within just two years—except that Chinese soldiers fought on Korean rather than Chinese soil.

ACTION AND REACTION BY STUDENTS AND OFFICIALS

Journalists and academics discussed these issues and the students responded. There were the usual activities: lectures, discussion meetings, street propaganda, wall newspapers, and so forth. On May 4, representatives from 120 Shanghai universities and middle schools gathered on the Chiaotung University campus and established the Shanghai Students Association to Oppose U.S. Support of Japan and to Relieve the National Crisis. Students in other cities soon joined in the protest activity. A similar North China protest association was set up in Peiping on May 30.

The mood of the academic community was reflected in a public opinion poll conducted on May 18 and 19 by the academic research department of the Student Self-governing Association of St. John's University in Shanghai. Nine hundred and forty students and faculty members replied. An overwhelming majority agreed that Japanese fascism had revived and that this would result in another Japanese invasion of China. As to what students and intellectuals could do about the situation, the majority response was in favor of mobilizing Chinese public opinion against U.S. policy towards Japan and demanding strong action from the Chinese Government.

A similar poll sponsored by the Law College of Futan University covered 1,613 persons with similar results. Students were particularly angered by reports that iron ore was being exported to Japan from Hainan Island, and that Okamura Yasuji, former Japanese Army Commander-in-Chief in China, had been appointed an adviser for the exploitation of economic resources in Kwangtung and Hainan Island.

In Peiping, students at Tsinghua University designated the week beginning May 23 as Oppose American Support of Japan Week. On June 1, 338 presidents and professors of Shanghai colleges and universities signed a telegram to President Truman and Secretary of State Marshall protesting U.S. policy toward Japan. Two days later, a relatively mild editorial in the official *Chung-yang jih-pao* requested the public to distinguish between the anti-American movement being instigated by "professional students who are Communist military spies," and the genuine suspicion of U.S. policy toward Japan entertained by some people in industrial, commercial, and educational circles. The latter group was asked to leave to the experts such questions as what level of industrial development would restore Japan's military capabilities and what level was necessary to maintain the livelihood of the Japanese people. In any case, admonished the paper, the anti-American movement must be brought to an end.

Meanwhile, Americans in China had also begun to speak out in a manner that did not ease the tension. On May 25, 26, and 27, the American-owned *Shanghai Evening Post and Mercury* published a series of articles denouncing the anti-American activities at St. John's University. The paper reminded the students that their university was financed by American funds and also that, were it not for America's military efforts against Japan, the students would not now be enjoying freedom in Shanghai. The American Consul General in Shanghai, John M. Cabot, expressed similar views. At Memorial Day services on May 30, Cabot was quoted as saying with reference to the activities at St. John's: "Many [in the U.S.] will bitterly retort that students getting their education through the beneficence of Americans who have contributed their mites to knowledge and understanding—students whose very food depends upon the labor of the American farmer and the generosity of the American taxpayer—should not spread calumnies against the U.S."

This brought a series of sharp retorts in the Chinese press, as did a statement by the American Ambassador. On June 4, Ambassador Stuart warned the students that the anti-American movement might have grave consequences at a time when the U.S. was preparing a new large-scale aid program for the Chinese Government. On the issue which had aroused the protest, he declared: "I defy anyone to produce a single shred of evidence that any part of Japanese military power is being restored or that there is any intention on the part of the U.S. other than to assure that it will never rise again."

Considering the state of student feeling about U.S. aid to the KMT Government, the threat was somewhat inappropriate. Some tried to explain it by suggesting that Ambassador Stuart had been forced to make the statement as the representative of the U.S. Government. They believed that were he still President of Yenching University—a post he held for over twenty-five years until he was named U.S. Ambassador in 1946—Dr. Stuart would never have made such inopportune comments. In reply, 437 professors from colleges and universities in Peiping addressed Dr. Stuart as their former colleague, offering evidence that the U.S. was indeed restoring Japan's military capabilities and rebuilding Japan without any regard for the lessons of history, which taught that China would be the victim.[45]

Initially, the Vice-minister of Education expressed public agreement with Ambassador Stuart's statement. But Sun Fo, President of the Legislative Yuan, had strong words of criticism, saying it was a mistake to lecture the Chinese people in a threatening tone, since this would only "antagonize rather than explain." General public criticism mounted. Finally even the *Chung-yang jih-pao* in an editorial on June 18, expressed the hope that the U.S. would look carefully at its policy of support for Japan.

During this anti-American campaign, there were fewer of the large-scale demonstrations and parades that had characterized earlier student protests. The students concentrated instead on educational activities such as street propaganda teams, press conferences, the circulation of protest statements, together with on-campus meetings, classroom strikes, cartoon exhibitions, and the like. One massive parade planned for June 5 in Shanghai, was thwarted by tight security measures. Students who managed to circumvent the police cordons around their schools found themselves contained by hundreds of police, mounted police, and armored cars in the vicinity of the Bund Garden where the parade was to have begun. Police fired on parading students in Peiping on June 9, and also attacked them with clubs and rocks. In Kunming, student protest growing out of arrests made during a parade on June 17 continued until mid-July.

AFTERMATH

The Government's apparent deference to public opinion on the issue of Japanese recovery did not mitigate its distrust of the students. On August 18, a Chung-yang News Agency release entitled "Irrefutable Proof of Communist Spies Instigating Innocent Students in Order to Create Student Unrest" was carried by virtually every Chinese-language newspaper in Shanghai. The statement declared that every past instance of "student troubles" had been organized and led by

45. *Hsin min wan-pao,* Shanghai, June 13, 1948 (*CPR,* June 14).

Communist agents. The emergency economic reform program, the Government's final effort to restore public confidence through the revitalization of the economy, was inaugurated the next day. Also on August 19, the Government announced that special criminal tribunals would deal with so-called political offenders. The tribunals immediately began issuing warrants for the arrest of students suspected of having instigated the most recent wave of protest activity. Ch'u An-p'ing, editor of the popular weekly *Kuan-ch'a,* denounced the timing of the action as a calculated attempt to gain social approval for the move against the students by carrying it out simultaneously with the widely applauded attack against unscrupulous merchants and profiteers under the economic reform measures.

It was initially rumored that the lists of those to be arrested or summoned for questioning contained the names of 300 students in Shanghai, another 300 in Nanking, 248 in Peiping, and scores in each of several other cities including Wuhan, Canton, Hangchow, Chungking, Chengtu, and Tsingtao. Communist publications later claimed that during the autumn of 1948 hundreds of students fled to the liberated areas from the Shanghai area alone. The accuracy of this claim is impossible to verify, but considerably fewer students were actually arrested or summoned than initial reports had anticipated.[46] By the end of September, between 80 and 90 students had been arrested in Shanghai, approximately 180 in Nanking, 100 in Peiping, and 80 in Kunming. Figures for other cities are less certain.

The period of investigation and questioning was prolonged. Two months after the initial arrests were made in Shanghai, no formal charges had been brought against any of the students. On October 16, parents of the arrested students held a press conference requesting that action be taken to settle the cases as soon as possible. Two days later, forty students were released for lack of evidence. Twenty-six others were formally prosecuted. Of these, varying reports indicated that about ten received light jail sentences of two years or less. The remainder were found innocent, again for lack of sufficient proof that the students were Communist agents. In addition, some twenty students could not be formally prosecuted, since the investigators had found their offenses to be "less serious." The authorities nevertheless felt that these students should spend some time in a reformatory. Unfortunately, Shanghai could boast no such institution, so the

46. There were numerous reports throughout the Civil War years of sympathetic friends and professors helping blacklisted students evade the police dragnet. A number of these students did.flee to the Communist side. In fact, everyone seemed to know of someone who had fled to the Communist areas rather than risk arrest by the KMT police. A typical story was told by the missionary educator, Ralph Lapwood, who returned to Yenching University in the summer of 1948. When the police stepped up their surveillance of the students in August, word leaked out that 38 Yenching students were on the blacklist. The 38 were able to escape while the Acting President of the University kept the police from entering the dormitories. According to the author's personal knowledge, his friend Liu Shih, a student leader and Christian whose name was on the blacklist, fled into the nearby Communist areas after hiding for three days on the campus grounds (Ralph and Nancy Lapwood, *Through the Chinese Revolution,* pp. 37-38).

students were detained in prison. In January, 1949, the Ministry of Justice ordered the dissolution of the special tribunals and the release of all political prisoners who had not yet been sentenced.

RESULTS

The student protest clearly had no effect on U.S. plans for the revival of the Japanese economy. But the movement did focus public attention in China on the issue of Japan's rehabilitation. Although little substantive effort was made to allay the fears expressed, the Central Government did eventually defer to public opinion on this issue. This was indicated by the June 18 editorial and others like it, as well as by a much-publicized visit to Tokyo in late summer by former Premier Chang Ch'ün. On his return to China, he announced his findings: that the U.S. had disarmed Japan, that militarism was being rooted out, and so on. The critics remained unconvinced.

In addition, the decision made the previous year to subdue the student movement by whatever means necessary continued to be implemented, and the Government's prestige to suffer accordingly. Its wisdom was sharply challenged in the press, as was the charge that all student protests had been organized and led by Communist agents. A common criticism of the Government at this time was that its tactics were only alienating the students further, and forcing many who would not otherwise have done so to turn towards the Communists.

THE STUDENT MOVEMENT AND THE POLITICS OF CIVIL WAR

In tracing the development of the student movement, the focus has been on the students themselves, their objectives, organization, activities, and achievements. These features combined in a series of confrontations with the KMT authorities. Their effect was not only to turn the student community more firmly against the Government, but also to discredit the Government in the eyes of other sectors of the population. What remains to be discussed is the students' relationship with the other half of the Civil War equation: the Chinese Communists. Toward that end, three issues are examined below: (1) the Communist view of the student movement in the KMT areas; (2) the Communist influence on that movement; and (3) the comparative orientation of the students toward the two contending parties.

THE COMMUNIST VIEW OF THE STUDENT MOVEMENT IN THE KMT AREAS

By comparison with the Government's intransigence, the Chinese Communist position on the student movement was a model of pragmatism and flexibility. The Communists actually had reservations of their own about the student demonstrators. A 1939 statement by Mao Tse-tung was often quoted during the Civil War years and was characteristic of the Party's attitude towards students and intellectuals in general. "Subjective and individualistic, impractical in their thinking and irresolute in action," was the way Mao described them. But he also

acknowledged the important contribution they could make to the revolution. [47]
The Communists therefore extended overt and covert encouragement to the
student movement as a means of mobilizing public opinion against the Government.

While both sides continued to rely on force as the most effective means of
safeguarding their respective interests, only the Communists seemed to recognize
the political capital to be gained by supporting popular sentiment against the
war. Mao indicated the course the Communists would follow when he wrote at
the time of the December First Movement: "We support the democratic movement now developing in the KMT areas (as marked by the student strike in
Kunming) in order to isolate the reactionaries, win numerous allies for ourselves
and expand the national democratic united front under our Party's influence." [48] Mao made no attempt to camouflage the political motives underlying
his statement of support for the peace movement. Nevertheless, that policy of
support represented an application of the twin principles of democracy and
centralism so important in Chinese Communist political thought and action. The
result was a policy stated in terms which paralleled, rather than mocked, the
prevailing demand for peace.

Yet the Party's reservations about intellectuals remained, even as it encouraged the student protest movement. In an article commending the students of
Kunming and elsewhere for their anti-war struggle, a *Chieh-fang jih-pao* writer
offered a few suggestions to the students for their future work. Fearing that they
underestimated the importance of workers and peasants, he emphasized the
significance of the worker-peasant contribution to the Anti-Japanese War. He
pointed out that they had constituted the most important force in the Resistance and in the creation of the base areas, and expressed the hope that "you
will be able to unite with the local workers, peasants, and soldiers and eliminate
the feeling that you are better than they are." [49]

A year later, commenting on the nationwide anti-American demonstration
following the alleged rape of the Peita student, the *Chieh-fang jih-pao* was more
outspoken in its praise for the students' efforts. But the words of caution and
advice remained: "You should value this experience, strengthen your unification, even more firmly believe in peace, independence, and the future democratic struggle, and develop your heroic spirit." [50]

47. Mao Tse-tung, "The Chinese Revolution and the Chinese Communist Party,"
Selected Works, 2:322.

48. Mao Tse-tung, "Policy for Work in the Liberated Areas for 1946," *Selected Works,*
4:78. The term "democratic movement" was used by the Communists to refer to all of the
popular protest activity which occurred in the Government areas. This included anti-war
demonstrations as well as protests against other aspects of KMT rule, by students and
others. A number of incidents occurred, for example, during the latter half of 1945 in
Chungking, Chengtu, and Kunming, involving student protests against the academic policies
of political and school authorities which Yenan summarized as "the democratic movement
of students under the Kuomintang's oppression," *CFJP,* Yenan, Nov. 24, 1945, p. 3.

49. *CFJP,* Yenan, Dec. 12, 1945, p. 4.

50. *CFJP,* Yenan, Jan. 9, 1947, p. 1.

Briefly stated, the Communist political credo during the Civil War was that "without the broadest united front of the overwhelming majority of the population, it will be impossible to win victory in China's new democratic revolution."[51] Whatever its deficiencies, Mao regarded the student movement as a vanguard in building such a united front. In the editorial he wrote for the Hsinhua News Agency on May 30, 1947, he asserted: "Public sympathy is all on the side of the students, Chiang Kai-shek and his running dogs are completely isolated. . . . The upsurge of the student movement will inevitably promote an upsurge of the whole people's movement. This is borne out by the historical experience of the May 4th Movement of 1919 and the December 9th Movement of 1935." The Communists therefore tried wherever possible to capitalize on the Government's misfortunes by expressing support for the protests of students and others, and by attempting to influence the direction of these activities.[52]

COMMUNIST AND OTHER INFLUENCES ON THE STUDENT MOVEMENT

What is to be made, however, of the specific KMT charge that the student protest movement was brought about by underground Communist "agents" and "spies" working among the students?[53] The Communists were of course noncommittal at the time, but in later years they too claimed that the Party and its underground cadre led and organized the student movement in the Government areas during the 1945-49 period.[54] Yet concrete details about such leadership activity remain scant.

A contemporary Peking University student recalled years later that a list of perhaps fifty underground workers at the University was made public shortly after the Communists took Peiping. A woman recollected that several students working with her as officers of their school's student self-governing association emerged as Communist cadres after liberation. A man later claimed that he had been a Communist and an underground worker during his college days in Shanghai. In another case, two recent graduates in geography from Chekiang University joined the teaching staff of a middle school in Fukien province in 1948. Soon afterward, they organized a study group, a folk dance group, and a singing group. Many of the younger students, at least, did not even understand the pro-Communist inferences of some of the songs they were taught at that time.[55]

51. Mao Tse-tung, "The Present Situation and our Tasks," *Selected Works,* 4:170.
52. For further discussion of the Party's policies toward students and intellectuals, see Chapters Six and Nine.
53. This is a charge which has continued to be made both officially and unofficially in Taiwan. See Szu-fa hsing-cheng-pu tiao-ch'a-chü, ed., *Kung-fei hsueh yun kung-tso te p'ou-shih, passim;* and Wang Chien-min, *Chung-kuo kung-ch'an-tang shih-kao,* 3:552-58.
54. Wang Nien-k'un, *passim;* and Hu En-tse, *passim.*
55. One student did not catch on until two years later when about twenty students were arrested at National Taiwan University in Taipei for singing one of the songs entitled, "Singing About the Coming of Spring." The notion of the advent of spring had long been used to symbolize a new society and a new China. But as in the case of this song, it was also used by the Communists to symbolize their own victory. (These recollections from interviews conducted during spring and summer, 1969.)

An article in the *Chieh-fang jih-pao* on June 29, 1951, outlined the history of the Communist cell at Chiaotung University. The branch had been established in the 1920s, destroyed in 1933, and reestablished in 1937. In August, 1945, it had only twelve members but was able to build on this base. The cell was reorganized into a general branch in August, 1947, in the aftermath of the Anti-Hunger Anti-Civil War Movement.[56] The article claimed that the Party branch not only organized social, academic, and welfare activities within the university, but was also behind virtually all of the protest activities that Chiaota students engaged in during the Civil War years.

The article also implied that the branch was in control of the Chiaota Student Self-governing Association. Specifically, Li Chün-liang, a student body officer, joined the Party in 1948 at the time of the movement protesting U.S. support of Japan. In early 1949, after the surrender of Peiping and Tientsin to the Communists, the Party organization at Chiaota underwent considerable expansion in preparation for the liberation of Shanghai. Four hundred Chiaota students had been drawn into the Communist-sponsored New Democratic Youth League by April, 1949. One of the final acts of the KMT in Shanghai was the execution of Mu Han-hsiang and Shih Hsiao-wen, the former a member of the Party's general branch committee at Chiaota, and the latter an officer of the Student Self-governing Association and member of the New Democratic Youth League. They had been arrested with about forty of their classmates during a raid on the campus on the night of April 26, just a month before Communist troops entered the city.[57]

Finally, if the All-China Students Association established in Shanghai in June, 1947, did not have close contacts with the Communists at that time, it acquired them shortly thereafter. The Association was forced to go underground soon after its formation, but was later said to have maintained a headquarters organization in Shanghai. This headquarters organization moved to the liberated areas at the end of 1948, its responsible members arriving in Shihchiachuang in mid-December. The immediate reason for the move was to prepare for the Fourteenth All-China Students Representative Conference held in Peiping in March, and the formal reestablishment of the All-China Students Association. Meanwhile, an "office" was maintained in Shanghai to "promote student activ-

56. According to the 1945 Constitution of the CCP, a general branch could be formed in any village with 50 or more Party members, and in any factory, office, or school with 100 or more Party members. This does not necessarily mean that there were 100 CCP members at Chiaota, however, since the organizational rules as provided in the Constitution could be modified in the case of underground Party organizations. See Articles 50 and 54 of the 1945 CCP Constitution. An English translation of the Constitution appears in Peter S.H. Tang, *Communist China Today: Chronological and Documentary Supplement* (New York: Praeger, 1958).

57. From a reprint of the article in Hua-tung jen-min ch'u-pan-she, ed., *Tsai tou-cheng li chuang-ta,* pp. 86-100. A similar pattern of Communist activity was reported among Chinese students in the U.S. One writer, for example, was able to name two Communists among the 150 Chinese students at the University of Wisconsin in 1948 (Robert Loh, as told to Humphrey Evans, *Escape from Red China,* p. 35).

ities in the KMT-controlled areas." [58] Within twenty-four hours after the liberation of the city, a Shanghai Students Association had emerged and was operating in the northern and central districts of Shanghai. A spokesman for the Association told a *Ta kung pao* reporter that about eighty of Shanghai's three hundred universities, colleges, and middle schools had been in "constant contact" with the Association—he did not say for how long—but that the remainder were still "comparatively backward." The task of the Association was to establish contact with all of them as quickly as possible. [59]

However sketchy and self-serving, such recollections and claims indicate that there was an underground Party organization among the students in the KMT-controlled areas. Its membership must also have increased sharply as the probability of a Communist victory grew more apparent. But lacking more substantive information, any estimate as to the overall numbers of such cadres is impossible to make. Their task was not easy. As we have seen, the Government itself had student informers in the schools. On the basis of the information they supplied, arrests of student activists were continuously carried out in most major cities. Students arrested or abducted were often never heard of again. Execution was the expected punishment for genuine Communist agents if their identity as such could be more or less established. Torture was a common means of extracting confessions and information. According to one informant, underground work was so dangerous that those engaged in it were obliged to concentrate on information-gathering, social activities, and surreptitious pamphleteering, while other students carried on the more prominent tasks of actual leadership. One is inclined to suspect, therefore, that there were relatively few underground Communist cadres among the students during most of the Civil War period, and that they remained reasonably circumspect in their activities.

This brings us to the more important question: what kind of influence did this Communist element have on the protest movement itself? Communist students within the Kunming Student Strike Committee could have exerted considerable influence during the December First Movement. Similarly, Communists in the History Society at Peita or at Tsinghua could have influenced the development of the anti-American protests in Peiping after the rape incident. The two later protest movements were so diffuse and widespread that it is difficult to locate the points at which Communist cadres could have actually "led and organized" them. Communists could, however, have played an important role in the efforts to form a national student organization.

Yet the general student response, even in the first two protests, was so immediate and spontaneous as to render the charge of Communist instigation almost meaningless. Such a charge implies that the student protest movement could not have developed as it did without the presence of underground Communist agitators. But this is a conclusion impossible to draw given the large number of non-Communist student leaders the movement also contained, and

58. U.S. Cons., Peiping, Hsinhua radio, North Shensi, Feb. 3, 1949.

59. *TKP*, Shanghai, May 28, 1949 *(CPR);* Peiping mandarin broadcast, May 29, 1949 *(Daily Report,* May 31).

the widespread support upon which each of the four major protests was based. The charge also implies that the rest of the students were misled into demonstrating against the Government and the Civil War. But the students knew well enough what they were doing, and admitted they did not care that the Communists were advocating many of the same things they were.[60]

Commenting on the Government's charge that a recent series of civil disturbances had been "stage-managed" by the Communists, the American Ambassador reported to the U.S. Secretary of State on February 5, 1948, that the question of Communist involvement was largely academic. The Communists were surely interested in exploiting them, but in each case the disturbances were due to popular dissatisfaction with the Government born of its own administrative ineptitude and its failure to provide effective arrangements for a redress of grievances.[61]

When they addressed themselves to the question of Communist involvement in the student movement, non-official Chinese sources almost without exception arrived at conclusions similar to Ambassador Stuart's. Their comments provide insight into the Government's failure to maintain credibility, and also give some indication as to the attitude of the intellectual community in general toward the students' activities. The following were all written between April and September, 1948.

One of the more conservative arguments appeared in the May 27 issue of the *Lih pao*. Recalling that those in the Government who were dealing with the present student unrest had themselves participated in the student movements of the past, it wondered that they were incapable of viewing the students' activities more sympathetically. The vast majority of the students were "pure and zealous," participating in anti-Government activities only because of their dissatisfaction with the political situation. Indicating that there were undoubtedly some Communist agents in the schools, the editorial went on to chastise the Government for sponsoring its own "professional students." Why not purge them all, it suggested, and in addition increase government appropriations for education, adopt progressive educational policies, and do away with the administration of education by bureaucrats and politicians.

The Shanghai *Ta Kung Pao* on April 15 expressed similar views, but was more inclined to view the student problem as a reflection of the larger political situation. Since the Government had resolved to crush the Communist rebellion, it could not very well let the CCP carry on its activities in the schools. But in dealing with student unrest, the Government should first try to learn its real nature rather than wrongly attribute everything to the Communists. A more strongly worded editorial in the same paper on July 16 declared: "Anyone who uses violence against youths does not understand their psychology nor does he know what education is. To consider all youthful students as [Communist] bandits is to force them to join the opposing camp."

---

60. Payne, *China Awake*, p. 222.
61. *China White Paper*, 2:842.

This last point was also expressed by the independent Peiping journal, *New Road*, and by the Shanghai journal, *Reconstruction Review*. The former suggested that since young people tend to be overly enthusiastic, they would merely persevere in the course they were following if force was used to try to divert them from it. When government officials were corrupt, it was only natural that young intellectuals should protest. This did not mean, however, that large numbers of students were working for the CCP. [62] Declared the *Reconstruction Review*, the current high-handed manner the Government is using against the students is actually being welcomed by the Communists because it is providing them with the best opportunity to recruit new members into their ranks.[63]

Finally, Chao Ch'ao-kou, writing in *Kuan-ch'a*, suggested that enemies usually infiltrated secret agents into one another's camp in wartime. Hence it was entirely possible that Communist agents were taking advantage of the situation to intensify student unrest. Nevertheless, it was unreasonable to give such persons credit for single-handedly creating and controlling the "student troubles" that the Government seemed to fear so much. If there were Communists participating, they were following the students, not leading them. In reference to the August 18 Chungyang News Agency release which claimed that each instance of student unrest had been led by Communist agents, Chao noted that people wondered how enemy agents working under difficult conditions were able to exert such great leadership over the students when the political and academic authorities remained unable to do so.[64]

The consensus which emerges from these opinions is that Communist cadres could not be held responsible, as claimed, for the student protest movement. This conclusion is also borne out by the few pieces of circumstantial evidence available. For example, the Government ultimately released most of the student activists arrested in Shanghai in May, 1947 and in the late summer of 1948, on suspicion of being Communist agents. Had there been any evidence at all, it seems fairly certain the Government would have prosecuted them or found them guilty as charged. One can only assume that there were either few Communist agents in Shanghai schools at the time the student movement was at its height, or that most of these agents managed to stay well underground beneath a far larger mass of student activists.

This is not to suggest the Communists had no influence on the student movement, but only that their chief influence should be sought at a different level. Again, unfortunately, there is only circumstantial evidence. The trial of three young men charged with conspiring to foment student unrest at Chekiang University under the direction of the Communists, provides one example of such evidence. On the night of October 25, 1947, Yü Tzu-san, Chairman of the Student Self-governing Association of National Chekiang University, was

62. *New Road*, Peiping, Aug. 28, 1948 (*CPR*, Shanghai, Sept. 17).

63. *Reconstruction Review*, Shanghai, Sept. 5, 1948 (*CPR*, Sept. 17).

64. *KC*, Sept. 4, 1948, p. 3. Professor Chang Chih-jang expressed a similar view in *KC*, Sept. 18, 1948, p. 3.

arrested along with a classmate and two friends recently graduated from the University. They were formally charged with conspiring to aid the Communist rebellion financially through the cultivation of a commercial peach orchard, and also of secretly plotting to gain control of the Student Self-governing Association in order to instigate student demonstrations at the University. The case took a sensational turn when Yü allegedly committed suicide while in prison under interrogation.[65] The other three were found guilty as charged and each sentenced to seven years imprisonment. After their conviction, the young men were referred to by officials as guilty Communist bandits.

Few students charged with aiding the Communists received public trials, but in this case there was a trial and a fairly detailed summary of the court proceedings appeared in the press. Among the most important pieces of evidence used against the accused were the fingerprinted but unsigned confession of the dead student, and a similar unsigned statement admitting the charges attributed to one of the defendants. The court was advised that he had refused to sign the document. In their testimony before the court, the three defendants denied all charges that they had been acting under the direction of the CCP.

According to their testimony and statements by the defense counsel, the young men were all members of the New Tide *(Hsin ch'ao)* Society, which bore no relation to a Communist society of the same name. The group had been founded in 1945 at Chekiang University, and had a total membership in November, 1947, of seventeen, all of whom were agronomy students in the College of Agriculture. Thirteen of the seventeen had recently graduated and were then living in seven different cities and Taiwan. Nevertheless, each member of the Society was pledged to contribute 5 percent of his monthly income to a fund for operating the peach orchard. The students were trying their hand at the cultivation of some newly planted trees not expected to bear fruit for three or four years. The Society also published a wall newspaper. This contained only articles on agriculture and was registered with the University.

The only substantiated link between the students and the CCP was some books and booklists seized from the young men at the time of their arrest. They admitted that the booklists were circulated among the Society members, who were urged to make reports on their studies of the suggested reading materials. Some of these were published by the Communists, as were some of the materials in the students' possession. The defendants maintained that all of the materials had come from bookstores recognized as legitimate by the Government and that some of the books had been purchased in Chungking. In defending themselves against the charge that they were promoting the Communist method of study, that is, writing reports after reading suggested materials, the defendants replied that no one ever looked at the reports and that the Society's program of learning

65. The background of the case to this point is described in Hsiao Yang, "Che-ta hsueh-sheng pei-pu ts'an-szu-an" [The arrest and death of a Chekiang University student], *KC*, Nov. 8, 1947, p. 16.

was actually based on an article entitled "The Problem of Studying Philosophy." The article had appeared in an academic journal unrelated to the CCP.[66]

Assuming that the facts presented here can be accepted at face value, this case probably offers a more realistic picture concerning the nature of Communist influence on the students than the verdict would imply. It seems likely that the young men were penalized for their interest in Communist reading matter rather than for any conspiratorial activities actually carried out under the direction of the CCP. According to a former student there, a Communist cell did exist at Chekiang University in the 1930s, and such an organization could be presumed to exist in 1947 as well. Also, the Communist underground did try to circulate reading materials among the students. Yet no evidence presented in the Yü Tzu-san case suggested that the defendants were actually secret agents. Nor did the sentences imposed support this. Considering the severity of the formal charges, the young men might have received death sentences—and without the niceties of a public trial. The authorities apparently made the case public to serve as a warning to others. But it did not have the appearance of an operation expected to rid Chekiang University's Agronomy Department of any secret links with the CCP.

The evidence did indicate, however, that the students were interested enough in the Communist alternative to pursue their studies of it knowing, as everyone did at that time, the consequences if their interests were discovered. KMT leaders were partially justified in their distrust of the student movement—but for the wrong reasons. That there was often similarity between the student protests and the line taken by Yenan radio or the Communist press was almost certainly due more to the Communists' political acumen in expressing support for the students' anti-Government anti-Civil War activities, than to Communist influence on those activities. In addition, the Civil War itself bred curiosity within the student community about the progress of the conflict and the nature of the Communist opponent, which the scarcity of information only enhanced. But it was at these more overt levels of interaction—expressed in terms of shared concerns for commonly acknowledged problems and curiosity about the Communist alternative—that the CCP probably exerted its greatest influence on the students at this time.

Because they persisted in the claim—and apparently believed—that a small but strategically placed group of Communist cadres was responsible for the student protests, KMT leaders never seriously attempted to explain why so many students participated in them. Had the Government done so, it would have been obliged to come to grips with the reasons for the failure of its own youth workers to acquire a mass following in favor of the war and the KMT. There seem to have been a number of reasons for the particular focus of the students' discontent and the intensity of their protest.

66. The Yü Tzu-san case received extensive press coverage. This account is based on: *TKP*, Shanghai, Nov. 2, 1947 *(CPR,* Nov. 3); *CYJP*, Shanghai, Nov. 21 *(CPR); Hsin-wen pao,* Shanghai, Nov. 20 *(CPR,* Nov. 21); *Hsin-wen pao,* Shanghai, Jan. 8, 1948 *(CPR).*

The highly politicized nature of the student community was rooted in the recent past of the Chinese student experience, and beyond that to the traditional role of the scholar as a man of public, not just academic, affairs. The students obviously believed they could mobilize public opinion and in this way pressure the Government into responding to their demands. Their belief was entirely consistent with the twentieth century tradition of student activism dating back to the May Fourth Movement of 1919 and before.

In addition, the more recent experiences of the Anti-Japanese War conditioned the students for their new roles as anti-war protesters. When the students of Peking, Tsinghua, Nankai, and other universities set out on the arduous journey to the Southwest, they marched in the vanguard of a patriotic war of resistance against the Japanese invader. [67] They left behind their families and the security of an ordered existence in some of China's top educational institutions. Having endured this uprooting experience and the uncertainties of refugee life—which included inadequate food, housing, educational facilities, and deteriorating educational standards—they had gained a keen awareness of the hardships of prolonged war. Commenting on how students had been toughened by their experiences during the Anti-Japanese War, Yü Ts'ai-yu, editor of the Peiping *Ching-shih jih-pao,* wrote: "Yesterday's students advocated 'democracy' and 'science' and opposed imperialism and feudalism. These ideals have not changed today . . . only the ideals of today's students have been tempered by society and their exuberance has been repressed, so that in their speech and actions they are now more determined and firmer."[68]

Nevertheless, the most radical edge of the student movement during the Civil War years was not in the Peiping-Tientsin area where the leading academic institutions had followed the Government to the Southwest, but in Shanghai and Nanking where larger numbers of schools and students had not done so. The Japanese occupation provided these students with a different set of experiences: the disruption of KMT influence within the schools; the disorder and disillusionment associated with the returning KMT administration; and the inequities of the Government's reconversion policies in education. Given the tradition of student activism, these two complementary themes of opposition to war and hostility to the KMT Government must have sustained the student protest during the Civil War years.

By 1947, these two themes had converged around the specific issues of economic hardship caused by the Civil War, and the repressive measures adopted by the Government against the protest movement. These latter were aggravated by the state-supported system of education and the consequent government interference in many aspects of academic life. Because they touched the students' lives directly, these issues disposed the young people to accept and act

67. On this period see John Israel, *Student Nationalism in China, 1927-1937,* Chapters Five and Six.

68. Yü Ts'ai-yu, "T'an chin-t'ien te hsueh-sheng" [Talking about today's students], *KC,* Apr. 24, 1948, p. 17.

upon the intellectual arguments of their elders as the latter assessed the nature of KMT rule and the price the nation as a whole should have to pay to maintain it.[69]

In the spring of 1947, the economic grievances were greatest in the Nanking-Shanghai area as a consequence of the Government's ill-fated reform measures.[70] However, the students' economic hardships included not only the immediate deprivations created by inflation and economic mismanagement, but the increasingly limited opportunities for employment after graduation. Before World War II, qualified liberal arts students, which China's universities turned out in the greatest numbers, could look forward to reasonably secure careers as teachers or bureaucrats. By the end of the war and certainly by 1947, the remuneration for such jobs had been reduced to subsistence level. Even more important, the number of jobs themselves were diminishing under the dual impact of spiraling wage costs and the ever-larger areas coming under CCP control.

In July, 1947, it was estimated that two-thirds of the year's college graduates in Peiping would be unable to find jobs, although the engineering students were still somewhat better off than those in literature or law. A year later, few of Chiaotung University's eight hundred engineering and technical graduates could entertain any hope of employment. Previously, the National Resources Commission had taken many Chiaota graduates. With the Communists in control of most of Manchuria and north China, the Commission had few job openings by the summer of 1948.[71] Economic hardship directly attributable to the war thus became a personal problem which gave reality to the "anti-hunger" themes running through the student anti-war movement. The economic insecurities engendered by the war must have contributed substantially to the students' protests against it.[72]

Equally important, however, were the methods used by the Government in its attempt to control the students. We have traced the progressive alienation of the student community that resulted. The assumption that the students were being manipulated by the Communists together with the policies derived therefrom were obviously counterproductive, creating more problems for the Government

69. The arguments appeared in liberal newspapers and periodicals throughout the period. The older generation's assessment of KMT rule, including the issue of Government intervention in academic affairs, is outlined in Chapter Five below.

70. Even though they probably did influence the development of the student movement during the period in question, the Japanese occupation and the economic disruption during the spring of 1947 are not sufficient explanations for the relatively greater radicalism of Shanghai youth. Since this phenomenon has also been found among Party intellectuals after 1949, the causes must run much deeper within the Shanghai intellectual milieu. They may have to do with Shanghai's position as the nation's major industrial center, but any real answer must await a more detailed analysis.

71. *Shun pao*, Shanghai, July 19, 1947 *(CPR);* and *TKP*, Shanghai, June 15, 1948 *(CPR).*

72. For a sensitive treatment of this question, see Fei Hsiao-t'ung, "Mei-yu an-p'ai hao te tao-lu" [There is no properly arranged path], *KC*, May 3, 1947, pp. 6-7; also *TKP*, Tientsin, July 10, 1947 (CPR, July 11).

than they were ever able to resolve. Of greatest significance in this respect were not those who fled to the Communist areas to escape arrest, for their numbers were relatively small. More important was the wider resentment engendered by the Government's indiscriminate treatment of all student activists as Communist suspects. As we shall see further on, this did not necessarily make the students in general pro-Communist. But it did intensify their opposition to the Government.

The students generally had no way of distinguishing the genuine Communist agents in their midst, for these dared not behave much differently than the average student activist. Yet all alike were threatened, beaten, and arrested for actions that reflected the prevailing sentiments of the student community. It was not surprising that the students scorned the Government for crying wolf too often, and cooperated time and again to help blacklisted student leaders escape without bothering to question whether they were Communists. Thus one of the Government's key errors in dealing with the students was the belief that their protest movement could be subdued if only the Communist agitators among them could be eliminated.[73]

The Government failed in its efforts to "pacify" the students because it could not bring itself to acknowledge certain facts about their protest movement: that it was spontaneous; that the radicalizing issues were the Civil War itself and the Government's repressive tactics; and that the most active students in the movement, unlike the KMT's youth workers, were genuine student leaders in terms of activism and intellect, who represented the prevailing aversion to the war and dissatisfaction with the KMT.

STUDENT POLITICAL ATTITUDES

Despite the widening of this gulf between the students and the Government, there is little indication, except of a superficial sort, as to what kinds of political alternatives the students favored. Little emerged from the rhetoric of the student movement, for example, concerning the students' attitudes towards the Chinese Communists. The lack of documentation on this forbidden subject is understandable. But the question becomes an important one in trying to estimate just how much support the Communists actually had among the students, and the extent to which the students' confrontation with the Government reflected a willingness to transfer their political loyalties to the CCP. Mao did, after all, suggest some months after the May 1947 demonstrations that the CCP had "won the support of the broad masses in the areas and big cities under Kuomintang control."[74] Was this a reasonably accurate evaluation, or was Mao perhaps

73. Doak Barnett's interview with Ch'en Li-fu, head of the KMT Organization Department and the powerful CC Clique, gives an indication of the reasoning that inspired the student arrests. Apparently, Government leaders authorized them not merely to intimidate the students, but also in the genuine belief that if the "real" Communists could be apprehended the movement could be controlled (*China on the Eve of Communist Takeover*, p. 50).

74. "The Present Situation and Our Tasks," *Selected Works*, 4:170.

indulging in a bit of rhetoric? Conflicting reports indicate that the question was a difficult one for foreign observers to answer even then.[75]

Strikingly similar conclusions emerge, however, from two surveys of student opinion conducted in 1948. One of these was made at the University of Shanghai on December 13, with approximately one thousand persons, both students and faculty, participating. There is no indication as to how these respondents were chosen or who conducted the poll. The results of the survey were published in the *Tung-nan jih-pao*, a KMT newspaper. In response to the question on the KMT-CCP conflict; 15.9 percent were for prosecuting the campaign against the Communists to the finish; 72 percent favored a coalition government; 8.4 percent answered that China should be partitioned; and 3.7 percent favored a Communist government.[76]

Similar results emerged from a more systematic survey of the opinions of Chinese students studying in the U.S. The survey was sponsored by the North American Chinese Students Christian Association and was conducted during March and April, 1948. Some 2,300 questionnaires were sent out to Chinese students then studying in various universities in the U.S. Answers were sent in by 714 students. Of that number, 48 percent had come to the U.S. in the fall of 1947 or later, and, 33 percent had arrived between 1944 and 1947. Their responses to five of the eight questions in the questionnaire were as follows:[77]

QUESTION 1: *What sort of changes do you feel should be made in the land system of China?*

	(% of those responding)
no answer	2.4
land to the tiller	33.0
organize cooperative farms	46.5
organize collective farms	9.8
no change	6.6
other	2.1

QUESTION 2: *What is the best way to achieve industrialization in China?*

	(% of those responding)
no answer	1.4
nationalization of light and heavy industry and of public utilities	6.8

75. A Peking University student told Barnett in March, 1948, that at least 50 percent of the students at Peita were sympathetic to the CCP, considering it "better" than the KMT. Yet a short time earlier, Ambassador Stuart had told Barnett that 90-95 percent of the students were opposed to communism in China—though he admitted that a similar percentage opposed the Government (*China on the Eve*, pp. 46-47). Tillman Durdin estimated in mid-1948 that 70 percent of the university students in Peiping "supported" the CCP, but only about half had done so the year before (*New York Times*, June 20, 1948).

76. *Tung-nan jih-pao*, Shanghai, Dec. 24, 1948 *(CPR)*.

77. The results of the survey were reprinted in *KC*, July 17, 1948, pp. 8-9.

nationalization of heavy industry and public utilities	51.5
private operation of light and heavy industry and public utilities	4.9
joint public and private operation of light and heavy industry and public utilities	10.8
joint public and private operation of heavy industry and public utilities	14.2
a cooperative system and nationaliza- tion of heavy industry and public utilities	0.9
a cooperative system	9.5

QUESTION 3: *I feel that peace in China must be sought by:*

	(% of those responding)
no answer	1.8
the Nationalist Government should eliminate the Communist Party	18.0
the organization of a coalition govern- ment to include the CCP, the Democratic League, other parties and independent elements	51.1
the adoption of a federal system	17.9
the division of the country into independent areas	3.2
national rule by the CCP	2.7
let the United Nations arbitrate	1.1
other	4.2

QUESTION 4: *What should the Chinese liberals do at the present time?*

	(% of those responding)
no answer	3.9
participate in the Nationalist Government as individuals	15.3
cooperate with the Communist Party as individuals	3.0
form a new party and cooperate with the Government	19.5
form a new party and cooperate with the Communist Party	4.4

form a new party and adopt an independent party line	39.7
take no political action	9.9
other	4.5

QUESTION 5: *Do you feel the recent elections held in China and the pro-mulgation of a Constitution indicate that the country is truly moving in the direction of democratic government?*

	(% of those responding)
no answer	1.7
yes	18.9
no	49.0
not necessarily	31.0

The results of these two surveys bore remarkable similarities despite the differing conditions under which they were conducted. The percentage of students favoring a Communist government in China was 3.7 in the Shanghai poll and 2.7 in the American. At the opposite end of the political spectrum, those favoring the Government's campaign to annihilate the Communists represented 15.9 percent and 18 percent respectively. The larger numbers favoring a coalition government in the Shanghai survey, 72 percent as opposed to 51.1 percent in the American survey, may in part be explained by the fact that the latter poll allowed for a greater choice of responses from those not committed to either party.

These findings are consistent with the dominant themes of the student movement throughout the Civil War period. The opposition to the war took positive form in the desire that both the KMT and the CCP come together in a coalition government. The students were apparently willing to accept the immediate political consequences, as they understood them, of their demand for an end to the war without a military decision on the battlefield. Thus Mao was in part correct, at least so far as the student population was concerned, when he asserted that the Communists had won mass support in the cities under Government control. That support nevertheless came in the form of a qualified mandate. Less than one-fifth favored the annihilation of the CCP; but even fewer favored national rule by the CCP alone. The Communists' underlying reservations about them seemed to be justified by the qualified nature of the students' commitment.

These were subtleties which Government leaders, on the other hand, either could not recognize or would not accept. They may have been more correct than not in their assumption that the students in general remained ideologically uncommitted to the principles of communism. The failure of these leaders lay more immediately in their refusal to acknowledge the reality of the general desire for peace and political reform. Nor could this failure be blamed on overzealous or shortsighted subordinates. The Central Government in Nanking, and Chiang Kai-shek himself, were responsible for both the style and substance of the official response to the student protests.

The Government's intransigence in dealing with the student movement was, moreover, indicative of a broader political strategy which seemed calculated to reduce popular support for the KMT to a minimum, even as the Communists were, in Mao's words, striving to create "the broadest united front of the overwhelming majority of the population." By adopting an all-or-nothing approach, the Government rejected the residual support which the students and others were also willing to accord to the KMT as a potential partner in a coalition government. The Communists on the other hand, were able to capitalize on their share of goodwill by avoiding demands for total commitment. Their policy of a united front served them well at a time when the KMT was squandering its own fund of popular support.

IV
The Political Costs of Economic Mismanagement

Monetary inflation was the dominant feature of urban economic life during the Civil War years. Because its effects were so extreme and so pervasive, manifesting themselves in ways that every city dweller could readily comprehend, the inflation did more than any other single issue to undermine public confidence in the KMT's ability to govern.

Inflation had commenced during the Anti-Japanese War, when the Government was cut off from the coastal cities, its main source of financial support. Public revenues were inadequate to support the war effort, and the Government turned to the printing press as a principal means of covering the deficit.

Measures such as the collection of land tax in kind, compulsory sale of grain to the government at below market prices, and compulsory lending of grain to the government, all were inadequate to close the gap between revenue and expenditure. Between 1942 and 1944, government income, not including bank credit, amounted to two-fifths to one-half of total government expenditures, the dominant proportion of which was allocated for military purposes. In 1945, such income amounted to only one-third of expenditures. After 1938, the deficit was made up almost entirely by expanded note issues. As a consequence, the average level of prices rose by over two thousand times between 1937 and August, 1945.[1]

Thus the pattern of inflationary finance was already set before the Civil War began. The gap between income and expenditure persisted between 1946 and 1948, as did the principal means of bridging it. Meanwhile, the logical consequences of relying on printing press money played themselves out to their final conclusion.

The KMT Government paid heavily for what must have initially seemed the most painless solution to its financial problems. It is commonly assumed that the

1. Arthur N. Young, *China's Wartime Finance and Inflation, 1937-1945*, pp. 20-21, 29-30, 33, 64, 162, 299. Military costs, according to one estimate, were about 60 percent of the Central Government's total expenditures between 1941-48 (Chang Kia-ngau, *The Inflationary Spiral: the Experience in China, 1939-1950*, p. 155). For the pattern of defense expenditure during the pre-1945 period, see Young, *Wartime Finance*, p. 16; and Chou Shun-hsin, *The Chinese Inflation, 1937-1949*, p. 70.

inflation at least cost the regime the support of the urban salaried middle class, which bore the major burden of soaring prices and depreciating currency. Economists who have studied the Chinese inflation, while neither analyzing the political implications in depth nor defining very carefully their conclusions, suggest that the inflation-caused impoverishment of this sector contributed to the general loss of support which ultimately caused the downfall of the KMT.[2]

The major salaried middle-income groups making up this urban minority were professors and teachers, military officers, and civilian government employees. But these groups, with the exception of the intellectual community, were among the least likely to demonstrate their disillusionment with the KMT in any politically meaningful way. As for the intellectuals as a whole, it is true that they were the primary source of the anti-civil war movement in the KMT areas, and that economic issues inspired one of the major themes of that movement. Nevertheless, as will be indicated in Chapter Five, the intellectuals' alienation from the Government and their opposition to its war against the Communists were based on a wide range of considerations, only one of which was their own impoverishment resulting from the inflation. Moreover, the intellectual community did not actually withdraw its support from the KMT until its defeat on the battlefield was certain. Nor is there any indication that military officers and civil servants in general behaved any differently. Hence the difficulty of isolating and tracing the direct links between the inflation and the Government's loss of support among these middle-income groups.

When "support" is defined in less ambiguous terms, however, the costs to the Government in terms of its loss were more clearly marked and they were many indeed. They ranged from increasing inefficiency and corruption among civil servants to the rebuffs the Government received from other sectors of the urban population. Labor, capital, and the public at large repeatedly flouted the authority of the Government by refusing to obey its decrees and cooperate with its reform measures. This was done even when these were clearly identified by the Government as necessary features of its war effort against the Communists. In case after case, the inflation, and the ensuing erosion of popular confidence in the Government's ability to cope with the deteriorating economic situation, lay at the root of its failure to induce compliance.

THE REVIVAL OF THE LABOR MOVEMENT

The direct relationship between labor's restiveness and the pressures of inflation can be easily established. Whatever the other intervening variables may have been, it therefore seems safe to conclude that the inflation was at least one of the causes responsible for the Government's inability to dominate labor in the

---

2. Chang, *Inflationary Spiral*, p. 66. In the words of Chou Shun-hsin: "This inequitable distribution of the burden produced widespread graft and corruption among the civil servants, and it undoubtedly was an important factor in the downfall of the Nationalist Government" (*Chinese Inflation*, p. 258). Even more ambiguously, Arthur Young states: "Inflation softened up China's intellectuals for communism" (*Wartime Finance*, p. 323).

same manner after World War II as before. Certainly, the deteriorating economic situation provoked labor's repeated "disobedience" and provided a ready-made issue around which to mobilize a movement independent of Government control.

THE BACKGROUND

When the KMT came to power in 1927, it undertook a systematic campaign to gain control of the labor movement. The Communists had been in the forefront of labor organizing activity during the 1920s and the labor movement grew rapidly in those years.[3] By 1927, there were some three million organized workers in China's industrial centers. Fearing the strength of the Communists, Chiang Kai-shek broke the KMT-CCP alliance and set about eliminating Communist influence within the labor movement.

After the first blunt move to suppress the unions in the spring of 1927,[4] the KMT acted to consolidate its victory by official sponsorship and supervision of all labor union activity. Unions were taken over by organizers whose allegiance was to the KMT rather than to labor. They became in effect "government-sponsored." In October, 1929, a labor union law brought all labor union activity under government supervision.[5] Within individual unions and factories, KMT labor organizers—often working with management—developed a variety of tactics aimed at the division and control of the labor force. Several groups might be organized within a factory or an industry, based on regional and/or occupational differences among the workers. Manual and non-manual workers in a single enterprise were not allowed to join the same union. Workers were sometimes divided arbitrarily by wage levels, and so on. This accentuated the conflicting interests between and among these groups, making it easier to play them off one against the other.

Strikebreaking was another useful tactic. Groups of ostensibly unemployed workers, such as those organized by the Shanghai underworld leader, Tu Yueh-sheng, and his protege, Lu Ching-shih, were used to break strikes by providing men to take over the striking workers' jobs. Armed force was also used when other methods proved ineffective.[6]

---

3. Jean Chesneaux, *The Chinese Labor Movement, 1919-1927, passim.*
4. On the events of 1927, see Harold R. Isaacs, *The Tragedy of the Chinese Revolution, passim;* and Chesneaux, *Chinese Labor,* Chapter Fourteen.
5. This law is translated in Fang Fu-an, *Chinese Labour: an Economic and Statistical Survey of the Labour Conditions and Labour Movements in China,* pp. 161-70.
6. *Ta ko-ming i-lai shang-hai kung-jen . . . ,* pp. 15-18. Strike-breaking was only one of many services which ingratiated Tu Yueh-sheng with the KMT authorities. As leader of the *Ch'ing-pang* (Green Gang), an underworld secret society, he helped Chiang Kai-shek seize control of Shanghai in 1927. Tu's close relations with the KMT Government continued for many years and he became one of the most influential men in Shanghai. With his new status, Tu sought a more respectable image. He therefore formed the Society of Perseverance, which his proteges joined as his students *(hsueh-sheng).* See Y.C. Wang, "Tu Yueh-sheng (1888-1951): a Tentative Political Biography," *Journal of Asian Studies,* vol. 26, no. 3 (May, 1967): 440.

Aided by the economic depression of the 1930s, the KMT Government succeeded in dominating organized labor with these methods. The Communist-controlled All-China Labor Federation was banned and went underground. It continued to exist until 1931, when the Communists abandoned their effort to maintain separate union organizations in KMT cities.[7] Sporadic strikes and labor disputes nevertheless continued to occur after 1927, causing one observer to predict that "given the opportunity, Chinese workers will demonstrate quickly enough that they have not lost the ability to organize themselves very effectively."[8]

The Japanese occupation of China's major industrial centers in 1937-38 disrupted the Government's "special" relationship with labor. The Government was able, from its wartime base in Chungking, to maintain some underground links with its labor organization in the occupied areas through the efforts of secret service chief Tai Li, Tu Yueh-sheng, and others. But the network of KMT controls over labor was effectively broken. In addition, the war provided an opportunity for the Communists to reestablish and/or strengthen their own underground contacts in a number of important enterprises within the Japanese-occupied areas. This occurred in Shanghai as Communist-led guerrilla fighting developed nearby in southern and northern Kiangsu and in eastern Chekiang. It also occurred in the North and in Hong Kong.[9]

In the hinterland, meanwhile, the Government sought to maintain its hold over labor while mobilizing it for the war effort. The Chinese Labor Association (CLA), more of a service organization than a federation of labor unions, had been set up in 1935 and moved with the Government to the Southwest after the Japanese invasion. In 1940, this organization and all labor affairs were placed under the jurisdiction of the Ministry of Social Affairs. A new national labor union law in 1943 reaffirmed the control of the Social Affairs Ministry over all labor unions. The CLA remained, until 1946, the official national labor organization and was recognized as the representative of Chinese labor by the International Labor Organization. All the labor federations in the Communist areas, with an estimated membership of from six hundred thousand to one million, were also nominally affiliated with the CLA, reflecting the KMT-CCP united front of the Anti-Japanese War years.

THE RECONVERSION PERIOD: FAILURE OF THE HARD-LINE APPROACH

When the Government reoccupied the coastal cities after the Japanese surrender, it set about rebuilding its labor organization. Before KMT labor cadres could

7. Eleanor H. Lattimore, *Labor Unions in the Far East*, p. 16; and Nym Wales (Helen Foster Snow), *The Chinese Labor Movement*, p. 178.

8. Wales, *Labor Movement*, p. 67.

9. A two-way traffic developed as contacts were established between the Communist underground in the cities and the guerrillas in the countryside. Shanghai workers fought with the New Fourth Army and with the South Kiangsu Anti-Japanese volunteers. Similarly, workers from Hong Kong and Peiping reportedly joined Communist guerrillas in nearby areas. See section below on "The Communist Underground." Also *Ta ko-ming i-lai . . .* , pp. 31-32; and Wales, *Labor Movement*, pp. 86-89.

accomplish their task, however, the workers had begun responding to the conditions, described in Chapter Two, created by the KMT's take-over from the Japanese. In late 1945 and early 1946, thousands of workers engaged in strikes and protest demonstrations demanding adequate severance pay or wage adjustments. Most of the strikes and work slowdowns violated officially established union procedures stipulating that workers must first make known their demands and request mediation or arbitration before resorting to any kind of job action.[10]

The immediate cause for the upsurge of labor agitation was twofold. As noted, the ranks of the unemployed swelled rapidly after August, 1945. This problem was soon compounded by a precipitous rise in prices. Immediately after the Japanese surrender, prices slumped sharply both in the interior and in the coastal areas. In Chungking, the wholesale price index fell from 179,500 (1937 = 100) in August to 118,417 in October. In Shanghai, the index, calculated in Chinese government currency at the official rate of exchange between *fapi* and puppet currency, fell from 43,200 in August to 34,508 in September. But by November, prices had begun their upward climb once more, rising sharply in Shanghai and somewhat more gradually in the interior. In December, the Shanghai wholesale price index was 88,544.[11] The trend was upward, with no end in sight, and labor responded accordingly. In 1936 just prior to the Japanese invasion, there were 278 strikes and labor disputes recorded for the whole country. In 1946, in Shanghai alone there were 1,716 strikes and labor disputes.[12]

Initially, the Government adopted a hard line; and industry, both public and private, generally held out against the workers' demands for wage adjustments. The Mayor of Shanghai announced that the workers' demands should be rejected if they exceeded the ability of management to meet them. He also threatened to use force if workers struck in violation of "lawful procedures." Meanwhile, the authorities resorted to strikebreaking tactics similar to those used against workers in the 1920s and 1930s (and soon to be directed against student demonstrators as well). Workers were attacked by organized groups of thugs acting in concert with local police and other law enforcement personnel. Officials charged that the labor unrest was the work of Communist agitators inciting the workers to make unreasonable demands.

10. *TKP*, Shanghai, Jan. 26, 1946 *(CPR); Chung mei jih-pao,* and *Shun pao,* Shanghai, Jan. 27, 1946 (both in *CPR,* Jan. 28).
11. Chang, *Inflationary Spiral,* p. 69.
12. *China Weekly Review: Monthly Report,* Jan. 31, 1947, p. 13; and *TKP*, Shanghai, Feb. 26, 1947 *(CPR,* Mar. 5). The Shanghai labor force was the most restive, its independence seeming to vary in direct relation to its size. Statistics of the National Economic Survey Commission and Ministry of Social Affairs in April, 1948, showed 7,738 factories in Shanghai, or 55 percent of the total number in China. Tientsin had 1,211 factories (8.6%), Taiwan 985 (7%), and Nanking 888 (6.3%). This survey showed Shanghai having 367,433 industrial workers, and a national total of 682,399 *(CYJP,* Nanking, Apr. 27, 1948: *CPR,* May 5).

The Shanghai Power Company strike of January, 1946, provided a typical example of the aggressiveness that marked labor's relations with the KMT authorities at this time. On January 23, some three thousand employees from the Company's three main branches went on strike to protest the dismissal of a number of workers' representatives who had been active in promoting the workers' demands. The strike lasted nine days and spread to several of Shanghai's largest factories and department stores. On January 31, plainclothes men and security forces converged at the gates of the Yangtzepoo Plant, which the workers had occupied when the strike began. A group of women began clamoring outside the gate for their husbands to return home for the Chinese New Year holiday. When the gates were opened to admit the women, the police rushed in, beat up a number of workers, and drove the remainder from the premises. Forced to submit their demands to mediation, the workers cut off the electricity supply. Negotiations between the workers' representatives and mediators at the municipal Social Affairs Bureau had to be conducted by candlelight.

Far from being intimidated, other workers organized a protest in support of the Power Company strike. On February 4, some one hundred representatives from forty Shanghai unions, primarily in the weaving and machine manufacturing industries and five other public utility companies, gathered to express sympathy for the Shanghai Power Company workers. The next day a similar meeting took place at the office of the Shanghai General Labor Union, a government-sponsored federation of unions within the city. Over two hundred persons attended, representing union organizations from more than seventy different enterprises and occupations. The meeting expressed full support for the Shanghai Power Company workers. The Chairman of the Shanghai General Labor Union, Chou Hsueh-hsiang, declared that by their struggle the Power Company workers were providing a model for all workers to follow. He expressed the hope that other unions in the city would support them so that they might achieve their demands.[13]

FAILURE OF THE CARROT-AND-STICK APPROACH

The Government's hard-line approach of early 1946 was clearly inadequate to control labor agitation, particularly when officers of government-sponsored unions were beginning to talk more like *bona fide* representatives of labor than of the political authorities they were supposed to be serving. Hence the new policy of April, 1946, which would characterize the Government's approach toward labor throughout the remainder of the Civil War period. Unlike its uncompromising attitude toward the students, the Government now assumed a more flexible posture *vis-à-vis* labor. While continuing its effort to weaken and subdue the labor movement, the Government also attempted to pacify the

---

13. Chung lo, "Tsai tou-cheng li chuang-ta: chi erh-shih-wu nien lai te chung-kung shang-hai tien-li kung-szu chih-pu" [Growing up in the struggle: remembering the Party branch in the Shanghai Power Company during the past 25 years], *CFJP*, June 30, 1951 (reprinted in Liu Ch'ang-sheng, ed., *Chung-kuo kung-ch'an-tang yü shang hai kung-jen*, pp. 30-34); *WHP*, Shanghai, Feb. 5 and 6, 1946 (*CPR*, same dates).

workers by acknowledging the legitimacy of their principal demands. New guidelines stipulated that workers were to be paid each month on the basis of their pre-war (1936) wages multiplied by the current cost-of-living index. Moreover, the base wage was set at a level intended to improve the general lot of the workers by comparison with their pre-World War II treatment. The base pay for unskilled workers was equivalent to the 1936 pay of skilled workers. The basic wages of the latter were scaled upward accordingly.

At the same time, new regulations were designed to bring labor firmly under the control of the Ministry of Social Affairs. On April 24, the Executive Yuan issued an order requiring that all labor-management disputes be submitted to government-sponsored arbitration. Strikes by workers and lockouts by management were prohibited prior to such arbitration. Arbitration committees would consist of nine to fifteen members, the majority to be government representatives. These moves were necessary, the Government declared, in order to control Communist agitators who were exploiting labor unrest arising from legitimate economic considerations. Such arguments were publicized in pro-Government newspapers, and the Minister of Social Affairs visited Shanghai as part of the campaign to promote the new approach toward labor.[14] The newly-appointed Mayor of Shanghai, Wu Kuo-chen, announced that his administration would act to settle disputes as quickly as possible, but that striking workers and their leaders would be punished.

The Demise of the Chinese Labor Association

An important element of the Government's plan to reestablish control over labor was the successful effort to break the growing independence of the CLA. The moves against the CLA were taken gradually, in a series of steps whose ultimate objective was not immediately apparent. The pattern of action was similar to that adopted during the students' anti-war movement: the early actions against the CLA were made by local officials acting in apparent contradiction of Central Government policy. In due time, however, the contradiction was resolved with the center formally adopting the same position as that initially taken by local authorities.

On August 6, 1946, a group of some two hundred armed police and members of the Chungking General Labor Union invaded and occupied the Chungking office of the CLA and its three affiliated agencies, the Workers' Welfare Club, the Workers' Hospital, and the Workers' Cultural Service Club. Over twenty CLA staff members were jailed.

The next day at a press conference, spokesmen for the Chungking General Labor Union charged CLA officials with corruption and maladministration; instigating workers' strikes; and engaging in political activities. Refusing to disclose the evidence for these charges, the spokesmen went on to state that the Chungking General Labor Union was the legal organization of the three hundred thousand workers of Chungking and was therefore entitled to take over the

14. For example, *Ch'iao-sheng pao,* Shanghai, May 31, 1946 *(CPR),* and *Shun pao,* Shanghai, June 1, 1946 *(CPR).*

office and agencies of the CLA. They claimed to have the approval of the Chungking municipal government, and said that the Chungking General Labor Union intended to appeal to the public for the dissolution of CLA offices in other localities. [15] Later in the month, the Honan provincial government ordered the Kaifeng office of the CLA to cease all activities and to turn over its office, together with the Workers' Hospital and the Workers' Dining Hall, to the local General Labor Union.

Chu Hsueh-fan, the head of the CLA, and Wu K'ai-hsien, director of the Social Affairs Bureau of the Shanghai municipal government, were subsequently summoned to an interview with Chiang Kai-shek at his summer residence in Kuling. When Chu returned to Shanghai on September 12, he announced that the affair had been settled, that President Chiang had ordered the Chungking office and agencies of the CLA restored to it, and that the imprisoned CLA staff members would be released on bail. The next day, nineteen of them were released although three others remained in detention. In late September, however, the Ministry of Social Affairs in Nanking issued the following order to the Social Affairs Departments of the provincial governments:

> The Chinese Labor Association, the Chinese Labor Promotion Association, the China Welfare Association, the Labor Problems Research Society and other organizations are all workers' organizations and their aim is either to promote the welfare of the workers or to study labor problems. However, it has been reported that recently those organs have been engaging in activities which are in violation of Government orders and regulations, and that they have been organizing the workers and instigating strikes. The Ministry demands that any labor organizations which . . . have already registered with the local authorities concerned, should strictly obey the law and statute of the Government and should not engage in activities of organizing the workers and should not do propaganda work among the workers. The authorities concerned should strictly supervise the activities of these organizations so as not to hinder the development of the labor unions in various localities.[16]

The affair had obviously not been settled. The Central Government had now legitimized the actions taken by the local authorities in Chungking and Kaifeng. Chu and the secretary-general of the CLA were soon forced to submit their resignations in a "reorganization" of the CLA. On November 10, Chu flew to Hong Kong en route to Paris to attend an executive committee meeting of the World Federation of Trade Unions. While in Hong Kong, he suffered serious injuries when an automobile rammed a rickshaw in which he was riding. It was common rumor that the "accident" was an assassination attempt by KMT agents in the British colony. When Chu returned from Europe, he went not to Shanghai but to the Communist areas. Meanwhile, the Government announced in March, 1947, that preparations were being made to organize the General Labor Union at the provincial and national levels. Henceforth the National General Labor Union

15. Chungyang News Agency, Chungking, Aug. 7, 1946 (*CPR*, Shanghai, Aug. 8).
16. *TKP*, Shanghai, Sept. 28, 1946 *(CPR)*.

would take over the CLA's role as the representative of Chinese labor at all international conferences.[17] By the end of the summer, the Government announced the inauguration of the Union at the provincial level in Kiangsu, Chekiang, Kwangtung, and Hupeh.[18]

The CLA affair remained something of a mystery, allegedly causing "great surprise" in all quarters because of Chu Hsueh-fan's standing as a member of the KMT and long-time supporter of the Government's labor policy.[19] A member of the Green Gang and "student" of Tu Yueh-sheng, Chu Hsueh-fan had begun his career as a postal clerk in Shanghai in the 1920s. Shortly after he joined the postal service, he began working with his friend, Lu Ching-shih, as an organizer for the Shanghai Postal Workers Union. After becoming a protege of Tu Yueh-sheng, Chu rose rapidly and was named chairman of the KMT-sponsored Shanghai General Labor Union in 1928.

In fact, the break between Chu and the KMT Government had been developing since at least the spring of 1944. At that time, the Chinese Laborers' Welfare Association was formed in Chungking. Chu Hsueh-fan was not among the government officials, social workers, and labor leaders originally named on the new organization's board of directors. Some two thousand workers staged a protest when the Welfare Association held its inaugural meeting on May 1, 1945. Chu was summoned to the Ministry of Social Affairs and reminded that the CLA must obey the Ministry's instructions. He was then instructed to sign a "letter of repentance" but refused to do so.[20]

Suddenly there had emerged two different government-sponsored labor organizations dedicated to the same task, a situation apparently necessitated by the growing independence of Chu and the CLA. The details underlying this development were never made public. But in view of what followed, Chu Hsueh-fan seems to have been co-opted by the interests he had originally been more than willing to help control. As he listened to labor's demands for increased wages and better working conditions, he found himself interceding more frequently with the Government on behalf of the workers than vice versa. In the opinion of one contemporary observer, economic and political pressures both at home and abroad were responsible for Chu's transformation. On the one hand, he chafed under international criticism of the CLA as a government-controlled organization which did not represent Chinese labor.[21] At the same time he himself desired, although perhaps for reasons of his own personal power, to serve as a genuine labor leader, a role made more immediately relevant by the economic deterioration in the KMT areas after 1943.[22]

17. *Tung-nan jih-pao,* Shanghai, Mar. 17, 1947 *(CPR).* Previously the union had been organized only at the municipal and *hsien* levels.

18. *Lih pao,* Shanghai, Sept. 27, 1947 *(CPR).*

19. For example, *Shih-tai jih-pao,* Shanghai, Aug. 10, 1946 *(CPR).*

20. *Hsin min wan-pao,* Shanghai, Sept. 5, 1946 *(CPR,* Sept. 7).

21. Some American unions objected on these grounds to contributions made to the CLA during WW II through United China Relief (Lattimore, *Labor Unions,* p. 20).

22. Israel Epstein, *Notes on Labor Problems in Nationalist China,* pp. 97-99.

Whatever his reasons, Chu soon had begun speaking out publicly on the liberal side of a number of issues and against the actions of the Government. In early August, 1945, he wrote a letter of sympathy to the Chungking edition of the *Shanghai Evening Post and Mercury* when it was temporarily banned for criticizing the KMT. During the Political Consultative Conference which met in January, 1946,[23] the CLA refused to associate itself with some 170 organizations mobilized by right-wing KMT elements to petition against one of the liberal proposals under discussion. When the name of the CLA was nevertheless included as one of the opposing organizations, CLA officials sent an open letter to local newspapers in Chungking denying their association with the petition.

Finally, on the closing day of the Conference, the CLA published its own list of demands including: realization of basic human rights; formation of a coalition government; elimination of the causes of the Civil War; land-to-the-tiller; repeal of regulations restricting workers' rights, and amendment of the Trade Union Law; the right to strike and collective bargaining; minimum wage rates based on the cost-of-living index; and protection of the workers' livelihood.[24]

With this open declaration in favor of the workers' demands, the CLA finally cast itself unequivocally in the role of labor's representative. The transformation in one of the KMT's most long-standing supporters was a clear harbinger of the course the post-war labor movement would follow. The particular circumstances underlying Chu Hsueh-fan's defection may remain obscure.[25] But, for the labor movement as a whole, the Government's efforts at control were thwarted at every turn by the state of the post-war economy. The Government was never able to reassert the hold it had maintained over the labor force during the decade prior to the Japanese invasion.

Additional Attempts at Labor Control

This replacement of the CLA by the General Labor Union was but one of several actions during this period. The broader picture of the Government's efforts to control the labor force only points up the extent of its failure.

The Shanghai Bureau of Social Affairs revised its regulations in early 1947 to allow any factory with one hundred or more workers to organize a factory labor union. Such small unions were encouraged to join industry-wide unions. District labor unions, made up of several small unions in different industries within a given district, were to be reorganized into factory and industry-oriented unions. The objective was to break the solidarity that had developed among workers in the district unions, where labor unrest in one factory often spread rapidly to

---

23. Regarding the Political Consultative Conference, see Chapter Five.

24. "Urgent Requests and Minimum Demands of the Chinese Labor Association on the Chinese Political Situation and Labor Movement" in Epstein, *Notes on Labor*, pp. 104-106.

25. Chu's old mentor, Tu Yueh-sheng, also left Shanghai for Hong Kong at about the same time. By the end of 1946, Tu's power was at low ebb, perhaps due in part to his inability to control Shanghai labor. But, despite some speculation, there is no proof of direct relationship between the declining fortunes of the two men. Tu soon returned to Shanghai. See *China Weekly Review: Monthly Report,* Feb. 28, 1947, p. 3; and Y.C. Wang, "Tu Yueh-sheng," pp. 449-50.

involve neighboring workers.[26] In October, 1947, a meeting of labor union officials called by the Shanghai Bureau of Social Affairs resolved that the formation of factory unions be speeded up and the reorganization of district unions be completed before the end of the year.[27]

By the end of August, about half a million Shanghai workers were organized into 453 unions (293 industrial unions and 160 vocational) with another 25 unions in the process of formation. Industrial unions accounted for 293,600 workers, almost half of whom were organized into the city's 74 textile labor unions. Among vocational workers, communications and transport workers formed the largest contingent with 86,200; repair and construction industries accounted for 43,125.[28] All these unions were affiliated with the Shanghai General Labor Union. Similarly in Tientsin, there were 60,000 unionized workers, all in organizations affiliated with the government-supervised municipal labor federation.

In addition to officially sponsored unions, the Government resorted, as it had in the pre-war period, to other tactics of organizational control. These now included the organization of branches of the KMT's San-min-chu-i Youth Corps among the younger workers; and an attempt to attract as many workers as possible, particularly the leaders and activists, into various KMT-controlled groups and associations. In Shanghai, the old labor organization of Lu Ching-shih, now under the immediate direction of Ch'en Li-fu and Wu K'ai-hsien, constituted the basis for the most important organizing effort of this sort, the Laborers' Welfare Association. A less ambitious undertaking was the Workers' Aid Society, organized among the workers by Government cadres under the leadership of Chi Yuan-p'u and Wu Kuang-yuan. Also, at the time of the second emergency economic reform program in August, 1948, a Greater Shanghai Youth Service Corps was organized among the workers to aid the Voluntary Investigation Battalion of the Woosung-Shanghai Garrison Command in the implementation of the program.

In Shanghai, the Laborers' Welfare Association engaged in a wide range of activities. Similar tactics were adopted in other cities as well, although it is unclear just how extensively they were implemented. In Shanghai, Association members were sent into districts and factories where their primary recruiting efforts were directed at the upper levels within the work force such as the foremen, staff personnel, union leaders, and younger activists. Chou Hsueh-hsiang returned to his old sphere of influence among the cigarette factory workers. There he revived and expanded his pre-war organization, the *Li she,* and used this to create a Cigarette Factory Laborers' Welfare Association. In this way he organized over two hundred people, all leaders in the city's cigarette factory unions. These people then undertook a broader organizing effort aimed at

---

26. *TKP,* Shanghai, Mar. 18, 1947 (*CPR,* Mar. 19); and Chung-kuo lao-kung yun-tung shih pien-tsuan wei-yuan-hui, ed., *Chung-kuo lao-kung yun-tung shih,* 4:1792-93.

27. *TKP,* Shanghai, Oct. 26, 1947 (*CPR,* Oct. 28).

28. *TKP,* Shanghai, Oct. 25, 1947 (*CPR,* Oct. 28). The ratio of men to women in the total figure was 3:2. See also, *Chung-kuo lao-kung yun-tung shih,* 4:1792.

recruiting workers into the KMT and also into factory protection teams. These teams were widely organized in Shanghai, and were usually headed by cadres of the Laborers' Welfare Association.

A Social Workers' Training School was set up in Shanghai on the lines of the Central Training Institute in Nanking. Workers recruited into the school had to join the KMT. After their training, all were commissioned as first, second, or third level cadres of the Laborers' Welfare Association. In the more important factories—that is, factories where the workers were most active—the Association sent its "secretaries" to enter the unions to observe the activities of union leaders and workers alike. In many factories, the Association also maintained secret agents and investigatory groups whose function was to gather information on left-wing elements among the workers, draw up blacklists, and the like.

Finally, there were a number of other workers' organizations, all with varying ties to the Government. These included the Hsiaofeng Society organized by the San-min-chu-i Youth Corps, the Hsieh-i Society controlled by the military, the Hsingsheng Society controlled by "certain authorities" in Nanking, and the Hsingchung Study Society. Some of these were small, tightly-knit organizations, while others were more in the nature of mutual aid societies with a fairly wide membership. So great was the KMT organizing effort that in one enterprise where the workers were particularly active—the Talung Machine Factory—there were said to be about ten different pro-Government groups and societies.[29]

Their number was not necessarily an indication of their support among the workers, however. According to one post-liberation source, the KMT's factory protection teams were often selected on the basis of predetermined namelists over which the workers named had no say. Those who objected were accused of being pro-Communist. Workers were also sometimes deceived into joining such groups. This happened to several women textile workers who thought they were joining a social organization, paid their dues, and did not bother to read what was written on the receipts they received. To their surprise, they later learned they had joined the San-min-chu-i Youth Corps. Some workers, on the other hand, knowingly joined these organizations, hoping to safeguard their jobs thereby. Others were told that if they joined they would not be conscripted into the army, or that if their factory staged a strike they would not be arrested, or that they would become important people in the factory and be allowed to carry weapons. Of the fifteen thousand Shanghai workers organized into factory protection teams, only a few hundred at most could be considered "backbone elements." Despite all its efforts at this time, concluded the same source, the KMT "was never able to send down roots among the Shanghai workers and could not grasp hold of them."[30]

29. Ch'en Ch'ing-mei, "Ying-yung chien-ch'ih ti-hsia tou-cheng te chung kung shang-hai ta-lung chi-ch'i ch'ang chih-pu" [The heroic support of the underground struggle by the CCP branch in the Shanghai Talung Machine Factory], *Kung-jen jih-pao*, June 27, 1951 (reprinted in Liu Ch'ang-sheng, ed., p. 77).

30. *Ta ko-ming i-lai . . . ,* p. 25.

The Failure of the Government's Efforts

Whatever the bias that underlay this particular evaluation, it was little different from many others at the time.[31] The degree of successful government control varied. Unions representing skilled workers generally maintained considerable independence; those representing unskilled and illiterate laborers somewhat less. Among the strongest unions were those of the postal, communications, and public utility workers. Those unions demonstrated their independence on almost all issues, whether political or economic, and were generally in the forefront of labor agitation. One example of this independence occurred in February, 1947, when the Shanghai Social Affairs Bureau ruled that the postal employees would henceforth be required to guarantee one another's behavior and report all "suspicious" actions on the part of fellow workers. The employees unanimously refused to comply.[32] In another instance, the Shanghai telecommunications workers demanded pay equal to that received by the postal workers. When this was refused in May, 1947, they went out on strike. Telecommunications workers in Kwangtung, Kwangsi, Hangchow, Sian, Peiping, and Tientsin responded with various actions of their own in support of their Shanghai colleagues.[33]

While the pattern of government control varied from union to union and was less successful overall in Shanghai than elsewhere, the trend toward independent union activity, open criticism of the Government's labor policy, disregard for its decrees, and leadership support for the demands of the rank and file was general. Thus in Tientsin, the inaugural meeting of the municipal labor union federation organized by the local authorities adopted resolutions opposing the Government on a number of key issues. The delegates had been selected in union elections under the supervision of the Tientsin KMT headquarters, the municipal Bureau of Social Affairs, and the preparatory committee for the organization of the labor federation.[34] But the meeting resolved that the police and judicial authorities should not intervene in labor disputes before these were submitted to competent authorities for settlement; decided to appeal to the central authorities for rigid restrictions against trade with Japan (such trade had already been agreed to in principle by the State Council); expressed dissatisfaction over the procrastination of the Tientsin Bureau of Social Affairs in solving a dispute between workers and the management of several hotels and restaurants over the dismissal of workers for participating in union activities; and asked the author-

31. One Shanghai manufacturer indicated in 1948 that the government had little influence over the union in his factory. A newspaper editor, commenting more generally, asserted that no one was really in control of the Shanghai labor unions (A. Doak Barnett, *China on the Eve of Communist Takeover*, p. 78). This view also emerged from a special report on labor prepared by *China Weekly Review: Monthly Report*, Jan. 31, 1947, pp. 12-16.

32. *WHP*, Shanghai, Feb. 28, 1947, and *Hsin min wan-pao*, Shanghai, Feb. 27, 1947 (both in *CPR*, Feb. 28).

33. *Hsin min pao*, Nanking, May 14, 1947 *(CPR)*; and *Yi shih pao*, Tientsin, May 13, 1947 *(CPR*, May 14).

34. *Kung-shang jih-pao*, Tientsin, May 12, 1947 *(CPR*, May 13).

ities to take action against any employer who dismissed workers for organizing law-abiding labor unions.[35]

Official statistics did show an abrupt decline in the number of strikes after May, 1946, from a high of sixty in March to only nine in June. This low level continued through November and was generally attributed to the decision to peg wages to the rise in the cost of living. But despite the decline in strikes, the number of labor disputes remained at about the same level, averaging well over one hundred per month.

Most sources tended to accept the Government's claim that labor as a whole was better off than it had been before the Anti-Japanese War, when Chinese workers were among the lowest paid in Asia. Despite the upward revision of pay scales which allowed the Government to make this claim, however, a few commentators agreed with labor spokesmen that the workers' living standards had not necessarily improved. Wages were never able to keep pace with prices, since the actual cost of living was usually higher than indicated by the officially compiled cost-of-living index.

A *Ta kung pao* writer on May 2, 1946, found five major problems still confronting Shanghai workers. He was writing specifically of those whose wages were tied to the cost-of-living index—workers in Shanghai's main industries and enterprises. (1) There was a severe shortage of housing. (2) Medical expenses were higher than the average worker could afford. (3) Educational facilities were inadequate and too expensive, leaving the majority illiterate. (4) Day nurseries were lacking for young children of working mothers. (5) The workers were unable to cope with the pace of inflation since they could not buy all necessities for the month when they received their pay, nor could they afford to keep the money and let its value depreciate.

Recession, Unemployment, and Labor Unrest As many commentators were also well aware, the decision to peg wages to the rise in the cost of living dealt with symptoms rather than causes. Without attacking the basic problem of currency inflation, automatic wage adjustments could only exacerbate the situation by leading to increased production costs, and in turn to increased commodity prices. In the process, the critics warned, some enterprises would be forced out of business and workers would lose their jobs.[36]

In fact, this is essentially what happened. The unhappy combination of rampant inflation and rising unemployment overtook urban economic life, providing a fertile field for continuing labor agitation. Rather than openly defy the ban on strikes during the summer and fall of 1946, workers adopted other methods to make their demands felt. They engaged in work slowdowns. Tram car operators gave free rides to passengers. Bartenders served customers free of charge. These actions tended to arise not over demands for increased wages but over such issues as the reduction of work hours by management, layoffs, and demands for severance pay.[37]

35. *TKP*, Tientsin, Aug. 30, 1947 (*CPR*, Sept. 2).

36. For one contemporary analysis of these dangers, see *Cheng yien pao*, Shanghai, Apr. 15, 1946 *(CPR)*.

37. *TKP*, Shanghai, Feb. 26, 1947 (*CPR*, Mar. 5).

Demands of this kind reflected the business downturn during the latter half of 1946. With local goods being undersold by those from abroad, hundreds of producers and commercial firms in Shanghai alone declared bankruptcy and closed down. The alternative was to reduce costs by cutting back production and discharging personnel. According to one estimate, the number of unemployed in the city at the end of 1946 totaled 250,000,[38] out of a population of 3,900,000.[39]

Nor was this recession/unemployment cycle confined to Shanghai. A recession was under way throughout the country. In Canton, one out of every five persons, or 228,038 in a total population of 1,152,408, were reported out of work at the end of 1946.[40] Business failures were common. As a result, the Canton Social Affairs Bureau was obliged to deal with an ever increasing number of labor disputes.[41] In Tientsin, 20 shops were said to have declared bankruptcy in one week alone, joining 250 others that had closed their doors during the final weeks of 1946. In Peiping, the Social Affairs Bureau reported that 1,600 shops had gone out of business between January and October, 1946. Similarly, in Hankow it was claimed that the number of shops and businesses known to have closed their doors during 1946 numbered in the thousands, and that close to 100,000 persons were out of work. An estimated 200,000 persons, or about three-tenths of the 650,000 inhabitants of Nanking, were unemployed at the end of the year.[42]

In December, the number of strikes in Shanghai rose again—this time to a level higher than that of any month since the Japanese surrender—and the Government was powerless to prevent them. The immediate cause seemed to be a ruling by the Shanghai Bureau of Social Affairs in response to worker agitation for traditional year-end bonuses. The Bureau announced that employers should pay such bonuses except in the cases of enterprises which had earned no profits during the previous year. Employers naturally exploited the loophole, and workers reacted accordingly. But the upsurge of labor unrest at the end of 1946, was only a prelude to events in 1947. According to the Shanghai Social Affairs Bureau, the number of strikes and labor disputes during that year reached an all-time high for the city of 2,538.[43]

Emergency Reforms and Labor Unrest. The rash of disputes in December, 1946, and January, 1947, over bonuses and year-end wage settlements was

38. *TKP,* Shanghai, Nov. 8, 1946 (*CPR,* Nov. 15); also *China Weekly Review: Monthly Report,* Jan. 31, 1947, pp. 5-6. Unemployment reached a high level during the immediate post-WW II period, declined during the first half of 1946, and then began to rise again. See Chi Chung-wei, "Random Notes on Labor in Shanghai", *TKP,* Shanghai, May 2, 1946 (*CPR,* May 23); and *TKP,* Shanghai, Feb. 20, 1948 (*CPR,* Feb. 21).

39. *Hsin min pao,* Nanking, May 1, 1947 (*CPR*).

40. *Hua-nan jih-pao,* Canton, Feb. 12, 1947 (*CPR*). The statistics are from the Canton Police Bureau, as of November, 1946.

41. *Chien-feng jih-pao,* Canton, Nov. 16, 1946 (*CPR*); *Ho-p'ing jih-pao,* Canton, Mar. 11, 1947 (*CPR*); *Hsi-nan jih-pao,* Canton, July 10, 1947 (*CPR*).

42. It must be emphasized: there is no way to verify these figures and they should be considered only as approximations. They appeared in *TKP,* Shanghai, Nov. 8, 1946 (*CPR,* Nov. 15), and *China Weekly Review: Monthly Report,* Jan. 31, 1947, pp. 5-6.

43. *Lih pao,* Shanghai, Jan. 7, 1948 (*CPR,* Jan. 12).

brought to a temporary halt by the Government's proclamation of an emergency economic reform program on February 16. All wages were frozen at their January levels, and ceilings were placed on the prices of essential commodities—rice, flour, cotton yarn and cloth, fuel, salt, sugar, and edible oil. The Government also planned to allocate essential commodities to factories for distribution to their employees at the fixed prices. In addition, government employees and teachers in state-supported schools in Nanking and Shanghai were to be supplied with these commodities. If successful, this practice was to be extended to other cities. The program prohibited trading and hoarding of gold and foreign currencies by private individuals. The Government also announced measures to check the growing flight of capital to Hong Kong from all of China's major cities.

Considering the rapid rate of inflation and its basic causes, the breakdown of this partial system of price controls was to be expected—particularly since it was implemented only in the larger cities. Production costs continued to rise, as did prices generally, while only the market prices of essential commodities remained frozen. The price of rice in the producing areas soon reached levels higher than those in the cities where the rice was marketed. The rise in the price of raw cotton made textile production unprofitable. Producers of coal and edible oil found themselves in similar difficulties. A rice shortage developed in late April, which could be partly blamed on transportation difficulties and heavy government requisitions for military purposes. But shortages were worst in cities where the emergency measures were most vigorously enforced, that is, in the Nanking-Shanghai area. Mobs raided rice shops, and the rioting often spread to those selling oil and cotton yarn. Among the cities where rioting occurred were Wusih, Wuhu, Chengtu, Shaohsing, Shanghai, Hangchow, Hsuancheng, Hofei, Chuhsien, Nanking, and Soochow.

The emergency measures were fully operative for only about one month. By mid-March, it was clear that the plan to issue supplies to teachers and civil servants on a nationwide basis could not be implemented. A black market in U.S. dollars was in existence by early April, and most of the essential commodities also emerged on the black market soon thereafter. The Government found itself unable to allocate basic necessities to workers through the factory distribution program and decided to pay each worker a subsidy corresponding to the value of the goods that would have been rationed to him. The workers then complained that they could not sustain their basic livelihood because the wage subsidy provided compensation only for a limited number of essential items while the cost of everything else continued to rise. During the month of May, the wholesale price index for Shanghai rose 54 percent as opposed to a 19 percent increase during the month prior to the imposition of the reform measures.[44]

Once again the workers chose to demonstrate in defense of their economic interests, and the Government had no choice but to give in to their demands.

---

44. On the February, 1947, reforms, see Chang, *Inflationary Spiral*, pp. 72-73, 350-52. Numerous accounts of the rice riots are in *CPR*, Shanghai, for April and May, 1947.

The number of strikes, work slowdowns, and protests multiplied daily toward the end of April—at the same time that the spring, 1947, student tide was also rising. The workers' specific demands varied from enterprise to enterprise; some asking for wage adjustments, others for subsidies to cover all food expenses, and so on. The basic objective, however, was that wages be unfrozen and pegged once more to the cost-of-living index. The workers' protests came to a head at the May Day celebrations in Shanghai. Several thousand laborers attended a government-sponsored rally and shouted their demands that the cost-of-living index be unfrozen as the Mayor and the Directors of the Shanghai General Labor Union and the Social Affairs Bureau tried to argue otherwise.[45] The days that followed saw a continuous series of worker demonstrations and parades while the student Anti-Hunger Anti-Civil War campaign was also gathering momentum.

Finally, under the combined pressure of labor unrest and the collapse of the rice market, all of the emergency reform measures were officially abandoned. Unable to afford its wage compensation plan, the Government announced that workers would henceforth be paid in accordance with the monthly fluctuation in the cost-of-living index. Industrialists, for the most part, were opposed to the automatic wage adjustments, and became more so as the economic situation worsened. Meanwhile, the Government was left with the onus of having promulgated a reform program which not only solved nothing but which, in its failure, actually created more disruption than the conditions it had been designed to correct.

Toward the end of 1947, escalating production costs combined with reduced demand, due to the general reduction in real purchasing power, led to a significant cutback in industrial production. This escalation of the trend apparent since 1946 contributed further to the problems of unemployment and underemployment. According to national statistics published in Nanking, some 45 percent of the labor disputes in seven major centers during the first half of 1947 arose over the discharge of workers.[46]

Under these conditions, business and industry continued to press for the right to negotiate on wages. The employer stood to gain from such an arrangement because of widespread unemployment and a continuous influx from the poverty-stricken countryside. The steadily growing labor pool served to depress wages for many different kinds of occupations, acting as a counterweight to the agitation of organized labor for improved treatment.[47] But the strength of the latter in

45. Chang Hui, ed., *Shang-hai chin pai nien ko-ming shih-hua,* pp. 194-96.

46. *Ta kang pao,* Nanking, Aug. 30, 1947 *(CPR).* The same source gives official figures for labor disputes in the seven cities during January-June, 1947: Shanghai 788, Chungking 53, Tientsin 39, Hankow 31, Tsingtao 27, Nanking 19, Canton 8.

47. There is no precise data on the proportion of the labor force that actually received automatic wage adjustments. *China Weekly Review* reported in January, 1947, that a "large number" of establishments did not pay their employees in accordance with the rise in the cost of living—mostly old-fashioned businesses and workshops in food, drug, metal, wool, and felt trades. These provided workers with little more than bed and board. In other small establishments, wages often depended on family or personal ties and were not uniform. Moreover, in some trades such as construction, the contractors and foremen often paid

terms of its disruptive potential was such that the Government now no longer dared respond primarily, as it had in the past, to the demands of employers and entrepreneurs.

Strikes were again banned under the general mobilization for war proclaimed by the Central Government in July, 1947. And again, the ban did little to ease the pressure of labor's demands. The economic burdens of the working class were becoming so great, wrote one analyst with personal knowledge of the period, that the municipal authorities warned it would not be "politically feasible" to change the system of automatic wage adjustments again.[48] Instead, the authorities resorted to such expedients as manipulating the cost-of-living index. The workers responded by demanding that the methods used in calculating the figures each month be made public. In 1948, as the rate of inflation accelerated, Shanghai workers began to agitate for twice-monthly wage adjustments, to which the municipal government ultimately agreed.

The Communist Underground

Commenting on the "totally new perspective" in labor-management relations after World War II, *The China Weekly Review* suggested that the new relationship must be due in part to the general feeling among the workers that improved treatment should be their share of victory. In addition, the workers were now better organized and had "professional trade union executives" to lead them.[49] The general consensus was, moreover, that some of these new-style labor leaders were actually members of the Communist underground whose immediate objective was not so much to promote the interests of the working class as to disrupt economic life in KMT cities.

As in the student movement, the authorities often arrested labor activists for whom little evidence could be found to substantiate the charges of subversion made against them. The Communists themselves later revealed, however, that underground Party branches were operating in several of Shanghai's most active labor unions and its largest industrial and commercial establishments. These included:

1. *The Number 12 Factory of the National Shanghai Textile Mills.* The Party branch had been reestablished in this factory in 1938 with only four members. By 1945, the number had grown to twenty. These Party members worked within

---

minimum wages to their labor—even though the contracts had been negotiated on the basis of wage rates that were often well above the official cost-of-living index. See *China Weekly Review: Monthly Report,* Jan. 31, 1947, p. 15.

48. Chang, *Inflationary Spiral,* p. 354. Banker, economist, brother of Carsun Chang (founder of the Democratic-Socialist Party), and member of the Political Study Clique, Chang Kia-ngau held a variety of posts in the KMT Government. He was Minister of Railways before WW II, Minister of Communications during the war, Chairman of the Northeast Economic Commission from 1945 to early 1947, and was appointed Governor of the Central Bank of China on March 1, 1947. He held this post for about a year, and left China in May, 1949.

49. *China Weekly Review: Monthly Report,* Jan. 31, 1947, p. 12.

the factory union and led the workers in at least two protests. During one in April, 1947, two Party members were wounded, and a third arrested. In March, 1948, the police arrested but later released thirteen activists, most of whom were Party members.[50]

2. *The Shanghai Customs.* A Party branch was formed in the Shanghai Customs Bureau in December, 1936, by three young trainees. Customs employees engaged in many economic protests during the Civil War years. These usually took the form of work slowdowns and culminated in the sixteen-day slowdown of November, 1948. All the Customs employees participated, demanding increased compensation for the soaring prices after the failure of the Government's second emergency economic reform program (described below). The Party branch was allegedly active in organizing this strike, which seriously disrupted trade and was claimed to have obstructed the flow of military supplies to the KMT armies at the front.[51] The front in question was not far off, for the Communists had just begun the decisive Huai-Hai Campaign in northern Kiangsu.

3. *The Talung Machine Factory.* The Party branch here was established in 1944. It reportedly led in demanding severance pay from the Japanese when it closed down in August, 1945, and also in seeking a relief allowance when production remained at a standstill for several months during the take-over period. By the time the factory began to return to production in February, 1946, the Party branch had become the backbone of a movement to organize all the workers in Shanghai's Western District into a joint labor organization. Several Party members from this factory were arrested during the Civil War years. One KMT labor leader was quoted as saying that if the Talung Machine Factory workers could be subdued, it would be possible to control labor unrest in all of western Shanghai. Ku Liang, a union leader in this factory and a Party member, became chief of the First Bureau of the Shanghai Municipal Labor Office after the Communist victory.[52]

4. *The Union of the French Tram, Power, and Water Company.* This union was one of Shanghai's most aggressive. Its Party branch had been in existence through the Japanese occupation. In 1945, the branch could claim to control about two hundred members and labor activists. Among other things, they infiltrated the various KMT-sponsored groups within the Company. One of the most "heroic" of these activists was a young man in his late twenties by the name of Chu Chün-hsin. He eventually came under the surveillance of the KMT police and had to flee to the liberated areas. He returned to Shanghai after liberation and resumed his work as a labor activist there.[53]

50. Ko Hsien, "Chung-kung shang-hai kuo mien shih-erh ch'ang chih-pu te kuang-jung tou-cheng shih" [A history of the glorious struggle of the CCP branch in the no. 12 factory of the National Shanghai Textile Mills], *CFJP,* June 28, 1951 (reprinted in Liu Ch'ang-sheng, ed., pp. 41-49).

51. Ch'en Shang, "Chi chung-kung shang-hai hai-kuan chih-pu shih-wu nien ying-yung tou-cheng te chi-ko p'ien-tuan" [Some paragraphs on the 15-year heroic struggle of the CCP branch in the Shanghai Customs], *CFJP,* July 2, 1951 (reprinted in Liu Ch'ang-sheng, ed., pp. 50-63).

52. Ch'en Ch'ing-mei, pp. 74-80 (see note 29).

53. *I-chiu-wu-ling jen-min nien-chien,* p. wu 9; *Ta ko-ming i-lai . . . ,* p. 36.

5. *The Shenhsin Number Nine Cotton Mill.* The Party branch was said to have played a major role in the January, 1948, strike at this mill. The strike made headlines in Shanghai when the authorities resorted to force to break it, claiming that Communist elements were responsible.[54] The strike involved all seven thousand workers, who were demanding that management supply a ration of coal and rice to .all employees, as was the practice in a number of other enterprises at this time. Party members were credited not with instigating the strike but with providing leadership as it developed. Management had turned down the workers' initial demands, and union leaders showed little willingness to press the matter further. The Party branch then persuaded the employees to continue their strike. Party members also organized a propaganda team, and several inspection teams to oversee the protection of equipment and materials.

Early on the morning of the fourth day of the strike, February 2, a force of three thousand soldiers and police surrounded the mill where the workers had barricaded themselves. When the police attacked, the workers stood by their defenses, hurling rocks, furniture, oil drums, and iron bars down from the roof, and at one point blocked the path of an armored vehicle with a factory truck. Among those identified as leaders at various stages of that day's battle with the police were four Party members.[55]

6. *The Shanghai Power Company.* A Party cell had existed continuously here since 1925 and was said to be the guiding force behind the January, 1946, strike of the Shanghai Power Company workers already described. The Party branch gained fifteen new members as a result of that strike. The Government tried to break the power workers union during the Fut'ung Incident in September, 1947. Claiming that it was the publicity agency of the CCP in Shanghai, the police raided the Fut'ung Printing Press on the evening of September 19. Fifteen shop employees were arrested, together with six members of the Shanghai Power Company union who were proofreading the forthcoming issue of a workers' journal published by the cultural section of the union.[56]

Four days later, most of the two thousand workers from the Company's three main branches gathered at the Social Affairs Bureau and remained there for eight hours while worker representatives negotiated for the release of their colleagues. The Bureau subsequently ordered the union to suspend all activities and await reorganization. In addition, the Bureau ordered the Power Company to discharge twenty-nine other employees designated by the Headquarters of the Garrison Command as suspected Communist agents. The city government and the Garrison Command then ordered the arrest of the twenty-nine "so as to have the root of the trouble removed once and for all."[57] Responding to these develop-

---

54. *Ho-p'ing jih-pao,* Shanghai, Feb. 3, 1948 *(CPR).*

55. The battle, between workers and police lasted for several hours. Many workers were injured and over 250 arrested—most being soon released. Public opinion seemed on the side of the workers, and the factory ultimately agreed to ration rice and coal to its employees (Hua-tung jen-min ch'u-pan-she, ed., *Tsai tou-cheng li chuang-ta,* pp. 33-40).

56. *CYJP,* Shanghai, Sept. 24, 1947 *(CPR).*

57. *TKP,* Shanghai, Sept. 26, 1947 *(CPR).*

ments, the workers of the French Tram Company went out on strike, followed soon thereafter by the workers of the British Tram Company, several textile plants, and machine-making factories. Reflecting city-wide sentiment in favor of the arrested workers, officials of 209 unions issued a joint statement of support for the sympathy movement and the protest strikes which continued for several days.

The Fut'ung Printing Press was indeed an "underground printing press of the CCP" in Shanghai. [58] Many activists in the labor movement fled Shanghai for the liberated areas as a result of this incident. In addition, Wang Hsiao-ho, an official in the Power Company union and Chairman of the Shanghai Electrical Workers Union, was arrested, sentenced to death by the Shanghai Special Criminal Tribunal, and executed. [59] It was later revealed that Wang Hsiao-ho was a Party member. [60]

7. *Shanghai's Largest Department Stores.* In one of these, the Wingon Emporium, a Party branch had been established in 1937. After the Japanese surrender, this cell joined with those in a number of other stores including Sincere's, the Tahsin Company, the Hsinhsin Company, and the China Native Products Company, in helping to organize the Department Store Employees Union of the Third District. Among the union's activities were the extension of medical and emergency loans, and educational loans for the children of union members. Also, the union set up six small libraries, a dramatic group, two bands, a chorus of 300 singers, and often held lectures and discussion meetings. The union had 4,500 members in over one hundred different stores at the time of the February Ninth (1947) Incident, another well-known labor confrontation with the KMT authorities during this period. The incident occurred when a large group of unidentified men armed with clubs and iron bars broke up the first meeting of the Preparatory Committee for the Promotion of National Products and the Boycott of U.S. Goods. The Committee had been initiated by the China Native Products Company as part of the fourteenth anniversary of the Company's founding, and was sponsored by the Union of Department Store Employees of the Third District.

The buy Chinese campaign had been inspired by the Central Government itself, which declared temporary restrictions on imports in November, 1946, in an effort to improve its balance of payments position. The Government had also extended new industrial production loans, and announced measures designed to encourage exports. In line with this policy, the National Chamber of Commerce launched a Buy Chinese Movement which was taken up by provincial merchants

58. Miu Yü, "Shang-hai kung-jen yun-tung te i-tso chien-ch'iang pao-lei: chi chung-kung fa-shang shui-tien kung-szu chih-pu te tou-cheng shih-chi" [A strong fortress in the Shanghai labor movement: recalling the history of the struggle of the Party branch in the French water and power company], *CFJP,* June 27, 1951 (reprinted in Liu Ch'ang-sheng, ed., p. 20).

59. U.S. Cons., Peiping, Hsinhua radio, North Shensi, Oct. 24, 1948.

60. Chung Lo, pp. 24-40 (see note 13); K'o Lan and Chao Tzu, *Pu szu te Wang Hsiao-ho.*

associations. In Shanghai, the Municipal Council issued a public statement urging people to purchase Chinese rather than foreign products.[61]

As it happened, the student demonstrations in late December and January, 1947, protesting the alleged rape of the Peita girl student by a U.S. Marine, coincided with the native products campaign and gave impetus to the developing anti-American tone within it. This embarrassed the Government in its relations with the U.S., some of whose businessmen had already protested the import restrictions. Thus a pro-Government newspaper reported that "ambitious politicians" were trying to turn the legitimate campaign to promote native products into an anti-American boycott. [62] Moreover, the first meeting of the Preparatory Committee was to have been addressed by Kuo Mo-jo and the economist Ma Yin-ch'u, both well-known leftists and outspoken critics of the KMT regime.

Of the several hundred union members who gathered for the meeting on Saturday morning, February 9, ten were seriously injured including Liang Jen-ta, an employee of the shoe department at the Wingon Emporium, who died as the result of a skull injury. The attack was generally assumed to have been the work of agents and hirelings of the secret police. [63] Predictably, it served only to create another incident around which to organize a new wave of protest. This time, management came out on the side of its employees. Representatives of some of the largest firms in Shanghai made public statements supporting the buy Chinese campaign and their employees' right to freedom of assembly. [64] Perhaps because of the widespread indignation aroused by the death of Liang Jen-ta, the authorities waited several months before making their final move against the Department Store Employees Union. Then on September 30, at least nine members and officers of the union were arrested including the chairman of its executive board, Ch'en Shih-chün. The Social Affairs Bureau simultaneously ordered the union to suspend all activities and await reorganization on grounds that "quite a number of responsible officials of the union have become affiliated with the bandit party and have repeatedly attempted to create disturbances in this city."[65]

According to later revelations, Ch'en Shih-chün, a young man in his thirties, was a Party member while he was an employee of the advertising department of the China Native Products Company. Other Party members active in this union

61. *WHP,* Shanghai, Feb. 10, 1947 *(CPR).* The Buy Chinese Movement was supported by Chinese manufacturers and merchants but does not seem to have caught on among consumers. In Shanghai, the largest firm dealing in native products reportedly had daily sales of CMC$10 million; the Wingon Company, dealing in foreign products, had four times that volume: *Hsi-nan jih-pao,* Canton, Dec. 28, 1946 *(CPR).*

62. *Ho-p'ing jih-pao,* Shanghai, Feb. 10, 1947 *(CPR).*

63. Shortly after Shanghai's liberation, three men were charged with responsibility for this incident: Mao Te-k'ang, an employee of Wingon's No. 1 Textile Mill; Wei Jung-lai, director of the personnel section of the mill; and Kuan Yun-k'ang, a worker in the No. 14 Factory of the Chinese Textile Industry. *TKP,* Shanghai, Oct. 20, 1949 *(CPR).*

64. *TKP,* Shanghai, Feb. 11, 1947 *(CPR).*

65. *TKP,* Shanghai, Oct. 1, 1947 *(CPR).*

included Ting Sheng-ya, an employee of the crockery department at Wingon's, and Han Wu-ch'eng.[66]

In light of this specific corroborating evidence, a number of other charges made by the KMT authorities at this time gain more credence. Among the charges was the "confession" of Chu Sung-mou, allegedly a Communist underground leader working in the labor movement in the Nanking-Shanghai area. He was arrested at the Wusih railway station on June 7, 1948. According to his statement as published in a government-supervised newspaper, there were some eight hundred underground Communist agents working at a variety of tasks in that area.[67]

Another charge involved Communist underground operations in the Tientsin area, where eighty-three suspects were arrested between December 3, 1947, and February 18, 1948. Forty of these were released because of insufficient evidence, but forty-three were turned over to the Tientsin Garrison Command. Many of the leading members of the Communist underground labor organization in Tientsin were allegedly arrested at this time, including Li Wang-ch'uan and Chang Yu-ch'uan. Yu Ta-sheng, the suspected leader of the underground operations in the city, fled to the liberated areas sometime in December, but his wife stayed behind and was among those apprehended. According to the charges made against them, the arrested had been engaged in transporting supplies to the Communist areas, creating labor disturbances in Tientsin, and disseminating Communist propaganda.[68]

As with the student movement, the extent to which Communist underground activities contributed to the Government's inability to control labor unrest is difficult to gauge. Communist agitation may well have been decisive in a number of strikes and labor disputes. But with these running into the thousands, and with large numbers of workers supporting them, the evidence does not seem to warrant the conclusion that the Communists deserve credit for all the unrest on the labor front. Certainly the workers, like the students, were advised often and bluntly enough that they were being exploited by the Government's mortal enemy. And like the students, the workers either did not believe it or did not care, so intent were they on pressing their demands. Moreover, the Government's

66. Chuang Ch'ing-hsün, "I-k'ao ch'ün-chung chien-ch'ih tou-cheng: chung-kung yung-an kung-szu chih-pu chieh-fang ch'ien te tou-cheng" [Relying on the masses to support the struggle: the struggle of the CCP branch in the Wingon Company before liberation], *CFJP*, July 1, 1951 (reprinted in Liu Ch'ang-sheng, ed., pp. 64-73).

67. *Shun pao*, Shanghai, June 15, 1948 *(CPR)*. In addition to work in the student and labor movements, the Communist underground also allegedly purchased and transported much-needed supplies such as gasoline and kerosene to the liberated areas. Contact with the liberated areas was assisted by secret radio transmitters in KMT territory. This information from interviews in 1969 and 1973. Also *Hsin-wen pao*, Shanghai, Oct. 30, 1947; *CYJP*, Shanghai, Nov. 3, 1947; *Shun pao*, Shanghai, Nov. 7, 1947, and Jan. 14, 1948 (all in *CPR*, same dates).

68. *TKP*, Tientsin, Feb. 18, 1948 *(CPR)*.

tendency to give in to labor's economic demands indicates a recognition, even on the part of KMT leaders, that these were not contrived and that they were the basic cause of labor's unrest.

Thus the Shanghai labor movement in the late 1940s would seem to exemplify the sort of situation in which the Communist role itself was more a symptom than a cause. The issues and grievances did not need to be manufactured: they were there ready-made and available for exploitation by anyone interested. Both the issues, and the climate facilitating their exploitation, emerged from the combined effects of: (1) the Japanese occupation, which effectively severed the KMT's control over labor; (2) the apparent anticipation among the workers at the end of World War II that victory would bring them economic betterment; and (3) the reality of a post-war economy disrupted by rampant inflation and the contraction of business and industry. The net result was an increasingly independent labor force that refused, on numerous occasions and in a variety of ways, to comply with the Government's pleas for cooperation and support in its struggle against the Communists.

ECONOMIC MISMANAGEMENT AND THE LOSS OF PUBLIC CONFIDENCE

Equally significant politically, the inflation undermined general public confidence in the KMT's ability to govern. This in turn hampered the Government's efforts to reduce the pressures of inflation. It produced a downward spiral, of political deflation and aborted reforms, which moved in inverse relation to the upward course of wages and prices. So long as the Government continued to rely on the printing press as its main source of revenue, the efforts to implement wage-price freezes, currency reform, and the like, could at best serve only as short-term palliatives minimizing the most harmful effects of the inflation. More often than not, however, such measures were ill-conceived, half-heartedly implemented, and coolly received by a skeptical public. Under the circumstances, they became positive liabilities—not only failing to achieve what the Government claimed they would, but in many cases even intensifying the conditions they were intended to ameliorate. While journalists and writers were wondering in print at the Government's "trial and error" approach to economics, various sectors of the public demonstrated their lack of confidence in more concrete ways.

THE DOWNWARD SPIRAL

In 1946, the industries suffering most from rising costs were those dependent on foreign markets and those that had to compete with the foreign products then coming freely onto the local market. Industries such as drugs, paper, cement, and tobacco were among the first to suffer from foreign competition, as were industries such as silk filature and silk knitting which depended largely on overseas markets.

Toward the end of 1946, the Government revised the exchange rate and undertook other measures to encourage exports and restrict imports. But these measures could have little effect given the overall problems created by the inflation. The producer faced: declining demand due to a general reduction in real purchasing power; high labor costs; high interest rates; continuing increases in fuel, water, electric power, and freight costs; and increasing trade and production taxes. [69] As noted, these conditions finally resulted toward the end of 1947 in a general contraction of industrial output at the same time that the real purchasing power of significant portions of the urban population sharply declined. This general contraction was felt first in the silk textile, rubber goods, cement, and tobacco industries; next in underwear, cosmetics, matches, and woolen textiles; and finally in the cotton textile industry itself.[70]

Unfortunately for the Government, it was obliged to bear the major burden of responsibility for virtually all of these problems and many others besides. This was so, first, because of the basic policy of inflationary finance; and second, because of the inadequacy of its efforts to bring some order to the resulting chaos. For example, monetary policies vacillated continuously between the expansion and suspension of credit. Unrealistic official interest rates encouraged the growth of an underground money market and thus increased the supply of funds available for speculative purposes. A government loan to Shanghai rice merchants in 1946 was used by them, apparently with official collusion, for speculative purposes thereby causing a further rise in the price of rice.[71]

In its effort to increase revenues, the Government permitted the continued existence of an irrational tax system, which placed numerous and often exorbitant levies on commodities, business operations, and the like, but left virtually untouched the personal incomes of speculators and profiteers. In addition, the Government's foreign trade policy resulted in an unfavorable balance of trade and harm to local producers, conditions which were only partially corrected by the reforms of November, 1946.[72]

The Government was also vulnerable to the charge that, in its attempts to promote economic development, it was only encouraging the growth of bureaucratic capitalism, that is, enterprises controlled by high government officials—either still in office or recently retired—and their associates. These men used their connections with the Government and the Central Bank to obtain foreign

69. Chi Chung-wei "A Thorough Analysis of the Industrial Crisis in Shanghai", *TKP*, Shanghai, June 25, 26, 27, 1946 (*CPR*, July 13).

70. Chang, *Inflationary Spiral*, p. 353.

71. The rice loan scandal received wide publicity in the Shanghai press. For example, *Hsin-wen pao*, June 12, 1946; *Shih-shih hsin pao*, June 14; *TKP*, June 19; and *WHP*, July 9 (all in *CPR* for same dates).

72. See Chang, *Inflationary Spiral*, and Chou, *Chinese Inflation*, for full discussion of these and other policies, including some that were relatively successful. Among the latter were the Government's gold sale program in effect from Mar. 8, 1946, to Feb. 17, 1947; and an effort to ration essential commodities in a few cities. This was started on a limited scale in Shanghai in July, 1947. Later the government undertook rationing of rice and flour in Shanghai, Nanking, Peiping, Tientsin, and Canton. The scope of these programs was limited, however, and had little impact on the overall situation. On the defects of the tax system, see Chou, pp. 64-67.

exchange, import commodities, and gain other advantages not granted to the ordinary entrepreneur.[73]

The public could hardly be expected to support the Government's reform efforts when experience had taught that withholding support was often the less harmful alternative. From the entrepreneur turned speculator, to the shop clerk who invested his savings in a gold ring rather than in the bank, the public was only responding to the realities of economic life. Thus when the Government offered bonds for sale during the first half of 1947, capitalists were reluctant to buy. Members of industrial, commercial, and financial circles backed off when questioned about newly issued bonds soon to go on sale in Kunming. Because of past experience with such bonds, they said, it would be unwise to risk purchasing them again without "careful consideration."[74]

There were signs by 1947 of an increasing unwillingness by the general public to entrust their savings to banks. Safer alternatives included gold, silver, and remittances to Hong Kong. The regulation that private banks were to offer interest rates no higher than those approved by the Central Bank of China was openly flouted, reflecting the gap that existed during most of the Civil War period between official and black market interest rates. The Government was never successful, except for very limited periods, in curbing the black market activities either of the banks themselves or of other institutions.

When it became more profitable to invest in hoarding and speculation than in industrial production, capital was so invested. The use of capital for speculative purposes was not a new phenomenon: it had already become a problem during the Anti-Japanese War. The incentives for such activity merely grew as the effects of the inflation intensified during the Civil War years—increasing the obstacles to production on one hand, and expanding the opportunities for speculation on the other. These latter included: buying, selling, and hoarding commodities; speculating on the securities market; investing in gold and foreign currencies; and lending at black market interest rates.

Indeed, the opportunities seemed limitless. For example, the Government made loans to productive enterprises to help them cope with the workers' demands for New Year bonuses at the end of 1946. Some observers maintained, however, that the loans accounted for the immediate rise in the stock market quotations. The root of the evil was not lack of money. Many billions were lying idle or being remitted to Hong Kong. Some businessmen were known to have large sums which they refused to invest in their own enterprises, where the profits were less than could be gained by speculation.[75]

The following is representative of the opinions which appeared in the press, including KMT newspapers, describing the activities of the business community:

73. The term "bureaucratic capitalism" was not generally used to refer to the large state-owned enterprises such as the China Textile Development Company, or the many operations of the National Resources Commission. It referred specifically to the use of public office and connections to promote private enterprise and profit.

74. *Yun-nan jih-pao*, Kunming, Apr. 9, 1947 *(CPR)*.

75. *China Weekly Review: Monthly Report*, Jan. 31, 1947, p. 6.

Businessmen . . . cannot shun responsibility for their contributions to the poor economic situation. First, and foremost, they have failed to change their attitude and policy toward business. . . . They have continued to borrow large sums at high interest rates in order to hold commodities, gold bars, American bank notes, government bonds, stocks and shares, in the hope that the inflation will move fast enough to allow them to sell out, pay the interest charges and still reap a large profit. Many have made substantial profits, while others have contributed to the bank and business failures by collapsing themselves when the market was against them.[76]

What was bad for business was not necessarily bad for the businessman. Lack of data makes it impossible to conclude that businessmen and industrialists, either individually or as a group, actually benefited as much from the inflation as they might have from more conventional operations. But the inflation provided ample scope and incentive for those willing to commit even small amounts of capital to speculative purposes, and many chose to do so ignoring the pleas both official and otherwise to "change their attitude toward business." Nor were these pleas normally followed up by visits from the tax collector or police inspector—an unfortunate omission that indicated where the final burden of responsibility rested.

AUGUST, 1948: THE LAST EFFORT

Of all its policies and programs during the Civil War years, the emergency economic reform measures announced in February, 1947, and August, 1948, were the two most ambitious and widely publicized of the Government's attempts to stabilize the economy. Because of this, they were also the most damaging to the Government when they failed. The major weaknesses of the 1947 reforms have been sketched above and need not be repeated. The cost of the second failure was greater not only because the objectives of the 1948 effort were more comprehensive, but also because, as KMT leaders themselves admitted, this was their last chance. The Government had no other means at its disposal with which to try to stabilize the economy and revive public confidence.[77] Yet it was evident from the start that the 1948 reform program could not succeed, because it contained the same flaws responsible for the failure of the 1947 effort. The new program could not, therefore, inspire the public confidence and cooperation necessary for its success.

The financial and economic emergency measures were announced on August 19. A new currency was inaugurated. The exchange rate between the new Gold Yuan and the old currency was fixed at GY 1 to CNC\$3,000,000. The total note issue of the new currency was restricted to two billion Gold Yuan. Strikes and protest demonstrations were again banned. Increases in wages and prices after August 19 were forbidden without prior government approval. Gold, silver, and foreign currency—all of which had become major objects of investment as a

76. *China Weekly Review: Monthly Report,* Dec. 31, 1946, p. 8.
77. John Leighton Stuart, *Fifty Years in China,* p. 194.

hedge against inflation—were to be turned in to the government in exchange for Gold Yuan.

Other measures included an increase in commodity taxes, an increase in the official rate of exchange for foreign currencies, credit controls, reduced interest rates, and strictures against hoarding. The Government appointed three high officials to supervise the enforcement of the emergency reform measures in north, central, and south China. They were Vice-premier Chang Li-sheng in the North; O.K. Yui, the Governor of the Central Bank of China, in central China; and T. V. Soong, Governor of Kwangtung Province, in the South.[78] Chiang Kai-shek's son, Chiang Ching-kuo, was given full control over the implementation of the emergency measures only in the Shanghai area.

Doubts about the reform program appeared almost immediately in the press, and grew more insistent once the pattern of enforcement became clear. The first measure to draw fire was the wage-price freeze. The critics pointed out that wages and prices varied in different parts of the country and that those obtaining on August 19 did not necessarily represent the most reasonable level in every case. Despite the provision for authorized increases, a rigid interpretation of this provision would lead to a recurrence of the disruption caused by the 1947 wage-price freeze.[79]

A second point to earn immediate condemnation was the requirement that everyone exchange their gold, silver, and foreign currency holdings for Gold Yuan notes, while those with assets abroad exceeding U.S.$3,000 were only required to register their holdings. The owners of foreign assets valued at less than that amount were not even required to declare them.[80] An article in the liberal weekly, *Shih yü wen* (Time and Culture), was particularly outspoken. The fundamental principle underlying the emergency reforms, it commented, was the maintenance of the status quo in the traditional manner of "effecting a nominal change to preserve an old order." No measures attempted to correct the unequal distribution of wealth. Salaries and wages were frozen, but capital which had fled abroad would not be touched. The official prices for gold and foreign currencies (held mostly by the well-to-do) had been fixed at a high level equal to or even above the black market quotations, but the rate for silver (held by the poorer classes) was well below the black market price. In addition, the increased commodity taxes would only harm legitimate business and industry, and would inevitably be passed on to the consumer—placing yet another burden on lower-income groups. Meanwhile, the income and properties of the wealthy remained untaxed.[81]

Finally, the early critics pointed out, the reform program contained nothing which would significantly alter the Government's basic financial situation. The

78. *Ho-p'ing jih-pao*, Shanghai, Aug. 20, 1948 *(CPR)*.

79. *TKP*, Shanghai, Aug. 21, 1948, and *Hsin-wen pao*, Shanghai, Aug. 23, 1948 (CPR, Aug. 21-23). The Government's first two experiments with freezing wages and prices were in 1938 and 1942, and were as unsuccessful as its third attempt in February, 1947.

80. *TKP*, Shanghai, Aug. 23, 1948 *(CPR)*.

81. *Shih yü wen*, Shanghai, Aug. 27, 1948 (CPR, Sept. 18-20).

only real guarantee against continuing inflation was some approximation of a balanced budget. Assuming the continuing level of military and other expenditures, a more balanced budget could not be achieved without a substantial increase in government revenues and in overall production. Without removing the basic causes of the inflation, the substitution of one currency for another could hardly be expected to have a stabilizing effect on the economy.[82]

It soon became apparent that whatever defects the reform program itself contained, the most urgent problem had to do with the nature of its implementation. For the emergency measures were being strictly enforced only in the city of Shanghai. Chiang Ching-kuo went about this task with a fervor reflecting the Government's awareness that this was its last chance and its hope that if China's commercial and financial center could be conquered, the rest of the country would somehow fall into line.

Maximum publicity surrounded Chiang Ching-kuo's activities in Shanghai. He was portrayed as a man moving fearlessly through the jungles of the city apprehending and punishing even the most powerful speculators and profiteers. For a time, Chiang's "tiger hunting" enjoyed widespread support among the people of Shanghai, who had seen themselves as victims of avaricious businessmen able to exploit the inflation to their own advantage. Over three thousand such individuals, including some of Shanghai's most prominent, were imprisoned. The Government sought to prove at last that its deeds were as good as its words, and that no one would be spared in enforcing the emergency measures. Within a month, however, enthusiasm for Chiang Ching-kuo's flamboyant tactics was turning to sarcasm as the defects in the reform program began to make themselves felt.

By August 28, the Central Bank had already issued GY 30 million to the public in exchange for gold, silver, and foreign currencies. But no measures had been devised to attract—or force—all this idle capital into productive or at least non-inflationary channels. [83] This would have been difficult in any case, since the public allegedly never had enough confidence in the new currency to make a campaign to encourage savings worthwhile.[84]

Even more serious were the pressures which threatened Shanghai from outside because of the failure to implement the program uniformly on a nationwide basis. The use of force in Shanghai did produce some immediate results. Prices were stabilized and remained so for about six weeks. Nevertheless, it required little sophistication in economic matters to understand that if conditions were not improved in the rest of the country, Shanghai could not long remain unaffected by them. [85] Yet this eventuality had apparently been overlooked by the economic planners in Nanking. Prices in the rest of the country, where the freeze was not so rigidly enforced, continued their upward climb.

82. *Ibid.; Chien-sien jih-pao,* Shanghai, Sept. 14, 1948 (*CPR,* Sept. 15); *Hsin lu,* Shanghai, Sept. 20, 1948 (*CPR,* Sept. 30).

83. *Chin-yung jih-pao,* Shanghai, Aug. 28, 1948 (*CPR,* Aug. 31).

84. *Hsin-wen pao,* Shanghai, Sept. 9, 1948 *(CPR).*

85. *TKP,* Shanghai, Sept. 15, 1948 *(CPR).*

By the end of September, Shanghai was becoming an economic island. Merchants either held back supplies bound for the city in anticipation of an eventual break in price controls there, or sent their goods elsewhere. Rice shipments were halted outside the city by merchants willing to pay prices higher than those prevailing on the Shanghai market. Food stocks dwindled and the replenishment of raw materials became difficult at a time when hoarding had been made a criminal offense. A number of flour mills curtailed production. The Shanghai Power Company sent an emergency appeal to the government when the Company was unable to obtain more than one-half its monthly requirement of coal.

Some concerns which depended on imported raw materials found that, due to the rise in import costs, the ceiling prices of their finished products were lower than production costs. For example, the ceiling price of a certain grade of cotton yarn was fixed at GY 707 per bale. But because raw cotton could not be purchased at its ceiling price, the yarn producer reportedly suffered a loss of GY 70 per bale of yarn produced.[86] The government had made no provisions for the continued flow of supplies into the city of Shanghai, for rationing necessary commodities and materials, or for the maintenance of a workable ratio between production costs and commodity prices.[87]

Added to these pressures was the revelation around the first of October that the government had issued an additional GY 220,000,000 to cover its budget. The amount of notes issued had already reached 50 percent of the maximum GY 2 billion limit announced in August. The meaning of this news was lost on no one. Public confidence was further shaken by the deteriorating military situation in Manchuria and Shantung, where Government forces lost the capital city of Tsinan in late September.

The event that finally shattered the surface calm in Shanghai seemed trivial by comparison with the problems at hand. On October 1, the Ministry of Finance announced an increase in the tax rates for seven kinds of goods including tobacco and wines. All the tobacco shops in Shanghai closed down and requested permission to raise their prices to cover the tax increase. The Government granted permission and, on October 3, tobacco shops reopened with their prices marked up by 100 percent.[88] Doubts as to the government's ability to enforce the price freeze seemed confirmed, and a buying spree began at once. People sought to hedge against the expected depreciation of the new currency by transforming their cash into commodities as quickly as possible. Crowds rushed to take advantage of the low ceiling prices while they lasted. Shopkeepers, fearing they would be unable to replace their stocks, began to shorten business hours, or to withhold goods from sale. In some cases they refused to do business altogether. The black market revived, and "travelling merchants" were

86. *Hsin-wen t'ien-ti* (associated with the KMT), Shanghai, No. 50, Oct. 16, 1948 (*CPR,* Oct. 20).

87. Liu Ti-yuan, "Lun wu-chia te chü-pu kuan-chih" [On the partial control of prices], *KC,* Oct. 2, 1948, pp. 4-7.

88. *Chien-sien jih-pao,* Shanghai, Oct. 7, 1948 *(CPR).*

said to be moving large quantities of goods out of the city.[89] While the average person's capital was being transformed into commodities, that of the wealthier and more astute was fleeing to havens such as Taiwan, Canton, Szechwan, and Hong Kong.[90]

Chiang Ching-kuo tried to stem the tide, but to no avail. Thirty to forty "patrol units" were set up by the Greater Shanghai Youth Service Corps, a group numbering several thousand recruited from workers, which was established in mid-September to aid in the implementation of the reform measures. These new units were to patrol the city daily, investigate black market activities, and receive information from local residents concerning violations of the emergency measures. Film companies in Shanghai received an order from the Central KMT Publicity Board that the new currency was not to be ridiculed in any film, and that violators would be punished for undermining public confidence in the Gold Yuan.[91]

Chiang Ching-kuo's authority was extended to the entire province of Kiangsu, as well as the provinces of Chekiang and Anhwei. A good idea, the critics said, but too late. Open criticism of Chiang's work began to appear in the press. As one writer expressed it: "Chiang is rather lonesome in Shanghai. With the exception of the common people who got a brief relief of pent-up feelings from his tiger hunting, Chiang has so far failed to get the cooperation and support of any really powerful group in Shanghai. His ideals and work have not yet taken root here." More specifically, Chiang owed this failure to his basic ignorance of how industry and finance operated. However impressive his political credentials, he had come to Shanghai unprepared for his economic tasks; had failed to investigate the production needs of the city; and had taken no action when presented with statistical data by industrialists in early October concerning their production difficulties.[92] By the end of October there were severe shortages of such essential commodities as rice, cooking oil, and fuel. Among the items that had disappeared entirely from the local market were medicines, milk powder, coffins, toilet paper, and cotton.[93]

A special meeting of the Executive Yuan on October 31 adopted "supplementary measures" for the economic reform program and in effect abandoned the ceiling price system.[94] On November 1, the president of the Special Criminal Tribunal in Nanking announced that merchants who had been detained on suspicion of raising prices in violation of the August 19 measures would not be prosecuted. Those who had been arrested, tried, and found guilty would be released on bail.

89. *TKP* and *Shang pao*, Shanghai, Oct. 6, 1948 *(CPR);* and *TKP*, Shanghai, Oct. 7, 1948 *(CPR)*.

90. *Shang pao*, Shanghai, Oct. 15, 1948 *(CPR)*.

91. *Hsin min wan-pao*, Shanghai, Oct. 16, 1948 (*CPR*, Oct. 19).

92. *Hsin-wen t'ien-ti*, Shanghai, No. 50, Oct. 16, 1948 (*CPR*, Oct. 20).

93. *TKP*, Shanghai, Oct. 28, 1948 *(CPR)*.

94. *TKP*, Shanghai, Nov. 1, 1948 (*CPR*, Oct. 30-Nov. 1).

By November 6, prices in Shanghai had jumped to over ten times their August levels.[95] On November 8, the price of pork rose from GY 6 per catty in the early morning to GY 12 by 11:00 A.M. Restaurants doubled and tripled their prices within a single day. Buyers fruitlessly mobbed the rice shops, while farmers in the countryside around Shanghai, who had harvested a bumper crop, held back their rice—unwilling to exchange it for currency they feared would soon be worthless. By the end of November, the government had printed GY 3.4 billion, having completely abandoned any pretense of adhering to the GY 2 billion limit originally announced.

The only achievement of the economic reforms that anyone could think of was that they had enabled the government to confiscate U.S.$170,000,000 worth of gold, silver, and foreign currencies from the people.[96] Yet even here there remained some question as to how large a part of the public's savings was actually confiscated in this way. It was estimated that the amount of gold, silver, and foreign currency turned in by the end of September, 1948, represented only 20-30 percent of the public's actual holdings.[97]

The most overtly indignant group in Shanghai was not the long-suffering "middle class," but the businessmen and industrialists. The Shanghai Chamber of Commerce and the Shanghai Industrial Association called a meeting on November 1 of responsible persons from local industrial and commercial organizations. Speaker after speaker rose to denounce the Government for the havoc that had been wreaked on business and industry, and for the unprecedented indignities to which so many entrepreneurs had been subjected. One speaker referred to the "quack doctors" who had treated the four million citizens of Shanghai as "specimens for an experiment." Others demanded the resignation of the Minister of Finance, and punishment of those responsible for the reform program.[98] Commentators elsewhere were somewhat more dispassionate. "This currency reform has been a lesson for students of politics," wrote one prophetically. "It is probably the last course the Nanking Government will offer."[99]

THE BURDEN OF INFLATIONARY FINANCE

It is difficult, as has been noted above, to isolate and trace the links between inflation and the Government's loss of support by the salaried middle-income minority. But there is no doubt that salaried employees bore, in relative terms at least, the major burden of the inflation. There is also no doubt that they suffered severe economic hardship as a result, although in absolute terms there were obviously many, such as low-income workers and the unemployed, whose deprivations were as great or greater.

95. Chang, *Inflationary Spiral*, p. 359.
96. *Ibid.*, p. 80.
97. *Tung-nan jih-pao,* Shanghai, Oct. 6, 1948 *(CPR).*
98. *TKP* and *Chung-hua shih-pao*, Shanghai, Nov. 2, 1948 *(CPR).*
99. "Chin-yuan ch'üan-hsia te hsi-sheng-che" [The victims of the gold yuan], *STPP*, Nov. 15, 1948, p. 2.

The major salaried groups were professors and teachers, military officers, and civilian government employees. Their impoverishment had begun during World War II, when inflation reduced their real income to between 6 and 12 percent of their pre-war salaries. This average figure varied within and between occupations and departments because of efforts, not uniformly made, to provide employees with housing, rice, fuel, and other basic necessities. By 1945, salaried workers had emerged as "a new depressed class" and remained so throughout the Civil War years.[100]

While the Government could at least decree that labor was to be compensated for the rise in the cost of living, the Government found it more difficult to do the same for its own employees. These included the majority of college and university professors, whose pay scales were comparable to those of regular civil servants.[101] When a *Ta kung pao* reporter examined the average monthly wages in Shanghai's main industries in May, 1946, he found that, however great the grievances of the workers, their pay scales were still higher than those of teachers and government employees. Despite variations ranging from CNC$50,000 for women workers in the hosiery industry to a high of CNC$180,000 for carpenters and CNC$200,000 for machine workers, the average monthly pay in Shanghai's major industries at that time was CNC$100,000.[102] But the average monthly salary of Shanghai's university and college professors at the end of February, 1946, ranged from CNC$52,000 to CNC$78,000.[103] The incomes of barbers, tailors, and bank clerks were higher. Even the office boys in government banks were earning about CNC$110,000 monthly during the first half of 1946. A pedicab driver in Shanghai could earn as much as CNC$20,000 a day.[104]

In December, 1946, primary and middle school teachers in Kunming's public schools issued a demand for increased salaries. The monthly income of primary school teachers was then CNC$80,000, said to be scarcely enough to support a family of two or three in that city.[105] The Shanghai University Professors' Association may not have been exaggerating when it declared, in a burst of self-pity, that "the remuneration of a professor is even less than that of a coolie in the employ of a dairy farm whose duty it is to remove cows' manure, or of a tram conductor, or of a servant in the employ of a government bank."[106]

100. Chang, *Inflationary Spiral,* pp. 63-65; and Chou, *Chinese Inflation,* p. 244. By mid-1946, a Kunming professor estimated that the real income of his colleagues had been reduced by 98 percent from the 1937 level. *TKP,* Shanghai, Aug. 30, 1946 *(CPR,* Aug. 31).

101. See Chapter Three, note 28. At this time there were approximately 180 institutions of higher learning in China. Of these, 122 were state schools with an estimated 10,000 faculty members. There were also a substantial number of government (provincial) middle schools. *TKP,* Tientsin, July 10, 1947 *(CPR,* July 11); and *Chung mei jih-pao,* Shanghai, Feb. 28, 1946 *(CPR,* Mar. 1).

102. Chi Chung-wei (see note 38).

103. *Chung mei jih-pao,* Shanghai, Feb. 28, 1946 *(CPR,* Mar. 1).

104. *Ho-p'ing jih-pao,* Shanghai, May 28, 1946 *(CPR);* and *TKP,* Tientsin, Apr. 2, 1946 *(CPR).*

105. *CYJP,* Kunming, Dec. 25, 1946 *(CPR,* Dec. 27).

106. *TKP,* Shanghai, Apr. 10, 1946 *(CPR).* At the end of 1947, Barnett found the income of Shanghai college professors about the same as rickshaw coolies, when business

The salaries of all public employees were revised upward on the average of once every three months during most of the Civil War years. But these adjustments never corresponded to the actual rise in the cost of living and so did little to alleviate the impoverished conditions of teachers and civil servants, whose real income remained in most cases insufficient to maintain their basic livelihood. [107] In April, 1947, a lower level government employee in Tientsin was earning CNC$200,000 monthly, which was sufficient only to pay for his meals and various miscellaneous expenses but not his rent. [108] In a joint statement, ten professors from Peking and Tsinghua universities asserted that public teachers and civil servants were unable to maintain even the lowest standards of living, cold and hunger having become facts of daily life for them and their families. These low and unjust salaries, warned the professors, were producing three evils: falling work efficiency, spreading corruption, and declining morale. [109]

According to a survey by the Shanghai municipal government in early 1948, approximately 69 percent of 1,942 civil service families surveyed were either in debt or in a position where "income falls short of expenditure." [110] In March, 1948, the head of one such family told of his difficulties in a letter to the *Ta kung pao*. As a "junior staff member of a certain government agency," he received a monthly salary of CNC$3,100,000. This was not enough to provide him and his parents with the basic daily necessities and pay the rent of three *tou* of rice per month for the hut in which they lived. They had just been able to make ends meet by subsisting on rice, vegetables, and one pound of pork per week for the three of them. At the end of January, however, the government had reduced the rice ration of employees at this man's level from eight to three *tou* per month. Now, he wrote, one cannot even buy enough cornflour to last a month. "During the past ten days we have filled our stomachs with thin gruel. Sitting at my desk for eight hours a day, I feel so hungry, that my head aches and eyes blur." [111]

One popular view at the time about the effect of their economic plight on the political orientations of salaried workers was that they had at least lost all fear of socialism. With salaries and savings consumed by the inflation, they had already been reduced to "proletarian" status and had little left to lose. This view was something of an exaggeration—since the adherence to socialist ideals among

was good, and that a number of organizations paid their professional employees "at about the same level" as their manual workers (*China on the Eve*, p. 19).

107. *Shun pao*, Shanghai, June 10, 1946 (*CPR*, June 11); *TKP*, Tientsin, Oct. 17, 1947 *(CPR); New Star* (independent), Tientsin, Aug. 21, 1947 *(CPR)*.

108. *Shang-wu jih-pao*, Tientsin, Apr. 6, 1947 (*CPR*, Apr. 9).

109. Wang Tsun-ming, *et al.*, "Wo-men tui-yü kai-shan kung-chiao jen-yuan tai-yü te i-chien" [Our opinion concerning the improvement in the treatment of public teachers and civil servants], *KC*, Oct. 18, 1947, p. 3.

110. *Shun pao*, Shanghai, Mar. 16, 1948 (*CPR*, Mar. 23).

111. *TKP*, Shanghai, Mar. 13, 1948 (*CPR*, Mar. 23). For a further analysis, see Wu Ch'i-yuan, "Kung-chiao jen-yuan te tai-yü tsen-yang ts'ai neng te-tao chen-cheng te kai-shan?" [How can the treatment of public teachers and civil servants be genuinely improved?], *KC*, Oct. 19, 1946, pp. 8-9.

academics, for example, seems to have been rooted in a wider range of intellectual considerations (as the following chapter will attempt to show).

Nevertheless, the impoverishment of the academic community did inspire one of the major themes of the student anti-war movement which enjoyed widespread support among the professors. As we have seen, the professors themselves apparently precipitated the Anti-Hunger Anti-Civil War demonstrations in 1947. At that time, they demanded, among other things, a reduction in military expenditure and an increase in the allocation for educational purposes, including pay increases for themselves. Thus the economic deprivations caused by the Government's use of the printing press to finance its war effort provided one important issue for those who argued against the war and obviously helped to undermine support for it within the intellectual community. But unlike the labor movement which fed directly on the economic chaos created by the inflation, the intellectuals' refusal to support the Government's civil war policy was based on a more complicated assessment of the Government itself together with the sacrifices that the nation as a whole should have to bear in order to preserve it. The intellectuals' own recent impoverishment was only one of the considerations evident in their assessment.

As for civil servants, they did not participate to any significant extent in the anti-Government protests of the period. They did not register their discontent in any politically meaningful way except by writing letters to newspaper editors or subscribing to the journal, *Kuan-ch'a,* if they could afford it. [112] And, like the intellectual community, they did not actually abandon the KMT until its fate was sealed on the battlefield. It is therefore difficult to determine just what their impoverishment may have cost the KMT beyond the obvious increase in corruption and reduction in efficiency. This may have been serious enough in terms of the damage done to the Government's image *vis-à-vis* the rest of the population. But in terms of the civil servants themselves, their orientation toward the KMT and the Civil War was probably not much different than that of the intellectual community.

Chang Kia-ngau seems to have summed up the situation most accurately when he suggested that the new depressed status of civil servants and teachers was "all the more dangerous politically because of their leftist intellectual leaning." [113] The implication of his statement was that the political-intellectual orientation of this group was already set and only reinforced by the harsh economic realities of the Civil War years. If this was in fact the case, the major political costs to the Government of the inflation were probably registered in areas other than the support lost as a result of the hardships it created for the urban salaried middle-class.

On the final balance sheet, then, the Government paid heavily for its mismanagement of the economy, the decision to rely on printing press money being only

---

112. See Chapter Five and the Bibliographic Notes on the popularity of this journal at this time.

113. Chang, *Inflationary Spiral,* p. 65.

the most glaring example thereof. Of all the consequences of that decision, perhaps the most dangerous for the Government was that it lulled those who made it into believing there could be a painless solution to their financial problems. The use of the printing press, combined with a similarly debilitating reliance on the continued flow of foreign aid, [114] did manage to tide the Government over the Anti-Japanese War. In the process, however, inflationary forces were set in motion that could not be checked without drastic and far-reaching revisions in the Government's way of operating. Then, without any past experience in implementing the hard decisions that such changes would have necessitated, the Government not surprisingly chose to finance its war against the Communists in the same manner. The net result was a Government with neither the will nor the capacity to do anything but preside over the deterioration of its economic position.

More specifically, the inflation provided a ready-made issue for a labor force suddenly freed at the end of World War II from the constraints of eight years of Japanese rule and ten years of KMT control before that. Within the context of rampant inflation, the Government could not reassert its pre-war hold over labor. During the first six months after the Japanese surrender, the Government was made fully aware of the disruptive potential of a labor force that ignored with impunity officially established procedures for the resolution of labor-management disputes. The Government had no choice but to accept labor's demand for automatic wage adjustments corresponding to the rise in the cost of living.

This decision not only accelerated the upward wage-price spiral, but also compromised the Government's long-standing alliance with business and industry, previously one of the main pillars supporting the KMT's structure of power. The Government was thus obliged to trade a fitful peace on the labor front for the resentment of entrepreneurs who argued that the concession to labor was contributing to their own soaring production costs. High wage payments were only part of the problem. But the Government seemingly could not win since it was responsible, either because of the inflation itself or because of the inadequate attempts to minimize its pressures, for virtually all other components of the problem as well. These ranged from reduced demand due to a general reduction in purchasing power, to irrational taxes on commerce and production,

---

114. The point here is not to criticize the KMT Government for accepting foreign aid, but to emphasize the Government's seeming unwillingness to face up to the harsh facts of China's economic situation. Both the Government's reliance on the printing press and its dependence on foreign aid were indicative of this weakness. And both ultimately placed it in the embarrassing position of having no recourse except to continue appealing to Washington as the economic crisis worsened. This weakness provided good material for editorial writers. For example, *STPP* (Jan. 15, 1948, p. 3) likened the Government to an old decaying family that had to borrow to eat—and to buy opium for its degenerate offspring. This weakness also provided significant contrast with the austerity and self-reliance which characterized the Communist effort. For details of U.S. aid, credits, sales, etc., to the KMT, see *China White Paper,* 1:360-409, 2:939-80, 1042-53. For an analysis of the American aid program, see Chou, *Chinese Inflation,* pp. 173-84.

and culminated in the disastrous August, 1948, reform. This finally brought the Shanghai Chamber of Commerce and the Shanghai Industrial Association to its feet in open condemnation of the Government's policies.

Meanwhile, business, industry, and the public at large had for some time been demonstrating their lack of confidence in more concrete ways. Commercial and financial circles refused to respond when the Government offered bonds for sale. The general public demonstrated an understandable tendency to invest its savings elsewhere than in the bank. Private lending institutions ignored regulations against offering interest rates higher than those approved by the Central Bank. Merchants held back supplies for cities where prices were controlled during the emergency reform programs of 1947 and 1948, thus contributing to their failure. Entrepreneurs indulged in hoarding and speculation when this became more profitable than regular business and productive operations. This led to cutbacks in production, closing businesses, and rising unemployment.

In summary, the Government's mishandling of the economy: contributed to the revival of a labor movement independent of Government control; was responsible for the recession-unemployment cycle which became pronounced in 1947; compromised the Government's relations with business and industry; contributed to the demoralization of the civil service and the intellectual community's intense aversion to the Civil War; and produced an erosion of public confidence in the KMT's ability to govern, which both fed upon, and in turn contributed to, the failure of most of the Government's efforts to reduce inflationary pressures. As a result, the Government could not induce compliance with decrees and reform measures, even when these were identified as necessary features of its struggle against the Communists. This deflation of authority occurred at a time when the Government needed a maximum degree of economic cooperation and sacrifice from everyone if it was to survive at all.

V

A Summary of the Indictment:
The Intelligentsia's Critique
of the Kuomintang

In the Kuomintang's eyes, its greatest enemy today is the Chinese Communist Party. But there is no talk about why the CCP's power has expanded so and in fact who has assisted it. Let us analyze this. Let us start with the young people. They are pure and at first are without fixed notions about politics. So long as politics is not corrupt, society is secure, everything is on the right track, and the nation has some future, they will of course support the Government. But the Government in its various activities can only cause people to lose hope. . . . Next let us discuss the older generation. The basis of the present regime's support has been the urban population: government employees and teachers, intellectuals, and business and industrial circles. At present, no one among these people has any positive feelings toward the Nanking regime. The KMT's tyrannical style of behavior is causing deep hatred among liberal elements; as for civil servants and teachers, the skimpiness of their salaries since the end of the Anti-Japanese War has caused them to lose hope in the present political regime; the government officials by indulging in corrupt practices and creating every kind of obstruction have caused extreme dissatisfaction in business and industrial circles; and the violent rise in prices due to erroneous financial and monetary policies and the continuation of the Civil War is causing sounds of resentment to be heard everywhere among the urban population.[1]

General George Marshall, in his farewell statement after the failure of the U.S. mediation effort between the KMT Government and the Communists, suggested that the situation in China might be saved if only the liberals could somehow gain power within the Government. However well-meaning, the suggestion was politically unsound because the liberal community was made up primarily of intellectuals. Being intellectuals first and politicians at best only second, they lacked the kinds of resources necessary to survive in the political environment of KMT China during the Civil War years. Yet there seems little doubt that liberalism was the dominant political current among intellectuals in the KMT-

1. Ch'u An-p'ing, "Chung-kuo te cheng-chü" [China's political situation], *KC*, Mar. 8, 1947, p. 3.

controlled areas, and that it inspired a critique of the KMT Government almost as devastating as that offered by the Communists themselves.[2]

It has been suggested that a Chinese tradition of humanism, Western missionary education, and the large proportion of teachers and professors who had received advanced training abroad in Europe and the United States, all contributed to the Chinese intelligentsia's acceptance of what were essentially Western concepts of political liberalism.[3] Whatever factors may have been responsible, a modern liberal climate was quite firmly established among the intellectuals, if not among political leaders, by the late 1940s. This was the intellectual milieu in which the student anti-war movement was able to develop in the manner described above. The students took to the streets in spontaneous bursts of opposition to the actions of the KMT Government, leaving to their elders the task of spelling out the intellectual arguments in finer detail. This the older generation did in a profusion of editorials and essays that were clearly the middle-aged equivalent of the students' activism.

During the late 1940s, intellectuals publicized their views in a number of newspapers and periodicals. These enjoyed varying degrees of popularity, as well as attention from the KMT authorities and secret police. Yet despite the harassment, the two most widely read liberal publications of the Civil War years survived more or less unscathed. These were the *Ta kung pao,* a daily newspaper with editions published in Shanghai, Tientsin, and Hong Kong,[4] and *Kuan-ch'a (The Observer),* a weekly journal published in Shanghai. It was popularly assumed that the *Ta kung pao* enjoyed political immunity not only because of its prestigious position as one of the nation's leading newspapers, but also because of its close association with the Political Study Clique of the KMT.[5]

The secret of *Kuan-ch'a's* success, on the other hand, remained something of a mystery. Despite periodic attacks from the right and the left, *Kuan-ch'a* generally succeeded in maintaining its credibility as an independent journal of liberal political opinion beholden to no political group. It was also reputed to be the most popular journal of its kind in the late 1940s. For these reasons, and because it was primarily a journal of political opinion with the majority of its articles contributed by college professors, *Kuan-ch'a* has been used here as the basic source of information on the political views of the intelligentsia in the KMT areas during the Civil War years.[6]

2. In Chinese Communist usage during this period, an intellectual was anyone who was receiving or had received anything above and including a middle school education or the equivalent: where Communist sources and views are cited, this is the definition that must apply. In non-Communist sources, the term tended to have a narrower meaning. Throughout most of this chapter, therefore, the term "intellectual" refers more specifically to those such as writers, journalists, college professors, and teachers who were contributing in a direct participatory sense to the intellectual life of the nation.

3. John K. Fairbank, *The United States and China,* pp. 196-200.

4. After WW II, the Hong Kong edition of the *Ta kung pao* was not revived until 1948, and was politically to the left of the other editions from that time.

5. See Bibliographic Notes.

6. A second major source was the journal, *Shih-tai p'i-p'ing* [Modern Critique], published in Hong Kong by Chou Ching-wen, former secretary to the Young Marshal,

The founder and editor-in-chief of *Kuan-ch'a* was Ch'u An-p'ing, a professor at Futan University in Shanghai who had studied in England. The journal first appeared on September 1, 1946, and was published weekly thereafter until December 24, 1948, when the Central Government banned it on charges of aiding and abetting the Communists. During the two years and four months of its existence, the journal's popularity grew steadily. By the end of 1948, its circulation was said to be sixty thousand with its actual readership estimated conservatively as double this figure. *Kuan-ch'a* circulated nationwide, the four cities of Peiping, Tientsin, Nanking, and Shanghai accounting for only some 20 percent of its total subscriptions. According to one former Peiping resident, the popularity of the journal was such that even the small group of rickshaw men who parked in the lane near his home often read it while waiting for customers. Literate rickshaw pullers were apparently a phenomenon confined largely to Peiping, however. According to *Kuan-ch'a*'s own statistics, the bulk of its readers fell about evenly into three main groups: the academic community, students as well as teachers; government employees, including middle and lower level civil servants and military officers; and industrial, business, and banking circles.[7]

Commenting on the success of his journal, Professor Ch'u related proudly how a majority of students taking the entrance examinations for Tsinghua, Nankai, and Peking Universities in the summer of 1948 had discussed *Kuan-ch'a* in response to a civics question asking them to write a critique of a newspaper or journal they read regularly.[8] By 1948, *Kuan-ch'a*'s military reports—allegedly based on leaks from within the Defense Ministry itself—had become famous as the only popularly available source of accurate information on the progress of the war. When it was banned at the end of the year, one of the few commentators left to write the journal's obituary suggested that the more than 100,000 faithful readers of *Kuan-ch'a* would now have even greater conviction that the KMT had no future before it. He concluded: "The Age of Professor Ch'u An-p'ing cannot be allowed to exist any longer, and the periodical may be considered to have fulfilled its mission. . . . [T]he present moment appears to be the last five-minute period in the existing order of things, and so more talking seems unnecessary."[9]

In September, 1946, however, talking seemed far from unnecessary. Issue number one of *Kuan-ch'a* contained a declaration of purpose. Noting the growing sense of public demoralization, the editor recalled how the nation had been able, not many years previously, to unite against a foreign aggressor. But today, he wrote, people seem to be more concerned with their own interests

---

General Chang Hsueh-liang. Unlike *Kuan-ch'a,* this journal contained articles and statements by Communist and Democratic League spokesmen. But despite Mr. Chou's reputed leftist sympathies at this time, and the fact that the journal was being published in the British colony beyond the control of the KMT Government, *STPP* did not differ markedly from *KC* in the tone of its editorials and much of its political commentary.

7. See Bibliographic Notes.

8. Ch'u An-p'ing, "Ch'ih chung, k'u tou, chin hsin" [Heavy burdens, bitter struggle, determined effort], *KC,* Aug. 7, 1948, p. 4.

9. *Chien-sien jih-pao,* Shanghai, Dec. 28, 1948 (*CPR,* Dec. 31).

than with the welfare of the nation as a whole. The purpose of his enterprise, therefore, was to arouse the people "in order to save the nation from disaster."[10]

Inherent in all the liberal writings of this period, and in the student demonstrations as well, was the belief that if only the arguments could be made compelling enough the Government would somehow be obliged to respond to the popular demands for peace, economic reconstruction, and political reforms. This belief seems to have been maintained until about the middle of 1948. By that time it had become fairly obvious that the Government was not going to respond, and indeed that it would soon not even be able to. Prior to that time, however, the students sought actively to mobilize public opinion by their parades, petitions, and various propaganda activities, while the older generation of intellectuals emphasized "public reflection and serious discussion." Toward this end, *Kuan-ch'a* was dedicated to the presentation of political opinions and arguments containing critical evaluations of the Government, the KMT, and the opposition parties, as well as positive suggestions for improvement. These opinions and arguments were based on the liberal view of politics and society which held that the interests of the nation and its people would best be served by the realization of democracy through freedom, progress, and rationality.

The ideals and expectations which this view encompassed were clearly drawn and represented a basic common denominator of contemporary liberal values. Of democracy, Ch'u An-p'ing wrote:

> We cannot agree that any group which represents the interests of a minority should dictate national affairs. . . . We cannot agree that all of the government's measures should serve only the power and interests of a minority. . . . The government's actions must be in accordance with the decisions of the people and in all that it does the government must be responsible to the people. Democratic government exists for the wellbeing of the people: to guarantee their freedom and promote their happiness.

Of freedom:

> We demand freedom, demand the various basic human rights. Freedom is not license, freedom must be law-abiding. But the law must first guarantee the freedoms of the people and must make everyone equal before the law.

Of progress:

> We demand democratic politics and industralization, but for democratic politics and industrialization to succeed, everyone must first have a scientific

10. It is unlikely that by "disaster" Ch'u was referring here to a Communist victory. He never wrote of the Communists in that vein. In addition, few people at this time believed that the Communists could actually defeat the Government's forces. The real disaster that everyone feared in mid-1946 was simply the Civil War itself. The mediation effort of General Marshall was still in progress, but it was becoming increasingly apparent that a peace settlement was not going to materialize. At this time, and for at least a year and a half thereafter, writers and journalists in non-official circles within the KMT-controlled areas seemed to be almost unanimous in their evaluation of the Civil War as a costly and hopeless venture which was likely to drag on indefinitely since neither side had the capacity to defeat the other. This argument is discussed at greater length in the text below.

spirit and a modern outlook. We demand full modernization in politics, economics, society, education, and military affairs.... For only with modernization can we seek greater and faster progress and only then can we advance on equal terms with the various nations of the world and exist together with them.

And of rationality:

Without rationality, society cannot be secure and culture cannot progress. Today in China, everywhere there is a reliance on force to resolve disorder, even young people presently receiving an education are repeatedly using force.... In the past ten years or so, education in China has failed completely in this area. We demand that government and the various sectors of society pay full attention to this point. Only with the development of rationality will society begin to be able to differentiate between right and wrong and begin to have peace and public morality.[11]

THE INTELLIGENTSIA'S CRITIQUE OF THE KMT GOVERNMENT

Liberal commitments found their most forceful expression in the intelligentsia's critique of the KMT Government. The liberals began by accusing the KMT of betraying the political mandate that, in principle, legitimated its right to govern. Liberal intellectuals did not necessarily subscribe to Sun Yat-sen's Three People's Principles as an act of political faith. Nor did they have any particular respect for Sun's program as a guide for the conduct of government. But as it happened, the three principles of nationalism, democracy, and the people's livelihood, while meaning different things to different people, summed up the three most basic political concerns of the intellectual community.

By officially adopting Sun's program as its political creed—including the concept of tutelage as a preparatory stage leading to constitutional government— the KMT intended to preserve for itself the mantle of Sun's prestige and authority as the founder of modern China. In so doing, the KMT of Chiang Kai-shek had pledged itself to the implementation of a program which in practice it was unwilling to pursue. The Party's nationalist credentials, and the fund of prestige derived therefrom during the Anti-Japanese War, were all but obscured in the post-war period by the KMT's inability to fulfill popular aspirations for peace, economic reconstruction, and some form of responsive government. The liberal indictment of the Government therefore contained two major charges. One had to do with the form, and the other with the output of KMT rule.

THE FORMS OF KMT RULE

The belief that government should exist not only for the people, but of and by them as well, was reiterated time and again. The only possible justification for

11. Editorial, "Wo-men te chih-ch'ü ho t'ai-tu" [Our purpose and attitude], *KC,* Sept. 1, 1946, pp. 3-4.

twenty years of KMT tutelage was, as Sun Yat-sen had indicated, to prepare the way for a constitutional form of government. The consensus was that the KMT had failed utterly in this task. Ch'u An-p'ing treated his readers to some cynical comments on the occasion of a hawkers riot in Shanghai on November 30 and December 1, 1946:

> Big shops were attacked as were dance halls and movie theaters and automobiles passing on the street. All of these brought forth the hatred of the poor for the rich. The unjust conditions between rich and poor are beginning to be understood by the poor and they are expressing their will which shows the progress of Chinese society. We have felt that there has been little achievement to speak of during the past twenty years of KMT tutelage, but now the people are daring to protest and to ask openly, "Why don't you give us food?" The KMT authorities should be proud because the objective of tutelage is to raise the people's political knowledge and to give them political power. . . . [P]erhaps after all, twenty years of KMT tutelage has not been without result.[12]

Wu Shih-ch'ang, a professor at National Central University in Nanking, was more blunt:

> The KMT one-party dictatorship is without doubt like that of the Soviet Union. KMT principles stipulate that, unlike the Soviet Union's long-term one-party dictatorship, the objective is a democratic polity and that tutelage is only a stage in that process. Unfortunately, that stage has lasted too long. The objective still has not been reached and has instead become corrupted.[13]

Constitutional Government

Liberal intellectuals viewed the institutions and procedures being established in the name of representative government with considerable skepticism. The original source of these was the Political Consultative Conference (PCC), a multi-party gathering which met from January 11 to 31, 1946, to seek a peaceful solution to the conflict between the CCP and the KMT. Thirty-eight delegates attended the conference: eight from the KMT, seven from the CCP, five from the Youth Party, two from the Democratic League, two from the Democratic-Socialist Party, two from the National Salvation Association, one from the Vocational Education Association, one from the Rural Reconstruction Association, one from the Third Party, and nine non-partisans. The conference reached agreement on five major areas of conflict between the KMT and the CCP, thus laying the foundation, in theory at least,

12. Ch'u An-p'ing, "Lun shang-hai min-luan" [On the disorders in Shanghai], *KC*, Dec. 14, 1946, p. 4.
13. Wu Shih-ch'ang, "Lun tang te chih-yeh-hua" [On the professionalization of the party], *KC*, Mar. 8, 1947, p. 10.

for a genuine coalition government. The agreements dealt with: reorganization of the national government; a political program to end the period of KMT tutelage and usher in constitutional government; revision of the 1936 Draft Constitution; membership of the National Constitutional Assembly which would adopt the revised constitution; and reorganization of Government and CCP armies into a united force.

Liberals were for the most part satisfied with these agreements. But the conference had no power to enforce them, and therein lay the crux of the problem. Right-wing elements within the KMT opposed many of the conference resolutions and succeeded in revising the Party's position on certain points at the KMT's Central Executive Committee meeting in March. The two most important revisions placed curbs on provincial autonomy, and provided for the continuation of presidential government, as opposed to the cabinet system approved by the conference.

After this blow from the KMT right wing,[14] the conference agreements continued to disintegrate more or less concurrently with the breakdown of the January ceasefire that had made them possible in the first place. In addition to the unilateral KMT revisions, the key points of disagreement that emerged during 1946 concerned the amalgamation of Communist forces into the National Army, and the KMT's refusal to grant the CCP and the Democratic League joint veto power in the forty-member State Council. This was to be the highest organ of state power pending the inauguration of constitutional government. The two parties, claiming that the KMT had violated both the letter and the spirit of the original conference agreements, refused to be bound by them or to participate in their implementation. The Government then proceeded unilaterally with the convocation of a National Constitutional Assembly on November 15, 1946, to adopt the revised draft of the 1936 Constitution; the promulgation of the new Constitution on January 1, 1947; the election in November of delegates to the First National Assembly; and the meeting of that Assembly during April, 1948, to choose the nation's President and Vice-president.[15]

14. These elements were also held responsible by liberal public opinion for the violent disruption of a meeting celebrating the successful conclusion of the Political Consultative Conference at Chiao-ch'ang-k'ou in Chungking on Feb. 10, 1946. Many participants were physically assaulted by thugs generally assumed to have been hired by right-wing KMT elements. The incident was often used thereafter to symbolize KMT obstructionism in the face of widespread popular demand for peaceful settlement with the CCP. For the commonly-accepted view of who was responsible for the incident. see John F. Melby, *The Mandate of Heaven*, pp. 88-89. For the KMT right-wing's version, see Chung-kuo lao-kung yun-tung shih pien-tsuan wei yuan-hui, ed., *Chung-kuo lao-kung yun-tung shih*, 4:1585-87.

15. On the PCC and the breakdown of the agreements it produced, see U.S. Department of State, *Foreign Relations of the United States, 1946, the Far East, China*, pp. 1-723; Carsun Chang, *The Third Force in China*, pp. 142-222; and Ch'ien Tuan-sheng, *The Government and Politics of China*, pp. 317-45, 375-81. The Constitu-

The poll of Chinese students studying in the U.S. (cited in Chapter Three) indicated the negative sentiments this activity evoked. Of those responding to the question "Do you feel that the recent elections held in China and the promulgation of a constitution indicate that the country is truly moving in the direction of a democratic government?" close to 80 percent answered either "no" or "not necessarily."

The letters-to-the-editor columns of *Kuan-ch'a* and other publications reflected a similarly negative attitude. One disillusioned young lawyer just out of law school wrote that the promulgation of the Constitution was something which should have pleased those in the legal profession, but instead the words "rule of law" had become a mockery for them. The judiciary may have been independent in the early years of the Republic, he remarked, but under the tutelage of the KMT it is no longer. He went on to cite a case recently brought to the attention of the Shanghai Court in which a local office of investigation had recommended that action be taken against a certain *hsien* magistrate suspected of wrong-doing. "Instructions from superiors" were received by the Court shortly thereafter and the case had to be dropped. Under such conditions, concluded the writer, how can one possibly speak of an independent judiciary.[16]

Another letter described the process whereby one *hsien* had chosen its representative to the First National Assembly in the general election held between November 21 and 23, 1947:

> Today all the nation's newspapers are carrying news about the opening of the National Assembly. But I still remember what a joke it was last year when Hsuan hua *hsien* elected its National Assembly representative.
>
> ... [T]he KMT's candidate for the National Assembly representative was T'ung Hsiu-ming; and there were a few others also contesting the election. One cold cloudy afternoon, T'ung Hsiu-ming gave a public election speech in the open-air theater grounds in the marketplace. In order to learn something about democracy, I braved the cold wind to listen. When I arrived, except for a few shop apprentices, all those seated in the audience were peddlers from off the nearby streets. When I asked them what they had come for, their answer was that the police had told them to come. ... Then three or four officers brought in over two hundred men who were said to be just then undergoing military training. Only then were all the seats filled. Mr. T'ung's speech was very simple and contained no election principles at all. ... After Mr. T'ung had concluded his speech, the *hsien* magistrate, Wang I-fang, took over and began to talk. To the "voters" in the audience he said: "I order you to elect Mr. T'ung Hsiu-ming. This order is the same as the order telling you that you should go to do repair work on the defense installations. It is wrong for anyone to disobey. ..." After the meeting, the *pao* and *chia* heads certainly obeyed the words of Magistrate Wang; they went to every household

tion adopted by the National Constitutional Assembly is translated in Appendix D of the latter volume. Conference resolutions and news releases concerning the March, 1946, meeting of the KMT Central Executive Committee are in *China White Paper* 2:610-21, 634-39.

16. Unsigned letter, Feb. 8, 1948, Shanghai (*KC*, Mar. 6, 1948, p. 2).

and spoke as follows: "The *hsien* magistrate has spoken. Whoever does not vote for T'ung Hsiu-ming will have to go out and work on the defense installations when they need repairs in the future." The result of the election was of course that T'ung Hsiu-ming received the most votes.

Today is the big opening of the National Assembly and I suppose Mr. T'ung Hsiu-ming is already sitting securely in a representative's seat. But with so much having gone on behind the scenes, is it any wonder that those representatives who have been elected but cannot obtain their election certificates have . . . gone to the National Assembly meeting place and are clamoring to be allowed to participate. Really what a joke it is.[17]

The meeting of the First National Assembly itself inspired equally caustic commentary. From Nanking where the Assembly was meeting, a *Kuan-ch'a* reader described the scene as one of confusion and disorder in which the Three People's Principles had become nothing but slogans. In his view, the Government's greatest failure had been in the promotion of democracy, where there had been no achievement whatever. That was why the Communists had broken out in rebellion and people everywhere were responding to them. "If the present Government continues not to care about the problems of the common people, and those on the political stage today continue to be so selfish," he concluded, "then these persons are going to fall from power and it will most certainly be their own fault."[18]

Of the National Assembly meeting, Ch'u An-p'ing wrote: "The pandemonium was such, I could think of nothing else to do except laugh." But he was unwilling to hold the representatives themselves responsible. Instead, he suggested that twenty years of KMT tutelage was to blame. The object of tutelage had been to teach the people how to hold elections, yet it was common knowledge that the elections for the National Assembly representatives had been a farce; that the quality of the representatives elected was uniformly low; and that in all of KMT-controlled China there was apparently no other leader of national stature, either within or without the KMT, to compete with Chiang Kai-shek for the office of president. For all these shortcomings, Ch'u placed blame directly on the KMT. "I say very frankly," he concluded, "that in terms of the elections for the National Assembly and the events that have transpired at its sessions, the KMT's past twenty years of tutelage have been a complete

17. Letter signed Ting K'e-shan, Mar. 30, 1948, Hsuanhua *hsien* (*KC,* Apr. 10, 1948, p. 2). The comment about representatives elected but unable to obtain election certificates referred to a problem arising from the KMT agreement with the Youth Party and Carsun Chang's Democratic-Socialist Party promising them 300 and 260 seats respectively for joining the Government. A number of KMT members, however, ran without Party endorsement in constituencies intended for the other two parties. These won only 70 and 68 seats, and threatened to walk out of the Assembly unless given the agreed number. The KMT thereupon tried to persuade those who had run without Party endorsement to yield their seats—but found most unwilling. The squabbles were still unresolved when the First National Assembly convened on March 29, 1948. On the elections, see *Tsai sheng* (Rebirth Weekly, organ of the Democratic-Socialist Party), Shanghai, no. 194, Dec. 14, 1947 (*CPR,* Nanking, Jan. 16, 1948).

18. Letter signed Hsu Shao-fu, Nanking, Apr. 3, 1948 (*KC,* Apr. 10, 1948, p. 2).

failure." Yet even at this late date, April, 1948, he still seemed to retain hope that the KMT leaders could learn from past mistakes. He therefore called on the Party to "come forward with good intentions and a courageous spirit to change completely its style of work and do something meaningful for the country."[19]

Civil Liberties

Perhaps more important to the intellectual community than the clumsy gestures in the name of representative government, were the official transgressions against civil liberties. These liberties were guaranteed by the Constitution, as well as by numerous official statements and declarations. In practice, they were often honored only in the breach, either arbitrarily ignored by local authorities or held officially in abeyance by a declaration of martial law or some similar emergency proclamation. Such measures were used expressly to silence those who criticized the Government, its policies, and the Civil War. Since students and intellectuals in the KMT areas continued to be the most persistent and articulate in this regard, they naturally bore the brunt of the Government's repressive measures. Hundreds of persons were watched, followed, threatened, harassed, and arrested, in the manner described in Chapter Three with reference to the students. Many persons "disappeared." Imprisonment, assassination, and torture became commonplace features of political life.

Official news censorship, in effect during the Anti-Japanese War, was not formally instituted during the Civil War years. But interference with the press took a number of forms. These included: temporary censorship; regional censorship; temporary suspension of an individual publication over some specific issue; permanent banning if the infraction was considered grave; physical assaults on printing establishments and editorial offices; arrest and imprisonment of journalists; and even the beating up of newsboys and hawkers. From the Government's point of view, however, these efforts were largely counter-productive. They did succeed in reducing the quantity and quality of news and political commentary available to the reading public. But because the ban on publications that criticized the Government was never total, it tended to intensify the criticism from those remaining.

Thus what was in the student movement a protest "against oppression," became among the older generation an open and persistent denunciation of the Government for its interference with due process of law, with the freedoms of the press and of assembly, and with the right to petition and protest. The criticism grew intense on several occasions—many of which involved the Government's treatment of student protestors, as we have already seen. Another such occasion was the arrest of over two thousand persons in the course of a so-called census investigation in Peiping. Most of the arrests took place between February 15 and 18, 1947. Those taken into custody included professors, teachers, doctors, publishers, some shop clerks, and a few students.

19. Ch'u An-p'ing, "Kuo-ta p'ing-lun" [Commentary on the National Assembly], *KC*, Apr. 24, 1948, p. 3.

Among the first to protest publicly were thirteen professors who issued a statement demanding a guarantee of human rights. The statement wondered at the duplicity of a government that could promulgate a constitution guaranteeing civil liberties in January and release a thousand prisoners from Peiping jails, only to carry out a wave of arbitrary mass arrests six weeks later.[20] The police issued a statement in reply declaring that the arrests had been necessary to guarantee public security. The police also maintained that the arrests had been made in accordance with the law, since local *pao* and *chia* officials had given prior evidence beforehand on those in their jurisdictions who were suspected of having "broken the law." Finally the police said that most of those involved had been released on bail within twenty-four hours after their arrest, except for about forty persons allegedly guilty of hiding firearms and plotting violence.

Far from mollified, 192 members of the teaching staffs of Peking, Tsinghua, Sino-French, Yenching, and Normal universities issued a "Declaration of Human Rights" on March 1. The professors denounced the "illegal behavior of the Peiping authorities," calling the arrests a betrayal of the newly-promulgated Constitution and of the Government's repeated proclamations guaranteeing civil liberties.[21]

In May, 1947, 130 journalists belonging to the North China Correspondents Association met in Peiping. The slogans adopted by the conference were "Freedom of the Press" and "Guarantee Civil Liberties." Even the official coordinator of the conference—a manager of the Government's Chungyang News Agency—responded to the prevailing mood. In an address, he deplored the recurrent attacks on newspaper offices, and incidents such as that on May 1, when a newspaperman, Chang Chin-wu, was arrested. "We should concentrate all our strength," he continued, "on the struggle for freedom and the guarantee of civil liberties. The arrest of Mr. Chang of the *Hua-pei jih-pao* is an illegal measure and all newspaper circles throughout the country should protest it."[22]

The correspondents' protest may have been instrumental in securing Chang's release, but it was not sufficient to keep similar incidents from occurring throughout the country. Within a month, three Shanghai newspapers *(Wen hui pao, Hsin min wan-pao,* and *Lien-ho wan-pao)* had been banned for printing news allegedly intended to undermine public order and overthrow the Government;[23] a fourth newspaper had been temporarily suspended; news censorship

20. Chu Tzu-ch'ing, *et al.,* "Pao-chang jen-ch'üan" [Guarantee human rights], reprinted in *KC,* Mar. 8, 1947, p. 21.

21. *Ibid.;* and Peiping correspondent, "Hsin wu-szu-yun-tung chih ch'ien-hsi" [The eve of a new May Fourth Movement], *KC,* Mar. 15, 1947, pp. 16-17.

22. Peiping correspondent, "Ts'ung mei-chün hsia-ch'i tao Chang Chin-wu pei-shih" [From the withdrawal of the American military to the release of Chang Chin-wu], *KC,* May 24, 1947, pp. 17-18. Chang was arrested on May 1, 1947, and held as a military prisoner on suspicion of being "a Communist and traitor." The correspondents sent an open letter to General Li Tsung-jen, head of Chiang Kai-shek's Peiping Headquarters, and Chang was subsequently released on bail. No specific charges were ever brought.

23. Ch'u An-p'ing denounced the banning of the three newspapers and the measures to subdue the student protests (see Chapter Three, note 32). The *Hsin min wan-pao,* owned like the other *Hsin min* papers by a group of Szechwan industrialists, was allowed to resume

had been imposed in Tientsin;[24] and about sixty journalists had been arrested in the cities of Chungking and Chengtu. Newspaper circles and other public groups made countless protests and appeals. Officials invariably replied that the freedom of the press would be maintained and the security of newspapermen guaranteed. Like Chang Chin-wu, most of the newsmen arrested were soon released. But the harassment and intimidation continued. The comments of Chou Shou-chang, editor of the Nanking *Hsin min pao,* were typical of the response:

> [A]side from killing students, the Government must also wave the red cap high in the air, seizing people everywhere and attacking them as "traitors and bandits." The freedom of the press especially has been destroyed with the banning of the three newspapers. Reporters are being seized everywhere and forced to acknowledge that they are Communists. In Tientsin, the system of news censorship has even been restored. Let us reflect coolly: after all, who is being irrational? What sort of thing is it to speak of rationality and of law, and then in practice to violate both reason and the Constitution?[25]

"Do you really mean to say," queried the *Ta kung pao* editorially, "that these people are all conspiratorial Communist elements? Is it really necessary to use such tactics against them? To arrest reporters, kill students, and create an atmosphere of terror, is this an intelligent method?"[26] Ko Szu-en, a professor at the National Social Education College, held up as a model the popular concept associated with the rights of a free press in the U.S.—that whatever the opinions of others, a person should defend to the death their right to express them. Governments which suppress public opinion and corrupt the press, he warned, do not survive.

One of the most blatant attempts to silence critics of the Government was the assassination of Wen I-to, a popular professor of Chinese literature at Southwest Associated University in Kunming. Outspoken, as were many of his colleagues, in his demands for reform, Wen was gunned down in front of the faculty dormitory as he was returning from a Democratic League press conference on July 15, 1946. His death followed by four days that of Li Kung-p'u, another prominent member of the League. Li was shot and killed on a Kunming street near his residence as he was returning from the theater with his wife.

The killings sent a wave of fear through the academic community in Kunming. About a dozen professors took refuge in the American Consulate, and

---

publication after the directors in Chungking agreed to dismiss some staff writers of the Shanghai evening edition—who were charged by the Executive Yuan's Information Bureau with "faulty reporting." *CYJP,* Shanghai, July 30, 1947 *(CPR).*

24. See Chapter Three, note 32. Censorship by the Tientsin authorities was imposed on June 1 and lifted on June 10, 1947. The purpose was to suppress news of student protests in progress throughout the country. But newspapers from Peiping, where there was no censorship, reached Tientsin by 10:00 A.M. daily and were sold in large numbers on the main streets (*KC,* June 28, 1947, p. 17).

25. Chou Shou-chang, "Feng-k'uang-le te chung-kuo" [China gone mad], *KC,* June 14, 1947, p. 7.

26. Quoted in Ko Szu-en, "Hsin-wen tzu-yu te ti-ch'ao" [Freedom of the press at low tide], *KC,* June 14, 1947, p. 9.

the affair eventually grew so embarrassing that the Central Government offered them safe conduct out of the city of Kunming. After a painstaking investigation on behalf of the Democratic League, Liang Shu-ming and Chou Hsin-min came to the conclusion that the assassinations had been planned and carried out either by, or with the knowledge and consent of, the Headquarters of the Yunnan Garrison Command. They alleged that middle and lower-ranking officers probably executed the deed including the extensive preparatory investigations and the cover-up work afterwards, and that their superior officers probably instigated it.[27]

The academic community never forgot the Kunming murders, which were regularly cited thereafter to exemplify the oppressive climate fostered by KMT rule. Almost two years after the event, in April, 1948, the head of the Peiping Municipal KMT Committee, Wu Chu-jen, issued a public warning to "three professors" accusing them of being used by the CCP to incite the students. Everyone knew that the three referred to were Hsu Te-heng, Fan Hung, and Yuan Han-ch'ing, who had addressed a student rally at Peita the previous month. Ninety of their colleagues from Peking, Tsinghua, Yenching, and Normal Universities immediately published an open letter of protest addressed to Chairman Wu, in which they wrote:

> [W]e want to inquire further: is a second Wen I-to incident being planned? Because we would like to enlighten the authorities. Wen I-to was killed but not only did this not eliminate dissatisfaction with the situation among academicians, it instead only deepened further their alarm and anger.[28]

The incident also evoked a characteristic expression from Ch'u An-p'ing:

> The Government cares for nothing but itself. All of its measures originate with this concern. If the Government wants to repair a railway or build a road, it will be because the Government needs the railway or the road to transport soldiers; if the Government wants to construct a telephone network, it will be for the purpose of strengthening its political control; if the Government makes some relaxation in the financial system, it is because in that way it can collect more taxes. . . . In general, everything is for the Government itself; this regime has no interest in anything that is not of direct benefit to it. . . . The people have nothing to eat, does it care? It does not.

27. Liang Shu-ming and Chou Hsin-min, *Li Wen an tiao-ch'a pao-kao-shu, passim.* This report provides a detailed reconstruction of the events surrounding the murders, and an equally interesting account of the investigation itself and the obstacles placed in its way at every turn by the authorities in Kunming. Two lower-ranking officers of the Garrison Headquarters were sentenced to death for the murder of Wen I-to; and the Garrison Commander, General Ho Kuei-chang, was relieved of his command. Some biographical information on Li and Wen is in Li Wen erh lieh-shih chi-nien wei-yuan-hui, ed., *Jen-min ying-lieh,* with a foreword by Kuo Mo-jo. See Chapter Three, under "The December First Movement," for the political situation in Yunnan at this time.

28. For the letter, with the names of the ninety signing professors, see *KC*, May 1, 1948, p. 2. For Professor Yuan Han-ch'ing's speech at the Peita student meeting in March, see "Chih-shih ch'ing-nien te tao-lu" [The way for intellectual youth], *STPP*, May 15, 1948, p. 6.

The people have no clothes to wear. Does it care? It does not. The people have no houses in which to live. Does it care? It does not care. The Government only protects the wealthy and cares nothing for the poor.

He concluded with a warning that if, in such an environment, the Peiping authorities instigated a second Wen I-to incident, then the Government should expect chaos to erupt immediately.[29]

The Wen I-to incident and the warning to the three Peiping professors was of course part of a broader issue, namely, the KMT's habit of injecting politics into education. Unlike the freedoms of speech, assembly, and the press, there were not even constitutional guarantees against political interference in education. The Central Executive Committee of the KMT on at least one occasion resolved to reform itself in this regard, but the resolution was never implemented. The Party and the Government continually offended against the liberal ideal that the latter's interference in the school system should be kept to an absolute minimum, and that partisan political activities therein should not be permitted at all. Liberals did not object to the independent political activities of the students themselves. On the contrary, these were supported and encouraged. The objections arose instead over: the KMT attempt to nurture activists of its own to work among the students and recruit for the San-min-chu-i Youth Corps; Government interference with the substance of what was taught; and attempts to intimidate and silence critics in the academic community.

Government interference was built into a system which relied so heavily on state support.[30] The Ministry of Education exerted a large measure of control over all spheres of academic life, from student body regulations to academic and administrative appointments in the national universities. This made conflicts between the Ministry and the universities over academic matters almost inevitable.[31] Given the liberal inclinations of so many Chinese intellectuals, the interference of the Education Ministry made it inevitable also that academic and political conflicts would become inextricably intertwined.[32] Such interference had intensified during the Anti-Japanese War when Ch'en Li-fu of the CC Clique was Minister of Education. By the late 1940s, the "intrusion" included government-edited texts bearing the officially-approved version of Chinese history, and civics books promoting KMT ideology.

Writing as the father of six children, Wang Yun-sheng, editor-in-chief of the *Ta kung pao,* admitted that, being a busy man, he had never bothered to look at

29. Ch'u An-p'ing, "Ti-erh-ko Wen I-to shih-chien wan-wan chih-tsao pu-te" [A second Wen I-to incident absolutely must not be created], *KC,* May 1, 1948, p. 4.

30. On the proportion of state-supported and private institutions of higher learning, see Chapter Three, note 28.

31. One such conflict arose, for example, over the Ministry's order to drop the courses in international law and jurisprudence at the Law College of National Tungchi University in Shanghai. *TKP,* Shanghai, July 29, 1947 *(CPR).*

32. For one such case at National Chekiang University, see S.Y., "Che-ta wen-hsueh-yuan ko-hsin yun-tung hsiang-chi" [A detailed record of the movement to reform the College of Liberal Arts at Chekiang University], *KC,* June 12, 1948, pp. 16-17. Another example was the conflict, mentioned in Chapter Three, over the Ministry decision to abolish certain departments at National Chiaotung University in the spring of 1947.

his youngsters' textbooks. When he finally did so in early 1947, he discovered that liberal colleagues had been only too correct in their criticism. He expressed dismay at the irony of his own situation. The father attacks the rule of Ch'in Shih Huang-ti, he wrote, while the children are taught to praise the tyrant. The father writes about the Taiping Rebellion as the prelude to China's modernization, while the children are taught to treat the uprising with contempt. The father cries out for the withdrawal of parties from the schools and an end to the country's backward traditions, while the children pore over books that teach nothing but KMT doctrines and glorify the virtues of China's past.[33]

Typical of the Government's response to such criticism was an Education Ministry statement following complaints by school authorities in late 1946 about students being forced to participate in KMT activities. The Ministry agreed to "take steps to denounce it," if investigation proved the complaints to be justified. The Ministry did not, however, wish to interfere with the issue of KMT activities in the schools since this was a matter for the Party itself to decide.[34] There the matter rested. By 1948, the Government and the KMT had, if anything, increased their interference in the schools in a vain attempt to contain the students' protest activities. In consequence, liberal criticism had grown more strident, as in the following comment from *Shih-tai p'i-p'ing:*

> Most recently, the parties have all learned that the schools are a source of strength and therefore want to control thought and control the schools. They want to use the students for their own ends and so the schools have become big training camps for the parties. . . . We therefore cry out: get the parties out of the schools; give the schools the freedom to teach; give professors the freedom to teach; and give the students the freedom to learn; give China the freedom for a new life![35]

THE OUTPUT OF KMT RULE: POLICIES AND PERFORMANCE

The second major charge in the intelligentsia's indictment of the KMT Government tended to be stated in even harsher terms than the first. The liberal creed held that government existed not only of and by the people, but for them as well. Yet few in the late 1940s any longer believed that the Government was even concerned with, let alone actually acting to promote, the interests and well-being of the population. The case against the Government's policies and

33. *TKP,* Shanghai, Jan. 28, 1947 (*CPR,* Jan. 30).

34. *TKP,* Shanghai, Dec. 20, 1946 (*CPR,* Jan. 16, 1947).

35. "Tuan p'ing: lueh-t'an tang-p'ai t'ui-ch'u hsueh-hsiao" [Short comment: on getting the parties out of the schools], *STPP,* June 15, 1948, p. 3. By "parties," the author meant to include the CCP as well as the KMT. The same issue had an account of the winter youth camp for Mukden university and middle school students during the February, 1948, vacation recess. Mukden was still under KMT control and the camp was sponsored by the military. Attendance was forced by threat of losing study subsidies and even expulsion. Students objected to the compulsory military training and political indoctrination. By the end of the camp, over 100 recalcitrant students had been arrested. Ch'un Sheng, "Shen-yang

performance was usually argued in terms of one or more of three interrelated issues: corruption, the Civil War, and incompetence.

Corruption

It is virtually impossible to ascertain which of these three issues occupied the more central position. Except for the first months of the take-over period when official venality reached truly unprecedented proportions, corruption seemed to inspire relatively less critical comment than the other two. Yet people often found it difficult to distinguish where the one left off and the others began, so closely intertwined did they appear—in terms of cause and effect—at all levels of public life. Rarely did a political essayist fail to mention the problem of corruption, but just as rarely did he devote an entire article to it. One writer probably came close to the prevailing attitude when he suggested: "We have already heard so much about corruption that we have become numbed by it and neglect it as the source of all inadequacies."[36]

Ch'u An-p'ing summed up his own feelings in writing that the KMT regime's greatest crime was perhaps its "lack of virtue," which was in turn serving to demoralize the entire society. Under such a government, he wrote, life was much easier for those who were immoral and did not obey the law. As a consequence, most people had turned toward speculation, were not to be trusted, and refused to take responsibility for anything.[37]

From all the reports and commentaries as a whole there emerges the impression of a bureaucracy permeated with corruption—in the sense of a willful perversion of formal laws and procedures by the holders of public office for the sole purpose of their own and their families' private gain—from the center down to the lowest *pao* and *chia* official.[38] Essentially, money and favors greased the wheels that made the KMT political system move, ensuring also that it moved less effectively. In terms of its costs, corruption alienated the liberals. It was resented by the large numbers who could not, or would not, compete successfully in the corruption game, and so saw their legitimate interests harmed by the favors sold to others. It demoralized the bureaucracy and reduced its capacity to function. It had a debilitating effect on the morale of the fighting forces. And it

---

erh san shih" [Two or three things about Mukden], *ibid.*, p. 35. Also, Kao Ch'ao. "Shen-yang tung-ling ying te feng-po" [The tempest over the Mukden winter camp], *KC*, Mar. 6, 1948, p. 16.

36. Yang Jen-keng, "Kuo-min-tang wang ho-ch'u ch'ü?" [Where is the Kuomintang headed?] *KC*, Mar. 15, 1947, p. 6. Yang was a professor at Peita.

37. Ch'u An-p'ing, "P'ing P'u-li-t'e te p'ien-szu te pu chien-k'ang te fang hua pao-kao" [A critique of Bullitt's biased unhealthy report on his visit to China], *KC*, Oct. 25, 1947, p. 5.

38. Among the clearest and most unself-conscious statements of this phenomenon are the sketches of six twentieth-century "gentry" families compiled by Chow Yung-teh from 1943-1946 in one *hsien* near Kunming. The image of pervasive corruption that emerges from

gave away valuable political capital to the Communists, who, as we shall see below, worked assiduously to keep their own reputation clean.[39]

Corruption: the Consequences. Consistent with their humanistic concerns, liberal writers tended to focus on the consequences of official malfeasance for those who suffered most from it. The most glaring examples in this regard were almost always reported from the rural areas. But here especially, the consequences of official corruption were fully realized only within the larger context of rural poverty, the inadequacies of the Government's rural policies, and the additional hardships created by the Civil War.

For example, a report from *Kuan-ch'a*'s correspondent in Nanchang, Kiangsi, focused primarily on the toll which the assorted disasters of the twentieth century had taken in the province. These included the Northern Expedition of the 1920s, the KMT's Communist extermination campaigns of the 1930s, floods, droughts, and the Japanese. He estimated that the population in 1947 was 40 percent less than at the turn of the century. In some areas, cultivated land amounted to only 70 percent of the land under cultivation before World War II. But the land taxes and government requisitions continued unabated, taking into consideration neither the reduction in the labor force nor the decrease in cultivated land. Yet however bad conditions were in Kiangsi, they did not explain the extreme poverty that existed there. Responsibility for that he placed more specifically on corrupt officials or, in his own words, the local "bloodsucking devils."[40]

Similar pictures emerged from the pen of virtually every liberal writer who investigated conditions in the rural areas. The impoverishment of the peasantry,

---

these sketches is not relieved by the examples of official honesty which are also cited therein. Thus Chairman Wang had served in various official capacities for thirty years and still had "empty sleeves" (*liang-hsiu ch'ing-feng,* literally, two sleeves full of wind, a term used with reference to honest officials); yet he condoned extensive graft on the part of *hsien, hsiang,* and *pao* officials in apparent disregard of the popular sentiments against them. *Hsien* magistrate Chao was removed from office on charges of corruption and inefficiency; but one of his chief accusers was also one of the most unscrupulous grafters in the *hsien.* The one incorruptible official of the lot—the only one among all the *hsiang* and *chen* heads "who dared to offend the influential and to speak for the people"—was removed from his position after the *hsien* magistrate had accepted a bribe for that purpose (Chow Yung-teh, "Life Histories," in Fei Hsiao-t'ung, *China's Gentry: Essays on Rural-Urban Relations,* pp. 145-87).

39. A considerable literature on political corruption has been produced in recent years, some of it suggesting that corruption in public office is not necessarily a bad thing. The Chinese experience does not appear to support this particular hypothesis. For a useful analytical pro and con summary, see J. S. Nye, "Corruption and Political Development: a Cost-Benefit Analysis," *American Political Science Review* 61 (June 1967): 417-27. Most of the arguments are in Arnold J. Heidenheimer, ed., *Political Corruption: Readings in Comparative Analysis* (New York: Holt, Rinehart, and Winston, 1970).

40. Wang K'e-lang, "Ts'ung shu-tzu k'an chiang-hsi" [Looking at figures in Kiangsi], *KC,* Oct. 18, 1947, pp. 17-18.

compounded by the twin evils of corruption and war, we,re obviously the first cause of concern. Land tenure problems, as such, did not draw comparable fire from these writers. This emphasis may have indicated as much about their own ideological predispositions and immediate political concerns as it did about actual conditions in the countryside. But whatever the case, the term "blood-sucking devil" was a common epithet, and it was used primarily with reference to the *hsiang, chen, pao,* and *chia* officials, who constituted the basic levels of administrative authority.

These were the officials responsible for the actual collection of taxes and the requisitions of men, money, grain, and materiel ordered by all of the higher political and military authorities. Some of the impositions derived from the Central Government's tax system, some from the requirements of troops garrisoned in the vicinity, some from the needs of the *hsien* government, and some from the budget of the village militia—to name the most common sources. What made the exactions truly extortionate, however, was the practice of collecting more than the stipulated amount of each requisition. This accounted for the considerable gap between what was exacted from the peasants and what actually was received by the government.[41]

Nor was there any court which could guarantee unprotected and illiterate peasants a redress of grievances. Peasants had only three options open to them when the exactions grew too great. They might send representatives to petition the *hsien* or provincial authorities for relief. But experience had proved that this course was not often effective and could be dangerous as well. The higher officials often sided with the lower who, in any case, had ways of avenging themselves against troublesome peasants. Second, the peasants might refuse to cultivate their fields, a course with unfortunate consequences for everyone. It was taken only when the exactions levied against them grew so great that the peasants would have had to go into debt in order to meet them. Finally, the peasants might simply run amuck. When they did so, the full force of their wrath was vented on the local officials who were lucky to escape with their lives. But such rioting subsided as quickly as it flared, once the peasants' anger had spent itself. Since the peasants lacked the means to sustain and consolidate their strength, the officials soon returned and reprisals commenced.

Liberal writers recorded all these alternatives as occurring in the KMT areas during the Civil War years. They viewed as both callous and shortsighted the Central Government's failure to check the excesses of those acting in its name, who were enriching themselves at the expense of an already impoverished peasantry.

In southern Shensi, for example, local officials ran "guest houses" and protection rackets for gamblers and prostitutes. The officials purchased arms and

41. For a typical statement of this problem, see *Shih-chi p'ing-lun* (Century Critic, associated with the KMT Political Study Clique), Nanking, Nov. 29, 1947 (*CPR,* Shanghai, Dec. 16).

hired body guards, and—like bandits—used threats and actual physical assault to extort money from the people. But unlike bandits, the Central Government authorized them to make requisitions and collect taxes in its name. Their exploitation of this power to their own advantage was regarded by the local inhabitants as their greatest crime. In some districts, local officials called upon families twenty to thirty times a month to make contributions on one pretext or another. People there said that much of what was collected went into the collectors' pockets.[42]

In September, 1945, the Central Government announced the formal suspension of the land tax and other requisitions for one year in all the former Japanese-occupied territories. This announcement was soon followed by others, however, authorizing requisitions for the support of local-level administration, and ordering the compulsory sale of rice for army use. In effect, this meant compulsory sale to the government at lower than prevailing market prices.

Sometimes the peasants received even less than the official rate of compensation to which they were entitled. The price fixed by the central Ministry of Food was CNC$5,500 per picul, but the Anhwei provincial government immediately reduced this to CNC$4,500 per picul. Knowing the "long process" of transferring the funds from the provincial government to the *hsien* level, and on to the *pao* and *chia* chiefs in the towns and villages, the correspondent who reported the story wondered how much of even the latter figure was actually reaching the peasants. He noted the resentment in some districts of northern Anhwei where the compensation received was said to be extremely low; and noted also that this was popularly attributed to corruption in the provincial administration of the Government's grain policy.[43] In Wuhu *hsien,* in the southern part of the same province, many areas remained uncultivated in the spring of 1946. The *hsien* magistrate himself acknowledged that the rural crisis there had been heightened by "irrational compulsory contributions" extracted from the people, and by the money extorted from them by "unscrupulous landlords and gentry."[44]

Administrative units in southern Shansi differed somewhat from those in most other parts of the country at this time. The basic-level units were the *lin* and *lü*, rather than the more common *chia* and *pao*. The *lin* or neighborhood was an organization of five families. Five *lin* formed a *lü* or 25-family unit, several of which comprised a *chü-ts'un*. Above this was the *chih-ts'un* or governmental village, also called the *pien-ts'un*. Official personnel at this level included the *pien-ts'un chang* or village chief, his four assistants, one secretary, one clerk, the chief of the local home guard unit, a special reporter, the officer in charge of the village company of soldiers, a dozen or so village constables, and assorted runners and messengers. These were the people one correspondent described as "wolves and tigers" preying upon the villagers.

42. *Hsi-ching ping-pao,* Sian, Aug. 31, 1945 (*CPR,* Chungking, Sept. 18).

43. Ch'ien Meng-chao, "Compulsory sale of rice for army use most hated by the people of Anhwei", *Shun pao,* Shanghai, Apr. 30, 1946 *(CPR,* May 1).

44. *TKP,* Shanghai, Apr. 30, 1946 (*CPR,* May 1).

During 1946, these village officials allegedly collected a land tax on three different occasions; requisitioned once each grain, raw cotton, and cotton cloth; and collected money three different times for a "village loan." The villagers were also called upon to provide the officials with whatever they needed for their personal use, or thought they could successfully extort. In the recent past, this had included such items as shoes, stockings, clothes, firewood, straw, rice, flour, oil, salt, soy sauce, and vinegar. In addition, the villagers still had to pay the customary "fees" to the officials for any services rendered, a practice apparently tolerated in normal times when other impositions were not excessive, but not in 1946.

In the correspondent's native village, a total of eight persons had, also within the recent past, occupied the position of *pien-ts'un chang.* All had been poor when they assumed the post, and well-off by local satandards when they left it. "Why go away to earn a living," the reporter's father had advised his son. "All you need to do is find some way to become a messenger in the local government office."[45]

The same correspondent wrote of an incident in Yühsiang *hsien,* where landowning peasants joined together in a novel form of protest against the exorbitant requisitions. They decided to turn their land over to the *hsien* government. But this plan miscarried because local officials treated it as a form of rebellion and locked up the first few representatives of the landowners to come forward with the proposed transaction.

Central Hupeh was yet another region with a devastated appearance and local officials who could still find ways to profit at the peasants' expense. The latter, returning to villages and fields that had been overrun by the Japanese, lacked the money to rebuild their houses or to purchase animals, tools, and seed grain. Aid which had been promised from the Hupeh office of the Chinese National Relief and Rehabilitation Administration (CNRRA) did not materialize in time for spring planting. *Hsien* and village officials managed to monopolize the agricultural loans made available by the Hankow branch of the Farmers Bank of China. Peasants who calculated that their income would be insufficient to cover the various local requisitions and the usurious interest rates charged by local moneylenders, let their fields lie fallow in the spring of 1946.[46]

Peasants everywhere were regularly trapped in a similar fashion. When harvests were abundant, grain dealers were in a position to capitalize on the situation and force down prices. When times were bad and the peasants could not make ends meet between spring sowing and the autumn harvest, they were thrown upon the mercies of the local moneylender.[47] The problem was a traditional one for the Chinese peasant, certainly not peculiar to the twentieth century. The fault of the KMT Government lay in its failure to ameliorate it. Not having implemented any basic reforms in the grain marketing system and

45. Southern Shansi correspondent, "Fa-wai t'ien-ti, jen-chien hsueh-lei" [Heaven and earth outside the law, tears of blood among the people], *KC,* Jan. 11, 1947, pp. 20-21.

46. *Ho-p'ing jih-pao,* Shanghai, Apr. 18, 1946 (*CPR,* Apr. 20).

47. *Tung-nan jih-pao* and *WHP,* Shanghai, Aug. 24, 1946 *(CPR).*

never having enforced its anti-usury laws, the most the Government could do when the need arose was to provide relief funds and emergency loans. Yet even these seemed to have difficulty reaching those who needed them most, at least in the form ostensibly intended. Such measures were often altered beyond recognition by the implementing officials. One widely known case concerned the 1946 Hunan famine.

Famine conditions were reported in many parts of Hunan in 1946, the central and southern parts of the province being the most seriously affected. The area had suffered a drought the previous year, but that was only one contributing factor. Others were the requisition of food by the Japanese in 1944 and 1945; similar requisitions by Government troops after the Japanese surrender; the sale of food to buyers from Hupeh province where food shortages had forced up prices immediately after V-J Day; the compulsory sale of 1,600,000 piculs of rice for army use; and the post-war proliferation of local government offices which had to be locally financed. But people complained of still other grievances. Army requisition officers were reported to have collected rice from the peasants and refused to pay the stipulated price for it. Troops travelling through the province had purchased food not for their own use but for sale elsewhere, thus contributing to the shortages in Hunan and tying up vital transport facilities, already disrupted by the Hunan motor vehicles take-over scandal described in Chapter Two. Finally, the food shortages in Hunan, evident from the time of the Japanese surrender, had been neglected by the incoming KMT officials, who were preoccupied with their various take-over activities.[48]

Local resentment was assuaged somewhat by the Central Government's withdrawal of an order for two million additional piculs of rice from Hunan, and by the police effort to halt unauthorized food shipments by the military. The positive effect of these actions, however, was soon neutralized as news spread of the corruption in the relief program. Relief work included emergency rice shipments from Kiangsi, loans financed by the United Nations Relief and Rehabilitation Administration (UNRRA), and the distribution of free flour and clothing from the U.S. Officials responsible for distributing the flour often sold it instead. In Ch'iyang *hsien,* they were selling it to restaurants and flour shops. In Liling *hsien,* one relief worker had sold seventy sacks on the open market. In Hengshan, *pao* and *chia* officials hoarded large amounts of it. In Yungan municipality, they were charging people CNC$50 per catty for their share. There were even cases where the officials substituted Chinese flour for the U.S. relief flour, which could then be sold at a profit.

As for the emergency loans, the men responsible for administering these seemed to favor their relatives and friends. The officials also charged ordinary people exorbitant rates of interest despite the regulations against this. In Hengyang, the local government received a CNC$30 million construction loan, of

48. *TKP,* Shanghai, Feb. 26, 1946 *(CPR);* and *TKP,* Shanghai, Mar. 8, 1946 *(CPR,* Mar. 9).

which ten million went to the contractor and twenty million disappeared. Instead of aiding the needy, relief materials were being monopolized by the rich, the influential, the *hsiang* officials, and the *pao* chiefs.[49]

These and many other forms of graft were described by *Kuan-ch'a*'s correspondent in Lanchow, Kansu, also in 1946. Many districts of the province had suffered from drought during the previous year. The officials turned the situation to their advantage by declaring a need for more relief funds than were actually required, and also by lending the funds to the peasants at high rates of interest. This was known to have occurred in Lunghsi *hsien* and Weiyuan *hsien*. Another incident involved extortion from laborers on a public works project. For repairing a section of highway, laborers conscripted from a number of nearby *hsiang* were required to work in three-day shifts. Each man was promised CNC$3,000 for this work. When it came time to pay, a *hsien* official spoke to the laborers telling them that while they were getting 3,000 *yuan*, the local KMT committee members and the heads of various offices in the *hsien* government were not receiving a cent. He therefore asked each man to turn back 1,000 *yuan* for the Party and government officials and everyone did.

In T'ungwei *hsien*, the head of the *hsien* government took out a public loan of over CNC$10 million and disappeared without a trace. At one time it was common knowledge that a number of such absconding officials were living in Lanchow. Yet there was no investigation. Occasionally some villagers would band together and come into town intending to settle accounts with a culprit; but invariably a special committee would be formed and rush to the official's defense. The local people thus learned the truth of the old saying that "officials protect one another" *(kuan kuan hsiang wei)*, and that the so-called "will of the people" did not count for very much. They understood also why men would go to the lengths that many did to become a *hsien* magistrate, despite the meagre official salary of the post.

On at least one occasion, however, peasants in Kansu had made their presence felt, although nothing came of it in the end. Their protest had occurred in 1943. It was initially regarded as a bandit disorder *(fei luan)*, but soon had to be acknowledged as a popular insurrection *(min pien)*. It started in three *hsien:* Lint'ao, K'angle, and T'aosha; then spread to Yüchung, Tinghsi, Weiyuan, and Huining. The disturbance grew so great that Lanchow itself became tense. The rebels were said to have reasons for their action, and slogans as well (one of them: "the freedom to resist hunger"). They killed *pao*, *chia* and *hsiang* officials; then turned on *hsien* magistrates, as well as other officials and outsiders who had come to exploit the resources of the area. But the rebellion was finally put down, and the usual executions and punishments followed. Except for the removal of a few officials, things became again as they had been before. Some officials even managed to profit from the disorders. The local people were afraid

49. Paraphrasing a comment in *Hsin-wen pao*, Shanghai, Apr. 15, 1946 *(CPR,* Apr. 24); also *Hsin-wen pao*, Shanghai, July 11, 1946 *(CPR,* July 12).

of being implicated in them; to ensure against accusation, money began its upward flow once more.[50]

A similar story of peasant insurrection came from northern Chekiang during the first half of 1946. Both Communist and non-Communist guerrillas had been active in much of this area during the Anti-Japanese War. Moreover, by turning first against *hsiang, pao,* and *chia* officials who had collaborated with the Japanese, rebellious peasants here did adopt a pattern of action similar to that promoted in some areas by the Communists. Nevertheless, the uprising also bore all the characteristics of a traditional peasant riot and thus appeared to be the spontaneous effect of people pushed beyond the limits of their endurance.[51] The underlying problem was rural poverty aggravated that year by near-famine conditions in many villages and heavy requisitions of rice, food, money, and labor for the support of the returning KMT administration. The peasants complained that there was little difference between the heavy burdens placed upon them by the Chinese government and those suffered under the Japanese occupation.[52]

Initially, several thousand men, women, and children journeyed to Hang-chow, the provincial capital, to petition for relief. These people came from districts nearby (including Ch'ungte, T'unghsiang, T'unglu, Fuyang, Chuchi, Shaohsing, and Hsiaoshan). The provincial government took no action. Suddenly, in January, 1946, violence erupted in Ch'ungte, T'unghsiang, Tech'ing, and Wuhsing, affecting some twenty *hsiang* and *chen*. In March, the same thing occurred in Chiahsing *hsien* and Hsinch'eng *hsien*. The rioting spread from *hsiang* to *hsiang* throughout the month of April. In each place, the violence subsided or was suppressed almost as quickly as it had flared. But not before *hsiang, pao,* and *chia* officials had been made to feel the peasants' wrath.

These officials were the primary targets of the uprising, not merely because they had collaborated with the Japanese or even because they were responsible for the collection of grain and other levies, but because in addition to these their "cruelty and corruption" continued unabated. Not all the tales the local people

50. Lanchow correspondent, "Yu-huan chung-chung te hsi-pei chiao" [Manifold troubles in the Northwest], *KC*, Dec. 21, 1946, pp. 14-16.

51. For a discussion of peasant riots in China during the nineteenth century, and of anti-extortion riots in particular, see Hsiao Kung-chuan, *Rural China: Imperial Control in the Nineteenth Century,* pp. 433-53. Professor Hsiao asserts: "By far the most fertile and important source of riots was official extortion in connection with tax collection." He notes that anti-extortion riots were most frequent during the last half of the nineteenth century, the declining years of the Manchu dynasty.

52. According to the account book of a peasant in Wuhsing *hsien*, where rioting occurred in January, he had paid out between August, 1945, and August, 1946: money for victory bonds; money for savings bonds; a tax in kind for the *hsien* administration; a tax in kind for the *hsiang* administration; rice and uniform fees for the local defense corps; rice for the district administration; rice for wounded soldiers; rice for the supplementary personnel of the *hsien* police; rice for conscripted laborers; rice as deposit for rifles lent to the people; fees for buying ammunition; travelling expenses for the staff of the district administration; and fees for the temporary facilities set up for the reception of armies passing through the *hsien*. *WHP*, Shanghai, Aug. 1, 1946 *(CPR)*.

told about these "merciless" creatures could have been untrue, even allowing for the exaggeration that must have crept into the telling. According to one such story, the *pao* chiefs would as soon see an impoverished peasant commit suicide—and had indeed done so—as try to mitigate the burden of the requisitions levied against him. Large sums had been collected, sometimes at gunpoint, for which no accounting was ever made. The peasants could see that for every *tou* of rice collected for the government, *hsiang* and *pao* chiefs took a share for themselves.

Those who protested often received a beating for their audacity. The *hsien* magistrates and district heads habitually sided with the *hsiang* and *pao* officials. It was no accident that the groups of petitioners who journeyed to Hangchow contained women and children. The men were reluctant to leave their families at home, they said, for fear of the reprisals the village officials might carry out against them. So, after petitioning the provincial government in vain, peasants in northern Chekiang took matters into their own hands—beating their oppressors, setting fire to their homes, and smashing their belongings. Local officials and their families, here as in Kansu in 1943, were fortunate if they escaped unharmed. Many died in a most brutal fashion.[53]

Corruption: Causes. The prevailing tendency among liberal writers was to suggest that morality followed the economy, and that corruption was therefore a function of scarcity. But scarcity like the insecurity it creates, is a relative condition. No one seemed inclined to grapple with the problem of how much was enough to turn it into an independent variable at any given time or place. The inevitable skeptics could not resist pointing out that the most corrupt people were also the richest.[54] The Communists, as we shall see, could not resist joking about the economically determined rationalization for the KMT's problem; as well they might, since the poverty of the territory they controlled was well known and tales about the integrity of their officials were widespread. Despite their own professed adherence to the ideals of socialism, however, liberal writers seemed unready to analyze corruption as the outgrowth of a system wherein personal security depended primarily on the acquisition of private wealth and the ownership of private property—as was the case in KMT China, and in imperial times as well.

Indeed, liberal writers were not inclined to view the problem in historical perspective at all. This might have deflected some responsibility from the KMT by portraying it as the inheritor, rather than the perpetrator, of a bureaucracy containing certain endemic weaknesses of structure and custom. The phenomenon was ancient enough, and the similarities between the traditional problem and the system of graft under the KMT great enough, to warrant such a

53. From a lengthy investigative report on the peasant riots in Chekiang by Tang Shu-chung, *Shih-shih hsin pao,* Shanghai, May 1, 2, and 5, 1946 (*CPR,* May 25).

54. Fu T'ung-hsien, a professor at St. John's University in Shanghai, was one of these. He attributed the problem to the social climate and saw the solution in education: "I chiao-yü chiu Chung-kuo" [Save China through education], *KC,* May 17, 1947.

conclusion. In the 1940s, as in the 1800s for example, local officials received unrealistically low salaries. Similarly, one of the most common complaints with respect to Chinese officials in the eleventh century was their venality, particularly among the lower ranks—a phenomenon "traceable in large measure to inadequate pay."[55]

In addition to "starvation salaries," Professor Hsiao Kung-chuan found other institutional features inherent in the nineteenth century Chinese bureaucracy which increased the opportunities and incentives for graft. These included the custom of sending gifts to superiors, the practice of selling official posts, and the *hsien* magistrate's lack of practical training for his post. This last, together with the impermanence of tenure, made it necessary for him to rely on the "hordes of unscrupulous underlings" who populated local government offices.[56] Most of these features were also present in one form or another in the 1940s. Although the reasons for their existence during the two periods were not necessarily the same, the response of the officials themselves was.

The customs with regard to such practices were well established and appear to have been generally condoned unless they became "excessive." The conception of what was excessive naturally varied over time and space. According to conventional wisdom, the problem was most often recognized as such during periods of internal disorder or dynastic decay. The declining years of Chinese dynasties were traditionally marked by increasing fiscal instability, administrative inefficiency, and military weakness. These conditions, which were conducive to and in turn intensified by increased venality among officials, were all present in the 1940s.

The attitude of tolerance "within limits" was also still operative in KMT China.[57] Yet the tradition itself, which accepted graft as a problem of degree rather than of kind, was rarely blamed. This was so even though liberal critics might acknowledge human nature to be such that corrupt habits once formed were difficult to break, and that the habit once established could easily get out of hand. Writing in the early 1940s, two sociologists, for example, recognized the persistence in the rural areas of "a deeply rooted traditional idea," reinforced by contemporary practice, "that to be an official leads to wealth." But they viewed the problem essentially as a product of the closed village economy. They therefore concluded with a plea for the development of rural industry to

55. E. A. Kracke, Jr., *Civil Service in Early Sung China: 960-1067*, p. 196.

56. Hsiao, *Rural China*, pp. 414-15. See also Chang Chung-li, *The Chinese Gentry: Studies on Their Role in Nineteenth Century Chinese Society*, pp. 43-51.

57. Martin C. Yang recalled that no one in his native village in Shantung province ever complained about the "commissions" taken by the village officials for services rendered so long as the amounts remained small. Commenting on the costs of rural construction projects, Yang wrote: "The *chwang-chang* [village head] and his chief assistant collect their village's share and here, too, they make a commission for themselves. This is an open secret. Within limits, the villagers tolerate it, but sometimes the exploitation becomes so flagrant that they are forced to take action." Martin C. Yang, *A Chinese Village: Taitou, Shantung Province*, p. 181.

provide "other outlets for ambitious young men" in search of security and wealth.[58]

In the more acrimonious climate of the Civil War period, such pleas were transformed into accusations. Critics wasted little time on analytical rationalizations. Instead, they held the KMT directly responsible for the conditions that were allowing corruption to assume excessive proportions. One of the most thoughtful of these accusations combined the economic argument with a second common complaint concerning the proliferation of administrative offices. Comparing conditions during the late 1940s with those prevailing during the early 1930s, the writer recalled that in the earlier period corruption and incompetence had not been commonly associated with the KMT. "Not that there were no cases of corruption in the KMT Government between 1931 and 1937," he wrote, "but who would have thought of calling it a corrupt government? . . . Who would have denied its actions and achievements?" The same government was still in power, with the same men occupying the most responsible positions. Yet they seemed to be conducting the nation's affairs in a very different manner than a decade earlier, and the feeling of the people toward them was completely different.

First, the writer blamed the impoverishment caused by the Anti-Japanese War and the Civil War which followed. The ensuing inflation had reduced the salaries of public servants to a fraction of their pre-war levels. With their wealth and property thus wiped out and their incomes insufficient to sustain them, they naturally resorted to graft and corruption, which was like an infectious disease. If the conditions were right, its very existence was sufficient cause for its perpetuation and growth.

Second, the writer blamed the phenomenon of bureaucratization. The fewer their accomplishments, he wrote, the less vigorous bureaucrats become, and the more firmly do they hang on to their positions. The highest officials had not just grown old. They had become bureaucrats. They had allowed the proliferation of governmental organs at the center, in the provinces, and at the *hsien* and municipal levels. Everywhere there were more government offices and units than there had been before World War II. The more organs there were, the less unified the authority within them, and the less responsible the people who staffed them. Nor was it enough to speak of proliferating organizations. Rather there were systems of organizations: a new examination system, a personnel system, an accounting system, an auditing system, a statistical system, and a national treasury system—all recently established. With every new system came a new set of laws and regulations, in addition to all of the old ones that were continually being revised. Was it any wonder, then, that ordinary people felt confused and the powers of the *yamen* seemed more threatening to them. And the more threatened people felt, the greater was the opportunity for corrupt officials to enrich themselves.

58. Fei Hsiao-t'ung and Chang Chih-i, *Earthbound China: a Study of Rural Economy in Yunnan,* pp. 277-79, 306-13.

Finally, as the cycle fed upon itself, more organizations meant more public servants. Given the state of the national treasury, the more there were of them, the poorer they were, thus augmenting the conditions in which corruption flourished. For these key factors in the political crisis, concluded the writer, the Government can and must bear responsibility.[59]

The Civil War

The inclination to focus on the economic causes of corruption was a two-edged sword. It did not cast the Government in any better light, but only shifted the locus of its responsibility. The policy of inflationary finance *per se* was not automatically singled out for special condemnation. Inflation may have been the immediate cause of everyone's poverty, but as such it was only one of several considerations that bolstered anti-war sentiment. There seemed to be more or less general agreement that, once committed to fighting the Communists, the Government had little choice but to adopt such a financial policy—from which, even if it had been more carefully implemented, adverse consequences could not have been avoided. Thus the Civil War itself became the central focus of everyone's attention, the most basic cause of everyone's misfortunes. The public appeal for peace issued by 585 professors in the Peiping-Tientsin area during the student demonstrations in the spring of 1947 read in part:

> During recent weeks commodity prices have steadily soared, thus causing a great deal of uneasiness among the people. In Nanking, Shanghai, Peiping, and Tientsin there have been disturbances. There have been rice riots, and labor and student strikes in these cities. We, the undersigned, have been devoting ourselves to cultural and educational work and have never entertained any political ambitions. However, today, we see with our own eyes the angry waves of civil war and economic collapse. The situation is not surpassed in seriousness even by that which obtained in France around the time of the French Revolution and in Russia around the time of the October Revolution.
>
> We know full well that all the unsettled phenomena today are rooted in the economic crisis, that the economic crisis has resulted from the prolonged Civil War, and that all the labor and student strikes are inevitable results of the existing situation. A study made by us convinces us that China is now on the brink of collapse; politically, militarily, economically, and culturally.

59. Hao Jan, "Lun cheng-chih shang te hsin ping-t'ai" [On the new malaise in politics], *Shih-chi p'ing-lun*, Nanking, vol. 3, no. 14 (reprinted in *KC*, Apr. 10, 1948, pp. 18-19). With respect to the bureaucratization problem, there were specific demands for the elimination of the many-tiered local administrative structure and for a streamlined tax-collection system. One writer proposed that taxes and requisitions be paid directly to the *hsien* government to bypass the *hsiang, chen*, and *pao* officials. See *Hsi-ching ping pao*, Sian, Aug. 31, 1945 (*CPR*, Chungking, Sept. 18). Sun Feng-ming, secretary of the government of Luan *hsien*, Hopei, advocated the same solution, declaring that ten catties of millet per *mou* paid directly to the *hsien* treasury annually would be sufficient to meet all of the taxes and expenditures of the *hsien*. But he acknowledged that such a reform was easier proposed than realized, since the local officials, whose interests it was designed to undercut, would do all in their power to obstruct its implementation. *TKP*, Shanghai, Aug. 11, 1947 (*CPR*, Sept.3).

... If the Party, Government, and military authorities want to save themselves as well as the people, the only course open to them is to stop the Civil
War immediately, to negotiate with the CCP sincerely and then to achieve
peace and to establish a coalition government.[60]

Ch'u An-p'ing expressed an identical view a year later, commenting on the
cabinet of the new Premier, Weng Wen-hao, formed in May, 1948:

We feel that whoever takes office today will have no way of improving the
present situation unless he has a way of ending the Civil War. . . . The
conscription of men and the requisition of grain is causing the greatest
bitterness in the rural areas. This is due to the Civil War. In the cities, the
greatest hardships suffered by the people are due to inflation. This, too, is
because of the Civil War. Production must be increased and there must be
large-scale construction, but these things cannot be done while the war
continues. Nor can there be overall reform. The Civil War is the cause of all
our illnesses and difficulties.[61]

Liberal intellectuals opposed the Civil War because they reasoned it was too
high a price to pay in order to keep in power the KMT regime as it was then
constituted. This reasoning was based on the view, widely held until about the
middle of 1948, that the Civil War was likely to continue indefinitely because
neither side had the capacity to defeat the other. According to one statement of
this view, the KMT had been trying since 1927 to destroy the CCP, but there
was nothing to indicate that it could be any more successful now than in the
past. The KMT armies had gained victories in northern Kiangsu, southern
Shantung, and had even occupied Yenan in early 1947. Still, the Communists
were not really wavering. They were relying instead on the guerrilla strategy they
had developed during the Anti-Japanese War, which would make it difficult to
destroy them. Moreover, inflation in the Government areas was great enough to
suggest that economic collapse was imminent.

On the other hand, the CCP could not easily defeat the Government. This was
so because the CCP did not have the support of all the people any more than did
the KMT; and also because the CCP was economically weak. By comparison with
the CCP, the KMT was regarded as the stronger party despite the debilitating
effects of corruption and inflation. Finally, the Communists would not be able
to defeat the KMT because the Soviet Union was unlikely to give them aid in
amounts comparable to that being supplied by the U.S. to the Central
Government.[62]

60. This statement was signed by 144 faculty members from Tsinghua University, 141
from Yenching, 105 from Peking, 89 from Nankai, 77 from Peiyang, 17 from Sino-French,
6 from the Fine Arts College, and 6 from the Teachers Training College. *TKP*, Shanghai,
June 1, 1947 (*CPR*, June 2).
61. Ch'u An-p'ing, "P'ing Weng Wen-hao nei-ko" [Comment on the Weng Wen-hao
cabinet], *KC*, June 5, 1948, p. 3.
62. Ch'i Chung, "Kuo kung ying-kai hsieh-shou ho-tso" [The KMT and CCP should
join hands and cooperate], *STPP*, Aug. 1, 1947, pp. 23-25; Wu Shih-ch'ang, "Ts'ung mei su
shuo-tao kuo-nei" [A discussion about the U.S., U.S.S.R., and internal affairs], *KC*, Apr. 5,

As for the costs of the war, these were calculated both in terms of the inflation, which had completely disrupted the urban economy, and the further impoverishment of the rural areas. The printing press may have been the Government's chief source of revenue; but, as already indicated, the Government depended also on a land tax, compulsory purchase of grain at lower than market prices, and collection of grain on loan. These levies, together with the requisitions to support local needs, the abuses associated with conscription, and the disruptions caused by a poorly disciplined and underpaid army in the field, created in many areas an insupportable burden for the peasantry. It was within this environment that the corrupt practices described above were able to assume the proportions they did. The many wartime requisitions meant increased opportunities for official graft, while inflation increased the incentives. As a result, some critics argued, the war was actually counterproductive in terms of the Government's primary objective, since it was creating the very conditions most favorable for the growth of the CCP. Finally, an increasingly militaristic government, and increased political alienation among the populace, were also condemned as direct results of the war.

For all of these reasons, the Government's insistence on fighting so costly a war, while refusing to implement any of the reforms that might have made it seem worthwhile, provided perhaps the strongest evidence to support the liberal charge that the KMT Government did not exist "for" the people: that, instead, it was willing to sacrifice the interests of the nation as a whole in pursuit of its own selfish aims, but was basically incapable of serving even that end effectively.

The War: Economic Consequences. The inflation-induced deprivations brought upon the urban salaried middle class—of which they were themselves a part—were not the only consequences of the war that urban intellectuals regularly denounced.[63] They turned just as often to the rural areas for their illustrations of the excessive burdens being imposed upon the people by the Civil War. It is difficult to ascertain the extent to which their own economic plight influenced their perception of the war. One can only be certain that their situation could not have influenced them favorably. But if the writings they left behind are a true reflection of their thinking, then the costs of the war for the rural areas contributed as much to their negative evaluation as did the havoc wrought by inflation upon the urban economy and the living standards of the middle class.

1947, p. 4; and Yang Jen-keng, "Lun nei-chan" [On the civil war], *KC,* Mar. 20, 1948, p. 5. Many probably agreed with Wu Shih-ch'ang's contention that if the Communist armies could really be destroyed within a few months, everyone would tolerate the hardships and support the war effort. In his view, most people would not oppose the war "if by the next New Year, they could see the nation united, reconstruction begun, an end to the conscription of soldiers, requisitioning of grain, and collection of miscellaneous taxes, and also if there could be freedom and democracy." But it was obvious to all that this would be an impossibility. Wu Shih-ch'ang, "Lun ho-p'ing wen-t'i" [On the problem of peace], *KC,* June 14, 1947, p. 4.

63. These deprivations are discussed in Chapter Four under "The Burden of Inflationary Finance." See also Chapter Three under "The Anti-Hunger Anti-Civil War Movement."

This emphasis on the rural areas in the thinking of liberal intellectuals actually derived only in part from humanistic considerations. It also reflected a pragmatic assessment of the relationship between the countryside and the conduct of politics and war in a non-industrialized society where 80 percent of the population lived in the rural areas. The economist Yang P'ei-hsin offered one of the clearest statements of this assessment. In June, 1946, the Government decided to reinstitute land taxes, government purchase, and the collection of grain on loan, in most of China's provinces and the five cities of Nanking, Shanghai, Peiping, Tientsin, and Tsingtao, during the coming fiscal year to begin in October. Of the total amount of grain requisitioned and borrowed, about 60 percent was to go to the center, 15 percent to the provinces, and 25 percent to the *hsien*. In addition, there was a fixed requisition of "public grain" which remained in the local areas. The total amount of grain requisitioned in fiscal 1946, including the local public grain, was fixed at 69,971,411 *tan,* divided in specific proportions between rice and wheat. Some 30 million *tan* of this was turned over to the Central Government.

Nevertheless, the system of grain finance failed completely in 1946. The 30 million *tan* waš insufficient to meet the Central Government's needs. These had apparently been underestimated by about 15 million *tan.* This was the result, concluded Yang, of Nanking's failure to comprehend the seriousness of the war and the strength of its enemy. By March, 1947, four million men were on the Government's military payroll, each of whom was issued, in theory at least, twenty-five ounces *(shih liang)* of rice per day. In addition, supporting personnel in the rear were estimated at about two million. Their needs, together with those of civil servants, brought the Central Government's total grain requirements in fiscal 1946 to 45 million *tan.*

As a consequence, the Government had to resort to an additional grain requisition, as well as the expenditure of foreign exchange for the purchase of rice from abroad. And as a further result, the price of rice rose sharply, aggravated by the ineptness with which the Government's 1947 emergency economic program was handled. Because of the large concentration of troops in the North, grain requirements there were particularly large. Local governments were obliged to purchase grain at the officially stipulated rate well below the market price, as was the custom with government purchases. The Hopei provincial grain office, for example, purchased rice from a certain trading company at the stipulated rate of CNC$1,300 per catty when the market price was over CNC$3,000 per catty. The merchants naturally responded by raising prices. In the town of Yülin, two hundred grain shops actually had to stop doing business entirely in early July because the government requisitions had completely depleted their stocks. In Szechwan, the Central Government sent personnel out to requisition rice in early May, 1947, and the price rose from CNC$120,000 per *tan* to CNC$400,000 almost immediately.

Yet the troops did not have sufficient grain, nor did the peasants themselves. It was estimated at this time that the combined total of all central and local requisitions averaged out to about 30 percent of what each peasant produced. A conference in late July to fix grain policy for the coming fiscal year resolved, over the objections of some provincial governors, to increase the total amount of grain tax and purchase from the 70 million *tan* figure of 1946-47 to 87 million *tan* in 1947-48. The dissenting governors argued that the burden of the peasants could not be increased further, for they had already reached the limits of endurance. Indeed, in some areas they had been forced to subsist on grass and the bark of trees. Yang estimated that perhaps thirty million people had been adversely affected by the failure of the grain supply system. But, he concluded, "it is not the grain policy as such that is at fault; it is the Civil War . . . that has made a disaster of the Government's grain policy."[64]

To give its readers some idea of what these wartime burdens meant for an average village, *Kuan-ch'a* published a letter written in May, 1948, by a resident of Ch'ench'iao *hsiang*, Nanhui *hsien* in Kiangsu province near Shanghai. The *hsiang* had a population of 15,000 persons, who cultivated a total of 32,000 *mou* of land. The letter listed some fourteen different taxes and contributions, including 192 *tan* of rice for the salaries of sixteen soldiers in the regular army, 10 *tan* for their uniforms, 15 *tan* for their ammunition, and 126 *tan* for the *hsiang's* contribution to the self-defense forces of Nanhui *hsien*, in addition to 12 *tan* for the support of the *hsiang* administrative offices. These were regular annual expenses.

Temporary levies imposed during the previous year only included 22 *tan* of rice for 560 pairs of army boots, 200 *tan* for the construction of two pillboxes, 20 *tan* for the *hsiang's* contribution to Nanhui *hsien's* sea defense installations, 525 *tan* to cover conscription expenses (in Ch'ench'iao *hsiang* each new recruit was supposed to receive 35 *tan* of rice and his family an additional compensation of 15 *tan*), another 75 *tan* to cover the cost of conscripting five men into the provincial security forces, 24 *tan* to provide compensation to the dependents of four local men reported to have died in battle (although local units were known to have engaged in battle with CCP units on only one occasion); an additional 30 *tan* contribution to the national armies and to the local security forces, plus other miscellaneous sums to cover certain administrative expenses of conscription and the National Assembly election.

In addition, the *hsiang* was expected to supply firewood, food, rice, cigarettes, and other necessities to units of the KMT armies and the local security forces whenever they were in the vicinity. The grand total came to something like 1,250 *tan* of rice. When adjusted for corruption, the total burden of the people of this *hsiang* during one year was about 1,500 *tan* of rice or ten catties per person. Concluded the writer, "this burden is enough to make people cry out in bitterness."[65]

64. Yang P'ei-hsin, "Ching-chi tsung tung-yuan hsia te chia-chin cheng-liang" [Increased grain requisitions under the general economic mobilization], *STPP*, Sept. 1, 1947, pp. 24-26.

65. Letter signed Chu Shu-chin, May 26, 1948 (*KC*, June 5, 1948, p. 2). Another similar, though less detailed, letter was from a resident of the fifth district of Mo *hsien* near Tsingtao (*KC*, May 8, 1948, p. 2).

This theme of the hardship caused by the requisitions for war-related purposes, or at least on the pretext thereof, was reiterated constantly in news dispatches, editorials, and essays.[66] A somewhat less common argument was that of Professor Wu Ch'i-yuan, who decried the Communists' emphasis on economic warfare as a major element of their military strategy. The Communists destroyed the Government's communications and productive capabilities, to which Government forces often responded in kind. "The results of such a war," he wrote, "must be the impoverishment of the people and the dissipation of wealth. No matter who wins and who loses, the Chinese economy will suffer damage that will take years to recoup."[67]

The War: Conscription. Another mark against the Government and the war was the "conscription farce." A comment by the *Kuan-ch'a* Kansu correspondent summed up the image of the conscription process that emerged from all liberal publications of the period. Referring to the order for twenty-four thousand recruits received by provincial officials in 1946, he wrote: ". . . as soon as the news arrived, the people felt it to be a great disaster but the *hsiang, pao,* and *chia* chiefs ran about happily. Good fortune had arrived for them once again since they would now have an opportunity to rake in a few more dollars."[68]

Writers described the conscription process in considerable detail, revealing a system formally designed to spread the burden of military service more or less equally, but in practice doing just the opposite. The problem originated in the traditional unwillingness to join the army. Those who could afford it bought their way out—a transaction easy enough given the state of official morality. The poor fended for themselves as best they could.

Ideally, conscription proceeded in the following manner, described here with specific reference to Chekiang province. First, *pao* officials drew up namelists of

66. For additional examples, see note 52 above. A *TKP* correspondent listed the compulsory contributions by the people of Luan *hsien* in eastern Hopei in addition to their regular taxes: (1) 200 catties of millet per month to each officer of the local militia and 150 catties monthly to each of its members; (2) daily food allowances for railway guards; (3) materials and labor for the repair and construction of railway fortifications; (4) straw, fodder, vehicles, etc., collected by the Military-Civilian Cooperation Stations on behalf of Government troops; (5) purchase and replacement of arms and ammunition for local defense units, and the repair and construction of local defense installations; (6) payment of salaries and purchase of arms and ammunition for special forces attached to some of the police stations in the *hsien;* (7) payment, mostly in kind, of all the *hsiang* and *pao* officials' salaries; (8) payment of a special subsidy of 150-200 catties of millet per person per month to all policemen and civil servants receiving fixed monthly salaries, to help them sustain the burdens of inflation. *TKP,* Shanghai, Aug. 11, 1947 (*CPR,* Sept. 3). For a listing of such exactions in the months preceding the Japanese surrender, see "Some Concrete Instances of Illegal Exaction", *Chin-feng jih-pao,* Sian, Aug. 30, 1945 (*CPR,* Chungking, Sept. 18). This article dealt with Sanyuan *hsien* near Sian.

67. Wu Ch'i-yuan, "Ts'ung ching-chi kuan-tien lun nei-chan wen-t'i" [Talking about civil war problems from an economic viewpoint], *KC,* Sept. 7, 1946, p. 3. Wu was a professor at Tsinghua at this time. Kao Ch'ao laments the destruction of Manchurian industry, mining, and grain production caused by the war, in, "Lei-yen k'an tung-pei" [Looking at the Northeast with tearful eyes], *KC,* Feb. 28, 1948, pp. 17-18.

68. Lanchow correspondent, p. 14 (note 50 above).

all able-bodied men in the *pao* from twenty to thirty-five years of age. The lists were then made public and the men had two weeks in which to try to find some way of having their names removed. At the end of that time, members of the *Pao* Representative Committees (which generally included the *pao* and *chia* chiefs, the head of the primary school, a district secretary, and assorted local "gentlemen") met to consider the petitions for exemption and decide which could be accepted. Then a revised list of potential recruits was drawn up and each man given a number, duly registered on a bamboo tally. The names and numbers were sent from each *pao* to the *hsien* government. At a meeting in the *hsien* town, important persons such as the *hsiang* chiefs and town mayors drew the tallies.

The exact method of the drawing depended on the number of men to be inducted from each *hsien* and the number of *pao* therein. For example, if seven hundred men were needed and the *hsien* had altogether seven hundred *pao,* then two men would be selected from every *pao:* one man as the new recruit, and the second as alternate. According to one method used, if the first tally drawn was number 73, then number 73 in every *pao* was the new recruit. If number 49 was pulled in the second drawing, then number 49 in every *pao* became the back-up man. In this way, the full complement of seven hundred men could fairly quickly be delivered by the *hsien* government to the nearest induction center.

In practice, all manner of unauthorized activities went on beneath the surface of this textbook operation. The price of a recruit varied from place to place. In one *hsien* in Chekiang, it might be anywhere from three to five million *yuan*. A man willing to pay such a sum, to be divided up among a number of local officials and the substitute, could ensure that the substitute would report and be accepted for induction in his place. Often such "professional recruits" disappeared soon thereafter. The induction center then reported that they had either died or escaped. In the latter case, the man was officially sought throughout the province. If he was not found, his name was removed from the army rolls and the alternate in his *pao* had to come forward to take his place. There was usually a considerable length of time between a man's disappearance and the removal of his name from the rolls. The vacancies were camouflaged by paying local peasants CNC$50 or so to substitute for the missing men during roll call should some high official turn up for inspection.[69]

Reports on conscription in Peiping indicated even more irregularities. In 1946, the formalities were abandoned altogether. The conscription order for the city was issued on August 30, and the first recruits inducted on September 11. The process was to have been carried out on the basis of namelists and the random drawing of tallies. However, owing to lack of manpower, financial resources, and adequate planning, the recruiting could not be carried out in the officially prescribed manner. Local officials therefore decided to meet their quota by seizing a given number of men from each district in the city and

69. Hangchow correspondent, "Che-chiang te cheng-ting cheng-shui" [Chekiang's conscription and tax collection], *KC,* Nov. 16, 1946, pp. 14-15.

suburbs. The plan was kept secret, adding to the atmosphere of fear and disorder. But as local officials moved through the districts rounding up recruits, the usual distinctions between rich and poor made their appearance. Those with one or two million *yuan* could buy their way off, despite the warning military authorities had issued to all district officials and *pao* chiefs against such practices.

Public criticism grew so great that municipal government officials met with members of the local KMT organization to investigate some of the charges. Many of these were subsequently declared to be without foundation and denounced for having created "false impressions" among the people. The criticism nevertheless persisted. Admitting that the events of September and October, 1946, had done little to enhance the Government's prestige in Peiping, one municipal official suggested that he and his colleagues would learn from the experience.[70]

Yet the formal procedures continued to be violated, as they had been during World War II. During the first half of 1948, *Kuan-ch'a* published a series of letters on the conscription issue. Letters from Chengtu, Tsingtao, Nanchang, Hsuchow, Hsienyang, and Shanghai, all told the same story. Military units regularly took it upon themselves to fill the vacancies in their ranks. Armed soldiers, usually in the company of a local civilian official (such as the *pao* chief) who could identify the households with draft-age men, would move from door to door in the dead of night. Recruiting parties also seized passersby on the road. Sometimes even students—officially exempt from military service—were abducted in this manner. When families of men seized in Tsingtao petitioned the military commander in the area, the authorities responded that they had no knowledge of any such occurrence. When the troops are allowed to behave in this way, concluded one letter, why should we even bother to speak of constitutional guarantees and human rights?

Everywhere there were stories about how lucrative was the trade in ablebodied substitutes; of how obliging the local officials could be if enough cash was forthcoming; and of how they would collect from the villagers three times the amount of grain actually turned over to the dependents of newly conscripted men.

Even though the local officials said that the treatment of recruits had improved, noted one letter from Chengtu, men there still had to be seized by force since no one wanted to be a soldier. A man would flee if he could, and not return home until the recruiting party had moved on—the poor man's method of avoiding conscription. It was said in Chengtu that peasants in the vicinity had run away leaving their fields to lie fallow; that some had resorted to armed force to resist induction; and that others had even sold their labor to landlords in return for guarantees against conscription.

No one wanted to be a soldier in Mukden either. In May, 1947, the lot-drawing of recruits could not be carried out because, of the four thousand men called to take part, only eighty-two showed up at the appointed time and

70. Peiping correspondent, "Pei-p'ing te cheng-ping hsi" [Peiping's conscription farce], *KC,* Nov. 9, 1946, pp. 17-19.

place. Of these, thirty-nine passed the physical and were enlisted without drawing lots.[71]

This reluctance to join the ranks did not necessarily reflect opposition to the war against the Communists—although it obviously did not indicate any great enthusiasm for it. The men were not afraid of fighting, noted one correspondent after talking with villagers in central Anhwei. Rather their enthusiasm was dampened first and foremost by the maltreatment that was the conscript's lot. The condition of recruits and of enlisted men in general was notorious. Americans in China, and Chinese themselves, had commented on this during World War II, [72] and there was no evidence to suggest much improvement during the Civil War years. In June, 1945, a Sian newspaper discussed three main reasons for the poor record of Free China's conscription efforts: (1) the irrationalities of the conscription process itself, in which money was too often the only deciding factor; (2) the extremely poor treatment of the men once inducted; and (3) the neglect of the soldiers' families.

In mid-July, 1945, five officers of the Eightieth Army were executed for the murder of a hundred and five recruits. At this time, the press printed many specific charges. There were allegations of recruiting officers who required conscripts to pay for their rations; of officers selling rice and coal allotted to the recruits, while the latter went hungry; of the rich, the intellectuals, and young merchants going free, and the poor being press-ganged; of the *hsiang, chen, pao,* and *chia* officials and unit commanders all profiting from the sale of substitutes; of new recruits being issued summer uniforms in winter and vice versa; of cruel and inhuman treatment; of large numbers of conscripts dying due to maltreatment and being buried secretly to hide the fact; of wounded conscripts being buried alive; and of news censorship being used to keep conscription abuses from being publicized. The Minister of Conscription was publicly confronted with these accusations, but the demand for a "fundamental revolution" in the administrative apparatus of conscription went unheeded.[73]

Allegations of cruel punishments and inadequate supplies of food, clothing, and medical care continued into the Civil War period. Officers sold rice intended

71. The series of seven letters appeared in the letters-to-the-editor section of *KC*, Feb. 28, Mar. 13, Apr. 24, May 8, and 22, 1948. The Mukden newspaper report on the failure of conscription is in U.S. Department of State, *Foreign Relations of the United States, 1947, the Far East, China,* p. 144. The irregularities in the implementation of conscription orders for 1946 and 1947, and the resistance to them, were widely reported in the Shanghai press during the last three months of 1946 and August, 1947.

72. For some American views, see Barbara W. Tuchman, *Stilwell and the American Experience in China, 1911-45;* and Theodore H. White and Annalee Jacoby, *Thunder Out of China.* Agnes Smedley, *Battle Hymn of China,* was particularly concerned about the treatment of the wounded, noting both positive and negative aspects.

73. *Ch'ing-nien jih-pao,* Sian, June 11, 1945 *(CPR,* Chungking, July 19); *Hsin min pao* and *Hsin hua jih-pao,* Chungking, July 11, 1945 *(CPR); Shih-shih hsin pao* and *CYJP,* Chungking, July 11, 1945 *(CPR,* July 12); *CYJP,* Chungking, July 19, 1945 *(CPR); Shih-shih hsin pao,* Chungking, July 22, 1945 *(CPR,* July 23); *Shih-shih hsin pao,* Chungking, Aug. 24, 1945 *(CPR).* The live burial story was often repeated. For an eyewitness account as told to Robert Payne in 1945, see his *China Awake,* pp. 103-104.

for the men and pocketed the profits. New recruits were roped together on the march, and confined in various ways to prevent their escape. Many reports told of the neglect of the wounded; too often medical facilities were primitive or non-existent.[74] From Anhwei came the story of a man who had been conscripted but managed to escape. He finally made his way back to his village, weak and in poor health. He told of being locked together with many other men in a small room in the heat of summer. They were not allowed to wash, and the daily food ration was usually little more than a few bowls of rice gruel. At night, the men were bound together with ropes to prevent their escape.[75]

In Chekiang, a reporter was present when officials met with representatives of the people, members of the KMT organization, and *hsien* magistrates to discuss local military matters. Everyone responded favorably to questions put by the investigators, except for one old man who spoke out against the hardships suffered by the recruits. He told how they had neither sufficient food nor clothing, and how the platoon commanders beat the men and left them to die when they fell ill on the march. The old man later received a severe rebuke from a local military officer and was cautioned against speaking so foolishly in the future.[76]

The War: Military Discipline. Actually, the poor discipline of the KMT armies received as much publicity as the inhuman treatment to which they were subjected: both were examples of the demoralization afflicting the Government's military effort. Whether the poor peasant conscripted at gunpoint was the same man who turned to prey upon his own kind, once he found himself irrevocably in the ranks, is a question calling for more detailed study than is possible here. There might emerge, for example, distinctions between the conscript and the volunteer; or between these and the professional or mercenary; or between a man fighting in his home district and one garrisoned several hundred *li* away. But no such refinements appeared in contemporary accounts.

"If the common people love their lives," wrote a *Kuan-ch'a* correspondent in Paoting, "they must bring forth money. Bandits or soldiers, there is no difference between them. In ancient times it was so, and so it is even today." Whenever the troops returned, he continued, the city was thrown into a turmoil. They took grain, cloth, cattle, horses, and whatever else they needed, including even people's clothes and shoes. Those who dared refuse to hand things over were accused of being in league with the Communists. When people tried to lecture the soldiers about correct military discipline, they answered that they were risking their lives and their pay was insufficient. Moreover, they knew they

74. For example Liang Shih-ch'iu, "Shen-yang kuan-kan" [Impressions of Mukden], *Shih-chi p'ing-lun*, Nanking, vol. 3, no. 9 (reprinted in *KC*, Mar. 6, 1948, p. 19); Ho P'eng, "Tsai nei-chan tsui ch'ien-hsien" [At the very forefront of the civil war], *KC*, Sept. 27, 1947, p. 18.

75. Special correspondent, "Ts'ung chung-kuo hsiang-ts'un k'an chung-kuo cheng-chih" [Looking at Chinese politics from the Chinese countryside], *KC*, Oct. 19, 1946, p. 18.

76. Hangchow correspondent, p. 15 (see note 69 above).

would never be reprimanded because the Central Government needed them to fight the Communists. Discipline might well induce desertion.[77]

A more personal account came from a correspondent who returned in 1947 to his native village near Szupingkai in the Northeast after an absence of eighteen years. He found the family home in a dilapidated condition. His elder brother explained that if repairs were made, the soldiers garrisoned in the vicinity would want to live in the house. His mother was more outspoken: "When the Japanese were here, we waited for Chairman Chiang to come back and never did we think it would be like this. The Japanese at least did not enter houses and take things, but now it is much worse. They [KMT troops] come in at will to live in your house, or they take things and leave. This house is really no longer our own. They curse the CCP, saying it makes communal property of everyone's homes, but they themselves are doing the same thing every day." The author's visit came to an abrupt end after ten days when a group of soldiers came one night and tried to conscript him. His mother managed to intervene successfully, but fearing for his safety, forced him to leave the next day.

Meanwhile, he had talked with some of the soldiers who came each day to "borrow" things from the family. "I was on the battlefield fighting the Japanese for many years," he told them, "and at that time, although our discipline was not very good, still it was not as bad as yours is now. How is it that we have fallen into such a state?" They replied that during the Anti-Japanese War, if anyone went over to the enemy that man was regarded as a traitor. But today, they told him, no one dared discipline them too strictly for fear they would defect to the other side—and many would praise them as progressive elements.[78]

The War: Political Consequences. The political consequences of the war were generally thought of in terms of the political demoralization of the people, such as the above soldiers' comments indicated, and the increasing trend toward militarism in government. The former was illustrated by an incident during the summer of 1947. KMT soldiers were supposed to have asked some peasants in a village somewhere in north China who was better: the KMT troops or the Eighth Route Army. "You are both equally good," was the reply. "It is only we ordinary people who are not."[79] This story was repeated many times during the summer of 1947, and treated very seriously in intellectual circles. What sarcasm from our countrymen, lamanted one editorial writer, but who could deny the truth of the peasants' retort. The two warring parties were faring well enough in their exploitation of the people.[80]

Similarly, the *Kuan-ch'a* correspondent in Changchun reported his informal inquiry into the political attitudes of people in the surrounding countryside. He claimed to have been unable to find anyone who would even admit to caring

77. Ho P'eng, p. 19 (note 74 above).

78. Han Ch'i, "Tung-pei shih jih" [Ten days in the Northeast], *STPP*, August 16, 1947, pp. 25-28.

79. Ho P'eng (note 74 above).

80. *STPP*, June 16, 1947, p. 2.

whether the Communists took his village or not. "If the Eighth Route comes, it won't mean anything much," some said. Others retorted: "We have seen seven months of the Central Government's forces, two months of the Eighth Route Army, and over half a year of the big noses [the Russians]. Whoever comes, it is all the same. What should we fear!" Still others replied: "It is not even possible to hope for days as good as those after the surrender to Japan." The real tragedy, declared the writer, is that it is impossible to argue with people here, who are now recalling the good points of the Japanese in comparison with the KMT.[81]

Equally tragic, in the minds of these intellectuals, was the ever-increasing involvement of the military in political and administrative affairs, a phenomenon most apparent at the provincial level. They attributed the trend to prolonged wartime conditions, and pointed out that even the American, General Wedemeyer, had noticed and disapproved of it.[82] For them, the presence of military men in government represented the antithesis of democratic politics. A description of General Liang Hua-ch'eng's political "work-style" in Kirin province typifies this view.

The general was appointed governor of the province in 1946. Described as a Cantonese with small eyes and a "spirit which manifests itself in action," he spent much time and effort promoting his public image as a well-rounded, dynamic personality with everything under control. He soon announced that Kirin had no financial problems, a puzzling conclusion since there was much poverty in the province. The general, at least, had no financial problems for he had quickly acquired an automobile and had reportedly built himself a heated swimming pool, despite the severe coal shortage in the province.

He had also placed under the management of the provincial government all factories and enterprises formerly owned by the Japanese. Small businessmen soon felt the effects of this, since the provincial government's monopolies were able to control the local market for many of Kirin's products. Meanwhile, no serious attempt was made to dislodge the Communists, who controlled most of the *hsien* in the province. The writer concluded on a note of resignation: "If China cannot progress to the point of having democratically elected provincial chairmen, then at least we hope the Central Government will not again place a military man in an official administrative position."[83]

In a more analytical vein, Professor Ch'ien Tuan-sheng outlined the historical development of military influence on the KMT, tracing it back to Sun Yat-sen's original alliances with various warlords of the Peiyang government. What was at that time strictly a marriage of convenience soon grew into a force within the

81. Changchun correspondent, "Ling-hsia san-shih tu te jen-hsin" [People's hearts are 30 degrees below zero], *KC*, Mar. 1, 1947, p. 18.
82. *KC* correspondent, "Wei-te-man tsai chung-kuo so liao-chieh te, so fan-nao te, ho k'o-neng chien-i te" [What Wedemeyer understood when he was in China, what bothered him, and what he probably proposed], *KC*, Aug. 30, 1947, p. 16.
83. Changchun correspondent, "Liang Hua-ch'eng tsai chi-lin te tso-feng" [Liang Hua-ch'eng's work style in Kirin], *KC*, Dec. 7, 1946, pp. 16-17. For other comments on militarism and democracy in Changchun, see Changchun correspondent (note 81 above).

Party not easily eliminated. When the KMT was reorganized in 1924, it tried to cut itself off from the Peiyang warlords but, at the same time, placed great emphasis on military training and established the Whampoa Military Academy. The Party also allowed a number of old warlords into the revolutionary army. After the Northern Expedition, the military period should have come to an end. In fact, the period of political tutelage had no way of beginning: the KMT had become the prisoner of the forces it had co-opted to accomplish its revolutionary objectives. Thus Chiang Kai-shek, the chief military figure, was able to secure for himself the position of political leadership as well.

The Military Reorganization Conference of 1929 was convened to reduce the size of the armies; but the top military leaders, including Chiang, were unwilling to reduce their own forces. Then Chiang began to fight the CCP, which made military control seem a continuing necessity. It was this military control that eventually was responsible for the Civil War. A symbiotic relationship developed between the success of the Chinese Communists as they gained control of more and more territory, and the expansion of Chiang's power within the KMT Government. The Whampoa Academy men loyal to him constituted the core of the military clique within the KMT. Because of their access to Chiang and their control of the Government's troops, they became the most important element within the KMT, thus becoming involved in politics at every turn.

Once a military faction becomes dominant in politics, Ch'ien continued, opposition political parties have no recourse except to arms. Nor can the people's rights be guaranteed except by a similar resort to force. Administratively, civilian tasks become subordinated to military. Moreover, the military in China respected no law and had no concept of responsibility to act in the public interest. Professor Ch'ien expressed the feelings of many when he declared that if the military could not be removed from the political sphere at every level and brought under the unified control of a national civilian government, then there could be no hope for the salvation of the Chinese people.[84]

The War: Responsibility. The Communists managed to avoid sharing full responsibility with the KMT for the war, although they did not emerge entirely unscathed. There were many who suggested that both the CCP and the KMT were equally responsible for the war, and that the Communists probably did not want peace any more than did the KMT. There were also many bitter comments condemning both Parties for pursuing their own selfish ends at the expense of the nation as a whole.[85] Nevertheless, the main thrust of the anti-war movement was always directed against the KMT Government. There were several reasons for this.

84. Ch'ien Tuan-sheng, "Chün-jen pa-hu te chung-kuo cheng-fu" [China's government usurped by military men], *STPP*, Dec. 15, 1948, pp. 21-23.
85. For example, Chou Shou-chang (note 25 above); Yang Jen-keng (note 62); Fu T'ung-hsien (note 54); Wu Shih-ch'ang (note 62); and editorial, *STPP*, June 16, 1947, pp. 2-3.

For example, as Wu Shih-ch'ang suggested with respect to the student anti-war protestors, they took their petitions to the Government, and not to the CCP, because they were not yet ready to go over to the Communist side. They still recognized the KMT Government as the legitimate ruler of China with the power to make peace as well as war. Petitions, noted Professor Wu, were presented to recognized governments, not to opposition parties.

Second, there was a tendency to believe that the Communists had been sincere at the Political Consultative Conference in January, 1946, when they agreed, along with representatives of the KMT, to a number of compromises aimed at resolving the differences between them and avoiding civil war. Unfortunately for its case, the KMT gravely damaged belief in its own sincerity by unilaterally breaking a number of the Conference agreements (by action of the KMT Central Executive Committee) only a few weeks after they had been concluded. Suspicions about the Government's sincerity seemed to be confirmed by the disruption of a meeting at Chiao-ch'ang-k'ou in Chungking on February 10, 1946, to celebrate the successful conclusion of the Conference; and by the attack on the offices of the Communist Party newspaper in Chungking a few days later. Both incidents were commonly thought to have been the work of thugs hired by right-wing elements within the KMT.[86]

Perhaps the most important reason for directing anti-war sentiment primarily against the Government was the belief that the strength of the CCP was being built on the weaknesses and shortcomings of the KMT. Liberal critics held the Government responsible for not having acted to remedy these defects during its years in power. Because of that failure, the Government had to bear the main burden of responsibility for the growth of the CCP, and thus for the Civil War as well. This was a theme in Ch'ien Tuan-sheng's argument on the relationship between KMT militarism and the CCP's armed opposition. The theme was even more strongly emphasized by the economist, Wu Ch'i-yuan, who was more inclined to fault the Government directly for its inflationary policies than were many of his colleagues. "If we want to understand the nature of the Civil War," he wrote, "we must turn to the Government's economic policies and measures during the past nine years." He continued:

> The result has been nine years of currency inflation, price fluctuation, and the division of wealth so that the Chinese economy has been changed into a condition of sharp contrast with the rich getting richer and the poor poorer. Even before the [Civil] War, the middle classes except for cliques of corrupt officials were almost all impoverished under the pressure of inflation and low wages. The peasantry which occupied over 85 percent of the population was

86. For example, Ch'ang Ming, "Fan-lun chung-chien p'ai te cheng-chih lu-hsien" [Talking in general terms of the political line of the groups in the center], *STPP*, June 16, 1947, p. 33. On the Political Consultative Conference, the KMT Central Executive Committee meeting, and the Chiao-ch'ang-k'ou incident, see notes 14 and 15 above. On the *Hsin hua jih-pao* incident, see Chapter Six under "The Issue of Nationalism."

already in a state of hunger and was threatening to rise up due to the depredations caused by soldiers, bandits, grain requisitions, conscription, natural disasters, and all kinds of oppression. While the majority of our countrymen had no way of living, the policies of currency inflation were expanded which increased the power and wealth of a privileged group. . . . With society in such a state, would there not be a civil war whether or not there was a CCP? The expansion of the power of the Communists can be attributed directly to such economic policies.

Anyone in the position of the CCP could make use of the economic gulf between rich and poor and the fact that the Government favors the wealthy class, and also that the poor who are in the majority are in opposition to the Government.[87]

Ch'u An-p'ing expressed similar views in a stinging rebuke to the American ex-diplomat, William Bullitt, who visited China in 1947 and recommended that more U.S. aid be given to the KMT Government:

Mr. Bullitt advocates aid for this Government because it is anti-Soviet and anti-Communist. . . . Is it possible that Mr. Bullitt has not considered under what circumstances the CCP has risen to the position it occupies today? In this writer's view, the corrupt control of the KMT is the major factor which has created the rising power of the CCP. . . . If in the past twenty years, Chinese politics had been enlightened, how could so many people have been pressured to turn to the left, thus increasing the power of the CCP? If in the past twenty years, politics had not been so corrupt and incompetent, how could people have been made to feel that the future is so empty that they have turned and entrusted their hopes to the CCP? I say very truthfully that I feel the corrupt control of the KMT to be the mother of the CCP; it has created the CCP and nurtured the CCP.[88]

Incompetence

Volumes could be and in some cases have already been written exploring the specific charges of incompetence—political, economic, administrative, and military—that were leveled against the KMT Government. Among the many issues which aroused sustained critical comment were: the Government's handling of the student movement; economic mismanagement; the treatment of tens of thousands of refugees who fled either the battle zones or the Communist areas; and the complete failure of the Government's performance in Manchuria.

The questions raised about the rationality of the Government's attempts to suppress the student movement were outlined in Chapter Three. The basic argument was that the Government's repressive methods were actually increasing the students' hostility and driving them into the CCP camp, an effect opposite to that presumably intended.

87. Wu Ch'i-yuan, pp. 3-4 (note 67 above).
88. Ch'u An-p'ing, p. 5 (note 37 above). A similar point was made by Chin Feng, "Ma-shang te chih, ma-shang shou chih, ma-shang shih chih" [Hastily gained, hastily guarded, hastily lost] , *STPP,* Mar. 15, 1948, pp. 3-4.

The Government's lapses in the economic sphere have been discussed at length in Chapter Four, and need not be dealt with further here.[89] The tendency among liberal intellectuals was to blame the Government not for its policy of inflationary finance *per se,* but for its insistence on pursuing a course that made the policy necessary. There was, nevertheless, much criticism of the ineptitude with which the policy was implemented, including the fumbling efforts to minimize its worst effects.

Political Incompetence: Refugees. This particular problem developed as people fled their homes either for fear of the Communists or the dangers of war. Often fleeing with the aid and encouragement of retreating Government forces, the former category seems to have been the larger. In mid-1947, one writer noted that many people north of the Sungari River in Communist territory felt ill-at-ease with the strictures of Communist rule and had moved south to the KMT-controlled cities of the Northeast. These refugees included young people, mostly university and middle school students, who did not like the Communist system of education, and wanted to continue with their past form of study.[90]

In addition, small businessmen had also fled from the same area. Another report described many of the refugees in Changchun as children of wealthy landlords and merchants who had been liquidated, and young men who had run away for fear of being conscripted into the CCP army.[91] Landlords and small landholders made up another common category of refugee. Having heard "bloody tear-dripping stories" about the treatment meted out to their kind once the Communists gained control of an area, many landlords fled in panic rather than wait and find out for themselves whether there was truth in the rumors. These people constituted a natural source of political support for the KMT, and might have been used to good advantage by a more astute regime. There were scattered attempts to exploit the anti-Communist sentiments of the refugees. One such attempt was apparently behind an incident in June, 1946, when a group claiming to be refugees from northern Kiangsu beat up a petitioning peace delegation at the railway station in Nanking.[92]

For the most part, however, the Government abandoned the refugees to their fate. Many were quickly reduced to a state of abject poverty. With jobs scarce or non-existent, whatever savings they had been able to bring with them were rapidly eaten up by inflation. An estimated 100,000 such people had converged on Mukden by November, 1947. Those who gathered in Changchun were soon transformed into "pitiful refugees" without even enough to eat. Many of the students who had fled to that city in pursuit of "the freedom to study" were unable to continue their schooling due to lack of funds or space in government schools. Cut off from their families and without any means of support, the

89. Much of Chapter Four is based on accounts from liberal writers and publications.

90. P'an Tzu-ming, "Sung-hua chiang p'an te yin-yang-chieh" [Darkness and Light on the Sungari river frontier], *KC*, July 26, 1947, p. 19.

91. Changchun correspondent (note 81 above).

92. *Shih-shih hsin pao, Hsin-wen pao, CYJP,* and *Shih-tai jih-pao,* Shanghai, June 24, 1946 *(CPR); WHP* and *TKP,* Shanghai, June 25, 1946 *(CPR).*

young people became "free drifters in a free city." As a result, there were said to be many among them who had "lost hope" in the KMT authorities.[93]

Similarly, Derk Bodde described the plight of some two thousand refugee middle school students airlifted to Peiping from Taiyuan in June, 1948. Once deposited in Peiping, the students, many of whom were no more than twelve or thirteen years of age, were on their own except for a daily ration of steamed corn bread provided by the Social Welfare Bureau. The local academic authorities ignored them. Professor Bodde noted the demoralization of these young people, who were obliged to camp out in the parks, temples, and empty buildings of the city. They lacked books, adequate clothing, sanitary facilities, employment, or seemingly any personal initiative beyond that necessary for petty theft and the occasional slaughter of a stray dog to supplement their meagre diets.[94]

By September, 1948, an official of the American Embassy estimated that there were between twenty thousand and thirty thousand refugee students in Peiping, twenty thousand in Nanking, and ten thousand in Hankow.[95] The issue of the Government's responsibilities toward these young refugees in particular had reached an angry climax that summer. The outburst was inspired by an incident on July 5 in Peiping when an army unit opened fire on a group of demonstrating students, killing at least fourteen of them and injuring over one hundred. The demonstrators were part of a contingent of five thousand students encouraged to leave the Northeast, and flown at government expense to Peiping and Tientsin. This was part of a program to reduce the pressure on food and supplies in the cities of the Northeast, and to disperse the population in order to prevent as many as possible from joining the Communists (who, by 1948, controlled all of Manchuria except for a few major cities).

Each of the five thousand students was given a subsistence allowance for three months and then ignored. Those in Peiping soon were reduced to wandering the streets and sleeping in parks and temples. Unlike the Shansi student refugees, these from the Northeast began to complain. The authorities responded by suggesting they undergo military training. The students then organized a protest demonstration, during which they broke down the gate of the Peiping Municipal Council and marched on the residence of the council president. At

93. P'an Tzu-ming (note 90 above). One Mukden dispatch reported 5,000 refugee students in that city by summer, 1946. Some 2,000 of these demanded admission to schools in the fall term without sitting for the required examinations. This demand was prompted in part by the alleged sale of exam questions by clerks of the Matriculation Office. See *Min-kuo jih-pao*, Tientsin, Aug. 16, 1946 (*CPR*, Peiping-Tientsin). The total of 100,000 refugees in Mukden is in a U.S. Embassy report on Nov. 26, 1947 (*Foreign Relations of the United States, 1947*, p. 378).

94. Derk Bodde, *Peking Diary*, pp. 31-33, 65-68, 74-77, 100-103. Not all student refugees in Peiping were in quite so sorry a state, however. Bodde noted that in November, 1948, over 2,000 students were evacuated from Paoting and placed in temples in the outskirts of Peiping. They were accompanied by their teachers, who conducted classes and maintained relatively good morale and discipline.

95. Melby, *Mandate of Heaven*, pp. 281-82.

this point, the demonstrating students were surrounded by armored cars and halted with a barrage of machine gun fire. Editorial comment was bitterly critical.[96]

The reaction to this incident was different only in degree from the commentary deploring the pitiful state of peasant landholders from northern Kiangsu who had fled south to the Nanking-Shanghai area. A letter to *Kuan-ch'a* described one case involving three out of the many refugee families living in caves near Louhsiashan village near Nanking. Their only means of livelihood was cutting firewood, but conflicts often arose between the newcomers and the local people, who regarded the mountains as village property. On one occasion, three refugees were seriously beaten by villagers for collecting firewood from village lands. The refugees lacked the funds necessary for arbitrating the case so it was sent to court, but the magistrate refused to hear the case because there was no money to pay the court fees.

While these negotiations were in progress, the families of the injured men asked to be allowed to remain in jail because they had no means of supporting themselves. A college student living in the village contributed money to cover the men's medical expenses. The magistrate ultimately let them off with an admonition to be more polite to the local community, and a promise that the case would be dropped if they would leave the area. The three refugee families soon thereafter returned to their native village in the Communist areas. The letter pointedly concluded: "[The refugees] came south hoping for protection but instead were abandoned and made to suffer.... The two parties are now fighting; one is struggling for the people and the other is abandoning them."[97]

The Manchurian Debacle. Similar conclusions about the KMT's inability to govern were drawn from its performance in Manchuria. Communist gains there were rapid following the Japanese surrender, and the critics were willing to admit that the problems in the KMT-held areas were to some degree a product of the military situation. Nevertheless, the Government was blamed for its incompetent and irresponsible performance in virtually every sphere of activity, from the military to education.[98]

96. One of the bitterest was by Chou Ching-wen. From Manchuria himself, Chou regarded the incident as one of a long series of injuries inflicted on the people of the Northeast by the KMT government. Chou Ching-wen, "Wei ch'iang-sha tung-pei liu-wang hsueh-sheng k'ung-sung nan-ching cheng-fu" [Accusation against the Nanking government for the shooting of Northeast refugee students], *STPP,* July 15, 1948, pp. 1-2.

97. Letter from Louhsiashan village, Apr. 16, 1948 (*KC,* Apr. 24, 1948, p. 2).

98. Newspapers in KMT-held Manchuria cities were all controlled or supervised by the government, KMT, or military. Thus, as with the military progress of the war, few independent sources of information were available to the public. Nevertheless, a number of writers and journalists tried to investigate and report on developments in the Northeast. The sketch here is based on a comparative reading of the following selection.

KC:

(a)   Nov. 9, 1946, pp. 16-17, Shenyang correspondent
(b)   Dec. 21, 1946, pp. 17-18, Shenyang correspondent
(c)   Mar. 1, 1947, pp. 17-19, Changchun correspondent (see note 81)

Some critics were inclined to place the blame on a few of the top regional officials. At the same time, there also existed an awareness that one or two men could not possibly be responsible for a debacle as far-reaching as this was. The only alternative, then, was to damn the entire Government performance—and most liberal writers did so. They began quite naturally with the take-over period. The return of the Central Government after fourteen years of Japanese occupation was accomplished even later in the Northeast than elsewhere. This was due to the Russian presence and the Government's inability to move its troops more rapidly into the area. As the local welcome for the Russian liberators cooled, largely because of their poor discipline, the Central Government was blamed for their prolonged stay. When the Russians finally left in the spring of 1946, they were followed by the Government's take-over officials. As noted in Chapter Two, these behaved in the Northeast no differently than they had everywhere else in the former Japanese-occupied territories.

Nevertheless, the key to the situation, according to most critics, was Chiang Kai-shek's distrust of the Manchurians. The Central Government therefore acted, as it had in Yunnan, to assert firm military control over the region. The objective was to prevent the reemergence of the old semi-autonomous power base dominated by the family of the "Old Marshal," Chang Tso-lin. Nine of the ten armies sent to take over the region were made up of soldiers from other parts of China. Instead of reverting to the historical provincial demarcations in effect prior to the Japanese occupation, the Government divided the three original Northeast provinces into nine administrative units, and appointed outsiders to fill virtually all the top posts. [99] At the local level, the incoming KMT officials allied themselves with landlords, and others who had collaborated with the Japanese. These were the only elements in the region who could be counted on

---

(d) July 12, 1947, pp. 4-5, Ho Yung-chi

(e) July 26, 1947, pp. 19-20, P'an Tzu-ming (see note 90)

(f) Feb. 28, 1948, pp. 17-18, Kao Ch'ao (see note 67)

(g) Mar. 6, 1948, p. 19, Liang Shih-ch'iu (from *Shih-chi p'ing-lun,* vol. 3, no. 9; see note 74)

(h) Mar. 13, 1948, p. 15, *Kuan-ch'a* correspondent

(i) Mar. 20, 1948, pp. 17-18, Shenyang correspondent

(j) Mar. 27, 1948, p. 16, Ch'ien Pang-k'ai (from *Ch'ing-tao shih pao,* Tsingtao, Feb. 19, 1948; see Chapter Two, note 4)

(k) Apr. 3, 1948, p. 17, Kao Ch'ao

(l) Apr. 10, 1948, p. 12, Shenyang correspondent

STPP:

(m) Aug. 16, 1947, pp. 25-29, Han Ch'i (see note 78)

(n) June 15, 1948, p. 35, Ch'un Sheng (see note 35)

(o) July 15, 1948, p. 1, Chou Ching-wen (see note 96)

99. Li Tsung-jen indicates that the decision to divide Manchuria into nine provinces was based on suggestions of a committee led by Wu Ting-ch'ang and other members of the Political Study Clique, which Chiang Kai-shek commissioned to study the area preparatory to the Government's return after WW II ("The Reminiscences of General Li Tsung-jen," Chapter 46, p. 1). Members of this clique reputedly dominated bureaucratic appointments in the Northeast during this period.

to have loyalties neither to the Communists nor to the still popular "Young Marshal," Chang Hsueh-liang.

In Yunnan, the Government's efforts met with at least temporary success. In Manchuria, the strategy of asserting central control proved clumsy indeed, foiled by an active Communist opposition in alliance with resurgent regional loyalties. In the 1930s, these sentiments had been accentuated by the early Japanese occupation of the area, and the Central Government's initial acquiescence to that encroachment. These feelings were dramatized in the Sian incident. After the Japanese surrender, initial support for the Chiang Kai-sek Government appeared genuine. But localism soon reemerged with the resentment caused by the Government's take-over policies and the behavior of its officials. Like the Russians, "the southerners" wore out their welcome very quickly. The arrogance and greed of the officials and officers, and the poor discipline of the KMT troops—outsiders all—gave local people the impression they were again being forced into submission as a conquered people. "Mukden respects only wealth and power," wrote one correspondent, "and military men in particular have great influence. As for the common people, they feel on the one hand that all under heaven belongs to the southerners and on the other that life today is not as good as it was in Manchukuo times."[100]

Among the angriest expressions of this resentment was that of Chou Ching-wen in his above-cited commentary at the time of the July 5 student refugee incident in Peiping:

> The Government perhaps does not like local power, but it cannot because of this despise the local people. I recall the past twenty years of history and it alarms me. The Nanking Government from the beginning has hated the local powers in the Northeast and therefore did not mind using foreigners to destroy it, caring nothing about the land and looking on the local people as enemies. And so it is today; the power of the Northeast is being destroyed by the Nanking Government. The patriotic Chang Hsueh-liang has been under arrest for eleven years; and sovereign rights have now been granted to the U.S.S.R. in Manchurian territory, which was once sacrificed by the Nanking Government to Japan. . . .

Concerning the Government's use of outside administrators, one writer indicated his disagreement with the view that this was the cause of "the Northeast problem." "I do not have this local fellow-villager outlook," he wrote, "Chinese are Chinese, and a good man is a good man wherever he comes from." [101] Unfortunately, the Government stood to lose either way.

The past and present came together in the person of Chang Hsueh-liang. The Young Marshal had been the key figure in the detention of Chiang Kai-shek at Sian in December, 1936, over the latter's reluctance to fight Japan. Chiang submitted to the demands of the Young Marshal and his troops, but placed him

---

100. See note 98(a), p. 16. On the situation in Yunnan, see Chapter Three under "The December First Movement."

101. See note 98(g), p. 19.

under house arrest immediately after the incident. By early 1947, Chang Hsueh-liang had been removed to an even more secure confinement on Taiwan, although his release after World War II had been generally anticipated.[102] Chang's continued confinement was widely resented in the Northeast, a fact not without political significance. One report in March, 1948, asserted that Central Government leaders had made two crucial post-war miscalculations in the Northeast. First, they had closed their eyes to the facts that Chang Hsueh-liang and his father Chang Tso-lin had a special place in Manchurian history and were held in high regard because of it. Second, they had underestimated the strength which the Communists had built up during fourteen years of underground activity in the region.[103]

As to the first blunder, the Government maintained that it had acted in the interests of national unification, and that regional forces loyal to independent figures, whether Communist or not, could not be allowed to persist. The critics retorted that only Chang Hsueh-liang could have mobilized the people of the Northeast against the Communists. Certainly the Central Government alone was unable to do so. Its forces remained poorly disciplined and inadequately supplied, distrusted by and distrusting of the local population, pitted against locally supported and rapidly growing Communist units.[104]

As for the second error, the Government was criticized for having relied wholly on the assurances of the Japanese and the puppet Manchukuo government that they had eliminated all Communist forces in the area. Those forces had suffered severe repression during the Japanese occupation, but a few thousand were believed to have survived and maintained their organization intact. They were therefore in a position to take maximum advantage of the opportunity provided by the many months during which Soviet troops occupied the major cities and communications lines in Manchuria, and no one occupied

---

102. Rumors, all unsubstantiated, abounded at this time concerning negotiations for Chang's release. One of the more intriguing was that Chiang Kai-shek offered to release Chang in 1946 if he promised to "use his prestige to swing the Manchurian balance in the Kuomintang's favor"—an offer which the Young Marshal refused (Israel Epstein, *The Unfinished Revolution in China*, p. 375).

103. See note 98(h), p. 15.

104. For a comparative view of the Communist performance in the Northeast, see Chapter Six. Regional loyalties, and the continuing popularity of the Young Marshal, probably would not have weighed so heavily in the Manchurian political equation if the Government's record there had been less open to criticism. Under the circumstances, however, the importance of the localism issue probably cannot be overestimated. American consular officers stressed it repeatedly in their reports during 1947—describing the growing antipathy of the local people, and the Government's inability to defend the region against the Communists without their support. Yet the Government spurned even such help as was offered. For example, a locally formed Northeast Mobilization Commission, thought to enjoy considerable support, offered to organize a local defense force to fight the Communists. The offer was refused. General Ma Chan-shan, a cavalry officer who had served under both the Old and Young Marshals, agreed to work with the Government and was made Deputy Commander of the Northeast Command. But he was never given anything to do, nor any troops to lead. See *Foreign Relations of the United States, 1947*, pp. 141-42, 144-45, 152, 156-57, 175, 210-11, 232-35, 292-93, 307, 330, 398-99, 404, 708-9, 744.

the countryside. Even after General Tu Yü-ming and the Chinese forces took over in the Northeast, they continued to act upon the erroneous assumption that the local Communist base had been wiped out.

To these two errors might be added a third: the Government's overestimation of its own strength. Thus, instead of adopting the common strategy of compromising with one enemy to defeat a second, the Government chose to confront both regionalism and communism simultaneously, thereby driving them into an alliance with each other. As it happened, the Northeast became an important link in the Communists' strategy of victory. There could scarcely be a more clear-cut example of how poorly the Government was served by its calculated disregard of popular demands.

Still, this was only one element in the Manchurian debacle as portrayed by the KMT's liberal critics. They criticized the military establishment for faulty planning, and for relying on inadequate intelligence. They criticized the military for allowing its forces to become dispersed and surrounded in the defense of various key points, even after these had ceased to be of any strategic value. "Why doesn't the KMT concentrate its strength and launch a defensive attack? Why hasn't it sent more troops to the Northeast? Why haven't the masses been armed to form a real defense force?" Such were the questions that people were asking in 1947 and 1948. General Tu Yü-ming, Commander of the Northeast China Command, was criticized as grossly incompetent. There were persistent rumors that he and General Hsiung Shih-hui, Director of Chiang Kai-shek's Headquarters in the Northeast overseeing the civilian administration, did not get along and could not work well together. Reflecting this split, military and civilian officials were said to be at loggerheads and unable to cooperate with one another.

In August, 1947, both generals were replaced. General Ch'en Ch'eng was sent as overall commander to unify the Government's political and military efforts. Nevertheless, the military situation continued to deteriorate. His dictatorial work-style, and the passive behavior it produced in his subordinates, was criticized as yet another factor underlying the Government's weakening position in the Northeast. Certainly, he did nothing to inspire the cooperation or confidence of the local people. And although he himself was reputedly honest, the corrupt practices of the officers and men under his command continued unabated.

Prices in the Government-controlled areas of the Northeast were even higher, according to some reports, than those in other parts of the country by early 1948. The upward price spiral was blamed primarily on diminishing supplies due to the fighting in the region. The Communists were disrupting railway and electric power lines; seizing or destroying coal mines and food crops; and had won control of most of the Manchurian countryside by 1948. Yet, this was not the whole story.

The Government had issued a separate currency in the Northeast in the hope of isolating the region from the inflationary effects of KMT financial policy in the rest of the country after the Japanese surrender. The Government then proceeded to carry out policies that ensured the very result it was ostensibly trying to avoid. Its military and political expenditures in the Northeast in early 1948, were estimated at 200 billion per month in local currency. This figure was not made any more acceptable by the knowledge that a good portion of the political expenditures were going to support the top officials of seven provincial governments living "in exile" in Mukden. The newly-created provinces they nominally governed were in Communist hands, and in some cases had been so since 1945.[105]

Since its income in the Northeast was nowhere near adequate to cover these expenditures, the Government printed more money—thus defeating entirely the purpose of maintaining a separate currency. Moreover, the regulations governing the relationship between Manchurian currency and *fapi* invited speculation. Before the exchange rate between the two was fixed at 1:10 in March, 1948, it had fluctuated in practice between 1:11.50 and 1:6. This fluctuation, plus the regulation stipulating that *fapi* could circulate freely in the Northeast whereas Northeast currency was not allowed to circulate in the rest of the country, provided opportunities for profit-making too tempting to be ignored by those in a position to exploit them. These were primarily government officials with idle cash and time to spare, and a few other wealthy individuals. The traffic in gold and currencies between Manchuria and the rest of the country was allegedly great enough to affect the value of the *fapi* itself. At one point, the Government blamed the rise in the price of gold on speculative buying by the Communists in the Northeast. But if the Communists were engaging in this sort of economic warfare, they were not alone. So long as its own officials were carrying on there undisturbed, the critics noted, the CCP was not the only enemy the Central Government had to worry about in the Northeast.

Economic instability was such that within a few days after the exchange rate between Northeast currency and *fapi* was fixed at 1:10 in an effort to curb speculation, the black market rate was quoted at 1:7; the price of gold and silver had more than doubled; and the consumer price index had responded in kind. Between March 1 and March 19, the prices of soy beans, kaoliang, rice, and flour had more than doubled. In the midst of this particular crisis, "as if adding oil to the fire," the Central Bank of Mukden announced another issue of Northeast currency notes in the unprecedented denominations of $100,000, $500,000, and $1,000,000. Concluded one writer: "The Central Government keeps saying it wants to protect us in the Northeast, but we wonder if they have either the determination or the desire to do so."[106]

105. The seven provinces were Liaopei, Sungkiang, Hokiang, Heilungkiang, NunKiang, Antung, and Hsingan. Small portions of the two remaining provinces, Kirin and Liaoning, were still held by the Central Government in April, 1948. Also being supported in Mukden, with almost nothing to do, were several hundred Central Government supervisory and administration personnel for the whole Northeast. These included officers for finance, agriculture, irrigation, culture, education, and communications.

106. See note 98(k), p. 17. On the Government's military performance in Manchuria, see Lionel Max Chassin, *The Communist Conquest of China: a History of the Civil War, 1945-49*, pp. 57-68, 76-81, 114-21, 131-36, 165-67, 187-92; and O. Edmund Clubb, *Twentieth Century China*, pp. 260-90.

THE LIBERAL IDEAL: SOCIALISM AND DEMOCRACY

The intellectuals' critique of the KMT Government has been presented for a dual purpose: first, to illustrate their orientation toward the Government; and second, to cast further light, albeit through liberal eyes, on the nature of KMT rule. What follows is the positive expression of these intellectuals' political commitments as they debated among themselves the nature of state and society they hoped might emerge from the chaos of the Civil War. It was at this point, however, that their arguments broke down and the flaws in the underlying assumptions were most fully exposed—casualties of a predicament which was for these liberal intellectuals as unassailable as it was unacceptable.

They were, of course, more preoccupied with criticizing the KMT than with expressing their commitments in positive form. This preoccupation was nevertheless consistent with the assumptions upon which it was based, namely, that the war could not be fought to a conclusion by either side, and that the Government could be persuaded to reform itself. Being true liberals as well as representatives of China's intellectual elite, they seemed unwilling to believe that the Government could ignore their critique—well-intentioned and self-evident as their arguments were. Nor could they have a clear picture of the developing military situation, being cut off from the battlefield by a paucity of factual information and by their own inclinations as well. In any event, the futility of their cause became fully apparent only within the context of the positive solutions they proposed. Their sophisticated critique degenerated, finally, into naive generalizations when they addressed the specific question of how their solutions were to be translated into reality.

THE ENDS: GENERAL PRINCIPLES

The general principles they advocated were clear enough and enjoyed widespread support. Socialism and democracy constituted the liberal ideal. Beyond that, diversity began to emerge. Socialism and democracy meant different things to different people, which was at least one of the reasons for the seemingly endless controversies concerning the nature and application of these objectives within the Chinese context.

Of socialism, Ch'u An-p'ing declared: "at present the Chinese people in general and especially the intellectuals really do not oppose it but instead are positively disposed toward it."[107] Fu Szu-nien, who tended to emphasize the need for such conventional reform measures as the elimination of privileges for the so-called "favored families" and equalization of the tax burden through a graduated income tax system, nevertheless stated flatly that if socialism could be effectively achieved in China he would "approve 100 percent."[108] A typical

107. Ch'u An-p'ing, p. 6 (note 1 above).
108. Fu Meng-chen (Fu Szu-nien), "Lun hao-men tzu-pen chih pi-hsu ch'an-ch'u" [On the necessity of rooting out favored-family capital], *KC,* Mar. 1, 1947, p. 6. Fu, among many other posts, was director of the History and Philology Institute of the Academia Sinica. He created a minor sensation in Nanking political circles when he denounced T. V. Soong and H. H. Kung in a series of three articles in February, 1947. The first two were

view was that of Professor Cheng Lin-chuang, head of the Economics Department at Yenching University:

> In a capitalist society, although there is economic freedom there is no economic justice. But it does exist in socialist nations, and only because it does are those societies secure. There are two aspects of economic justice. One is the guarantee of the right to employment and the second is the guarantee to the right of a basic livelihood. The realization of these two objectives requires unceasing production and social organization for just distribution. These conditions can exist only in a planned economy. They will not be easily realized in capitalist nations unless the principle of free enterprise is changed. . . . We believe that economic justice and social security together constitute the main direction of society's present development. At the same time, we believe even more that everything which goes against this tide will in the end be washed away by it.[109]

Socialism was also seen as an appropriate model for economic development as well as an instrument of economic justice. Thus even as he deplored the territorial and organizational expansion of the U.S.S.R., fearing that China might be its next target, Professor Ting Su of National Central University advocated a Soviet-style economic system for China. It would, he declared, provide the most effective form of organization for the growth of China's economy.[110]

Given the diversity of understanding and commitment, it would be unfair to synthesize these views into some composite definition of the democratic socialist reform program advocated by Chinese liberals in the 1940s. It is not clear, for example, that when they advocated socialism everyone actually had in mind a "Soviet-style planned economy." Their most basic similarities and differences will become apparent in what follows and this should be sufficient for our purposes here.

Nevertheless, if one were obliged to piece together the most representative components of their reform program on the basis of the proposals most commonly advanced by members of the liberal community, it would probably approximate the demands made public on the eve of the National Assembly meeting in the spring of 1948 by a group of ninety-nine Nanking professors. They blamed the Civil War on the KMT failure to implement the Three People's Principles, and the CCP use of force to attain political power. They castigated the CCP for compromising its loyalty to the nation through its commitment to world revolution, and denounced the Government for its corruption and inefficiency. And they called for the following measures:

Political reforms
1. Recognition of the principles of political and economic equality

published in *Shih-chi p'ing-lun*, Nanking, vol. 1, nos. 7 and 8; the third in *TKP*, Shanghai. *KC* reprinted all three in this March 1, 1947, issue.

109. Cheng Lin-chuang, "Ching-chi cheng-i yü she-hui an-ch'üan" [Economic justice and social peace], *KC*, Mar. 15, 1947, pp. 9-10.

110. Ting Su, "Su-lien chi chiang tung ku" [The Soviet Union's imminent concerns in the East], *KC*, July 3, 1948, p. 7.

  2. Respect for the freedom of speech

  3. Absorption of talent into the government

  4. Observance of the law

  5. Elimination of superfluous organizations and the establishment of a sound civil service system

  6. Punishment for corruption on the part of public officials

  7. Decentralization of political power and the strengthening of local self-government

Economic reforms

  1. Liquidation of bureaucratic capital; requisition of private bank deposits abroad

  2. Equalization of land holdings on the basis of the land-to-the-tiller principle

  3. Nationalization of all banks

  4. Nationalization of all public utilities

  5. Currency reform and the curbing of inflation

  6. Revision of the tax system, and the institution of capital and inheritance taxes

  7. Improved treatment for civil servants and army personnel.[111]

The arguments began in earnest when the proposals were expanded beyond this common denominator of agreement, and particularly when the discussion included the question of how best to apply them to the Chinese situation. This was amply demonstrated in a series of exchanges by Shih Fu-liang, Yen Jen-keng, Chang Tung-sun, and Fan Hung which took place in the pages of *Kuan-ch'a* in late 1947 and early 1948.

Shih Fu-liang's ideas always seemed to elicit a response, perhaps because he had been one of the founding members of the CCP. He maintained that he had for the past twenty years been convinced that China's democratic revolution must culminate in the development of socialism. This was so because of the contradictions inherent in capitalism and the unequal distribution of wealth upon which it was based. In short, capitalism was incompatible with the basic concept of democracy.

Shih nevertheless argued that since China had not yet achieved a material base adequate for the implementation of socialism, it would not be possible to move directly from the "feudal" stage, then in the process of being destroyed, to socialism. For the transitional period, therefore, he advocated what he called the "new capitalism." The new capitalism would be the economic program of a "new democratic" political regime, led by the laboring classes, to be installed after the defeat of the KMT Government. It would entail: a full reform of the land system, and implementation of land-to-the-tiller; confiscation of all bureaucratic capital and the expansion of the nationalized sector to include banks, heavy industry, major communications facilities, and some light industry; the protection of national business and industry and aid for small producers; the

111. *Hsin min pao*, Nanking, Mar. 27, 1948 (*CPR*, Apr. 1).

implementation of a progressive labor law to guarantee a basic standard of living for all; and economic, financial, and social policies designed to discourage the accumulation of excessive personal wealth and to encourage the reinvestment of profits in productive enterprises.[112]

One might assume that this program, similar in broad outline to that spelled out by Mao Tse-tung's *On New Democracy*, would have satisfied the more radically inclined of Shih's colleagues. But it did not. For example, Yen Jen-keng, a professor at Chekiang University, took him rather severely to task in one article and then, in a second, rebuffed Shih's attempt to minimize the differences between them. Yen objected, first, to Shih's willingness to allow exploitative relations between capital and labor to continue, however modified, for the sake of increasing production. Yen's second main point of disagreement was Shih's willingness to entrust his hopes for a change in the economic system to some future type of "new democratic political regime." Yen doubted whether workers, peasants, rich peasants, the petty bourgeoisie, intellectuals, and national capitalists could unite in the struggle for socialism—particularly if the rich peasants, petty bourgeoisie, and national capitalists were allowed to revive. They may be exploited today, he asserted, but they all contain the character of exploiters within them. He therefore advocated moving directly to socialism because "I feel that we can perhaps solve the problems of production and distribution at one and the same time."[113]

Shih Fu-liang had more in common with Chang Tung-sun, and in this case was somewhat more justified in his protestations that the main differences between them were matters of emphasis and explanation. But differences there were. Chang, like Shih, emphasized the importance of developing and increasing production as the first step that China must take. Chang also felt that socialism was not the immediate solution because social reforms alone could never succeed in an impoverished nation. He also believed, and here he differed with Shih, that liberalism and its economic equivalent capitalism, however modified, could not ensure the development of production in a backward country such as China.

This was so because capitalism would only create new forms of injustice in such countries. Once the good things of Western culture enter China, they only increase the sufferings of the people because in China there are special interests who can make use of such things to oppress the people. These oppressive forces also stood in the way of developing productivity. They included privileged bureaucratic capital, landlords, usurers, and the cast-offs of a backward feudal society such as the vagrants and wanderers, tenant farmers and hired laborers who could produce little and often resorted to extortion and robbery in order to live.

112. Shih Fu-liang, "Fei-ch'u po-hsueh yü tseng-chia sheng-ch'an" [Abolish exploitation and increase production], *KC*, Mar. 20, 1948, pp. 7-9. Shih left the CCP in 1927.

113. Yen Jen-keng, "She-hui-chu-i? 'Hsin tzu-pen-chu-i' hu?" [Socialism? "New capitalism?"], *KC*, June 19, 1948, pp. 5-8. Shih Fu-liang's response was "Hsin chung-kuo te ching-chi ho cheng-chih" [The economy and politics of the new China], *KC*, July 24, 1948, p. 4. Yen replied in "Tsai ho Shih Fu-liang hsien-sheng t'an 'hsin tzu-pen-chu-i' " [Again discussing the "new capitalism" with Mr. Shih Fu-liang], *KC*, Aug. 7, 1948, p. 15.

Chang concluded that a "progressive" planned economy was China's only hope of developing its productive capacity. With a planned economy, everything else, including politics and education, had to be planned as well. This should be done in accordance with the principle that all exploitative relations which hinder production must be eliminated, while those which encourage production could be allowed to exist in the transitional period. Conversely, social reforms which benefit production would be encouraged, while those that interfered with it could not be supported. Chang was insistent that each nation must work out its own solutions on the basis of this principle. He suggested, however, that two models of its apparently successful application were the Soviet Union's New Economic Policy of the 1920s which made it possible for the U.S.S.R. later to move to socialism, and post-World War II economic policies in Sweden.[114]

Chang Tung-sun seemed to have more cause to argue with the Peita economist, Fan Hung, than with Shih Fu-liang. Professor Fan was straightforward and unequivocal in his diagnoses, as well as in his prescriptions for the realization of socialism:

> In terms of economics, . . . we must clearly understand that in today's world, all evil is due to the exploiting of the propertyless classes by those with property. Then what remedy is there? This of course has to do with changes in political power.
>
> In politics also, I feel that China, like other nations, has only two roads before it. One is that of revolution and the other is that of counter-revolution. The latter puts all political power in the hands of the exploiting class. To tell these exploiters to give up voluntarily their political power or to limit their exploitation and work for the welfare of the people: this is what is called the third road and is advocated by Jesus Christ, Confucius, and contemporary professors. . . .
>
> On the revolutionary road, the exploited classes are united with their exploiters either by peaceful or violent means. Political power is seized, the power of the exploiters is limited and the life, health, and freedom of the exploited are protected. . . .[115]

114. Chang Tung-sun was a frequent contributor to *KC* and other liberal journals. He was also a prominent member of the Democratic League until it was banned in the autumn of 1947, and a professor at Yenching University. This summary of his ideas on economic reform is based on the following of his articles. (a) "Kuan-yü chung-kuo ch'u-lu te k'an-fa: tsai ta Fan Hung hsien-sheng" [A view on the way out for China: another reply to Mr. Fan Hung], *KC*, Jan. 31, 1948, pp. 3-4; (b) "Cheng-chih shang te tzu-yu-chu-i yü wen-hua shang te tzu-yu-chu-i" [Liberalism in politics and culture], *KC*, Feb. 28, 1948, pp. 3-5; (c) "Ching-chi p'ing-teng yü fei-ch'u po-hsueh" [Economic equality and the abolition of exploitation], *KC*, Mar. 6, 1948, pp. 3-5; (d) "Tseng ch'an yü ko-ming: hsieh-le 'min-chu-chu-i yü she-hui-chu-i' i-hou" [Increasing production and revolution: after writing "democracy and socialism"], *Chung chien* [China reconstructs], vol. 3, no. 4 (reprinted in *KC*, Aug. 7, 1948, pp. 26-27).

115. Fan Hung, "Chih yu liang t'iao lu" [There are only two roads], *KC*, Apr. 10, 1948, pp. 3-4. Professor Fan's exchange with Chang Tung-sun actually preceded this particular statement by several months and revolved around a number of related issues. The debate between the two developed in the following articles. (a) Chang Tung-sun, "Wo i chui-lun hsien-cheng chien chi wen-hua te chen-tuan" [I seek an examination of constitutional

Professor Fan's hope was that China would be transformed into "the model of a free socialist nation." But he was careful to emphasize the word "free." The fear that a socialist China might become subservient to the Soviet Union was often expressed at this time. Many leftists, including the Communists, found themselves vulnerable on this point and went to some lengths to disavow the inevitability of any such relationship between China and the U.S.S.R. The common theme was that China must find an approach to socialism best suited to the particular Chinese context, and that the responsibility for changing China lay entirely within China itself.[116]

A more difficult problem for many of these intellectuals was that posed by their simultaneous devotion to the ideals of socialism and democracy. Sun Pao-i, who severed relations with Carsun Chang after the latter agreed to let his Democratic-Socialist Party join the KMT Government in 1947, criticized Chang for his excessive commitment to the Anglo-American style of political democracy. Chang had once said it would be virtually impossible for political democracy, as practiced in the West, ever to evolve from economic democracy, which he equated with the economic system of the U.S.S.R. For his part, Sun argued that evolution from political democracy to economic democracy, as Chang defined them, would be just as impossible since democratic political parties in the West were all controlled by capitalists.

What Sun really rejected, however, was Chang's either-or approach. We need both the vote and the rice bowl, declared Sun. Since neither the Anglo-American nor the Soviet systems can give us both, let us extract what we want from each and leave the rest.[117] Most liberals would undoubtedly have applauded such a neat summation of their ideals. But the questions remained: what to take, and what to reject, and how.

Chang Tung-sun was one of the few who addressed himself directly to the complexities inherent in the problem, but he too hedged on its solution. In emphasizing the importance of a planned economy for the development of production, he suggested that both equality and freedom would have to be circumscribed and could exist only within the limits set by the plan. In a

government and culture], *KC,* Oct. 11, 1947, pp. 3-6; (b) Fan Hung, "Yü Liang Shu-ming Chang Tung-sun liang hsien-sheng lun chung-kuo te wen-hua yü cheng-chih" [Discussing China's culture and politics with Messrs. Liang Shu-ming and Chang Tung-sun], *KC,* Nov. 29, 1947, pp. 5-8; (c) Chang Tung-sun, "Ching-ta Fan Hung hsien-sheng" [A respectful reply to Mr. Fan Hung], *KC,* Dec. 13, 1947, pp. 5-6; (d) Fan Hung, "Wo tui-yü chung-kuo cheng-chih wen-t'i te ken-pen k'an-fa" [My basic view of China's political problems], *KC,* Dec. 27, 1947, pp. 5-6; (e) Chang Tung-sun, "Kuan-yü chung-kuo ch'u-lu te k'an-fa: tsai ta Fan Hung hsien-sheng" [A view on the way out for China: another reply to Mr. Fan Hung], *KC,* Jan. 31, 1948, pp. 3-4.

116. Fan Hung, "Kuan-yü 'i p'ing-teng tai-wo chih min-tsu' " [Concerning "a nation which practices equality"], *KC,* June 26, 1948, pp. 7-8. This was Fan's response to criticism of him by Chou Tung-chiao, "Lun 'i p'ing-teng tai-wo te min-tsu' chien lun wo-men te tao-lu" [On "a nation which practices equality" and our path], *KC,* May 22, 1948, pp. 4-6.

117. Sun Pao-i, "Wu yu ai chen-li!" [I love truth more!], *STPP,* Dec. 16, 1947, pp. 10-11.

planned society which must eliminate all obstacles to production, need one even ask whether freedom will be limited and equality harmed? Nor did he seem overly concerned about this. "As for making the plan in such a way that freedom and equality might be preserved to the greatest extent possible," he wrote, "that is an affair for the planner and cannot be described in detail here." There was one point, however, beyond which he was not willing to go. He called it cultural freedom, or absolute freedom of culture and thought, which he posited as the guarantee of a progressive political system. Once the seed of cultural freedom is sown, he concluded, its growth cannot be stopped. It will be able to nurture a tradition of freedom in China.[118]

Chang's views concerning many of the institutions conventionally associated with democracy were consistent with his treatment of the principles of freedom and equality. He argued that an Anglo-American constitutional form of government could not exist in China. For example, it would be impossible to hold free elections because these would be manipulated by the existing powerful cliques to their own advantage. He maintained that the CCP, the KMT, and the Democratic League together represented all the interests in the country. Hence, "when such parties consult together, on the surface it may seem to be only a matter among parties, but in fact it can mean genuine democracy." Toward this end, he placed great emphasis on two concepts: compromise, and checks and balances. These he maintained were the prerequisites for the conduct of democratic politics.[119]

Another who shared some of these views was Liang Shu-ming, who argued that, in view of China's cultural traditions, an Anglo-American form of government could not be established there. He maintained that contesting elections was basically incompatible with the customs and behavior of the people and that a democratic constitution could never survive in China. Like Chang, however, Liang was not willing to dismiss the matter entirely. He suggested that a team of experts might be able to devise some other form of democratic political system which did not entail elections or a Western-style constitution, and which would therefore be more in keeping with China's national character.[120]

By and large, however, this degree of pessimism concerning the future of democratic principles and institutions in China was not shared by the majority of those who expressed their views on the subject in print. On the other hand, no one was willing to argue that the obstacles were not formidable. The economist Ku Ch'un-fan expressed a fairly typical view: although democratic

118. Chang Tung-sun, p. 5 (see above note 114b); and, Chung Tung-sun, pp. 4-6 (see note 115a).

119. Chang Tung-sun, "Chui-shu wo-men nu-li chien-li 'lien-ho cheng-fu' te yung-i" [Reflections on our intention to strive to establish a "coalition government"], *KC*, Apr. 5, 1947, p. 6.

120. Liang Shu-ming, "Yu-kao hsuan tsai, chui-lun hsien cheng" [A forecast of electoral disaster, a search for constitutional government], *KC*, Sept. 20, 1947, pp. 5-10, and Sept. 27, pp. 8-10. Liang's ideas on the inapplicability of Western democracy to China are also outlined in Chi Wen-shun, "Liang Shu-ming and Chinese Communism," *China Quarterly* 41 (Jan.-Mar. 1970): 64-82.

politics had deficiencies as a system of government for China, these could doubtless be overcome—albeit gradually.[121]

Another writer, Kuo Shu-jen, agreed. Arguing specifically against the ideas of Chang Tung-sun and Liang Shu-ming, Kuo reminded them that constitutional democracy was not just a form of government but a way of life and could not be developed overnight. He outlined the difficulties the U.S. had experienced in its own political development. Many of the States had clashed with the federal constitution even after it was ratified. The development of industry had created social injustices which the constitution was powerless to prevent. Politics and administration had often been corrupt, and elections controlled. Yet remedies were gradually and sometimes painfully worked out. On the basis of the American experience he therefore concluded: "We cannot because of someone's control, doubt the system itself and abandon our efforts to carry it out. . . . The ideals of this system must become a habitual part of the lives of the people so that the system can become a part of our culture. As for the deficiencies, we can continually work to overcome them."[122]

Actually, the tendency was to look to England rather than to the U.S. Many of these intellectuals saw in the British Labour Party the best model for China to follow. Its victory in 1946 provided a real-life example to support the contention that the goals of Western style democracy and socialism could indeed be pursued simultaneously. "If the British Labour Party succeeds in power," wrote Ch'u An-p'ing, "then it will be clear to the people of the world that it is not necessary to follow the way of Moscow in order to realize socialism. The Labour Party is on the one hand carrying out a policy of socialism, but at the same time still recognizes the free will of the people."[123]

THE MEANS: COALITION GOVERNMENT

Fan Hung may have been justified in his impatience with these "contemporary professors" who advocated a "third way," assuming that the exploiters, oppressors, and the KMT would voluntarily reform themselves and abandon the system that had nurtured them. But if they were politically naive, the professors were at least intellectually consistent. They also believed that the CCP could be persuaded, as Ch'u An-p'ing wrote, "to correct its policies" and abandon its role in the Civil War.[124] Not one among them was willing to argue that the ultimate or

121. Ku Ch'un-fan, "Ts'ung min-chu tao ti-kuo" [From democracy to imperialism], *KC,* Nov. 1, 1947, pp. 3-5. Ku was a bank official.

122. Kuo Shu-jen, "Hsien-cheng ho chung-kuo wen-hua" [Constitutional government and China's culture], *KC,* Mar. 13, 1948, pp. 6-8. The author was living in the U.S. when he wrote this article.

123. Ch'u An-p'ing, p. 6 (note 1 above).

124. Many expressed this view. The economist Wu Ch'i-yuan wrote that the Communists "should abandon their life-and-death struggle and the attempt to set up a proletarian dictatorship by armed revolution. They should learn to become a constitutional party within a constitutional government, be willing to promote democracy, and be satisfied with this." As for the KMT, he suggested that its officials should be willing to compromise and, "in accordance with the hopes of the people of the nation and the majority of the KMT's own members, immediately implement democracy and force the wealthy classes to make some sacrifices" (*KC,* Sept. 7, 1946, pp. 4-5—see note 67).

long-term objective of the CCP was anything but the realization of communism in China. As noted, however, most of them did not believe that the CCP would ever be in a position to do so. Thus to the liberal intellectual, committed to neither of the two warring parties, the perceived military stalemate was thought to provide sufficient incentive for voluntary compromises on both sides. As such, it also seemed to provide an ideal opportunity for the promotion of a centrist alternative.

There was also more or less general agreement concerning the political structure within which the liberal alternative might best be achieved. Liberals pinned their hopes on a coalition government as agreed upon by the Political Consultative Conference at its meeting in January, 1946.[125] Wang Yun-sheng described the PCC agreements in this way:

> Among them the reorganization of the government was primary. Because all of the various political parties were to participate in the reorganization of the government, it was to be coalition in nature. This government was then to be used in the convocation of a national assembly and the writing of a constitution. It would be a transitional government to be replaced by democratic general elections and a constitutional government. In this way, the line of the PCC could be transformed into the way of a democratic constitutional government.[126]

The idea of a coalition government also appealed to those not overly sanguine about the workability of constitutional democracy in China. Chang Tung-sun felt a coalition government to be the political form best suited to China's needs:

> I have seen some people cursing and others praying, but besides this I have seen nothing else being done. Yet the KMT is not afraid of curses and does not heed prayers. It thinks only superficial thoughts about changing itself and continues to hold its old privileged position. Because of this, we want to change the nature of the KMT, and to do so we must first create an environment in which there will be supervision and force on all sides, to force those who will not change voluntarily to reform themselves. And this . . . can only be realized through a coalition government. We obviously oppose the KMT, but we want to save it. Nor would it be easy to make a revolution against it. No one today can overthrow the KMT.[127]

THE PROCESS: PERSUASION

Thus, in the words of Professor Wu Shih-ch'ang, there were many reasons but only one way. The most basic problem, therefore, was how to induce the KMT and the CCP to respect the resolutions of the PCC and join together in a

125. Some criticized the PCC because only representatives of political parties had participated and the people were not directly represented. But, because it was a genuine multi-party meeting that—in principle, at least—had resolved all the chief obstacles to the peaceful evolution of a constitutional government, most liberals clung to the PCC resolutions as the basis for the political compromise they had in mind (see above, note 15).

126. Wang Yun-sheng, "Chung-kuo shih-chü ch'ien-t'u te san-ko ch'ü-hsiang" [Three directions for China's future], *KC,* Sept. 1, 1946, p. 5.

127. Chang Tung-sun, p. 6 (note 119 above).

coalition government. The only answer was a third party or group of some sort. This was conceptualized as a genuine third force based upon the support of the broad mass of the population, which deplored the war, was dissatisfied with the KMT, and did not quite trust the CCP. The reasoning was that if the strength of this hitherto unmobilized majority could be properly channeled, it could somehow compel the two parties to lay down their arms and accept a coalition government.

It was acknowledged that this might be easier said than done, and on one point there was almost universal agreement: the Democratic League and the various minor parties, as then constituted, were incapable of performing the task. The existing parties which made up the so-called "third force" were at best dismissed as weak, disorganized, and powerless. No one contradicted Ch'u An-p'ing when he presented his verdict. "Our criticism of the Democratic League," he wrote, "can be summed up in two phrases: 'its natural endowments are weak, and it is out of tune with reality.' " The people in the League were mostly "of another generation," old scholars, thinkers, and philosophers—without a real politician among them. Having diverse educational backgrounds, political viewpoints, and experience, the only thing holding them together was their spirit of opposition to the KMT. Concluded Ch'u, "the Democratic League is hardly even worth being criticized as the tail of the Communist Party."[128]

At worst, the members of these minor parties, whether avowed liberals or not, were ridiculed as opportunists and pawns of the two major parties. These men often tried to justify their political activities as necessary for the realization of their ideals. But in the eyes of their critics, they always seemed more preoccupied with the acquisition of wealth, position, and social recognition.

What then was to be done? How was a strong and independent third force to emerge, and what form should it take? Chang Tung-sun had suggested that such a force could serve as a "bridge between the CCP and the KMT, forcing each onto the right track, bringing them together, and achieving cooperation between them." But one writer wondered where such a force was to come from—since the forces which then existed between the Communists and the KMT were most certainly neither strong nor independent.[129]

In fact, the question represented the moment of truth for liberal intellectuals. In trying to answer it, the contradiction between their own ideals and the reality of the existing situation was fully exposed. For the most common response to the question of how a third force might emerge, was quite simply that this was the responsibility and the mission of the intellectuals themselves. Professor Chou Chung-ch'i stated this as well as any:

[T]here is only one road left to follow and that is to allow the middle parties to lead the revolution and to set up a new government. What are the third

---

128. Ch'u An-p'ing, p. 7 (note 1 above). For a similar but more detailed critique of the Democratic League, see Wen Fu, "Look out, China Democratic League", *The Weekly*, Shanghai, June 8, 1946 *(CPR, June 22)*.

129. Ch'ang Ming, p. 33 (note 86 above).

parties? They are the pro-peace elements among the intellectuals and liberals; they have intelligence, faith, and expertise; they understand the needs of the people and can get their support. If they can carry out socialism, lead the revolution, and organize a coalition government of many parties, it may take thirty years. But these are the kinds of people who must stabilize China and complete the final stage of the revolution. China today must rely on the efforts of the intellectuals.[130]

Not everyone subscribed to this view, of course. One writer scoffed at the "innocence" of so-called liberal elements who "delude themselves by believing that they have the power to reform the situation."[131] Another gave more detailed expression to such doubts in the process of discussing the rumor that Hu Shih was planning to organize a political party.[132] In his own ambivalence on the matter, Ch'u An-p'ing seemed to sum up these contradictions between the many who felt the intellectuals could "save China" and the few who understood that they could not. His views were developed most fully in an article, "China's Political Situation," which appeared in March, 1947:

> In addition to the Democratic League and the Democratic-Socialist Party, liberal elements can also be found in university and cultural circles. Their numbers are great but they are dispersed . . . their strength is hidden, it is not on the surface; it is the strength of moral not political power; it is limited to the influence of thought and speech and is not the strength of political action.
>
> When he was in China, Marshall said that the utmost effort should be exerted to encourage this group of truly liberal elements to organize themselves. But no matter how well Marshall may have understood the Chinese political situation, he is after all an American with an American point of view, and is therefore somewhat cut off from the situation here. Liberal elements do not easily form themselves into strong organizations and there are reasons for this.

Some of those reasons, Ch'u suggested, were inherent in the nature of Chinese intellectuals themselves, and some had grown out of the political environment of KMT China. Whatever their virtues, the inherent vices of Chinese liberals—for the most part literary men—were their narrow-mindedness and their individualism. Politics required farsighted individuals who would struggle for the big things

130. Chou Chung-ch'i, "Lun ko-ming" [On revolution], *KC,* Jan. 25, 1947, p. 10. Chou was formerly a professor at Lingnan University in Canton.

131. Nanking correspondent, "Ho-ch'u shih kuei-ch'eng?" [Where will the journey end?], *KC,* July 17, 1948, pp. 11-12.

132. This rumor was current for a time after Hu's return from the U.S. in 1946. The writer, noting that Chang Chün-mai (Carsun Chang) of the Democratic-Socialist Party was a "very learned Ph.D" but had little success in leading his party, commented that politics and education were not the same—nor were the requisites for engaging successfully in them. The writer felt that Hu Shih would be able to provide general ideas, but questioned whether he would be able to offer effective leadership when it came to the concrete programs essential to sustain a political party. See, Nanking dispatch, "Hu Shih te t'ai-tu" [Hu Shih's attitude], *KC,* Sept. 1, 1946, p. 21.

rather than quibble over the small, people who could concern themselves with the whole situation and could accept the principle of cooperation in the interests of political action. Such action required organization and discipline; but because liberals were more concerned with right and reason than with power, it was not easy to develop organizational strength among them. Political action also required leadership; but because of their pride and imprudence, it was difficult to produce leaders among liberal elements.

Beyond these inherent weaknesses, Ch'u listed three that had been imposed on the liberals by twenty years of KMT rule. First were the political restrictions resulting from the Government's refusal in practice to guarantee such basic rights as the freedoms of the press, speech, and assembly. Second were the economic restrictions resulting from the impoverishment of the intellectual community. Its members could just barely keep body and soul together, and lacked the time, energy, and resources necessary for political activities. Third were the restrictions on thought resulting from twenty years of KMT interference in education. Not only had this failed to produce loyal followers for the KMT among the youth but, more importantly, it had given them a poor education. Thus instead of being able to cope in a rational manner with their dissatisfaction, many young people were simply overcome by it, and turned blindly to the extremes of right and left.

Then suddenly, without warning or even a paragraph of explanation, Ch'u shifted the line of his argument and took up almost precisely where General Marshall had left off. He continued:

Although liberal elements have suffered from the above kinds of restrictions, objectively speaking their strength at present is growing daily. This growing strength is not due to their own efforts, however, but is a result of the times. From the viewpoint of morality and thought, it is not the Communists but this group of liberal intellectuals that can shake the KMT regime today. Because everyone fears the CCP, fears the violence of their killing and burning; and no matter whether or not this fear is misconceived, people are still afraid of the Communists. On the other hand, it is not the KMT that can repulse the Communists, but this same group of liberals. The corruption of the KMT is already luminously displayed for every eye to see and is being recorded by every tongue. So that even if it is a question of the Three People's Principles, it is difficult for the people to maintain hope and trust in the KMT. Given these two extremes, only if the liberal elements come forward as leaders can a stable mean be achieved which is compatible with the sense of rectitude of the general population. We have said that today in China, this group of liberal elements is very dispersed, and that morality is the source of their strength. The strength of morality is without form, nor can it be seen or grasped; but that strength is deep and can be long-lasting. This strength has its roots in the society and in the hearts of people. . . .

The absolute majority [of the people] hope that a new force can be produced outside the CCP and the KMT, in order to stabilize the present political situation in China. . . . In China at the present time, most all of the liberal elements are depressed and anxious about the nation's future. But they absolutely cannot stop there with their passive feelings of distress and anxiety. The liberal elements can and should rise up; this is not a question of whether or not they would like to do so, or are willing to do so. It is a question of their historical responsibilities.

Such a contradiction could only have been born of desperation. On the basis of his own analysis, Ch'u should have concluded that it was not a question of whether liberal elements were willing to rise up, but whether they would be able to do so. A year later, after the Democratic League had been banned and the Democratic-Socialist Party discredited by its alliance with the KMT, the intellectuals had progressed no further. They were still "suffering great mental anguish" over the future of the nation; still exhorting one another to trade passive criticism and despair for positive action; still reminding themselves that it was their duty to abandon academic pursuits if necessary in order to save the nation and bring it under civilian rule.[133]

The exhortations reached a climax during the National Assembly meeting in April, 1948. On March 26, Nanking professors made public the reform proposals listed above. Also in the capital, the preparatory committee for a Professors' Advisory Organization for National Affairs was formed at this same time, and intellectuals in the North organized an Association for Sociological and Economic Research.[134] Yet no one seemed very clear as to just what role these groups should play. They were supposed to be representing the "will of the people," but what that meant in concrete terms was never spelled out.

Party politics had fallen into such disrepute that the formation of a new political party was not even seriously considered. It would be difficult indeed, explained the *Hsin min pao,* for a few scattered liberals to form a new party that could overthrow both the KMT and the CCP. If such a party opted for a policy of compromise or appeasement with either of them, it could hardly remain neutral or independent. The power necessary to stop the Civil War lay instead with "the Chinese people." The solution therefore: let liberals act according to the wishes of the people, stand by the people, look for support from the people, and represent the will of the people, and the liberals would have nothing to worry about as regards their political influence.[135] In this version, the will of the people was conceptualized as a kind of organic force that liberal intellectuals were somehow supposed to embody. Formless and faceless, their political influence would then presumably rise up to be borne along by the tide of the general will.

Perhaps a last remnant of the ancient association in China between public affairs and men of letters, this "solution" of the intellectuals was hopelessly out

133. *Hsin min pao,* Nanking, Apr. 1, 1948 *(CPR).*

134. *Hsin min pao,* Nanking, Apr. 8 and 11, 1948 (*CPR,* Apr. 8 and 12).

135. From two editorials in the Nanking edition of the *Hsin min pao* on Apr. 11 and May 7, 1948 (*CPR,* Apr. 12 and May 7). This paper was permanently banned on July 8 under Article 21 of the Press Law, which stipulated that publications were not to disturb public order or injure the interests of the nation. The paper was charged with disseminating Communist propaganda, undermining the prestige of the Government, and criticizing the Government's bombing of Kaifeng after its capture by Communist forces.

of touch with the reality of Chinese politics in 1948. Not enough time was left to devise a liberal democratic solution for China. And even if there had been, one cannot but question whether these intellectuals would have been capable of participating effectively in it. The pages of *Kuan-ch'a* and other liberal publications of the period bore testimony to the feats of criticism and moral exhortation that liberal intellectuals performed during the Civil War years. But, as Ch'u An-p'ing and his colleagues sometimes pointed out, criticism however incisive and exhortations however forceful, were not enough. What was needed were practical solutions, and people with the resources necessary to implement them.

Given their own political commitments and the political environment in which they found themselves, it was inevitable that the liberals should fail in their effort to influence the course of the struggle between the KMT and the CCP. They were too far removed from the forces that defined the nature and meaning of the struggle and would therefore decide its outcome. By law and by custom, these intellectuals were exempt from military service. By inclination, they preferred the cosmopolitan environment of Shanghai or Peiping to the intellectual isolation of rural China. However great their concern and sympathy for the peasant's plight, they could express it only on paper—in abstract terms, as it were. So to others, less repelled by daily contact with war and village life, would go the privilege of deciding the issues these intellectuals had debated so eloquently. Perhaps their greatest tragedy was, appropriately enough, more intellectual than political: they failed to comprehend the fact of their own irrelevance.

Ch'u An-p'ing finally understood this in the summer of 1948. His concession of defeat appeared in the July 17 issue of *Kuan-ch'a* as a "farewell editorial." It was prompted by well-placed rumors that his journal was about to suffer the same fate that had befallen the *Hsin min pao* ten days before. Ch'u wrote in part:

> Finally, we are willing to say quite frankly that although the Government fears our criticism, in fact we now have no more interest in criticizing this Government. As for this journal, already in the past few months there have been few articles containing heated criticism of the Government because everyone is very despondent. What else is there to say? And what use would it be? We feel that when a government has reached a stage that the people are not even interested in criticizing it, then such a government is already in tragic enough straits. Unfortunately, the Government does not even have this much self-awareness, but is still pulling at heads and ears, planning to ban journals and newspapers. How really pitiful and laughable. We want to tell all our friends who are concerned about us: let them ban us or not, we are past caring. If we are banned, we ask that no one be sad. In this age of bloodshed, when untold numbers of lives have been sacrificed, buildings and property destroyed, families separated, and so many ideals and hopes have been shattered under this dark rule, what does it matter if this one small journal is banned. Friends, we should face the facts and the oppression and remain determined in our loyalty to the nation. If today one method does not work,

then tomorrow use another and continue the effort. Because although methods may be dissimilar, our loyalty to the nation will never waver.

As it turned out, twenty-one more issues of *Kuan-ch'a* were published after Professor Ch'u wrote his farewell editorial. The journal was finally banned in late December. But in the intervening months, it was clear at last that the time for talking liberal politics in China was finished. The tones of outrage and urgency that had given life to the arguments during the past two years were gone. "The Age of Professor Ch'u An-p'ing" had indeed come to an end.

In December just before the journal was banned, Shanghai newspapers reported that both Ch'u and his friend Wang Yun-sheng of the *Ta kung pao* had left the city for an unknown destination. In January, the mystery of their whereabouts was solved when the Communist radio reported that Ch'u and Wang and many others were in the liberated areas attending a meeting of the Political Consultative Conference at Shihchiachuang. Before the year was out, most of the liberal intellectuals who had raised their voices so persistently against the KMT Government would make a similar decision, either crossing into Communist territory as Ch'u had done or simply waiting with words of welcome for the victor.

PART TWO

The Communist Alternative

VI
The Intelligentsia's Critique of the Chinese Communists

By the late 1940s, there were few sectors of Chinese society that had neither experienced nor witnessed at close hand the adverse effects of KMT rule. Public dissatisfaction had been given overt expression in the form of recurrent student demonstrations, labor disputes, rice riots, civil unrest, peasant uprisings, and a steady stream of criticism from the intelligentsia. Authoritative pronouncements and decrees of the Central Government and its local representatives were openly defied by students, workers, businessmen, industrialists, financiers, and peasants, and held up for public condemnation by the liberal press and the academic community.

The KMT could have saved itself, in the eyes of its critics, but gave repeated evidence of being both unwilling and unable to do so. As a result, each group in its own way and for its own reasons withheld support and cooperation from the Government in its pursuit of the one objective that it deemed most essential to its survival, namely, the military defeat of the Chinese Communists.

An important question, however, remained: whether, and to what extent, the support and allegiance being withdrawn from the KMT could be transferred to the CCP. The question can be examined directly with regard to only one sector of the urban population—the liberal intelligentsia. We have already seen that both the students and their elders were more than willing to accept the CCP as a partner with the KMT in a coalition government. Liberal intellectuals openly advocated this alternative as being preferable to a protracted civil war. Nevertheless, if the student polls cited in Chapter Three are any indication, only a small minority favored national rule by the CCP alone. What considerations underlay this seeming contradiction? What prompted so little enthusiasm for the CCP among a group so obviously disillusioned with its chief antagonist?

Given the constraints under which they wrote and published in the KMT areas, an open and sustained examination of the Communist alternative was not possible. But occasional comments and evaluations—especially if they were in some way critical—were possible. What follows here is a summary of these views concerning the Chinese Communists. This may serve also as an introduction to the more detailed account in subsequent chapters concerning the manner in which the CCP approached the same types of problems that were undermining public support for the Government.

The intelligentsia's comments on the CCP were in many respects different from their critique of the KMT. Intellectuals in the KMT areas were naturally more familiar with the policies and performance of the Government than those of the CCP. Second, since they felt that the Government was in large measure responsible for the existing political situation, and that it still possessed the power to reform itself and end the war, they concentrated their efforts on the Government in the hope of compelling such action from it. By contrast, the CCP was relegated to the position of an opposition party which had yet to occupy any position of national power. This treatment of the CCP may have owed as much to the political restrictions under which the liberal press was operating as to the political biases of the liberals themselves. Nevertheless, their critique of the CCP, while admittedly based on less than ample information, gives the impression of having been made in good faith and was in all respects consistent with their fundamental ideological commitments.

As with their treatment of the Government, the liberals' discussion of the CCP revolved around two central concerns: the performance of the CCP in the areas it controlled, or occupied briefly; and the form of Communist rule. Whereas the KMT Government proved vulnerable on both counts, the CCP's rating on the liberal balance sheet contained only one unequivocal minus. The liberal reaction to major aspects of the Communists' program ranged from positive to mixed. Political life under Communist rule, on the other hand, drew a generally negative response.

Ch'u An-p'ing summed up the liberal view rather succinctly in March, 1947. Noting that he himself had never lived in any area controlled by the CCP, he nevertheless acknowledged that much good concerning the Communists' work was said by those who had. He acknowledged also that, in terms of economic principles, there was little to fear from the CCP. What was fearful, in his view, were Communist methods of political action. He continued:

> Frankly, although the CCP is today crying out loudly about its 'democracy' we would like to know whether, in terms of its basic spirit, the CCP is not really an anti-democratic political party. Because in terms of their spirit of control, there is actually not much difference between Communist and fascist parties. Both try to control the popular will by strict organization. Today in China's political struggle the CCP . . . is encouraging everyone to rise up and oppose the 'party rule' of the KMT. But in terms of the CCP's real spirit, what the CCP advocates is also 'party rule' *[tang chu]* and is certainly not rule by the people *[min-chu]*.[1]

1. Ch'u An-p'ing, "Chung-kuo te cheng-chü" [China's political situation], *KC,* Mar. 8, 1947, p. 6. Information about the CCP was a serious problem. *Kuan-ch'a* and other liberal publications did, however, publish a fair number of articles about the CCP areas. These were based on interviews with persons who had lived in some Communist area, or were reports of correspondents in the field who were able to spend some time in or close to a Communist-controlled region. These provided some alternative to the official Government version of Communist activities.

POLICIES AND PERFORMANCE

In terms of CCP policies and their implementation, the issues attracting the most attention and eliciting the most positive response were almost all related in some way to the war itself. As we have seen, one of the reasons the intellectual community refused to support the Government on the war was the heavy price being exacted from the population because of it. That price included the burdens imposed upon the peasantry in the form of taxation, government purchase and borrowing of grain, increased opportunities for official peculation, the abuses associated with military conscription, and the depredations of a poorly disciplined army in the field.

The Communists did not emerge entirely blameless in liberal eyes on all these counts. Nevertheless, some liberal intellectuals were aware that, however great the wartime sufferings of the people, the Communists—unlike the Government— were managing to increase their strength among the peasantry in the very process of fighting the war. Whereas KMT officials and their local allies continued to use the war as a source of personal gain, the Communists were using it to broaden their base of popular support in the countryside.[2] Liberal writers ascribed the Communists' success to: their social and economic policies; the relative competence and integrity with which those policies were being implemented; and the discipline of the Communist armies.

IN MANCHURIA

As noted in Chapter Five, the shortcomings of the KMT administration in the Northeast after World War II were widely known and discussed. It was also known, but not quite so freely discussed, that the Communists were skillfully taking advantage of the Government's mistakes. A key goal of the KMT's reoccupation policy in Manchuria was the extension of direct Central Government control over the area. To recapitulate, a number of measures were utilized to seek this end. The Government partitioned the three Northeast provinces into nine administrative units and filled virtually all the top posts therein with outsiders. Remaining suspicious of the Northeast troops, the Government refused to allow them to participate in the take-over there when the Russians withdrew in 1946. The Government's local allies included landlords and others who had collaborated with the Japanese, but were the only elements loyal neither to the Communists nor to the still-popular Young Marshal, Chang Hsueh-liang. In late 1946 or early 1947, the Young Marshal, still under arrest for his part in the Sian Incident ten years before, was moved to a more secure exile in Taiwan.

According to the Government's liberal critics, the Communists took full advantage of the widespread resentment these measures aroused. Because the Communists understood the importance of avoiding the. Central Government's arrogant attitude toward the people of the Northeast, they used local talent and personnel in as many political and military positions as possible. Most of the

2. Yang Jen-keng, "Lun nei-chan" [On the civil war], *KC,* Mar. 20, 1948, p. 5.

surviving men and units from the old Northeast Army of Chang Tso-lin and Chang Hsueh-liang went over to the Communists, as did one of the latter's younger brothers, General Chang Hsueh-szu. The Communists welcomed them as allies and allowed them to retain their identity as a non-Communist force under the overall command of Lin Piao. Chang Hsueh-szu also occupied a prominent position as Governor of Liaoning province and as a vice-chairman of the Northeast Administrative Commission, the highest administrative body for the Communist-controlled areas of Manchuria.[3]

Communist troops in the area contained a substantial proportion of Northeasterners. Lin Piao's forces there, said to total about 300,000 men by mid-1946, were known as the Northeast Democratic Allied Army. It contained three distinct components. One was the Northeast People's Self-Defense Army led by Chou Pao-chung. This was the former Northeast Anti-Japanese Allied Army, a Communist force that suffered heavy losses as a result of the Japanese campaign against it beginning in 1938. By 1940, the survivors had mostly been forced underground where they remained until 1945. A few small bands managed to sustain a low level of guerrilla activity from mountain hideouts. Some sat out the remainder of the Japanese occupation in prison camps. After the Japanese surrender, the remnants of this force emerged from underground and prison and promptly began operations in collaboration with the Soviet occupation troops. Re-named the Northeast People's Self-Defense Army, it numbered about 150,000 men by mid-1946 as a result of organizing efforts among the local population.

The People's Self-Governing Army made up a second contingent of Lin Piao's Manchurian force. This was the former Northeast Army of the Old and Young Marshals, units of which had been led by Chang Hsueh-szu in north China during the Anti-Japanese War. After 1938, these troops participated in guerrilla activities, cooperating with the Communists in central and southern Hopei, the Hopei-Shantung-Honan Border Region, and the Shansi-Chahar-Hopei Border Region. When they left north China for Manchuria in 1945, these Northeast troops numbered only about 3,000. Many former comrades rejoined the ranks, however, and by mid-1946 they contained an estimated 25,000 men.

The third element of the Communist force in the Northeast was the Eighth Route Army, actually made up of contingents from both the Eighth Route and New Fourth Armies. These units—some of them commanded by Northeastern generals—moved into Manchuria by junk from Shantung, and overland on foot via Hopei, Jehol, and Suiyuan in October and November, 1945.[4]

3. See these articles in *KC:* (a) July 12, 1947, pp. 4-5, Ho Yung-chi (see below note 9); (b) Mar. 13, 1948, pp. 15-16, "Pei wang man-chou" [Looking north to Manchuria] ; (c) Mar. 27, 1948, p. 16, Ch'ien Pang-k'ai (see Chapter Two, note 4); (d) Apr. 3, 1948, p. 17, Kao Ch'ao (see below note 8).

4. Hung Hsu, "The beacon fire of Changchun", *WHP,* Shanghai, June 11, 1946 (*CPR,* June 18 and 19). Also Lu Te-jen "Autumn in spring", *TKP,* Shanghai, Apr. 20, 1946 (*CPR,* Apr. 26).

Concerning the first component, some remnants of the Northeast Anti-Japanese Allied Army, including Chou Pao-chung himself, had fled across the border into Soviet territory

Correspondents in Mukden and Changchun were fond of writing that all the armies—Russian, Chinese Communist, and Central Government—were equally unpopular.[5] Nevertheless, different reports told different tales and while no one seemed to have a good word for either the Government or the Russian troops, the Chinese Communists enjoyed a somewhat better average. For example, there was the writer, quoted in the previous chapter, who had spent ten days in his native village about 120 *li* from the city of Szupingkai in early 1947. Government and Russian troops had made uniformly negative impressions upon the local people. But the Chinese Communists, who had occupied the area for a short time, apparently behaved rather well. They did carry off many items including X-ray and blood transfusion equipment from the 150-bed Japanese-built *hsien* hospital when they withdrew, although they did not touch the peasants' personal belongings.

Throughout the Japanese occupation, the local people had not been aware, they said, that there were two different kinds of Chinese troops. But they soon learned to recognize the difference; and about the Communists they now "maintained somewhat more hope." The writer expressed some cynical comments about how little it took to satisfy simple people, but nevertheless admitted that his mother was favorably impressed by a group of Communist soldiers who had been billeted with the family. They had respected her wishes, had not bothered her sixteen-year-old granddaughter, and had taken nothing that did not belong to them when they left.[6]

Similarly positive reports circulated about the Communist treatment of prisoners-of-war, whether military officers and men or civilian government

---

and returned to Manchuria with Soviet forces in August, 1945. Concerning the second and third components, Commander-in-Chief Chu Teh, on Aug. 11, 1945, ordered four generals to move their troops into the Northeast to cooperate with the advancing Soviet Army. The four were the non-Communist Chang Hsueh-szu, with forces then in Hopei and Chahar, and three Communist generals: Li Yun-ch'ang, in the Hopei-Jehol-Liaoning border area; Wan I, in Shantung and Hopei; and Lü Cheng-ts'ao, in Shansi and Suiyuan. Generals Lü and Wan were natives of Liaoning in Manchuria, and had served under both the Old and Young Marshals. See Hu Hua, *et al.*, ed., *Chung-kuo hsin min-chu-chu-i ko-ming shih ts'an-k'ao tzu-liao*, pp. 401-402.

The Northeast Democratic Allied Army was formed on Jan. 1, 1946, with four military regions. These regions, their military commanders, and political commissars were: (1) Jehol-Liaoning (western Manchuria), Lü Cheng-ts'ao, Li Fu-ch'un; (2) Kirin-Liaoning (eastern Manchuria), Chou Pao-chung, Lin Feng; (3) Kirin-Heilungkiang (northern Manchuria), Kao Kang, Ch'en Yun; (4) Liaotung (southern Manchuria), Ch'eng Shih-ts'ai, Hsiao Hua. Lin Piao had overall command, with P'eng Chen as political commissar. See Chou Erh-fu, "Yueh-liang shang-sheng te shih-hou" [When the moon rises], *Ch'un-chung* [Masses], Shanghai, July 7, 1946, p. 21.

5. See, for example, the following reports in *KC:* (a) Shenyang correspondent, "Shenyang wan han" [Mukden in late winter], Dec. 21, 1946, pp. 17-18; (b) Changchun correspondent, Mar. 1, 1947, p. 18 (see Chapter Five, note 81); (c) Kao Ch'ao, Feb. 28, 1948, pp. 17-18 (see Chapter Five, note 67).

6. Han Ch'i, "Tung-pei shih jih" [Ten days in the Northeast], *STPP*, Aug. 16, 1947, pp. 25-28.

personnel.[7] The good treatment was said to be particularly effective in encouraging the men to surrender. They were given a choice as to whether they wished to join the Communist forces or return home. Those who chose the latter were given cigarettes and travelling money and sent on their way.

Thus the same correspondent who deplored the hardships the war created for the people of the Northeast also acknowledged in April, 1948, that the Government was indulging in wishful thinking if it really believed it could win popular support for a military showdown with the Communists there. This was so, he wrote, because Communist troops there had already "entered deeply among the people."[8] Despite the thousands of students, civil servants, businessmen, and other people of means who did not wish to live under Communist rule and had fled to the KMT-held cities south of the Sungari River, many thousands more had joined the Communists. Hence it was often said after the Taiwanese revolt in February, 1947, that a similar uprising had not occurred in the Northeast because everyone there who wanted to rebel had already gone over to the Communist side.[9] One writer summed up the situation in the following manner:

It should be known that when the Chinese Communists pull up the railway tracks, or bury land mines, or explode bombs, it is not the Communists that are doing it; the common people are doing it for them. The Chinese Communists had no soldiers in the Northeast; now they have the soldiers not wanted by the Central Government. The Chinese Communists had no guns; now they have the guns the Central Government managed so poorly and sent over to them, and sometimes even secretly sold to them. The Chinese Communists had no men of ability; now they have the talents the Central Government has abandoned.[10]

AND ELSEWHERE

Manchuria was not the only place where Government forces suffered by comparison with the Communists. This turned out to be a familiar story in almost every field area with which inquiring correspondents came into contact. *Kuan-ch'a* published favorable reports concerning the behavior of Communist troops in many different localities, some by writers who disapproved of other aspects of the Communist program. The localities included the Kiangsu-Chekiang-Anhwei Border Region; T'aihsing *hsien*, Kiangsu, on the north bank of the Yangtze; central Hopei; western Shensi; Kansu; and southern Shansi.[11]

---

7. Shenyang correspondent, "Ha-erh-pin kuei-lai" [Return from Harbin], *KC*, Sept. 13, 1947, pp. 21-22; letter signed Yuan Yun-lan, Mukden, Feb. 17, 1948 (*KC*, Feb. 28, 1948, p. 2).

8. Kao Ch'ao, "Fa-pi ch'u kuan yü liu-t'ung-ch'üan pien-chih so chi-ch'i te po-lang" [Nationalist government currency enters the Northeast and the tide of Manchurian currency devaluation rises], *KC*, Apr. 3, 1948, p. 17.

9. Ho Yung-chi, "Ts'ung yin-tu fen chih shuo-tao chung-kuo ch'ien-t'u" [Talking about the partition of India and China's future], *KC*, July 12, 1947, pp. 4-5. On refugees in the Northeast, see Chapter Five under "Political Incompetence: Refugees."

10. Ch'ien Pang-k'ai, pp. 16, 14 (see note 3(c) above).

11. See the following articles in *KC*: (a) Oct. 5, 1946, p. 8, Chu Tung-jun "I have come from T'aihsing". Chu was a professor at National Central University in Nanking; (b) Nov. 9,

The correspondent who reported on the discipline of the First and Sixth Divisions of the New Fourth Army in the Kiangsu-Chekiang-Anhwei area was particularly impressed that there were no officers' wives and concubines following when the troops were on the march; that the Army did not impress civilians for military coolie service; and that officers and men received the same treatment. In addition, the New Fourth went out of its way to make friendly contact with the people, often even paying a bit more than the going price when they had to buy provisions off the local market. As a result, merchants in the area referred to the Army as fourth elder brother *(szu ta-ko)*. But just wait until he has a place securely garrisoned, the reporter cautioned. Then fourth elder brother brings out all of his methods one after another, first registering households, then levying taxes, and finally recruiting soldiers.[12]

Most writers who discussed the matter at all recognized that the Communist successes involved something more than good strategy, clever tactics, and troop discipline. Everyone knew that the Communists controlled entire areas while Government forces were hard put to hold the "points and lines," that is, major cities, towns, and communications arteries. Because they "identified themselves closely with the people," the Communists had plenty of food and manpower for their armies.[13] Similarly, an article in the liberal weekly, *Shih yü wen,* describing conditions in the war zone south of Tientsin, noted that Government forces could not requisition food without resort to armed force. The Communists, on the other hand, had no such difficulties. "Just a slip of paper" in the hand of one of their provisions collectors was enough to ensure that the items would be delivered wherever they were needed.[14]

"The reason is simple," declared another writer:

> The KMT cannot correct its weaknesses and defeat the Communists because the KMT is limited by its social and economic organization. Because the Communist armies have changed production relations and social and economic organization in the liberated areas, they have been able to establish the new social order they need. Grain requisitions, military conscription, and self-defense can therefore be carried out with a high degree of effectiveness. There is no need to use excessive military force to defend the villages and towns they control.[15]

It is not that the Government has not seen these things, asserted yet another correspondent. It knows that in dealing with the Communist armies, politics is

---

1946, pp. 19-20, Special correspondent "This too is a border region"; (c) Dec. 28, 1946, pp. 15-16, Chiangnan correspondent "Conditions in southern Kiangsu"; (d) Sept. 27, 1947, pp. 18-19, Ho P'eng "At the very forefront of the civil war"; (e) Mar. 6, 1948, p. 15, Li Tzu-ching "The struggle situation in the liberated districts of south Shansi"; (f) June 19, 1948, p. 16, Sian correspondent "After the fighting in east Kansu"; (g) July 17, 1948, p. 15, Lanchow correspondent "A report on the most recent situation in the Northwest".

12. See note 11(b) above.

13. *TKP,* Shanghai, Feb. 14, 1947 *(CPR).*

14. *Shih yü wen,* Shanghai, vol. 2, no. 12, Nov. 28, 1947 *(CPR,* Dec. 4).

15. Special correspondent, "K'ung-hsin chan yü ch'üan-hsin chan" [Empty-hearted war and whole-hearted war], *KC,* May 8, 1948, p. 13.

more important than the military. But the Government is not willing to overturn the old society and its tragic fate is thus being sealed.[16]

One of the most positive views of the Communist effort to overturn the old society came from a KMT civil servant who spent three months in Hotse, Shantung, in the Shansi-Hopei-Shantung-Honan Border Region during the summer of 1946. He went there in an official capacity to participate in relief work associated with the rechanneling of the Yellow River. Having little to do, he spent the time talking politics and trying to find out what he could about the Communists. He came away obviously impressed by things he had seen, such as the equalization of wealth, the austere conditions under which Communist officials lived, and most especially by their "administrative work style." "They are completely different from us," he marvelled, noting their sincerity, their sense of responsibility in performing any task, and the meetings afterward at which errors were openly admitted and frankly criticized. Unlike some among us, he wrote, they do not say one thing while knowing in their hearts that it is not so. Of course, he admitted, "the lower-level cadres cannot avoid shallowness and mechanical answers . . . but better they have that ideology than none at all, and better to be conscientious and self-confident as they are than negligent and self-deceiving as we are."

He was impressed by the simplicity of their accounting procedures and their method of handling official documents. Unlike "our rotten accounting system" with its false reports and false accounts, he wrote, they only record actual income and actual expenditure. Since they were not required to waste time and energy on reams of useless official documents and records, Communist officials and administrators could concentrate on the substance of the jobs they had to perform.

He also noted the apparent willingness with which the local people cooperated with the Communists, participating in public works projects, helping with military transport, and the like. He regretted that he had not made a greater effort to discover the exact methods the Communists used to activate, organize, and lead the people. He concluded, nonetheless, that the Communists were able to develop the strength of the common people by adopting the unusual practice of treating them like human beings, explaining things patiently to them, and allowing them to talk back in return. He was especially surprised by the way poor men and women dared to stand on a platform at the struggle meetings and speak out openly against those who had insulted, cheated, and oppressed them. He had witnessed many such meetings while he was in Hotse, including several directed against the German priest and the nuns from the town's Catholic church.

By his observation, the only people in the town and the surrounding district who actually disliked the Communists, in addition to the landlords and rich peasants most of whom had by this time disappeared, were the businessmen.

16. See note 11(g) above. For similar comment specifically on western Honan, see Yeh Chün, "Chieh-k'ai yü-hsi te nei-mu" [Behind the scenes in western Honan], *KC*, Nov. 15, 1947, p. 17.

Many of these had been hurt by the Communists' efforts to control trade with the KMT areas. This had resulted in an "import" ban on many nonessential items such as cigarettes, cosmetics, foreign consumer goods, etc. The leather shoe business had declined due to the demise of its primarily gentry clientele and the growing popularity of cloth shoes. Restaurant owners were doing well, since there was little else to spend extra money on. Some merchants did carry on black market dealings with nearby KMT areas. Because they were trying to be "especially polite" to businessmen, the Communists usually kept "one eye closed" with respect to this trade. Occasionally a merchant was punished for such activities by being paraded through the streets wearing a tall green cap with the words "big bad egg" written on it. As for the peasants, the majority of them seemed to support the Communists whole-heartedly.[17]

Land Reform

Land reform was most often acknowledged as the basis of the CCP's success in changing the social and economic organization of the rural areas.[18] Despite their misgivings about the way it was being implemented, liberal writers tended to accept the Communists' claim that land reform was the source of their strength in the countryside.[19] One school teacher, interviewed in Shanghai shortly after leaving the Communist area in northern Kiangsu, remarked that, although he had never heard them say so, he felt certain the Communists would not have turned so quickly to land reform from the more moderate policy of rent reduction had the Civil War not created the necessity for such a change. "After the farmer receives his share of land," this observer pointed out, "he will naturally think that the only way to preserve his share of land is to follow the CCP to the very end. As a matter of fact, farmers are fearful of measures of revenge from the landlords, and it is highly probable that they will plunge in with the CCP."[20]

One of *Kuan-ch'a's* correspondents expressed the view that the primary objective of the Communists' land reform program was the development of their political and military strength in the countryside. In any event, the results were obvious:

In the liberated areas, land has been changed both in terms of its military uses and in terms of social life. This change has shaken people out of their old ideas about the land. And the deep military strength of the liberated areas has

17. Chiang Sha, "Tsai ho-tse chieh-fang-ch'ü so-chien" [What was seen in Hotse liberated area], *KC,* Mar. 6, 1948, pp. 13-16, 18; and Mar. 13, pp. 12-13.
18. For example, P'u Hsi-hsiu, "Kuo-min-tang san-chung-ch'üan-hui niao-k'an" [A bird's-eye view of the KMT Central Executive Committee's Third Plenary Session], *KC,* Mar. 22, 1947, p. 15; Wu Ch'i-yuan, "Ts'ung ching-chi kuan-tien lun nei-chan wen-t'i" [Talking about civil war problems from an economic view point], *KC,* Sept. 7, 1946, p. 4; and Wu Shih-ch'ang. "Ts'ung mei su shuo-tao kuo-nei" [A discussion about the U.S., U.S.S.R. and internal affairs], *KC,* Apr. 5, 1947, p. 4.
19. See Chapter Seven.
20. Cheng Yueh-chung, "Three stages of the land problem in northern Kiangsu", *Economics Weekly,* Shanghai, vol. 3, no. 18, Oct. 31, 1946 (*CPR,* Jan. 4, 1947).

come as a result of this great change. Under their new social order, they [the Communists] have no problems about sources of grain and manpower.

If the CCP really wants to control the rural areas, he concluded, the land reform movement will enable it to grow roots in the villages and to grow strong, and the KMT is doing nothing to meet this challenge.[21]

The liberal intellectual's willingness to acknowledge the nature of Communist strength in the countryside nevertheless contained a large measure of ambivalence. Indicative of this were the repeated appeals to the Government to find a solution of its own for the problems in the rural areas. Indicative also was the tone of desperation that appeared along with the realization that no such solution was even being sought. "There must be a way out," declared one writer in February, 1948. But at the same time, he acknowledged that the Government had yet to come forward with a concrete program and that, even if it did, there was no one in the rural areas who could be relied upon to implement it.[22]

A few criticized the Communist program of land division and redistribution as economically unsound. Professor Wu Shih-ch'ang wrote that each person would receive only two or three *mou* and no one would be able to earn enough to live. He maintained that only with industrialization, mechanization of agriculture, and collectivization could agricultural production be increased and the standard of living raised.[23]

Nevertheless, the main problem was not so much *what* the Communists were doing in the countryside as *how*. It was not the class struggle movement and the land reform program themselves, but the manner of their implementation that bothered liberal intellectuals most. Expressing this view, an editorial in the *Ta kung pao* asserted that people throughout the country wanted two things. They wanted the CCP to remain faithful to its promise made during the Anti-Japanese War to eschew the path of violent land reform. And they wanted the Government to implement the principle of the people's livelihood which meant limiting private capital and equally distributing land.[24] The sensational reports of struggle meetings, liquidations, beatings, and executions were too numerous and too widespread to be dismissed as the work of a few overzealous or misguided local cadres. Violence apparently had to be calculated as part of the cost of the Communists' rural program, and it created serious misgivings in many minds about the CCP.

One of the few who neither overlooked this cost nor seemed to feel too uncomfortable with it was the civil servant quoted above who had visited Hotse.

21. *KC* correspondent, "Tu-ti kai-ko, ti-tao chan" [Land reform, tunnel warfare], *KC,* Apr. 3, 1948, p. 14.

22. *KC* correspondent, "Ts'ung chan-chü k'an cheng-chü" [Looking at political conditions from the military situation], *KC,* Feb. 28, 1948, p. 16.

23. Wu Shih-ch'ang, p. 5 (see note 18 above). Chu Tung-jun (see note 11a above) was also critical. He did not think much of "dividing shops"—distributing the shop owner's assets and stock among the employees—which he claimed was being done in villages in T'aihsing *hsien,* Kiangsu.

24. *TKP,* Shanghai, Aug. 1, 1946 *(CPR).*

"As for the method of struggle and the killing incidents," he wrote, "I felt it was not quite right. But after rethinking the matter, I also feel that it cannot be avoided." Social organization in China was such that the local officials and gentry had always controlled affairs in the villages, while the peasants stood in an inferior position and had no one to protect their interests. He himself had not witnessed any killings while he was in the liberated areas. But the local newspaper did report such incidents during his stay, and an official told him that those among the landlord class who had abused and harmed the people were sometimes killed.

Thus an urban intellectual could look upon such violence as a form of social justice. The more common response, however, was one of disapproval and apprehension. The reaction of one of *Kuan-ch'a*'s readers to Communist activities in southern Shansi was more typical, albeit more extreme than most. Mentioning briefly the events that had transpired there, which included the physical mutilation and death of a number of landlords at the hands of the peasants, he concluded his letter: ". . . Sir, I want to cry. I can scarcely write down such things. Please print this piece of news. I know your publication is neither KMT nor rightist, nor am I a rightist. But I am speaking bitterness for the people of southern Shansi. My head is all confused with what I see and hear. I stand with the people."[25]

A few months later, *Kuan-ch'a* published a story from the same area describing in fuller detail the events to which this letter had referred. In March, 1947, General Hu Tsung-nan had, as the writer explained, made the strategic mistake of moving troops garrisoned in southern Shansi to attack Yenan—in effect trading thirty reasonably prosperous *hsien* in southern Shansi for forty-five poor and emaciated ones in Shensi. The writer then described how order was quickly established in the districts of southern Shansi after they were taken by the Communists; how the soldiers were withdrawn shortly thereafter; how grain was distributed to the people and the beggars disappeared; and how life became much more calm and peaceful as compared with conditions under Yen Hsi-shan's rule. Most of the teachers fled, so the children were not in school, but they had been assigned to work in the fields or to do other tasks.

After the soldiers withdrew, people's governments were set up at the *hsien,* district, and *ts'un* levels. Cadres were sent out to conduct census investigations with three to five political workers assigned to each village. They sought out the poorest peasants and inquired about the names, occupations, property holdings, family background, and so forth of everyone in the village. The next step was to set up a peasant association with the non-property owners in the village as the basic members. Then all families in the village were formally designated as rich, middle, or, poor peasant with each grade being subdivided into three levels— upper, middle, and lower. Finally came the class struggle movement in which the peasant association, under the guidance of a peasant cadre, played the leading role.

---

25. Letter signed Chang Ch'iang-li, Sian, Oct. 30, 1947 (*KC*, Nov. 8, 1947, p. 2).

The peasant association generally met in the evenings, although there were sometimes several meetings a day. The topics discussed were secret and members generally refused to divulge their nature. But according to the village grapevine, the cadres would speak about how ferocious the rich peasants were, how they exploited the poor, and how the cadres had come to pull the peasants up from poverty and help them to overthrow their exploiters. At the meetings, poor peasants also made reports telling who in the village had money, what they had done in the past, and so forth. Eventually, these people would be brought before a general meeting of the entire village where the most extreme acts of violence usually occurred.

Rich peasants were the first objects of attack. Their property was confiscated and their buildings sealed for future distribution to the poor. Sometimes mistakes were made and people were wrongly classified as rich peasants. Some of these families were said to have been reduced to destitution. The writer claimed that his village contained very few rich peasants, but the property of more than thirty families was confiscated. In another village with only one hundred families, the property of forty was confiscated. Many of these so-called rich peasants could not even run away since members of the village youth or women's brigades stood guard outside the village and refused to let anyone in or out who did not have a pass from the peasant association. In many places, also, confiscated lands, grain, and other property remained undistributed and idle for many months.

The peasants association singled out for public censure those among the wealthy who could be charged with particular instances of abuse and exploitation. Such persons were brought before general village meetings to be struggled against and were often physically assaulted by the villagers. The punishment included stoning, clubbing, beating, and stabbing, and the victims sometimes died as a result. What seemed to disturb the writer more than the specific acts of violence, however, was the arbitrariness with which they were carried out. The village peasant association conducted the class struggle movement and not even village administrative personnel could interfere. He wrote that in the Communist areas, there seemed to be no rule of law, no lawyers, no courts of law, nor any legal safeguards for the individual. The power of life and death was not even held by the local government, but lay instead in the hands of the peasant association cadres.[26]

Equally disquieting were reports from northern Kiangsu. Proximity and the presence of several thousand refugees from the area made information about conditions there relatively accessible to the Shanghai-Nanking intellectual community. And if repeated references are any indication, conditions in northern Kiangsu were responsible for many liberal misgivings about the Chinese Communists. The class struggle movement began in some districts there shortly after the Japanese surrender. Those who had collaborated with the Japanese were brought before the villagers for punishment. Peasants were also encouraged to

26. Li Tzu-ching, p. 15 (see note 11(e) above).

"settle accounts" with landlords and local despots who had accumulated large areas of land at the peasants' expense, charged excessive rentals, exploited tenants and farm laborers, and the like.

One observer who claimed to approve of this liquidation movement "in principle" nevertheless found much to criticize in the manner of its implementation. The problem, he said, was that Chinese society lacked social organization. The peasants had "a characteristic love of revenge," and once such a movement began, it could easily go too far. Thus, despite the work teams that the CCP had sent to guide the class struggle, many people had been unfairly treated and many "deplorable" incidents had occurred.[27]

As indicated in the CCP's key land reform directive of May 4, 1946 (to be analyzed in the following chapter), the Communists were well aware of the unflattering image created by the presence in KMT cities of so many refugees from the liberated areas. Aware, too, of the Central Government's neglect of the refugees, the Communists sought to neutralize some of the criticism directed against them and at the same time capitalize on the Government's failures. The method was a well publicized campaign welcoming back all who cared to return to districts held by the Communists.

A lengthy article in a leftist Shanghai journal undertook to analyze the refugee problem. Acknowledging that many imagined the North Kiangsu Liberated Area to be some sort of "hell" because of the thousands who had fled, the article divided the refugees into six different categories according to the reasons for their flight. Some left because they feared they would be automatically conscripted into the New Fourth Army. Some middle-class people and educated youths fled because they believed the stories that the Communists killed and burned, and shared property and wives. These two groups had obviously been deceived by the KMT's false rumors and anti-CCP propaganda. A third type of refugee was the ordinary landlord who had refused to accept the principle of reduced rent and interest. Evil bullies and bad gentry who had exploited and oppressed the people comprised the fourth type. Those who had been traitors and puppets during the Japanese occupation made up the fifth. Finally, there was a sixth kind of refugee; people who had been frightened off by inexperienced local cadres who had made mistakes in the implementation of Party policies, thus giving people an erroneous impression about the New Fourth Army and the democratic government.

The article emphasized that the Party would welcome the return of refugees from categories one, two, and six. Even landlords would be welcome if they agreed to the reduction of rent and interest. Only traitors and bad elements were warned that they faced punishment should they return and be apprehended.[28]

In the summer and autumn of 1946, a few thousand small and middle landlords, having been rendered penniless by the inflation and other hazards of KMT-controlled Shanghai, did apparently return to the liberated areas in north-

27. See note 20 above.
28. Fan Chang-chiang "Let's start with with the northern Kiangsu refugees", *Wen tsui tsa-chih*, Shanghai, no. 36, June 27, 1946 (*CPR*, July 6).

ern Kiangsu. The local governments there extended relief to them and helped them to find housing and a means of livelihood. Some were given portions of land to till in their native villages equal to that of the average peasant. A few of the returnees were allowed to retain ownership of their own lands once they agreed to adhere to the policy of rent and interest reduction. Earlier in the year, the *Ta kung pao* in a dispatch from Peiping had reported the success of a similar program in north China intended to encourage refugees to return to their native places in the liberated areas there. Landlords were also among the returnees, having been promised protection of their interests if they agreed to abide by the policy of rent reduction.[29]

Knowledge of these Communist efforts (which grew into a major anti-leftist campaign in 1948) probably did ameliorate to some extent the intellectuals' misgivings about the means the Chinese Communists were using to achieve their ends. But there is no evidence to suggest that the misgivings were eliminated. Rather, the ambivalence inherent in the response of liberal intellectuals to the Communist land reform program was related to their more fundamental reservations about political life under Communist rule. Before turning to that concern, however, there was one other that evoked feelings of ambivalence among liberal intellectuals.

The Issue of Nationalism

As mentioned in the preceding chapter, liberals who advocated some form of socialism for China sometimes found themselves criticized on nationalistic grounds. There was a fear, expressed by a number of writers, that a socialist China might in some way become subservient to the Soviet Union. Others who did not share this fear were nevertheless sensitive to the charge and often went to some lengths to disavow the inevitability of any such relationship.

The Chinese Communists, of course, were criticized on the same grounds. Nationalism became a key feature in the Central Government's propaganda campaign against the Communists during this period. One of the main issues in the campaign was the presence and activities in Manchuria of the Soviet Army during 1945-46, and the relationship of the CCP to it.

In accordance with the Yalta Agreement of February 11, 1945,[30] the U.S.S.R. entered the war against Japan on August 9, 1945. Russian troops had just begun entering Manchuria when the Japanese surrendered on August 14, the same day that the Soviet and Chinese Governments announced the conclusion of

29. *TKP*, Shanghai, Mar. 23, 1946 *(CPR)*.

30. Roosevelt, Stalin, and Churchill agreed, without consulting China, that the conditions for Soviet entry into the war against Japan should include the return to Russia of old rights and privileges in Manchuria lost to the Japanese in the Russo-Japanese War. These included: the lease of Port Arthur as a Russian naval base; preeminent interest in the commercial port of Dairen; and shared control of the Chinese Eastern and South Manchurian railways. Chiang Kai-shek was notified in June of this Yalta agreement, and subsequently ratified it in a series of agreements and the Sino-Soviet Treaty of Friendship and Alliance in August, 1945. The Yalta agreement itself was not made public until February, 1946. See Robert C. North, *Moscow and the Chinese Communists*, pp. 215-22.

a Treaty of Friendship and Alliance between the two countries. During the negotiations, Stalin had allegedly assured the Chinese representative, T. V. Soong, that Soviet forces would be withdrawn from Manchuria within three months after a Japanese surrender.

As noted, the Chinese Communists were in a position to take maximum advantage of the period from mid-August to mid-November while the Russians occupied the cities and major lines of communications in the Northeast and no one controlled the countryside. During this period, CCP forces entered Manchuria with the acquiescence if not the active cooperation of the Soviet occupation forces. It is unlikely that the latter could have prevented this penetration even had they tried, which they apparently did not. In addition, they adopted delaying tactics at a number of points thus frustrating the American effort to transport KMT troops to the Northeast as quickly as possible.

By November, 1945, Soviet withdrawal from Manchuria would have meant the immediate occupation of much of the region by the Chinese Communists. The KMT Government therefore negotiated with the Soviets, ultimately obtaining their agreement to extend their stay and also to allow the Americans to transport Government troops to the major cities of Manchuria. January 3, 1946, was set as the new target date for the Soviet withdrawal. The date was extended again to February 1, and extended yet a third time, with the approval of the Chinese Government. The Soviet evacuation of Manchuria was not completed until May, 1946.[31]

While the Manchurian "crisis" was thus developing, the KMT Government, or at least elements within it, launched a propaganda campaign against alleged Soviet cooperation with the Chinese Communists. The Soviets were also denounced for removing and shipping to the U.S.S.R. supplies, equipment, and machinery from Manchurian industrial and mining enterprises. This was an accepted means of extracting war reparations from a defeated country, except that all such installations and equipment in the former Japanese-occupied areas of China were supposed to revert to Chinese ownership. The issue reached a climax in February, 1946, with the publication of the complete text of the Yalta Agreement, and the murder of Chang Hsin-fu, a special commissioner sent by the Government to Manchuria to take over the Fushun coal mines. He and members of his party were dragged from a train and killed in an area garrisoned by Soviet troops.[32]

Criticism of the U.S.S.R. was not limited to official and KMT circles. Public opinion was particularly shocked over the provisions of the Yalta Agreement which restored to the Soviet Union the same sort of special rights and privileges

31. Tang Tsou, *America's Failure in China, 1941-50,* pp. 324-40.
32. The motive and assailants remain a mystery. The Chinese Communist called it "a nationwide conspiracy of reactionaries with Japanese and puppet remnants": *Hsin hua jih-pao,* Chungking, Feb. 27, 1946 *(CPR).* Many others including the leftist *WHP* claimed that Chang Hsin-fu was stabbed to death by Soviet soldiers: *WHP,* Shanghai, Mar. 8, 1946 *(CPR,* Mar. 12). Chiang Kai-shek later implied that the Chinese Communists were responsible: *Soviet Russia in China: A Summing-up at Seventy,* p. 170.

that the young Soviet Government had renounced shortly after the October Revolution. With the exception of the Communist *Hsin hua jih-pao* (Chungking), the leftist *Wen hui pao* (Shanghai), and the Soviet-backed *Shih-tai jih-pao* (Shanghai), expressions of anger erupted in the Chinese press over the readiness of the U.S. and Great Britain to give in to Russian demands that violated China's territorial integrity.

In Chungking, students from fourteen colleges and middle schools went on strike in an appeal for the preservation of China's sovereignty. Professors at National Central University in Nanking met on February 18 and drafted a protest to Great Britain and the U.S. On February 19, a statement issued in the name of three thousand students at the National Provisional University in Nanking urged Soviet troops to withdraw from the Northeast and expressed opposition to the Yalta Agreement. In Shanghai, the entire student body of National Chiaotung University resolved to strike classes in protest.[33] On February 22, the Shanghai General Students Association held a meeting attended by over two hundred students representing Chiaotung University, Aurora University, St. John's, Soochow University, Hangchow Christian College, and other schools. The meeting set up a Shanghai Students Association for the Defense of National Rights.[34]

The anti-Soviet movement within the academic community collapsed almost overnight, however, after it became known that a group of demonstrating "students" had attacked the business office of the *Hsin hua jih-pao* in Chungking, and that the action had apparently been instigated by right-wing elements within the KMT.[35] On February 26, the student body of the Provisional University in Shanghai resolved to call off a planned strike on grounds that it had been "entirely instigated by some agitators who were endeavoring to use the students as tools." Similar action had already been taken by the Shanghai Students Association for the Defense of National Rights, and all strikes and demonstrations were cancelled.[36]

The spontaneity with which the academic community initially responded was nonetheless illustrative of the extent to which feelings could be aroused over the perceived violation of China's national sovereignty. Nor was the CCP able to escape public censure. In an editorial bristling with anti-Soviet barbs, the *Ta kung pao* directed its anger against the Chinese Communists as well. Inasmuch as Government troops have met with such great difficulties and restrictions in the Northeast, the editorial noted, let us ask how Chinese Communist armed forces have managed to enter the Northeast so easily.[37] Similarly, the liberal *Hsin min*

33. *TKP*, Shanghai, Feb. 22, 1946 *(CPR)*.
34. *Ho-p'ing jih-pao*, Shanghai, Feb. 23, 1946 *(CPR)*.
35. This rumor was well substantiated. Even the *Ho-p'ing jih-pao* stated that "it was a portion of the reactionaries who had tried to provoke such an incident to undermine President Chiang's prestige and overthrow the decisions of the People's Consultative Conference." *Ho-p'ing jih-pao*, Shanghai, Feb. 27, 1946 *(CPR)*.
36. *Lih pao* and *Shih-tai jih-pao*, Shanghai, Feb. 27, 1946 *(CPR)*.
37. *TKP*, Shanghai, Feb. 22, 1946 *(CPR)*.

pao maintained that the dispute between the Government and the CCP over the latter's demand that it be allowed to maintain the autonomy of its regional governments was an internal problem. Foreign powers should not intervene. Just as the Government should not use the Manchurian problem as an excuse to ignore the democratic measures recommended by the Political Consultative Conference, so the Chinese Communists owed it to the public to make known their attitude toward the Soviet Union. Sympathy in political concepts, concluded the paper, should not be allowed to override national interests.[38]

Obviously on the defensive but unwilling to criticize the Soviets, the Chinese Communists responded with lengthy analyses that sought to distinguish between patriotism and "anti-alienism." They compared the anti-Soviet movement to the anti-alien Boxer Rebellion, instigated by reactionary elements and manipulated by the Government. The objective of such a movement, claimed the Party paper in Chungking, is not to defend China but to take a blindly antagonistic attitude toward foreign nations.[39]

When reporters in Mukden questioned him about the removal of equipment from Manchurian factories by Soviet troops, Lin Piao's Chief-of-Staff, Wu Hsiu-ch'üan, replied as did all official Party spokesmen at this time that he knew nothing of such activities.[40] The Chinese Communists also reminded their critics that during the fourteen years of Japanese occupation, it had been the Chinese Communists and the people of Manchuria who struggled together, while the troops of the KMT never fired a shot against the enemy in the Northeast. When they finally did arrive, one editorial remarked pointedly, they managed to take over everything they could lay their hands on.[41]

The *Ta kung pao*'s Mukden correspondent verified the truth of the latter assertion, but he also reported that the prestige of the CCP had suffered by reason of its association with the Soviets. "Those who have helped foreigners to remove things from the Northeast have made a bad impression upon the people," he wrote.[42] Yet however bad the impressions were, the heat that the issue generated, particularly as directed against the CCP, did not persist long after the withdrawal of the Soviet Army.

An undercurrent of criticism did remain, as reflected in the recurrent suggestion that the Chinese Communists were rather too closely tied to a foreign power. A typical comment was that attributed to a National Assembly representative. Both the KMT and the CCP were talking about implementing the Three People's Principles, he said, but the KMT was only carrying out the first half of the Principles, and the CCP the latter half. Thus what the people had in either case was only *"min pan chu-i"*—half the People's Principles. The CCP was forgetting nationalism, the KMT had disregarded the people's livelihood, and the

38. *Hsin min pao*, Chungking, Feb. 22, 1946 (*CPR*, Feb. 23).
39. *Hsin hua jih-pao*, Chungking, Feb. 25, 1946 *(CPR)*.
40. *Hsin-wen pao*, Shanghai, Apr. 19, 1946 (*CPR*, Apr. 25).
41. *Hsin hua jih-pao*, Chungking, Apr. 4, 1946 *(CPR)*.
42. Lu Te-jen "Autumn in spring", datelined Mukden, Mar. 27, *TKP*, Shanghai, Apr. 20, 1946 (*CPR*, Apr. 26).

two parties each were doing only about half of what they should in terms of democracy.[43]

But perhaps because the issue of nationalism was such an important element in the KMT propaganda campaign against the Communists, and was also sometimes turned against them as well, liberal writers tended to eschew it. The undercurrent of criticism seemed to be about equally matched by another theme which suggested that the Communists were, after all, Chinese and therefore unlikely to compromise the national interests of China. Thus in their evaluation of the Chinese Communists after the Soviet withdrawal from Manchuria, the liberals tended to look inward focusing primarily, as the Party itself was doing, on issues of immediate domestic concern.

THE FORMS OF COMMUNIST RULE

Whatever they may have thought of the achievements of the CCP, liberals were almost by definition opposed to the political practices and institutions associated with Communist rule. If they criticized the KMT's dictatorial style of politics, the CCP fared no better. Most writers criticized both parties for violating the principles of democracy and indulging in one-party rule. Indeed, this was one reason—probably second only to their desire to see an immediate end to the Civil War—why liberals were so anxious to bring both parties together in a coalition government. They viewed such a government as a means whereby one party could serve as a check upon the excesses of the other. Both might thus be induced to change from special "revolutionary-type" organizations into ordinary political parties more in keeping with the liberal ideal. Hence the willingness to have the CCP participate in a coalition government, and the apparent lack of enthusiasm for a national government dominated by the CCP alone.

Because these intellectuals had little direct experience with political life under Communist rule, they were much less specific in their criticism of the CCP than of the KMT. But this did not appreciably reduce the level of their opposition. They objected to the all-powerful position of the CCP in the liberated areas and to the restrictions placed upon individual freedoms, particularly those related to the expression of political dissent.

Among the least critical views was that of the KMT civil servant quoted above. "I feel that the democracy of the KMT is the form of democracy without its substance," he wrote, "and the democracy of the CCP is democracy under Party control." He felt that because there were no more bureaucrats and local bullies, because of the way everyone was allowed to speak out at public meetings, and because of the equality that was practiced there, a kind of democracy did exist in the liberated areas. For the most part, however, the liberal view of democracy as practiced by the Chinese Communists was considerably more critical.

43. See note 11(c) above.

Chang Tung-sun, who was willing to relinquish a large measure of freedom and various other of the components of liberal democracy, nevertheless asserted: "As for the CCP, we feel that its organization is too strong to be appropriate in a democratic nation." [44] Professor Chou Chung-ch'i acknowledged that, in line with Mao's theory of the New Democracy, the CCP advocated first the realization of the Three People's Principles, and maintained that communism could only be a future goal to be sought after industrialization had been achieved. But when all we want is the Three People's Principles, queried Professor Chou, will it not be overdoing things somewhat to entrust this to the CCP? [45]

Another writer tried to explain why liberals had so many doubts about the Communists. "Some people say," he wrote, "that in opposing feudalism the task of the liberals and the CCP is the same and their objective is as one. Truly, with respect to the destruction of the old China, today's students and the CCP are of the same will, and sympathy is related to this. But sympathy is not the same as support. There is a great distance between them and the CCP on the question of building a new China. This is because the CCP places too much emphasis on the masses and overlooks the individual." Because of this, he concluded, the Communists' style of democracy raised as many doubts as did that of the KMT. [46]

An editorial in *Shih-tai p'i-p'ing* was more explicit. Denouncing rightist groups for their transgressions against civil liberties, the editor then turned on the leftists: "If they see someone cursing the KMT Government in speech or action, then they applaud. But no matter what the CCP says or does, it is evaluated as being good and those who disagree are subject to 'liquidation' and attacked as reactionaries, accomplices, running dogs, KMT secret agents and the like, and all fall into the category of criticizers of the CCP." [47]

Many, however, were not so even-handed in their criticism. The more common tendency was to suggest that if the KMT was bad in this respect, the CCP was worse. Professor Yang Jen-keng fell into this category. Under Communist control, he wrote, because of the Party's discipline and the "infantile leftwing disorders" of its cadres, the will of the people has no way of expressing itself. The CCP basically denies freedom, he declared, and its strict intervention is even greater than that of the KMT. [48]

Their concept of democracy and ours are two different things, asserted another writer, pointing out that even though there was no formal news censorship in the liberated areas, the Communists exerted even stricter control

44. Chang Tung-sun, p. 7 (see Chapter Five, note 119).

45. Chou Chung-ch'i, "Lun ko-ming" [On revolution], *KC*, Jan. 25, 1947, p. 10.

46. Yü Ts'ai-yu, "T'an chin-t'ien te hsueh-sheng" [Discussing today's students], *KC*, Apr. 24, 1948, p. 18.

47. *STPP*, Aug. 1, 1947, p. 1.

48. Yang Jen-keng, "Tzu-yu-chu-i-che wang ho-ch'u ch'ü?" [Where are the liberals headed?], *KC*, May 10, 1947, p. 5. Professor Yang also expressed his views on the CCP in "Lun nei-chan" [On the civil war], *KC*, Mar. 20, 1948; and "Kuan-yü 'chung-kung wang ho-ch'u ch'ü?' " [Concerning "Where are the Communists headed?"], *KC*, Nov. 1, 1947. Professor Wu Shih-ch'ang had an almost identical view in "Lun ho-p'ing wen-t'i" [On the problem of peace], *KC*, July 14, 1947, pp. 4, 6.

over the news than did the Central Government.[49] CCP leaders control the entire Party with iron discipline, complained Chou Shou-chang, editor of the Nanking *Hsin min pao*. Even worse, Mao the political leader had become the arbiter of literature and art as well. His essay, "On Literature and Art," had become the highest creative principle for writers and artists. Chou recalled a report he had heard about certain writers in Yenan who developed differences with the political leadership, but were required to continue their work in accordance with principles that were considered politically correct.[50]

On this, as on other matters, Ch'u An-p'ing seemed the most outspoken. There can be no democracy without freedom of thought, he declared, so how can the CCP defend itself on this point? We liberals have been influenced by Anglo-American traditions yet we still criticize England and the U.S. "But have we ever heard the CCP criticize Stalin or the U.S.S.R.? Have we ever seen leftist newspapers criticize Mao and Yenan? Do you mean to say that Stalin and Mao are saints among the saintly with no points to criticize, and that Yenan and Moscow are heavens among the heavenly...?" At least, he concluded, under KMT rule we can still struggle for freedom; however circumscribed, this freedom is still a question of "more or less." But if the CCP were in power, it would then become a question of "having and not having."[51]

THE LIBERAL-COMMUNIST ALLIANCE OF 1949

What then must have been in the minds of people like Ch'u An-p'ing and Wang Yun-sheng when they finally decided to cross over into the liberated areas in late 1948 and 1949, or like Chang Tung-sun to remain at their university posts with words of welcome for the victor? Their misgivings about the CCP were deep-rooted and they had made no secret of them. They had not for the most part supported the Communist-led revolution and they did not relish the idea of a government dominated by the CCP. Indeed, they had argued consistently and conscientiously against it, and did not go over to the Communists until all hope of a liberal compromise had been extinguished.

Under the circumstances, what sort of an accommodation did these liberal intellectuals hope to make with the new regime? What kinds of compromises did they anticipate they would have to agree to? They did not, of course, address this question directly, but possible answers can be inferred from two different themes that appeared in their writings. One had to do with their response to Mao's concept of the New Democracy and to the Party's policies toward the intelligentsia derived therefrom. The second theme had to do with the intellectuals' general recognition of the kinds of compromises which might be necessary if the task of destroying the old society was to be accomplished.

49. Ch'en Yen, "Kuo kung wen-t'i ho-i pu-neng ho-p'ing chieh-chueh te chui-so" [Why KMT-CCP problems cannot be resolved peaceably], *KC*, Aug. 9, 1947, p. 15.

50. Chou Shou-chang, "Lun shen-hua cheng-chih" [Of myths and politics], *KC*, Jan. 18, 1947, p. 6.

51. Ch'u An-p'ing, p. 6 (see above, note 1).

THE NEW DEMOCRACY

During the Civil War years, the ideas outlined by Mao in his "On New Democracy" (January, 1940), provided the basis of the Party's policies and ideological pronouncements. Intellectuals in the KMT areas were conversant with Mao's ideas in this respect, thanks to the more tolerant spirit of the anti-Japanese united front period when they first appeared in print. The intellectuals were also aware that their own misgivings about the Party were paralleled by the Party's equally fundamental reservations about them.

In Theory

As noted, Mao's 1939 statement on intellectuals was quoted and reprinted frequently throughout the subsequent decade as the essence of the Party's position on intellectuals. In this statement, Mao categorized them as petty bourgeois by reason of their family background, standard of living, and political viewpoint. He warned that because they were inherently individualistic, impractical, and irresolute, some would withdraw, become passive, and even hostile to the revolution. He suggested further that they could overcome such shortcomings "only in mass struggles over a long period." At the same time, however, he also noted that they were politically alert, dissatisfied with conditions in China, and often lived in fear of unemployment. Hence they could play an important role as a revolutionary vanguard and as an instrument for linking the masses with the main forces of the revolution. As proof of this assertion, Mao cited the tradition of political activism developed by Chinese students and intellectuals since the turn of the century.[52]

This view of the intelligentsia was contained within Mao's conceptualization of the New Democracy. Communism, he maintained, was a distant goal to be achieved only after the old feudal society had been destroyed and replaced by a new one wherein the Three People's Principles would at last have been realized. The proletariat, the peasantry, and the intelligentsia together with other sections of the petty bourgeoisie, would be the "basic forces" of the new transitional society. It would be ruled by a coalition of all anti-imperialist and anti-feudal classes under the leadership of the proletariat. A mixed economy, and land-to-the-tiller in the rural areas, were to constitute the major elements of the new society's economic policy. This new system would be called the New Democracy.[53]

When the Seventh National Party Congress met in April, 1945, the Party and the nation looked forward to Japan's impending defeat. In his political report to the Congress, "On Coalition Government," Mao again outlined the principles of the New Democracy as the basis of the Party's program and future tasks. "We Communists do not conceal our political views," he wrote. "Definitely and beyond all doubt, our future or maximum program is to carry China forward to socialism and communism." But he noted that some people were suspicious,

52. Mao Tse-tung, "The Chinese Revolution and the Chinese Communist Party," *Selected Works,* 2:320-22.
53. Mao Tse-tung, "On New Democracy," *Selected Works,* 2:339-84.

fearing that if the CCP gained political power, it would immediately abandon its notions about New Democracy and follow the example of the Soviet Union. Attempting to allay such fears, Mao declared that "throughout the stage of New Democracy, China cannot possibly have a one-class dictatorship and one-party government and therefore should not attempt it." The state system of the New Democracy was suited to the present stage of China's historical development, as distinguished from that of the Soviet Union, and would continue to exist "for a long time to come."[54]

In short, the Party's post-war line was to be unity, democracy, peace, and the construction of a new China under a coalition government. Mao called for an immediate end to KMT one-party rule and for its replacement by a coalition government—a united-front democratic alliance, which would include "representatives of all the anti-Japanese parties and people without party affiliation." And to build a new-democratic China:

> . . . we need large numbers of educators and teachers for the people, and also people's scientists, engineers, technicians, doctors, journalists, writers, men of letters, artists and rank-and-file cultural workers. . . . Provided they serve the people creditably, all intellectuals should be esteemed and regarded as valuable national and social assets. . . . Therefore, the task of a people's government is systematically to develop all kinds of intellectually equipped cadres from among the ranks of the people and at the same time take care to unite with and re-educate all the useful intellectuals already available.[55]

In Practice

Just how much liberal intellectuals knew about the New Democracy in practice—particularly as it applied to them—remains unclear. What follows in this section is a more systematic outline of the Party's policies toward intellectuals during the 1945-49 period than a reliance on liberal writings alone would allow.

In January, 1948, Mao issued a warning that the Party must keep its reservations about intellectuals within limits. He cautioned against "adventurist policies" towards intellectuals, noting that only a very small minority were actually determined counter-revolutionaries. Instead, the Party should adopt a "careful attitude" toward intellectuals, and "unite with them, educate them and give them posts according to the merits of each case." [56] This was perhaps an indication as to why, during the Civil War years, there were at least as many reports of teachers and students fleeing the Communist areas as of movement in the opposite direction.[57] According to one *Kuan-ch'a* correspondent writing

54. Mao Tse-tung, "On Coalition Government," *Selected Works,* 3:282-85.

55. *Ibid.,* pp. 304-5.

56. Mao Tse-tung, "On Some Important Problems of the Party's Present Policy," *Selected Works,* 4:184.

57. On students fleeing from the Communists, see Chapter Five under "Political Incompetence: Refugees." A comparison of the numbers of students and intellectuals fleeing the Communist and KMT areas is almost impossible to make. Contemporary accounts seem to indicate larger numbers leaving the Communist areas: these tended to be reported in tens of thousands, while those moving into the Communist areas were reported by the Commu-

from southern Kiangsu, among the Communists' biggest failures in that area was their treatment of intellectuals and members of the middle class, who were "one after another fleeing the control of the New Fourth Army."[58] Similarly, Wu Shih-ch'ang listed as one of his major points of opposition to the CCP the fact that it had ᴄut itself off from the petty-bourgeoisie and that, as a consequence, the intellectual level within the Party was "unfortunately limited."[59]

Nevertheless, those intellectuals who fled to the liberated areas from the Government side were treated with every consideration. However many refugees their own take-over may have generated, the Communists—unlike the Central Government—did not allow the treatment of those who fled to them to become a political liability. The Communists welcomed refugee intellectuals: in newspaper editorials, over the airwaves, and doubtless by more covert means as well. Moreover, the statements of welcome and support were reinforced in practice. Students from the KMT areas were given free board and tuition at liberated area schools, and sometimes free clothing, blankets, and other daily necessities as well.[60]

In May, 1946, Yenan radio claimed that universities and middle schools in north and central China, although not yet ideal places for study, had nevertheless become havens of refuge for thousands of students from Shanghai, Peiping, Tientsin, and other KMT cities. Over 300 students from Peiping and Tientsin were said to have enrolled in the North China United University in Kalgan. Several hundred students, who had made the journey from Shanghai after the Japanese surrender, were attending classes in schools in northern Kiangsu. Many of these students had become disillusioned with the Central Government's discrimination against the so-called "puppet-students" who had remained in Japanese-occupied China and studied in schools and univȩrsities there.[61] By August, 1946, there were fourteen universities and technical schools in the Shansi-Chahar-Hopei Border Region with a total enrollment of 6,225 students, many of whom had come from the KMT areas.[62] Professors and lecturers from the KMT areas were given administrative and academic positions in liberated area schools, and were actively encouraged to come and staff them.

---

nists themselves only in hundreds and thousands. Some of these reports will be cited in the text; for other references to students entering the liberated ' areas, see Chapter Three, especially notes 46, 62, 63. Any figures may be misleading because refugees in KMT areas were usually concentrated in a few urban centers, while refugees in the liberated areas were much more widely scattered. Also, as indicated in Chapter Five, the refugee status of large numbers of students in KMT cities was not always voluntary—particularly during the later stage of the war. Many such students were required to leave, by assigned transportation, areas threatened by the Communists.

58. See note 11(b) above.
59. Wu Shih-ch'ang, "Chung-kuo hsu-yao ch'ung-chien ch'üan-wei" [What China needs is the reconstruction of authority], *KC,* Oct. 19, 1946, p. 7.
60. Hsinhua News Agency, Yenan, Jan. 29, 1946 (*FYI,* Jan. 30).
61. Hsinhua News Agency, Yenan, May 28, 1946 (*FYI,* May 29).
62. Hsinhua News Agency, Yenan, Aug. 9, 1946 (*FYI,* Aug. 10). This border region claimed 134 educational institutions, including middle and vocational schools, with total enrollment of 26,000.

The effort to unite with and reeducate intellectuals in the liberated areas did not become an object of serious concern, however, until the end of 1947, when the Party inaugurated a wide-ranging effort to overcome "leftist errors." Mao's January, 1948, warning against adventurist policies toward intellectuals was issued within the context of the anti-leftist campaigns developing at that time. They were designed to overcome certain problems in the land reform movement and in the Party's nascent urban policies.[63]

Jen Pi-shih included a statement on intellectuals in his widely-quoted discussion of land reform problems, also dated January, 1948. His message was essentially the same as Mao's, except that Jen's specific reference point was the intellectual offspring of landlord and rich peasant families. We must not reject all intellectuals related to the feudal system, he said, just because we want to destroy feudalism. Many students, including some sons and daughters of landlords and rich peasants, were favorably inclined toward the revolution and did not oppose land reform. They were gradually realizing that land reform was a basic element of the democracy they desired. Besides, he continued, within three to five years the revolution is going to be victorious throughout the country and we are going to need large numbers of medical personnel, agronomists, accountants, specialists of all kinds, teachers, and civilian railway technicians. It took many years to train such people and as yet the liberated areas did not contain many of them. Jen emphasized the necessity of using existing talent but, at the same time, reeducating it politically and training it to serve the people.[64]

One of the first regional directives to reflect the new conciliatory emphasis of 1948 was issued by the Party's Northeast Bureau on January 15. This document, like all the others of its kind, began with a statement emphasizing the contribution intellectuals could make to the Chinese revolution despite their inherent weaknesses. Two incorrect tendencies had nevertheless occurred in the Party's dealings with such people in the Northeast. On the one hand, nothing had been done to reform those who had managed administrative offices, factories, mines, and railways during the Japanese occupation and now continued in the same positions under the new Communist dispensation. On the other hand, some cadres had adopted the "poor and hired peasant line." They had not only applied it erroneously in the village land reform movement, but had moved it mechanically into schools and offices as well. In the process, many educated people were discriminated against on the basis of their family backgrounds alone.[65]

63. See Chapters Seven and Eight.

64. Jen Pi-shih, "T'u-ti kai-ko chung te chi-ko wen-t'i" [Some land reform problems], in *Chih-shih-fen-tzu yü chiao-yü wen-t'i*, pp. 15-16. For an example of what Jen was cautioning against, see Isabel and David Crook, *Revolution in a Chinese Village: Ten Mile Inn*, pp. 143-49. A village teacher was suspended and made to wear a badge proclaiming him a "first class struggle object," because he was of rich peasant origin, although he himself had not engaged in any anti-social activities.

65. See Hsia Cheng-nung, "Chih-shih-fen-tzu ch'u-lu wen-t'i" [On the problem of the way out for intellectuals], *An-tung jih-pao*, May 8, 1948, reprinted in Hsin hua jih-pao tzu-liao shih, ed., *Lun chih-shih-fen-tzu: hsüeh-hsi ts'ung-shu*, p. 36. There were cases of

To correct such errors, the Northeast Bureau issued a seven-point directive. The investigation of class origins, thought, attitude, and work style should continue in all units and organizations in order to root out landlord and rich peasant thought, corruption, and bureaucratism. Nevertheless, people should not be dismissed simply because of their class origin. The educated sons and brothers of landlords and rich peasants should be investigated and reformed, but so long as their work was good and they did not oppose land reform, they should be allowed to continue at their jobs. And, provided that they were receptive to progressive ideas and willing to be reeducated, the relatives of landlords and rich peasants should be accepted in cadre schools.

Students in ordinary middle schools should participate in thought reform programs, but there should be no general refusal to enroll the children of landlords and rich peasants. This was especially true in schools already under the control of the local Party organization. Teachers should not be dismissed because of their class origin, unless they opposed land reform and engaged in counter-revolutionary activities. Similarly, technical experts, engineers, doctors, and the like, should all—with the exception of the few counter-revolutionaries among them—be allowed to continue their work so long as they admitted their past errors.

Finally, except for government offices at the *ch'ü* and village levels and the peasant associations, from which they were to be temporarily excluded, intellectuals should be allowed to participate in the work of all public organizations and government units at the *hsien* level and above.[66]

Comrade Hsia Cheng-nung was almost apologetic at the "May Fourth" Youth Conference in Antung when he tried to explain the reason for the temporary injunction against assigning intellectuals to posts at the district and village levels. We are just now at the peak of the land reform movement, he pointed out, and the families of many intellectuals either have been or are now the objects of struggle. If we put them to work in such places, land reform will not be properly implemented. But this does not mean, he told his young audience, that we do not want you. So long as you understand that your individual family has been struggled with so that the people of the entire country can be saved, so long as you firmly support land reform and do not oppose it, the Party and the democratic government still need you.[67]

By the autumn of 1948, the tone of conciliation had grown more insistent as the Party found it more and more difficult to meet the escalating demand for all kinds of basic level work cadres—military, administrative, political, economic,

---

intellectuals being dismissed from office jobs; of factories requiring introduction by a union before hiring intellectuals in managerial and staff positions; and of teachers not being allowed to teach. This article summarized an address by Hsia at a "May Fourth" Youth Conference held in Antung during early May, 1948. The reprinting, a year and a half later, was to make it available to intellectuals throughout the country.

66. CCP Northeast Bureau, "Kuan-yü tung-pei chih-shih-fen-tzu te chueh-ting" [Decision on intellectuals in the Northeast], Jan. 15, 1948, in Cheng pao ch'u-pan-she, ed., *Kuan-yü chih-shih-fen-tzu te kai-tsao*, pp. 1-2.

67. See note 65 above.

and cultural—created by the unexpectedly rapid advance of the Communist armies. This was reflected in the directive on policy toward intellectuals issued by the Party's Central China Bureau on September 29, 1948. The intellectuals are important resources for us, the directive began, but there are not a few among them who harbor doubts about us. This was partly because of the KMT's anti-Communist propaganda. But the Party itself had been careless about its intellectual and youth work, and there had been errors in the Party's policy. In order to overcome the intellectuals' doubts as well as their shortcomings, the Party outlined a specific program of education and thought reform.

Party and government organs at all levels were to use meetings and literary activities, as well as newspapers, official statements, notices, pamphlets, cartoons, et cetera, to publicize the Party's policy toward intellectuals and thus help quiet their fears. In addition, various kinds of short-course schools and training classes were to be opened for teachers and students. Each class would last for three or four months and concentrate on current events, problems of the Chinese revolution, and the basic policies of the CCP. In carrying out this work, local cadres were to pay attention to four specific points. First, in the various training classes and cadre schools, undisciplined and anarchical attitudes were to be avoided, as were liberalism and particularism. Second, intellectuals newly arrived in the Communist areas or in areas newly taken over by the Communists were to be allowed some privileges as regards food, clothing, and study materials. But cadres responsible for the training work were called upon to live austerely and to make examples of themselves in order to influence the intellectuals.

Third, a free democratic work style was to be adopted to induce the intellectuals to be completely open and candid concerning their doubts and reservations. Fourth, the short-course schools were instructed to rely on discussion meetings, debates, wall newspapers, and various forms of mass activity as the means of resolving all problems of thought. Specifically, the methods of the three inspections, Party rectification, and cadre investigations were to be eschewed in dealing with non-Party intellectuals in newly liberated areas.[68]

The directive concluded that it was impossible to avoid getting a few counter-revolutionary elements mixed in with these students and teachers who had lived for so long under KMT control. But the ordinary KMT and San-min-chu-i Youth Corps members, who were forced to join in order to safeguard their jobs and their studies, and who did not determinedly oppose the revolution, were to be treated no differently than those who were not members of those organizations. All should be allowed to study and once they had gained an elementary knowledge of CCP policies, and their doubts had been eliminated or at least reduced somewhat, they were to be given jobs in various organizations where they were most needed.[69]

68. The "three inspections" were of class background, ideology, and work style. For more on the differences at this time between cadre and non-cadre education, see Chapter Nine under "The Victors and Others."

69. CCP Central China Bureau, "Cheng-ch'ü, t'uan-chieh, kai-tsao, p'ei-yang chih-shih-fen-tzu" [Win over, unite, reform, and train intellectuals], in Hua-pei hsin hua shu-tien, ed.,

THE INTELLECTUALS' RESPONSE

Despite its misgivings about them, the Party was clearly offering the intellectuals a place in the life of the new-democratic society. Still, most of the intellectuals whose writings have been analyzed here could not have been expected to be overly enthusiastic about the sort of "reform and reeducation" they were all expected to undergo—however elementary and superficial it might initially be. And they entertained no illusions as to the long-term implications of the Communist program for a new-democratic society. Many even criticized it as a deception, since it placed major emphasis on the new-democratic phase and was perhaps purposely vague about what was to follow. "The CCP has not abandoned Marxism-Leninism," commented one writer, "nor has it given up anything else; it is only a tactic. Therefore, no matter what democracy the CCP advocates, it can never be a democratic party."[70] Everyone agreed that, whatever their immediate plans, the long-range goal of the CCP was the transformation of China into a Communist state. But for some, there were intervening considerations. One of these had to do with timing and "objective conditions."

Thus when Chang Tung-sun argued in favor of bringing the CCP into a coalition government, he acknowledged that the CCP had never concealed its belief in Marxism or in the necessity of a Communist revolution. But I myself have talked to them, he wrote, and they say that only their sons or grandsons will live to see it. The problem of a Communist revolution was therefore not one of the present but of the future, and who could predict that the objective conditions would be ripe for revolution in fifty or sixty years? Perhaps by then, he continued, people would have enough to eat and the standard of living would have risen and every household would be self-supporting. The CCP is now at the stage of carrying out the New Democracy, he concluded, "and since they do what they say, that is what they will do." There was no need to be afraid of the CCP's brand of "futuristic revolutionary theory."[71]

Shih Fu-liang was another who shared this view. As he saw it, the CCP did not want to carry out communism at that time, nor even socialism, because conditions were not yet appropriate. The most they wanted to achieve for the time being was a new-democratic state. With specific reference to the CCP's expressed support for a coalition government, he wrote:

> Some say this is just a strategem and that when the time is right, the CCP will carry out a Soviet system and a proletarian dictatorship. I do not dare to say they will not and that this is not a possibility. But "when the time is right" is an objective question. . . . Perhaps China can go its own road and we will be able to move peacefully to socialism from the new capitalism and the new democracy.

Kuan-yü ch'eng-shih cheng-ts'e te chi-ko wen-hsien, pp. 37-39. The implementation of this and similar directives in the newly liberated areas during 1949 is discussed in Chapter Nine.

70. Tung Ch'iu-shui, "Lun hsin min-chu-chu-i chi ch'i ts'e-lueh" [On the new democracy and its policies], *STPP,* Jan. 15, 1948, p. 20.

71. Chang Tung-sun, p. 7 (see Chapter Five, note 119).

At any rate, he concluded, no democratic person nor democratic party today need fear the threat of communism.[72]

There is no way of knowing how widespread this particular belief may have been. Perhaps Chang and Shih were speaking only for themselves, but perhaps not. Moreover, there existed one additional consideration which may have contributed to the willingness to accept the CCP's New Democracy "under the leadership of the proletariat," despite a certain apprehension about the manner in which aspects of it were already being implemented in the Communist areas. This was a recognition that it might be necessary to compromise certain liberal principles at least temporarily in order to lay the foundations for a new and progressive society.

As we have seen, this was a theme which appeared in some liberal proposals for the achievement of socialism and democracy. Not surprisingly, it appeared also among those who allowed themselves to be genuinely impressed with what the Communists were doing. These were people like the KMT civil servant who felt that perhaps the violence was unavoidable; and felt also that the Communists had achieved a certain kind of democracy because they had done away with local bullies and had given the peasants the right "to stand on a platform and say the things that someone should say."

Finally, this theme appeared in a student's rebuke to Professor Yang Jen-keng, who had written emphasizing the distance that existed between the liberals and the CCP. It was true, the student wrote, that middle-class liberals had difficulty accepting the violent methods of the CCP, and that they placed highest value on the free development of the individual. But liberals also had a social conscience and their sense of social justice had been aroused by the inequities inherent in Chinese society. This could provide the basis for at least a temporary reconciliation of the contradictions between the freedom of the liberals and the equality of the Communists, especially since the Communists were for the most part from the middle class themselves and would therefore probably accept the well-intentioned criticism of the liberals.

From the point of view of the liberals, he went on, such a compromise must take place because, however great an influence they may have exerted culturally, their tragedy lay in their ineffectiveness. They had not been able to overturn the old society because they had concentrated too much on the freedom of the individual and overlooked the welfare of the majority. They had not put down roots among the people, nor did they understand that land reform and the awakening of the peasants were the necessary conditions for the destruction of the privileged interests that controlled Chinese society. The liberals, he asserted, should therefore join with the Communists in order to destroy their common enemy. After that key task had been completed would be time enough to resume the old relationship of mutual opposition.[73]

72. Shih Fu-liang, "Lun 'kung-ch'an-chu-i te wei-hsieh'" [On the "threat of communism"], *STPP*, Oct. 1, 1947, p. 16.

73. Li Hsiao-yu, "Tu 'kuan-yü chung-kung wang ho-ch'u ch'ü?' chien lun tzu-yu-chu-i-che te tao-lu" [On reading "Where are the Chinese Communists headed?" and on the way of the liberals], *KC*, Jan. 3, 1948, pp. 7-9. Li was a student at National Central University.

This, then, was the process whereby, to paraphrase Jack Belden, a decisive minority of the population came finally to embrace the Communist program.[74] The political arguments that dominated intellectual life during the Civil War years indicated a degree of commitment to liberalism which has perhaps been underestimated because of the political weakness of its adherents. The strain that the acceptance of the Communist program entailed was clearly apparent in the anger and frustration which marked their political commentaries as the intellectuals began to realize that their ideas were not going to influence the conduct of the KMT in any way. Their dilemma was intensified by the simultaneous realization that the KMT was about to be replaced by a new political elite that was likely to be as intransigent as the KMT with respect to certain fundamental tenets of the liberal creed.

The Communist military victory in fact eased this dilemma for Chinese liberals. Prior to that time, they had been confronted by a choice between the KMT, which they had found wanting on virtually all counts of political principle and performance, and the CCP, whose political principles were regarded as the negation of some of the liberal community's most deeply-held commitments. All that remained of their loyalty to the KMT was the distant possibility that their struggle for a liberal democratic society might someday succeed. Abandoning this possibility was the price that would doubtless have to be paid if they were to go over to the Communists, whose performance otherwise was by and large admired. The force of this dilemma was eased once it had been reduced, by the KMT military defeat, to a choice between immediate and indefinite exile, or acceptance of a national government led by the CCP in its new-democratic phase.

Not everyone was willing to accept the CCP even in its new-democratic phase. Although the majority of China's liberal intellectuals were, some chose otherwise. Hu Shih was one of these. His opposition to the KMT had never reached the level of intensity displayed by so many of his colleagues. Nevertheless, he had spoken out on the liberal side of a number of issues during the Civil War years, most notably the student movement. After flying out of beleaguered Peiping in January, 1949, Hu was reported to have told George Yeh, Vice-minister of Foreign Affairs of the Central Government, that there was really very little to be said for the KMT. "The only reason why liberal elements like us still prefer to string along with you people," he told Yeh, "is that under your regime we at least enjoy the freedom of silence."[75]

Most liberals obviously did not place so high a price on their own personal freedom of silence.[76] Or perhaps they did not think that they would want to avail themselves of it. In his conversations with the anthropologist Robert

74. Jack Belden, *China Shakes the World*, p. 398.
75. Quoted in *Hsin-wen t'ien-ti* (associated with the KMT), Shanghai, no. 68, Apr. 28, 1949 (*CPR*, May 3).
76. One of Pa Chin's friends advanced this same argument, but could not get the novelist to say he agreed with it. Although his anarchist philosophy did not endear him to the Communists, Pa Chin remained in China in 1949. See Olga Lang, *Pa Chin and His Writings*, p. 217.

Redfield, Fei Hsiao-t'ung, for example, indicated that he felt he could work effectively under a Chinese Communist government, albeit as a member of its "loyal opposition." Although his views on certain matters had been attacked by the Communists, as had the views of most prominent liberals, Fei nevertheless spoke in late 1948 of his hope that he would be able to contribute to China's industrial and agricultural development—meanwhile criticizing the Communists when he felt criticism was necessary.[77]

Whatever else they may have been, then, these intellectuals should not be dismissed as political opportunists—a favorite theme in many circles since 1949. Liberal intellectuals were indeed johnny-come-latelies to the revolutionary cause. But they were also committed enough to the path of liberal reform to pursue that goal until the possibility of achieving it no longer existed. Only after the military defeat of the KMT became a certainty, did the orientation of the intelligentsia toward the Communists shift from something like reserved disapproval to qualified acceptance.

However the liberals may have rationalized their decision to accept Communist rule, there is no indication that they extended anything like unequivocal support to the new regime, or that the compromises they were willing to make were in any sense fundamental or permanent. Their commitment extended to the Communist program of the New Democracy and beyond that to the development of a socialist economy, but certainly not to a one-party or one-class dictatorship. Just as the CCP never tried to conceal its long-range objectives for Chinese society, so liberal intellectuals did not hide their opposition to them.

Communist reservations about the Chinese intelligentsia were thus as well-founded as were the misgivings of the latter about the CCP. The strain that the alliance with these intellectuals created within the Party was clearly reflected in the admonitions reminding Party members to avoid adventurist policies toward intellectuals, to unite with them, and win them over. The deep-rooted nature of the differences between the intellectual community and the CCP, obscured by their alliance in 1949, must therefore go a long way toward explaining the tension that has existed in the relationship between them ever since.

77. See Introduction by Robert Redfield in Fei Hsiao-t'ung, *China's Gentry: Essays on Rural-Urban Relations,* pp. 2-3.

VII

The Return to Land Reform

Winning over the liberal intellectual community was not, of course, the foremost concern of the Chinese Communists in 1945 and 1946. That objective would assume greater importance with the second major change in Chinese Communist strategy during the Civil War years, namely, the move from the countryside back to the cities. Before that could be seriously contemplated, however, the CCP needed to consolidate and expand the base it had won in the countryside during the Anti-Japanese War. To accomplish this task the Party turned once again to land reform, abandoning the more moderate Anti-Japanese War policy of rent and interest reduction.

We have already seen that one element in the liberal intellectuals' critique of the KMT Government was its failures in the countryside. They described how the agricultural economy was often not even able to sustain itself, let alone underwrite the expenditures of the Central Government and its armies in the field. Perhaps because of their ideological predisposition, their criticism fell most heavily on the effects of government corruption and neglect in the countryside, and the increased burdens created by the war for an already impoverished peasantry. Liberals generally supported the principle of land-to-the-tiller, but the problem of landlord-tenant relations did not draw comparable attention from them during the Civil War period.

The "agrarian problem"—the backwardness of Chinese agriculture and the poverty of the peasants—had nevertheless been a subject of investigation and debate by scholars and politicians from the 1920s onward. Their diagnoses and prescriptions tended to divide into two categories. One emphasized the exploitative nature of the urban-rural relationship in general, and of rural socio-economic institutions in particular. The other focused on the more technical aspects of agricultural production. Leftists, by and large, adhered to the former view and rightists to the latter, while liberals fell somewhere in between by combining elements of both.[1]

---

1. Ramon H. Myers summarizes both arguments in *The Chinese Peasant Economy: Agricultural Development in Hopei and Shantung, 1890-1949,* pp. 13-24. For a cross section of the work on agrarian problems by Chinese liberal and leftist writers during the 1930s, see *Agrarian China: Selected Source Materials from Chinese Authors.*

The two positions were sharply juxtaposed at the eighth annual conference of the Chinese Agricultural Association held in Shanghai in October, 1946. This non-partisan group of some 4,000 persons was dedicated to the promotion of agricultural development, democracy, and national modernization. Its 1946 convocation was noteworthy only in that representatives of various political parties attended to explain their respective policies on the agrarian question.

The Government's views were presented by representatives from the Ministry of Social Affairs, the Shanghai municipal Bureau of Social Affairs, central KMT headquarters, and the Shanghai KMT organization. The address of the latter representative provided some insight into the sort of obscurantist mentality that could render meaningless even the most enlightened of national policies. In an emotional statement the gentleman asserted that there were no points of conflict in the villages of China. He declared that unlike city dwellers, who customarily did not even know the names of their next-door neighbors, country folk were very sociable. Even landlords and tenants remained on friendly terms with one another. Moreover, urban intellectuals could never be sure that their analyses of rural conditions were correct. He advocated educating the peasants so that they might be able to judge their situation for themselves. The main KMT theme was that improved techniques of agricultural production would solve China's problems in the countryside. Referring pointedly to the Communists, the speakers denounced both the use of violence in attempting to cope with the agrarian problem, and the exploitation of the problem for political purposes.[2]

These statements were indicative not so much of official KMT policy as of the prevailing attitude toward its implementation. In 1926, before the KMT-CCP split, rent reduction became an official plank in the KMT party platform. This was the 25 percent rent reduction plan upon which the Communists' own policy for the Anti-Japanese War years was modeled. The original KMT version recognized 50 percent of the main crop as the maximum rent then being collected. The 25 percent reduction was to be made on this 50 percent maximum. After reduction, the maximum rent would thus be 37.5 percent of the main crop, while any subsidiary crops would not be subject to rent payments. Despite their being written into the national Land Law of 1930, these provisions were never widely implemented.

The Land Law was revised in 1937 with the intention of reducing rents further and of gradually transferring ownership of land to the tenant who tilled it, as advocated by Sun Yat-sen. According to the 1937 revisions, rents were not to exceed 8 percent of the land value. Again little effort was made to enforce this provision, the Japanese invasion being the immediate excuse. After World War II, the objectives of rent and interest reduction, and of land-to-the-tiller, were written into the program for national reconstruction adopted by the Political Consultative Conference in January, 1946. The same objectives were embodied in the Government's 1946 Land Law and the Constitution adopted that same year.

2. *Economics Weekly*, Shanghai, vol. 3, no. 16, Oct. 17, 1946 (*CPR*, Jan. 31, 1947).

The reform of tenancy conditions was also among the recommendations made by the joint China-United States Agricultural Mission for improving China's agriculture.[3] But despite some prodding by the Americans, the Government did not push the implementation of tenancy reforms beyond the experimental stage until it was too late—after the retreat to Taiwan.

By contrast, Hua Kang, the Communist representative at the Chinese Agricultural Association meeting, asserted that agricultural reform was the prerequisite for industrialization, and that a change in production relations constituted the essence of agricultural reform. Improvements in agricultural productivity and in farming technology depended, first, on the transformation of the "feudal system of production" wherein a non-productive "small minority" owned the land and controlled the livelihood of the peasants who tilled it. The peasant remained poor, and his agricultural techniques backward, because his surplus went to the landlord, moneylender, merchant, and official in the form of high rents and interest rates, controlled prices, and unfair tax burdens.

Hua went on to list the actual steps that had been and were being taken in the Communist areas to bring about the requisite village reforms. During the Anti-Japanese War, the Communists had abandoned land reform in the interests of creating a united front with the KMT against the invader. During the war, however, the Communists had carried out a 25 percent reduction of farm rentals, levied a single progressive tax, made available agricultural loans at low interest rates, encouraged productive activities on the part of rich peasants, increased production through the opening up of waste lands, increased cotton acreage, started to coordinate the use of labor by organizing labor exchange or labor service teams *(pien kung tui)*, and promoted cultural and educational activities in the villages.

After the war, Hua continued, the Communist areas abandoned the rent reduction policy for the more advanced one of abolishing tenancy altogether and transferring the ownership of land to the peasant who tilled it. The methods being used to accomplish this included the confiscation and distribution to the peasants of land taken over by the Manchus during the last dynasty, land seized by the Japanese, land taken over by traitors, all land forcibly or illegally occupied, and "black land" or land left unregistered so as to avoid taxation. Landlords were also being required to make restitution to peasants who had been the victims of various other kinds of feudal exploitation. Fields lost through inability to meet mortgage payments were being returned to the original owners. In addition, some landlords were voluntarily transferring land ownership to their tenants, and the authorities in Yenan were considering a program of government compensation to landlords.[4]

Nor could there be any doubt that the Communists were actually carrying out the sort of land reform their representative described. The dispossessed

---

3. *Foreign Relations of the United States, 1946, The Far East, China*, pp. 1284-86.
4. See note 2 above.

landlord families collecting in KMT-held cities throughout north China and Manchuria attested to its implementation.

The contrast between the agrarian practices of the two parties could not have been more clearly drawn. Indeed, the sharpest observation by the KMT's representatives was their charge that the Communists were exploiting the agrarian problem to their own political advantage. Regardless of individual political attitudes, those who understood what the Communists were doing in the countryside understood the political implications as well. According to intellectual observers, land reform was making it possible for the Communists "to put down roots in the villages and to grow strong." They said that because of land reform the Communists could effectively carry out three important tasks: grain requisitions, military conscription, and local self-defense.

Unfortunately, contemporary observers did not trouble to analyze in any detail the process to which their conclusions referred. As a result, they left behind a host of questions that the student of history can, in the final analysis, answer only by inference and conjecture. There are three key interrelated questions, from which many others derive.

1. In much of north China, where the Communists built their major base areas during the Anti-Japanese War and where they carried out land reform immediately afterwards, an absolute majority of the peasants already owned the land they tilled. What did liberal intellectuals mean, then, by their assertions that the Communists were growing strong in the countryside because of their land reform program? What did the Communists themselves mean by their oft-repeated claim—made both publicly and in the relative privacy of intra-Party documents—that only through land reform could they mobilize mass peasant support for their struggle with the KMT? What was the meaning of statements such as the following:

> The experiences of the past hundred years have shown that the democratic liberation movement of the Chinese people failed because it was only a movement of a handful of people. Only after the carrying out of land-to-the-tillers in which peasants forming 80 percent of the Chinese population are really liberated, can the liberation movement stand rocklike against any storm. Three times during the War of Resistance, peasants in the liberated areas demanded the carrying out of the land-to-the-tillers. When they demanded this for the fourth time after the victory over Japan, the Central Committee of the CCP agreed to this legitimate demand of the peasants while guaranteeing a decent living to the landlords. And it is precisely this land-to-the-tiller which has strengthened the popular liberation army.... If the Communist Party had not agreed to this demand of the peasants while Chiang received external aid from the U.S., it would not be impossible for the Chinese people's movement for independence, peace and democracy to meet again with failure like that of 1927.[5]

2. In the spring of 1948, the tide of battle was turning in their favor and the Communists began planning seriously for their move southward into areas where

5. Hsinhua News Agency, Yenan, Sept. 14, 1946 *(FYI)*.

tenancy was more prevalent than in north China. If land reform was as important as they claimed, why did the Communists suddenly call a halt to its
implementation in newly liberated areas at this time?

3. Finally, Mao himself has indicated that it was the Japanese invasion that
taught revolution to the Chinese people and provoked them to fight.[6] Yet the
Party's agrarian policy was at its most moderate during the Anti-Japanese War
years. What, if any, is the relationship between this statement and the assertion
that only land reform could guarantee a base of mass support for the revolutionary war against the KMT? Specifically, if tenancy was not a major problem
in north China, what role could rent reduction possibly have played in mobilizing the peasants there during the Anti-Japanese War?

What follows in this chapter is an attempt to answer these three questions in
order to define more precisely the nature of the CCP's appeal to the Chinese
peasantry.

THE SOCIO-ECONOMIC ROOTS OF THE CCP'S SUCCESS

The general pattern of land tenure in China during the first half of the present
century is well known. Tenancy was, with some exceptions, low in north China
and high in the Northeast and in the South. Accurate statistics are hard to come
by. For the most part, those that exist should be treated as approximations. The
automatic assumption, furthermore, is that such figures may also reflect the
political biases of those who compiled them. Despite the problems they may
contain, however, the tenancy figures are in basic agreement. The most widely
quoted are those published by the National Agricultural Research Bureau of the
Ministry of Industry of the KMT Government. They show that in the 1930s,
approximately 30 percent of China's farm families were tenants cultivating
rented land. An additional 24 percent owned a portion of the land they tilled.
Forty-six percent were landowners, presumably holding title to at least enough
land to support themselves. Thus 70 percent of China's peasants owned some
land, but over 50 percent of China's peasants rented either part or all of the land
they tilled.[7]

LAND TENURE: NORTH CHINA

These national averages obscured wide regional variations. For instance, in
Szechwan province in the Southwest an estimated 56 percent of all farm families
were tenants; but in Hopei and Shantung in the North the tenancy rate was the
lowest in the country, averaging only about 12 percent. The provincial land
tenure averages for the six years 1931-36, in areas of north and east China where

6. Mao Tse-tung to Edgar Snow, "A Conversation with Mao Tse-tung," *Life*, Apr. 30,
1971, p. 47.

7. A number of scholars have used the National Agricultural Research Bureau statistics. For example, Albert Feuerwerker, *The Chinese Economy, 1912-1949*, p. 34; Dwight
Perkins, *Agricultural Development in China, 1368-1968*, p. 91; T. H. Shen, *Agricultural
Resources of China*, p. 96; and Chang Yu-i, ed., *Chung-kuo chin-tai nung-yeh shih tzu-liao*,
hereafter *Nung-yeh shih* (Peking, 1957), 3:728-30.

TABLE 1. LAND TENURE, 1931-1936
(percentage of total farm families)

Province	Tenants	Owners	Owner-Tenants
Chahar	35	38	27
Suiyuan	26	56	18
Ningsia	27	63	11
Kansu	22	59	19
Shensi	23	55	22
Shansi	17	62	21
Hopei	12	68	20
Shantung	12	71	17
Honan	22	57	22
Kiangsu	33	41	26

the Communists carried out rent reduction and land reform between 1937 and 1948 are given in Table 1.[8]

By comparison, statistics published by the National Land Commission of the KMT Government's National Economic Council classified a slightly greater proportion of the peasantry in the two key provinces of Hopei and Shantung as landowners. Landlords who rented out all or a major portion of their land accounted for approximately 3 percent of the peasantry, while the vast majority—over 70 percent in both provinces—fell into the owner-cultivator category. These statistics showed an additional 10 percent of the peasants as owning a part of the land they tilled. About 5 percent were full tenants. Agricultural workers accounted for 4 percent in Hopei and 2 percent in Shantung.[9]

Figures compiled in these provinces by the Government's Agricultural Experimental Station, by the Japanese, by John Lossing Buck,[10] and by Sidney Gamble[11] all told roughly the same story as these two sets of statistics. And so did those compiled by the Communists. The categories and definitions they used were not entirely the same as those used by other investigators making comparison difficult. But a number of village surveys can be cited.

The village investigations were conducted by local cadres in Communist-controlled areas of Shantung and Hopei under conditions which would have made accurate statistical reporting a dubious proposition at best. The surveys represented selected village samples, and the findings were circulated among

8. Based on NARB statistics for 1931 through 1936 as reprinted in Chang Yu-i, ed., *Nung-yeh shih,* pp. 728-30. The survey covered 1,120 *hsien* in 22 provinces, excluding Manchuria.

9. Myers, *Peasant Economy,* Appendix A, Table A-6, p. 303.

10. All in *ibid.*

11. Gamble found that more than 92 percent of the families in Ting *hsien,* Hopei, owned some land; that 30 percent rented some land; and that only 4.8 percent were full tenants. *Ting Hsien: A North China Rural Community,* pp. 209-11.

Party members and cadres for the specific purpose of publicizing land tenure relationships as a preparatory step in the land reform campaign. Nevertheless, the local surveys all indicate that tenant-farmers or full tenants could have made up only a relatively small minority of the peasants in the villages investigated, and that the owner-tenants and full tenants combined still only represented a minority of the population. But before presenting these findings, the criteria used by the Communists for differentiating rural classes should be explained.

Communist documents from the Civil War period indicate that local cadres committed many errors of classification and were often confused by the reality they were obliged to define in this way. One must simply assume, therefore, a certain margin of error. Yet, despite some modifications and some temporary and local variations, the basic categories used and the criteria for differentiating them remained essentially the same from 1933 onward. This consistency was reinforced by repeated clarifications and explanations issued in an effort to minimize and correct errors. Under the circumstances, one may also assume that a given classification approximated rural socio-economic conditions in the following manner:

1. A landlord family was one whose members did not labor or did so only incidentally, relying on the exploitation of others for its main income. Land rent constituted the principal means whereby the family exploited the labor of others, although it might also invest in business, industry, and moneylending.

2. Members of a rich peasant household did engage in labor but, in addition, such a family regularly derived a substantial and sometimes the major portion of its income from the exploitation of others. A rich peasant might rent out some of his land or invest in business, industry, or moneylending; but a primary form of his exploitation was the hiring of long-term farm labor. A rich peasant might rent a portion of the land he tilled. He might even be a full tenant, but such rich peasants were "in the minority."

3. A middle peasant household might own all the land it tilled or it might not, but in general it neither exploited others nor was it exploited by them. The livelihood of such a family depended wholly or at least primarily on the labor of its members who probably owned both land and the implements necessary to farm it.

4. A poor peasant household owned little or no land and few if any farm tools. In general, the poor peasant family was exploited by others because its members had to rent land, borrow money, and hire themselves out as laborers in order to live. (Note: This poor peasant classification generally, but not necessarily, contained the full tenant category used by non-Communist investigators.)

5. Workers, including hired farm laborers, lived entirely or at least primarily by selling their labor to others.

In all of the above categories, the term *labor* referred not just to productive agricultural activities but also to important *(chu-yao)* subsidiary and handicraft work such as cutting firewood, transport, spinning, the practice of medicine, etc. It was not meant to include less important *(fei chu-yao)* or incidental *(fu-tai)* labor such as weeding, tending draft animals, helping to cultivate vegetables and the like. Households which engaged in handicrafts as a primary source of income were not strictly speaking farm families and presented something of a problem. In practice, such households were sometimes treated as rich, middle, or poor peasants depending on their circumstances, and sometimes they were simply placed in a separate category. Officially, those whose livelihood depended either entirely or in large part on their own labor and perhaps also on a small amount of capital, could be regarded as poor people *(p'in-min)*. These included self-employed or independent producers, peddlers, small shopkeepers who did not hire help.[12]

Instructions and directives issued locally embellished and elaborated upon these general criteria for the individual cadre-investigator, helping him to define what constituted family labor; to distinguish between big, medium, small, and evil landlords; to refine the middle peasant category into upper, middle, and lower grades; and to understand that not all families engaging in handicraft production were by definition poor. [13] There is no way of knowing which of these specific standards the local cadres were using when they compiled their data; but the general classification outlined above formed the basis of five separate village surveys in Shantung. The findings were appended to a report made at a provincial mass work conference in September, 1945. The report was made by Li Yü, Chairman of the CCP-sponsored Shantung provincial government that came into existence on August 13, 1945.[14]

The most detailed of the studies, the only one to distinguish farm and non-farm households, claimed to show 1937 tenancy ratios in twelve villages (Village Group A, Table 2), near Tatien in the present Chünan *hsien*. The survey found that 473 families or 19 percent out of a total 2,491, rented land from others. Altogether 931 families, or 37 percent in this village sample, were designated poor peasants, the group within which the full tenant would generally be placed. Since only 232 of these families rented land, then at most only

12. According to the officially revised versions of two documents originally issued in 1933: "Tsen-yang fen-hsi chieh-chi" [How to analyze classes], and "Kuan-yü t'u-ti toucheng chung i-hsieh wen-t'i te chueh-ting" [Decisions concerning some problems in the land struggle]. These were reissued as "reference documents" to local Party committees in December, 1947; and then as "formal documents" by the CCP Central Committee on May 24, 1948. See *Ch'ün-chung,* Hong Kong, June 17, 1948, pp. 2-9. The 1933 versions are translated in Hsiao Tso-liang, *The Land Revolution in China, 1930-1934: A Study of Documents.*

13. For one such document from the Chiao-tung District of Shantung, see *Kuan-yü ch'üeh-ting chieh-chi ch'eng-fen ch'u-shen wen-t'i.*

14. This government superseded the Communist wartime administration of the province and incorporated the five military-administrative districts formed during the war (*Shan-tung sheng cheng-fu chi shan-tung chün-ch'ü kung-pu chih ko-chung t'iao-li kang-yao pan-fa hui-pien,* p. 6). The five districts were: Chiao-tung (Chiaotung Peninsula), Po-hai (northern Shantung along the Pohai Gulf), Lu-chung (central Shantung), Lu-nan (southern Shantung), and Pin-hai (coastal area from Tsingtao south to the Kiangsu border).

one-quarter of the poor peasants, or about 9 percent of the total number of families in these villages, could have been full tenants. There might have been additional full tenant families, but if so, they were rich or middle peasants.[15]

In another group of twelve villages (Village Group B, Table 2) located like the first group in the Pin-hai District, a total of 2,265 families owned 30,028 *mou* of land. Of these, 251 families rented out some 3,000 *mou* to 540 tenant households. Over half the total number of families were classified as poor peasants. But with only 326 of these renting land, the percentage of full tenant households in this village sample was probably in the region of 14 percent.[16]

A third Pin-hai survey of twelve small villages (Village Group C, Table 2) in the present Linshu *hsien*, found 1,909 families owning a total of 38,461 *mou* of land. Of these, 197 families rented out some 5,300 *mou* to 627 tenant households. Of the tenant households, 446 were designated poor peasants. They represented half the total poor peasant population and accounted for the relatively high rate of tenancy, perhaps as much as 23 percent, in this village sample.[17]

Despite the probable biases and errors in these findings, they still show tenancy as affecting only a minority of peasant families. These findings reinforce the impression given by the Shantung provincial averages, namely,.that tenancy in itself was not a problem that concerned the village masses. The local surveys did show, however, a large ratio of poor peasant families in the villages investigated and a wide inequality between rich and poor.

THE "POOR PEASANTS"

In fact, the poor peasant category effectively obscured actual tenancy relations. As a rural classification, it apparently had its origin in the Russian countryside, where tenancy alone was not a realistic indicator of the peasants' living conditions. This was so because tenancy tended to be a condition of the more, rather than the less, affluent.[18] In China this was not the case. But if tenancy was

15. Li Yü, *Lun ch'ün-chung lu-hsien yü shan-tung ch'ün-chung yun-tung* (hereafter cited as Li Yü, *Report*), chart on tenancy relations following p. 91. One obvious problem is that this survey shows 261 families renting out 33,000 mou; but the 473 tenant families are credited with renting only 11,000 mou. This apparent discrepancy is not explained. If not an error, it suggests that an unusually large proportion of land was rented to households outside the twelve villages surveyed, or to units other than the households listed. This report was made at the Second Representative Mass Work Conference in Sept., 1945.

16. *Ibid.*

17. *Ibid.* The fourth survey covered only three small villages on the Chiao-tung peninsula. Of the 185 poor peasant families in these villages, ninety-one families, or 18 percent of the total 500 families, rented the land of others. Altogether 159 families rented some land. The fifth survey covered an even smaller sample, 327 households in Chanhua *hsien*. The figures are almost certainly incomplete or selectively compiled, since all of the seventy-four middle and 226 poor peasant families are shown to own no land at all.

18. V. I. Lenin, "New Economic Developments in Peasant Life," 1893, *Collected Works,* I (Moscow: Foreign Languages Publishing House, 1960), pp. 13-73.

TABLE 2. LAND TENURE, SHANTUNG

Classification	Households	Land owned (mou)	Average mou per household
Village Group A, 1937			
landlord	169	34,404	204
rich peasant	173	6,084	35
middle peasant	717	11,158	16
poor peasant	931	5,555	6
farm worker	157	176	1
handicraft	124	333	3
merchant	163	388	2
professional	9	51	6
vagrant	48	85	2
absentee		153	
Totals	2,491	58,387	
Village Group B			
landlord	67	3,838	57
rich peasant	178	6,671	37
middle peasant	708	11,756	17
poor peasant	1,245	7,424	6
other	67	339	5
Totals	2,265	30,028	
Village Group C			
landlord	66	6,677	101
rich peasant	108	4,708	44
middle peasant	775	17,267	22
poor peasant	898	9,548	11
farm worker	57	248	4
other	5	13	3
Totals	1,909	38,461	

SOURCE: See note 15.

Households renting land to others	Land rented out (mou)	"Tenant" households	Land rented (mou)
162	32,238		
18	329	44	3,425
24	312	167	5,564
25	164	232	2,162
1	4	16	112
2	28	8	40
10	63	5	27
1	13		
5	34	1	3
13	147		
261	33,332	473	11,333
50	1,595	3	23
56	527	6	85
77	534	197	892
65	335	326	1,709
3	50	8	21
251	3,041	540	2,730
58	4,015	1	16
40	428	7	121
72	729	146	1,103
24	158	446	3,662
2	11	25	155
1	1	2	12
197	5,342	627	5,069

really divided between the middle and poor peasants in anything like the proportions indicated in the few surveys above, and if it often affected only a minority of the peasants in any case, then tenancy was not always a necessary— or at least not a sufficient—indicator of the peasants' living conditions in China either. Hence the utility of the poor peasant category for both the Russian and the Chinese Communists. By focusing on the uneven distribution of wealth, it produced a realistic profile of socio-economic conditions and problems in the countryside. In the process, it indicated quite clearly which proportion of the rural population the Communists regarded as their natural base of support.

In Shantung and Hopei, for example, at least 50 percent of all farms were between 10 and 50 *mou* in size. An additional 40 percent of the farms were 10 *mou* or less.[19] The amount of land necessary to support the average farm family of five persons in this region varied from village to village, but it was probably well above the 10 *mou* limit in most districts.[20] Thus, if 40 percent of all the farms in Hopei and Shantung were 10 *mou* or less, then at least that number of farm families did not own sufficient land to support themselves, and had to supplement their income by other means. Very often they had to go into debt, as well, in order to make ends meet. The National Land Commission's statistics showed that the yearly income of close to 40 percent of all rural families in Hopei and 25 percent of such families in Shantung was not sufficient to cover their expenditures. The same source showed that in 1936, 43 percent of the rural families in Hopei and 28 percent in Shantung were actually in debt.[21]

If these non-CCP figures and estimates (of farm size, land needed to support a farm family, and indebtedness) are reasonably accurate, they indicate that a substantial proportion of the rural farm families in these two provinces did not own sufficient land to be self-supporting without borrowing, renting land, working as hired labor, or engaging in subsidiary production. And this is about the same proportion that made up the poor peasant category on the Communists' classification tables. In the first of the three village surveys described above, 37 percent of the households fell into the poor peasant category. The proportion grew to 43.6 percent with the addition of the hired peasant families. The percentage of poor peasant families in the other two surveys was 54.9 percent and 47 percent (50 percent with hired peasants) respectively.

Comparable proportions appear in another survey of twenty-five villages in nine *hsien* within the Pei-yueh District of the Shansi-Chahar-Hopei Border

19. Myers, *Peasant Economy*, Appendix A, Table A-5, p. 302.

20. *Ibid.* Appendix A, Table A-1, p. 299. Myers found that 10 *mou* was estimated to be enough to support a family in only one of the sample villages in nine different *hsien* for which such information was available. Estimates for the other nine villages ranged from 25 *mou* to 75 *mou*. The actual average size of the farms in these villages ranged from 5.5 *mou* to 28 *mou*. In six of the villages, the average size was less than 10 *mou*.

21. *Ibid.*, p. 242.

TABLE 3. OWNERSHIP OF LAND AND DRAFT ANIMALS,
PEI-YUEH DISTRICT, SHANSI-CHAHAR-HOPEI

	Percent of Population	Percent of land	Average land per person	Percent of draft animals
Landlords	3.11	9.00	7.62	2.80
Rich peasants	7.42	17.48	6.22	15.60
Middle peasants	50.12	50.94	2.68	58.00
Poor peasants	35.32	20.58	1.54	22.00
Hired peasants	1.65	0.99	1.40	0.46
Workers	1.04	0.31	0.78	0.46
Others	1.26	0.79	?	0.33

Region. Although conducted in 1941, the survey findings were included in a Party work report by P'eng Chen in November, 1944, on the grounds that socio-economic conditions had changed little in the interim. There was no indication of changes before that date.[22] The survey, covering 4,177 families (18,401 persons), is summarized in Table 3.[23]

Conceding that these figures did not seem to indicate serious landlord-rich peasant domination, P'eng Chen pointed to other indicators of the unequal distribution of economic power. For example, the landlords and rich peasants owned the most fertile land and the best animals. More important, they alone had a surplus of grain and cash, making it possible for them to control the grain market and the village economy. He also noted that another investigation of

22. P'eng Chen's report circulated as an intra-Party document. A contemporary report, issued for general consumption and emphasizing the achievements of the Anti-Japanese War land policy, claimed that there had been changes in a sample group of thirty-five villages in this same District between 1937-42. During those years, landlord families fell from 2.4% to 1.9% of the total farm families, and the land they occupied from 16% to 10% of the total. Rich peasants rose from about 5% of the families with 22% of the land, to 7.8% with 19.5% of the land. Middle peasants rose from 35.4% to 44.3% of the households, and the land they occupied from 41.6% to 49%. Poor and hired peasants fell from 47.5% of the population to 40.9%, and the land they occupied from 41.6% to 49%. Poor and hired peasants fell from 47.5% of the population to 40.9%, and the land they occupied rose from 19% to 20%. "Chin-ch'a-chi pien-ch'ü shih-shih t'u-ti cheng-ts'e te ching-yen" [The experience of the Shansi-Chahar-Hopei Border Region in implementing the land policy], Jan. 15, 1945, in Li Keng, ed., *Chieh-fang-ch'ü te t'u-ti cheng-ts'e yü shih-shih* (hereafter *T'u-ti cheng-ts'e*), p. 49.

23. P'eng Chen, "Chin-ch'a-chi pien-ch'ü tang te kung-tso ho chü-t'i cheng-ts'e pao-kao [Report on Party work and concrete policies in the Shansi-Chahar-Hopei Border Region], in *T'u-ti cheng-ts'e chung-yao wen-chien hui-pien* (hereafter *Chung-yao wen-chien*), pp. 98-101. The nine *hsien* were: Laiyuan, Fup'ing, Ch'üyang, I, Ting, P'ingshan, and Lingshou (all in Hopei); Yü and Lingch'iu (in Shansi).

seven *hsien* in central Hopei found 46.8 percent of the population to be poor peasant; 38.6 percent were middle peasants and 6.3 percent rich peasants.

Conditions in two additional villages may be cited. In the village in Luch'eng *hsien*, southeastern Shansi, where William Hinton conducted his investigation, the pre-liberation classification was as follows: 46.8 percent poor peasant; 6 percent hired laborer; and 40 percent middle peasant. This village of approximately 250 households contained only one full tenant family.[24] In Yuanch'ü village, She *hsien* (then in northern Honan), 600 of the total 979 households in the village were either middle or new middle peasant before land reform and 300 families were classed as poor peasant. Land reform began in this village in 1946, when it had already been liberated for several years. The village had experienced at least two rent reduction drives and other struggles, accounting for the presence of new middle peasants.[25]

THE NORTHEAST

Statistics for the Northeast, where the Communists also carried out land reform after 1945, are even less available than for the rest of the country. One 1927 estimate, whose origins are obscure, classified a total of 2,549,699 farm families: 28.6 percent tenants, 27.6 percent part-tenants, and 43.9 percent landowners or owner-cultivators.[26] After September, 1931, the Northeast came under the control of the Japanese. They estimated that about 30 percent of the Chinese farmers there were tenants, and that another 20 percent were owner-tenants. As to the living conditions of these people, one Japanese source noted that "the majority of the Manchurian tenant-farmers can barely manage to earn a living by cultivating small strips of arable land they lease from landlords," and that the conditions of owner-tenants differed little from this norm.[27]

These tenancy estimates do not include migrant and other hired laborers, who reputedly formed a much larger segment of the rural population in Manchuria than in north China. In a survey conducted by the Japanese-sponsored Manchukuo government in thirty selected villages, the average percentage of rural households classified as hired peasant in 1936 was about 20. The percentage of tenants cited above, when combined with this hired peasant figure, does correspond to the proportion of landless families, roughly 48 percent, given in another Manchukuo survey.[28] However unsatisfactory these estimates, it is probably safe

24. William Hinton, *Fanshen: A Documentary of Revolution in a Chinese Village*, p. 209.

25. "Lo Ching t'ung-chih lai-hsin" [Letter from Comrade Lo Ching], in *Chin-chi-lu-yü yuan-ch'ü tzu-chueh t'uan-chieh yun-tung te ching-yen* (hereafter *Yuan-ch'ü tzu-chueh*), pp. 18-20.

26. H. G. W. Woodhead, ed., *China Year Book, 1928* (Tientsin: The Tientsin Press, 1928), pp. 1011-12.

27. *Japan-Manchoukuo Yearbook*, 1939, p. 788.

28. The hired peasant survey is cited in Chang Yu-i, ed., *Nung-yeh shih*, p. 551. The villages were selected from each of the three main geographic regions—south, central, and

to conclude that as much as half the rural population in the Northeast belonged in the poor peasant category.

THE IMPLICATIONS

These figures suggest that the Chinese Communists directed their main appeal not to tenant farmers as such, but to a much larger group of poor peasants and farm workers. Together they made up that sector of the rural population that, by definition, did not own enough of the means of production to remain self-supporting without suffering exploitation in the sense of having to rent land, sell their labor, or pay interest on loans. In practical terms, these were the people whose living conditions were by common agreement the lowest in any given village. And these were the people who provided the base of support for the Chinese Communists in the countryside. The elimination of tenancy alone could not have created a base of "mass" support for the Communists in north China, because tenancy was not a problem that concerned enough of the village masses. A substantial majority of the peasants there already owned the land they tilled.

The figures also suggest, moreover, that while the poor and hired peasants probably did constitute a majority in the Manchurian countryside, they did not necessarily do so in the villages of north China. In any given district there, the poor and hired together may have yielded to an absolute middle peasant majority; or they may have shared primacy of place with a near-equal middle peasant minority. If Manchuria represented the classic case for land reform as the Communists described it, north China did not. In addition, Manchuria contained, by conservative estimate, 16.7 million hectares (approximately 41.3 million acres) of uncultivated but arable land in 1945, including that vacated by Japanese settlers.[29] North China had no such wealth of untapped resources. Our main problem, then, is to explain the nature and significance of the Communists' appeal to the peasantry in north China. For it was there that the claims concerning the relationship between the CCP's land reform policy and the rural support it mobilized during the Civil War must have met their severest test.

The argument I will develop is that the Communists' key land reform slogan, "land-to-the-tiller" *(keng-che yu ch'i t'ien),* obscured as much as it revealed, since popular usage understood it to refer primarily to the elimination of

---

north—corresponding roughly to the three original provinces, Fengtien (the present Liao-ning), Kirin, and Heilungkiang. The hired peasant ratios were 13.5%, 17.9%, and 34.4% respectively. The survey of landless families is cited in the same source (p. 552). This survey covered 37 selected villages in 36 different *hsien* in the three regions. Landless households were 32.5%, 48.9%, and 63.2% respectively. However, a word of caution is in order. Frontier conditions in much of Manchuria during the early decades of this century meant that land registration was less precise than in the rest of China. Unregistered may have actually exceeded registered land in the early 1930s: see F. C. Jones, *Manchuria Since 1931,* pp. 169-70. Other differences between the Northeast and the rest of China are mentioned below under "Radical Land Reform: 1946-47."

29. Kungtu C. Sun, *The Economic Development of Manchuria in the First Half of the Twentieth Century,* p. 55.

tenancy. Tenancy *was* eliminated. But it was only one of several issues in north China. In addressing them, the Chinese Communists attacked simultaneously the more basic fact of socio-economic life in the countryside, namely, the inequality of wealth. This culminated in the October, 1947, Outline Agrarian Law, which stipulated not just the elimination of tenancy but the equalization of all village land and property.

At its most elementary level, land reform within the context of the Civil War represented a simple political equation. "Our Party must bring tangible material benefits to the people," wrote Mao, "only then will the masses support us and oppose the Kuomintang attacks. Otherwise, the masses will be unable to see clearly which of the two parties, the Kuomintang or the Communist Party, is good and which is bad."[30]

However, land reform was politically significant beyond this positive economic appeal to the poor. Equally important was its negative force. Together with the economic superiority of the landlords and rich peasants, land reform effectively destroyed the political power structure which supported them and which they supported. The Communists could then replace this with a political authority loyal to them and sustained by the active support of the poor peasants.

"Land-to-the-tiller" thus assumed a much broader meaning in Communist practice than in the minds of the liberal intellectuals who also advocated it. The Communists undoubtedly kept the slogan precisely because of its wide appeal and its capacity to encompass a range of meanings. In any case, the Communists could still argue that they were operating within the framework of Sun Yat-sen's third principle, the People's Livelihood—although in a somewhat different manner than his writings seemed to anticipate. Land for the tiller was only a part of his general land policy, which he labeled the "equalization of land rights" (p'ing-chün ti-ch'üan).[31] Whatever Sun himself may have meant by it, "equalization of land rights" would have made a more accurate, albeit less popular, slogan for the Communists' land program.

LAND REFORM: THE LESSONS OF
THE ANTI-JAPANESE WAR

The first official indication of a shift away from the policy of rent and interest reduction was the CCP Central Committee's May 4, 1946, "Directive on Liquida-

30. Mao Tse-tung, "Build Stable Base Areas in the Northeast," Dec. 28, 1945, *Selected Works*, 4:82-83.
31. Sun Yat-sen, *San Min Chu I: the Three Principles of the People*, trans. by Frank W. Price (Shanghai: Commercial Press, 1929), p. 456. Also see Harold Schiffrin, "Sun Yat-sen's Early Land Policy," *Journal of Asian Studies*, vol. 16, no. 4 (Aug., 1957): 549-64. However much Sun's formulation owed to the West, the concepts of land-to-the-tiller, and the equalization of land holdings, had ancient roots in Chinese thought on agrarian reform, extending back at least to Wang Mang's interregnum (A.D. 9-23). See, for example, Wan Kuo-ting, "The System of Equal Land Allotments in Medieval Times," in E-tu Zen Sun and John De Francis, eds., *Chinese Social History: Translations of Selected Studies* (Washington: American Council of Learned Societies, 1956), pp. 157-84.

tions, Rent Reductions, and Land Problems." Though widely cited as the source of the Party's new land policy, it circulated only as an intra-Party document. Its content was neither excessively radical nor very systematic. But the announced aim of the policy was to destroy existing patterns of land tenure and transfer the ownership of land to the peasants who tilled it. The ensuing land reform campaign took a number of different forms, some more radical than others, in the areas where it was implemented.

This seemingly experimental phase came to a close with the promulgation by the CCP Central Committee on October 10, 1947, of the Outline Agrarian Law. This authorized a systematic land reform program aimed at abolishing landlords as a class and equalizing land ownership. Toward those ends, the Law laid down a single set of principles and procedures to be followed in the expropriation and redistribution of land.

On May 25, 1948, the Party center directed that land reform should not be carried out unless the area in question was militarily secure; unless a majority of the peasants demanded land redistribution; and unless enough cadres were on hand to keep the task from being overwhelmed by the "spontaneous activity of the masses." These conditions did not generally obtain in areas liberated after the summer of 1947, the "new liberated areas." These areas were therefore directed to abandon land reform temporarily in favor of the more moderate policy of reducing rent and interest rates.

The shift back to land reform in 1946 should not have come as too great a surprise. In 1940, Mao had mentioned such a policy as part of the interim New Democracy. Mao wrote at that time:

> The republic will take certain necessary steps to confiscate the land of the landlords and distribute it to those peasants having little or no land, carry out Dr. Sun Yat-sen's slogan of "land-to-the-tiller", abolish feudal relations in the rural areas, and turn the land over to the private ownership of the peasants.[32]

Nevertheless, the shift was unexpected, coming as it did just one year after Mao's widely publicized report to the Seventh Party Congress in April, 1945. Mao indicated at that time that the Party would continue the rent reduction policy after the conclusion of the Anti-Japanese War:

> The Communist Party has made a major concession in the anti-Japanese war period by changing the policy of "land-to-the-tiller" to one of reducing rent and interest. This concession is a correct one, for it helped to bring the Kuomintang into the war against Japan and lessened the resistance of the landlords in the Liberated Areas to our mobilization of the peasants for the war. If no special obstacle arises, we are prepared to continue this policy after the war, first extending rent and interest reduction to the whole country and then taking proper measures for the gradual achievement of "land-to-the-tiller."[33]

32. Mao Tse-tung, "On New Democracy," *Selected Works*, 2:353.
33. Mao Tse-tung, "On Coalition Government," *Selected Works*, 3:298; also *Chung-yao wen-chien*, p. 8.

In October, Chou En-lai publicly reaffirmed this position in Chungking. The reduction of land rent and interest rates continued to be the chief objective of the Communist land policy, he said, while land-to-the-tiller and land nationalization should be left to the future.[34]

The only possible explanation for the sudden shift, in the opinion of many observers, was the Civil War itself. In October, 1945, negotiations were in progress between the CCP and the Central Government; in May, 1946, war was imminent. That summer, the Government began a major offensive against the Communist areas. The Communists never formally announced that the war was the cause of the change in their land policy. But in 1946, they began to argue that only land reform could mobilize the peasants to support them against the KMT. The causal relationship seemed clear.

Nevertheless, a few perceptive observers pointed out that the Communists' land policy had been moving "to the left" for some time prior to May, 1946. An intra-Party directive drafted by Mao in early November, 1945, reflected a militancy which the CCP was not yet willing to admit to the outside world:

> Rent reduction must be the result of mass struggle, not a favor by the government. On this depends the success or failure of rent reduction. In the struggle for rent reduction, excesses can hardly be avoided; as long as it is really a conscious struggle of the broad masses, any excesses that have occurred can be corrected afterwards. Only then can we persuade the masses and enable them to understand that it is in the interest of the peasants and the people as a whole to allow the landlords to make a living so that they will not help the Kuomintang. The present policy of our Party is still to reduce rents, not to confiscate land.[35]

Actually, land was already being "confiscated" in the Communist areas although it was called "settling accounts"; and rent reduction had become a euphemism for a long list of scores being settled in the process. The May Fourth Directive only affirmed and formalized a policy that had been developing in practice even prior to the Japanese surrender. In this respect, the new directive both pointed the way forward, and indicated what had been taking place under the guise of rent reduction for several years.

THE MAY FOURTH DIRECTIVE[36]

The Directive began by noting that a mass movement was developing in Communist-held areas of Shansi, Hopei, Shantung, and central China. In dealing with

34. *Hsin hua jih-pao*, Chungking, Oct. 20, 1945 *(CPR)*.

35. Mao Tse-tung, "Rent Reduction and Production Are Two Important Matters for the Defence of the Liberated Areas," *Selected Works*, 4:72.

36. "Chung-kung chung-yang kuan-yü ch'ing-suan chien tsu chi t'u-ti wen-t'i te chih-shih" [CCP Central Committee directive on liquidations, rent reduction, and land problems], in *Chung-yao wen-chien*, pp. 1-7. This directive was never issued for general circulation. It was reprinted in a Taiwan publication in 1950: Nei-cheng-pu tiao-ch'a-chü, *Chien-fei hsien-chuang hui-pien: t'u kai*, pp. 40-45. Differences between the Taiwan version and that summarized here are more of form than substance. Except for a few minor discrepancies, the wording is identical. But the numbered items appear in different sequence, and the contents of some items have been rearranged.

traitors, reducing rent, and liquidating old debts, land was being taken from the landlords and given to the peasants. A few places had even gone so far as to equalize land ownership with each person being allotted three *mou* of land. Because some people, Party members included, had begun to express doubts about this mass movement, the leadership had decided to affirm the policy line. The various local Party committees were directed to implement it, conditions permitting, before the year was out. The local committees must understand, declared the directive, that this historic task was the most basic of all work. The instructions for leading the movement were outlined as follows:

1. In the struggle against traitors, and in the struggles to liquidate old debts and reduce rent and interest rates, take land from the landlords and put it in the hands of the tillers.

2. Absorb the middle peasants into the movement. See that they, too, benefit from it and do not encroach upon their land. If their land is taken from them, it should be returned or compensation paid to them.

3. In general, do not touch the land of rich peasants, but if it cannot be avoided in the process of liquidating debts and land reform, then do not attack them too severely. There should be a difference between landlords and rich peasants. If the latter are treated too harshly, it will cause the middle peasants to waver and affect production adversely.

4. Distinguish between the core districts, those where our political authority has been established, and border districts that we do not yet occupy firmly. In the latter, carry out rent reduction, but in order to minimize confusion and losses do not, in general, activate the masses to demand land.

5. The above principles must be followed or divisions will occur among the peasants; the poor and hired, together with our Party, will be isolated; and the reactionaries will be strengthened. To avoid this, the local Party committee should issue this directive and explain it in light of local conditions before the cadres are sent to the districts to do the actual land reform work. Explain to people outside the Party that this directive represents the demands of over 90 percent of the rural population, that is, the hired, poor, and middle peasants, handicraftsmen, and other poor people, as against the interests of the landlords and rich peasants. Also explain that these demands are the same as those advocated by Sun Yat-sen and the Political Consultative Conference.

6. Distinguish between landlords with much land, bad gentry, and local tyrants *(o-pa)*, on the one hand, and medium and small landlords on the other. Be rather more considerate of the latter, using methods of arbitration and agreement to resolve their problems with the peasants.

7. Concentrate on traitors and local tyrants. Isolate them completely. Take their land and leave them just enough to sustain themselves.

8. Except in the case of the very worst traitors, the industrial and commercial enterprises of rich peasants and landlords should not be encroached upon, so as to avoid adversely influencing the development of business and industry. Our treatment of the feudal landlord class is different in principle from our treatment of capitalist business and industry. In some places, methods used in the

villages to liquidate feudal landlords have been erroneously used in the cities to liquidate business and industry. This should be stopped.

9. If the people support it, the most traitorous elements and the worst public enemies may be tried in court and executed. But except for such people, do not seize many others, or beat or kill them. This will frighten the masses and provide the reactionaries with the pretext for a counterattack.

10. Adopt a conciliatory attitude toward all intellectuals who can be educated; toward enlightened gentry, urban capitalists, and people outside the CCP who approve of our democratic principles; and toward landlords and others who have run away and now wish to return home.

11. Some of the latter wish to return home in order to create disturbances in the liberated areas. Let them return to the surveillance of the masses. This will reduce the strength of those elements in the [KMT-held] cities who are maligning us.

12. Many forms have been devised for solving the land problem, such as:

a. Outright confiscation and redistribution of land belonging to traitors with large holdings.

b. Voluntary sale of land, after rent reduction, with the tenant having first right of purchase.

c. Voluntary donation by the landlord to his tenants.

d. The sale of land in order to liquidate the landlords' debts incurred through the receipt of [excessive] rent and interest, forcible take-over of property [foreclosures], unpaid taxes, and "other unreasonable exploitation."

These forms are legal and reasonable and very different from those used during the 1930s. The various places can adopt different forms in accordance with the different targets of their struggles.

13. The property obtained must be fairly distributed to the poor families of war dead, to anti-Japanese fighters and cadres, and to peasants with little or no land. After the land problem has thus been resolved, concentrate on other work such as developing production; building the peasant associations, the people's militia, and the CCP organization; recruiting cadres; improving the *ch'ü* and *hsiang* political organization; and educating the masses to protect themselves and the land they have received.

14. The land policy of the Party center as formulated in 1942, activated a broad mass movement in support of the Anti-Japanese War. The rent reduction policy has not been completely abandoned; but, in view of the developing movement to liquidate debts and reduce rent, the present change could not be avoided.

15. Both rightist and leftist deviations on land policy have occurred within the Party. These should be corrected locally on the basis of this directive.

THE BACKGROUND OF EXPERIENCE

The May Fourth Directive did not mark a sharp break with the past—for two reasons. First, it derived from the previous rent reduction policy, which when enforced was said to have inspired land sales and contributions, and when violated provided one of the grounds for calculating the landlords' debts. Second, such sales, contributions, and punishments had been associated with the Communist rent reduction policy from its inception. Moreover, they had been accompanied by a number of other methods designed to transfer wealth from those who had it to those who did not. The difference between rent reduction in practice, and land reform in its 1946 formulation, was more of degree than of kind.

The similarities were reflected in Liu Shao-ch'i's recommmendations as to the course the Party's land policy should take during the Anti-Japanese War. So similar in spirit were Liu's proposals, made in 1937, with the May Fourth Directive, that the Shansi-Chahar-Hopei Party Bureau reprinted them in 1946 and circulated the two documents together. Given the necessity of the anti-Japanese united front, Liu had approved the Party's decision to stop the violent confiscation of landlord holdings. But he wrote that the transferral of property from landlords to peasants should not be similarly abandoned. He suggested the Party issue certain laws and decrees aimed at achieving that objective. Such action was necessary to ensure the peasants' participation in the resistance. While the landlords might not like it, they should be willing to sacrifice for the national interest.

Liu offered ten proposals. Besides reducing rent and interest, they included recommendations: (1) that the land of traitors be confiscated and distributed to peasants with little or no land; (2) that land belonging to runaway landlords be distributed to peasants to cultivate rent-free; (3) that local public lands be distributed to the peasants; (4) that tenant peasants be guaranteed perpetual tenancy rights to the land they tilled; (5) that local rascals and bad gentry who had exploited the peasants be punished; the peasants directly elect their own village political authorities, and organize their own armed self-defense force; and (6) that exorbitant interest rates be prohibited.[37]

As will be indicated below, most of these six proposals were being implemented in one form or another by 1945. Yet not one of them had been written into the Party's most widely publicized statement on peasant land policy during the Anti-Japanese War period. This was the "Decision on Land Policy in the Anti-Japanese Base Areas," passed by the Political Bureau on January 28, 1942.[38] The Communist base areas had suffered major losses as a result of the Japanese campaigns against them in 1941-42. The Decision's conciliatory tone, as compared with Liu's proposals, seemed to reflect the difficulties of those years, and the leadership's consequent desire to minimize class friction. The Decision did not even acknowledge the desirability of gradually transferring land from landlords to peasants. In order to avoid a reduction of credit, interest rates

37. Liu Shao-ch'i, "K'ang-jih yu-chi chan-cheng chung ko-chung chi-pen cheng-ts'e wen-t'i" [Various questions concerning the basic policies of the Anti-Japanese guerrilla war], Oct. 16, 1937, in *Chung-yao wen-chien,* p. 27; also Liu Shao-ch'i, *Collected Works,* 1:41.

38. "Chung-yang kuan-yü k'ang-jih ken-chü-ti t'u-ti cheng-ts'e te chüeh-ting," in *Chung-yao wen-chien,* pp. 29-37.

on loans contracted after 1937 were to be freely determined in accordance with local conditions. No mention was made of punishment for local bullies who had exploited the peasantry.

But despite its moderation, the Decision seemed to stress rightist errors of omission more heavily than the commission of leftist excesses. It pointed out that, while the Party's rent and interest reduction policy had been in effect since 1937, "many base areas" had not yet carried it out "extensively, conscientiously, or thoroughly." In some base areas, the policy was nothing but a propaganda slogan. Local governments had promulgated laws without enforcing them, so the reductions were carried out in name only. Leftist mistakes had occurred "only in some places."

Two years later, however, Mao spoke of "a kind of ultra-left deviation" that had developed within the Party during 1941-42. It occurred, he said, in response to the progressive breakdown of the united front with the KMT that paralleled the intensified Japanese campaigns against the Communist areas. As a result, "excessive attacks were made on the landlords."[39]

The Shansi-Chahar-Hopei
(Chin-Ch'a-Chi) Border Region[40]

"Excesses" did occur, but probably not only for the reason that Mao gave. Nor did they first appear in 1941, although that may have been about the time the Party began to recognize them as such. For example, in February, 1941, Liu Lan-t'ao, a Party official in the Pei-yueh District of the Chin-Ch'a-Chi Border Region, sought to bolster the spirit of the united front by admonishing local cadres that the present was not the time for a thorough resolution of the land problem. He advised them, among other things, to respect the landlords' ownership rights; to stop temporarily the return to the original owner of lands lost at any time during the past thirty years due to defaulted mortgage contracts; and not to confiscate the land of runaway landlords. In dealing with temple and grave lands, he warned that the temple accusation movement carried out in some places was wrong and that the forceful levelling of grave mounds, and felling of trees surrounding grave sites, had caused much dissatisfaction.[41]

All such practices fell into the category of excesses when judged by united front land policy standards. Such practices had obviously occurred in this district prior to February, 1941. And even Comrade Liu noted that landlords had resorted to a variety of tactics to avoid rent reduction in places where it had been attempted. Where landlords had acutally taken revenge against tenants and

39. Mao Tse-tung, "Our Study and the Current Situation," Apr. 12, 1944, *Selected Works*, 3:169.

40. The Chin-Ch'a-Chi military area was formed in November, 1937; the Border Region government in January, 1938 (James P. Harrison, *The Long March to Power: A History of the Chinese Communist Party, 1921-72*, p. 299).

41. "Liu Lan-t'ao t'ung-chih tsai chung-kung chin-ch'a-chi pien-ch'ü pei-yueh-ch'ü tang wei erh-yueh k'uo-kan-hui shang te pao-kao" [Comrade Liu Lan-t'ao's report to the February (1941) enlarged cadre conference of the Pei-yueh District Party Committee Chin-Ch'a-Chi Border Region], in *Chung-yao wen-chien*, pp. 56-61.

created disorders, he declared that the peasants should strike back and "struggle according to reason and law."

P'eng Chen's 1944 report on Party work in the Border Region brings these apparent discrepancies into somewhat better focus. Like everyone else, he described the anti-Japanese resistance as both a national and a peasant war. Unless the Party could improve the peasants' lives politically, culturally, and especially materially, they would have no energy or desire to participate in the resistance. But the landlords were hostile to any improvements in the peasants' living conditions, and this had already resulted in sharp struggles when reforms were attempted. The contradiction was critical because the war required the cooperation of landlords and peasants.

He outlined the history of landlord-peasant relations in the Border Region as follows. When the Party first began implementing the double reduction policy, the landlords opposed it. At this time, the cadres' inclinations seemed to be more left than right, but those of the "basic masses" seemed just the opposite. During the second stage, which lasted about two years beginning with the Japanese invasion of north China in July, 1937, the Party's power developed rapidly, as did the struggle against reactionaries. The peasants stood up with great sound and fury to attack evil landlords. In some places, peasants refused to pay rent or interest. They cancelled debts and transformed the land sales movement by expropriating land without compensation.

Village struggles intensified and the landlords' opposition took new forms. They started marrying their daughters to tenants and poor peasants, and sought other means of coopting them. But at the same time, the landlords also began conspiring with the Japanese against the peasants, attacking them, seizing village personnel, and the like.

According to P'eng, this struggle was a necessary phase in the development of landlord-peasant relations. Pushing the reforms further than was immediately necessary presumably helped to achieve the landlords' acquiescence to the policy they opposed, once the "excesses" had been corrected. The correctives began with a directive from the Party center in Yenan on the third anniversary of the Marco Polo Bridge Incident. A Border Region directive was issued a month later. These 1940 directives outlined the same principles that would be reaffirmed in the final summation of the Party's united front land policy in January, 1942. They stipulated that landlords and creditors should reduce rent and interest, but that tenants and debtors must pay them. They also guaranteed everyone's civil liberties including the right to make and terminate contracts.[42]

Actually, P'eng was describing a policy that had yet to be widely enforced within the Border Region. As of October, 1943, rent reduction had been "thoroughly" implemented in only a few *hsien* at the heart of Pei-yueh District; in most of the Seventh and Ninth Sub-districts in central Hopei; and in small portions of the Sixth and Eighth Sub-districts. Elsewhere in Pei-yueh and central Hopei, rent reduction had only been "basically" achieved. In P'ing-pei, the

42. P'eng Chen, pp. 43-55 (see note 23 above).

region to the north of Peiping, the policy was still in the first stages of implementation. Even that stage had not been reached in more than a thousand villages drawn into the base area in Pei-yueh and eastern Hopei during the preceding year. Finally, there were several districts which had carried out the policy but where everything gained had been lost with the shifting fortunes of war.

However, the criteria for determining "thorough" implementation in Chin-Ch'a-Chi encompassed a good deal more than the Party's official rent reduction policy seemed to indicate. Thorough implementation meant 25 percent rent reduction; *the elimination of all excessive economic exploitation;* the full activation of the masses; the consolidation of the benefits won; the seizure of political power by the "basic masses"; and the formation of local militia forces. "Basic" implementation meant that the 25 percent rent reduction had been carried out and economic exploitation attacked, but that neither had been done thoroughly. In some villages and in many households, rent had been reduced in name only, while tenants secretly paid landlords at old rates. The peasants had not been fully activated and could easily lose the benefits won.

All of this information was contained in a Border Region directive in mid-October, 1943.[43] It followed one from the Party center on October 1, outlining the "Ten Great Policies" of the Anti-Japanese War in their final formulation. Rent and interest reduction was only one of the policies, but the directive called specifically for its thorough implementation following the autumn harvest.[44]

Reiterating the policy statement from the Party centèr, Border Region authorities called for the immediate, thorough, and extensive implementation of rent reduction. In addition, the regional directive also listed the three prerequisites for initiating rent reduction or reintroducing it in newly opened districts or those retaken from the enemy. The three conditions were: (1) the removal of pro-Japanese political authorities and the reform of the village political structure; (2) the ability of anti-Japanese armed forces to operate in the vicinity; and (3) the preliminary construction or restoration of a party organization, peasant associations, and other mass organizations in the villages. The directive ordered

43. "Chung-kung chung-yang chin-ch'a-chi fen-chü kuan-yü ch'e-ti shih-hsing chien tsu cheng-ts'e te chih-shih" [Directive of the CCP Central Committee Chin-Ch'a-Chi Sub-bureau on the thorough implementation of the rent reduction policy], Oct. 18, 1943, in *Chung-yao wen-chien,* pp. 83-88.

44. "Chung-yang cheng-chih-chü kuan-yü chien tsu sheng-ch'an yung cheng ai min chi hsuan-ch'uan shih ta cheng-ts'e te chih-shih" [Central Political Bureau directive on rent reduction, production, support-the-government-and-cherish-the-people, and propagandizing the ten great policies], Oct. 1, 1943, in *Chung-yao wen-chien,* pp. 78-81. This directive is attributed to Mao Tse-tung in his *Selected Works,* 3:131-35, which, however, omits section four listing the ten great policies. In the version cited here, the ten policies are: struggle with the enemy; streamline troops and simplify administration; unify leadership; support the government and cherish · the people; develop production; rectify the Party; investigate cadres; carry out current events education; implement the three-thirds united front system in government; reduce rent and interest. Most of these policies are described in Mark Selden, *The Yenan Way in Revolutionary China.*

that rent reduction be carried out wherever those conditions existed, and that the conditions themselves be prepared everywhere else. In districts where the struggle with the enemy still threatened, all work should be subordinated to it and to the maintenance of a united front.

The intensifying campaign that followed in the wake of these October directives provided the immediate context of P'eng Chen's concern about leftism. In his November, 1944, report, he noted that leftist inclinations tended to come to the fore only after an area had been basically consolidated and the peasants activated to the point where they would stand firm against landlord opposition. The excesses were dangerous, however, and could threaten the long-term survival of the base area. P'eng listed six inclinations among cadres which encouraged the commission of leftist excesses by the peasants:

1. The cadres genuinely doubted that the landlords were capable of opposing the Japanese.

2. Some cadres refused to distinguish between different kinds of landlords. Every time an anti-Communist upsurge occurred and some of the landlords began to waver, these cadres felt betrayed by the entire class and advocated its destruction.

3. Many cadres felt that the moderate provisions of the united front land policy were wrong and therefore continued to encroach upon the landlords' rights as guaranteed thereby. The peasants were allowed to violate the terms of tenancy agreements and mortgage contracts—sometimes refusing to pay rent and interest altogether, cancelling old debts, and taking back lands lost when mortgage terms had not been fulfilled. The cadres also took the peasants' side when disputes arose over such problems as permanent tenancy rights, and the exchange rates for paying rent and interest—originally fixed at pre-war levels but now payable in the inflated wartime Border Region currency.

4. Some local Party authorities simply refused to accept the united front land policy and continued to implement the previous one, confiscating landlord holdings and distributing land to the peasants.

5. There was a tendency to treat landlords and rich peasants alike, and to implement the land policy so as to weaken the latter as well as the former.

6. There was also a tendency to neglect production while concentrating almost exclusively on distribution, that is, on improving the peasants' livelihood and changing landlord-tenant relations.

The foregoing outline of developments in Chin-Ch'a-Chi shows that several basic components of the land reform campaign were associated with the more moderate rent reduction policy, both in the "thorough" and the "excessive" phases of its implementation. This association occurred only where rent reduction was actively pursued. In terms of the base area as a whole, however, the dominant concern throughout most of the period of the policy's implementation was with rightist errors of omission, P'eng Chen's protestations to the contrary not withstanding. Thus our outline has also begun to suggest the nature of the lessons the Chinese Communists learned during the Anti-Japanese War. The threads of the argument emerge with greater clarity in the data available from other base areas.

The Shansi-Hopei-Shantung-Honan
(Chin-Chi-Lu-Yü) Border Region[45]

In this Border Region, too, Party documents listed the "elimination of exploitation" as a separate objective in addition to rent and interest reduction. Moreover, Party authorities indicated specifically what other kinds of exploitation they had in mind, and sanctioned attacks against them where excessive rent and interest were not effective in arousing peasant interest. In so doing, the regional authorities indicated the difficulties they were experiencing in trying to adapt central policy to local conditions so as to mobilize the widest possible base of popular support.

Here, too, the implementation of the rent and interest reduction policy did not get off to a particularly fast start. The promotion of the campaign was further complicated by the drought and subsequent famine that ravaged much of Honan and surrounding areas between 1942-44.[46] Efforts were made to combine relief measures with the basic reform program. The Party committee of Hopei-Shantung-Honan (Chi-Lu-Yü), a sub-region within the larger Border Region, issued a directive in June, 1943, on interest rate reduction. Many peasants had been forced to take loans as a result of the disaster and interest rates had risen accordingly. The directive stipulated that interest on loans taken the previous winter or spring, and payable after the autumn harvest, should total only 30 percent of the amount borrowed—though 50 percent would be permissible in districts immediately threatened by the enemy. If actually implemented, this directive resulted in a considerable saving for the peasants since interest on such loans at this time was reputedly over 100 percent.[47]

Across the Peiping-Hankow Railway in the T'aihang Sub-region, a Disaster Relief and Spring Cultivation Movement was launched at this same time, and efforts made to control the market price of grain. In one village in Wuan *hsien*, famine relief measures included the search for and seizure of grain being hoarded by landlords and rich peasants. The grain was distributed free to the poor.[48]

The first attempt to liquidate past debts of exploitation also began in this region at this time. But despite these initial undisguised attacks on the wealthy, achievements were limited in all respects. A Party cadre, Lo Ching, described the history of these efforts in She *hsien*, just to the southwest of Wuan. With specific reference to Yüanch'ü village, Comrade Lo admitted that before 1942 the Party's work there had been backward in the extreme. The masses had not been mobilized, and nothing could be done without the approval of gentry and landlords. In 1942, the great mass campaigns began with the "settling old debts

45. This Border Region government was formed in July, 1941 (Harrison, *Long March to Power*, p. 301).

46. An eyewitness account of the famine in KMT-controlled areas of Honan is in Theodore H. White and Annalee Jacoby, *Thunder Out of China*, pp. 166-78.

47. Chi-lu-yü ch'ü tang wei, "Chien hsi ch'ing chai kung-tso chih-shih" [Directive on interest reduction and debt liquidation work], June 8, 1943, in *Ch'ün yun chih-shih hui-pien* (hereafter *Chih-shih hui-pien*), p. 5.

48. Isabel and David Crook, *Revolution in a Chinese Village: Ten Mile Inn*, pp. 56-59.

movement," the famine relief and anti-traitor campaigns of 1943, and two drives to further the implementation of rent and interest reduction in 1944 and 1945. Still the activation of the peasants had not been "even, or deep, or widespread."[49]

The Activation of Mass Struggle. As Comrade Lo's remarks suggest, the campaign to promote "mass activation" through rent and interest reduction was intensified in this Border Region, too, following the October 1, 1943, directive from the Party center. The recapitulation of the Ten Great Anti-Japanese War Policies was part of the CCP's overall effort to consolidate its strength against the Japanese pacification campaigns. As noted, these accelerated in 1941-42, with the adoption of scorched earth tactics by the Japanese army in the form of its notorious "kill all, burn all, destroy all" policy.[50] The enemy's pacification campaigns reduced the population from which the Communists could collect taxes by half, to under 50 million, and the Eighth Route Army to about 300,000 men.[51] But having strengthened its internal organization with the Party Rectification Movement (1942-44),[52] and having developed its Ten Great Policies to a point of maximum readiness, the Party was in a position to apply them with increasing effect as the Japanese offensive began to recede in 1943.

A directive from the Hopei-Shantung-Honan Sub-region Party Committee in November cautioned against deceiving "ourselves and others" by blindly claiming that the Party had improved the peasants' lives. In accordance with the Party center's directive of October 1, it ordered local Party committees to spend one month assessing the peasants' living conditions, particularly in the areas the Japanese had occupied and in districts not yet fully liberated. Answers were to be sought to several questions. Had rent and interest reduction been thoroughly implemented? Had the wages of farm workers been raised? Had anti-corruption and anti-black land struggles been carried out and the fruits obtained thereby distributed to the poorest peasants? Was the Party's progressive tax system being enforced?[53]

After the investigations had been completed the following spring, the sub-region launched a campaign attacking formalism in the implementation of rent reduction, a problem also addressed by the center's October 1st directive. Mao Tse-tung's 1927 "Report on an Investigation of the Peasant Movement in

49. "Letter from Comrade Lo Ching" (see note 25 above).

50. Chalmers A. Johnson, *Peasant Nationalism and Communist Power*, pp. 55-56.

51. Mao Tse-tung, *Selected Works*, 3:167-68.

52. The Party reform movement of 1942-44 aimed at both the "sinification of Marxism" and the "Bolshevization" of the CCP. Its purpose was to teach Party members to apply Marxism to Chinese problems, and to inculcate Stalinist methods of organization and discipline in a party that had grown from forty thousand in 1937 to several hundred thousand in 1942. Many of these new recruits had been drawn to the Party more in its role as leader of the anti-Japanese resistance than as vanguard of the Chinese revolution. On the reform movement, see Boyd Compton, *Mao's China: Party Reform Documents, 1942-44.*

53. "Ch'ü tang wei (yuan chi-lu-yü) kuan-yü shen-ju chien-ch'a ch'ün-chung kung-tso te chih-shih" [The Regional Party Committee (originally Hopei-Shantung-Honan) directive on deeply investigating mass work], Nov. 16, 1943, in *Chih-shih hui-pien*, pp. 8-9.

Hunan" was reissued in keeping with the spirit of the times. "Why are the masses so cold toward us?" queried Huang Ching, head of the Sub-region Party Committee, in a statement marking the start of the campaign. According to reports from even the most secure districts in the region, the peasants were generally hesitating and passive, the cadres isolated, and production not progressing satisfactorily.

The reason for this, said Huang Ching, was that the cadres were afraid of hurting the landlords, afraid that the peasants would go too far. Instead of mobilizing them to struggle with the landlords, the Party committees had simply decreed the reduction of rent, and moved on to production work. Production should not have become the main preoccupation until the peasants could be guaranteed some immediate improvements in their living conditions. But such improvements depended on weakening the landlords who monopolized the surplus within the village economy. Until that had been accomplished, they would continue their resistance, and continue taking back the benefits that Party decrees had bestowed upon the peasants. The answer was to raise the peasants' political consciousness in the course of the struggle to improve their livelihood. They had to be mobilized to stand firm against the landlords' opposition. We must change our attitude, challenged Huang, we must not fear that the masses will commit errors and we must not limit their actions.[54]

As indicated, rent and interest reduction were not the only targets of the intensifying campaign to reduce the political and economic power of landlords and others. In the Twelfth Sub-district, for example, struggles against unregistered or black land, corruption, and *o-pa* (local tyrants), were found to be particularly effective means toward that end.[55]

It seems impossible to find a precise definition of the term *o-pa*. As a general rule of thumb, an *o-pa* was a local man of some power who used it not just once but habitually to do evil to others. His immediate source of power might be political or economic, to the extent that the two could be distinguished within the context of a Chinese village. Thus he might be a landlord pure and simple; he might be a secret society member; or he might be a political official, albeit with close links to landlords or other men of means. Because of his political and economic connections, neither law nor social custom could readily be invoked against him. He probably, although not necessarily, had access to instruments of violence which he used to enforce his designs. The criminal acts that could inspire this appellation varied from place to place, but were generally in the nature of murder, physical assault, rape, extortion, or the illegal seizure of property. His victims might be drawn from any class, but his actions were such that they were condemned by all.

54. Huang Ching, "Kuan-yü fa-tung ch'ün-chung chi mu-ch'ien chung-hsin kung-tso wen-t'i te fa-yen" [A statement on activating the masses and problems in current core work], Apr. 25, 1944, in *Chih-shih hui-pien*, pp. 20-26.

55. "Fen-chü kei shih-erh ti wei te chih-shih-hsin" [A letter of instruction from the Sub-bureau to the Twelfth Sub-district Party Committee], Jan. 18, 1945, in *Chih-shih hui-pien*, p. 30.

In practical terms, the attack against these local tyrants, and especially against tyrant landlords, was used as a catalyst to activate peasant hostility against the landlord class as a whole. But in villages without landlords, cadres used the *o-pa* campaign as an initial issue around which to mobilize peasant support. Hence the warning to the Party Committee of the Twelfth Sub-district against mechanically commencing mass work in any area by trying to mobilize support for rent reduction. Cadres were advised to investigate local conditions and begin with the most pressing demands of the peasants.

However, when mass work began with struggles against corruption, black land, or *o-pa*, leadership tended to be quickly monopolized by middle peasants. The Party therefore warned cadres not to overlook the economic welfare of poor and hired peasants at this stage, but to try to resolve some of their problems, develop their political consciousness, and nurture leadership elements among them. Then, as soon as the "democratic struggles" had been concluded, the cadres should turn to the "struggles for the people's livelihood," that is, the reduction of rent and increase of wages. It was only through these measures that the "basic masses" could be fully mobilized, effectively organized, their leadership established in the village, and their superior strength consolidated.

In all cases, moreover, the settling accounts method was to be adopted. The liquidation struggle, or the struggle to settle accounts of past exploitation, became an important instrument of the Party's land policy after 1943 and remained so throughout the land reform period. This method entailed calculating the debts owed the peasants by landlords and others from the take-over of mortgaged land, unpaid labor, deliberate attempts to circumvent rent reduction, and the like. On the basis of the peasants' claims and accusations, the amount of past exploitation was fixed and calculated in terms of cash, grain, or other property. When the debts added up to more than the accused could readily pay—a regular occurrence—he was obliged to sell some of his land in order to make up the balance. The proceeds were turned over to the exploited party. The distribution of such property—often referred to as the struggle fruits—became progressively more direct, more egalitarian, and less prone to abuse as time went on.

This method was important, particularly while the united front land policy was still officially in effect, because it allowed the Party to avoid the onus of outright land confiscation. More significant, it involved the peasants directly in the struggle by forcing them to state their claims openly, and schooled them in the diverse manifestations of exploitation by encouraging them to recall every past injustice. Both before 1945 and after, in this Border Region and others, the struggles covered the gamut of issues and grievances. Lastly, settling old accounts was an effective means of transferring wealth from those who had more to those with less. The latter did not have to wait for the next harvest or the next time they needed a loan to realize tangible benefits; nor did they even have to be tenants or debtors. Settling old accounts did not rely on the promise of future gains; it provided them directly in the immediate present.

Party cadres in the Twelfth Sub-district were instructed to calculate and settle "old" grievances in the course of the struggles against corruption and local tyrants. In exposing black land, reducing rent, and increasing wages, old accounts were not to be calculated, but only those accumulated since the establishment of the anti-Japanese government of the particular *hsien*. In addition, owners of black land could be fined from one to five times the amount owed in back taxes.

As for interest rate reduction, the core areas of the sub-district had had little experience with such work. Only tyrannical landlords *(o-pa ti-chu)* should be made to return to their debtors the amount of excessive interest charged on loans made before the Anti-Japanese War began. Otherwise, accounts were to be settled only on high interest loans made after the start of the war. The methods of liquidating such accounts were to vary according to the class background of the creditor and debtor households involved.[56]

Actually, the use of the black lands campaign as a device for activating peasant hostility against landlords dated back at least to the beginning of 1943. In February of that year, the Sub-region Party Committee directed that everyone, whether rich or poor, should participate in the campaign to report voluntarily and search out unregistered land. "In general," the poor and middle peasants were not to be punished even if they refused to report their unregistered holdings. But they were required to turn over all or part of the back taxes owed, according to their economic situation. Rich peasants and medium and small landlords were ordered to pay their back taxes in full. Big landlords who refused to report were to pay the full amount of taxes owed plus a fine.

This last course was recommended especially for villages where the peasants' class consciousness had not been well developed. Where it had been, the cadres should anticipate more voluntary reporting, fewer fines, and a minimum of class friction over this issue. Where the peasants had not yet been aroused, the proper approach was to isolate the most reactionary landlords, mobilize the peasants to investigate their land holdings, and see that some benefits accrued to the peasants. "The stage of development of the mass movement and class policy in a village should determine whether a fine is heavy or light and back taxes paid in part or in full."[57]

Of Excesses and Middle Peasants. The pattern of leftist deviations in this Border Region was similar to that described by P'eng Chen in Chin-Ch'a-Chi. They occurred with the intensifying rent reduction campaign during 1944, in areas where it was most thoroughly developed. Hua *hsien* (Honan) and Fan *hsien* (Shantung) were two such areas, where the following tendencies had been observed: (1) Some cadres cherished a blind faith in the masses to the point of denying the validity of leadership by refusing to follow the provisions of Party policies and government decrees. (2) In villages that had no landlords, middle

56. *Ibid.,* pp. 30-32.

57. Chi-lu-yü ch'ü tang wei, "Ch'ing-ch'a hei-ti chih-shih" [Directive on investigating black land], Feb. 25, 1943, in *Chih-shih hui-pien,* pp. 1-2.

peasants were attacked instead. This had occurred in Fan *hsien* and was the "most serious and dangerous" deviation, "a grave violation of the Party's class policy." In such villages, middle peasants had become so fearful and insecure as a result of being struggled against and economically weakened, that they had adopted a passive attitude toward production. They even hoped for the return of the KMT army. As a further result, the attack on middle peasants also dealt a blow to poor peasants' hopes for improved living conditions. (3) Elsewhere, cadres failed to distinguish between wealthy and less wealthy landlords, between law-abiding landlords and *o-pa,* between the enlightened and the reactionary, and even between landlords and rich peasants. All were attacked indiscriminately. Some good landlords were not just weakened economically, but destroyed and left with no means of supporting themselves. (4) During 1944 there had been a great expansion of the liberated districts and the Party's strength therein. Some comrades had begun to wonder whether the time for returning officially to the more radical policy of outright expropriation had not arrived. They were reminded that it had not, and that the Party's land policy was still to weaken the landlord class politically and economically, not to destroy it.[58]

Some of these deviations, especially the third and fourth, could not have been entirely unwelcome in light of what would soon follow. Moreover, the Party's instructions seemed calculated to bring about such results, so thinly did the line continue to be drawn between thorough and excessive implementation. This was particularly true with respect to the middle peasant problem. For example, a regional Party directive in late 1944, encouraged a line of action that seemed to make almost inevitable the weakening of middle peasants. It also hinted at the probable origins of the diverse struggle targets emerging within the rent reduction program.

According to the directive, middle peasants controlled villages where there were no landlords or rich peasants. Middle peasants constituted a basic force within the present democratic revolution. But they had their "weaknesses." They were not as determined in the struggle against landlords as were the poor and hired. When middle peasants controlled a village, there were local tyrants and corrupt officials among them. Methods of political struggle should therefore be used in dealing with this kind of "feudal exploitation." Indeed, when a majority of the peasants genuinely hated such individuals and demanded a confrontation with them, local cadres were advised not to "pour cold water" on the masses, or inhibit them for fear of alienating the middle peasants. Economic struggles, or the policy of economic weakening, should not be adopted, although appropriate economic compensation could be demanded from them in liquidating their debts of political exploitation.

The potential contradictions were obvious since middle peasants lived, by definition, with little surplus to spare. Also, the incentives for abusing the latter provision were great, in view of the "weaknesses" of middle peasants as emphasized, and the necessity of producing some tangible benefits for the poor. The

---

58. Fen-chü, "Chih-hsing ta-tan fang-shou te p'ien-hsiang" [Deviations in courageous action], Feb. 8, 1945, in *Chih-shih hui-pien,* p. 32.

directive noted that in villages without landlords, the cadres had initially emphasized agricultural production. When they found that the poor had no means of
increasing their production, they had turned on the middle peasants who did.[59]

Given these conflicting goals, the problem could hardly have been expected
to resolve itself. In May, 1945, another Party communication began:
"Recently ... punishment of middle peasants has been very great causing them
to become terrorized and social order insecure. The main problem is the middle
peasants' fear which has had a demoralizing effect making it difficult to turn
toward production and to consolidate our work."[60]

The Shantung Base Areas

Guerrilla fighting in Shantung followed at once on the heels of the invading
Japanese in late 1937. Administrative and political bodies were organized at the
hsiang level as early as 1939 in a few relatively secure districts dominated by
Communist forces and their local allies. *Hsien,* multi-*hsien,* and regional level
organizations were soon built around these isolated but expanding guerrilla
bases. Communist forces gradually gained control of the resistance movement in
the province and went on to organize the five military-administrative districts
mentioned above.[61] Some province-wide political coordination was achieved by
the Shantung Sub-bureau of the CCP through a number of provincial representative and work conferences (the first held in 1940), a provisional consultative
council, and a provincial wartime administrative committee. Nevertheless, the
local "organizations of political power" were not joined under a single provincial
government until 1945, reflecting the relatively insecure state of the Communists' military and political base in Shantung throughout most of the Anti-
Japanese War.

The initial Japanese offensive in the province came to a halt in 1939, when
the enemy began "sweeping his rear." The objective was to consolidate the area,
secure key points and communications lines, occupy secondary cities and large
villages, and in general wipe out guerrilla resistance. Pro-KMT guerrillas were
competing with the Communists for control of the resistance movement at this
stage, but sometimes joined with the Japanese in their mopping up operations
against the Communists. Despite initial losses, Communist units were able to
expand their bases in the wake of the drives against them during 1939-40. But
from the winter of 1941, the pacification campaigns intensified with the inauguration by the Japanese of their "three-all" policy. By the end of 1943, Japanese
and puppet troops had secured over 400 key points in the mountain districts of
central Shantung where pro-Communist forces had gained an initial foothold.

According to one summary of wartime work, the Communist districts in
central Shantung alone were subjected to nine large-scale mopping up campaigns

59. "Fen-chü kuan-yü tui chung-nung cheng-ts'e te chih-shih" [Sub-bureau directive on
policy toward the middle peasants], Dec. 28, 1944, in *Chih-shih hui-pien,* pp. 28-29.

60. Fen-chü min-yun-pu, "Ch'ün yun t'ung-pao: ti-erh-hao" [Mass movement notifica-
tion, no. 2], May 7, 1945, in *Chih-shih hui-pien,* p. 37.

61. See note 14 above.

and several smaller attacks during 1943. During that year, 137 days, or one day out of three, were devoted to military operations, and all other work suffered accordingly. While some political organizations managed to "maintain their existence" during this period, many others were destroyed. However, 1943 marked the highpoint of the Japanese campaigns, and Communist forces moved quickly to recoup their losses. In the Central Shantung District, the counter-attacks began in July 1943. By the middle of 1945, Communist forces had regained the areas lost and the Central Shantung Administrative Office could claim control over more territory than when it was established in 1942.[62]

Rent Reduction. Under such circumstances, rent and interest reduction remained little more than propaganda slogans during most of the Anti-Japanese War. A few districts made some efforts to carry out the policy in 1940-41, but with little result. In the spring of 1942, a provincial wartime work conference called for its implementation, and the same pattern noted elsewhere began to unfold. That year the various base areas embarked upon their first concerted drive to carry out rent reduction where conditions permitted. A second impor-tant feature of the movement in Shantung was wage increases for hired farm labor. There is no indication that interest rate reduction was attempted, except on a limited basis, until 1944-45.

Village level cadres were left largely alone with respect to their methods and style of work. Rent reduction was handled primarily by work teams, whose efforts were of necessity both temporary and brief. Not having been seriously weakened to begin with, landlords and others began to resist as soon as the work team moved on to another village. Any gains that had been won by the peasants soon dissipated "like smoke and clouds." Party leaders nevertheless professed themselves satisfied with the superficial achievements of the rent reduction movement.

Like other regional Party organizations, the Shantung Sub-bureau responded to the October 1, 1943, directive from the Party center by issuing one of its own calling for the investigation and more thorough implementation of rent reduc-tion. The Sub-bureau also called a mass work conference which confronted the failure of the Party in Shantung to grasp the principles of mass movement work. From January to June, 1944, various localities called cadre work conferences of their own, the first time that a serious effort to correct rightist tendencies actually reached the lower-most rung of the Party in the province.

Still, only a few *hsien* (among them Chünan and Inan), actually implemented the October rent reduction directive. In most Communist-dominated districts, the work either was not done at all or was done very carelessly. Part of the

62. *Lu-chung-ch'ü k'ang-jih min-chu cheng-ch'üan chien-she ch'i nien lai te chi-pen tsung-chieh chi chin-hou chi-pen jen-wu*, pp. 1-17. At the Japanese surrender, the Central Shantung District included 26 *hsien* spread across the T'ai, Lu, I, and Meng mountains. The liberated areas contained about 3.5 million people, with another million in contested or guerrilla areas. Japanese control had been reduced to slightly over a million people living in 1,600 villages.

reason for this was that the cadres were overwhelmed with other work: an army recruiting drive in March and April; the "support the government and cherish the people campaign"; a production drive; the rectification of leadership organizations; and defensive measures, including the protection of the summer crop and preparations for another Japanese mopping-up campaign. Only after a directive in mid-1944 declaring rent and interest reduction and the investigation thereof to be the key tasks for the four months from July to October, did it develop into a "comparatively broad movement." According to a report in September, 1945, the investigation of rent reduction had been thoroughly conducted in 17 percent of the 23,417 villages in the liberated areas of Shantung. Rent and interest reduction had not yet been undertaken in 36 percent of these villages. Work in the remaining 47 percent was somewhere in between, a state defined vaguely as "not thorough."[63]

The Problems. The pressure of other work was not the only reason for the slow development of the rent reduction movement in Shantung. However incomplete, the investigations revealed three basic problems among the cadres. The first, and most important, was labeled the "special characteristics theory" *(t'e-shu lun)*. Party cadres in Shantung tended to believe that rent and interest reduction were not important revolutionary tasks, since they could neither activate a majority of the peasants nor weaken the "forces of feudalism" in the countryside. The reason for this was that landownership was not concentrated and interest rates were not high. Shantung's rural economy was of a special nature being dominated by small landholders and small merchants. Some villages had no rented land at all, while landlord-tenant and debtor-creditor relations in general were few and insignificant. Instead, some cadres had found that alleviating the tax burden was "the most pressing demand of the masses." Others felt that corruption and local tyrants were the most important local issues. These cadres differed little in their evaluation of the peasants' demands from urban liberal intellectuals. The similarity was not lost on Party leaders, who denounced their "petty bourgeois" orientation.

A second problem arose in districts that had landlords. Here some cadres, even if they understood the significance of the rent reduction policy, felt it dangerous to risk losing the landlords' support for the resistance. Other cadres simply thought the policy wrong, arguing that rent reduction was not in accord with the new democratic economy because it involved "activating class struggle." Besides, it was only "a technique for buying off poor people."

A third major gap in the cadres' understanding may have been contingent upon the others, but concerned specifically the manner of its implementation rather than the policy itself. This was the common rightist tendency we have seen elsewhere criticized as formalism, bureaucratism, and mechanically decreeing rent reduction. The Party organization as a whole still had not grasped the principles of mass movement work, of educating and organizing the peasants, and activating them for the struggle.

63. Li Yü, *Report*, pp. 42, 56.

Mass struggle was necessary because the forces of feudalism had countless ways of nullifying any attempt to curb their power. Fearing the consequences of the accelerating struggles, over two thousand landlords and rich peasants living in coastal areas were thought to have fled Shantung by sea in 1944-45. Others went over to the Japanese or joined secret KMT organizations and armed bands. But for all those who fled, many more stayed behind. The actions that the latter were said to have taken included:

1. Spreading rumors and in general playing upon the peasants' anticipation that the KMT would soon return.

2. Taking back land officially sold or given away.

3. Threatening tenants with eviction and sometimes actually doing so. Under this and other threats, tenants agreed to pay the old rates surreptitiously. In one group of ten villages where rent reduction was declared completed, investigators subsequently found that only 40 percent of the tenant families had actually achieved rent reduction. In the region around the town of Tatien in Chünan *hsien,* investigations revealed that those paying less rent were primarily rich peasants, while the poorer tenants continued to pay the old rents.

4. Taking advantage of the cadres' inexperience to create dissension and discredit the new mass organizations. In one such case, for example, an attempt was made to break up the literacy training class for women by circulating the rumor that the cadres were making use of it to "wear broken shoes," that is, consort with loose women.

5. Infiltrating the people's militia and using it to create disorders.

6. Sending a son to join the army so as to gain the privileged status of an army family.

7. Inciting army dependents to discredit the cadres by claiming insufficient support.

8. Invoking clan loyalties to inhibit the struggle between rich and poor members.

9. Allying with all alienated elements including middle and poor peasants who had been struggled against.

10. Bribing cadres and new village officials. As could have been expected with so pervasive and long-standing a habit, corruption continued to be an "important" problem at the local level during the early years of Communist-sponsored administration. Investigations revealed that in the vicinity of Tatien, landlords had successfully bribed two village heads, three peasant association leaders, three women's association leaders, two mutual aid team leaders, and two heads of other village-level organizations.

Because of this resistance, in Shantung as elsewhere, the Party seemingly could not over-emphasize the point: the reduction of rent and interest could not be realized except through "mass struggle." If the peasants had any grievances at all, it would not be difficult to mobilize them. But unless they could be organized and educated to recognize and resist counterattacks, victories could only be temporary. The power of the traditional elite could not be broken until the peasants had learned to exercise voluntarily their new right to struggle against it. The cadres' failures in this regard were a source of major concern to Party leaders.

According to Li Yü, Chairman of the Shantung provincial government, the origin of the erroneous attitudes toward rent and interest reduction lay in the non-proletarian orientation of "very many comrades," who still did not understand the mass line of the Party and never thought of their work in terms of promoting the wellbeing of the peasants. For most of these comrades, the revolution meant resistance to Japan and little else, except perhaps an official position. Their "independence" also derived from this. As a result, they had not yet grasped the organizational concept which held that the lower echelons must obey the higher and that all of the Party must obey the center. They did not even bother to discuss, study, or disseminate directives from the Party center and the Shantung Sub-bureau.[64]

Solutions: Cadres. As an antidote for these failings, Shantung Party leaders prescribed rectification and study procedures as developed in Yenan during the 1942-44 Party reform movement. The Shantung case was a clear example of some of the problems that the rectification movement was designed to combat. The rectification movement thus provided models that all local Party units in Shantung were called upon to emulate as the Party endeavored to reassert its revolutionary identity. Had it not done so, its long-term goals stood in danger of being diluted, and even inundated, by the diverse assortment of people that had been drawn to the Party as leader of the resistance. But this identity could not be reasserted in the abstract, simply by recourse to small-group study sessions, self-criticism, class purification, exhortations to organizational discipline, and lectures on the "mass movement method" of activating peasants. The principles propagated in this way had to be applied in practice in order to be learned. These were, in effect, means toward the single end of translating the Party's revolutionary goals into reality. By 1944-45, rent reduction had become one of these objectives.

At this point, the Party came up against the ultimate problem of adapting this particular goal to the socio-economic conditions of rural Shantung. For all its talk about changing the attitudes and orientations of its cadres, the Party simultaneously sought concrete solutions to this most concrete of problems. The task was to discover what issues, in addition to rent and interest reduction, could be used to generate peasant support.

Solutions: Issues. The Party's response was twofold. First, it conducted investigations into the nature of tenancy and credit relationships in Shantung, defining them to include the widest possible range of practices associated with the payment of rent and interest. Second, the Party admitted that landownership was widespread, and explicitly redefined the double reduction policy to

---

64. These problems with cadres and landlords are discussed in Li Yü, *Report*, pp. 7-11, 52-53; and *T'u-ti tsung-chieh pao-kao (ts'ao-an)* (hereafter *Ts'ao-an*), pp. 1-6.

mean the reduction and elimination of "all the most flagrant exploitations," both political and economic, in the countryside.

The "extra burdens" that cadre investigators found associated with tenancy, particularly in the Pin-hai, Central, and Southern Districts of Shantung, included customary obligations to present gifts to the landlord on certain occasions, and similar obligations for the tenant and/or his wife to work a given number of days each year for the landlord, called *po-kung* or unpaid labor. Another form of unpaid labor was called *tai-chung ti* or *pai-chung ti,* land cultivated without compensation. A tenant who rented a certain amount of land tilled an additional few *mou* for the landlord without payment. In the Chiao-tung District, the practice of paying a deposit, *ya-tsu,* to the landlord when renting land was still followed, as was that of paying a part of the rent in advance.

As for interest rates, the cadres cataloged a wide variety differentiated according to the nature and size of the loan and the time period involved. They found that the interest rates for short-term cash loans averaged 3 to 5 percent per month. Other types of loans were more exploitative not only because the "interest" was higher but because these were the kinds of loans taken by the poor who often could not make ends meet between spring sowing and autumn harvest. These peasants most commonly took small scale short-term loans the terms of which were governed by custom and demand. One type involved food grain borrowed in the spring when the price was dear and returned in the autumn when it was cheaper. But two or three *tou* of grain might have to be returned for every *tou* borrowed. This kind of loan was taken primarily by peasants who had to borrow in order to eat. Also, cash borrowed in the spring could be returned in the autumn in the form of grain or other agricultural produce, the value of the latter being calculated at one-half to one-third the market price. In yet another variation of the seasonal loan, money or grain borrowed was repaid through labor, its value being calculated at about one-half the going wage for short-term farm work.

An additional area where Communist investigators found fertile grounds for reform was the transfer of land ownership. There were two basic categories here, legal and illegal. As regards the latter, cadres discovered that in certain "backward mountain districts," local power-holders had devised various techniques for extorting land from the peasants. In the Japanese-occupied districts, Chinese collaborator officials had used their power to seize land. The return of lands lost in these ways was found to be among the "pressing demands" of the peasants and became an issue in the struggles against *o-pa* and traitors.

Other methods of transferring land rights involved forms of borrowing but were different from the typical mortgage agreement. According to one such arrangement, called *szu-ch'i-huo-wei* or partially sold title deed, the seller of a piece of land could buy it back within a given period of time for the same price he had received. This was usually about two-thirds the market value of the land. If he could not do so, the sale became final unless the buyer agreed to an extension. Another arrangement called *tien-tang,* or mortgage sale, was actually a commercial transaction. Title to the land and cultivation rights were transferred immediately to the buyer in return for a sum equal to about one-half the actual selling price. The seller could redeem his land within two or three years for the same sum. Otherwise the sale became final although he could negotiate for the repurchase of a portion of his land. So great was the desire to retain land that most peasants chose to gamble on a future upturn in their fortunes by resorting to the above commercial transfers or to a straight mortgage arrangement.

One final source of grievance in this area, falling somewhere between the legal and illegal, was of recent origin. It arose out of the landowner's fear of the Communists and his attempts, mentioned above, to circumvent reforms real or anticipated. In order to escape the burdens of the progressive tax, landowners sold land. When tax rates were reduced at the end of the war, the previous owners often pressed to buy back the land from the new owners. In order to circumvent rent reduction, landlords also pressured their tenants into participating in false sale agreements. The "tenant" continued to pay "rent" in lieu of compensation and became responsible for paying the land tax or public grain assessment as well.[65]

Having discovered, catalogued, publicized, and ordered the elimination or modification of all these practices and more, the Party nevertheless admitted that the landlord-tenant relationship still constituted only a minority problem in Shantung. Rather than completely discount the "special characteristics theory," the Party sought to place it in proper perspective. Landownership was "in general" not concentrated. But in villages where tenancy existed, families renting some land averaged from one-fifth to one-fourth the total number of households. It was estimated further that in the five administrative districts, from 30 percent to 90 percent of all the villages contained some rented land. The percentage was lowest in the Po-hai District where landlords were few. At the other extreme, in Chünan *hsien,* one of the areas where the land policy had been most thoroughly implemented as of 1945, 430 of the 513 natural villages contained some rented land. There were, after all, "not a few" tenant households in the province. Landlord-tenant relations could be used as one issue, albeit only one, around which to activate the Shantung peasantry.

"The problem," explained Chairman Li Yü, "does not lie in the number of tenant households." "Feudal control" referred not merely to the concentration of landownership but to political and economic exploitation in its entirety. And while the two types of exploitation might appear to be disparate in any given village, they were in fact inextricably linked within the system as a whole. Some cadres felt that the struggles against corruption and local tyrants could best mobilize a majority of the peasants; so they mechanically separated these issues from rent reduction. This tendency derived from the peasants' natural inclinations to strike back only against those who had directly abused, cheated, and intimidated them. In the process, the variety of targets had grown so great that the main direction of the movement was often lost. Li Yü warned that struggling

65. *Ts'ao-an,* pp. 14-35; Li Yü, *Report,* p. 39; and *Ta-tien ch'a chien tou-cheng tsung-chieh,* pp. 2-5.

against thieves and loose women, for example, was relatively insignificant except that the peasants could be easily mobilized to do so. Such targets should be attacked only if the peasants demanded it.

Corrupt officials and local tyrants were another matter. Together with landlords, they constituted the "forces of feudalism" and were to be attacked as such. In Chünan *hsien,* there were local tyrants who were not landlords, but rich and even middle peasants. Yet they identified their interests with those of the landlords in the context of the local power structure that protected them all. Hence the double reduction movement was one way of challenging the economic power of all of them, while the political struggle against corruption and tyrants was an integral part of the same revolutionary task.

However difficult the theoretical problems created by the realities of the Shantung countryside, this pragmatic elaboration of the Party's land policy derived from the immediate experience of the cadres in the field. The goals remained everywhere the same. The ultimate objective, the second revolutionary task, was to increase production and move toward collectivization. Prior to that, the existing economic system had to be weakened, and those exercising political control overthrown. The Party held that this primary revolutionary task could only be achieved by mobilizing the peasants to join in the struggle, and that they would not do so unless they could see the immediate benefits to be gained thereby. "Empty words" and theoretical abstractions meant nothing to them. "As soon as the masses' lives have been improved, their consciousness is also raised and they are willing to act," declared Li Yü, as if anticipating Mao's statement on tangible material benefits quoted above. There were "many kinds of revolutionary work," and many different ways of providing material benefits for the peasants. The cadres were encouraged to use all of them, so long as they understood that the Party's land policy constituted the theoretical basis of their mass mobilization work in the countryside. This was the meaning behind Li Yü's reminder that "the reduction of rent and interest is the mother of all other work."[66]

Solutions: Process. Li Yü also meant that, at the most basic level, the work of providing benefits for the masses had to come first. Rectifying the Party branch, building a village political structure, developing mass organizations, all of this work was important in mobilizing the peasants. But providing material benefits, he asserted, was the first and most important step in that process.

Actually, this was something of an exaggeration. Li went on to outline the specific procedure to be followed. The first step was to educate the cadres, especially the new ones, in the spirit and meaning of the Party's policies and methods of mass action. The second step was to send them out into the villages where they were to begin work by investigating the peasants' living conditions, starting with those of the poorest and most oppressed. After preliminary investigations, the cadres were to begin educating and organizing the villagers. This meant laying the groundwork for the organization of a peasant association,

66. Li Yü, *Report,* pp. 44-48, 61; *Ts'ao-an,* p. 3.

farm workers' union, women's and children's associations, and the like. It also meant organizing literacy classes and winter schools, and using them to propagandize the peasants. The cadres were to explain that each person's hardships were manifestations of class oppression and exploitation.

As a third step, after the peasants had gained some understanding, the cadres could pay more attention to discovering and recruiting new activists among them. Such persons should be among the most oppressed, the most alert, and the best able to get along with their fellow villagers. Fourth, after the ground had been thus prepared in terms of a certain basic level of village organization, leadership, and mass consciousness, the struggle could begin. To the greatest extent possible, the peasants were to understand the reasons for it, the benefits to be gained thereby, and the limits beyond which they should not go. The most oppressive and the most unjust individuals were to be exposed and accused publicly. The struggle against them would take both non-violent and violent *(wen-tou* and *wu-tou)* forms. The former included lectures, discussions, and accusation meetings. The more violent phase would follow as the peasants avenged themselves against those who had killed, injured, and oppressed them. At this stage, the culprit might be paraded through the village streets, forced to wear the green cuckold's cap, beaten, et cetera. Then rent and interest rates could be reduced and accounts settled generally.

Finally, in the aftermath of the struggle, its achievements had to be consolidated. This meant: distributing the fruits of the struggle "in accordance with the demands of the majority"; discussing and correcting errors; absorbing into the Party the best activists who emerged during the struggle; rectifying the Party branch; establishing leadership cells; recruiting for the militia and other mass organizations; remaining alert to the landlords' counterattacks; reforming village government; and finally, developing production.[67]

A useful variation of this procedure, in an area where landownership was not concentrated, was the multi-village struggle meeting. In the case of a very wealthy landlord or notorious *o-pa,* several thousand people from as many as a hundred villages might gather for the accusation and settling accounts meetings.[68]

Whether or not they knew its exact details, this work outline suggests what liberal intellectuals meant when they pointed to land reform as the Party's key instrument for "putting down roots" in the villages. By 1945, the developing struggle movement had become the cornerstone of the Party's most basic work at the village level, namely, the activation *(fa-tung)* of the peasants to destroy the existing economic and political system, and to create a new one.

Results. In Chünan *hsien,* it was recorded that 1,782 instances of struggle occurred during 1944-45, when most of the "obstacles to the activation of the masses" were finally overcome. Local tyrants and corruption led the field, while

67. Li Yü, *Report,* pp. 12, 57-59.
68. *Ibid.,* p. 12. The Crooks (*Revolution in a Chinese Village,* pp. 110-13) also describe one such meeting in Wuan *hsien,* Honan.

rent and interest ran a poor fourth. In Laitung *hsien,* corruption and local tyrants were also the most frequent targets. The targets and instances of struggle in these two *hsien,* and in Shantung as a whole are listed in Table 4.[69]

In Laitung *hsien,* the "fruits" of these struggles were catalogued as follows: 2,763,986 *yuan* in cash (currency unspecified); 209,999 catties of grain; 10,066 *mou* of land; 1,667 *mou* of mountain land; 306 mules; 206 pigs; and houses or parts thereof totaling 1,656 rooms.

Unfortunately, there is little information on how this property was redistributed. Criticism of the work suggests that it was done somewhat carelessly, and that families of military men were the principal beneficiaries. This latter conclusion is also supported by Li Yü's preoccupation with the immediate results of the 1944 struggle movement which he expressed in terms of the 1945 recruiting campaign. He pointed to the experience of Kuangjao *hsien,* Po-hai District, to illustrate his point.

He described the northern part of this *hsien* in particular as having been "extremely backward." In 1944, the local government and Party committee expended a good deal of effort on the recruiting campaign but were unable to fill the *hsien's* quota. Most of those who did join up ultimately deserted. Then toward the end of the year, the Party and government launched the campaign to reduce rent and interest and to struggle against corruption and local tyrants. A total of 3,145 men volunteered during the subsequent army recruiting campaign even though it was carried out in only a few districts of the *hsien.* This particular development was what prompted Li to write that "as soon as the masses' lives have been improved, their consciousness is also raised and they are willing to act." In terms of the province as a whole, 11,000 men joined the army in 1944. But in the recruiting campaign around the lunar New Year, 1945, some 40,000 young men allegedly volunteered, while the people's militia expanded to include over half a million men.

As for the larger organizing effort developing out of the struggle movement, some 4 million people had been drawn into the growing network of military and civilian organizations by 1945. This was about 26 percent of the total population of the old liberated areas of Shantung.[70]

The Question of Excesses. In Shantung, too, the line between the thorough and the excessive implementation of rent reduction remained a hazy one. Li Yü's commentary suggests that the haziness was intentional, as was the leftism it

69. Sources of this data are: Li Yü, *Report,* pp. 12, 47; and *Lai-tung hsien cheng-fu: i-chiu-szu-liu-nien shang-pan-nien min cheng kung-tso tsung-chieh,* unpublished report, 1946, no pagination. Laitung *hsien* was created during the Anti-Japanese War in the T'ai Mountains Sub-district of Central Shantung District. In 1946, this *hsien* contained 44,838 households with 241,435 people, living in 430 villages. The data presented here is drawn from 357 of these villages. By Li Yü's own admission, statistics were difficult to obtain and those provided in his report could only indicate "conditions in general." Chünan *hsien* figures are likely to be the most accurate, since that was one of the areas where the Party's land policy had been most thoroughly implemented at this time.

70. Li Yü, *Report,* pp. 15, 60-61, 84-85.

TABLE 4. STRUGGLE TARGETS, SHANTUNG

Shantung Liberated Areas (1945)		Chünan hsien (1945)		Laitung hsien (first half of 1946)	
Targets	Instances of struggle	Targets	Instances of struggle	Targets	Instances of struggle
Local tyrants	5,201	Local tyrants	589	Corruption	187
Rent reduction	4,672	Corruption	433	Local tyrants	180
Raising wages	3,369	Wrecking*	184	Settling accounts	154
Corruption	3,186	Rent & interest reduction	180	Rent reduction	109
Black land	518	Black land	139	Secret agents	80
Spies	215	Superstition	127	Broken shoes	27
Aiding the enemy	192	Secret agents	39	Interest reduction	6
Others (broken shoes, bandits, thieves, etc.)	1,954	Ill treatment	10	Other	142
		Other	81		
Total	19,307	Total	1,782	Total	885

SOURCES: See note 69.
*"Wrecking" here apparently refers to attempts to disrupt and discredit the new Communist-sponsored village organizations.

fostered. He indicated that such excesses were necessary at a certain stage of the movement's development.

Approximately 13,000 persons bore the brunt of the 1944-45 struggle movement in Shantung. A campaign directed against such a variety of issues could not avoid cutting across class lines. Middle peasants were well represented among the ranks of "struggle objects." The class backgrounds of these were as follows:[71]

	Shantung province	Chünan *hsien*
landlords	3,589	418
rich peasants	5,028	595
middle peasants	3,379	534
poor peasants	859	213
others	519	—

To a certain extent, Li found cause for concern in the confused class structure of the movement. He noted that the attacks against rich and middle peasants were "in some ways" wrong, to say nothing of the attacks against poor peasants. Middle and poor peasants who had become bandits, vagrants, and the "dogs' legs" (henchmen) of landlords, had not only been criticized. They had also been punished and fined, creating economic hardship for them and their families. Middle and poor peasants were all part of the basic masses and should therefore be persuaded to admit their wrongdoings. They should not be made the objects of struggle, "unless the masses demanded it" in which case it was "not absolutely wrong."[72]

Li was equally ambivalent on the various excesses that had occurred in Shantung. These had been numerous. They included indiscriminate attacks and arbitrary punishments. Wages had been raised excessively, weakening rich peasant employers. The landlord and rich peasant families of men who had joined the army often did not receive the preferential treatment to which they were entitled. Excesses in some border or guerrilla districts had directly harmful consequences, pushing many people into collaboration with the Japanese or other reactionary forces. And this was not all.

According to Li, the 1944-45 investigation of rent and interest reduction, carried out under the slogan of "weakening feudalism," developed rapidly into a movement to destroy economic exploitation altogether. This occurred in the course of settling accounts. The fruits were used to "root out poverty," or more accurately, redistribute wealth. By 1945, the function of the settlement was clear. The amount paid did not necessarily bear any relationship to the amount owed. Rather than repayment for a debt incurred through past exploitation, the clearing of accounts had become an alternative to the outright confiscation and redistribution of property.

There were places in Chiao-tung District where the abacus was simply handed over to the peasants, who settled accounts as they wished. Elsewhere, the

71. *Ibid.*, p. 12.
72. *Ibid.*, p. 49.

punishment for having once boxed a man's ears was fixed at 100 *yuan*. Since wage increases for hired labor was an important reform in Shantung, settling accounts for past unpaid labor became the corresponding punishment as the investigation movement accelerated. The method of *ch'i-che-pa-fan*, cut at seven and increase by eight, was used in many villages. Literally, this meant that a peasant could claim compensation for unpaid or underpaid labor performed up to seven years previously; the sum was then multiplied by eight, the number of years since the Japanese invasion. By the time it was translated into inflated 1945 currency, the sum had expanded still further. In Shuangshan *hsien*, South Shantung, a man was required to pay 8,000 *yuan* in compensation for having underpaid a laborer by 20 *yuan*. In another case, a wage claim of 4 *yuan* was settled for 1,000 *yuan*. Tenants were encouraged to settle accounts in the same manner even though the practice of *t'ui-tsu*, or returning rent to the tenant, had been intended primarily as a punishment for landlords who tried to circumvent rent reduction.[73]

In each case, the movement had gone "too far." But this was an "unavoidable phenomenon" as the masses became aroused and the struggle sharpened. Analyzing the phenomenon, Li distinguished between excesses that issued from the cadres, and those that came from the masses themselves. The latter were not only permissible but necessary; the former were to be avoided. "If it is an action issuing self-consciously and voluntarily from the masses and not from a minority," he wrote, "the order from the center is that, 'this kind of mass leftism not only is not harmful, but has its beneficial nature because in this way the objective of weakening the forces of feudalism can be achieved.' "[74] Quoting from the section on excesses in Mao's 1927 "Report on an Investigation of the Peasant Movement in Hunan," Li continued in a similarly radical vein.[75] He challenged anyone who worried lest such an upsurge of mass anger endanger law and order.

If the masses lack consciousness of this kind, how can they turn themselves around *[fan-shen]*? How can they overthrow a feudal system several thousand years old? The masses will treat as a struggle object anyone who wants to stop or change this revolutionary activity of theirs. If you are afraid of the

73. *Ibid.*, pp. 13-14, 31-32.

74. *Ibid.*, p. 33. Li did not cite the central directive to which he made reference. His statement, made in September, was similar in tone to the November, 1945, intra-Party directive, quoted above, in which Mao wrote: ". . . as long as it is really a conscious struggle of the broad masses, any excesses that have occurred can be corrected afterwards."

75. The sentence quoted was the famous one concerning the difference between making a revolution and inviting guests to dinner. Sections of Mao's Hunan report were widely reprinted at this time, with this passage invariably included. In the same paragraph Mao also wrote: "Frankly, a state of terror must be created in every village for a short period. Otherwise, it will be absolutely impossible to suppress the activities of counter-revolutionaries in the villages, or to overthrow the gentry's power. In correcting wrongs, it is necessary to go to extremes or else the wrongs cannot be righted [Chiao-wang pi-hsu kuo cheng, pu kuo cheng pu neng chiao-wang]," from *Chung-yao wen-chien*, p. 19.

leftism of the masses, try to contain it, do not dare to activate them, or pour cold water on their activity, that is inclining toward right-wing opportunism.[76]

As for leftism on the part of the cadres alone, this could not be allowed because it isolated them from the masses. Li explained this in terms of the "law of the mass movement." In the initial or preparatory phase, cadres tended to be inhibited by rightist thoughts. Nevertheless, the cadres sometimes allowed their leftist inclinations to get the better of them, and launched the attack too early. Because the masses were not thoroughly aroused at this stage, the landlords were able to intimidate the peasants, oppose rent reduction, and wreck the peasant associations. Only after organizations had been basically established, cadres trained, activists discovered, and the peasants propagandized, was the stage set for the second or struggle phase of the movement.

During the struggle stage, leftism could not be avoided. The cadres were to "help the masses attack the landlords, smash the reactionary control of the landlord class in the countryside, and establish the superior power of the masses." Landlord counterattacks had to be resisted repeatedly until the landlords would understand that they had no alternative but to acquiesce. This was the third stage when unity became the guiding principle. Li asserted that it was "impossible to unite peacefully with the landlords." Unification had to come through struggle. If unity was sought too early, the masses would not be able to stand up and the situation would devolve into one of basic defeat.

Li's only other word of caution was that during the struggle stage, it would be unwise to attack indiscriminately or to struggle with "a majority of the enemy" since this would create too much instability. If "a minority or even a minority of the very worst" were attacked in each place, the influence of this act would be sufficient to root out the reactionary forces in the area. For the rest, education and the superior strength of the masses would be sufficient to overcome the opposition.[77]

In order to verify his claim concerning the utility of leftism, Li pointed to the achievements of the wage settlement campaign in Laopo District, Chünan *hsien*. The settlement struggles ran full cycle in this district and when the new level of "unity" had been reached, 776 households (63 landlords; 407 rich peasants; 304 middle peasants; and 2 poor peasants) were poorer by 537,267 *yuan*; 4,197 *mou* of land; 122,701 catties of grain; and seven draft animals. These struggle fruits had been distributed as compensation to 2,182 households (506 middle peasants; 1,489 poor peasants; and 187 farm workers).[78]

The results for Chünan *hsien* as a whole were stated in equally significant terms. After the settling accounts movement had run its course, there were virtually no landlords left in many villages, and at least 6,000 peasants had received some land. By 1945, there could be little doubt; leftist excesses were a deliberate feature of the land policy. They were encouraged for the specific

76. Li Yü, *Report*, p. 33.
77. *Ibid.*, pp. 33-37.
78. *Ibid.*, pp. 13-14.

purpose of transforming the "investigation of rent reduction" campaign into land reform. This was the development that was formalized in the May Fourth Directive. Land reform in its May, 1946, manifestation was nothing more nor less than the multi-featured struggle movement described above. Its key objectives were not just land-to-the-tiller, but the political and economic destruction of the existing rural elite, and the mobilization of peasant support for the creation of a new one.

SUMMARY: THE LESSONS OF THE ANTI-JAPANESE WAR

Despite the documentary gaps that remain in our knowledge of this period, the events outlined above suggest an answer to the last of the three questions raised in the introduction to this chapter, and lay the groundwork thereby for answering the other two. The third question concerned the nature of the revolutionary lessons learned during the Anti-Japanese War, and the role of rent reduction in mobilizing the peasants at that time. The answer begins with the attempt to unravel the seeming contradictions in the Party's "moderate" united front land policy.

The fact of first importance was that the policy, even by 1943-44, had been implemented in far fewer districts than the Party was willing to acknowledge openly. Where the policy had been carried out, it was probably done in name only as often as not. This accounts in part for the dominant preoccupation throughout the 1942-45 period with rightist errors of omission in its implementation.[79] Leftist excesses could appear only where the policy was being vigorously pursued.

In the mass movement method of policy implementation as practiced by the CCP, moderate lines are typically the corrective of choice for excesses of the leftist variety. Similarly, a preoccupation with rightist errors indicates the perceived necessity of moving in a more radical direction. From 1942, the Party's land policy was carried out in the form of a mass movement. The foregoing outline of developments during the Anti-Japanese War seems to explain the contradiction of the moderate 1942 rent reduction policy being accompanied by a preoccupation with rightist errors. This contradiction cannot be explained simply in terms of the Party's desire to promote a land policy modified to confoim to the dictates of the anti-Japanese united front.

If leftist excesses appeared in districts of the Chin-Ch'a-Chi Border Region where rent reduction was carried out in 1937-39, as P'eng Chen indicated, then these must have been among the few districts to which the 1942 Party decision also referred. In such districts, the experiment with rent reduction showed how far ideologically committed cadres and self-interested peasants would go when conditions permitted. In the process, the experiment demonstrated simultaneously the potential dangers of the rent reduction policy for the anti-Japanese united front, and the potential for agrarian revolution that existed in north China.

79. *Chieh-fang jih-pao* (the Party newspaper in Yenan), emphasized such problems as late as Feb. 9 and Apr. 4, 1945.

Given this potential, the moderate 1940-42 line on rent reduction did represent a corrective step backward, as P'eng also indicated. It served as a corrective for the excesses that had been committed, and as a restraint against the radical inclinations the policy's more extensive implementation would set in motion.

Nevertheless, the key 1942 decision on rent reduction also called for the economic liquidation of "unrepentant traitors" who had exploited the peasantry. Furthermore, the 1942 decision listed the reduction of exploitation by all landlords, and the reduction of rent and interest, as two separate goals. In addition, if the Political Bureau in Yenan meant the same thing as did Chin-Ch'a-Chi leaders when it ordered the "thorough" implementation of the 1942 rent reduction policy, then attacks against other kinds of exploitation were sanctioned and encouraged by the "moderate" united front land policy.

Thus the policy appears to have been intentionally formulated and officially promoted so as to make the practical distinction between thorough and excessive a narrow one indeed. This conclusion is reinforced by the radical direction the policy took after 1944, when the distinction as drawn up to that time virtually ceased to exist. This development was marked by the statements of Li Yü and Mao Tse-tung in September and November, 1945, respectively, explicitly sanctioning excesses that occurred in the "conscious struggle of the broad masses." This allows the preoccupation with rightist errors to assume its appropriate role within the context of the developing mass movement. The Party center, and certainly the regional bureaus, were promoting not just the more extensive implementation of rent reduction, but a qualitatively more radical interpretation of that policy wherever military and political conditions permitted. Hence the Party's united front land policy contained in practice much more than the simple reduction of rent and interest.

Under the circumstances, it is not quite accurate to dismiss the varying interpretation of the term "basic masses" as local deviations during this period. Statements from the Party center invariably included middle peasants as part of the basic masses, whereas regional documents sometimes did not. But the necessity of implementing central directives to develop the mass movement meant that in some places, at one stage or another, middle peasants would have to be the targets of the attack. This was so because tenancy alone was not a mass issue, and the issues that were could not always be solved by attacking only landlords and rich peasants. The interests of the middle peasants therefore continued to be encroached upon until the equalization of land ownership had been basically enforced in broad areas across north China. Only at that point in early 1948, was a concerted effort launched to correct this particular leftist excess, although it had been recognized as a problem by regional Party leaders at least three years previously.

Finally, it is also impossible to conclude on the basis of the few contemporary documents available and analyzed here, that Liu Shao-ch'i was at odds with other Party leaders at this time. His "leftist" proposals were made in 1937, whereas the Party center apparently did not formulate an explicitly moderate land policy until 1940. Moreover, the Party's land policy in practice seems to have developed very much as Liu suggested: to support the united front officially and as needed, while undermining it wherever possible by finding other ways, barring outright confiscation, to take from the rich and give to the poor.

The rightist error of mechanically decreeing the Party's policy of rent reduction without thoroughly implementing it was at least partly the result, as both Li Yü and P'eng Chen suggested, of the initial preoccupation with the Japanese, and the diverse assortment of people drawn into the resistance movement primarily for that reason. But such errors also reflected the ongoing problem of survival. The 1942 policy statement had indicated that rent reduction might be de-emphasized in areas immediately threatened by the enemy. It stipulated: "In guerrilla areas or places near enemy strongholds rent reduction . . . may be a 20, 15, or 10 percent reduction, to be decided in accordance with the general goal of increasing the enthusiasm of the peasants for the struggle against the Japanese and rallying different classes for the war of resistance."

All of the rent reduction directives contained similar cautionary stipulations. The 1943 Chin-Ch'a-Chi directive was only the most explicit with its flat declaration that when the enemy threatened, the united struggle against him took precedence over everything else. The enemy threatened a good deal. And before the land policy could be effectively implemented in any district, the enemy had to be expelled militarily, his political hold broken, and the nucleus of a new power structure created.

It was no accident that of the Party's Ten Great Policies as formulated in 1943, the first concerned the struggle with the enemy, and the last the reduction of rent and interest, while six of the eight intervening dealt with political and administrative tasks.[80] In terms of the overall development of the Communist base areas, the first was primary, the intervening essential, and the last dependent upon all of the preceding. Together, they represented the sum total of the lessons the Communists learned about how to fight a revolutionary war in the Chinese countryside. The land policy and the class friction it engendered could become the "mother of all other work" in a village only after certain military and political preconditions had been met in the area as a whole. The anti-Japanese resistance mobilized the manpower and the CCP provided the leadership necessary to establish these preconditions on a significant scale as the Japanese tide began to recede after 1943.

With respect to rent and interest reduction alone, however, the policy apparently played a very subordinate role in the initial development of the Communists' anti-Japanese base areas because it had not been widely implemented at that time. But the united front land policy, by eschewing the violent confiscation of land, obliged the Communists to look for new ways of transferring wealth from those who had it to those who did not. This was a significant occurrence in an area where tenancy alone was not the dominant problem in any case, but where poverty and the unequal distribution of wealth were universal phenomena.

80. See note 44 above.

As a result of their search, the Communists' rural land policy had expanded by 1945 to encompass the range of issues that could provide, through the tactic of settling old accounts, benefits for the "basic masses" of north China. In addition to the material incentives provided by the distribution of struggle fruits, the Communists could also offer a solution for what the peasantry as a whole apparently perceived as its most immediate grievance: the corrupt and arbitrary use of political power and social position within the village community. In exploiting these issues—together with all the others associated with the ownership and use of land, unpaid labor, and indebtedness—the CCP had found the means to destroy the rural system of economic and political power, and to mobilize peasant support for the creation of a new one. Strictly speaking, the target was not the landlord class but the ruling class. The Communists had discovered the formula for "mass activation through class struggle" even in areas where landlords were not necessarily a problem that concerned the village masses.

The land reform program was the Communists' key revolutionary effort of the Civil War period. The development of that program in north China, together with the experience gained in the manner of and conditions for its implementation, must be counted among the most important revolutionary lessons the Communists learned during the Anti-Japanese War. Perhaps one of the reasons the May Fourth Directive was never publicized was that it mirrored those lessons so precisely. The directive may have contained the formula for success with its emphasis on evil in the form of traitors, local tyrants, bad gentry, and settling accounts. But in its pragmatism, the May Fourth Directive contributed little to the development of a theoretically consistent solution for China's land problems. It stood in sharp contrast both to earlier and later ideas concerning class struggle and the redistribution of wealth.[81]

RADICAL LAND REFORM: 1946-1947

The radicalization of the CCP's united front land policy can be dated from the Party center's October 1, 1943, directive on rent reduction and the Ten Great Policies cited above. During the years from 1944 to 1947, "rent reduction" developed into a mass movement to equalize rural land holdings, formalized in the 1947 Agrarian Law. The most important method used in the initial confiscation of property was the multi-featured struggle and settling accounts movement already described. As the May Fourth Directive indicated, at least four other methods of transferring property were being used simultaneously in 1946. These were: (1) direct confiscation applied primarily to the property of Japanese and their collaborators, but also to black lands and land acquired through mortgage foreclosures; (2) the sale of landlord holdings to tenants and others; (3) a land contribution movement; and (4) the equal redivision of village land and property.

81. On earlier ideas, see Hsiao, *Land Revolution in China.* The 1947 Outline Agrarian Law is discussed below.

One commentator suggested in September, 1946, that the Communists were experimenting with these different methods of returning land to the tillers as a preparatory step in the formulation of a general land law.[82] General Yeh Chien-ying told reporters the same thing in February, 1947. He explained that the Party center was sending investigators to the Border Regions to incorporate their diverse experiences into a set of uniform land reform measures.[83]

Unfortunately, the record is far from clear concerning the intra-Party debates that must have occurred during this transitional period. Land sales and contributions were clearly holdovers from the Anti-Japanese War years, and did not subsequently progress much beyond the stage of officially-sponsored border region experiments. Equal redistribution and direct confiscation, except in the case of Japanese property, were rarely carried out in the absence of mass struggle or settling of accounts. The typical sequence that developed during 1946-47 was the settling accounts struggle followed by increasingly egalitarian efforts to redistribute the struggle fruits. This process culminated in the complete expropriation of the landlords, including their land, houses, and all moveable property; and the more or less equal redivision of all village land and other means of production.[84]

DIRECT CONFISCATION

This method was particularly important in Manchuria, where it became the principal feature of the Communists' first attempts at land reform. According to a Party directive of April 17, 1946, all property and land in Manchuria owned or occupied by the Japanese and collaborators, and all *k'ai-t'o ti* and *man-t'o ti*, was to be confiscated at once and distributed to peasants with little or no land.[85]

Anna Louise Strong reported that Lin Piao assigned twelve thousand organizers from the army to serve as land reform cadres and guide the peasants in confiscating such land. The Northeast being much less densely populated than other parts of the country, no action was initially taken against landowners with less than seventy-five acres. Those who owned more tended to be defined automatically as collaborators in some degree.[86]

The rationale for this approach lay in the special nature of land concentration and ownership in Manchuria. A relatively small number of individuals had been able to take advantage of the new opportunities for land investment when the Northeast was first opened up by the Manchus to Chinese settlement. A 1927

82. Li Keng, "Chieh-fang-ch'ü tsou hsiang 'keng-che yu ch'i t'ien' " [The liberated areas are moving toward "land-to-the-tiller"], Sept. 10, 1946, in Li Keng, ed., *T'u-ti cheng-ts'e,* p. 18.

83. *TKP,* Shanghai, Feb. 13, 1947 *(CPR).*

84. This is the process described by the Crooks in *Revolution in a Chinese Village,* and by Hinton in *Fanshen.* Both books provide eyewitness accounts of land reform in villages in the Shansi-Hopei-Shantung-Honan Border Region.

85. "Chung-kung tung-pei chung-yang-chü kuan-yü ch'u-li jih wei t'u-ti te chih-shih" [Directive of the CCP Northeast Bureau on the management of Japanese and puppet land], Apr. 17, 1946, in Li Keng, ed., *T'u-ti cheng-ts'e,* p. 64.

86. Anna Louise Strong, *Tomorrow's China,* pp. 90-91.

study found that in 11 different *hsien* in northern Manchuria, individual land-lord holdings ranged from 1,000 to as much as 200,000 acres.[87] In order to protect their holdings, many landlords either actively united with the Japanese or acquiesced in their invasion. Landowners who were not so compliant often found their lands subject to confiscation or were forced to sell out at low prices. The expropriated land was called *k'ai-t'o ti* and *man-t'o ti.* Some of it was given to Japanese settlers; some was given to Koreans to cultivate; and some was rented to Chinese tenants. Hence the claim that land in the Northeast was concentrated in the hands of the Japanese and their puppets.

Another feature of land use which set Manchuria apart from the rest of China was the *pang-ch'ing* or dependent system. It had developed when the early Chinese settlers found themselves with more land than they had manpower to till. Neither tenant nor hired laborer, the dependent person worked the year around for the landowning family, lived with them, and received a specified percentage of the harvest in return. This was known as *nei pang-ch'ing. Wai pang-ch'ing* was an arrangement where a dependent person who had accumulated a little money to buy some tools, a separate house, and maybe an ox of his own, was given a piece of land by the landlord or rich peasant landowner. The dependent person thus became a landowner in his own right. He did not have to pay rent for his land but was obliged to work for the original landowner without compensation a certain number of days, ranging from sixty to two hundred, per year. Persons who received land in this way were sometimes referred to as secondary landlords *(erh ti-chu)* because they often rented out a part of their holdings and acquired tenants of their own.[88]

Sources vary as to the prevalence of the *pang-ch'ing* system, but it probably did contribute to the initial difficulties the Communists experienced in trying to apply their rent reduction program in the Northeast. Thus outright confiscation and redistribution may have been easier to administer, although even this approach seems not to have met with wholehearted approval.

At a July, 1946, meeting of the Provisional People's Congress of Nunkiang province held in the city of Tsitsihar, a "lively discussion" developed over the agrarian program. Communist members made up only one-fourth of the delegates, who represented a broad cross section of the local population. Some of the delegates, although agreeing in principle with the Party's announced goal of giving land to the tiller, felt that confiscated Japanese and puppet lands should be owned by the municipality and rented out to those who would till it. Other delegates, including the farmer representatives, argued in favor of the Party's policy that such confiscated land should be distributed to the poor and landless without payment. The latter view finally prevailed.[89] The next month it became

87. The study was titled "The Colonial Problems of Northern Manchuria and Its Future Development," and written by a member of the Chinese Eastern Railway Bureau's Economic Office. It is quoted in "Chung-kung tsai tung-pei chieh-chueh t'u-ti wen-t'i te fang-chen yü pan-fa" [The CCP's policy and methods for solving land problems in the Northeast], in Li Keng, ed., *T'u-ti cheng-ts'e,* pp. 62-63.

88. *Ibid.,* pp. 63-64.

89. Hsinhua News Agency, Yenan, July 23 and 26, 1946. (*FYI,* July 24 and 27).

part of the official agrarian program for the entire Northeast, adopted by the Provisional Supreme Administration for a Democratic Manchuria after "heated discussion."[90]

LAND SALES

Both during and immediately after the Anti-Japanese War, the Communists encouraged landlords to sell land to their tenants. Land sale was voluntary at this stage, albeit under the pressure of rent reduction, and subject to abuse in the form of the false sale arrangements mentioned above. This particular effort culminated in a set of Draft Regulations for the Government Purchase of Land from Landlords, promulgated in the Shensi-Kansu-Ningsia Border Region in December, 1946. Yeh Chien-ying had noted specifically that the new compulsory purchase program in Shen-Kan-Ning was "merely experimental in nature." It never progressed much beyond that stage. But in one sense, the experiment was indicative of the course the Party's land policy was taking everywhere. Compulsory purchase was directed against landlords as a class without any of the distinctions that had officially been maintained between good and evil.

According to the Draft Regulations, a landlord was entitled to retain, for each member of his family, one and a half times the amount of land held by each person in the family of the average middle peasant in the district. All land over this amount had to be sold to the government. Landlords who had distinguished themselves in the Anti-Japanese War were allowed to retain, for each member of their families, twice as much land as the average middle peasant. The land of rich peasants was not subject to compulsory purchase. The *hsiang* government, together with the *hsiang* peasant association and the landlord, were to fix the sale price, which was not to exceed the value of two years' average harvest for the area in question, nor to be less than the value of one year's harvest.

Land thus purchased by the government was to be sold to those with little or no land at one-half the purchase price, the peasants being allowed ten years to pay for their land. If a peasant was too poor to pay, the *hsien* government could petition the border region government for permission to waive payment. The amount of land purchased by the poor peasant, together with any lands already owned by him, was not to exceed the average amount of land held by middle peasants in the district. Poor peasants and hired laborers, as well as poor families with relatives in the army, were to be given first choice in the purchase of such land.[91]

On December 24, 1946, Hsinhua News Agency announced the first successful implementation of land reform through government purchase in Hochiashih village, Suite *hsien,* about a hundred miles north of Yenan. The purchase of land

---

90. "Tung-pei ko sheng shih min-chu cheng-fu kung-t'ung shih-cheng kang-ling ch'üan-wen" [The joint administrative program of the various provincial and municipal democratic governments in the Northeast], in Hsin hua jih-pao kuan, ed., *Tung-pei wen-t'i,* p. 159; and Hsinhua News Agency, Yenan, Aug. 20, 1946 (*FYI,* Aug. 21).

91. "Shen-kan-ning pien-ch'ü cheng-kou ti-chu t'u-ti t'iao-lieh ts'ao-an" [Shensi-Kansu-Ningsia Border Region draft regulations on the government purchase of land from land-lords], in Li Keng, ed., *T'u-ti cheng-ts'e,* pp. 57-60.

by the government and resale to poor families had begun on November 25, and was completed in nine days. Sixty-one families with little or no land in the village bought something over two hundred acres for about 8,000 pounds of grain, financed by the Border Region bank.[92]

In 1948, after the CCP had formally adopted a more radical land program, two sympathetic commentators remarked that there had been no effective way of implementing the compulsory purchase program because the amount of land involved was very great. It would have created grave problems of "financial administration" for the border region governments at a time when they were already hard pressed by the war. Since the program did not apply to them, small landlords and rich peasants would not have been destroyed; indeed, their numbers would probably have increased. In addition, the local money market would have been disrupted. The landlords would doubtless not have invested their newly acquired capital in industry as had originally been hoped, due to the low potential for industrial development in rural areas. Finally, the sale of land on the installment plan to the poor and landless would only have added to their indebtedness.[93]

Regional intra-Party documents denounced both the sale and contribution of landlord holdings in 1947, on the grounds that they violated the principle of activating the peasants through class struggle, and left the landlords in control of the villages.[94] Why the sale and contribution movements were undertaken at such a late date is not entirely clear, since the expropriation of landlords was already well advanced in many areas. Presumably these experiments were related to the military situation as part of the brief attempt (described below) at a united front with the landlords against the invading Government armies.

THE LAND CONTRIBUTION MOVEMENT

During the Anti-Japanese War, the Communists appealed to landowners to donate their surplus land for distribution to the poor, or to their tenants. After the war, the land contribution movement as such seems to have originated in the Kiangsu-Anhwei Border Region during the summer of 1946. At that time, the area was the target of a major KMT military offensive. Local landowning members of the Border Region People's Congress, the government, and the Party—among them Chou En-lai—took the lead in contributing their holdings.

---

92. Hsinhua News Agency, Yenan, Dec. 24, 1946 (*FYI*, Dec. 25); Hsinhua News Agency, Peiping, Dec. 26, 1946 (*CPR*, Peiping-Tientsin).

93. Shih Mei, "Lun hsien chieh-tuan te chung-kuo t'u-ti kai-ko" [On the present stage of China's land reform], in Shen Chih-yuan, *et al., Chung-kuo t'u-ti wen-t'i yü t'u-ti kai-ko*, p. 26; and Hsu Ti-hsin, "Chung-kung t'u-ti cheng-ts'e chih shih te fa-chan" [The development of the Chinese Communists' land policy], in *ibid.*, p. 19.

94. (a) "Hua-tung-chü kuan-yü shan-tung t'u kai fu-ch'a te hsin chih-shih" [A new directive from the East China Bureau on land reform reinvestigation in Shantung], July 7, 1947, in *Kung-tso t'ung-hsun, 24*, p. 2; and (b) "Kuan-ch'e kuan-hsing keng-che yu ch'i t'ien chi-ko chü-t'i wen-t'i te chih-shih" [Directive on some concrete problems in the thorough implementation of land-to-the-tiller], in *I-chiu-szu-ch'i-nien shang-pan-nien lai ch'ü tang wei kuan-yü t'u kai yun-tung te chung-yao wen-chien* (hereafter *I-chiu-szu-ch'i-nien*), p. 14.

The movement then spread to the Chin-Ch'a-Chi, Shen-Kan-Ning, and Chin-Chi-Lu-Yü Border Regions, as well as to Shantung and Manchuria.[95]

The hope was often expressed, at least in the English language service of the Hsinhua News Agency, that the program could make an important contribution to the land reform effort. There is no indication that it ever did so. The land contribution program seems to have been used primarily as a device for expropriating the surplus land of Party members, military men, and officials of the border region governments. This conclusion is indicated by the roster of important people who reportedly contributed land and other property.[96] Furthermore, the Hopei-Shantung-Honan Party Committee, in early 1947, instructed land reform cadres not to adopt the contribution method except where the families of such persons were involved. The reason was that land contribution eliminated struggle and therefore inhibited the political overthrow of landlords, as well as the political and psychological liberation of the peasants.[97]

EQUAL REDISTRIBUTION

In some liberated districts of northern Kiangsu, the settling of accounts with collaborators began immediately after the Japanese surrender and soon expanded to include local bosses and evil landlords. In such districts, the May Fourth Directive marked a shift, not from the reduction of rent and interest to settling accounts, but from the latter to the more or less equal division of property. Land was distributed on an equal basis according to the number of persons per family. All those who earned their living from the land, including former landlords, were entitled to an equal share. The amount each person received varied from place to place, depending on the arable land and the density of population. In one district, the average allotment per person was 2.5 *mou*.[98]

Northern Kiangsu was not the only region where equal distribution was basically achieved in 1946. It developed in many areas under the slogan *"t'ien-p'ing pu-ch'i"* ("fill-in-the-holes"). The method followed was one that had been formulated in the 1930s: *"ch'ou to pu shao; ch'ou fei pu shou"* ("take from those with more and give to those with less; take from those with better and give to those with worse"). The results of these initial equalizing efforts were nevertheless uneven, probably because they were not yet being uniformly promoted. A common practice in 1946 was to leave the landlord with a slightly greater than average share of land on the condition that he and his family cultivate it themselves.

95. Hsinhua News Agency, July 26, 1946 (*CPR*, Peiping-Tientsin); Hsinhua News Agency, Yenan, July 26, 1946 (*FYI*, July 27); and Lu Feng, *Kang-t'ieh te tui-wu: su-pei chieh-fang-ch'ü shih-lu chi i*, p. 255.

96. See, for example, Hsinhua News Agency, Yenan, Dec. 11, 1946 (*FYI*, Dec. 12); Sidney Rittenberg dispatch for Agence France Presse, Dec. 5, 1946 (*FYI*, Dec. 6); and Hsinhua News Agency, Yenan, Dec. 24, 1946 (*FYI*, Dec. 25).

97. See note 94(b) above.

98. Cheng Yueh-chung, see Chapter Six, note 20; and Lu Feng, *Kang-t'ieh te tui-wu*, p. 255.

In Wuan *hsien,* northern Honan, in the Chin-Chi-Lu-Yü Border Region, when the levelling slogan was advanced in 1946, the property of middle peasants had to be used to make up the deficiencies of the poor peasants because landlords and rich peasants had already been basically expropriated. After this levelling effort had run its course in a village in southeastern Shansi within the same Border Region, only one of the seven original landlord families remained. The poor peasant families in the village averaged 5.5 *mou* per person; the middle peasants 6.2 *mou* per person; and the rich peasants 6.9 *mou.* The one landlord family averaged 9 *mou.* [99] In yet another *hsien* in the Region, poor peasants had received an average of 4.5 *mou* per person. Landlord families were allowed to keep 11 *mou* per person which they were required to work themselves. [100]

These equalizing efforts progressed through a variety of interpretations before a single formula was agreed upon, in early 1948, with the revised version of the Outline Agrarian Law. Equal redistribution was obviously rooted in the ideological commitments of Chinese Communist leaders who had experimented with it in the early 1930s in Kiangsi. In 1946-47, however, it seemed to develop as much from strategic considerations as by ideological design—a mutually reenforcing exercise dictated by the perceived requirements for mobilizing north China's land-poor peasants to fight against the KMT. The KMT offensives in Chin-Ch'a-Chi, Chin-Chi-Lu-Yü, Shen-Kan-Ning, and east China (Shantung and Kiangsu), provided the immediate context for this mobilizing effort. They created an urgent need on the Communist side for more recruits, more militiamen, and more civilians willing to participate in the war effort as the KMT armies struck deep into the Communist base areas during the latter half of 1946 and early 1947.

Assessment and Reinvestigation

The argument used to promote equalization was that even where land reform had been carried out, poverty still existed and the lives of the poor and hired had not improved. In some places, landlord and rich peasant families still enjoyed a higher standard of living than the poor, as did military families who had been favored in the original redistribution of the struggle fruits. These were the basic conditions that the reinvestigation and levelling drives of 1946-47 were intended to correct.

Noting that there was not one *mou* to spare on the north China plain, the Hopei-Shantung-Honan Sub-region Party Committee, in late 1946, directed all political and military units to give up land allotted to them for production. The land of traitors and runaway landlords, and public land, had been distributed to the army and the civilian bureaucracy to cultivate, in conformity with the self-sufficiency campaign inaugurated during the Anti-Japanese War. [101] But the

99. Crook, *Revolution in a Chinese Village,* p. 127; Hinton, *Fanshen,* p. 209.

100. Hsinhua News Agency, Yenan, Oct. 20, 1946 (*FYI,* Oct. 21).

101. Ch'ü tang wei, "Kuan-yü chi-kuan pu-tui sheng-ch'an t'u-ti kuei nung te chih-shih" [Directive on the return to the peasants of the production lands of organizations and troops], in *I-chiu-szu-ch'i-nien,* pp. 1-3.

redistribution of such land to the poor could in itself contribute only marginally toward solving their problems.

Comrade P'an Fu-sheng and the Sub-region Party Committee analyzed the situation at a Party work conference in January, 1947, and in a series of subsequent directives.[102] First, land had not been thoroughly distributed to the peasants, nor had the landlords been thoroughly overthrown. Some districts were still "relatively polite" to the landlords, allowing them to remain in their fine houses, retain good land, and hide away their valuables. Meanwhile, everytime the peasants rose up, some of the middle peasants' interests were harmed. Finally, the cadres had not adequately carried out the directive from the Party center calling for the unification of land reform and the military effort. Since the start of the "patriotic war of self-defense," there had been a "comparatively widespread decline in the morale of the masses." This was attributed to the cadres' preoccupation with the war effort to the exclusion of land reform. Because the peasants' lives had not yet improved, they responded with little enthusiasm to the recruiting drives and requests to participate in military support work.

As usual, the problems were traced to a combination of subjective and objective causes, that is, to the "insufficient energy and understanding" that had so far been applied to the realities of poverty and war. The Party committee blamed itself first and foremost for lacking confidence in the possibility of simultaneously carrying out land reform, guerrilla war, and rear service work. Hence the concentration on the war effort alone under the immediate pressure of the KMT offensive.

In addition, there still existed among Party members in the region some erroneous ideas about land reform. The comrades seemed not to understand that land-to-the-tiller meant resolving the problems of land-poor peasants and eliminating the forces of feudalism. This meant, in turn, the complete economic and political destruction of the landlord class. Many cadres did not hate landlords; some even pitied them, saying that this or that landlord was not evil and that it was wrong to take land and grain by force. Such cadres had not yet understood: landlords were by definition evil, and the property they owned represented their exploitation of the peasants. Nor did such cadres seem to notice that many of the peasants still did not have land. Finally, some comrades were still saying that landownership was not concentrated and there was no class conflict in the countryside, or at least no serious exploitation. They claimed that this was the reason for the persistent attacks on middle peasants. The cadres could not otherwise fulfill the demands of the poor.

102. The following discussion is based mainly on three documents: (a) "P'an Fu-sheng t'ung-chih te tsung-chieh fa-yen" [Comrade P'an Fu-sheng's summary speech], at a Hopei-Shantung-Honan Region Party Committee people's movement work conference on Jan. 17, 1947; (b) See note 94(b); (c) "Ch'ü tang wei kuan-yü shen-ju t'u-ti kai-ko ch'ün-chung yun-tung te chih-shih [Regional Party Committee directive on penetrating deeply into the land reform mass movement], March 12, 1947: all in *I-chiu-szu-ch'i-nien*, pp. 4-7, 8-16, and 22-25 respectively.

To cope with these problems, the Hopei-Shantung-Honan Party Committee directed as follows: (1) where land reform had not been carried out, it was to be done immediately in conjunction with the army recruiting campaign and war support work; (2) in guerrilla districts, the same instruction applied, to be carried out under the slogan *"i shou na ch'iang, i shou fen t'ien"* ("take up a weapon in one hand and divide land with the other"); and (3) where land reform had already been carried out, the work should be investigated and corrections made according to the principle of "filling-in-the-holes." Land problems were to be thoroughly resolved, "not missing even one person or one *mou* of land."

Concerning certain specific questions, landlords' houses were to be distributed to the poor, not destroyed as had been done in some places. As regards business and industry, the Sub-region Party Committee distinguished, as did the Party center's May Fourth Directive, between capitalist enterprises in the cities and landlord-owned establishments in the countryside. The former were to be treated in accordance with the Party's policy on urban commerce and industry. Landlord enterprises in the countryside, however, were regarded as part of the "landlord feudal economy." They were therefore to be distributed to the neediest according to the "filling-in-the-holes" principle used to redistribute land and moveable property. But those persons unwilling to hold shares or participate in the cooperative management of such enterprises should not be forced to do so. [103] The cadres were not to initiate the economic liquidation of rich peasants, but if the masses demanded, it could be carried out. Old rich peasants should be allowed to keep the land they tilled themselves; new rich peasants were not to be expropriated. "In general," the commercial and industrial interests of rich peasants were not to be touched.

The middle peasant problem, on the other hand, remained as intractable as ever. The basic line enunciated in these directives was summed up in yet another motto: *"chung-chien pu tung liang t'ou tung"* ("leave the middle untouched while evening up the two ends"). This meant leaving untouched the property of middle peasants while equalizing the holdings of landlords, old rich peasants, poor peasants, and farm workers.

Typically ambivalent, the directives forbade local cadres to encroach upon the middle peasants' property, and at the same time made it difficult for them not to do so. Thus as a general rule, the property of middle peasants was not to be touched and if anything had been taken from them, they were to receive some form of compensation during the reinvestigation and levelling drives. As an additional measure aimed at mollifying the middle peasants and gaining their support, P'an Fu-sheng recommended that grain, cash, and other moveable property confiscated during the struggles be shared with them, leaving the land

103. These two specific issues were subjects of two further directives from the Sub-Region Party Committee: "Tsai t'u kai chung t'ing-chih ch'ai fang shih-hsing fang-tzu hui chia te chih-shih" [Directive on stopping the destruction of houses during land reform and turning them over to families], May 1, 1947; and "Tui ch'u-li ti-chu ching-ying chih kung-shang-yeh te chih-shih)" [Directive on the disposition of industry and commerce managed by landlords], May 22, 1947, in *I-chiu-szu-ch'i-nien*, pp. 28-30.

and other means of production for equal distribution to the poor. Finally, large villages were asked to try and adjust their redistribution so as to share some land with poor peasants in small villages where rich or middle peasants, rather than landlords, tended to predominate.

Nevertheless, there were exceptions to this general line. Middle peasant traitors and *o-pa* could be liquidated. Similarly, Party cadres should take the lead in liquidating those guilty of corrupt and oppressive behavior if the peasants wished it, although political rather than economic liquidation should be stressed in these cases. Most significant, in small villages where landownership was not concentrated, "a little land" could be taken from middle peasants. This had to be allowed because the cadres were also ordered to "guarantee the elimination of destitute peasants" by distributing land, grain, farm tools, animals, and buildings to them. Clearly, the basic problem was not always tenancy but insufficient wealth—or, alternatively, too many poor people.

The Party's East China Bureau advanced a more literal interpretation of the "equalize the two ends" slogan in its July, 1947, directive on land reform in Shantung.[104] This directive, too, asserted that the poor had not yet received enough land, while landlords and rich peasants had been allowed to retain relatively more. Here, too, regional Party leaders assumed full responsibility for the problems within their jurisdiction. The East China Bureau traced the erroneous "rich peasant line" to its own directive of September 1, 1946, denouncing it as "completely opposite" to the Party center's basic line on land reform. The objective of that line was not merely to carry out land-to-the-tiller, but "to cause those with little or no land to receive sufficient land, and at the same time to cause the laboring self-sufficient middle peasants' land not to be encroached upon."

The East China Bureau's September, 1946, directive may have been at variance with the center's line in July, 1947, but it did not seem so very different from that line in the summer of 1946. The September directive allegedly stipulated that middle and small landlords could retain half again as much land as the average middle peasant; that landlord families of army men and cadres could keep twice as much land as average middle peasants; and that methods of arbitration were to be used in liquidating the feudal exploitation of rich peasants. The September directive also sanctioned peaceful methods of land contribution and government purchase of surplus landlord holdings. All of these measures were criticized as erroneous in July, 1947.

Each of them, however, seemed to derive from the center's May Fourth Directive which approved the sale and contribution of landlord holdings; stipulated that methods of arbitration and mutual agreement be used in resolving problems between the peasants and medium and small landlords; and advised against touching the land of rich peasants unless it could not be avoided, in which case they were not to be treated "too severely."

Whatever the ultimate origin of the "rich peasant line," the East China Bureau reversed itself in July, calling for the confiscation of all the means of

104. See note 94(a) above.

production owned by landlords, who should be allowed to retain no more than the average amount of land held by poor and hired peasants in any given village. *O-pa*, reactionary landlords, and those whom the masses hated, were to be left with nothing at all, although their dependents might be allowed a certain amount of land if the village peasant association agreed. The surplus land, animals, and implements of rich peasants were to be expropriated. The land and property of middle peasants was "absolutely not to be touched" and if it had been, they were to be compensated. If the village did not have sufficient public or confiscated lands for this purpose, then middle peasants were to receive some other form of compensation.

If some tenants had already received more land than others in the recent liquidation struggles, they should be persuaded to part with the extra portion or at least exchange it for something else. Cadres, military men, and families of war dead should not be allowed to keep more land than other peasants. Land taken from landlords and rich peasants should be distributed first to poor and hired peasants according to the number of persons in their families. Where these standards had not been applied, the distribution of property was to be corrected so as to rectify the diverse errors of "surrender-ism" and adventurism committed in 1946.

Finally, this directive institutionalized the principle of mass participation in land reform, ordering governmental and Party organizations to defer to the village peasant associations. At the village level, the peasant association, the poor peasant small group within it, and land reform work teams were to carry out land reform. Moreover, they were also to participate in the reform of the local Party branch, organizations of political power, and the people's militia, this being necessary for the thorough and correct implementation of the land policy.

Liu Shao-ch'i, in charge of the Central Committee's land reform department at this time, was apparently associated with the warnings against both surrender-ism and adventurism, as well as with the issue of direct mass participation in the criticism of cadres. Liu was quoted by Ching Hsiao-ts'un, a leader of the Po-hai District (Shantung) Party Committee, as having warned that "with respect to the middle peasants, a careless attitude has been adopted and their wellbeing has been harmed, causing them to become frightened and to waver. The various places must pay careful attention to the middle peasants' attitude so as to catch any wavering on their part, and must adopt a policy of unifying closely with them. So long as the middle and poor peasants remain together, serious adventurism cannot occur. . . ."[105]

Comrade Ching referred also to a letter sent by Liu Shao-ch'i to Po I-po, Party Secretary of the Shansi-Hopei-Shantung-Honan Border Region, instructing that the masses should be allowed to criticize and expose cadres who had appropriated the fruits of the struggle for themselves. In addition, the letter

---

105. "Ching Hsiao-ts'un t'ung-chih tsai ch'ü tang wei k'uo-ta-hui shang te tsung-chieh" [Comrade Ching Hsiao-ts'un's summary at an enlarged meeting of the Regional Party Committee], in *Kung-tso t'ung-hsun*, 24, p. 15.

advocated the same line as did the East China Bureau's directives to the Po-hai District and to Shantung as a whole with respect to the treatment of landlords. In land reform and in the investigations thereof, all of the landlords' land should be taken and redistributed equally among the poor and hired peasants. Only after the landlords had yielded to the peasants should the latter bestow upon their former masters a minimum amount of property, not to exceed the average owned by the peasants themselves.[106]

The Outline Agrarian Law

The trend toward equalizing wealth evident in these directives culminated in the Outline Agrarian Law promulgated on October 10, 1947. According to Mao, the new law reaffirmed the policy enunciated in the May Fourth Directive, but also "explicitly corrected a certain lack of thoroughness in that directive."[107]

The Outline Agrarian Law abolished the landownership rights of all landlords, and of all ancestral halls, temples, monasteries, schools, and other organizations. The Law also cancelled all debts incurred in the countryside prior to the reform of the land system. Article 6 of the Law was perhaps the most significant, spelling out in unequivocal terms the goal of equal land distribution:

> Except as indicated in Item B of Article 9 of this Law, all land in the village belonging to landlords and all public land is to be taken over by the village peasant association and *together with all other land in the village,* is to be equally divided up among the total population of the village without distinction between men and women or young and old. In terms of quantity, land is to be taken from those with more and given to those with less; and in terms of quality, it should be taken from those with better and given to those with worse, so that all the people in the village will receive a comparable amount of land. . . . [emphasis added]

Only traitors and Civil War criminals were not to receive a share of land, although their dependents might if they were innocent of such crimes and willing to cultivate the land themselves. Landlords and their families were to receive land equivalent to those of other peasants in the village. As for property other than land, the landlords' animals, agricultural implements, houses, grain, *et cetera,* were to be taken over, as was the surplus property of rich peasants. All such items were to be distributed to peasants and other poor people who lacked them, with an equal portion being distributed also to the landlords and rich peasants. All expropriated property, including land, was to become the private property of the person to whom it was distributed.[108]

The provision that everyone in the village was to receive an equal share of property contained within it both moderate and radical elements. As regards the former, this provision was advertised as a safeguard against the leftist errors that had allegedly marred the Party's earlier land reform efforts in the 1930s. At that time, the landlords were left with no means of support, while rich peasants were

106. *Ibid.,* p. 16.
107. "The Present Situation and Our Tasks," Dec. 25, 1947, *Selected Works,* 4:164.
108. "Chung-kuo t'u-ti fa ta-kang" [The Outline Agrarian Law of China], in Shen Chih-yuan, *et al., Chung-kuo t'u-ti wen-t'i yü t'u-ti kai-ko,* pp. 73-75; and Hinton, *Fanshen,* Appendix A.

allotted only the poorest land. But given the scarcity of land in north China and the large number of middle peasants, this provision also made it necessary to encroach upon them if everyone in the village was to receive a comparable share of land. The contradictions, both in theory and in practice, that had characterized the Party's treatment of middle peasants seemed finally to have been resolved with this implicit demand to include them in the levelling process. However, it was resolved in a way that contradicted the principle of not moving the middle while evening up the two ends, which had been emerging in regional Party directives prior to October, 1947.

CIVIL WAR AS CLASS STRUGGLE: STRATEGIC NECESSITY OR LEFTIST EXCESS?

Landlords and liberals may have quailed at the violence; and pro-KMT writers may have been correct more often than not in their tedious arguments that China's agrarian system was not really "feudal." Even more correct perhaps were those who argued that parcelling up land into small plots for individual farmers made no sense. Such critics maintained that China's population density and agricultural backwardness should have made collectivization and modernization the top priorities in the countryside.[109] Nevertheless, these arguments overlooked the basic fact that land reform in the 1940s was not an end in itself, but only the first phase of the Communist-led agrarian revolution. As such, land reform was also a policy calculated to serve the immediate interests of the CCP in its struggle for political power, as the Communists themselves indicated. In exploring if and how it actually did so, we return to the main question posed in the introduction to this chapter.

In October, 1946, Mao Tse-tung summed up the experience of the first three months of the Third Revolutionary Civil War, dated by the Communists from the start of the KMT offensives in July. Evaluating the role of land reform in the Communists' defense strategy, Mao wrote:

> The experience of these three months has proved that the peasants stood with our Party and our army against the attacks of Chiang Kai-shek's troops wherever the Central Committee's directive of May 4 was carried out firmly and speedily and the land problem was solved radically and thoroughly. The peasants took a wait-and-see attitude wherever the "May 4th Directive" was not carried out firmly or the arrangements were made too late, or wherever this work was mechanically divided into stages or land reform was neglected on the excuse of preoccupation with the war. In the coming few months all areas, no matter how busy they are with the war, must resolutely lead the peasant masses to solve the land problem and, on the basis of the land reform, make arrangements for large-scale production work next year.[110]

109. The Communists were sensitive to the attacks from right, left, and center; and went to some pains to answer them. See, for example, Shen Chih-yuan, "T'u-ti kai-ko yü fa-chan sheng-ch'an li" [Land reform and the development of the forces of production], in Shen Chih-yuan, *et al., Chung-kuo t'u-ti wen-t'i yü t'u-ti kai-ko,* pp. 7-11.
110. "A Three Months' Summary," Oct. 1, 1946, *Selected Works,* 4:116.

Unfortunately, Mao did not describe the process to which he made reference. It seems to have been not quite so simple and straightforward as his statement implied, but the documents currently at hand do not permit a definitive analysis of the political-military significance of land reform. Here we can only evaluate the claims made for land reform; the arguments regional Party leaders used to convince the cadres of its validity; and the consequences of the policy in two different regions where it was implemented in 1946-47.

THE CLAIMS

The Hsinhua dispatches poured out of Yenan describing the progress of the land reform movement in concrete political and military terms. The theme was consistent throughout: the poor and the landless were rallying to the Communist side in an effort to protect their new-won gains against the advancing KMT armies. From Hantan in southern Hopei came a report that, following land reform, 100,000 farmers had joined the ranks of the Eighth Route Army in the Shansi-Hopei-Shantung-Honan Border Region. Land had been distributed to an estimated 10 million peasants, or one-third of the total peasant population in the Region, by the time the Government offensive against it began in the autumn of 1946. This land reform, the report commented, is welding the peasants together in an effort to defend their homes and land against the KMT attacks.[111]

Victories are greatest and most numerous wherever land reform is linked with the war, claimed another report. In Iyuan *hsien,* Shantung, the Communists had experienced some initial difficulty in hiring peasants to help with military transport. After land reform, large numbers of peasants volunteered for such work, and some of them even offered to return the wages they had received.[112] In a small village near the town of Kaomi, Shantung, along the Tsinan-Tsingtao Railway, land reform had been completed within earshot of Chiang Kai-shek's guns. When KMT troops attacked Kaomi, one of the landlords from the village threatened reprisals against the peasants there who had taken his land. In response to this challenge, the peasants called another meeting to settle accounts further, distributing land and grain to thirty-two of the poorest among them. The villagers then joined together to defend the area as best they could, sending children and old people to a safer place nearby and posting volunteer guards to patrol the approaches to the village.[113]

Peasants in central Shantung were simultaneously carrying out land reform and mounting a guerrilla campaign against the invading KMT forces. In the Po-hai District of northern Shantung, several thousand young men had volunteered for military duty. Following the redistribution of land in the Chiao-tung District, the self-defense units were said to have doubled in strength.[114]

111. Hsinhua News Agency, Yenan, Oct. 20, 1946 (*FYI,* Oct. 21).

112. Hsinhua News Agency, Yenan, Dec. 16, 1946 (*FYI,* Dec. 17).

113. Hsinhua News Agency, Yenan, Nov. 23, 1946 (*FYI,* Nov. 24).

114. "News Extracts," Hsinhua News Agency, Peiping, Nov. 26, 1946 (*CPR,* Peiping-Tientsin, Nov. 27).

After land reform, 20,000 farmers joined the local armed forces in northern Kiangsu, where peasant volunteers were reported fighting in every village.[115] In the Shansi-Chahar-Hopei Border Region, land reform was expected to stiffen local resistance despite the fall of Kalgan, the principal city of the Region, in October, 1946.[116] In western Jehol province, land reform had been conducted in the path of the advancing KMT armies. Thousands of peasants subsequently joined the army and many thousands more joined local volunteer units to defend their new-won lands.[117] A report from Yenan outlining preparations for the defense of the Shen-Kan-Ning Border Region—Yenan fell to Government forces in March, 1947—declared that military enlistment and training would go hand-in-hand with thorough-going agrarian reform.[118]

The journalist Sidney Rittenberg described the process in Mengpa, a village near the western edge of Shen-Kan-Ning. In this village, more than 160 tenant families had settled accounts with a tyrant landlord. Most of his land had been distributed to his tenants and he had fled to the KMT side of the border, letting it be known that he intended to fight his way back and reclaim his lost property. "When we fight back to Mengpa we will slaughter those tenants and I myself will open a restaurant with human meat," was the way he was supposed to have put it. Volunteers for the Eighth Route Army and the local self-defense unit suddenly increased. One peasant, a former tenant of fifteen years' standing, organized a stretcher brigade for the army, while another set up a food station when Communist troops came to defend the border.[119]

ARGUMENTS AND INSTRUCTIONS

Party documents told roughly the same story as did Radio Yenan, with two exceptions. The documents presented the relationship between land reform and peasant participation in the war effort in considerably more complex terms. And the claims were frequently interspersed with "must" and "should", making it difficult to ascertain where exhortation left off and declarations of achievement began.

The Tasks

The style of warfare developed by the Chinese Communists is well known. The reliance on an extensive network of popular support for their military operations continued after 1945, even though guerrilla warfare as such played a much less important role during the 1945-49 period than during the anti-Japanese resistance. Virtually all of the claims concerning the relationship between land reform and the peasants' participation in the "patriotic self-defense war" came from areas threatened by the advancing Government armies. In such areas,

115. Hsinhua News Agency, Yenan, Sept. 22, 1946 (*FYI*, Sept. 23).
116. See note 114 above.
117. Hsinhua News Agency, Yenan, Jan. 13 and 17, 1947 (*FYI*, Jan. 14 and 18).
118. Hsinhua News Agency, Yenan, Nov. 9, 1946 (*FYI*, Nov. 10).
119. Hsinhua News Agency dispatch by S. Rittenberg for Agence France Presse, Dec. 5, 1946 (*FYI*, Dec. 6).

peasant participation referred to the mobilization of the population to guarantee the supply of grain and manpower needed to sustain the war effort. Such mobilization called for the following:

1. The organization of several thousand men per *hsien,* ideally between 20,000 and 25,000, into militia units. The people's militia performed a direct supporting role for the front line units of the regular army, being responsible for sentry duty, diversionary activities, harassing the enemy's rear, garrisoning newly occupied areas, surrounding small points occupied by the enemy, and assisting civilians in the war zones with transporting military supplies, moving the wounded, escorting prisoners-of-war, and the destruction or construction of local installations. The militia was also responsible for protecting local Party and government organizations, guarding prisoners, suppressing local reactionary activities, exposing enemy agents, and keeping communications lines open.

2. The chief task of the local self-defense corps was to guarantee the transport of grain, ammunition, and other military supplies to the front, and the transfer of captured war materiel and the wounded to the rear. The self-defense units were organized in the war zones at the village and *ch'ü* levels, with the *hsien* governments responsible for overall coordination and direction. In each village, the self-defense unit was responsible for investigating the manpower, animal power, and material capabilities of every household and, on the basis thereof, for organizing military transport teams, teams of stretcher-bearers, mules, carters, boats, et cetera. All able-bodied civilian men between the ages of sixteen and fifty-five were obliged to participate in such transport work as needed by the regular army.

3. The women's associations were, among other things, responsible for maintaining a sentry post system for the interrogation of inter-village travellers. The women were also supposed to help with first aid and hospital work, to develop handicraft and other production in support of the war effort, and to encourage young men to volunteer during military recruiting campaigns.

4. Skilled workers were responsible for the maintenance of postal and tele-communications systems and public roads.

5. Cultural teams did front line and rear propaganda work aimed at developing the understanding and willingness of the people to support the war effort.

6. The youth associations mobilized their members to perform rear service work and to join the army.

7. In addition to land reform, the village peasant associations were responsible for the successful completion of army recruiting drives, and for ensuring that planting and harvesting were done on time so as to maximize production.

8. Finally, all the inhabitants of the war zones were expected to obey the orders of the front line military units and local political authorities in such matters as repairing defense installations; levelling blockade walls, ditches, and block houses; aiding the wounded; voluntarily reporting the activities of enemy agents, and the like.[120]

120. This outline of wartime support tasks is based on three proclamations of the Shantung government and military region immediately after the Japanese surrender. "Shan-

Radio Yenan portrayed the relationship between land reform and the peasants' performance of these wartime tasks in direct terms. Material incentives and fear of revenge were the chief explanations offered for the peasants' rising political consciousness and their consequent support for the Communists' war effort. Yet, however valid Mao's general claim that the poor would "support" the Communists in return for tangible material benefits, it did not necessarily follow that the poor would automatically respond with the specific kinds of military support the Communists needed at this time. The causal relationship was not so direct, nor the result so easily achieved.

Radio Yenan's claims to the contrary notwithstanding, intra-Party reports and instructions suggest four basic reasons for this. (1) The peasant had an ingrained reluctance to leave land and family to participate in the war. This was compounded and reinforced by; (2) the heavy losses suffered during the KMT's 1946-47 offensives against the liberated areas; (3) lack of resolution on the part of cadres; and (4) fear that the KMT would return, and that those struggled against would be able to seek revenge.

Local Recalcitrance: Cadres and Peasants

Sung Jen-ch'iung, a military commander and political commissar in the Shansi-Hopei-Shantung-Honan Border Region, reported in 1947 that after land reform a large group of liberated peasants had joined the army. This had given a considerable boost to the class consciousness of the troops, but he expressed concern about the lingering "landlord and rich peasant thought" among army cadres. This made it impossible for them to maintain a high level of class consciousness among the rank-and-file, many of whom had already been divorced from agricultural production for several years.

By "landlord and rich peasant thought," Sung referred specifically to a problem left over from the Anti-Japanese War. A majority of the military cadres had entered the army at that time and the primary motives of many in doing so had been to resist the invader and protect their families, or at least to get some benefits for them. Many of these cadres were of landlord and rich peasant origin. They had never thought of destroying feudalism, much less actually turning over their own lands to the peasants. The cadres also recalled that landlords had helped them during the anti-Japanese resistance, providing information, trading in needed commodities, hiding and caring for the wounded, and the like. As a consequence, the old cadres entertained no genuine class hatred. On the contrary, many even pitied the landlords and tried to protect them. Sung main-

---

tung sheng jen-min tzu-wei tui chan-shih ch'in-wu tung-yuan pan-fa" [Wartime logistics mobilization methods of the Shantung people's self-defense corps], Aug. 17, 1945; "Chan-shih jen-min chin-chi tung-yuan kang-yao" [Wartime emergency mobilization outline], Aug. 18, 1945; and "Min-ping hsien ta-tui kung-tso kang-yao" [Work outline of the *hsien* militia brigades], all in *Shan-tung sheng cheng-fu chi shan-tung chün-ch'ü kung-pu chih ko-chung t'iao-li kang-yao pan-fa hui-pien*, pp. 18-26, 40-42.

tained that in 1945 in southern Hopei, this had been a great obstacle to the successful activation of mass struggle.[121]

Nor was sympathy for landlords the only problem. Party leader P'an Fu-sheng in the Hopei-Shantung-Honan region declared that land reform constituted the basic condition for evoking a genuine mass response to the army recruiting drive. His assertion seemed to be borne out by a report that some 50,000 young men had volunteered in 12 different *hsien* along the Shantung-Honan border in April, 1947. Land reform had intervened between this experience and another recruiting drive in the same area in 1946, which had failed to develop into a "large-scale mass movement." [122] But Comrade P'an also noted that as soon as the cadres had heard about the recruiting campaign, the news "gave them a headache." And as soon as the peasants heard about it, "they sent their young men off to visit relatives." There were several reasons for the cadres' headaches.[123]

First, the cadres objected to the *quid pro quo* aspect of the land reform program, or the rather crass way in which the Party seemed to be trading land for recruits. As noted, Chairman Li Yü had also found this a problem in Shantung, where some cadres objected to the 1945 liquidation struggles as a technique for buying off poor people. According to P'an Fu-sheng, some comrades felt it wrong to "make joining the army the objective of land reform" by launching a recruiting drive immediately after property had been redistributed. The cadres "often did not understand" that the war against the KMT Government was an armed struggle of the peasants against the forces of feudalism, and that the peasants would not be able to keep their land if Chiang Kai-shek and U.S. imperialism were the victors. It is unclear from Comrade P'an's remarks whether the cadres literally could not grasp the link between the struggle to improve the peasants' lives and the war against the KMT, or whether in a more abstract sense their difficulties in implementing the policy led them to question its general validity. The latter seems more plausible since P'an indicated his awareness of the cadres' dilemma: they had to overcome the peasants' initial reluctance to struggle with the landlords, born of the fear that the KMT would return; and then immediately ask the peasants to defend their new-won land against the invading KMT army.

Related to this problem, the cadres also complained that the class consciousness of the masses was not very high, that they neither demanded land nor

121. *Sung Jen-ch'iung t'ung-chih liu-yueh shih-wu-jih tsai chung-yang-chü tang hsiao kuan-yü cheng-chih kung-tso te pao-kao*, pp. 1-2.

122. Hsu Yun-pei, "Ts'an chün yun-tung chien pao" [A brief report on the army recruiting movement], in *I-chiu-szu-ch'i-nien*, pp. 69-74.

123. According to *ibid.*, pp. 69-70, and two articles by P'an Fu-sheng in the same source: "P'an Fu-sheng t'ung-chih tsai yang-ku kan-pu ta-hui shang kuan-yü hsien-ch'i pao t'ien ts'an-chün yun-tung te fa-yen" [Comrade P'an Fu-sheng's statement at the Yangku cadre conference on raising up the movement to protect the fields and join the army], Apr. 11, 1947, p. 55; and "Ken-chü yang-ku nung-min ta-hui chung te t'i-yen tui-yü ch'ün-chung-hsing ts'an-chün yun-tung te chi-tien chü-t'i i-chien" [A few concrete opinions on the mass army recruiting movement according to the first-hand experience of the Yangku peasant conference], Apr. 25, 1947, pp. 63-64.

wanted to take up arms to defend it. Thirdly, some cadres complained that army recruiting was even more difficult after land reform than before. The peasants wanted to stay at home and enjoy the fruits of the struggle, especially when these included a plot of land.[124] Finally, where the cadres, for whatever reason, had failed to activate an enthusiastic upsurge of volunteers, "all kinds" of old-fashioned methods—including bribery and coercion—had been used to procure the required number of new recruits. This had occurred as recently as 1946 in the above-mentioned *hsien* along the Shantung-Honan border, for example. The cadres were fearful, when another recruiting drive was announced for early 1947, that they would again be forced to resort to the same kinds of unpopular techniques.

The Hopei-Shantung-Honan Party Committee addressed itself to these problems in an effort to correct the defects in the military recruiting policy before they adversely affected the war itself. The "protect the fields and join the army" movement should not be regarded as a burden imposed upon the masses by the Party. Joining the army was as essential to the peasants' wellbeing as land reform. The cadres must treat the village struggle against the forces of feudalism as a manifestation of the nationwide struggle against the forces of Chiang Kai-shek. The cadres were wrong to conclude that the peasants did not demand land. Land was a matter of life and death for them. But they were afraid Chiang's army would come and that they would suffer reprisals. The cadres must cut through these doubts and make the peasants understand that they would be able to keep their land only if they were willing to fight for it.

Comrade P'an also reiterated the importance of the mass line method of army recruiting. The objective was to develop a true mass movement, since neither compulsion nor the enthusiasm of a few activists would suffice. Thousands of new soldiers were needed; but they had to be genuine volunteers, not unwilling victims who would look for the first opportunity to desert. The first step in arousing this mass spirit should be a *hsien* cadres meeting and a subsequent meeting of the village Party branch to ensure that the cadres understood these principles. After these meetings, the task of army recruiting might be presented to the masses at *hsien* or district meetings of mass leaders, and in subsequent village mass meetings when these activist peasants returned to their villages. At these meetings, they were to explain the significance of the recruiting campaign, acknowledge that errors of coercion and compulsion had been committed in the past, encourage the masses to ask questions, and patiently respond.

At the same time, a large-scale propaganda campaign should be developed with the objectives of overcoming the peasants' doubts, convincing them that joining the army was a glorious thing to do, and destroying the backward tradition which held that good men did not become soldiers. All village organizations should contribute to the campaign. The peasant association was to discuss who should and should not volunteer, and the women's group to consider how

---

124. This particular problem is highlighted in Chou Li-po's novel about land reform in the Northeast: *The Hurricane [Pao-feng tsou-yü]*.

to send off husbands and sons. Primary school teachers were to write essays and run blackboard newspapers, and teach the children to sing army recruiting songs.

After the understanding of the villagers in general seemed to be sufficiently developed, a "revolutionary competition" or emulation campaign could be launched using the example of progressive villages to influence the more backward, and within villages establishing model families and model peasant volunteers for others to emulate. If necessary at this stage, CCP members themselves should take the lead in joining the army. Finally, all the village must join in paying tribute to the volunteers and in giving them a glorious send-off. Cadres were instructed to treat seriously the peasants' fear of death and their reluctance to leave land and family. Village and district cadres were to assume responsibility for the recruit's family, offering a written guarantee that his land would be tilled in his absence. They were also directed to ensure that progressive villages with many men in the army did not suffer hardship for lack of manpower during busy seasons.

However, in villages where land reform had not yet been thoroughly carried out, and especially if the village was backward in its response to the recruiting campaign, then land reform should be treated as the central task when the activists returned from the district meetings. The recruiting campaign could then be developed in conjunction with the division of land and property.

Local Recalcitrance: The Power Holders

P'an Fu-sheng expanded on the theme of land reform as the core task in a March, 1947, report detailing the inferior quality and quantity of Party members in the region. At the time, CCP members totaled 1.5 percent of the region's population as against a 3 percent target. Many villages had no Party branch and in those that did, district cadres arriving in a village often ignored the Party branch in going about their work.

Like Li Yü in Shantung, P'an emphasized that Party-building work, as well as army recruiting, must develop around the primary task of land reform. He reiterated the basic formula: after dividing land, property, and grain, the peasants had food to eat and clothes to wear, and their consciousness was therefore raised. Other tasks could not be successfully achieved until land reform had been carried out. P'an also noted that this was entirely different from the "egalitarianism" practiced at the start of the Anti-Japanese War. Then every unit did its own work in isolation from every other without any coordination or differentiation between primary and supporting tasks. Everyone had behaved as though their own unit's work was the most important. Little was accomplished until the Party learned to make mass activation through class struggle the core task.[125]

Perhaps because the issue was understood, P'an omitted one obvious step in the causal relationship of land redistribution, the rising consciousness of the

125. "P'an Fu-sheng t'ung-chih tsai ti wei tsu-chih-pu chang lien-hsi hui shang te tsung-chieh fa-yen" [Statement by Comrade P'an Fu-sheng at a joint conference of organization department heads of the Sub-district Party Committees], Mar. 8, 1947, in *I-chiu-szu-ch'i-nien*, pp. 35-51.

peasants, their demand for arms to protect their land, and village Party-building efforts. Only in passing did he point to an "even more important" result of land redistribution, namely, the peasants' emergence as the political masters in the village. We must control landlords and secret agents, he wrote further on, so as to prevent their wrecking the army recruiting drive.

Another writer was more explicit. Calling the army recruiting campaign the "continuous upward movement of land reform," Hsu Yun-pei emphasized that more peasants would volunteer where land reform had been thoroughly implemented. This was not merely because the landlords' property had been distributed to the peasants. In addition, the most evil landlords had either been killed or imprisoned. Having undergone both violent and non-violent struggle, the struggle objects had ceased to dominate their villages, and the Party could assume leadership. Here the rumors and disruptive influence of landlords and enemy agents could be controlled and the CCP's policy could reach the masses. Here the peasants understood more readily the importance of joining the army to protect their fields.[126]

Despite the emphasis of Party pronouncements, the provision of material benefits was not land reform's sole function; equally important was the destructive force the movement generated. "The objective of land reform is to destroy the feudal village landlords," declared another writer. "In this destruction, it is necessary to destroy their feudal control. If we only attack them politically and do not divide their lands, we absolutely cannot complete the task of land reform. Experience proves that only if the landlords' land and grain are all distributed and he falls to the level of a middle peasant . . . will it be impossible for him to resume his old attitude in the village."[127]

The peasants did not automatically demand arms to defend a new-won plot of land. Nor was the key motivation simple fear of the landlord's revenge, as Sidney Rittenberg and other observers suggested at the time. Indeed, far from emboldening the peasant, that fear probably had more of an intimidating influence. The peasants' fears about a "change of heaven" or the return of the KMT, are cited throughout the sources as an initial obstacle to the implementation of land reform itself. One of the surest ways of overcoming those fears, on the other hand, was to demonstrate to the peasants that the Party had the power to intimidate if not eliminate local tyrants and landlords. The peasants could somewhat more confidently throw in their lot with the new order having witnessed its ability to remove the most immediate source of potential retaliation.

CONSEQUENCES: THE KMT OFFENSIVES OF 1946-47

All of the peasants' fears and the cadres misgivings were realized in the areas that fell to the advancing KMT armies in 1946-47—the very areas where Radio Yenan

126. Hsu Yun-pei, pp. 72-74 (see note 122 above).
127. Li Chen-yang, "Chia-chi pien yu-chi ch'ü t'u kai te chi-tien t'i-hui" [Understanding a few points about land reform in the Chiahsiang-Tsining guerilla area], in *Kung-tso t'ung-hsun, 32: yu-chi chan-cheng chuan-hao*, supplement, p. 15.

had claimed the greatest successes in mobilizing the peasants through land redistribution.

During the Anti-Japanese War, as noted above, Party directives, both central and regional, invariably called for a de-emphasis of rent reduction and a minimum of class friction in areas immediately threatened by the enemy. This long-standing practice may well have been behind the cadres' misgivings, cited in the above section on equal land redistribution, as to the feasibility of simultaneously carrying out land reform, guerrilla war, and rear service work. In 1946-47, however, the condition of relative military security was abandoned as a prerequisite for initiating class struggle. This change reflected a fundamental difference between the two periods. During the anti-Japanese resistance, rent reduction struggles became a means of consolidating the Party's strength within the developing base areas. In 1946, virtually all of those areas became the targets of the Government's general offensive. The condition of military security surrounding class struggle was suddenly eliminated as district after district fell to the advancing KMT armies.

The struggle against the ruling class had already been set in motion in many of those districts. In some it had been in progress for at least two years. The option of reverting to a united front with the class enemy against the invader no longer existed for the Communists. Landlords and struggle objects could hardly have been expected, as a general rule, to unite with the Communists or even to have remained neutral in the struggle. Having already created their own enemy within, the Communists had little choice but to try to eliminate its influence altogether as the Civil War developed. Hence the intensification of the land reform movement in 1946-47, and Mao's injunction to Party cadres to solve the land problem radically and thoroughly no matter how busy they also were with the war.

But Communist leaders failed to distinguish between the loss of military security in areas where land reform had already been carried out, and the loss of military security in areas where it had not. The cost of land reform under both conditions was heavy in terms of social disruption, mutual reprisals, and civilian casualties. The consequences of land reform in the former areas were largely unavoidable, given the shifting fortunes of war and the unanticipated strength of the KMT's 1946 offensive. This could not be said of insecure areas where land reform was initiated under the slogan, "a weapon in one hand, land division with the other."

What follows refers to land reform under both conditions. One account comes largely from non-Communist Shanghai correspondents reporting on the situation in Su-pei or Kiangsu province north of the Yangtze River. The second is based primarily on intra-Party reports in the Hopei-Shantung-Honan region, and also on Jack Belden, who visited this same area in early 1947. First the Kiangsu story.

Northern Kiangsu

By early 1946, twenty-nine *hsien* in the area were entirely in Communist hands. The Central Government committed an estimated 150,000 troops to drive the

Communists from northern Kiangsu. The offensive began in July, 1946, advancing north from the Yangtze and east from the Tientsin-Pukow Railway. Government forces, moving eastward, penetrated the *hsien* towns along the Grand Canal which bisected the Communist area. By the following spring, they had retaken all of the *hsien* towns in northern Kiangsu. Communist guerrillas continuously disrupted the Government's communications lines between the Grand Canal and the railway, however, and large sections of the Canal remained in Communist hands despite the Government's occupation of the main towns along its banks.

One writer noted a number of differences between the Communist position in northern Kiangsu in 1946-47, and during the Anti-Japanese War. The KMT armies were not superior to the Japanese and puppet troops, while Communist forces, both regular and local, were considerably stronger than they had been in organization, training, and experience. Second, because of their superior strength the Japanese had been able to occupy not only large points or towns, but also the area surrounding them and the small points as well. By contrast, Government forces could not move freely in the countryside from one point to another. Finally, the Communists had needed considerable time to develop the capacity to launch counterattacks against the Japanese. But within less than a year after the KMT offensive began, the New Fourth Army was already beginning to retake lost areas. Underlying this new strength of the Communists, it was said, was the political consciousness of the people raised by many years of political training, by the complete destruction of the *pao-chia* system, by the establishment of elected political authorities in the villages, and by land reform.[128]

Nevertheless, the Government victories did make it possible for all of the *hsien* administrations to be reestablished under KMT control, for local KMT administrators and magistrates to return to their old bailiwicks, and for some landlords and merchants who had fled the area to return and attempt to resume their former way of life. This movement by the Government back into northern Kiangsu was at its height in the spring of 1947 and lasted for about a year. During that time, the local officials and their landlord allies rose to the Communists bait, so to speak, ignoring the orders and decrees issued in Nanking ostensibly to guide their actions in the recovered territories.

In early 1947, a Shanghai correspondents' inspection group spent nine days touring Nant'ung, Haimen, Jukao, and Tungt'ai, and returned with foreboding reports. The roads only one or two *li* outside the towns were unsafe and the Communists were already beginning to launch fairly large-scale attacks. Their ability to move swiftly and avoid the main forces of their enemy was attributed to the success of their political activities. And if "political activities" were recognized as a source of the Communist resilience, they were emphasized also as the key to the KMT's weakness. The *Ta kung pao* focused on the land problem, noting that it had caused deep fissures in the rural areas. Under the Communists land was distributed, the rich were persecuted, and even some of the middle class was made to feel uneasy. But under the Central Government, there was no land policy at all in the areas it had recently recovered and many people were dissatisfied. It seems, concluded the article, that the Government's

128. Lu Feng, *Kang-t'ieh te tui-wu*, pp. 269-70.

only objective in its dispute with the CCP is to regain the power to govern; all else is left unattended.[129]

A KMT-supervised paper was more explicit. Owing to its "unhealthiness" at all levels, noted the *Shun pao,* the local KMT administrative machinery in northern Kiangsu cannot function properly. *Hsien* and village administration is in the hands of evil men, and the lives of the people are truly miserable. They are subjected to a variety of extortionate taxes, and corrupt members of the gentry and other rascals have taken advantage of the situation to exploit and oppress them.[130] What was in progress in northern Kiangsu was a systematic effort at extortion and revenge by local officials in alliance with returning landlords.

The most notorious effort of the officials was the "voluntary surrender and repentance" program. People who had been active or held some office in the various organizations set up by the Communists such as the labor unions, peasant associations, chambers of commerce, women's groups and the like, were arrested and forced to repent. At this time, it was not uncommon to find seventy or eighty of these "surrendered elements" in the *hsiang* lock-up, and two to three hundred in a district gaol. Once there, they were required to write statements of guilt and repentance, produce a string of guarantors, and hand over their arms. Since many of these people had no weapons to turn over, the price of obtaining their freedom was often a tael of gold. If the gold was not forthcoming, the individual might be put to death depending on the whim of the official in charge. If the gold was forthcoming, it usually went into the officials' pockets instead of being used to arm the self-defense militia—the announced purpose of such "fines."

Incidents of revenge and retaliation abounded. One night, officials in a village in T'aihsing *hsien* executed twelve persons who had surrendered voluntarily. At dawn, the village chief summoned the families, confronted them with the bodies, and declared that the Communists were responsible for the deaths. In another incident, however, over a hundred persons who had surrendered to the authorities in Chouchia village, Jukao *hsien*, managed to escape and disarmed the district office. They then killed some seventy people including local officials and members of landlord families.

In addition, returning landlords organized "local administration promotion associations" and "rent collection committees." Under the authority of the former, landlords escorted by armed guards proceeded from house to house "settling accounts" with their old tenants. In the spirit of an-eye-for-an-eye, the landlords sought to avenge their treatment at the hands of the CCP. If the peasant fled rather than face his former landlord at such a settlement confrontation, the peasant was likely to find his dwelling stripped bare when he returned. The landlords also began, with the aid of local officials, to collect their rents once more. Some did so with an escort of soldiers. This was the "rent collection committee." Although the harvest was poor in the autumn of 1947, the combination of rent and the land tax in parts of the area controlled by the

129. *TKP,* Shanghai, Apr. 16, 1947 *(CPR).*
130. *Shun pao,* Shanghai, Apr. 11, 1947 (*CPR,* Apr. 16).

Central Government created such a burden that some tenants reportedly could not sustain themselves and their families.[131]

The Central Government in Nanking had promulgated land reform regulations for the "pacification areas" designed to wean the peasants away from the CCP. But the peasants could only learn from experience and most of them did not even know such regulations existed.[132]

For their part, the Communists at first were said to have meted out harsh punishment to those who voluntarily surrendered to the returning KMT authorities. Later, the Communists adopted a more lenient attitude, encouraging people to "surrender but do not repent, and enlist again in the New Fourth Army."

The Hopei-Shantung-Honan Area

Party reports from this area provide an insider's view of similar, although not necessarily identical, conditions created by the KMT advance northward across the Lunghai Railway into the Shansi-Hopei-Shantung-Honan Border Region. In a five-month summary covering the period from September, 1946, to January, 1947, the Party Committee revealed that of the thirty-five *hsien* towns in Communist hands within the Hopei-Shantung-Honan Sub-region at the start of the offensive, twenty-four had fallen to Government forces. Of the sixty-four secure *hsien* or portions thereof in the Sub-region, forty-nine were occupied and at least partially controlled by the enemy. In January, 1947, Communist forces reoccupied fourteen *hsien* towns and twenty-two *hsien.* They also claimed to have killed, wounded, or captured eight thousand of the enemy. But KMT forces soon recaptured much of this territory.[133]

Gloom pervaded the local Party organization. There were many who concluded that the Communist base within the Sub-region had been for all intents and purposes wiped out. In November, the Party Committee tried to relieve the general depression with the claim that the regular army and militia remained intact, while eight enemy brigades had been destroyed in the Border Region. With 80 to 90 percent of his forces on the front line and engaged in the offensive, Chiang Kai-shek had no source of replacements. "So long as we keep up our spirits and continue to destroy Chiang's forces coming into our territory," declared the Party Committee, "then we will not only stop the enemy's offensive, but must also change from the defensive to the offensive and restore all of our lost area."[134]

131. Hsiang Shao, "Su-pei shih-ti shih-ch'a lu" [An account of actual observations in northern Kiangsu], *KC,* Jan. 3, 1948, pp. 15-16.

132. Cheng Yueh-chung (see Chapter Six, note 20).

133. Ch'ü tang wei, "Chi-lu-yü wu-ko yueh lai yu-chi chan-cheng te tsung-chieh yü mu-ch'ien jen-wu" [A summary of the past five months of guerrilla war in Hopei-Shantung-Honan and present tasks], Feb. 2, 1947, in *Kung-tso t'ung-hsun, 32,* p. 37.

134. Ch'ü tang wei, "Kuan-yü k'ai-chan ti-hou yu-chi chan yü chun-pei yu-chi chan te chih-shih" [Directive on developing and preparing guerrilla warfare in the enemy rear], Nov. 20, 1946, in *Kung-tso t'ung-hsun, 32,* p. 49.

There were apparently three reasons for the low morale. First, the Government's gains were extensive. Second, they were unexpected. The Party committee wrote that initially it had thought the Government's forces would not penetrate north of the Lunghai line, but they did. Initially, it had anticipated that the enemy could be defeated in one or two battles, but the situation had not developed that way. Communist forces withdrew—actually this was a retreat planned as a temporary action. But after waiting several months, the enemy was still occupying their territory. Because of this, wrote the Party Committee in November, we have had to revise our plans and are now preparing for a long-term guerrilla war. This led to a third problem. The greatest concern among the cadres in developing guerrilla warfare was the difference between the war against the Japanese and that against Chiang Kai-shek. This latter was a class war with all of the landlords and struggle objects arrayed as the enemy, providing Chiang with a "broad social base."[135]

The Communists followed the principle of withdrawing before the advance of a superior force. The main army retreated together with most of the militia, the Party cadres, and their families. For example, seven to eight thousand persons withdrew from the Third and Fifth Sub-districts before they fell in August, 1946. This strategy of survival was essential to the Communists' ultimate victory, but the cost of having saved their main forces in this manner was a heavy one.

Material Benefits, Revenge, and the Withdrawal of Support. Ideally, the principle of withdrawal as a tactic of guerrilla warfare included the evacuation of the local population as well as the military and political units, the objective being to save both human life and the grain stores. In 1946, however, the Government's advance into the region was unanticipated and the villages unprepared for the sudden reversion to conditions of guerrilla warfare. As a result, cadres and defense units fled, and unarmed peasants paid with their lives while a third of the autumn harvest was lost to the enemy.

Following KMT forces back into such districts were the return-to-the-village corps *(hui hsiang t'uan),* armed units led by landlords and others bent on reestablishing their position in the countryside. As in Kiangsu, they began settling accounts of their own, seizing the land and grain that had been distributed to the peasants. Similarly, activists were killed, women raped, and village organizations smashed. Local KMT-sponsored governments were quickly established in their place.

Jack Belden reported that by early 1947, a total of four hundred men, women, and children had been killed in the 423 villages in Anyang *hsien* that had been taken by KMT forces. The killing of these peasants was conducted in as brutal a fashion as the executions of tyrant landlords. Live burial was a common punishment in this area and Belden heard many accounts about peasants who were killed in this manner. In one village, a peasant who had helped lead the struggle against a landlord and had taken back four *mou* of land lost through inability to repay a loan, fled when KMT forces returned. In retaliation, the

135. *Ibid.,* p. 50.

landlord had the man's wife, brother, and baby shot; and his son, uncle, nephew, and a married daughter buried alive. The worst case of retaliation that Belden was able to investigate personally occurred in a small village containing only twenty-eight families. When an expropriated landlord returned to this village with fifteen armed men, he killed someone in each of twenty-four families. In this way, according to Comrade P'an Fu-sheng, several thousand peasants were killed in nine *hsien* in the Third sub-district. In fact, close to ten thousand persons were killed by returning KMT forces in that one Sub-district, wiping out a base of eight to nine years' work there within a few months.[136]

Without cadres to lead them or armed forces to defend them, the peasants had little choice but to submit. However great their desire for revenge, they had no means of satisfying it. Their worst fears about a "change of heaven" had been realized and, according to Party reports, they retained little enthusiasm for the Communists as a result. In recaptured districts, returning Communist forces were cursed by the peasants for having abandoned them. The peasants were willing to talk secretly with individual cadres, to express their sense of grievance and their desire for revenge. But having abdicated its responsibility, the Party had lost its leadership and its "eyes and ears" as well. The peasants were reluctant to restore the peasant associations, or to form new militia units, or even to attend an open meeting, so little faith did they have in the staying power of the Communists.

"Facts prove," concluded the Party Committee in November, 1946, "that the retreat and withdrawal method is wrong and that we should not resort to it again." The regional Party Committee therefore determined to reenter the areas lost, to sustain independent guerrilla warfare therein without relying on the main force of the army, and to remain "together in life and death" with the peasants. Sub-district and *hsien* Party Committees were ordered to form armed work teams and guerrilla units. The new instructions were: "Those in the *hsien* must not leave the *hsien* and those in the region must not leave the region, nor is it permissible to withdraw from any place."[137] When Jack Belden visited this area in the spring of 1947, he found that guerrilla operations conducted by local militiamen had only just begun in Anyang *hsien*. He did not report on their development elsewhere.

The Intensification of Class Struggle. In November, 1946, at the height of the Communist retreat, the Party had tried to quiet fears of landlord strength with the claim that the class enemy was not united. Only a minority were actually joining the return-to-the-village corps. Most did not believe that Chiang's army could hold out against the Communists, and did not wish to risk exile or death when they returned. All such people could be neutralized or induced "to strive together with us."[138] At this time, too, the peaceful land sales and contribu-

136. Jack Belden, *China Shakes the World,* pp. 224, 260-61; "Chi-lu-yü wu-ko yüeh ...," p. 42 (see note 133 above); and, "P'an Fu-sheng t'ung-chih tsai ti wei ...," p. 38 (see note 125 above).

137. "Kuan-yü k'ai-chan ...," pp. 48-52 (see note 134 above).

138. *Ibid.,* p. 50.

tions methods of redistributing property were still being officially encouraged, as we have seen, in many of the Border Regions threatened by the KMT advance.

Already in January, however, regional Party leaders were moving away from this position. In a directive concerning areas recaptured during the regional counteroffensive then in progress, the Party Committee identified revenge, liquidation, and thoroughgoing land reform as the key tasks. It pointed, by negative example, to the experience of the Second Sub-district where the local Party committee had concentrated on relief and reconstruction in retaken areas while advocating a united front with the class enemy. Yet the peasants were hungry and demoralized. They wanted the land and grain that had been taken from them, and compensation for their losses. They allegedly did not trust the idea of an anti-Chiang united front and were unwilling to participate in Communist-sponsored village organizations on that basis. "The masses lose hope in us because we do not give what they want, and what the masses do not want we perversely give," asserted the Party as it outlined the correctives:

1. Support the peasants in their demand for revenge. Lock up those who have killed and harmed them, and if the peasants demand that such people be killed, then kill a few.

2. Hold memorial services for dead village cadres, activists, peasant association members, and peasants, explaining that they "sacrificed themselves gloriously in the patriotic self-defense war" and would be avenged.

3. Mobilize the peasants to take back their land and grain.

4. Because the old village organizations were overthrown by the enemy and the masses still had many doubts, do not try immediately to restore the peasant associations, women's groups, and so on. These could be reconstructed during the revenge, liquidation, and land reform struggles.

The peasants naturally feared Chiang's army, the directive concluded. But what they feared most was the class enemy in the village, the "landlords, *o-pa,* secret agents, and bad eggs." If these could be attacked and suppressed, the peasants would rise up again; only on that basis should an anti-KMT united front be attempted in recaptured villages.[139]

The next step was to abandon the concept of a united front under any circumstances, including guerrilla warfare and by May, 1947, regional Party leaders had done so. Guerrilla war was no longer just armed force against armed force. In the villages, it was a struggle between the peasants and their enemies. At first, explained the Sub-region Party Committee, we were confused on this point, but the past nine months have enlightened us. "It is basically impossible to come up with a united front of peaceful coexistence between them." The Party blamed the KMT Government for carrying the conflict into the villages and changing it into a class war by giving direct support to the local forces of feudalism there. If villages did not fall to the advancing KMT armies, they fell to

---

139. "Ch'ü tang wei kuan-yü shou-fu ch'ü kung-tso chih-shih" [Regional Party Committee directive on work in retaken districts] Jan. 20, 1947, in *I-chiu-szu-ch'i-nien,* pp. 19-21.

the returning landlords and officials who immediately set about restoring the old reactionary order.[140]

This was the context within which the Party's line on land reform changed— as noted above—from the "lack of thoroughness" apparent in the May Fourth Directive of 1946 to the radical egalitarianism of the October, 1947, Agrarian Law.

Class Struggle and Guerrilla War. The rationale for minimizing class conflict in militarily insecure areas had been destroyed, and the Party responded with the order to carry out guerrilla war and land reform simultaneously. The new argument—indeed it was more a declaration of faith—was that if guerrilla warfare served land reform, land reform would serve guerrilla war. Whereas previously the ability to sustain guerrilla war, or better yet to secure an area against it, had been the condition for initiating class struggle, suddenly class struggle became the condition for sustaining guerrilla warfare. The Party now instructed: when organizing guerrilla operations, implement land reform thoroughly. Our objective is to suppress the landlords and arouse the masses. When the peasants rise up to struggle with the landlords, at the same time teach the peasants how to dig tunnels, bury grain, lay land mines, develop intelligence networks, and evacuate their homes. So long as we dare to use our armed force to overthrow the landlords, the peasants will dare to divide the land and defend it.

In such areas, the primary objective was clearly to control the landlords, the most important condition for reestablishing and consolidating village bases. The conference on guerrilla warfare (in May, 1947) was reminded that a village military base referred to the condition where "the peasants under the leadership of the CCP can rise up and control the landlords," and that to consolidate meant "that the peasants can control the landlords under any circumstances." Experience during the Government offensive had proved that wherever village bases had been consolidated, guerrilla warfare could be sustained. We must thoroughly suppress the landlords and their running dogs, individually and as a whole, declared the Party. We must destroy them economically, politically, and organizationally. Only then can we destroy their power of resistance, ensuring that they will neither be able nor dare to attempt another restoration. Not surprisingly, the most violent treatment·of landlords, as reflected in Party documents, occurred during this period.

The instruction to unite guerrilla war and land reform was taken so literally that regional Party leaders advocated land redistribution even in districts where guerrilla bands were operating entirely on a hit-and-run basis. The southwest corner of Shantung contained many such districts in early 1947. Government forces twice invaded this region and twice the Communist main force withdrew.

140. Chang Erh, "Chiu-ko yueh yu-chi chan-cheng tsung-chieh yü chin-hou jen-wu" [A nine-month summary of the guerrilla war and future tasks], in *Kung-tso t'ung-hsun, 32,* p. 10. This is an outline, edited by Lu Feng-hsiang, of a report by Chang Erh at the Hopei-Shantung-Honan Region Party Committee guerrilla warfare conference, May 30-31, 1947.

Landlords and others returned to towns and villages spreading "fear, doubt, and confusion" among peasants and cadres. "Can land reform be carried out in such a district?" queried Li Chen-yang, referring to the countryside around Tsining which was at this time entirely in the enemy's rear and heavily garrisoned. "It can," was the emphatic reply, even though it had to be done in a single day by armed work teams with no previous experience in dividing land under such circumstances.[141]

The methods used were not particularly refined. In comparatively secure guerrilla areas, the procedure was to lock up two landlords and let two off for every one killed. Those who went free had to give guarantees and write pledges of repentance and reform.[142] In less secure districts, even these refinements were not possible. Anchü district in Tsining *hsien* was such an area.

"Class Struggle" and Guerrilla War in Anchü. The district lay just to the southwest of Tsining city, and contained seventy-four villages with sixty thousand people. Several hundred Government soldiers were garrisoned at three keypoints in the district. By early 1947, after Tsining had fallen a second time to Government forces, Anchü district could boast only "four or five" cadres. Helping them were three *hsien* cadres and nine other *hsien*-level activists. Anchü was devoid of any defense forces and had to rely on a twenty-man armed work team from the sub-district. This group was later supplemented by Tsining *hsien's* own armed work team, formed around a nucleus of ten men transferred from the *hsien* public security bureau.

Three months after Tsining had fallen the second time, the Party reported that guerrilla operations were being sustained in Anchü district, that the enemy's *hsiang* political organization was under attack, that a local self-defense corps had been formed, the *pao-chia* system destroyed, and that taxes were being collected once more. Land redistribution had been started in twelve of the district's seventy-four villages.

According to the Party's account, the cadres and work team members began their task with consciousness-raising sessions, reporting good news, enthusiastically encouraging one another, and believing in victory. Small group discussion meetings were held both inside and outside the Party, with the cadres taking the lead in expressing such attitudes. Problems were investigated, and plans made for the development of organization, intelligence, propaganda, and military work. The primary objective was to cut the enemy's supply of grain and manpower in the villages. Toward that end, the armed work teams struck first at the *pao-chia* system and the enemy's *hsiang* administration, the quickest and most effective means being to intimidate the *hsiang* chiefs and *pao* heads. One *hsiang* chief was assassinated and when others began forming local self-defense corps, the work team circulated a message: "Whoever joins enemy organizations will be killed and it will be a member of his own family who kills him." To back up such threats, team members abducted the son and daughter-in-law of another

141. Li Chen-yang, supplement, p. 13 (see note 127 above).
142. "Hu-hsi yu-chi chan chung te t'u kai yun-tung" [The land reform movement during guerrilla war in southwest Shantung], in *Kung-tso t'ung-hsun, 32,* supplement p. 9.

hsiang chief who had already recruited an eight-man group. The day after the kidnapping, he sent word that he would disband the corps.

Land reform was addressed in an equally straightforward fashion. When the work team entered a village, it simply ordered the landlords to hand over their property. Many were attacked in order to force them all to comply quickly. The work team also sometimes adopted the tactic of changing into Government army uniforms a few days after land was divided in a village, to test the landlords. The murder of anyone who fell for the ruse was reported to be "very effective" in intimidating others.

But if Government forces could not prevent the armed work team from entering a village, neither could the team prevent KMT patrols from entering the village afterward. Our problem, concluded the Tsining work team's report, is that we have worked too fast. We have not consolidated our area and our work is not "of a mass nature."[143]

By May, 1947, however, the overall Communist strategy was beginning to bear fruit. The enemy's advance had come to a halt and his weaknesses were becoming apparent. Government forces were now spread too thinly across the vast area into which they had advanced in pursuit of a quarry that had largely eluded them. The Party committee pointed out that while the armament of the Communist forces was neither heavy nor strong, the enemy was not dispersing to occupy minor keypoints as had the Japanese.

Conversely, the Communists' main force had stopped retreating and had launched a number of small counterattacks. Nationwide, the Party was claiming that ninety enemy brigades had been destroyed and that when the figure reached one hundred, the military balance would favor the Communist side. Further difficulties could be expected in Honan where the enemy was increasing his strength. But in Shantung, the Communists were beginning to seize the initiative and in Manchuria they had already done so, a prelude to the developing nationwide counteroffensive.[144]

SUMMARY: THE POLITICAL-MILITARY SIGNIFICANCE
OF LAND REFORM

During the Anti-Japanese War, the Communists de-emphasized rent reduction and class friction in areas immediately threatened by the enemy. In 1946-47, the condition of relative military security was abandoned as a prerequisite for initiating class struggle. This change reflected the difference between the two periods. During the anti-Japanese resistance, rent reduction struggles became a means of consolidating the Party's strength within the developing base areas. In 1946, virtually all of those areas became the targets of the Government's general offensive. The condition of military security surrounding class struggle was suddenly eliminated as district after district fell to the advancing KMT armies and the return-to-the-village corps.

143. Yang P'ei, "Chi-ning wu kung tui" [Tsining's armed work team], in *Kung-tso t'ung-hsun, 32,* supplement, pp. 18-23.

144. Chang Erh, p. 19 (see note 140 above).

De-emphasizing land reform and reverting to a united front with the class enemy against the invading KMT forces was no longer a possibility. Having created their own enemy within, the Communists had little choice but to try to eliminate its influence altogether as the Civil War developed. Hence the intensification of the land reform movement in 1946-47, and Mao's injunction to Party cadres in October, 1946, to "solve the land problem" no matter how busy they were with the war.

Nevertheless, having been deprived of the requisite military security across a broad front, Communist leaders apparently made one mistake: they failed to distinguish between the loss of military security in areas where land reform had already been implemented, and the loss of military security in areas where it had not. According to an informant who was living in the Shansi-Hopei-Shantung-Honan Border Region at this time and who is today of cadre status, the policy of attempting to carry out land reform in guerrilla areas was an erroneous one and was subsequently criticized as such. The main reason was the heavy cost in human life due to the retaliatory activities it generated in villages that could not be adequately protected by Communist forces.

A second consideration must have been reduced agricultural output. As Party leaders emphasized at the time, the war was not just a contest of men and arms but of wealth as well. In guerrilla districts, both landlords and peasants, fearing each other and uncertain of the future, left their fields uncultivated. Calling this a great danger and a key problem directly related to military victory, regional Party leaders worried in the spring of 1947 about the increasing amount of uncultivated land in the guerrilla districts.[145]

Moreover, these costs were apparently not matched by comparable gains. This verdict doubtless would have been altered—as would various features of the policy itself—had the Communist counteroffensive failed and the military situation devolved into a genuinely protracted guerrilla war. In Anyang *hsien,* where land reform had been carried out prior to the return of the KMT, guerrilla-type operations were developing by the spring of 1947, as they were in northern Kiangsu. According to Belden, they were inspired in Anyang *hsien* primarily by the interest of the peasants in protecting the results of land reform. Had such local peasant bands subsequently received training and leadership from members of regular army units as occurred during the anti-Japanese resistance, a similar kind of guerrilla war could presumably have developed around the class struggle in the rear of the KMT armies.

In 1946-47, however, the Communists' main objective was to preserve their regular armed forces and the Party organization intact for the nationwide counteroffensive aimed at the annihilation of the KMT armies. For that reason, Anyang *hsien* and Anchü district were devoid of Communist army units in early 1947, while the Central Government was reestablishing its own structure of political power with the support of the enemies the Communists had created during the struggle movement. The vengeance wrought by the return-to-the-village corps may have done as much to arouse the peasants' class consciousness

145. *Ibid.,* p. 23.

as any liquidation meeting. Yet ironically, the military and political conditions that made this possible, also contrived to demoralize peasants in some districts to a point of inaction, if the reports from the Hopei-Shantung-Honan Party Committee are any indication. The gains that could accrue from the peasants' heightened class consciousness could not become effective until a few cadres had begun to return and a minimal guerrilla infrastructure had been re-created.

Even then, the position of the armed work teams and the militia was so insecure that the next step—the intimidation of the local power holders—could be accomplished only by resort to terrorism in the form of isolated threats, kidnappings, and assassinations. This could have been, and in some instances was, carried out without the costly attempt to involve unarmed peasants in the process. But to initiate land reform, as was also done, in villages behind the KMT lines, where the armed work teams could not remain long enough to protect the beneficiaries from the returning KMT patrols, invited retaliation against peasants who had not yet been organized to defend themselves. So, too, did the practice of carrying out land reform in the immediate advance of the KMT armies as described in many of the above-cited dispatches of the Hsinhua News Agency.

The lessons learned during the Anti-Japanese War in this respect would probably not have been cast aside in 1946-47 had it not been for the sudden KMT intrusion into the Communists' main base areas in north and east China. That the most basic condition for the successful implementation of land reform was the capacity to protect it against its enemies was acknowledged by Mao Tse-tung and the Party center in May, 1948. The error of trying to pursue land reform under conditions of inadequate security was tacitly admitted in Mao's directive issued at that time which reestablished essentially the same criteria developed during the Anti-Japanese War. [146] This, then, is the answer to the second question, posed in the introduction to this chapter, as to why the Communists temporarily halted the implementation of land reform when they were about to move southward into areas where tenancy was more prevalent than in the North. Land reform may have been essential in mobilizing peasant support for the CCP, but that potential could not be realized in any given area until certain preconditions had been established.

Those conditions as reiterated in the Party's 1948 directive were: (1) The area had to be militarily secure, the enemy's armed force completely eliminated, and the possibility of having to revert to guerrilla warfare must no longer exist. (2) A majority of the basic masses must demand land redistribution. (3) Land reform cadres should be sufficient in number and training to be able to lead the work and not allow the masses to proceed on their own. The directive referred explicitly to insecure and newly liberated areas where these three conditions did not generally obtain. It emphasized that the first precondition had not been

146. "Chung-kung chung-yang kuan-yü i-chiu-szu-pa-nien t'u-ti kai-ko kung-tso ho cheng tang kung-tso te chih-shih" [CCP Central Committee directive on 1948 land reform and Party rectification work], May 25, 1948, in Chieh-fang she, ed., *Lun hsin chieh-fang-ch'ü t'u-ti cheng-ts'e,* p. 9; and Mao Tse-tung, *Selected Works,* 4:254-55.

established in districts bordering on enemy territory and that land reform should not be attempted in such areas.

An editorial in a local Honan newspaper explained the importance of establishing these preconditions:

> Have we done the preparatory work in the newly liberated areas of central China? Clearly, we have not done it well. In some of our newly liberated areas, the great majority of the peasants in terms of their thought and organization, are certainly not well prepared. In general, the peasants' political consciousness has not been raised, and their belief in the revolution is not firm. Although they are very poor, they lack a clear understanding of where their poverty comes from; although they need land, they do not firmly understand that the land should be returned to their families; they enthusiastically support the People's Liberation Army, but they are not firm in their determination to stand by it for a long period of time; they truly hate the control of the KMT and the oppression of Chiang's bandits, but they have many doubts about overthrowing his control and his basic forces. Organizationally, peasant associations of genuine hired, poor, and middle peasants have not been formed in the area, and mass cadres have not been recruited in large numbers.[147]

Nevertheless, the implementation of land reform in guerrilla areas and in newly liberated districts was a relatively specific problem. To conclude that land reform produced largely negative consequences where the three preconditions did not exist should not be misconstrued as an evaluation of the land reform program elsewhere.

First, it is necessary to point out what land division did not do. In the short-run, the only period that concerns us here, a resulting increase in production must be eliminated as a factor of any consequence. In 1934, Mao wrote, with reference to the Communists' first major attempt at land redistribution, that land reform often resulted in a temporary reduction of agricultural output. A note appended to this comment explained that there was usually a decline in farm production primarily because it took a year or two to settle the issue of landownership and fully establish the new economic order. During the interim period of uncertainty, the peasants "could not yet set their minds fully on production."[148] Given the disruption and uncertainties that accompanied land reform from 1944 to 1948, it is unlikely that the Communists' wartime financial problems were eased substantially as a result of any consequent increase in agricultural production.[149]

147. *Yü-hsi jih-pao* (editorial), "T'ing-chih hsin ch'ü t'u kai shih-hsing chien tsu chien hsi" [Stop land reform in new districts and carry out rent and interest reduction], Aug. 24, 1948, in *Lun hsin chieh-fang-ch'ü t'u-ti cheng-ts'e,* pp. 12-13. Communist forces were renamed the People's Liberation Army in 1946.

148. Mao Tse-tung, "Our Economic Policy," Jan. 23, 1934, *Selected Works,* 1:142, 145.

149. Production figures from this period are virtually non-existent. However, the production campaigns and organization of mutual-aid groups must have helped to offset the economic losses in the liberated areas. These efforts are outlined in S. Pepper, "The Politics of Civil War: China, 1945-1949," Ph.D. dissertation, Department of Political Science, University of California, Berkeley, pp. 361-70.

Mao wrote, however, that between 1946 and 1948, the Party had "mobilized some 1,600,000 of the peasants who obtained land to join the People's Liberation Army."[150] As we have seen, the redistribution of land and property was carried out in conjunction with the army recruiting campaigns from 1945 through 1947. It must therefore be concluded that redistribution contributed to their success. Intra-Party criticism nevertheless suggests that the process was probably never so simple as portrayed by the Hsinhua News Agency.

The poor young peasant who rallied to the colors in order to defend his family's land was the model whose image was transmitted to impress and inspire. Even so, it took more than that image to overcome the peasant's innate reluctance to join the army, and to leave a new-won plot of land. The data we have been able to present here does not allow us to conclude that the peasants automatically responded to the Communists' call-to-arms either from a sense of commitment to the new order or from fear of landlord revenge. The evidence indicates instead that fear of revenge was an initial obstacle that had to be overcome before the peasants would even accept the land, and that local cadres felt uncomfortable about asking them to join the army immediately after doing so. Hence the significance of land reform must be explained in somewhat different terms.

It is true that the Communists sought and undoubtedly received "support" in return for the tangible material benefits that property redistribution provided. But what the land reform struggles also made possible was the institutional capacity to transform this nascent class consciousness into the specific kinds of support necessary to fight a war. The primary component of the land revolution in this regard was the overthrow of the existing rural elite. Whether it was really feudal, whether it was even made up of landlords in any given village, were not the issues. The key consideration was that the struggle movement with its many targets destroyed the political and economic domination of the ruling class, an essential step in the creation of a new village power structure.

The construction of that new order was the real fulfilment of land reform as "the mother of all other work." Peasants who participated most actively in the multifeatured accusation movement provided new recruits for the Communist Party and new village leadership. Recipients of land and property added their numbers to the peasant associations and other village organizations. This was the institutional structure, manned by the peasants themselves, that the Communists could then rely on to assume responsibility for collecting the grain tax, organizing military transport teams, and exerting social pressure on reluctant peasants during the recruiting drives.

In answer to the main question posed in the introduction to this chapter, these were the "roots" the Party had been able to put down in the countryside as a result of land reform. Conditions permitting, those roots could indeed ensure a reliable supply of grain and manpower, and sustain the Chinese Communists in their struggle with the KMT.

---

150. Mao Tse-tung, "On the September Meeting–Circular of the Central Committee of the Communist Party of China," Oct. 10, 1948, *Selected Works,* 4:271.

TWO STEPS FORWARD, ONE STEP BACK:
CONSOLIDATION AND RECTIFICATION

Anna Louise Strong visited the Shansi-Hopei-Shantung-Honan Border Region in November, 1946. She learned that Border Region officials, many of whom were college graduates, worked without salaries for two meals a day, two cotton summer suits and one-third of a padded winter suit a year, and austere accommodations in peasant homes. One evening at dinner with some of the top officials of the Border Region government, she remarked that her American friends tended to excuse the notorious corruption of KMT officials because their salaries were so low that they had to steal to make ends meet. Everyone grinned, and someone retorted: "That's not the reason why they graft. KMT officials have to graft because if one of them should work hard and refuse to steal the people's money, Chiang Kai-shek would arrest him as a Communist!"[151]

The joke obscured the effort underlying the storied integrity of Communist officials. An example of the sort of effort required was the Party rectification campaign of 1947-48. One of its objectives was to check corruption among basic level Party members and work cadres then in the process of implementing the land policy. Unlike the KMT's repeated declarations in favor of reform and self-regeneration, the rectification movement was not a mere face-saving gesture. The campaign began some time in 1947, when the dominant concern in the land reform campaign was still with rightist errors. This was the period when land reform was, as noted, at its most radical in terms of equalizing wealth. Soon after the promulgation of the Outline Agrarian Law the emphasis shifted, in conformity with the "law of the mass movement," to a preoccupation with leftist problems. Party rectification continued into this phase and was conducted simultaneously with a campaign to consolidate land reform and correct excesses. An ideological education campaign within the People's Liberation Army was also carried out at this time.[152]

PROBLEMS ON THE RIGHT

As indicated in the section on land equalization, Party leaders were already calling for rectification as an antidote to certain rightist problems during the first

151. Strong, *Tomorrow's China,* p. 79; and Hsinhua News Agency, Yenan, Nov. 10, 1946, dispatch by A. L. Strong (*FYI,* Nov. 11). At the time she visited the Border Region, some 600 people were directing civil administration, the army, and mass organizations. When the Border Region capital, Hantan, fell to KMT forces in the autumn of 1946, these 600 people moved into the countryside and directed work from three nearby villages.

152. For a discussion of the rectification campaign at this same time against Party intellectuals, see Merle Goldman, *Literary Dissent in Communist China,* Chapter Four. The ideological education campaign in the PLA began in the winter of 1947-48 as "the reflection in the army of the movements for land reform and Party consolidation then vigorously proceeding in all the Liberated Areas." It was intended to strengthen discipline, improve combat effectiveness, and raise political consciousness of officers and men. One objective was the integration into the PLA of several hundred thousand former KMT troops who opted to change sides after their capture. Efforts were made to enhance democracy within the army by giving soldier representatives the right to participate in managing supplies; by

half of 1947. At the National Land Conference in September, the achievements as well as the difficulties of the land reform movement to date were discussed at length. In keeping with the previous assessment, the difficulties were blamed on "landlords, rich peasants, and riffraff" who had infiltrated into the Party, particularly at the local level. Their faults included graft, influence peddling, nepotism, arrogance, maneuvering for personal advantage, and stealing from the public stores. Impurities of class composition and improper work style were therefore identified as the two main problems obstructing the thorough implementation of land reform. Besides passing the Outline Agrarian Law, the Land Conference also adopted a resolution calling for a concerted Party rectification campaign, thus advocating for general application a course of action already begun in some liberated areas.

Following the National Land Conference, regional conferences were called to discuss the Agrarian Law and Party rectification. During this period, Party conferences were relied upon at all levels throughout the liberated areas as the main instrument for transmitting directives and instructions, for gathering information about local conditions, and for training local Party members and cadres. In the Chin-Chi-Lu-Yü Border Region, 1,700 people met at Yehtao in the T'aihang Mountains for eighty-five days. The Border Region land conference included examining sessions which investigated the class origin, thought, and behavior of every participant. A number of Party members received punishment for having violated the Party's land reform policy, and at least two of those punished were expelled from the Party for their transgressions.[153]

At the conclusion of the conference, the participants returned home and convened county land conferences attended by all full-time *hsien*-level political workers. In Luch'eng *hsien,* Shansi, the land conference lasted throughout the month of February, 1948. Each cadre attending was required to make a statement of his class origin and a self-criticism of his past work. Here, too, some were punished for their shortcomings with warnings or suspensions, and a few were expelled from the Party. Most, however, left the conference ready to carry out the purification of the village Party branches and the thorough and equal redistribution of the land. These reeducated *hsien*-level cadres were organized into work teams and sent into a selected number of representative villages in the county to begin the work of investigation and reform.[154]

In late November and December, 1947, a series of editorials in the Shansi-Chahar-Hopei Border Region newspaper indicated that a similar course of events was underway in that Border Region as well. In mid-October, about a thousand of the Region's leading cadres gathered for a month-long examination of the Agrarian Law and National Land Conference resolutions. The main concerns expressed in the Chin-Ch'a-Chi Border Region, as elsewhere, were that the initial

holding regular sessions between officers and men for mutual instruction; and by giving soldiers the right to criticize errors and shortcomings of cadres.

153. U.S. Cons., Peiping, Hsinhua radio, North Shensi, Jan. 17, 1948.

154. Hinton, *Fanshen,* pp. 263-64.

effort had not been carried out thoroughly and that as a result many of the poor had not yet been able to throw off the feudal yoke.

After the conference, the faults of cadres and Party members were widely publicized, as were the methods to be used in correcting them. In order to purge the Party's ranks of landlords, rich peasants, and other evil elements, the registration of new members was halted until the investigation of existing members could be completed. The work of all cadres born into landlord and rich peasant families was carefully scrutinized in order to determine whether they had obstructed land reform, particularly when their own families and friends were being struggled against.

A major innovation in 1947 was the opening up of Party rectification to the village masses, as mentioned. The names of all Party members in the villages were made public. Cadres and Party members who had committed errors were required to acknowledge them publicly and accept the criticism of the assembled villagers. Cadres and Party members who had taken for their own use confiscated property that should have been distributed to the poor, were forced to return such property to the people. Cadres found guilty of more serious crimes were relieved of their responsibilities and given appropriate punishment. One editorial went so far as to declare that the villagers themselves should elect village cadres; and that the poor peasant league *(p'in-nung t'uan)* and peasant association should investigate village Party members and recommend their explusion from the Party.[155]

When the Pei-yueh District Party Committee opened its land conference, poor peasants and farm workers who were not Party members were invited to participate. Similarly, when the Party Committee of Fup'ing *hsien* held its land conference, it searched the villages for poor and hired peasant representatives to participate in the conference sessions. At both conferences, the peasant participants were hesitant to speak out at first but soon rose to the occasion. Some of the cadres reportedly wept when their errors and weaknesses were revealed in public. When the Border Region Party Bureau called a conference of local Party committees, Comrade P'eng Chen himself was said to have consulted non-Party peasant representatives before presenting his report.

This method of reaching outside the Party in an effort to correct internal Party problems—advocated as we have seen by Liu Shao-ch'i—was apparently deemed successful, for it would be used during the Party rectification of 1957 and again a decade later when the prime target would be Liu himself. The method was not, however, greeted with unbounded enthusiasm by Party members in the Shansi-Chahar-Hopei Border Region in 1947. They questioned how persons who were themselves neither Party members nor even cadres could participate in a Party rectification meeting. But, admonished the Border Region newspaper, our Party's principles clearly stipulate that we are to maintain a close relationship with the people and are not to separate ourselves from them. Therefore, when we carry out the equal division of land and Party rectification,

155. *Chin-ch'a-chi jih-pao* (editorial), Nov. 27, 1947, in Chin-ch'a-chi jih-pao she, ed., *Ch'üan-t'i nung-min ch'i-lai p'ing-fen t'u-ti*, p. 7.

why should not hired hands and poor peasants participate in Party conferences? When the peasants discuss the Agrarian Law, continued the paper, their talk is all of village affairs and you Party members may feel that they are far off the mark. In fact, it is an education for you. They are telling you things which will be useful in implementing the Agrarian Law. You can only know which of its articles are appropriate to the local situation if you listen to the opinions of the local masses.[156]

At the village level in Chin-Ch'a-Chi, the holding of land conferences or meetings for land reform and Party rectification was ideally divided into a three-stage process: (1) a general meeting of the village Party branch; (2) a general meeting of all poor and hired peasants in the village; and (3) a general meeting of the entire village. The suggested procedure was as follows.

Upon their arrival in a village, the cadre work team was to call a general meeting of the village branch to brief local Party members on the new policy of equally dividing the land and purifying the Party's ranks. The branch was instructed to ensure that henceforth decisions made by the poor peasant league and the peasant association would be implemented. The branch was also advised that Party members whom the peasants truly opposed would be relieved of their responsibilities in the village. All arms in the village not in the hands of the poor peasant league were to be turned over to a higher-level and were not to be reissued until thorough investigations had been concluded.

After the Party branch meeting, the work team cadres were to call a general meeting of all genuine poor and hired peasants in the village. None of the original village cadres or Party members were to participate in this meeting, at which the work team cadres would explain the main points of the new Agrarian Law and methods for implementing them. The poor peasant league and peasant association, after being reorganized or newly established as the situation might require, would be the controlling force in the village.

Finally, a general meeting of all the villagers was to be called at which the Agrarian Law and proclamations of the Border Region government would be explained to everyone. Particular emphasis was to be placed on the new principle that all important matters in the village had to be discussed and agreed to by the poor peasant league and the peasant association before any action could be taken. Everyone in the village must be made to understand that the decisions of these bodies were to be obeyed.

This general pattern of events did not, of course, unfold as smoothly as the above outline might imply. Many places were congratulated for the "planned and prepared activization of the masses" which had been achieved. But in many others, conditions were just the opposite. Toward the end of December, it was reported that some villages had completed the three meetings in a single day. In one *hsien,* a cadre working alone claimed to have organized poor peasant groups and new peasant associations in six or seven villages within the space of a few days. In another *hsien,* the Party organization itself had announced that this was the proper procedure. Reports from many different villages indicated that land

156. *Chin-ch'a-chi jih-pao* (editorial), Dec. 2, 1947, in *ibid.,* p. 10.

reform and Party rectification had indeed been attempted in this manner. Finally, in some places, "evil" people were said to be organizing false poor peasant leagues (which contained elements other than genuine poor peasants, laborers, and lower-middle peasants), and peasant associations that contained middle peasants who still engaged in exploitation.[157]

Everyone must be aware of these problems, warned the Border Region newspaper. With the appearance of the false poor peasant leagues, all would now have to be examined closely; some would have to be disbanded while others would have to be reorganized and their worst members expelled. The key to all of the problems was leadership; responsibility for them lay primarily with local Party leaders. Three different types were said to exist, any one of which could spell defeat for the movement. Good comrades enthusiastic about land reform made up the first type. Their work was marred by inadequate planning and preparation, and even by a degree of rashness. This type of leader was basically incapable of activating the masses, putting the peasant association in order, or accurately demarcating classes. The second type of comrade was the individualist, primarily concerned with his position and reputation. This sort of person forced orders on the peasants, sent false reports to higher levels, and looked after himself at the expense of others. The third type of leader was the landlord-rich peasant type whose only goal was to seize power and undermine land reform.[158]

PROBLEMS ON THE LEFT

Unexpectedly, the Shansi-Chahar-Hopei Border Region newspaper had added a new problem to the list, and moreover had put it in first place. When the Party rectification campaign began, the main problems had been identified as rightist: class impurities and errors in work style such as commandism and bureaucratism. The editorial criticism of unplanned enthusiasm was one of the first indications of a general shift in the land reform and Party rectification movement. This became fully apparent in January, 1948, when the official line changed abruptly and leftist errors became the object of central concern. The old rightist deviations continued to be attacked, but the spotlight was focused on a different set of problems which included, in Mao's words, "the partial but fairly numerous encroachments on the interests of the middle peasants, the damage done to some private industrial and commercial enterprises and the overstepping in some places of certain lines of demarcation in the policy for suppressing counter-revolutionaries."[159]

Within three months after its promulgation, one of the most extreme provisions of the Agrarian Law, namely the equal redistribution of village land and property, was modified in deference to the middle peasants. If they did not

---

157. *Chin-ch'a-chi jih-pao* (editorials), Dec. 10 and 26, 1947, in *ibid.*, pp. 22-23, 29.
158. *Chin-ch'a-chi jih-pao* (editorials), Dec. 21 and 26, 1947, in *ibid.*, pp. 28-31.
159. "On the September Meeting," pp. 270-71 (see note 150 above).

agree to the equal division of land, they were to be allowed to keep more land than the average poor peasant in the village.[160]

The reasons for the timing of this modification remain unclear. The problems that precipitated the shift in January, 1948, may not have been fully appreciated by Party leaders the previous autumn due either to their own ideological predispositions or to a lack of adequate information. But these problems had been developing throughout 1947. They were neither solely nor even primarily the result of excesses committed immediately after the promulgation of the 1947 Agrarian Law, as some writers have suggested, since the Law—like the May Fourth Directive—only formalized a line that had been developing in practice for some time. Moreover, at least one of the problems—the encroachment on the middle peasants—had been acknowledged as such by regional Party leaders for at least three years.

Lacking verifiable information concerning the intra-Party debates that occurred at this time, the January, 1948, shift can therefore only be analyzed as a function of the total range of problems that developed during 1946-47, when the land reform movement was at its most radical. In January, Party leaders still seemed to be groping for an across-the-board solution to all of their various difficulties in the countryside. In formulating a general line for the developing land reform movement, the Party center seemed to be at the stage alluded to by Li Yü in 1945, when he warned the Shantung cadres that the key consideration was to judge correctly the point at which the limits of one phase had been reached and the next should begin. Unity should not be sought too early, but struggle could not be allowed to continue until it became counterproductive. This impression of uncertainty within the context of the developing mass movement during the winter of 1947-48 is reinforced by the way the two main policy lines finally came together in the Central Committee directive of February 22, 1948. This directive systematized the shifting patterns of land reform and Party rectification work by distinguishing between areas where it had been satisfactorily accomplished and those where it had not.

The first explicit statement of the change in the Party's line on land reform came in a lengthy speech by Jen Pi-shih before a meeting of the Northwest Field Army's Party Committee on January 12. There had been an intimation of things to come in Mao's report presented to a meeting of the Central Committee on Christmas Day, 1947. Mao had commented that it was necessary to listen to the opinions of middle peasants and make concessions to them if they expressed objections to the equal division of land. He also warned that in determining class status, care must be taken not to wrongly classify middle peasants as rich

160. According to Jen Pi-shih's report, "T'u-ti kai-ko chung te chi-ko wen-t'i" [Some land reform problems], Jan. 12, 1948, in *T'u-ti kai-ko chung te chi-ko wen-t'i ho san-ko tien-hsing ching-yen* [hereafter *San-ko tien-hsing*], pp. 17-18. This modification was formalized in the Feb. 22, 1948, directive (discussed below), and written into subsequent editions of the law. See, for example, Chung-kung chung-yang wei-yuan-hui, *Chung-kuo t'u-ti fa ta-kang.*

peasants.[161] Yet this was a theme that had been expressed before in official Party documents, even in the May Fourth Directive itself. And in his report, Mao had reiterated the Party's concern that the satisfaction of poor peasant demands should remain the most fundamental task of land reform. He also pointed out that although the decisions of the National Land Conference were being implemented everywhere, the problems of work style and impurities in class composition of the Party at the basic level remained unsolved.

Nevertheless, this same Central Committee meeting discussed the land reform and Party rectification movement in some detail. On the basis of this discussion, Mao drafted three weeks later, on January 18, 1948, an intra-Party directive which set the guidelines for the emerging land policy. He covered the abrupt shift from a preoccupation with rightist deviations to those of the left, by emphasizing that both existed within the Party and that the policy for coping with them would have to be decided on the basis of a given set of concrete circumstances. In land reform, the problem of right deviations was now seen as a danger primarily in areas where the masses had not yet been fully activated.

His main concern, however, was clearly with leftist mistakes as he outlined key features of the new line that would be adopted during the coming months. Commenting on the slogan "the poor peasants and farm laborers conquer the country and should rule the country," Mao called it erroneous. The hired hands, poor peasants, middle peasants, and other working people should rule the country. He went on to explain this in terms of a concrete policy designed to avoid rash and adventurist tendencies, particularly in dealing with middle peasants. Those found to have been wrongly classified and treated as rich peasants were to have their class status corrected and their property returned to them wherever possible. The property of rich middle peasants was not to be confiscated without the owner's consent, and middle peasants were not to be excluded from peasant associations and committees.

Concerning policies toward medium and small industrialists and businessmen, Mao asserted that the practice of encouraging landlords and rich peasants to invest in industry and commerce, adopted during the earlier period of rent and interest reduction, was correct and should still be followed. Also, the most important objective of land reform was the distribution of the land, grain, animals, and farm implements of landlords and the surplus property of rich peasants. Undue effort should not be placed on searching out other valuables buried or otherwise hidden by these people.

Mao made two final points. Both could have been holdovers from the previous effort to rectify work style, although the points also fit neatly into the new anti-leftist line. The first was an unequivocal demand for an end to unnecessary violence. "We must insist on killing less and must strictly forbid killing without discrimination," he wrote, noting that otherwise the Party would become isolated from the people. He insisted further that when crimes had been committed, suspects were to be tried before the people's courts as stipulated in the Agrarian Law. Death sentences were to be carried out only after it had been

161. Mao Tse-tung, "The Present Situation and Our Tasks," *Selected Works*, 4:165.

approved by the local government at the county or sub-regional level. Second, Mao emphasized the continuing need to struggle with cadres and Party members who had committed errors, and with "bad elements" among the workers and peasants. It must be made clear to all that the masses had the right to criticize cadres and Party members, to dismiss them from their posts, and to recommend their expulsion from the Party.[162]

Jen Pi-shih's January 12 speech was essentially an elaboration of the same points summarized in Mao's January 18 directive. Jen indicated the nature of the difficulties and concerns which had led the Party to adopt its new posture of striving to "unite firmly with the middle peasants." When we were fighting the Japanese, he noted, the middle peasants contributed much to our efforts, as they are doing in our struggle against Chiang Kai-shek. "Our People's Liberation Army is now 30 to 40 percent middle peasant. If we destroy the wellbeing of the middle peasants, it will cause us to be defeated in war." He also pointed out that in the old liberated areas where land had been equally and thoroughly divided, the majority of the people had now become middle peasants. The development of cooperative work and of the economy therefore depended on the new and old middle peasants whose production experience, together with the agricultural implements they owned, made them a valuable resource in the rural areas. But instead of being treated as such, there was evidence in all the liberated areas that the interests of the middle peasants had been encroached upon and that as result they were becoming alienated from the Party. This tendency Jen denounced as "very dangerous" and an instance of "extreme left-wing adventurism."

In many places, middle peasants had been wrongly designated as rich peasants and landlords, their lands and property had been expropriated, and some had even been beaten. He cited as an example the case of Ts'aichiayai, a village in Hsing *hsien,* Shansi (in the Shansi-Suiyuan Border Region), where some 50 households out of a total of 551 had been wrongly designated as rich peasants or landlords. Most of the 50 were middle peasants and a few were poor peasants.

Second, the poor peasants had not only become the leadership backbone of the land reform movement as was right and proper, but often monopolized everything that was done in the village, which was not. No middle peasants were elected as representatives in the peasant representative congresses, nor were middle peasants allowed to participate in any of the important decisions concerning the demarcation of class status, the distribution of confiscated property, or the assigning of responsibility for public work, grain requisitions, and the like.

Third, the greatest share of burdens such as public work and grain requisitions tended to be placed on the shoulders of the middle peasants who naturally resented having to make the heaviest contributions in the village. Jen Pi-shih emphasized that since the objectives of land reform had now been basically achieved, the excesses would have to be corrected if those achievements were not to flounder in a welter of confusion, hostility, and declining support for the Communists—if not outright defections to the enemy camp.

---

162. Mao Tse-tung, "On Some Important Problems of the Party's Present Policy," *Selected Works,* 4:182-86.

Jen discussed at length the standard to be applied henceforth. He elaborated upon the major points, with some modifications, of the two 1933 documents on class analysis which had just been reissued by the Party for research purposes.[163] The Party's good faith in compromising with the middle peasants was demonstrated by the new Central Committee decision allowing those who earned as much as 25 percent of their incomes from exploitation to be classified as middle peasants. In 1933, the figure had been fixed at only 15 percent. A number of other admonitions and prescriptions included recent changes in class status, the position of middle peasants in the peasant representative congresses, and the necessity of distributing the tax burden fairly.

Jen also explained the necessity of protecting business and industry, even when owned by landlords and rich peasants who lived by exploiting both producers and consumers. There was to be no repetition of errors such as had occurred, for example, in Kaochiapao, Shenmu district, northern Shensi. When Communist forces took this village, even small traders were expropriated. As a result, the marketing system virtually collapsed and people had to sneak out into the fields to buy and sell needed items in secret. Jen warned that this was a suicidal policy when the government trading company had not yet been widely established and the marketing cooperatives were not yet well run.

Finally, Jen—like Mao—went to some lengths to denounce the indiscriminate beatings, killings, and use of multilation as a form of punishment, all of which had been widely reported in the course of the land reform movement. However, Jen expanded the issue of violence by criticizing cadres for using force against the masses as well as against their class enemies. Now that the masses were to participate in the investigation and criticism of local cadres and Party members, peasants who had been beaten or otherwise harmed by them were likely to turn to violence as a means of revenge. Before the investigation meetings begin, he warned, we must explain clearly to cadres and masses alike that there is to be no more violence and no revenge on either side in the future.[164]

THE NEW SYNTHESIS

In the latter part of February, the two policy lines were formally reconciled by the Central Committee in its Directive on Land Reform and Party Rectification Work in the Old and Semi-old Liberated Areas (February 22, 1948).[165] This directive and Jen's address were thereafter circulated as the two basic documents of land reform and Party rectification work, together with the revised 1933 articles on class analysis and three essays summarizing typical land reform and

163. See note 12 above.
164. Jen Pi-shih, pp. 10-31 (see note 160 above).
165. Chung-kung chung-yang kuan-yü tsai lao ch'ü yü pan-lao ch'u chih-hsing t'u-ti kai-ko kung-tso yü cheng tang kung-tso te chih-shih," in *San-ko tien-hsing,* pp. 1-8. The English translation by Hsinhua News Agency (in *Daily Report,* Mar. 2, 1948) has errors and deletions. This central directive was actually preceded by a similar policy statement by the Chin-Chi-Lu-Yü Border Region Party Bureau on Feb. 6, 1948, in Liu Shao-ch'i, *et al., T'u kai cheng tang tien-hsing ching-yen,* pp. 32-33.

rectification experiences. [166] In a brief statement, Mao himself instructed that the three case studies should be given to every village work cadre. These cases, he wrote, will be more valuable than all the directives and instructions from the Party center in helping those who lack experience to grasp the proper work methods.[167]

The Consolidation of Land Reform

The Directive on Land Reform and Party Rectification Work in the Old and Semi-old Liberated Areas officially modified the principle of absolute equality in the redistribution of land as stipulated in Article Six of the Agrarian Law. In addition, the directive clarified some of the confusion surrounding the shift from a primary concern with the needs of the poor to the emphasis on pacifying the middle peasants. This was done by drawing a distinction between those areas where land reform had been basically completed and those where it had not. In the latter, the needs of the poor would continue to be of paramount concern.

Having arrived at this basic distinction, the Party was then able to indicate in a rather more systematic fashion the future course that land reform and Party rectification work should take. The directive outlined the three typical situations existent in the old and semi-old liberated areas.

Types One and Two. In the first situation, land reform had already been carried out in a relatively thorough fashion. Middle peasants and new middle peasants were in the majority, making up 50 to 80 percent of the village population. Poor peasants (including those who had not yet received their full share of the fruits of land reform, and landlords and rich peasants reduced to poor peasant status) represented from 10 to 40 percent of the village population. In such an area, the land could be regarded as having been equally divided. Any remaining problems could be solved by methods less drastic than reinvestigation and redivision. If it was deemed necessary to take some land from the new rich peasants or rich middle peasants for the poor, this should not be done without the owners' consent.

In the second typical situation, the liquidation struggles and the May Fourth Directive had been carried out. The peasants had been mobilized and organized, but the land had not been thoroughly divided. This might be due to any number of reasons, for example, poor leadership, class impurities within the Party, bureaucratism, or the military situation. In such an area, poor peasants were in the majority making up from 50 to 70 percent of the village population, and there were still old landlords and rich peasants who retained on the average more property than the middle peasants. Unless a majority of the villagers demanded

166. For other editions of these documents, see Liu Shao-ch'i, *et al., T'u kai cheng tang tien-hsing ching-yen;* also *T'u-ti kai-ko yü cheng-tang.*

167. Mao Tse-tung, "Hsu-yen" [Preface], Mar. 12, 1948, in *San-ko tien-hsing,* pp. 32-33. Mao's comments referred to all three case studies, but his preface was written specifically as an introduction to T'an Cheng-wen, "Shan-hsi kuo hsien shih tsen-yang chin-hsing t'u-ti kai-ko te" [How Kuo *hsien,* Shansi, carried out land reform], originally issued by Hsinhua News Agency, North Shensi, between March 18-21, 1948, and reprinted herein, pp. 34-50.

it, however, the process of land redistribution should not be undertaken again. But land and property should be rearranged as equitably as possible. The reason for the caution, the directive acknowledged, was that there was not always enough land in the hands of landlords and rich peasants to meet the needs of the poor. And taking land from middle peasants was now officially discouraged, unless the middle peasant's holding was twice as much as the average poor peasant holding in the village. If such was the case, no more than one-fourth of the middle peasant's land could be taken from him, and that not without his consent.

In organizational terms, the effort to conciliate the middle peasant was marked by the decline in importance of the poor peasant league. This was particularly true in the first type of area described above where new middle peasants had become the dominant class. In such an area, the poor peasant league was not to be abolished immediately but was to be transformed gradually into a poor peasant small group within the more broadly representative peasant association. In the second type of area where the poor peasant league still had an independent leadership function to perform, it should be maintained but new middle peasants were to be allowed to participate in its work. And here, too, after the work of land redistribution had been completed, the poor peasant league was to be transformed into a small group within the larger peasant association.

The Case Study. In solving problems characteristic of these two typical situations, the Central Committee advised that the experience of Huang-chiach'uan in Suite *hsien,* Shensi, be studied as the model for use in other areas. This was a village of seventy-five households and some 333 persons. By early 1948, land reform had been more or less satisfactorily completed. In terms of quantity, the land problem had been essentially solved. There were no households in the village without land. But inequalities remained between the forty-one middle peasant households and the thirty-one poor peasant families. In this village, therefore, the reinvestigation of land reform which followed the promulgation of the Agrarian Law concentrated on resolving the relatively minor disparities in the quantity and quality of land held by these two groups. The process took twenty-one days. The first nine were spent reinvestigating and registering the land holdings which was done by groups of twenty to thirty villagers who went out into the fields each day with five peasant arbitrators experienced in local land problems. Particular attention was paid to the quality of land holdings, their fertility, distance from the village and so forth.

After these initial investigations, seven days were spent in redistributing the land, taking from those with some surplus and giving to those whose deficiencies were greatest. Seventeen *hsiang* of land (according to the standards of this place, one *hsiang* was the equivalent of about three *mou*) were taken from the three old landlord families who had already been reduced to poor peasant status. But this was insufficient even when augmented by some public and cooperatively managed land. It was at this point that the middle peasants began to show much less enthusiasm for the whole undertaking. When this became apparent, the work team cadres went from door to door encouraging the middle peasants to discuss their misgivings. The cadres sought to allay the middle peasants' fears by explaining that they would not be forced to give up land against their will since the Party's policy was to unite with, them as well as to aid the poor. Those with some surplus were then invited to give it up voluntarily.

Under this sort of social pressure, seventeen middle peasant households turned over several *hsiang* of land but a few families with some surplus still held back. The work team cadres, bearing in mind Mao's injunction not to use force, organized discussion meetings which continued for most of three days. Everyone criticized the selfishness of Huang Wei-chih and Huang Hsien-ts'eng, both middle peasants with some surplus land who refused to give up any of it. Another middle peasant, Huang P'eng-liang, agreed to give up some land but later regretted it and the peasant association let him take it back. Then another member of his family gave up the land, which he again took back. Ultimately, some fifty-five *hsiang* of land was accumulated in the village. Most of this was redistributed to supplement the holdings of twenty-eight poor peasant and eight middle peasant households. After an additional five days devoted to making official reinvestigations and final adjustments, the land reform was declared finally to have been thoroughly and satisfactorily completed.[168]

Type Three. In the third type of situation, land reform work either had been done very poorly or, as in some recaptured border districts, not at all. In these areas, security permitting, land reform was to be carried out thoroughly. The surplus property of all landlords and rich peasants was to be confiscated. And *only if the land of a middle peasant exceeded the average peasant holding in the village by less then one-tenth, should the middle peasant be allowed to keep his surplus.* The land was not to be taken from him without his consent, however. If there was not enough land in the village, large households could be given relatively less land *per capita* than that allotted to smaller families. The great mass of poor peasants were to be given land, but "the error of agreeing to an absolutely equal division of land must not be committed."[169]

Party Rectification

On the important issue of Party rectification at the basic level, the Directive on Land Reform and Party Rectification Work in the Old and Semi-old Liberated

---

168. "Huang-chia-ch'uan shih tsen-yang tiao-cheng tu-ti kai-ko te" [How Huangchia-ch'uan consolidated land reform], Hsinhua News Agency, Feb. 28, 1948, in *San-ko tien-hsing,* pp. 57-60.

169. In this third type of village where the land had not been properly distributed, Mao endorsed the experience of Kuo *hsien,* Shansi, as the model to follow. Indicative of the problems in this *hsien* were the errors of class demarcations made in some 30 administrative villages: 43 rich peasant households had been wrongly designated as landlord; 106 middle peasant families had been wrongly designated as rich peasant; 31 middle peasant families had been wrongly designated as landlord; and 51 other households had been wrongly classified as "bankrupt" landlord. See note 167.

Areas recommended the general adoption of the method used in P'ingshan *hsien* in the Shansi-Chahar-Hopei Border Region. This was Party rectification combined with land reform consolidation, which included the public criticism of Party members and their work by the peasants themselves. In his recommendation of the three case studies, Mao identified Liu Shao-ch'i as the author of the study summarizing P'ingshan *hsien*'s experience with Party rectification.[170]

Party rectification was necessary because there were still some Party members in the villages who were using their positions to harm the peasants, thus negating the achievements of land reform. However, this basic-level rectification was to be carried out not only in the villages, but also in towns, factories, schools, the army, and other organizations as well. The only prerequisite for the successful adoption of the prescribed method was strong upper-level leadership and a few good backbone members in each individual branch. In the event that the latter condition was non-existent, upper-level Party leaders were to disband the branch, mobilize the masses directly, and rely on the poor peasant leagues, poor peasant small groups, and peasant associations to carry out land reform, criticize local Party members, and ultimately reconstruct the local branch.

In P'ingshan *hsien,* land reform had been more or less successfully implemented by the end of 1947, but as usual the *hsien* was not without problems. The indicators of trouble were manifold. In some villages, the peasants had risen up spontaneously to struggle with bad cadres and Party members. Cadres had been attacked and beaten. Also, the behavior of work team cadres sent into the villages often only made matters worse. Some had obstinately separated land and Party reform. Others had hampered the solution of local problems in various ways, even to the point of transferring people the peasants opposed to other villages.

Following the September, 1947, decisions concerning land reform and Party rectification, however, a serious effort to implement them was undertaken, particularly in the old liberated areas of the *hsien*. Initially, when the village Party branches began their investigations into the class backgrounds and work styles of their members, this was done behind closed doors. But this was soon changed, and the local branches opened their meetings first to non-Party poor peasants and then to middle peasants as well. Often there were twenty to thirty Party members and seventy to eighty non-Party peasants taking part in the investigation meetings. In this manner, every local Party member's work methods came under the close scrutiny of the villagers.

The past secrecy of the basic-level Party organs, wrote Liu Shao-ch'i, made it possible for individual Party members to alienate the Party as a whole from the local people. It was indeed a serious matter to open up the Party to public criticism, but such a democratic rectification movement had incontestable advantages. First, non-Party peasants would have more respect for the Party if

---

170. Liu Shao-ch'i, "P'ing-shan cheng tang ho fa-tung ch'ün-chung hsiang-chieh-ho te fan-li" [The pattern of Party rectification and activating the masses to unite in P'ingshan], originally an unsigned Hsinhua News Agency report from the Chin-Ch'a-Chi Border Region on Feb. 27, 1948, in *San-ko tien-hsing*, pp. 54-55.

the Party respected them enough to listen to their grievances and opinions. Moreover, the critical spirit of the public investigation meetings usually provided an effective substitute for the revenge which many peasants hoped to exact from those who had wronged them. Also, once the Party demonstrated its willingness to deal sternly with its members in order to resolve outstanding problems, this encouraged the peasants to reveal all their concealed doubts about the Party. This in turn gave the Party greater opportunity to gain insight into the attitude of the peasants and to respond appropriately to them.

In this way, concluded Liu, local Party members could learn to accept criticism, to correct their errors in due time, and to educate and activate the masses more deeply. Most significantly, the masses would not be left to search one-sidedly for the faults and weaknesses of cadres and Party members.

On the Function of Excesses

William Hinton provides us with one additional case study of the land reform and Party rectification process. His observations in Luch'eng *hsien,* Shansi, illustrate how difficult the process could be in its actual implementation, even after the Party center had worked out theoretical solutions for all of the typical problems. In the Shansi-Hopei-Shantung-Honan Border Region of which Luch'eng *hsien* was a part, the distinction between the three types of land reform situations, formalized by the Party center in its February 22 directive, had been outlined in early February and apparently served as the guideline for the Luch'eng *hsien* land conference held during that month.[171]

Changchuang, the village where Hinton conducted his observations, was classified as a type three village where land reform had not yet been thoroughly implemented. The cadres then adopted what they thought was the appropriate poor peasant line and set about eliminating rightist errors. First came the efforts to weed out class impurities within the Party; to chastise those cadres and Party members who had abused their power; and to reinvestigate and redistribute land and wealth as equally as possible. But all of this was soon followed by an abrupt shift to an attack on "left adventurism."

This shift came in April, the same month that the Border Region Party Bureau issued a "Directive on the Correction of Left Adventurism."[172] The directive instructed that: (1) excesses committed against middle peasants be corrected and their property returned; (2) the practice of "sweeping everything out the door" (the confiscation of all the personal property of evil landlords) should only be regarded as a temporary educational measure and such people should be allowed to keep enough property to sustain themselves; (3) the extreme restrictions which had been placed on the democratic rights of the people be abolished; (4) the people's courts alone had the right to impose a death sentence and the sentence was to be carried out by shooting, all other

171. On the Chin-Chi-Lu-Yü Border Region directive, see note 165.

172. "Chin-chi-lu-yü chung-yang chü chiao-cheng tso-ch'ing mao-hsien-chu-i te chih-shih," Apr. 23, 1948, in Ch'en Po-ta, *et al., Kuan-yü kung-shang-yeh te cheng-ts'e,* pp. 42-45.

forms of physical mutilation and punishment being henceforth forbidden; and (5) all business and industry, including that owned by landlords and rich peasants both in the city and in the countryside, was to be protected and not subjected to liquidation, confiscation, or distribution.

In Luch'eng *hsien*, work team cadres were obliged to assume a large measure of responsibility for the sudden shift, on the grounds that they had underestimated the progress of land reform two months previously. At the *hsien* land conference in April, village work teams were also criticized for having placed too much emphasis on trying to satisfy all the demands of the poor, for having neglected the interests of middle peasants, and for having dealt with basic-level Party members as though they were class enemies. After every family had been reclassified according to the Party's standards, middle peasants were to be compensated for any property illegally expropriated from them.[173]

That the shift to an attack on left adventurism occurred simultaneously in Luch'eng *hsien* and in the Border Region as a whole suggests that primary responsibility for leftism did not in fact originate with the work team cadres. This conclusion is reinforced by the relatively late date at which the shift occurred in the Border Region—more than three months after Mao had identified leftist excesses as the central concern. Some might argue that it simply took that long for the Party center to assert its authority and enforce its line in the Chin-Chi-Lu-Yü Border Region. A more plausible explanation, however, seems to be that the Border Region officials were proceeding in accordance with local conditions and the dialectic of the developing mass movement. That process, moreover, was clearly spelled out in the Party center's February 22 directive on the three different types of land reform situations. In the third type, where land reform had not yet been thoroughly implemented, the Party center did still sanction the near-equalization of village landholdings.

In his 1927 report on the Hunan peasant movement, Mao wrote that in order to correct errors, it was necessary to go to extremes.[174] This was as concise a statement of the "law of the mass movement" as one could hope to find. This law informed the mass struggles and land reform movement of the 1940s. P'eng Chen, Li Yü, and finally the Central Committee itself, all indicated that rightist deviations constituted the greatest obstacle during the initial stages of a movement, and that a left line had to be developed to overcome them before a new level of unity and moderation could be achieved.

For Party leaders, the most serious error lay neither in being excessively right nor excessively left, but in misjudging the point at which the limits of one phase had been reached and the next should begin. Li Yü warned the Shantung cadres in 1945, that the key point in developing the mass movement was to gauge correctly these two tendencies in relationship to the concrete situation in any given place. If peaceful reunification was attempted too early, local resistance would not yet have been thoroughly overcome, the peasants would not be able to stand up as a result, and the situation would devolve into one of basic defeat.

173. Hinton, *Fanshen*, pp. 243-415.   174. See note 75 above.

The function of excesses in Shantung in 1945 was to transform the rent reduction campaign into a genuine mass assault against the "forces of feudalism." And as Mao wrote with respect to the developing radicalism of rent reduction at this same time, any excesses committed in the process could be corrected afterwards.

The decision to attempt the equalization of village wealth, as stipulated in the first edition of the Agrarian Law, may have been erroneous in the absolute sense. But it was also part of the leftist phase of the land reform movement; and, far from being repudiated, that phase as such was basically reaffirmed in the February 22 Central Committee directive. It stipulated that, conditions permitting, landholdings should be thoroughly, if not absolutely, equalized where land reform had not yet been carried out and the peasants had therefore not been mobilized. While middle peasants in such areas were allowed a slightly greater portion of land than the poor, and while the middle peasants' surplus could not be taken without their consent, the directive did not state—as had the East China Bureau in mid-1947—that the land of middle peasants was absolutely not to be touched. The most serious efforts to conciliate middle peasants and reintegrate them into the village administrative structure were still reserved for areas where land reform had already been thoroughly implemented and land had been distributed to the village poor.

Thus the "excesses" that were committed against middle peasants seemed an unavoidable consequence of the compulsion inherent in the mass movement as it interacted with the socio-economic realities of the Chinese countryside. The function of this particular excess was to attack economic inequality as a source of village power and to ensure the distribution of material benefits to the poor peasants of north China.

SUMMARY

The answers to the three questions posed in the introduction to this chapter can now be summarized. Concerning the Communists' moderate land policy during the Anti-Japanese War and the nature of the revolutionary lessons learned therefrom, rent and interest reduction apparently played a minimal role in the initial formation of the base areas. Rent reduction did not begin to be implemented on a mass scale until 1942, and it could not be successfully carried out until a basic level of military and political security had been established.

Through no choice of their own, the CCP's main forces found themselves confined to north China at the start of the Japanese invasion. In the interests of a united front of resistance against the invader, the CCP abandoned the violent confiscation and redistribution of land which it had been using to mobilize peasant support and destroy the existing rural power structure. The united front land policy of rent reduction thereupon presented the Communists with a major dilemma: either they look for new ways of transferring wealth from those who had it to those who did not; or they suspend for an indefinite period their identity as a revolutionary party. The choice of the former alternative was doubly fortuitous for the Communists, since it enabled them both to preserve the nature of their party and enhance their chances of success in north China, where tenancy was not a dominant problem in any case.

As a result of their search for new ways of transferring wealth, the Communists' rural land policy had expanded by 1945 to encompass the range of issues that could provide, through the settling of old accounts tactic, benefits for the "basic masses" of north China. And in addition to the material incentives provided by the distribution of the struggle fruits, the Communists could also offer a solution for what the peasantry as a whole apparently perceived as its most immediate grievance: the corrupt and arbitrary use of political power and social position within the village community. In exploiting these issues together with all the others associated with the ownership and use of land, unpaid labor, and indebtedness, the CCP had discovered the formula for "mass activation through class struggle" even in areas where landlords were not a problem that concerned the village masses. This formula was the first revolutionary "lesson" the Communists brought with them from the Anti-Japanese War.

The second lesson concerned the process of the formula's application. For the Chinese Communists had not only found the means of destroying the rural system of economic and political power; they had also discovered how to mobilize peasant support for the creation of a new one. They had learned how to make the struggle against the ruling class the central task, the "mother of all other work." As P'an Fu-sheng put it, every unit had worked in isolation from every other at the start of the Anti-Japanese War. There had been no coordination or differentiation between primary and subordinate work. Little was accomplished until the Party had learned to make mass activation through class struggle the core task. In Shantung, Li Yü described the struggle movement as the starting point of all other village work including Party building and military recruiting.

A third crucial lesson from the Anti-Japanese War years concerned the conditions necessary for the successful initiation of the struggle movement. Before the Party's land policy could be thoroughly implemented in any district, the enemy had to be expelled militarily, his political hold broken, and the nucleus of a new power structure created. All Party directives, both central and regional, stressed the importance of minimizing class friction in districts immediately threatened by the enemy. The land policy and the intra-village conflict it generated could become the focal point of village work only after certain military and political preconditions had been met in the area as a whole. The anti-Japanese resistance mobilized the manpower, and the CCP provided the leadership necessary to establish these preconditions on a significant scale across north China as the Japanese tide began to recede after 1943.

The land reform program was the Communists' key revolutionary effort of the subsequent Civil War period. The development of that program in north China, and the experience gained in the manner of and conditions for its implementation, must be counted among the most important revolutionary lessons the Communists learned during the Anti-Japanese War. These lessons were formalized in the Party's directive of May 4, 1946, which marked the official shift from rent reduction to land reform. In fact, the May Fourth Directive signaled not the inauguration of land reform, but the culmination of the multi-featured struggle movement that had been developing in practice throughout the Anti-Japanese War.

The most basic condition for the successful implementation of land reform was the military capacity to protect it against its enemies. This was proven in the wake of the unanticipated advance of KMT forces into the Communist base areas in 1946-47. This advance eliminated all of the prerequisites as defined during the Anti-Japanese War, for instigating intra-village class friction. Communist forces could no longer operate freely, and the Central Government began rebuilding its own structure of political power in the rural areas, with the support of the enemies the Communists had created during the struggle movement.

The dangers of trying to carry out land reform under such circumstances were acknowledged in the May 25, 1948, directive from the Party center which reestablished essentially the same prerequisites adopted during the Anti-Japanese War. The Party did so even as it prepared to move southward into areas where tenancy was generally more prevalent than in north China. Land reform was not to be carried out unless the area in question was militarily secure; unless a majority of the peasants demanded land redistribution; and unless enough cadres were on hand to lead the work. These conditions did not generally obtain in areas liberated after the summer of 1947, the "new liberated areas." These were therefore directed to abandon land reform temporarily. In answer to the second of the three questions posed above, the Chinese Communists ceased their attempts to carry out land reform in such areas because the preconditions for its successful implementation had not yet been established.

Where the conditions for its implementation permitted, however, land reform made possible the mobilization and organization of the "basic masses" into a new structure of rural political power led by the CCP. The standard explanation was that as soon as the peasants' lives had been improved, their consciousness was also raised and they were willing to act. Certainly the Communists sought, and undoubtedly received, "support" in return for the tangible material benefits property redistribution provided. But the process was considerably more complex. Intra-Party criticism suggests that the nascent class consciousness engendered by the struggle movement and redivision of property did not, as claimed during 1946-47, result directly in the specific kinds of support necessary to fight the war against the KMT.

The primary component of the land revolution in this regard was the overthrow of the existing rural elite. Whether or not it was dominated by landlords in any given village was not the issue. The key consideration was that land reform destroyed the political and economic control of the local power holders, an essential step in the creation of a new order. The construction of that order marked the second crucial component of land reform as the "mother of all other work," thus making it possible, as one writer noted, for the Party's policies to touch the masses. Peasants who participated most actively in the multi-featured accusation movement provided new recruits for the Communist Party and new village leadership. Recipients of land and property added their numbers to the peasant associations and other village organizations. And this was the institutional structure, manned by the peasants themselves, that the Communists could then rely on to assume responsibility for organizing military transport teams and exerting social pressure on reluctant recruits. This was what liberal commentators meant when they referred to the "roots" the Party was putting down in the countryside as a result of land reform.

Initially, the struggle movement cut across class lines. This was an inevitable consequence of the many objects of attack as the Communists sought new ways of transferring wealth and mobilizing the peasants of north China. Until 1945, moreover, this feature of the movement was also apparent in the distribution of the struggle fruits, despite the general emphasis on taking from the rich and giving to the poor. After 1945, class lines were drawn more sharply with the increasingly concerted effort to transfer property to poor and hired peasants in particular. This effort resulted in the first edition of the Outline Agrarian Law. In stipulating the equalization of village wealth and property, the Law demonstrated that the CCP's interpretation of "land-to-the-tiller" went well beyond the elimination of the landlord-tenant relationship. For the scarcity of wealth and the large number of middle peasants, both new and old, made it necessary to encroach upon them if property was to be absolutely equalized. The contradictions that had characterized the Party's treatment of middle peasants seemed finally to have been resolved with this implicit demand to include them in the levelling process.

That the issue had not been resolved became apparent in early 1948 when absolute equality was abandoned in deference to the middle peasants. The attempt to eliminate poor peasants as a class was clearly too advanced an objective in 1947. But it was also too important a goal, within the context of the mass movement, to be abandoned outright— despite the danger of alienating the middle peasants. Hence the continued ambivalence towards them even in the final formulation of the Party's Civil War land policy. The most serious efforts to conciliate middle peasants were reserved for areas where land reform had already been thoroughly implemented.

VIII
The Return to the Cities

In March, 1949, Mao issued an historic statement. "The period of 'from the city to the village' and of the city leading the village has now begun," he wrote. "The center of gravity of the Party's work has shifted from the village to the city."[1] Forced to abandon its classic base of support after 1927, the CCP had devoted most of the next two decades to the task of gathering strength in the Chinese countryside. Then in 1948, the Party suddenly found itself in possession of an increasing number of towns and cities as Communist military successes accumulated with unanticipated speed. The time had come to resume its role as leader of the Chinese proletariat, a role for which the CCP was no longer entirely prepared.

The cities accounted for no more than 20 percent of the total Chinese population. Nevertheless, that 20 percent held a monopoly of the intellectual, technological, and administrative resources necessary to maintain a national government and build a socialist economy. In addition, the cities remained major strongholds of KMT power. By contrast, their enemies ridiculed the Communists as country bumpkins. Foreign observers continued to maintain, even as late as 1948, that the Communists would not try to take the large coastal cities because Party leaders were intelligent enough to recognize their inability to cope with urban problems.[2]

If Mao had any serious qualms, he kept them to himself. But he did issue a blunt warning in March, 1949: if the Party could not learn how to manage the cities and win the struggle against its urban enemies, the Party would be unable to maintain its political power, and it would fail. Thus the Chinese Communists

1. Mao Tse-tung, "Report to the Second Plenary Session of the Seventh Central Committee," Mar. 5, 1949, *Selected Works,* 4:363.
2. According to one American Foreign Service officer, this was the prevailing view among his colleagues in Shanghai. For similar views expressed by Prof. Nathaniel Peffer of Columbia University, the economist Ch'en Han-seng, Ambassador J. Leighton Stuart, and the U.S. Consul in Peiping (quoting hearsay confirmation from the Communists themselves), see U.S. Dept. of State, *Foreign Relations of the United States, 1947, the Far East, China,* pp. 46-47, 161, 220.

set about urbanizing themselves with the same determination they had applied to land reform. In fact, they had been at work on the former task since at least 1945.

By mid-1948, the Communists held, according to their own reckoning, 586 cities *(ch'eng-shih)*. The term *ch'eng-shih* in this case referred to all units down to and including the *hsien* town.[3] Most of the larger cities were located in Manchuria. These included seven provincial capitals (dates in parentheses are those on which the cities were taken by the Communists): Harbin (April 28, 1946), Peian, Hulun, Tsitsihar (1946), Chiamuszu (November, 1945), Antung (June 10, 1947), and Szupingkai (March 13, 1948); and the cities of Mutanchiang (1946), Kirin (March 9, 1948), Liaoyang (February, 1948), and Yingkow (February, 1948; subsequently lost but retaken before the year was out). Other cities in Communist hands by mid-1948 included Shihchiachuang, Hopei (November, 1947), and Loyang, Honan (April 7, 1948).

Of these cities, Harbin was the largest with a population of some 760,000.[4] Occupied by the Chinese Communists as Soviet troops withdrew, Harbin became the center of the CCP's most important experience in coping with urban problems during the 1946-49 period. Nevertheless, the first real-life challenge came not in Harbin but in Kalgan (Changchiak'ou), a city northwest of Peiping in what was then Chahar province within the Shansi-Chahar-Hopei Border Region.

The Communists held Kalgan for a little over a year, from the end of August, 1945 to early October, 1946. At that time it contained an estimated 150,000—200,000 people. Kalgan was not the only medium-sized city the Communists were able to occupy immediately after the Japanese surrender. The administration of Weihaiwei and Chiamuszu must have been equally challenging tasks. But probably because of its more central location, the Communists chose to try to develop Kalgan into a second capital. Information about their experience in Kalgan is sketchy. But it is possible to piece together some of the facts concerning the genesis of Chinese Communist urban policies in 1945-46.

---

3. "Chieh-fang-ch'ü liang nien fa-chan t'ung-chi" [Statistics for two years of development in the liberated areas], in Hsin hua she, ed., *Jen-min chieh-fang chan-cheng liang chou-nien tsung-chieh ho ti-san nien te jen-wu*, pp. 49-50. For a summary of cities won and lost between July, 1946, and the end of 1947, see *I-chiu-szu-pa-nien shou-ts'e*, pp. chia 33-35.

4. Except for the largest cities, population estimates for the 1940s are not readily available. Below are figures for most of the largest cities held by the Communists in mid-1948 (and Weihaiwei, which was lost in 1946). Sources are: (a) *Orient Year Book, 1942*, p. 508; and (b) *China Handbook, 1950*, at pages indicated.

Antung[a]	315,242	Mutanchiang[a]	179,217
Chiamuszu[a]	128,667	Shihchiachuang[b,46]	217,327
Harbin[a]	661,984	Szupingkai[a]	68,418
Harbin[b,17]	760,000	Tsitsihar[a]	133,495
Hulun[a]	39,877	Weihaiwei[b,60]	222,247
Kirin[a]	173,624	Yingkow[a]	180,871
Liaoyang[a]	100,165		

THE KALGAN EXPERIMENT

After January, 1946, correspondents sometimes travelled to Kalgan aboard the planes of the Peiping Executive Headquarters teams assigned to oversee the KMT-CCP truce. During interviews, Communist authorities emphasized their lack of experience in urban administration. They often said that their performance in Kalgan would help to determine whether rural cadres would be able to work effectively in the cities.[5]

The visitors were impressed with the same kinds of changes that have attracted all first-time visitors to Chinese Communist cities ever since. Beggars had disappeared from the streets. The number of rickshaw coolies had dwindled—like the prostitutes, they were being encouraged by the new city government to find other employment. The policeman's baton had also disappeared, and with it the threat to the backs of disobedient rickshaw pullers and cart drivers. The city gave the appearance of being well run. Streets were cleaned regularly and were well-lit at night. Buildings were being maintained, as were the city's buses which were owned and managed by the municipal government.

The early visitors were also impressed by the apparent efficiency with which the Communists had handled the collaborator problem. The Central Government was then embarked upon its own ill-fated efforts to reoccupy the former Japanese-controlled areas. The Communists avoided similar controversy by immediately arresting about three hundred persons known to have collaborated most actively with the Japanese in running the city. Twelve of these including the former mayor and the head of the secret police were executed. The remainder were freed after having been made to attend a three-month training course.[6]

The behavior of many cadres, however, left something to be desired. As of March, 1946, there were twenty thousand military and civilian personnel in Kalgan.[7] The Shansi-Chahar-Hopei Border Region newspaper expressed concern about the arrogance hampering some of them in their work. The cadres seemed not to understand that the new revolutionary order had to be based on the interests of the people. Nor were the cadres taking seriously enough the peacetime tasks of municipal reconstruction. The paper warned: "Every revolutionary warrior and member of the staff must develop the high degree of discipline he has manifested during the war and observe and obey the order and discipline of a peaceful city."[8]

5. *TKP,* Shanghai, Mar. 7, 1946 *(CPR).*
6. "Kalgan Prosperous, Peaceful after Communist Occupation," *China Weekly Review,* Mar. 30, 1946, p. 102; and Hsinhua News Agency, Yenan, June 16, 1946 *(FYI,* June 17).
7. *China Weekly Review,* Mar. 30, 1946, p. 102, citing Sung Shao-wen, head of the Kalgan Administrative Committee.
8. *Chin-ch'a-chi jih-pao,* Kalgan, Jan. 14, 1946 *(CPR,* Peiping-Tientsin, Jan. 23).

Despite the obvious difficulties in shifting from rural guerrilla warfare to the more mundane and complex tasks of urban reconstruction, the new municipal administration of Kalgan took shape fairly rapidly. This was possible in part because Kalgan could be incorporated into the already-existing structures of the Chin-Ch'a-Chi Border Region. Shortly after the Communist take-over, a civilian administrative committee was set up under Sung Shao-wen, a non-Party intellectual who had majored in history during his student days at Peking University. Also shortly after liberation, representatives of various organizations already established on a Border Region basis began preparatory work aimed at setting up branches or subordinate organizations in the city. These groups included the Border Region General Labor Union, Youth League, Students League, Teachers Union, and Peasants Association.

In mid-October, the Chin-Ch'a-Chi Border Region government and the People's Political Council—a popular advisory body corresponding to the organization of the same name in the KMT areas—resolved that formal governments should be established for the two provinces of Chahar and Jehol. Both were almost entirely in Communist hands at this time. It was also decided that people's representative conferences should be convened by the end of October in both provinces to inaugurate the provincial governments and discuss reconstruction policies.[9] Popular elections were held shortly thereafter in Kalgan to choose the city's representatives to the Chahar Provincial People's Representative Conference.

About the same time, elections were also held in Kalgan to select leaders for street organizations being formed in all districts of the city. These elections were part of the campaign to eliminate the unpopular *pao-chia* system.[10] The labor unions reportedly played an important role in this "election movement." According to figures made public in December, 112 workers were elected to lead street organizations in six of the city's nine districts.[11] Elections were held again the following April to choose the members of the Kalgan Municipal People's Political Council which held its first meeting toward the end of that month. According to a member of the Chin-Ch'a-Chi Border Region Party Bureau, about 80 percent of the city's population participated in this election which selected some ninety Council members and thirty alternates.[12]

More significant in terms of its immediate impact on the daily life of Kalgan's populace, was the Party's attitude toward business, industry, and labor. This was

9. *T'ien-chin tao pao* [pro-Communist], Tientsin, Nov. 8, 1945 (*CPR*, Nov. 16).

10. A traditional Chinese form of local organization and control, the *pao-chia* system was revived by the KMT and promoted by the Japanese. Under the Japanese, ten households formed a *p'ai*. Ten *p'ai* formed a *chia*, and ten *chia* formed a *pao*. See Franz Schurmann, *Ideology and Organization in Communist China*, p. 369.

11. Hsiao Ming, "Chang-chia-k'ou ch'üan shih kung-jen shou chieh tai-piao ta-hui te pao-kao" [Report to the first Kalgan all-city workers representative conference], in *Chang-chia-k'ou ch'üan shih kung-jen shou chieh tai-piao ta-hui*, (hereafter *Chang-chia-k'ou ch'üan-shih*) p. 11. Hsiao was head of the preparatory committee of the Kalgan General Labor Union.

12. Hsinhua News Agency, Peiping, Apr. 30, 1946 (*CPR*, Peiping-Tientsin, May 1).

the unknown quotient in the program of a Communist party that had concentrated for some twenty years on the peasant farmer and his problems. In the countryside, the Chinese Communists were reaffirming the principle of private land ownership, but not the existing system of land tenure. And at the village level, landlord-owned commercial and industrial enterprises were officially treated as part of the rural feudal economy. They were being taken over and placed under cooperative management. This was the practice in well-managed districts. In others, even small traders were expropriated and their stocks distributed. Central and regional Party documents cautioned against a similar liquidation of urban capital. But reports and subsequent directives indicated that urban liquidations were occurring during this period with the approval of local officials.[13]

The only other indicators of what policies the Communists might attempt in Kalgan were quite different, being a few well chosen phrases on the economy of the New Democratic state system. As indicated previously, this was part of the general program the Communists advocated for the period immediately after the end of the KMT one-party dictatorship. In general terms, the economy of the New Democracy was to be based on public, private, and cooperative enterprise with the exclusion only of monopoly capital. Large commercial and industrial enterprises were to be owned and operated by the state.[14] To summarize, the Communists' urban economic program in 1945 called for the abolition of bureaucratic capital (the large monopolistic-type enterprises controlled by KMT bureaucrats); a check on inflation; assistance to private industry (in the form of loans, procurement of raw materials, and marketing of products); and the improvement of the workers' livelihood.[15] This program was reflected in the slogan widely publicized by the CCP during the Civil War years: "Develop production, make the economy prosper, care for both public and private, benefit both labor and capital." But the question remained as to how such a policy, promising something for almost everyone, would be implemented in a city surrounded by a sea of rural upheaval.

LABOR

According to a report in mid-1946, the strikes and work slowdowns then plaguing factories in Shanghai had been largely eliminated in Kalgan.[16] If this

13. There was a discussion of this in Chapter Seven. The May 4, 1946 land reform directive (note 36) made the town-country distinction in item no. 8. Directives of the Hopei-Shantung-Honan Party Committee (notes 102 and 103) called, among other things, for the liquidation and cooperative management of landlord-owned commercial and industrial enterprises in the countryside. And Jen Pi-shih (preceding note 164) noted the suicidal consequences of dividing rural commercial property. Isabel and David Crook, *Revolution in a Chinese Village: Ten Mile Inn*, pp. 112-13, refer to confiscations of landlord-owned commercial and industrial property in *hsien* towns. The Crooks (pp. 138-43) and William Hinton (*Fanshen*, pp. 154-55) also refer to cooperatively managed enterprises at the village level after land reform. Additional references to urban liquidations are cited below.

14. Mao Tse-tung, "On New Democracy," Jan., 1940, *Selected Works*, 2:353.

15. Mao Tse-tung, "On Coalition Government," Apr. 24, 1945, *Selected Works*, 3:287.

16. Hsinhua News Agency, Yenan, June 16, 1946 (*FYI*, June 17).

claim had any validity, credit for the achievement belonged to the combination of wage increases, improved working conditions, labor discipline, and the extensive union organizing work done by the Communists during their first months in Kalgan.

Union Organizing

As in most cities under Japanese occupation, there had existed individual underground Party members and cadres in many of Kalgan's factories and workshops. After Japan's surrender, these cadres hastily organized workers into protection teams to safeguard plants and machinery from destruction in the immediate post-surrender period. The first labor union was said to have been established in Kalgan on August 23, five days before Communist forces fully occupied the city.

Labor organizing activity began in earnest after the meeting of the Provisional Kalgan Workers Representative Conference in mid-September. By mid-December when the First Kalgan All-City Workers Representative Conference was convened and the General Labor Union formally established, 13,933 workers had been organized into eighty commercial labor unions (6,325 members) and eighty-one factory unions (7,608 members).[17] According to the regulations of the new General Labor Union, unions could be established in any enterprise with fifteen or more employees who earned their living through physical or skilled labor. This included ordinary laborers, technical or skilled workers, shop clerks, apprentices, and lower ranking staff or managerial personnel in factories.[18]

In conjunction with this initial organizing activity, a "struggle movement" was launched, similar to the settling accounts struggles then under way in the countryside. According to Hsiao Ming, head of the General Labor Union Preparatory Committee, the workers often did not even wait for the cadres sent by the Committee to lead the struggle meetings. A total of one hundred and thirty-one instances of struggle were recorded during the months of September and October, directed against a variety of targets. The most prominent of these were people accused of having oppressed the workers and of having collaborated with the Japanese. Apparently attacks were made against factory owners and businessmen who fell into these categories, and reparations demanded of them in the same manner that exactions were being made from landlords. In addition to twenty-seven "liquidation struggles" and twenty-four "accusation struggles," the confrontations included fifty-six struggles over demands for wage increases, ten for reduction of rent payments, and five for various fringe benefits. Hsiao Ming claimed that the struggle movement aroused the workers, thus strengthening the

17. Hsiao Ming, p. 10 (see note 11 above).
18. "Chang-chia-k'ou shih tsung kung-hui tsu-chih chang-ch'eng" [Regulations on the organization of the Kalgan general labor union], Section 2, article 3, in *Chang-chia-k'ou ch'uan shih*, p. 12. Individual factory and enterprise unions were grouped by location into district unions.

development of the labor movement and facilitating the union-organizing effort. Some five hundred new activists reportedly emerged within the Kalgan labor force.[19]

Many of the functions of the struggle campaigns, which apparently continued for only a short time, were incorporated into the procedures of the new unions. Workers in each factory or enterprise where a union was organized elected a union committee to represent them in collective bargaining with management. The workers were encouraged to voice their opinions and demands freely, in small-group discussions and at general union meetings, on matters such as wages, working conditions, fringe benefits, and the like. Beating, scolding, and other means of intimidation that in the past might have been used by management to discourage discussions of this sort, were strictly forbidden.

Wages and Benefits

Even before the unions were organized, the Communists acted on their pledge to improve the workers' livelihood. One of the first decrees of the new administration ordered that all wages be doubled. Despite the inflationary consequences of such action, wages were increased again a month later by 25-30 percent. By October, many unions had been set up and were actively discussing the wage situation. The graduated pay scales used by the Japanese were abolished. These had been based on a complicated system of grades and levels within grades. New general wage standards for workers in public enterprises were announced by the Border Region Administrative Committee on October 26, 1945.

Wages were calculated in terms of catties of millet per month but paid in cash. They were adjusted upward each month in order to keep pace with living costs as indicated by the prices of certain basic necessities such as foodstuffs, coal, and cloth. According to the new standards, (1) the wages of youths, women, and apprentices were to range from 100 to 200 catties of millet per month; (2) ordinary workers were to receive from 200 catties to 280 catties; (3) experienced workers from 250 catties to 330 catties; and (4) skilled workers from 300 catties to 450 catties.

Distinctions were also drawn between heavy and light industry. In general, ordinary workers in light industries (such as cigarette manufacturing and oil pressing), postal workers, sweepers, and flagmen on the railroads were to receive between 200 catties and 250 catties of millet per month, with experienced workers receiving from 250 catties to 300 catties. Skilled workers in heavy industries came at the top of the pay scale but were not to receive more than 450 catties per month.[20]

By the end of October, inflationary pressures had clearly set in. Wages had to be revised upward in November, and in December labor again demanded pay

19. Hsiao Ming, p. 10 (see note 11 above).
20. "Kuan-yü chang-chia-k'ou hsuan-hua kung-ying kung-ch'ang kung-jen kung-tzu te piao-chün" [On the standards for wages of workers in publicly-owned factories in Kalgan and Hsuanhua], in Chin-ch'a-chi pien-ch'ü hsing-cheng wei-yuan-hui, *Chin-ch'a-chi fa-ling hui-pien*, pp. 129-30.

increases in order to compensate for the rise in the cost of living. As a result, basic wage rates were increased 10 percent for workers in light industries and 15 percent for those in heavy industries. According to one report, inflation in Kalgan was such that by March, 1946, the price of millet per catty had risen from 28 to 65 dollars in Border Region currency.[21] Basic wage rates nevertheless seem to have been stabilized in early 1946. The actual average take-home pay of workers in publicly owned industrial establishments remained at roughly the same level from April until the Communists were driven from Kalgan the following autumn. The levels ranged from about 300 catties of millet per month for ordinary workers, to 500 catties for the highest-paid skilled workers. The factory manager remained in a class by himself, and could receive up to 900 catties per month. Anna Louise Strong, who visited the city shortly before it fell to Government forces, maintained that the wages of Kalgan's workers were the highest she had encountered anywhere in China at that time.[22]

According to the Border Region Administrative Committee, however, the basic wage standards announced in October were intended only as general guidelines. Actual wage rates were to be fixed in accordance with the specific conditions obtaining in any given enterprise. In fact, three different wage systems based on these guidelines were introduced in Kalgan's publicly managed industries and in some private ones as well. Two of these methods of labor remuneration were based on the piece rate system and were designed to increase output by offering material incentives. The third method was based on the technical competence of the workers.

The progressive piece rate wage system was introduced in factories where wages could be calculated in terms of output per person. A standard output per person during a certain time period was established for which a fixed basic wage was stipulated. Output in excess of the standard rate was rewarded by progressive wage increments. The bonus or reward system was adopted in factories where output could only be estimated on a collective basis. In this situation, the standard collective output for a group of workers during a given time period was fixed along with the basic wage level. Total output in excess of the fixed standard was rewarded by a progressively increasing percentage of the basic wage rate for all of the workers in the group. The dividends wage system was adopted in enterprises with a mixed output. A division of profits between owners and employees was fixed after deducting costs, waste, and depreciation, with the workers' share of the profits being distributed among them on the basis of their level of technical competence.[23]

In all cases, the standards for fixing output, wage levels, bonuses, and dividends were to be determined by the employer and the employees together. The standards could be evaluated and re-evaluated by the workers and their

21. *TKP*, Shanghai, Mar. 7, 1946 *(CPR)*.

22. Chin-ch'a-chi pien-ch'ü tsung kung-hui kung-jen pao she, ed., *Chin-ch'a-chi pien-ch'ü kung-jen wu-i chi-nien hua-ts'e*, no pagination; and Anna Louise Strong, *Tomorrow's China*, pp. 65-66.

23. Hsinhua News Agency, Yenan, Aug. 28, 1946 *(FYI*, Aug. 29).

unions if it was felt that injustices existed. The workers did not hesitate to take advantage of their new bargaining power. In one small soap factory where there had already been sizable wage increases, some of the workers requested yet another. The plant had been set up as a joint enterprise with both public and private capital. It employed thirty-six workers who were reportedly earning several times the amount they had been receiving during the Japanese occupation. The union committee in the factory examined the company's books and concluded that the business might go bankrupt if higher wages were paid. This was explained at a general union meeting and the workers did not receive a further increase.[24]

It is difficult to ascertain just how many of Kalgan's workers were paid according to the standards obtaining in publicly managed industrial enterprises. For example, wage rates in one privately-owned tea company ranged from only 120 to 160 catties of millet per month in June, 1946.[25] According to the resolutions passed by the First Workers Representative Conference, the issue of wage increases in private enterprises was to be settled on the basis of conditions within the individual establishment. Wages should be raised appropriately but the employer should also be allowed a profit, this being in the interests of the workers themselves and the economy as a whole.

The Conference also acknowledged that it would be difficult to set city-wide wage standards for some types of work such as carpentry and bricklaying, recommending instead that the issue be resolved by the individual districts in the city. Similarly, the widely divergent conditions in Kalgan's commercial establishments made it impossible to fix wage standards for shop clerks and other employees, except in terms of the general principle of striving to improve their livelihood. In addition, labor union cadres were chided for not having paid sufficient attention to commercial workers.[26]

Besides wage increases a number of other efforts were made to improve the living conditions of the working class. The unions were encouraged to establish consumer cooperatives through which workers could purchase necessities such as fuel and clothing. Many such cooperatives were set up, serving both to protect the workers from the fluctuations of the market and to dampen the pressures of inflation. During the winter, workers in public enterprises were also given a special allowance to cover their coal expenditures. To help minimize food expenses, workers were encouraged to form voluntary eating groups managed by the workers themselves, with the factory paying the cook's salary.

The employer was made responsible for the medical expenses of workers who became ill or were injured on the job. The worker was to remain on the payroll during recuperation. For other illnesses, the workers were granted time off with pay and could receive treatment in municipal hospitals. A resolution was passed

24. Strong, *Tomorrow's China*, p.,67.
25. Hsinhua News Agency, Yenan, June 9, 1946 (*FYI*, June 10).
26. "Chang-chia-k'ou ch'üan shih kung-jen shou chieh tai-piao ta-hui i-an" [Proposals of the first Kalgan all-city workers representative conference], in *Chang-chia-k'ou ch'üan shih*, pp. 15, 19.

at the First Workers Representative Conference requesting the government to establish out-patient clinics where workers might receive treatment for lesser health problems.[27] By the following September, the city had four public hospitals in addition to a number of private ones, and thirteen out-patient clinics where the poor could receive free medical treatment.[28]

The new administration also tried to cope with the problem of unemployment which plagued all Chinese cities at this time. The employer was forbidden to fire a worker unless and until the action had been discussed by the factory management committee (if one existed), [29] and agreed to by the factory union. On October 5, 1945, the Preparatory Committee of the Kalgan General Labor Union set up a hostel for those already unemployed. During the first two months of its existence, it cared for close to 1,000 persons while the employment bureau of the city government assisted them in trying to find work. Unemployed workers from as far away as Peiping and Tientsin soon appeared in Kalgan seeking assistance.[30] By the following June, the employment bureau was said to have found jobs for about 1,700 people.

In addition, some 8,000 workers such as coolies, bricklayers, and carpenters who suffered seasonal unemployment during the winter months, were encouraged to organize themselves into cooperatives. Twelve of these were formed to engage in spinning and weaving, coal transport, flour grinding, and other occupations. The city government also provided loans and relief. But since all of these efforts were still insufficient to solve the problem of Kalgan's hard-core unemployed, they were encouraged to leave the city wherever possible. About 3,500 did so after receiving travelling expenses from the government to return to their native villages.[31]

A tendency to hold the line on labor's demands began to be apparent in Kalgan by the end of December, 1945, and seems to have gained strength thereafter. For instance, sixteen unions brought forward a proposal at the First Workers Representative Conference that the employer should be made to provide work clothes for the employees. The government's October instructions on basic wage standards had specifically denied that this was the employer's responsibility. The final resolution of the Conference reaffirmed the governments's position, stipulating that with a few exceptions such as post office employees, railway, electrical, and telephone workers, the conditions created by the war made it difficult to comply with this demand. Cloth was in extremely short supply in the liberated areas at this time.

Housing was another scarce item in Kalgan. In response to a proposal from member unions for a resolution of the housing problem, the Conference decided

27. *Ibid.,* p. 17.

28. Hsinhua News Agency, Yenan, Sept. 3, 1946 (*FYI,* Sept. 4).

29. The General Labor Union advocated that administrative and union cadres organize management committees in all publicly-owned factories, in which workers were to outnumber staff and management personnel. In private enterprises, meetings were to be held to acquaint workers with production and management conditions. See note 26 above.

30. Hsiao Ming, p. 10 (see note 11 above).

31. Hsinhua News Agency, Yenan, June 7, 1946 (*FYI,* June 9).

only to suggest that factory owners arrange dormitory housing for their employees if possible. Because of the war, there could be no general effort to meet housing needs. The Conference also resolved that because of wartime hardships, employers could not be expected to carry on the old custom of doubling wages for the last month of the year or giving New Year's bonuses.

Labor Conditions and Discipline

The eight-hour work day was adopted in principle for adults and a seven-hour day for younger workers. But in production directly related to the war effort, workers could "voluntarily" extend their work day. This happened on a number of occasions. Immediately after the liberation of the city, railway employees worked day and night to restore the badly damaged Peiping-Suiyuan Railway. Similarly, textile and garment workers undertook a crash program and agreed to work ten hours a day to turn out several thousand uniforms for the Army. In January, 1946, the New China Iron Works located in the nearby town of Hsuanhua, launched a crash program to increase production—as had the workers at the Border Region printing press in December. The latter more than doubled their output in going from an eight-hour to an eleven-hour day.[32]

In addition to the incentives provided by the piece rate system, workers were encouraged to increase both the quantity and quality of their output through various labor emulation and competition drives. As in the case of rural labor heroes, local newspapers gave maximum publicity to the labor champion who held the highest factory output record or kept the boiler running the longest.

Many workers also found themselves attending class each day. All factories were encouraged to establish, with union help, training classes for their workers. These classes concentrated on political studies, although there was a plan to expand the subject matter to include literacy training and technical education. By December, 1945, about fifty enterprises in Kalgan had set up study sessions for their employees, usually an hour per day either in the morning before the regular work day began or in the evening. The classes could not be conducted during work hours and the workers were not always as enthusiastic as those who initiated the program might have hoped. Union representatives at the December Workers Conference sought a solution to the problem, noting that "due to the cold weather" some workers were showing little interest in their studies. The Conference resolved that workers should be made to understand the importance of attending class but that the method of reducing wages should not be used to force them to do so.

Finally, new standards of labor discipline were introduced. This meant arriving at work on time, working actively and responsibly, and showing concern for company property. The method of criticism and punishment was prescribed for those who did not live up to these standards. Among the workers disciplined in this manner were some employees of a tobacco company who were caught

32. Hsiao Ming, pp. 10, 11 (see note 11 above); and *Chin-ch'a-chi pien-ch'ü kung-jen wu-i chi-nien hua-ts'e* (see note 22 above).

pilfering the company product. First a small-group criticism meeting was called, followed by a partial mass meeting to criticize and hear the confessions of the accused. Finally, a third gathering—a full mass meeting—was called to decide upon a suitable punishment for the culprits.[33]

INDUSTRY AND COMMERCE

Efforts to increase production required more, however, than piece rates, emulation campaigns, and labor discipline. The Border Region Party Bureau in its January, 1946, "Directive for the 1946 Production Campaign" called for an increase in agricultural production, particularly foodstuffs and cotton, as the main goal. Industry and commerce were secondary objectives. As regards industry, primary emphasis was to be placed on the spinning and weaving of cotton and wool. The towns of Kaoyang and Paoti in central and eastern Hopei, were to be restored as quickly as possible as centers of the spinning and weaving industry in the region. The directive also called for the restoration of other light industries, particularly those engaged in the production of daily necessities, and the mining industry. Private industrialists who wished to invest in or manage industries were to be welcomed, as were all scientists, engineers, and technicians who cared to work there. With respect to commerce, the objective was to encourage trade and restore the markets of the Border Region. Among those singled out for attention were the mule market of Kalgan, the medicinal herb market of Ankuo (Chichou), and the fur trade centered in Hsinchi.[34]

The Border Region's official production goals emphasized agriculture over industry, and light rather than heavy industry. The immediate aim was to achieve a level of production which could maintain basic living standards and sustain the war effort. These general principles informed the industrial production program for Kalgan, also outlined in January at a Conference of Managers and Directors of Various Companies and Factories, which was called by the Border Region Industry and Mining Administration.

The production outline for Kalgan contained three major points. Of primary importance was the development of factories which had resumed operations during the previous four months, and the immediate restoration of those still idle. Among the factories and workshops that had been destroyed or forced to suspend operations during the Japanese occupation, light industries were the first to be restored. Almost all of these had resumed operations by January, 1946, but a number of heavy industries still had not.

The second point in the industrial production program concerned the need for the large-scale development of the mines in the Kalgan area which included coal, lead, and other metals. Greatest emphasis was placed on the exploitation of the coal mines. Finally, the industries of Kalgan were to concentrate on the production of farm implements and light industrial machinery such as that required by the textile factories.[35]

33. Hsinhua News Agency, Yenan, June 16, 1946 (*FYI*, June 17).
34. *Chin-ch'a-chi jih-pao*, Kalgan, Jan. 26, 1946 (*CPR*, Peiping-Tientsin, Feb. 9).
35. *Ibid.*, Jan. 10, 1946 (*CPR*, Peiping-Tientsin, Jan. 26).

According to the Director of the Industry and Mining Administration, one of the main difficulties in the realization of these objectives by Kalgan's industries was their lack of competent managerial personnel. The Director noted that production statistics were inadequate and chided factory managers for not carrying out the necessary investigations and studies. We should be more businesslike, he warned, and should set up adequate management systems and learn to calculate production time with precision.[36]

Besides the labor policy—certain aspects of which were designed to increase output—specific measures to encourage industrial production in Kalgan included: (1) government loans to private as well as public industry, (2) extensive tax incentives, and (3) government assistance in the supply of raw materials and marketing of finished products. These measures formed the basis of an overall industrial incentives program which was put into effect throughout the Border Region in August, 1946. All factories and workshops (whether public, private, or jointly-owned) which produced cotton yarn, wool yarn, sheet glass, electricity, iron and steel, agricultural implements, machinery, and industrial raw materials were entitled to the most preferential treatment. This included: (1) an exemption from all business and income taxes for from two to five years depending on the amount of capital invested in the enterprises; (2) the right to apply for loans from the Border Region bank in case of a shortage of working capital; (3) government assistance in overcoming transportation difficulties involving raw materials and finished products; (4) the assistance of the Border Region trading company and all other government enterprises and cooperatives in surmounting difficulties involving the purchase of raw materials and disposal of finished products; and (5) government relief to compensate for damages incurred as a result of unavoidable calamities.

A second category of enterprises included cotton and woolen textile producers, flour mills, printing shops, and producers of daily necessities. Such enterprises were entitled to an exemption from all business and income taxes for from one to four years and all of the above-listed privileges with the exception of government relief in the event of unavoidable calamity.

Producers of cosmetics, toys, and other non-essential items made up a third category. Such enterprises were to be exempted from business and income taxes for from one to four years and were entitled to assistance in overcoming difficulties associated with the purchase of raw materials and sale of finished products. Liquor and cigarettes were among the few items to receive no tax exemptions.[37]

There is little information concerning the ratio of public and private enterprise in Kalgan. Initially, the government seems to have taken over a wide range of enterprises. These included not just public utilities, transportation, heavy industries, and mines, but many light industries as well. The sources do not indicate whether this represented a conscious attempt to expand the public

36. *Ibid.*

37. *Ibid.,* Aug. 5, 1946 (*CPR,* Peiping-Tientsin, Aug. 13); Hsinhua News Agency, Yenan, Aug. 11, 1946 (*FYI,* Aug. 12).

sector of Kalgan's economy beyond the formal outline of the New Democratic economic system, or whether it was simply a result of the initial take-over of enemy property. But the Border Region government, apparently in need of outside capital, announced in March, 1946, the transfer of twenty-three publicly-owned factories and mines to private ownership. Among these enterprises (the majority of which were located in Kalgan and Hsuanhua) were producers of cigarettes, matches, paper, textiles, leather goods, alcohol, and machinery. All of the shares in the New China Industrial Company which operated the twenty-three enterprises, were bought up within three months by merchants and industrialists from both the Communist and KMT areas.[38]

At the end of the Communists' year in Kalgan it was estimated that the municipal government had extended the equivalent of about $200,000,000 Chinese Nationalist currency (CNC) in low interest loans to private enterprise.[39] In addition, six local private banks had resumed operation in the city, each with capital of about CNC$100,000,000. By the summer of 1946, CNC$436,590,594 had been deposited in them and a total of CNC$207,676,000 extended by them in low interest commercial and industrial loans.[40]

Also contributing to what many visitors described as the economic boom in Kalgan was the revival of old trading patterns disrupted by the Japanese occupation. Shortly after liberation, the Communists removed all trade restrictions within the Border Region, as well as the ban on the export of foodstuffs from the Region. Kalgan had traditionally been a major marketing center for goods, particularly furs, food, and cattle from northern and southern Chahar. By the autumn of 1946, the number of fur dealers in Kalgan had grown from about fifty to more than three times that figure. Many of these dealers had been forced into bankruptcy during the Japanese occupation and were able to resume operations only with the aid of government loans. In addition, some thirty transport companies handling goods from Inner Mongolia resumed operations, and the municipal Kalgan government assisted other new companies to purchase camels and trucks.

The Kalgan food market was reopened in the spring of 1946. Grain from northern Chahar was exchanged for cloth from the textile centers in Hopei. Grain was also reportedly being purchased on the Kalgan market by merchants from the KMT cities of Peiping and Tientsin.[41] Throughout the Border Region, county fairs, temple fairs, and markets were reopened, reviving the movement of commodities not only to Kalgan and other points within the liberated areas but between them and the KMT areas as well. Travelling merchants attending these markets were said to be playing an important role as indirect commercial links

38. Hsinhua News Agency, Yenan, May 11, 1946 (*FYI*, May 12); Hsinhua News Agency, Yenan, June 6, 1946 (*FYI*, June 7).

39. Hsinhua News Agency, Yenan, Sept. 3, 1946 (*FYI*, Sept. 4).

40. Hsinhua News Agency, Yenan, July 22, 1946 (*FYI*, July 23).

41. Hsinhua News Agency, Yenan, June 9 and July 30, 1946 (*FYI*, June 10 and July 31).

between the two sides, despite the Central Government's ban on trade between them.[42]

INFLATION

The paucity of information makes it difficult to gauge the success of the Communists' attempts to cope with inflation in Kalgan. Officials there claimed that they did not resort to the printing press, but relied instead on a policy of extensive borrowing to meet their commitments. Yet Kalgan could not remain isolated from the effects of the inflation then developing in KMT cities, given the partially successful effort to circumvent the Government's economic blockade. Added to these external pressures were those generated by the Communists' initial wage policy. The combined effect was such that, as noted, the price of millet, which served as the basis of Border Region currency, more than doubled during the first six months of Communist rule in Kalgan.

Nevertheless, a number of countervailing influences served to dampen these pressures and to mitigate their consequences for Kalgan's citizens. After the initial round of wage increases, an attempt seems to have been made to hold basic wage rates steady. The Border Region trading company and a government foodstuffs company in Kalgan curbed price rises for some essential commodities. In addition, approximately 100 producer and consumer cooperatives shielded workers and others from the worst effects of the inflation. These trading organizations also reduced the capacity of merchants and speculators to engage in the sort of practices that were aggravating inflation in KMT cities.[43] The emphasis on reviving industry, trade, and transport also served to ameliorate many of the same conditions which were contributing to the Government's inflationary spiral.

Thus while the Communists in Kalgan were not able to avoid inflation, it seems to have been kept within manageable limits. Probably more fundamental to that achievement than any of the above, however, was the CCP's basic economic strategy. This was rooted in the non-monetary economy of the rural areas, and in a relatively conservative economic philosophy which emphasized strict austerity and self-sufficiency.

SOCIAL REFORMS

The most innovative undertaking in the realm of urban social problems centered on the programs to rehabilitate prostitutes, opium-addicts, thieves, and other so-called feudal remnants. The methods combined coercion and persuasion, and were essentially the same as those developed earlier in Yenan to cope with the rural equivalents of these non-productive elements.[44] The objective was to cause

42. *Chieh-fang jih-pao,* Peiping, May 7, 1946 (*CPR,* Peiping-Tientsin); and *Chin-ch'a-chi jih-pao,* Kalgan, Jan. 9, 1946 (*CPR,* Peiping-Tientsin, Jan. 24).

43. Hsinhua News Agency, Yenan, Sept. 3, 1946 (*FYI,* Sept. 4).

44. The objects of this effort were generally called *liu-mang,* a term denoting hoodlums, thieves, drug addicts, and the like. In 1937, there were an estimated 500 in Yenan. By 1945, the vast majority throughout the rural areas were claimed to be reformed and

the individuals concerned to realize that it was in their own best interests, as well as that of society as a whole, to change their ways of living.

The government did not ban prostitution outright, but a campaign to discourage it was begun almost immediately. All prostitutes were given the right to leave their brothels unconditionally if they wished. Many of the women chose not to avail themselves of this opportunity, however. It took "months of patient work" to enlighten minds "warped by many years of bondage." The months of patient work centered around the weekly medical examination all prostitutes in the city were required to undergo. In the waiting room of the medical ward set up for this purpose, female cadres regularly talked with them both individually and in small groups. The prostitutes were told that the city government would do its best to send them back to their families or assist them in finding other work. The message was reinforced by a steady decline in business, the result of social pressure designed to discourage potential customers. By the autumn of 1946, 463 of the 562 prostitutes in Kalgan's brothels at the time of Japan's surrender had either returned home to their families, found husbands, or were engaged in other employment.[45]

The problem of drug addiction was attacked in much the same manner, although the Eradicate Opium Smoking Campaign was part of a larger Border Region plan to convert poppy fields to food production. According to estimates made between 1940 and 1945, about 13 percent of the population, or something over 300,000 people, in Chahar and northern Shansi smoked opium. Opium cure centers were set up in many towns in the Chin-Ch'a-Chi Border Region, and various organizations such as youth groups, womens' associations, and the local newspapers undertook propaganda campaigns aimed at convincing addicts of the evils of opium. They were persuaded, and probably also coerced, into joining the opium cure centers where they were organized into small "mutual aid groups." These were ideally placed under the leadership of former addicts who had themselves been successful in breaking the habit. The Communists claimed some success for these centers as places where addicts were able to conquer their craving for opium. After an unspecified period spent in them, the former addict was encouraged during the second phase of the rehabilitation program to turn to farming or some other form of productive labor. By the summer of 1946, authorities in Kalgan claimed that the anti-opium campaign had been successful in rehabilitating perhaps a third of the total number of addicts in the Communist areas of Chahar and northern Shansi.[46]

Prison reform was also begun on a Border Region basis at this time and was undertaken in many small towns as well as in Kalgan. During the Communists'

---

absorbed into productive work—as their urban counterparts would be in the years that followed. A related group in the villages were the *erh-liu-tzu*, a term for loafers, idle gossips, and petty thieves at worst. The method used with this group was somewhat less severe, relying primarily on social pressure in varying combinations of scorn, ridicule, struggle, and moral exhortation. See Li Keng, *Chieh-fang-ch'ü te sheng-ch'an yun-tung*, pp. 20-24.

45. Hsinhua News Agency, Yenan, Sept. 3 and 24, 1946 (*FYI*, Sept. 4 and 25).

46. Hsinhua News Agency, Yenan, July 19, 1946 (*FYI*, July 20).

year there, prison officials claimed success with a group of about fifty thieves who had gone to work at "respectable" jobs following their release from prison. Another group was in the process of reform when the Communists were forced to withdraw from the city. In Hsuanhua, authorities reported that 150 prisoners had responded positively to the rehabilitation program and were released before the expiration of their sentences. Many of these criminals had also been drug addicts when they were imprisoned and were allegedly cured by the time of their release. For the ordinary prisoner, the reform process entailed humane treatment, bonuses and prizes for outstanding work done in prison workshops, education in political affairs, and self-criticism during small group discussion sessions. The prisoners were also given help in finding jobs after their release.

The most famous reformed prisoner in Kalgan was twenty-two-year-old Chu Yuan-chai, alias "Little Shantung," who was appointed warden of the city prison in May. Orphaned at the age of seven, he had turned from begging to stealing. After a varied career which included drug addiction and a prison term in Dairen by age fourteen, Chu settled in Kalgan during the Japanese occupation. Shortly after the Communists took the city, he was rounded up along with other known criminal elements and sentenced to a year in prison by the new city government.

Although he was apolitical and understood little about the "New Democracy" that he was told was giving him a chance to start anew, he responded positively to the treatment accorded him. Among the things that impressed him most, he told reporters, was the practice of allowing model workers—elected by the prisoners from their own ranks—to attend meetings, make speeches, and receive awards on the same platform with other labor champions in the town. He resolved to become a model worker himself and was eventually elected as a labor squad leader by his fellow inmates. He was released during the spring of 1946, several months before his sentence expired. Soon after requesting help in finding employment, he was notified of his appointment as prison warden. His success story was widely publicized as a model for others to emulate, demonstrating what could be achieved by even the most backward elements under the new regime.[47]

THE GENESIS OF CHINESE COMMUNIST URBAN POLICY, 1945-46

However fragmentary, this sketch of the Communists' experience in Kalgan reveals an urban policy still dominated by the overall rural orientation of the Party. The goals for Kalgan's economy were an integral part of the larger Chin-Ch'a-Chi Border Region production campaign which emphasized agriculture over industry and light over heavy industry. The objective was to achieve a basic level of self-sufficiency within the context of the war effort and the Central Government's economic blockade of the liberated areas.

Nevertheless, the attempt to develop Kalgan as an industrial and commercial center was premature, indicating that here, too, the Communists underestimated the strength of the Government's military offensive in 1946. Hence Kalgan was

47. Hsinhua News Agency, Yenan, Aug. 6 and Sept. 12, 1946 (*FYI*, Aug. 7 and Sept. 13).

treated differently than towns the Communists knew they could not hold permanently. Such places were also used to support the military effort, but not as sites for the development of commerce and industry. Instead, the practice at this time was to dismantle and carry off whatever machinery and equipment might be of use to Communist forces or to economic development in more secure areas. Such was the case, for example, in the Manchurian village described in Chapter Six, where Communist forces carried off equipment from the local clinic, although they did not touch the private property of the peasants themselves.

The practice of removing needed equipment eventually became counterproductive as the Communists began taking and keeping an increasing number of towns. But habits developed during long years of guerrilla war could not be changed overnight. As the Communists' capacity to sustain their victories increased, campaigns had to be launched to protect industrial and commercial enterprises in all cities from the moment of their capture. Both civilian and military personnel were chided for the unnecessary persistence of their "guerrilla mentality" in this regard.[48] In due time, the Communists began to pursue everywhere the same policy of safeguarding property and promoting trade and production that they had adopted in Kalgan.

Later, however, they referred to errors of over-confidence that had been made there.[49] The immediate context of the remark is unclear. But aside from the strategically premature decision to develop the city into a second capital, the new administration did seem ambitious in its attempts to provide something for everyone in Kalgan. Subsequent changes indicate that the main problem areas probably included the tax incentive program, the expansion of the public sector, the relatively high wage levels, and the adoption in principle of the eight-hour work day. Many of the changes began to occur during 1946 both in Kalgan and elsewhere.

All of the Border Region governments adopted forms of taxation intended to encourage the growth of trade and industry. Nevertheless, some anticipated future Communist taxation policy by not going quite as far as did the Chin-Ch'a-Chi Border Region. According to the tax regulations introduced in Chin-Chi-Lu-Yü in 1946, only public enterprises which supplied certain raw materials, producers of agricultural implements, printers, and non-profit charitable undertakings, were exempt from all taxation. Otherwise, taxes were levied on a progressive basis running from 2.5 percent to a maximum of 33 percent of net profits. The graduated income tax exempted only the very poor and ranged from about 10 to 30 percent of total income.[50]

As noted, the revision of the initial balance struck between public and private enterprise occurred in Kalgan itself during the spring of 1946. Similar measures

48. See Chapter Nine.

49. Anna Louise Strong, *The Chinese Conquer China*, p. 142.

50. *Chieh-fang jih-pao*, Peiping, May 15, 1946 (*CPR*, Peiping-Tientsin, May 16); and Hsinhua News Agency, Yenan, Nov. 10, 1946, dispatch by A. L. Strong (*FYI*, Nov. 11).

were taken elsewhere in the liberated areas. In May, the Chin-Chi-Lu-Yü Border Region government announced the transfer to private ownership of the Fengfeng and Chiaotso coal mines, two of the largest in north China. Six other coal mines in southern Hopei and northern Honan, and the T'aihang Implements Factory in southeastern Shansi were also transferred to private ownership at the same time.[51]

In June, the government of Jehol issued provisional regulations designed to encourage the mining industry, private as well as public, in a province known for its gold, silver, coal, and mineral deposits. The regulations stipulated, among other things, that all privately-owned mines taken over by the Japanese must be turned back to their original owners, and that privately-owned mines which had been rented to the Japanese would be returned to the owners as soon as the leases expired. Otherwise, all mines owned or operated by the Japanese or their puppets were to be run by the government. Private industrialists would nevertheless be encouraged to lease and operate mines in the province.[52]

In fact, all of the Border Region governments officially encouraged private businessmen and industrialists to invest in many different kinds of enterprises with offers of loans and other assistance. For example, the establishment of the privately-financed Juihua Bank in Hantan was announced with much fanfare in May, 1946. Another well-publicized case was that of Wang Ying-ku, an industrialist who had allegedly lost two chemical factories after twice running afoul of the KMT authorities in Kansu province. Finally in the autumn of 1945, he fled to southern Hopei. The Chin-Chi-Lu-Yü Border Region government gave him a low interest loan to finance a new factory, and turned over to him spare parts and equipment "collected" from various towns and villages.

The desire to assuage the fears of private capital was articulated clearly in the 1946 May Day editorial of the *Liberation Daily* in Yenan:

> Private capital is an indispensable force in the reconstruction of the liberated areas. Under the grave oppression of monopoly capital at home and abroad, the growth of Chinese national industry is faced with huge difficulties. To conquer such difficulties and reach the goal of developing production and economic prosperity, mutual concession and concerted cooperation between capital and labor are completely essential. Such cooperation is beneficial to the nation as well as to both capital and labor. Trade unions must on the one hand persuade capital to improve the workers' treatment so as to raise the enthusiasm of the workers . . . and on the other persuade the workers not to demand overmuch from the capitalists and to save materials, to strengthen labor discipline and improve the organizational management to attain the

51. Hsinhua News Agency, Yenan, May 27 and June 7, 1946 (*FYI*, May 28 and June 9). In a later account, the labor union official, Liu Ning-i, reported that the Fengfeng and Chiaotso mines had been transferred from public to joint public-private management. See Liu Ning-i, "Chieh-fang-ch'ü kung-yeh cheng-ts'e" [Industrial policy in the liberated areas], in Ch'en Po-ta, *et al., Kuan-yü kung-shang-yeh te cheng-ts'e* (hereafter *Kung-shang-yeh*), p. 30.

52. Hsinhua News Agency, Yenan, June 26, 1946 (*FYI*, June 27).

reduction of costs, to raise the quality of output and increase the profits of the whole factory.[53]

As the editorial indicated, the cooperation of the work force became an indispensable component of the effort to attract private capital and to promote economic development in general. Thus Yenan radio reported that over 800,000 unionized workers in the liberated areas of northern and central China had attended May Day meetings expressing support for the speed-up of economic reconstruction. They pledged to cooperate with capitalists, increase output, improve quality, and reduce costs, so that factory and mine owners would be able to operate their enterprises on a profit basis. Our task, Chu Teh told a meeting of trade unionists in Yenan, is to cooperate with the capitalists in developing production so that the living standards of the workers may be improved and the capitalists will be able to earn profits.[54]

These themes for May Day, 1946, were all indicative of the direction Chinese Communist labor policy would more self-consciously assume by the end of 1947. Similarly, the practice of expanding the work day in order to fulfill certain production tasks; the use of labor competition and crash programs to increase production; the promotion of material incentives designed to increase the output of the individual worker; an apparent effort to hold the line on some of labor's demands; and official emphasis on labor discipline, all existed at least in embryonic form during the Communists' year in Kalgan.

THE RETURN TO THE CITIES: 1947-1949

The changes which marked the development of Chinese Communist urban policy between 1947 and 1949 were threefold. First, there was a shift toward a more conservative position on several interrelated issues. This developed in the form of a campaign to correct leftist excesses, coinciding with the anti-leftist campaign in the land reform movement described in the preceding chapter. Second and related to the concern about left adventurism, came a new interest particularly evident in the Northeast in learning from the experience of the Soviet Union. Finally, urban administration became a major preoccupation in its own right rather than a low priority item overshadowed by the war, land reform, Party rectification, and the rural production campaigns.

The widely-circulated July 30, 1948, Hsinhua editorial on the achievements of the first two years of the Civil War officially acknowledged the new emphasis on the cities. According to the editorial, the capture of several important cities during the second year of the war, together with the Army's shift from the defensive to the offensive, had changed the military, political, and economic situation of the liberated areas. Second only to the military effort itself would be the task of implementing the Party's policy for newly-liberated areas, and particularly for newly-liberated cities, in the coming year.

53. Hsinhua News Agency, Yenan, Apr. 30, 1946 (*FYI*, May 1).
54. Hsinhua News Agency, Yenan, May 3, 1946 (*FYI*, May 4).

The major points of that policy for the cities were: the elimination and disbanding of the enemy's armed force; the arrest of all who continued to resist after the liberation of a city; the confiscation of property controlled by bureaucratic capitalists; and the establishment of a system of popular control. Arrests and confiscations were to be limited specifically to the above. Otherwise, all private property and all capitalists regardless of the scale of their enterprises, were to be protected—as were all cultural, educational, and religious organizations, and all foreigners. Wherever possible, productive enterprises were to remain in operation.

Unlike land in the semi-feudal rural areas, private property in the cities was not to be confiscated for redistribution to the poor. "The task and methods of social reform in the cities are completely different from land reform in the countryside," declared the editorial. "The opponents in the cities today are in general limited to the reactionary KMT power structure and genuine bureaucratic capitalists; as for the national bourgeoisie, our task is not revolutionary but rather to unite with it and reform it."[55]

The emphasis in the July 30 editorial on protecting urban business and industry, avoiding unnecessary disruption, and uniting with the bourgeoisie, reflected the anti-leftist line that had been developing since the previous autumn.

LABOR: THE ANTI-LEFTIST CAMPAIGN

The nature of the changes then under way on the labor front was publicized in another Hsinhua editorial issued on February 7, 1948. It marked the intensification of the anti-leftist campaign begun in late 1947, justifying that effort in the following terms:

> It must be pointed out that at present there still are within the CCP not a few Party members, cadres, labor union work personnel, and even leading members in high level leadership positions who simply do not understand the Party's industrial policy and the line of the trade union movement. They only see the trees and not the forest. They only know about the one-sided, narrow, near-sighted so-called "benefits for the workers," and cannot see even a little beyond that. They have forgotten how the excessively left adventurist industrial policy and labor movement line carried out during the 1931-1934 period harmed the working class laborers and the revolutionary government! They simply have not done any research into the CCP's correct industrial policy and labor movement line of the past eleven years. They stubbornly oppose the Party line, and many local leadership organs have for a long time not even formally discussed and propagandized the line of the Party center, thus causing labor movement work comrades to be completely unclear about the Party center's line. They are in a paralyzed state and this cannot continue. All of the Party's local leadership organs must seriously discuss the center's line, industrial policy, and the labor movement line, and determinedly correct all left adventurist thought, policy, and methods.[56]

55. Hsin hua she, ed., *Jen-min chieh-fang chan-cheng liang chou-nien tsung-chieh ho ti-san nien te jen-wu*, pp. 3, 9-10.

56. *"Chien-ch'ih chih-kung yun-tung te cheng-ch'ueh lu-hsien fan-tui 'tso'-ch'ing mao-hsien-chu-i"* [Firmly support the correct line of the labor movement and oppose "left-wing"

A few weeks later Mao reiterated this line in an intra-Party directive:

A sharp distinction should also be made between the correct policy of developing production, promoting economic prosperity, giving consideration to both public and private interests and benefiting both labor and capital, and the one-sided and narrow-minded policy of "relief," which purports to uphold the workers' welfare but in fact damages industry and commerce and impairs the cause of the people's revolution.[57]

The general objectives remained unchanged. Since 1937, they had been to promote cooperation between labor and capital and to benefit both. The May Day speeches of 1946 reaffirmed these same objectives: trade unions must persuade capital to improve its treatment of the workers, and persuade the workers not to demand overmuch from the capitalists. Nevertheless, the separate components of the general line were open to a range of emphasis and interpretation. And economic conditions were such that, like giving land to the poor without encroaching upon the middle peasants, the goals of benefiting both labor and capital were often contradictory when it came to implementation. Thus instead of trying to do both as was apparently attempted in Kalgan, or concentrating primarily on the needs of labor as was done in some cases, the emphasis shifted explicity in 1948 towards production and industrial development.

The Problems Defined

The two main problems were defined as an excessive preoccupation with the demands of labor while neglecting its responsibilities; and the tendency to promote struggle and discord within the labor force itself.

Concerning the first problem, Ch'en Po-ta wrote that in the old liberated areas, enterprise circumstances had often been ignored. Wage increases and improvements in working conditions had sometimes pushed production costs so high that goods could not be sold and industrial expansion came to a halt. Some enterprises were unable to sustain themselves and a number of publicly-owned factories required excessive amounts of financial aid from the government just to continue in operation.[58] In Harbin, privately-owned factories were said to have been especially hard-hit by such leftist excesses.[59]

---

adventurism], in Tung-pei shu-tien, ed., *Chih-kung yun-tung wen-hsien* (hereafter *Chih-kung wen-hsien*), 1:20. This editorial commemorated the twenty-fifth anniversary of the Feb. 7, 1923, strike on the Peking-Hankow Railway, which was suppressed by Wu P'ei-fu.

57. Mao Tse-tung, "On the Policy Concerning Industry and Commerce," Feb. 27, 1948, *Selected Works*, 4:203.

58. Ch'en Po-ta, "Fa-chan kung-yeh te lao-tung cheng-ts'e yü shui-shou cheng-ts'e" [Labor and taxation policies for the development of industry], May 1, 1948, in Chieh-fang, she, ed., *Mu-ch'ien hsing-shih ho wo-men te jen-wu*, p. 99.

59. Erh chieh ha shih chih-kung tai-piao ta-hui hsuan-pu" [Announcement of the second annual Harbin workers and staff members representative conference], May 13, 1948, in Tung-pei shu-tien, ed., *Chih-kung yun-tung ts'an-k'ao tzu-liao* (hereafter *Ts'an-k'ao tzu-liao*), p. 10.

Ch'en Pao-yü, head of the Central Hopei District General Labor Union, declared that similar problems had existed in that district since at least 1945. In October of that year, a Central Hopei Workers and Staff Members Representative Conference had passed a labor maintenance law which set excessively high standards for wage rates, labor insurance, and fringe benefits. According to Ch'en, the law tried to meet every conceivable demand, including that for the provision of clothing by the employer. In the Central Hopei District of the Chin-Ch'a-Chi Border Region the preoccupation with workers' benefits was reaffirmed at conferences in March and September, 1946. During this period, labor union work cadres allegedly concentrated on improving the workers' livelihood to the virtual exclusion of productivity and discipline.[60]

As for the "erroneous struggle model" within the labor movement, Ch'en Pao-yü also described its consequences. Labor union cadres not born into the working class were arbitrarily removed from their positions. The relationship between skilled workers and apprentices, and between master craftsmen and ordinary workers, was defined as one of exploitation. Skilled and non-manual workers were treated as a sort of labor aristocracy and often not allowed to join the unions. The difficulty, as Ch'en described it, was that many labor movement leaders and general cadres did not understand the special characteristics of urban labor work. Instead, they moved the rural class struggle into the factories. This divided the ranks of the working class, setting one group against another.

This problem was so prevalent in Manchuria that the Party's Northeast Bureau issued a directive condemning it. According to the directive, too much emphasis had been placed on manual laborers while others were attacked indiscriminately. The opposition which this created between the two groups made cooperation between them difficult and ultimately interfered with production.[61]

One additional feature of this same problem was the practice of basing wages on a worker's political activism rather than on ability and experience. This was denounced as a manifestation of vulgar one-sided "egalitarianism, mass viewpoint, and economic viewpoint." In May, 1948, the North China Liberated Area Industrial and Commercial Conference held it to be one of the most serious defects in the wage systems of publicly-managed enterprises in north China.[62]

60. "Chi-chung-ch'ü shou-tz'u kung-yeh hui-i: chien-t'ao chih-kung yun-tung te tso-ch'ing mao-hsien-chu-i" [The First Central Hopei Industrial Conference: an examination of left-wing adventurism in the labor movement], Apr. 28, 1948, in Ch'en Po-ta, *et al.*, *Kung-shang-yeh*, p. 46.

61. "Chung-kung tung-pei-chü kuan-yü kung-ying ch'i-yeh chung chih-yuan wen-t'i te chueh-ting" [The CCP Northeast Bureau's decision on the problems of employees in public enterprises], Aug. 1, 1948, in Hua-pei hsin-hua shu-tien, ed., *Kuan-yü ch'eng-shih cheng-ts'e te chi-ko wen-hsien*, p. 32.

62. "Hua-pei chieh-fang-ch'ü kung-shang-yeh hui-i" [The North China Liberated Area Industrial and Commercial Conference], in *Hsin kung-shang cheng-ts'e* (hereafter *Hsin kung-shang*), p. 106.

Tentative Solutions: Experiments
in Labor Reform

In Harbin, the General Labor Union began to correct these problems in individual factories as early as October, 1947.[63] The publication of the February 7, 1948, Hsinhua editorial quoted above, marked the extension of the movement to all the Border Regions. The editorial's injunctions to the workers were as explicit as its criticism of the cadres. For their own long-term welfare, the workers would have to tolerate a certain degree of exploitation since this would enable private enterprise to develop production and support the war effort. The workers should understand that production in both public and private enterprise was their responsibility, just as it was the responsibility of the peasants to turn over to the government large quantities of public grain. As members of the most advanced class, the workers should be willing to make sacrifices for the revolution, to work ten hours a day if necessary, and to refrain from making extravagant wage demands which contradicted the general line of developing production, enriching the economy, and benefiting both labor and capital.

During the spring and summer of 1948, a number of specific measures were introduced in line with these injunctions. Toward the end of the summer, most of these measures (or at least the experience derived from the attempts to implement them) were incorporated into the resolutions of the Sixth All-China Labor Conference. As with all such major undertakings, this one was first carried out on an experimental basis in a few key enterprises. The Northeast and particularly Harbin were important centers of experimentation during the first months. This labor reform campaign included a graduated piece rate wage system, with basic wage rates set at relatively low levels but containing some safeguards against the effects of inflation; increased work hours; a modest package of fringe benefits; and production competition or labor emulation campaigns.

Piece Rates. Undoubtedly the most difficult—and probably the least successful—of these experiments was the attempt to institute the piece rate and reward systems of wage payment. As in Kalgan where these methods were also introduced, they were based on a formal set of wage standards. These wage levels, differentiated by skill and experience, determined base pay. This was supplemented by piece rate or bonus incentives tied to the productivity of the individual worker or group of workers.

This system of wage payment based on a combination of ability, seniority, and effort, was an institutionalized feature of labor policy in the Soviet Union. The Chinese Communists never relied as heavily on piece rates as did the U.S.S.R.[64] But in 1942 when the liberated areas were experiencing grave

63. Wang Kang, "Kai-cheng kuo-kao hung-li i-hou te ha shih hsing-tung chi-ch'i yu fang" [The Harbin Hsingtung oil plant after correcting the payment of excessive bonuses], in Tung-pei shu-tien, ed., *Ts'an-k'ao tzu-liao,* pp. 33-34.

64. In 1956, 42 percent of the Chinese industrial work force was on piece rates; the ratio declined thereafter. In 1953, 77 percent of Soviet industrial workers were on piece rates. See Audrey Donnithorne, *China's Economic System,* pp. 206-7; and Abram Bergson, *The Economics of Soviet Planning* (New Haven: Yale University Press, 1964), p. 110.

economic hardship, Mao had recommended this method of wage payment as a means of encouraging labor activism and increasing production.[65] Whatever the fate of his proposal then, considerable effort did go into the attempt to introduce it in Manchurian factories six years later on the same grounds.

The value of this type of wage, according to the many reports and editorials lauding it in 1948, was its effectiveness in tying wage increases to increases in productivity. It could induce workers to raise output and maintain labor discipline voluntarily, without undue compulsion from management. Even the most "backward" members of the working class could understand the logic of the principle "the more work the more pay."

Such inducements were necessary, it was said, to overcome the habits workers had evolved in order to survive under the oppression of the Japanese and the KMT. It had become commonplace for workers to steal from the employer, waste materials, and take a half-hour to go to the toilet. In such a work environment, Ch'en Po-ta argued, excessive wage increases could neither raise the political consciousness of labor nor encourage it to economize and increase production. Unconditional wage increases would only lead down the path of unprincipled economism, causing the workers to assume that they automatically deserved special rights and privileges. When wages were fixed at the lowest possible level, on the other hand, there was also no encouragement for workers to reduce costs and increase production. And when wages were equalized, giving skilled workers and staff members the same pay as ordinary laborers, the former tended to lose their enthusiasm for production. Under the circumstances, the only solution was a wage policy based on the graduated piece rate system.[66]

In Harbin, the Second Annual Workers and Staff Members Representative Conference launched the promotion campaign for this wage policy in its "Provisional Methods for the Implementation of Wartime Wage Standards." This resolution called for the introduction of the progressive piece rate and reward system based on graduated wage levels. It also called for payment in terms of work points valued in kind so as to protect the workers from inflationary price rises.[67]

Many local cadres and Party members disapproved of the piece rate system. Most fundamental were their misgivings about its propriety in a society which, if not socialist, was at least headed in that direction. Just as excessively high wage rates tended to produce an "economic viewpoint" among the workers, they feared this system would have a like effect. They also feared that differences in take-home pay would lead to conflicts and disunity within the labor force. In addition, the piece rate system was questioned on practical grounds. Many

65. See the 1949 Hong Kong edition of Mao Tse-tung, *Ching-chi wen-t'i yü ts'ai-cheng wen-t'i,* p. 115. Mao wrote this in 1942.

66. Ch'en Po-ta, pp. 96-101 (see note 58 above).

67. See note 59 above. This conference, from May 1-13, 1948, was attended by 397 worker representatives. It approved a draft wartime labor law, a charter for the Harbin General Labor Union, and resolutions on fringe benefits and worker education. There were 549 branch unions in the city at that time with total membership of about 68,000.

doubted the feasibility of implementing it except in a relatively small number of enterprises where the output of individual workers could be measured.

The general lack of technical knowledge also contributed to the reservations of cadres responsible for implementing the complex and unfamiliar system. In some Harbin factories, management and labor union work cadres, lacking experience and adequate statistical information, were finding it difficult to fix correct production standards. As a result, production standards were set at inappropriate levels, as often too high as too low.[68]

To deal with these misgivings and related problems, Harbin's two major newspapers, the *Ha-erh-pin jih-pao* [Harbin Daily News] and the *Tung-pei jih-pao* [Northeast Daily News], published a series of articles and editorials during the first half of 1948. They described in detail the experience of factories which had successfully introduced the piece rate system. A key theme was that the system had to be introduced on a factory-by-factory basis. Wage standards and work hours need not be the same everywhere. They should be decided in accordance with conditions existing in individual enterprises. The cadres' fears about the complexity of the tasks confronting them would seem to have been confirmed rather than eased by the experiences publicized in this series, however.

The example of a shipyard that had begun switching over to the reward system in November, 1946, is a case in point. By the spring of 1948, all production workers in the enterprise were operating under this variant of the piece rate system. The organizational structure which the system necessitated included a Production Standards Department, a Statistical Department, and a Department for Matters Related to Production, all operating under a General Department for Labor Affairs. Directly linked to the Production Standards Department were groups within each of the shipyard's divisions, for example, carpentry, metal casting, electrical work, et cetera. These groups were responsible for investigating and determining standards.

The technique for fixing standards involved the distribution by the General Department for Labor Affairs of overall plans and designs for manufactured items to the shipyard's divisions. The plans were then broken down and distributed to the workshops within the divisions. The head of each shop together with its technical personnel were responsible for drawing up specific estimates of the work time necessary to complete the job in question, the technical level required for the job, the materials needed, et cetera. These estimates were then turned over to the Production Standards Department and its subordinate groups for investigation, evaluation, and final acceptance. Before production materials were issued to the workships and work could begin, however, management was responsible for ensuring that the workers understood the standards and the work plan on an hourly and monthly basis. Opportunities were given to the workers to express their opinions at various stages of this process.

68. "T'ui-kuang chi-chien kung-tzu chih yü ch'ao-o chiang-li chih" [Extend the piece rate wage system and reward system], *Ha-erh-pin jih-pao,* reprinted in Tung-pei shu-tien, ed., *Ts'an-k'ao tzu-liao,* pp. 17-20.

Finally, this wage system required a many-tiered inspection system: (1) inspections of one another's work by the workers themselves at the most basic level within the work group and shop; (2) inspection by a master craftsman responsible for an entire division within the shipyard; (3) inspection by a master craftsman responsible to the General Department of Labor Affairs; and, (4) the approval by the individual who had placed the order and whose signature was required before wages could be paid.[69]

Labor Emulation. Known variously as labor competition campaigns, model labor campaigns, and achievement campaigns, these attempts to induce increased productivity through competitive effort relied on both normative and material rewards. Labor emulation, too, was an institutionalized practice in the Soviet Union. Nor was it a new concept for the Chinese Communists, who had already put it to use in their efforts to boost agricultural production.

In industry, however, these campaigns were often associated with the introduction of piece rates and required an equally complex administrative structure when properly implemented. Indeed, both the introduction of piece rates and labor emulation performed an important function in the development of factory-wide production plans, a first step in the movement toward economic planning. The description of the achievement campaign carried out in a textile factory in the city of Antung even suggested that the primary purpose of the campaign was to ensure that labor and management learned how to devise and implement such a production plan.[70]

As with other of the Communists' labor reforms at this time, the workers did not respond with automatic enthusiasm. In one machine-making plant, when the model labor campaign was introduced in September, 1947, only about 10 percent of the workers were willing to participate. Most were either not interested or actually ridiculed the idea. But toward the end of October, interest began to pick up and ultimately about 70 percent of the workers participated. Output gradually increased and production plans were in some cases over-fulfilled, making it possible for the factory to introduce the piece-rate system. As the system operated within this factory, all who exceeded the fixed production standards and goals (in terms of quantity, quality, production time, economy, et cetera) were rewarded with progressive wage increases. These increases were calculated according to a scale which ranged from a 10 percent increase of the basic wage rates for workers who had exceeded their production plan by 5 percent, all the way up to a 100 percent increase for those exceeding their plans by 70 percent or more.[71]

69. (a) Liu Yun-kuang and Chu Li-ming, "I-ko tsao-ch'uan ch'ang te chi-chien kung-tzu chih" [The piece rate wage system in a shipyard], *Ha-erh-pin jih-pao*, reprinted in Tung-pei shu-tien, ed., *Ts'an-k'ao tzu-liao*, pp. 20-23; and (b) Liu Yun-kuang and Chu Li-ming, "I-ko chi-hsieh ch'ang te an-chien lei-chin kung-tzu chih" [The progressive piece rate wage system in a machine factory], *Ha-erh-pin jih-pao*, reprinted in *ibid.*, pp. 24-30.

70. "An-tung fang-chih ch'ang sheng-ch'an li-kung yun-tung te chi-ko wen-t'i" [Some questions about the production achievement campaign in an Antung textile factory], *Tung-pei jih-pao*, reprinted in *ibid.*, pp. 51-55.

71. See note 69(b) above.

Base Pay: Wage Levels. Also in accordance with Soviet practice, the Chinese instituted a system of seven grades differentiated by skill and experience, as the means of determining base pay. The pay scales fixed by the government for ordinary manual laborers in Manchuria ranged from 11.5 *yuan* per hour for grade one to 36.5 *yuan* per hour for grade seven. A separate fifteen-grade pay scale for technicians and staff members ranged from 3,500 *yuan* per month for grade one, up to 17,000 *yuan* per month for grade fifteen.

Both the job and the workers were categorized on the basis of the seven grades. In the above-mentioned shipyard, for example, it was calculated that the standard time for a given number of workers in the iron foundry to cast an anchor of a given weight should total 480 working hours; the men should be paid for the job according to the basic wage scale of grade three, or 16.70 *yuan* per hour. This particular group of workers could be rewarded with pay increases if they completed the job in less than the average estimated time, or devised some improvements in the work process.[72]

The Mass Line: Worker Participation. As with many Chinese Communist undertakings, it was often difficult to determine where the means used to implement this labor reform campaign left off and the ends began. Thus one writer explained that fixing wage standards was not just a matter of deciding on the grades and levels into which work and workers should be divided in any given factory. The process was in addition "a kind of mass movement" capable of activating the workers and developing a spirit of mutual criticism among them.[73] Certainly the methods used to institute wage reforms were designed to contribute toward that end.

Ideally, the process began with careful preparatory work. This meant explaining to the workers the rationale for instituting a new wage system and soliciting their criticisms in order to determine the extent of their opposition to it. Cadres were advised that the workers' most basic doubts should be overcome before explaining to them the concrete details of the new system. Once wage standards had been determined in an enterprise, these were to be presented by the union to the rank and file for evaluation. Experience had proven that if it was conducted at a large mass meeting, such evaluation was sure to fail. The workers should therefore be divided into small groups where their criticism and suggestions could be freely aired.

The workers were to indicate which grade and level of work they felt they should be placed in on the basis of their skill and experience. Then the small-group members could decide collectively whether to let each worker's self-evaluation stand. Small-group leaders were advised to select an average worker as the first in the group to be evaluated. The others would then stand out more clearly as being comparatively better or worse, and errors would be

---

72. Liu and Chu, pp. 24-25 (see note 69[b]); and p. 22 (note 69[a]).
73. Kuo Lin-chün, "Kuan-yü kung-tzu te min-chu p'ing-chia" [On the democratic evaluation of wages], *Ha-erh-pin jih-pao*, reprinted in Tung-pei shu-tien, ed., *Ts'an-k'ao tzu-liao*, p. 38.

minimized. The results of the small-group evaluations were turned over to the union for reevaluation, with the final decision being taken by a high-level salary evaluation committee. In this way, the workers' doubts could be effectively overcome and their sense of personal participation in the new system maximized.[74]

Benefits and Discipline: Government authorities nevertheless acknowledged that the wage levels, particularly for ordinary manual laborers, were not high enough to meet the declared objective of providing a basic livelihood for two people. Prices were rising continuously in the spring of 1948. The government therefore devised a grain rationing scheme, supplying factories with grain to be sold to their employees at a fraction of the market price. In the above-mentioned machine-making factory, each manual laborer was allowed to purchase sixteen kilos of grain per month and each non-manual worker twelve kilos. Besides this basic ration, all employees could purchase nine kilos of grain for each of their dependents who was unable to work. This automatically included parents over fifty years of age and children under sixteen.

The workers, however, did not readily accept what was often apparently a substantial reduction in take-home pay. In one soybean processing plant, union cadres relied primarily on the pressures that could be brought to bear in small-group discussions, buttressed by the threat of imminent unemployment should the business shut down completely. The workers eventually agreed not only to work for less pay—supplemented by guaranteed supplies of inexpensive food and fuel—and to give up their New Year's bonuses, but also to improve their work habits. Helping to sustain the general agreement was a production inspection committee formed among the workers themselves, and a number of small groups organized to promote labor competition and maintain labor discipline. By summer, 1948, the business was able to report a reduction in costs and a 30 percent rise in output as compared with the preceding autumn. As a result, the employer made needed repairs, expanded capital equipment, and hired an additional fifty workers. In this plant, it was only after all of these changes had been effected that the piece rate and reward systems were introduced.[75]

Similar efforts were made to solve the problems plaguing eight small privately-owned iron works in Kirin. These were engaged in the manufacture of agricultural implements such as hoes, sickles, axes, and the like. In this case, the government of the commercial district in which the foundries were located, initiated the negotiations by first explaining official business and labor policy, and then holding separate discussion meetings for the two sides while acting as mediator between them. Labor ultimately agreed that excessively high wages were unjust. And representatives of management acknowledged that the workers should receive somewhat higher pay than those in publicly-owned enterprises who received a number of extra benefits including dormitory accommodation on the factory premises. Thus wage levels were to be no higher than 10 percent

74. *Ibid.,* pp. 36-38.
75. Wang Kang, pp. 33-36 (see note 63 above).

above those in publicly-owned iron works, and twenty-five rather than the usual twenty-six days were to be regarded as a full month's work. In addition, workers' wages were to be calculated in terms of the price of grain on payday itself; a system of bonuses for excess output was worked out; and agreements were reached on the firing of workers during slack seasons, as well as on demands for wage increases during the busy months.[76]

The problems in a Harbin plant engaged in the manufacture of trolley cars were somewhat different. In this plant, there was little difference in the pay of experienced and inexperienced workers. Some apprentices were even earning more than skilled craftsmen. Shortly after the May Workers Representative Conference, small-group discussions were organized to evaluate factory conditions and study the proposed reforms. The workers were forthright in expressing their objections to the latter. Lengthy discussions, evaluations, and research were required before a majority could be convinced that pay scales really should not be the same for manual laborers and skilled technicians; that there should be a substantial difference between the wages of apprentices and those of master craftsmen; and that technical skills and productivity should be weighted more heavily than political views in determining wage classifications.[77]

An additional problem emerged as a direct consequence of the labor reform campaign. Some private employers in particular took advantage of the anti-leftist tenor of the campaign and used it to enrich themselves at the expense of their employees. It became necessary to remind local cadres to maintain a two-sided struggle against both rightist and leftist deviations. As regards the former, cadres were advised to "persuade, induce, or order" capitalist entrepreneurs to respect the laws and policies of the liberated areas. Actions taken against the privately-owned Hsingyuan Bedding and Uniforms Factory in Harbin were of that order.

The business began as a small self-sufficient operation and grew into one of the top producers in the city. The workers had participated in labor competition campaigns and the business received government aid and low-cost public grain. Profits increased, but the owners were unwilling to share them with the workers and even reduced the quality of the food served at mealtime. The workers repeatedly took their grievances to the factory owners but verbal promises were not carried out. Several workers quit and the remainder, by this time organized under union leadership, set about dismantling the company's machinery, some of which had by now fallen into disuse. The workers' plan was to set up shop on their own. At this point, the owners gave in and agreed to sell the factory to the

76. Su Ning, "Chi-lin ch'uan-ying-ch'ü t'ieh-chiang lu-yeh te kung-tzu wen-t'i shih tsen-yang chieh-chueh-te" [How wage problems were resolved in the iron works industry of Kirin's shipyard district], *Tung-pei jih-pao*, reprinted in Tung-pei shu-tien, ed., *Ts'an-k'ao tzu-liao*, pp. 30-33.

77. Wang Chih-i and Huang Chi-yun, "Tien-ch'e ch'ang ting kung-tzu te wen-t'i" [The problems of fixing wages in a trolley car plant], *Tung-pei jih-pao*, reprinted in *ibid.*, pp. 38-40.

workers collectively for 3,650,000 *yuan.* The sale was concluded with the help of a 2,500,000 *yuan* loan from the government.[78]

The Sixth All-China Labor Congress

The experiences gained during the months of experimentation with labor reform were brought together and standardized for use throughout the liberated areas in the resolutions of the Sixth All-China Labor Congress. The Congress, attended by 504 delegates from both liberated and KMT-held areas, met in Harbin from August 1 to 22, 1948. The meeting had originally been scheduled as the All-Border Region Workers and Staff Members Representative Conference, the culmination of the lower-level representative conferences held in many localities during the spring and summer. Shortly before it convened, the name of the meeting was changed and its tasks expanded. The objective was to establish it more firmly within the tradition of the Chinese labor movement, which had reached its height during the 1920s when the first five congresses were held.[79]

In addition to passing a wide range of resolutions specifying the divergent tasks of the labor movement in the KMT areas and in those held by the Communists, the Congress reestablished the All-China General Labor Union. In 1922, the CCP had played a key role in initiating the Union. Now in 1948, the Sixth All-China Labor Congress passed a new set of regulations for the All-China General Labor Union and elected the members of the Union's new Executive Committee.[80]

The resolutions of the Congress, as they applied to the liberated areas, dealt with management as well as labor. The rules that were set down for the former will be discussed in the following section. With respect to labor, the Congress adopted a line similar in tone to the Party's decisions of February, 1948, on land reform. The tone seemed to represent a compromise between the manifestations of leftism that had occurred and the recent concerted attempts to overcome

78. "Cheng-ch'ueh chih-hsing lao tzu liang li fang-chen" [Correctly carry out the policy of benefiting both labor and capital], Sept. 21, 1948, in Hua-pei hsin hua shu-tien, ed., *Kuan-yü ch'eng-shih cheng-ts'e te chi-ko wen-hsien,* pp. 25-26; Ch'en Po-ta, p. 99 (see note 58 above); and "Ho-ying hsing-yuan pei-fu ch'ang" [The cooperatively managed Hsing-yuan bedding and uniforms factory], *Tung-pei jih-pao,* reprinted in Tung-pei shu-tien, ed., *Ts'an-k'ao tzu-liao,* pp. 40-42.

79. *I-chiu-szu-chiu-nien shou-ts'e,* p. chia 26. Li Li-san emphasized the importance of this tradition in his opening speech to the Congress, tracing the history of the first five congresses and of the Chinese labor movement. See Hua-pei tsung kung-hui ch'ou-pei wei-yuan-hui, ed., *Ti-liu tz'u ch'üan kuo lao ta chueh-i,* pp. 1-6.

80. "Chung-hua ch'üan kuo tsung kung-hui chang-ch'eng" [Regulations of the All-China General Labor Union], in Tung-pei shu-tien, ed., *Chih-kung wen-hsien,* 3:32-37; and "Chung-hua ch'üan kuo tsung kung-hui chih-hsing wei-yuan-hui chih-hsing wei-yuan ming-tan" [Name list of members of the executive committee of the All-China General Labor Union], in *ibid.,* pp. 45-50. Fifty-three regular members and twenty alternates were elected to the Executive Committee. Also see U.S. Cons., Peiping, Hsinhua radio, North Shensi, Sept. 5, 1948.

them. Many concrete issues remained unsolved and a number of the proposed solutions were admittedly tentative in nature. But the Congress did mark a plateau in the development of the Communists' orientation toward labor. The preliminary experiences of the 1945-47 period were behind them and the "errors of over-confidence" had been fully evaluated. The Party's labor policy settled on a more production-oriented course, geared toward achieving the full and final military victory now within sight.

The Resolutions. [81] The key theme running through the Congress resolutions was the need to sacrifice for the war effort and the victory of the revolution. Concerning work hours, the resolutions advocated an eight- to ten-hour work-day, with a maximum of twelve hours in special circumstances. A supplementary document, issued by the Executive Committee of the All-China General Labor Union in September, explained that these special circumstances included small enterprises with no means of reducing work time immediately to ten hours. It also included enterprises operating on a twenty-four-hour basis that would experience difficulty in switching at once to three shifts per day. The Committee recognized that conditions in various enterprises were dissimilar and that uniform regulations could not yet be stipulated. The Committee also asserted that there were too many holidays in the liberated areas and that enterprises should try to operate three hundred days or more per year. [82]

Concerning wages, the Congress resolutions stipulated that a worker's pay should normally be sufficient to maintain a basic standard of living for two perons. At the absolute minimum, wages must be sufficient to sustain one person in terms of food, clothing, shelter, and daily necessities. The method of remuneration should be one that encouraged labor enthusiasm, ideally a system of graduated and overlapping wage scales based on piece rates as well as time standards.

However, more emphasis was placed on graduated wage scales than on the piece rate system, apparently reflecting the difficulties encountered in trying to adopt it. By contrast with the earlier attitude which tended to view piece rates as the best of all possible solutions, the Congress resolutions stipulated that the piece rate system should be adopted only where it could spur production. Where lack of experience or the production process itself made the system impracticable, it should not be introduced. And unlike the Kalgan labor leader who had denounced the complex grading system used by the Japanese to divide the railway workers, the Executive Committee of the All-China General Labor Union now found the same type of system "worthy of investigation."[83]

---

81. "Kuan-yü chung-kuo chih-kung yun-tung tang-ch'ien jen-wu te chueh-i-an" [Resolutions concerning the present tasks of the Chinese labor movement], passed by the Sixth All-China Labor Congress, in Tung-pei shu-tien, ed., *Chih-kung wen-hsien,* 3:6-21; also in Mao Tse-tung, *et al., Hsin min-chu-chu-i kung-shang cheng-ts'e* (hereafter *Kung-shang cheng-ts'e*), pp. 69-86.

82. "Kuan-yü chih-kung yun-tung tang-ch'ien jen-wu chueh-i-an chung te wen-t'i te shuo-ming" [An explanation of questions concerning the resolutions on the present tasks of the labor movement], Sept., 1948, in Tung-pei shu-tien, ed., *Chih-kung wen-hsien,* 3:23-24.

83. *Ibid.,* pp. 26-27; and Hsiao Ming (see note 11 above). The Executive Committee suggested that large enterprises with many kinds of employees investigate the old graduated

The Congress condemned the principle of egalitarianism in the payment of wages. Erroneous practices, such as the fixing of uniform wage standards for dissimilar enterprises, for apprentices and experienced workers, and for manual and non-manual labor, were to be corrected. The Congress also condemned the use of such criteria as family background, political activism, and number of dependents, in determining a worker's wage level. The wages of technical and managerial personnel were to be determined on the basis of their competence, education, and past experience; those of craftsmen and artisans on the basis of their technical ability and experience; and those of manual laborers on the basis of the labor process itself as well as the seniority of the worker. Local governments in the various liberated areas were instructed to fix relatively uniform wage standards and rates for similar industries, after which each factory was to evaluate the actual wages of each of its employees.

In newly liberated areas, the basic wage levels of all employees in publicly-owned enterprises were to remain unchanged, with increases permitted only in the supplementary cost-of-living allowances. The pay of workers in handicraft industries, shop clerks, and agricultural laborers, was also to remain at pre-liberation levels. This stipulation was indicative of the change that had overtaken the Communists' labor policy since 1945, when basic wages for all workers were more than doubled immediately after the take-over of Kalgan.

The Congress acknowledged that inflation could not be avoided as long as the war continued. Under the circumstances, wages could not be continuously increased in order to keep pace with the rise in the cost of living—another objective which the Communists had initially pursued in Kalgan. Measures would be taken, however, to minimize the adverse effects of inflation on the workers' living standards. Where price fluctuations caused serious hardship, a supplementary cost-of-living allowance could be granted with a minimum of difference in the amount received by workers at various grades and levels of the pay scale. Second, wages might be paid partly in cash and partly in kind, but were to be calculated on the basis of the current prices of certain necessary items such as food and fuel. In addition, publicly-owned enterprises were instructed to experiment further with the program of providing daily necessities at low cost to their employees. The program might then be extended for the benefit of other workers.

Congress resolutions guaranteed equal pay for equal work to men, women, and children. Women were granted forty-five days paid leave for childbirth, plus fifteen days during the first three months after giving birth and thirty days thereafter. Apprentices had to be guaranteed adequate food and clothing; but they were not to participate in wage deliberations. New Year's bonuses, presents, and other such customs could be continued where they were deemed beneficial to production and technical progress.

The Congress also resolved that, because of the war, the liberated area governments could not yet guarantee employment and social security for every

---

wage system of the Peking-Hankow Railway. This divided ordinary workers into twenty-eight levels; skilled workers into three grades, with several levels for each grade; managerial and medical personnel into four grades and various levels; and technical personnel into five grades and various levels.

worker. The employer must therefore assume responsibility for the health and safety of his employees, although cities with large concentrations of industrial workers might initiate labor insurance programs. The Executive Committee of the General Labor Union later noted that the Congress had been unable to reach agreement as to how the issues of labor insurance and fringe benefits should be settled. The Executive Committee itself outlined three different methods for possible experimentation by individual localities, but the one labor insurance program that was introduced some months later differed from all three. Meanwhile, the government was to assume responsibility for aiding the unemployed.

Publicly-owned enterprises in particular were called upon to promote labor competition and model labor movements as a means of reducing costs and raising the quantity and quality of production.

After August, 1948, Chinese Communist labor policy continued to develop along the lines laid down at the Sixth Labor Congress. Cooperative stores were set up wherever possible to supply the needs of workers and government employees. One such consumer cooperative was established in Shenyang (Mukden) in early 1949. With branches in each of the city's districts, the cooperative was intended to supply daily necessities to over fifteen thousand municipal employees including teachers of middle and primary schools.[84] In May, preparations began for the establishment of consumer cooperatives to serve the workers of the city's textile and clothing factories. Stocks were to be provided by the local state stores set up after the liberation of Mukden the previous November. At the same time, about fifty thousand industrial workers in the city began receiving their wages half in cash and half in commodity coupons redeemable only at the workers' consumer cooperatives and the state-run stores.[85]

Emergence of the Soviet Model. There were reports of increasing numbers of "support-the-front" production campaigns, model labor campaigns, merit campaigns, and the like. A directive by the Northeast General Labor Union in mid-March, 1949, called on all public enterprises where operations had been restored to normal to begin production competitions. Winning groups and individuals would be honored at model labor meetings on Labor Day, and given honorary titles and cash prizes.[86]

The most widely-heralded development in the area of labor policy during this period was the institution of labor insurance in the Northeast. This was said to mean for the workers what land redistribution meant for the peasants.[87] Financed by the employer with a monthly contribution amounting to 3 percent of the total wage outlay, the insurance program was first introduced in seven

---

84. U.S. Cons., Peiping, Hsinhua radio, Peiping, Mar. 30, 1949.
85. U.S. Cons., Peiping, Hsinhua radio, Mukden, May 31 and June 3, 1949.
86. U.S. Cons., Peiping, Hsinhua radio, Peiping, Mar. 26, 1949; and Hsinhua radio, Mukden, June 6, 8, 20, 1949.
87. *Tung-pei jih-pao,* Dec. 31, 1948, editorial, reprinted in Tung-pei shu-tien, ed., *Chih-kung wen-hsien,* 4:41.

major industries and enterprises within the public sector: railways, mines, textiles, electricity, post and telegraph, munitions, and military provisions. The program provided benefits and compensation for workers and employees in the event of death, injury, illness, old age, and pregnancy. Any surplus in the individual enterprise insurance fund could be used for projects such as the expansion of medical and child-care facilities. The program also included a general insurance fund to be used by the Northeast General Labor Union for the construction and maintenance of workers' sanitoria, homes for the disabled, orphanages, and the like.[88]

A set of principles drawn up to guide union cadres in their propaganda work pointed out that, while the new program could not yet solve the difficulties of all the workers, it was the most the government could do in wartime. Moreover, it was indicative of the improvements that would be forthcoming once the entire country was liberated, the ultimate objective being a system of labor insurance as comprehensive as that of the Soviet Union. This was lauded as the most advanced in the world in that it had resolved all the material difficulties of the working class.[89]

No matter how carefully conceived and well-intentioned these programs were, the key to their success lay in the effectiveness with which they were implemented. Perhaps the most critical problem the Communists faced at this time was the scarcity of cadres with the experience and training necessary to work in the newly liberated cities.[90] The rectification campaign of 1947-48 was the Party's response to the deficiencies of cadres responsible for land reform. But no great input of new technical skills was necessary for the implementation of their tasks. In the cities, on the other hand, the problems created by inexperienced cadres, often of rural origin, were far more complex. Nor were they capable of immediate solution.[91]

By the end of 1948, a plan to augment the supply of cadres in the Northeast by transfers from north China had been abandoned. Instead, preparations were

88. "Tung-pei kung-ying ch'i-yeh chan-shih chan-hsing lao-tung pao-hsien t'iao-li" [Temporary wartime labor insurance regulations for public enterprises in the Northeast], Dec. 27, 1948, in *Chih-kung wen-hsien*, 4:3-12; and "Tung-pei kung-ying ch'i-yeh chan-shih chan-hsing lao-tung pao-hsien t'iao-li shih-hsing hsi-tse" [Details concerning implementation of the temporary wartime labor insurance regulations in public enterprises in the Northeast], Feb. 28, 1949, in *ibid.*, pp. 13-33. Also U.S. Cons., Peiping, Hsinhua radio, North Shensi, Feb. 12, 21, Mar. 18, 1949; and Hsinhua radio, Peiping, Mar. 27 and 31, 1949.

89. "Tung-pei kung-ying ch'i-yeh chan-shih chan-hsing lao-tung pao-hsien t'iao-li te tsung hsuan-ch'uan yuan-tse" [General propaganda principles of the temporary wartime labor insurance regulations in public enterprises in the Northeast], Jan. 1, 1949, in *Chih-kung wen-hsien*, 4:39; and *Tung-pei jih-pao*, Dec. 31, 1948, editorial reprinted in *ibid.*, p. 42. A supplement outlining the thirty-year history of social insurance in the U.S.S.R. was appended to and circulated with the basic labor insurance documents. This was from the November, 1947, issue of the Soviet journal, *Trade Union*, translated in *Chih-kung wen-hsien*, 4:46-54.

90. *Tung-pei jih-pao*, Nov. 9, 1948, editorial, reprinted in Tung-pei shu-tien, ed., *Hsin te jen-wu yü hsin te li-liang*, p. 1.

91. See notes 129-132 below.

under way to move cadres from the Northeast southward, where they were even more urgently needed for the take-over of newly liberated areas. In an attempt to cope with the crisis, new emphasis was placed on cadre recruiting and education. The Northeast Party Bureau issued a directive ordering that all *hsien* and district level cadres should, with a few exceptions, be new cadres. The same directive also stipulated that provincial, *hsien,* and municipal Party organizations undertake large scale development of Party schools, training classes, and other special schools in order to prepare large numbers of new cadres to assume increased responsibilities.[92]

On the labor front, specifically, the Northeast Party Bureau and the Northeast Administrative Commission issued a joint directive on February 20, 1949, that the development of class consciousness among the workers and the training of large numbers of working class cadres were major responsibilities of labor unions and Party organizations in all urban districts. The directive called for the establishment of workers' spare-time schools, technical training classes, recreation clubs, workers' libraries, and workers' political schools. By June, 2,130 workers were said to be enrolled in such classes in the city of Harbin alone.[93] In this area, too, Party leaders in the Northeast began looking to the Soviet Union as a model—presumably because their own experience was so limited.

Russian articles describing the Soviet Union's experience with union work were translated for use as reference materials to aid the new working class cadres. One volume, compiled by the Sino-Soviet Friendship Association in Harbin, described the work of a labor union cadre in the U.S.S.R.; explained how labor unions had contributed to the victory of the cultural revolution there and to the quality of the Soviet workers' lives; and outlined the importance of socialist emulation campaigns in fulfilling production plans and developing the Soviet economy. [94] Another pamphlet described the role and accomplishments of labor unions both in the Soviet Union and in the "new democratic" nations of Central Europe where unions were not only promoting the welfare of the working class but helping to build socialism. In this way, the Chinese cadre learned that China was embarked upon the same course as countries like Hungary, Rumania, and Czechoslovakia where the number of workers participating in labor emulation campaigns was said to be continuously on the increase, where working and living conditions were constantly improving, where social insurance programs had been instituted, and where workers received free medical treatment while their children could be properly cared for in nursery schools.[95]

BUSINESS, INDUSTRY, AND MANAGEMENT

Whatever doubts the workers may have had, businessmen and industrialists had many more. Their fears were based on the general antipathy of communism for

92. See note 90 above.
93. U.S. Cons., Peiping, Hsinhua radio, Mukden, June 6, 1949.
94. Ha-erh-pin chung su yu-hao hsieh-hui, ed., *Chih-kung ts'an-k'ao wen-hsien,* pp. 124.
95. *Hsin min-chu-chu-i kuo-chia te chih-kung-hui.*

private enterprise, and on certain actions and statements of the Chinese Communists in particular. First, Communist rule had already proved unhealthy for certain kinds of businessmen in the liberated areas due to the ban on trade in many types of non-essential consumer items. We have already noted the resentment this caused among merchants in and around the town of Hotse, Shantung, even though the Communists were trying to be "especially polite" to the business community there.[96]

Second, we have also noted that landlord-owned commercial and industrial properties in the countryside were regarded as part of the feudal economy during 1946-47. As such, they were expropriated and transformed into cooperative or government managed enterprises. Third, the Chinese Communists had not refrained—or at least were not able to ensure that their basic-level personnel refrained—from liquidating landlord-owned urban enterprises. Similarly, the Communists had not initially restrained the urban labor force from making extravagant demands upon employers, just as hired farm hands had initially demanded wage increases from landlord and rich peasant employers. These practices had occurred despite the distinction almost universally drawn in Party directives between the rural feudal economy and capitalist urban enterprise, and pledges of support for the latter.[97]

Unlike the middle peasant problem which seems to have been allowed to develop in the interests of promoting the mass land reform movement, available sources are even less suggestive concerning the reasons for the contradiction between policy and practice with respect to urban enterprise. Thus the contradiction may have been tolerated as a necessary expedient arising from the clash between political and economic goals at a time when the former were of crucial importance; or the contradiction may have represented a genuine mistake or failing on the part of local cadres. The serious shortage of cadres experienced in urban work makes it impossible to discount the second alternative. Yet the pattern of continuing radicalism on the labor front described in Chapter Nine, suggests that the first consideration must also have been at work.

Regardless of the reasons, however, the contradiction between announced policy and actual practice only compounded the misgivings of capitalists. The root cause, of course, lay within the Party's own assumptions about businessmen and industrialists, as indicated by the editor of a liberal Hong Kong journal:

> [B]usinessmen and industrialists also are an element of the Chinese people; they have duties and rights as citizens of the nation. But at present, some political theorists want to put businessmen and industrialists at opposite ends from the people. If one says he welcomes the cooperation of business and industry with the people . . . then it is as if the businessmen and industrialists were not the same as the people. This kind of concept also is arousing opposition in business circles.[98]

96. See Chapter Six.
97. See note 13 above.
98. *STPP*, Dec. 15, 1948, p. 1.

Well aware of this opposition, the Chinese Communists went to some lengths from the end of 1947 onwards in trying to mitigate it. The protection of business and industry, and cooperation with private enterprise, became corner-stones of the Party's urban policy as the military balance shifted ever more decisively in its favor.

The Anti-Leftist Campaign: Cooperation with Private Enterprise

One of their most original ideas was the greeting cards the Communists sent to business firms in Tientsin for lunar New Year, 1948. The cards read: "We wish you long life and prosperous business. If we should take the city in this new year, do not be alarmed. We shall restore order quickly and welcome your business." [99] Many in Tientsin, particularly in the foreign community, were amused at the bravado of peasant guerrillas who dared to speak in such a a manner.

During the spring and summer, directives and conference resolutions affirmed the seriousness of the Party's purpose. The tone throughout was consistent with two widely-circulated statements, one an excerpt from Mao's December 25, 1947, report, "The Present Situation and Our Tasks," and the other from Jen Pi-shih's January 12, 1948, talk, "Some Land Reform Problems." Mao empha-sized that "unduly advanced labor conditions, excessive income tax rates, encroachment on the interests of industrialists and merchants during the land reform" and other such ultra-left policies must not be allowed to occur again, as they had during the 1931-34 period. "Industrialists and merchants" he defined as "all small independent craftsmen and traders as well as all small and middle capitalist elements." [100]

Jen Pi-shih seemed to go further. His comments on the suicidal error of expropriating even small village traders were noted in Chapter Seven. Without making the usual distinction between urban and rural or capitalist and feudal enterprise, he went on to state that landlord and rich peasant business and industry should not be confiscated. Although he did not explicitly say so, the implication was that this injunction should be applied in the countryside as well as the cities. [101] Whether the Party actually began to encourage the continuation of landlord-owned commerce and industry at the village level is unclear. In at least one Border Region, the policy does seem to have been so changed at this time. [102] But in his February 27 intra-Party directive, Mao reiterated the urban-rural distinction, as had earlier directives, saying that, "Precautions should be taken against the mistake of applying in the cities the measures used in rural

99. Strong, *The Chinese Conquer China*, pp. 259-60.

100. *Selected Works*, 4:168; and Mao Tse-tung, *et al.*, *Kung-shang cheng-ts'e*, p. 5.

101. See Chapter Seven, note 164; and Mao Tse-tung, *et al.*, *Kung-shang cheng-ts'e*, pp. 7-9.

102. The directive against left adventurism issued by the Shansi-Hopei-Shantung-Honan Party Bureau in April, 1948, stipulated that all business and industry—including that owned by landlords and rich peasants, in both town and country—was to be protected and not subject to liquidation, confiscation, or distribution. See Chapter Seven, note 172; and Hinton, *Fanshen*, pp. 404-5.

areas for struggling against landlords and rich peasants. . . ." And Mao did not specify that village commerce and industry should actually remain under private landlord ownership.[103]

The line on capitalist commerce and industry in the cities, however, was clearly drawn: such enterprises were to be protected, and labor must abandon its preoccupation with its own immediate gains for the sake of overall economic production. The confiscation of urban commercial and industrial properties belonging to otherwise law-abiding landlords, such as had occurred in some *hsien* towns during the land reform movement, was contrary to the Party's policy and would not be allowed to continue. Only the village land of such persons could be confiscated. In cities and towns, only genuine war criminals, counter-revolutionaries, and bureaucratic capitalists were to be deprived of their holdings. And in these cases, peasants or other unauthorized persons were forbidden to seal factories and shops, this being the exclusive right of the municipal government. All such confiscated commercial and industrial establishments were to be managed cooperatively, run by the government, or sold. They were to continue regular operations wherever possible and were not to be dismantled or harmed in any way.[104]

Regulations also covered the management of business and industrial establishments whose owners "did not understand" the Party's policy and had fled to the KMT areas. The property rights of such refugees were to be guaranteed, and personnel were to be appointed by the government to manage their shops and factories. Operations were to continue, but the concerns would be returned to the owners should they choose to return. The liberated area governments broadcast messages of welcome to all businessmen and industrialists who wished to do so, and pledged full support for their lives and properties.[105]

Individual questions on business and industry were resolved at the North China [106] Liberated Area Conference on Business and Industry in mid-1948. Among the most important resolutions passed by the Conference were those concerning the relative positions of public and private enterprises; financial policy; and the relationship between capital and labor.[107] On the first issue, state ownership was to be concentrated in heavy industry, munitions, machine manufacturing, and production materials for important industries. The Confer-

103. "On the Policy Concerning Industry and Commerce," *Selected Works*, 4:203.

104. See, for example, regional directives in Ch'en Po-ta, *et al., Kung-shang-yeh; I-chiu-szu-chiu-nien shou-ts'e,* pp. *chia* 65-66; and the various military orders discussed in Chapter Nine.

105. U.S. Cons., Peiping, Hsinhua radio, North Shensi, Apr. 21, 1948.

106. The Chin-Ch'a-Chi and Chin-Chi-Lu-Yü Border Regions were joined, in the spring of 1948, to form the North China Liberated Area. A unified north China government was not formally established until some months later.

107. The Conference met from May 17-June 27, 1948, attended by 320 persons—including representatives of unions, public enterprise management, cooperatives, and 36 representatives of private enterprise. This outline of some of the key issues dealt with is based on: *Hsin kung-shang,* pp. 31-32, 105-12; Mao Tse-tung, *et al., Kung-shang cheng-ts'e,* pp. 55-62; *I-chiu-szu-chiu-nien shou-ts'e,* pp. *chia* 66-68; and U.S. Cons., Peiping, Hsinhua radio, North Shensi, Aug. 11, 15, 17, 1948.

ence was somewhat vague on commercial enterprises, noting that the function of publicly managed commerce was to serve production and the war effort by stabilizing the prices of essential commodities and their supply to consumers and producers. It was emphasized, moreover, that a public system of unified procurement and supply would serve those ends by ensuring that producers, both public and private, receive needed supplies of materials and equipment.

The Conference adopted a progressive taxation system with commercial and industrial taxes ranging from 5 percent to 25 percent of net profits. In Kalgan in 1946, almost all industrial enterprises had been at least temporarily exempted from taxation. The new resolutions stipulated that all profit-making industrial and commercial establishments, public or private, would be taxed at rates not to exceed 25 percent of net profits. Only rural handicraft industries, cooperatives, certain state-operated enterprises, enterprises deemed essential to the development of business and industry, and enterprises which had suffered major losses due to the war would be tax exempt. In general, industries would be taxed at lower rates than business, and some industrial enterprises would benefit from a tax incentive program to encourage the growth of certain key industries.

As for their military labor service *(chan ch'in),* businessmen and industrialists were granted the right to request permission to pay a military assistance fee in lieu of actual labor service. This entailed such duties as stretcher-bearing at the front, assistance with military transport, and the like. These basic principles concerning financial and military obligations to the state were reaffirmed at the North China Liberated Area Financial Conference in September, 1948.[108]

Concerning the relationship between labor and management, the Conference on Business and Industry outlined the same moderate labor policy soon to be formalized in the resolutions of the Sixth All-China Labor Conference.

The Chinese Communists liked to quote the statistics of industrial and commercial development in the cities of Manchuria as proof of the soundness and sincerity of their policies in these fields. Impressive growth statistics for commercial and industrial enterprises, both public and private, were cited for Harbin, Mutanchiang, and Antung, as well as cities and towns in other liberated areas.[109] The Communists' intentions toward business and industry were put to one of their sorest tests, however, when Kirin was captured in March, 1948. At the time, the population of Kirin was about 200,000. The city had a fairly well-developed industrial sector including some heavy industries as well as

108. The Conference met from Sept. 3-19, 1948. Conveners were Jung Tse-ho and Wu P'o, director and deputy director of the Financial Bureau of the North China People's Government. The approximately eighty participants included the heads of administrative bureaus and financial departments, and the director of the North China Tax Affairs Bureau. Resolutions passed concerned liquor and tobacco taxes, grain procurement, the military labor service system, revision of the progressive agricultural tax, and the collection of commercial and industrial taxes. A draft budget for the North China Liberated Area for 1949 was also drawn up. See "Hua-pei chieh-fang-ch'ü ts'ai-cheng hui-i t'ao-lun nung-kung-shang-yeh shui-tse" [The North China Liberated Area Financial Conference discusses agricultural, industrial, and commercial taxes], in *Hsin kung-shang,* pp. 33-34; and U.S. Cons., Peiping, Hsinhua radio, North Shensi, Oct. 14, 1948.

109. *I-chiu-szu-chiu-nien shou-ts'e,* pp. *chia* 68-69.

textiles. It contained a total of 3,632 factories, workshops, and commercial establishments. Virtually all of these had, for one reason or another, ceased operations by the time the Communists entered Kirin.

Close on the heels of the retreating Government forces, peasants from surrounding villages invaded the city and began seizing landlords who lived there, "liquidating accounts" with factory and shop owners, dismantling machinery, and looting shops. The disorders continued for a number of days before the full force of the Party's policy toward business and industry began to be effective.

Orders were issued to bring a halt to the looting, and the policies they were supposed to be implementing were reiterated at a large gathering of municipal administrative cadres. Once order was restored, more than ten different meetings were held with members of business and industrial circles. Here, too, the Party's policies were explained and the local capitalists invited to express their views. These meetings were said to be "very useful" in allaying the capitalists' fears. But at the same time, problems continued to arise between labor and management as a result of the workers' demands for wage increases.

In fact, the workers behaved generally as if the time for collecting the spoils of victory had arrived. Management apparently did not dare intervene. In one shoe factory, workers even dismantled some of the machinery and carried it off. Eventually, the government began sending around administrative and union personnel to meet with the workers and explain the Party's policies to them. The municipal government also acted as mediator and arbitrator in a number of individual disputes between labor and management.

In addition, the government sponsored a loan program to help business and industry resume operations. But the loans were granted mainly to certain high-priority enterprises such as the iron works, railways, textiles, the garment industry, and shoe manufacturers, the latter three being military supply industries. The new municipal government also assisted enterprises in obtaining necessary supplies such as coking coal, cotton, and lumber. By the end of April, it was reported that 92 percent of the commercial and industrial establishments in Kirin had reopened their doors for business.[110]

Stories such as this were not enough to allay the fears of the business community, of course. The campaign of reassurance continued, the words of the economist Hsu Ti-hsin being typical of this effort:

> Inside the country and in Hong Kong, our countrymen in business and industrial circles retain not a few doubts concerning the urban social reforms in the liberated areas. These doubts can be divided into three points. Firstly, they worry that the PLA is going to transfer rural land reform into the cities and apply it to business and industrial enterprises; secondly, they worry that after liberation, the workers will oppress the owners; and thirdly, they worry that once it is established, the new democratic government will not be hospitable to private enterprise.

110. "Chi-lin hui-fu ho fa-chan szu-ying kung-shang-yeh te chi-ko wen-t'i" [Some questions about the restoration and development of private industry and commerce in Kirin], *Tung-pei jih-pao*, reprinted in Tung-pei shu-tien, ed., *Ts'an-k'ao tzu-liao*, pp. 44-48.

Hsu reiterated the Party's reassurances on each point. On the third item which questioned whether the protection of private enterprise was but a temporary gesture, Hsu acknowledged that this doubt was widespread and did his best to dispel it. China's area was great, its population large, its economy backward. Hence the necessity of developing production and the economy in the shortest possible time. If we abandon the general policy of the New Democratic revolution and deny private capital the right to exist, he wrote, we will surely fail.[111]

It is true, wrote Li Li-san a year later, that we do advocate communism. But a long time must pass before we can realize it because our level of economic development is so low. In this respect, he continued reassuringly, our situation is not like that of Russia at the time of the October Revolution or of the East European countries. It would be impossible for China to begin to move directly toward socialism as they were doing, or to carry out a socialist revolution as Russia had done.[112]

Another effort at reassurance was made by the *Hua shang pao* of Hong Kong, which published the first regulations to reach the British Colony issued by the liberated areas on import-export trade. These were the Shantung Liberated Area Provisional Methods for Managing Import-Export Trade, as well as a set of regulations dealing with customs duties. Hong Kong businessmen were interested in establishing trading ties with the areas under Communist control, but were uncertain of how to proceed or what to expect. Nor did the first regulations dispel their misgivings. Toward that end, the *Hua shang pao* also published in early 1949 answers to a series of questions found to be most current among local businessmen.

The paper's correspondent explained that the underlying goals on which the Communists' foreign trade policy would be based were the development of agriculture and industry and the support of the war until complete victory had been achieved. Foreign trade would therefore be managed so as to encourage the import of essential goods and to discourage the import of luxuries and goods produced in the liberated areas themselves. These principles were virtually identical to those which had previously guided the individual Border Regions in their "import-export" trade with the KMT areas. As for public trading organizations, they would control the import and export of five vital commodities: rice, cotton, oil, pig bristles, and gold. Trade in all other commodities would be left to private enterprise.[113]

All trade, however, was to be based on the principle of strict equality between imports and exports. The Chinese Communists went to extreme lengths

111. Hsu Ti-hsin, "Lun ch'eng-shih te she-hui kai-ko" [On social reform in the cities], Aug. 9, 1948, in his *Chung-kuo ching-chi te tao-lu*, pp. 307-9.

112. Li Li-san, "Kuan-yü fa-chan sheng-ch'an lao tzu liang li cheng-ts'e te chi-tien shuo-ming" [Explanation of a few points concerning the policy of developing production and benefiting both labor and capital], Liu Shao-ch'i, ed., *Hsin min-chu-chu-i ch'eng-shih cheng-ts'e* (hereafter *Ch'eng-shih cheng-ts'e*), p. 13.

113. Hua shang pao tzu-liao shih, ed., *Chieh-fang-ch'ü mao-i hsü chih*, pp. 36-43. The early external trade regulations of the Shantung and north China liberated areas were also reprinted in *Hsin kung-shang*, pp. 36-83.

in this respect, so intent were they on avoiding unfavorable trade balances such as the KMT Government had built up. This determination, compounded by a lack of experience in foreign trade, led them to stipulate that importers of foreign goods and materials were responsible for exporting goods and materials of an equal value. The result was a sort of barter system which proved so inconvenient that it soon had to be abandoned, although the principle of maintaining a strict trade balance was not.

The Chinese Communists were never so inexperienced in the fields of trade and finance, or so eager for the support of the business community, as to abandon their own economic self-interest. This they viewed in terms of the strategy of self-sufficiency developed during the years of economic isolation in the Border Regions. Their single-mindedness in this regard was always apparent, which helps to explain why all of their efforts to mollify private enterprise were never entirely successful. The editor of *Shih-tai p'i-p'ing* probably summed up the feeling of the business community as accurately as any when he wrote, in December 1948: "Hopefully, the new political regime will not be as bad for the capitalists as Chiang Ching-kuo has been. But we should not forget that most of China's businessmen . . . are afraid that future changes will only be worse."[114]

Industrial Management: the Challenge of Public Enterprise

Another area in which the Chinese Communists were anxious to overcome their acknowledged lack of experience was that of industrial management. This deficiency was the more serious because of their desire to develop certain key industries within the public sector. Thus one additional task of the North China Liberated Area Industrial and Commercial Conference was the formulation of a Draft on Economic Discipline in Publicly-Owned Factories. A statement on industrial management by Po I-po at the Conference was indicative of the key debate developing within the Party at this time. As if paraphrasing Lenin's famous comment on the same subject,[115] Po declared: "Our economic workers should study management and moreover must study all of the scientific and rational features of the capitalists in their management of enterprise; this work of learning rapidly about management is one of the most important of our Party's tasks at the present time."[116]

Among the problems that most disturbed Party leaders in the summer of 1948, was the "anarchical and undisciplined state of affairs" in many units,

114. *STPP*, Dec. 15, 1948, p. 1.
115. Lenin, with specific reference to the Taylor system, wrote: "The possibility of building socialism depends exactly upon our success in combining the Soviet power and the Soviet organization of administration with the up-to-date achievements of capitalism." See V. I. Lenin, "The Immediate Tasks of the Soviet Government," April, 1918, in *Collected Works* (Moscow: Progress Publishers, 1965), 27:259. The Taylor system, developed by Frederick W. Taylor, gained international renown in the early decades of the twentieth century as the epitome of scientific efficiency in the organization of work—with little regard for the human element contained therein.
116. Quoted in *Hsin kung-shang*, p. 109.

resulting in the waste of manpower, materials, and financial resources. A second serious problem was irrational organization and work-style.

One example of waste was that of a coal mining company which opened up a new coal shaft without first calling in the mining engineers to conduct a preliminary survey. Only after the shaft had been opened and over 300,000 *yuan* invested, was it discovered that the vein of coal was very thin and that the new shaft had little potential. Similarly, in the Chin-Chi-Lu-Yü Border Region the army built several air raid shelters without consulting construction engineers. As a result, the shelters all collapsed, wasting an investment of some 400,000 to 500,000 *yuan.*

Examples of irrational organization and work style abounded. There were often too many non-productive personnel on factory payrolls; industrial cadres were chosen and promoted on the basis of their political activism, family backgrounds, and seniority rather than technical competence; little effort was made to calculate costs nor was much attention paid to the relation between profits and losses; the objective pursued was often not the development of production but the provision of assistance and relief for the workers.

The resolutions of the North China Industrial and Commercial Conference were explicit in their intent to correct these shortcomings. Industrial projects were not to be undertaken without the approval of higher levels of authority and detailed investigation, research, and planning by competent technical personnel. In addition, all industrial enterprises were called upon to rationalize their operations.[117]

Similar goals for industrial management were formulated by the Sixth All-China Labor Congress two months later. The principle of rationalization as outlined by the Congress entailed drawing up a detailed plan of the production process in each enterprise, from the input of raw materials to the distribution of the finished product. It also entailed the adoption of specific standards for personnel management; the implementation of an inspection system in each factory to guarantee production standards as well as reasonable working conditions; and the adoption of a system of strict individual responsibility requiring each worker to assume personal responsibility for assigned work tasks.[118]

The system of individual responsibility, in particular, was a key feature of industrial management in the U.S.S.R. but was an innovation within the Chinese labor force, where collective responsibility was more familiar. The new responsibility system was first introduced into the administration of the Manchurian railways in 1948. The Manchurian railway system (or, the Chinese Changchun Railway) was one of the few areas where the Russians had a direct presence in China after the withdrawal of the Soviet Army from Manchuria in 1946.[119]

---

117. *Ibid.,* pp. 107-9. The Chinese term translated here as "rationalize" is *ch'i-yeh-hua.* It is also sometimes translated: "to be more businesslike."

118. See note 81 above.

119. This Soviet presence resulted from the August, 1945, Sino-Soviet Treaty of Friendship and Alliance and a series of supplemental agreements. The Changchun Railway Agreement put the Chinese Eastern and South Manchurian railways under Soviet-Chinese

Experiments with the responsibility system were first carried out among railway personnel based in the city of Mutanchiang. On the basis of this experience, the Party committee concerned with railway affairs in the Northeast issued a resolution directing that the responsibility system be adopted by all railway engineers in the Northeast. Previously they had worked in rotating crews, as was the practice everywhere except the U.S.S.R., with no one crew responsible for any particular locomotive. This practice was abolished and replaced by the responsibility system which assigned two or three crews to a locomotive and held them responsible for its operation.[120]

Po I-po's comments aside, the debate was apparently still in progress at this time as to whether the U.S.S.R. or the advanced capitalist nations of the West should be taken as the model in the field of industrial management. Addressing itself to this debate, the Party railway committee in the Northeast suggested that the railway management experience of the capitalist nations could supply reference materials useful in understanding their defects and good points. But the committee concluded that the experience of the U.S.S.R. should be adopted as the primary model for the new China since the Soviet Union had already evaluated and absorbed everything of value from the management experience of the capitalist nations.[121]

Whatever the model adopted, the rationalization of industry was a major undertaking that would take months and years of concentrated effort to accomplish. Administrators in Harbin readily acknowledged their difficulties. Scientific management in industry is a new thing for us, commented the *Tung-pei jih-pao* in the summer of 1948. The paper noted that progress had been made in the railway administration, but that the industrial affairs section of the municipal government still had many problems to overcome in estimating costs, allocating resources, and maintaining standards for manufactured goods. The structure of

joint ownership, stipulating that a Soviet citizen was to be manager of the joint system (also known as the Chinese Changchun Railway). See Robert C. North, *Moscow and the Chinese Communists*, pp. 219-20.

120. For a discussion of the Chinese experience with the responsibility system in the early 1950s, and its ultimate rejection, see Schurmann, *Ideology and Organization,* pp. 242-53.

121. "Hsin min-chu kuo-ying ch'i-yeh ying hsueh-hsi su-lien te ching-yen" [New democratic national enterprises should study the experience of the Soviet Union], in Hua-pei tsung kung-hui ch'ou-pei wei-yuan-hue, ed., *Ti-liu tz'u ch'üan kuo lao ta chueh-i,* pp. 58-60. The nature and extent of Soviet involvement in Manchuria after 1946 remain to be studied. It is generally accepted, as Anna Louise Strong emphasized after her journey through the Communist areas in 1946-47, that there were no official links between the two Communist Parties and that the Soviets did not provide military assistance to the Chinese. But the presence of Soviet personnel in the Manchurian railway administration, the organization of the Sino-Soviet Friendship Association in Harbin, and the publication of a number of Soviet writings in Chinese translation as the Chinese Communists set about learning from the Soviet experience in labor and management, suggest links of some sort. In 1948, the Chinese Changchun Railway also established the Harbin Industrial College, an institution of higher learning devoted to the training of engineering personnel. The College offered degrees in architectural engineering, transportation, electrical engineering, civil engineering, and economics. See U.S. Cons., Peiping, Hsinhua radio, North Shensi, Aug. 16, 1948.

research, investigation, and planning was still only in the first stages of development.[122] The following November, an editorial in the same paper noted that
after the Sixth All-China Labor Congress in August, many publicly-managed
enterprises in northern Manchuria had taken the first steps toward rationalizing
managerial procedures. But genuine and complete rationalization had yet to be
achieved in even one industrial enterprise.[123]

The same editorial also pointed out that publicly-run factories in Manchuria
were not yet paying enough attention to democratic management. According to
the resolutions of the Sixth All-China Labor Congress, factories were to form
management committees made up of the head of the factory, top level technical
personnel, other responsible persons in the factory and its union, and representatives elected by rank and file union members. The head of the factory was to be
chairman of its management committee. Its function was to make the major
decisions related to factory management. If the committee found the directives
issued by the higher levels of public management within the government to be
inappropriate, the chairman had the right to report the committee's resolutions
upward and request additional instructions.

In addition, large factories with five hundred or more workers were to form
factory representative committees made up of representatives of the various
kinds of workers and apprentices in the factory. Under the leadership of the
factory management committee, the representative committee was to propagandize factory decisions and production plans, summarize experience, and
gather the suggestions and criticisms of the workers. But in 1948, industrial
democracy, like scientific management, remained goals for the future rather than
accomplishments of the present.

FROM THE COUNTRYSIDE TO THE CITIES:
THE CCP IN 1949

Such was the background of the Party's experience with urban work when the
second session of the Seventh Central Committee issued its resolution declaring
the Party's shift from the countryside to the cities. In March, 1949, the Chinese
Communists had behind them not quite four years' direct experience with urban
management, limited primarily to Kalgan, Harbin, and a few other medium-sized
cities in Manchuria.

During that time, however, Chinese Communist thinking on urban problems
had overcome many of the idealistic impulses characteristic of newly-empowered
leftist parties, and some additional ones besides. In the first flush of their
enthusiasm to solve the problems of urban China as manifested in the city of
Kalgan, the Communists made commitments both to labor and management that
they soon found necessary to repudiate. The inflationary practice of increasing
all wages, adopted immediately after the take-over of Kalgan in 1945, was set
aside by mid-1948. Also set aside were efforts to keep wage increases parallel

122. Reprinted in Tung-pei shu-tien, ed., *Ts'an-k'ao tzu-liao,* pp. 49-50.
123. Reprinted in Tung-pei shu-tien, ed., *Chih-kung wen-hsien,* 3:3.

with the rise in the cost of living, and to provide workers with a maximum amount of benefits in an attempt to resolve their material difficulties. Other examples of the "over-confidence" displayed in Kalgan were the adoption in principle of the eight-hour work day, the expansion of the public sector, and the generous tax incentive program for public and private enterprise.

Also evident during the Communists' year in Kalgan, were labor emulation campaigns; the use of piece rates and material incentives to increase individual output; the practice of increasing work hours in order to complete essential tasks; attempts to hold the line on some of labor's demands; emphasis on labor discipline; and efforts to encourage private investment.

All these latter measures were indicative of the direction Chinese Communist urban policy would more resolutely assume in 1947-48. That direction began to take shape during the last half of 1947, with the advent of the campaign against left adventurism. At this time, the Party's orientation toward business, industry, and labor, shifted explicitly toward maximizing production for the war effort and economic reconstruction. The new line emphasized cooperation with private capital and the rationalization of management in public enterprise. The practice of remunerating labor according to need or political criteria was officially put aside in favor of wage differentials based on skill, seniority, and effort. The goal of resolving the material difficulties of the working class was not abandoned but deferred, being limited in the immediate present to certain basic guarantees and to minimizing the effects of inflation on the workers' living standards. Meanwhile, the promise of future gratification was symbolized by the experimental labor insurance program for public enterprise workers, introduced in Manchuria early in 1949.

Although similar in timing and in form, the urban and rural manifestations of the anti-leftist campaign were quite different in their respective functions. In the countryside, the anti-leftist campaign marked the culmination of a genuine mass movement that had destroyed the existing rural elite both politically and economically and equalized land ownership. This was not the case in the cities, where the anti-leftist campaign of 1948 signaled a new departure for the Chinese Communists. Urban policy became at that time a major and qualitatively different preoccupation, rather than a mere extension of the land reform movement as it had been until then. In the cities, the anti-leftist campaign was imposed in order to safeguard at least temporarily the position of the capitalist exploiter against the demands of a relatively advanced labor movement. The resistance of the workers to the Party's urban policy in its anti-leftist phase was reflected in the radicalism, described in Chapter Nine, that continued on the labor front during the first months after the liberation of China's major cities.

Thus, in mid-1949, Li Li-san admitted that some workers still had doubts about the principle of benefiting both capital and labor. They wondered why the Party gave top priority to the development of production and relegated the improvement of the workers' lives to second place. More to the point, they wondered why the Party was not distributing the property of capitalists to the workers in the same way that it was distributing the landlords' property in the countryside to the peasants. Second, since the capitalists relied on the exploitation of labor to make their profits, some workers questioned why they should produce more when it only meant more profits for the capitalists and therefore greater scope for exploitation.

To the first question, Li answered that it was possible to divide up and distribute land and still achieve increases in agricultural production. But when factories and shops and the equipment and stocks they contained, were distributed to the workers as had been done in some places, the results were quite different. Production and business came to a halt and the workers lost their jobs as well. The distribution of urban property served the interests neither of production nor of the workers.

Responding to their second question, Li argued that in the past the workers had actually been subjected to exploitation from three different sources, namely, imperialism and bureaucratic capitalism, private enterprise, and the backwardness of China's industry. The imperialists and bureaucratic capitalists were now defeated. Exploitation by private enterprise was being curbed by government laws protecting the interests of the workers. Eventually, this form of exploitation, too, would be completely eliminated. Only the extreme backwardness of the economy remained; and nationalized capital alone was still too weak to assume the entire task of developing industrial production. Hence the necessity not only of using private capital, but of mobilizing as much of it as possible for investment in productive enterprise. Under the circumstances, private capitalists would have to be allowed to earn their profits; but the national livelihood would benefit and so would the working class.[124]

The anti-leftist campaign in the cities also presaged a reordering of developmental priorities. In 1945-46, the production goals of Kalgan's economy still reflected the predominantly rural orientation of the Party. The goals were part of the larger Border Region production plan which emphasized agriculture over industry and light over heavy industry. By 1949, the historic redefinition of the Party's tasks signaled the emergence of a new strategy of economic development emphasizing heavy industry over light industry and agriculture.

Originally Marxism-Leninism had taught that the proletarian revolution entailed first the occupation of key cities and with them the political power of the nation. Afterwards, the revolutionary forces could enter the countryside, lead and organize the peasants, and set up a worker-peasant alliance. But working within the particular Chinese context, "Marxism-Leninism's best student," Mao Tse-tung, had created a revolutionary strategy which turned to the countryside and used it to encircle the cities. The strategy had been necessary because the strength of the enemy in the cities was great and the armed forces of the revolution weak. If the Chinese Communists had clung mechanically to the cities, they could not have gathered enough strength to defeat the enemy.

Then why turn to the city and use it to lead the countryside, some critics asked, questioning the sudden reorientation of the Party's work. Because, came the reply, the revolutionary forces were now powerful enough to seize even the

124. Li Li-san, pp. 9-12 (see note 112 above).

urban bases of the enemy. And because, also, the enemy's urban bases represented the most advanced sector of the Chinese economy while the CCP's primary goal was to build a modern industrial nation.[125]

The Party's rural base may have been the necessary ingredient of its victory, but without the cities the victory was not complete. The countryside was used to surround the cities, but in dialectical fashion the cities were needed in turn to penetrate the countryside and consolidate the victory that had originated there. When Mao Tse-tung arrived in Peiping on March 25, 1949, the move symbolized not merely the Communists' occupation of the nation's northern capital, but the reemergence of the CCP as an urban-based party. After more than twenty years, the CCP intended to resume its role as leader of the urban proletariat.

For the benefit of those who found this new course difficult to grasp all at once, the leadership function of the cities was outlined in some detail. It meant the city providing the countryside with a scientific revolutionary spirit. It meant the leadership of the working class and not of the urban populace as a whole. It meant that the workers with their class consciousness, collectivist concepts, organization, discipline, and scientific farsightedness, would lead the peasants and help them to overcome their backwardness and conservatism. It meant that industry would lead agriculture in the direction of mechanized production and scientific management, providing the technological and material basis for modernization, collectivization, and ultimately for the progression to socialism. What the new relationship between town and country did *not* mean was the "charming but useless" objective of "developing rural handicraft industry and urbanizing the countryside" while "planting flower gardens in the cities and rural-izing the towns."[126]

For all of these reasons, industrial construction was identified as the heart of the Party's urban work—the new core task. According to Mao's report to the second session of the Seventh Central Committee, the primary focus of city work henceforth would be the restoration and development of production, especially industrial production, with emphasis on public enterprise, private enterprise, and handicraft production, in that order. All other urban tasks such as the construction of political power, Party organization work, union organizing, mass organizing, security, culture, education, and propaganda, were to center around the core task of developing industrial production. Toward that end, Mao called on all Party members to exert the greatest possible effort in learning the techniques and methods of industrial production and management, as well as those of business and banking.[127]

Given this new orientation and their own inexperience, the Chinese Communists turned increasingly toward the Soviet Union for guidance despite the acknowledged differences between them in terms of revolutionary strategy and level of economic development. The Soviet experience thus provided models for

125. Yang K'uei-chang, *Ch'eng hsiang kuan-hsi wen-t'i,* pp. 16-18.
126. *Ibid.,* pp. 13, 37-38.
127. Mao Tse-tung, *Selected Works,* 4:364-65; U.S. Cons., Peiping, Hsinhua radio, North Shensi, Mar. 24, 1949; and Liu Shao-ch'i, ed., *Ch'eng-shih cheng-ts'e,* pp. 3-4.

the early Chinese efforts to develop scientific management and planning, the responsibility system in industrial management, methods of labor remuneration, the labor insurance program, the labor emulation campaigns, labor union work, and ultimately the strategy of economic investment which placed primary emphasis on heavy industry.

In Manchuria, a region fully liberated by the end of 1948, Party leaders outlined their concrete tasks for 1949 on the basis of the new orientation. Industrial construction required, first, the formulation of a general economic plan emphasizing certain keypoints. In the Northeast, this meant the immediate restoration of heavy industry, especially iron and steel, machine manufacturing, and electricity. It meant also the related development of railway transport, agricultural production, finance, and trade. In order to formulate and implement such a plan, all Party members were advised to strengthen their understanding of such concepts as administrative coordination, keypoints, the part serving the whole, and the backward serving the advanced.

Second, the Party was to become the propagandist for the construction plan, educating cadres and masses concerning the new economic tasks, criticizing erroneous thoughts, overcoming doubts, and studying the past thirty-year experience of the U.S.S.R. Party members were asked to remember that the labor movement, youth work, the mass organizations, et cetera, all must serve the central task of economic construction.

Third, the Party must pay more attention to the workers themselves, in order to ensure that they received a fair wage and did not suffer undue hardships from inflation. But this labor movement work must not be allowed to interfere with economic construction and the fulfillment of the production plan. Adequate numbers of cadres must be prepared to undertake union and Party organization work among the labor force, and to lead the factory management and workers' representative committees in promoting the rationalization and democratization of management.

Finally, local Party organs were instructed to set up supply and purchasing cooperatives in the countryside. These cooperatives were described as the best structure for uniting the urban nationalized economy and the rural small producer, within the framework of the city leading the countryside. They were intended to supply necessities such as cloth, salt, oil, and fuel to the rural areas, and to purchase their agricultural products in return.[128]

Perhaps the greatest problem, however, continued to be the scarcity of cadres experienced in city work and capable of implementing the Party's urban policies. This lay at the heart of the "undisciplined" and "irrational" behavior condemned in conference resolutions during the summer of 1948. Official statements decried the cadres' rural guerrilla mentality and their propensity to transplant village work styles into an urban environment. According to the above

128. *Ju-ho kuan-ch'e tung-pei ch'üan tang te chuan-pien?*, pp. 4-9.

outline of its work in the Northeast, the Party there was successfully embarked upon the move from the countryside to the cities in terms of leadership and thought. But the changeover was neither complete nor had it been done very well. Commented another writer:

> Now that we are moving from the countryside into the cities, the greatest difficulty is the backward, conservative, agrarian socialist thought of some people who have worked for a long time in the countryside. They are saturated with peasant consciousness and unable to comprehend the great leadership function that the cities can perform for the revolutionary enterprise. . . . Most of these people are accustomed to the methods of handicraft industry, and with their narrow guerrilla experience, they have no means of grasping city work in a systematic way.[129]

Some cadres, accustomed to the hard work and austerity of rural living, were easily corrupted after moving into an urban environment. But the main difficulty was the lack of knowledge concerning the management of a modern city's economy and especially of its industrial sector. Cadres and Party members lacked the ability to plan and to work systematically. They could not grasp the concept of a city as a concentrated and unified whole. Their work was fragmented, uncoordinated, and decentralized, as it had been in the villages. Production in many a plant and factory was disrupted before these deficiencies could be remedied. For example, one leading cadre in the Peikuan district of Shenyang ordered the closure of a textile mill due to a temporary lack of cotton yarn. The premises were then used for making bean curd and parking rickshaws. Such improvisation may have been an essential ingredient for survival in the rural areas during wartime, but was hardly conducive to the long-term development of major urban industries.

Another case was that of Chang Jih-hsin, head of a Shenyang copper foundry capable of turning out several thousand tons of copper per year. Comrade Chang had little technical knowledge and stopped routine repairs on the plant's smelters, declaring them to be in working order. The two main smelters subsequently broke down and the work of the entire foundry came to a halt, after which he sent in a simple report to the Department of Industry without even making an investigation.[130]

In Sian, industrial work cadres, fearful that handicraft workers might lose their jobs, refused to allow certain mechanized industries to resume operations after the Communist take-over of the city. In a number of places, cadres refused to let women work in factories and diverted large quantities of cotton for their use at home working on hand-operated spindles. As a consequence, many spinning mills were unable to operate at full capacity due to the lack of cotton. In the Northeast, union leaders even had to issue a special directive on collecting dues. The cadres, until recently preoccupied with rural work, did not seem to

129. Yang K'uei-chang, pp. 35-36 (see note 125 above).
130. *Ju-ho kuan-ch'e,* pp. 2-4.

understand the importance of collecting dues, much less of issuing receipts and keeping accounts.[131]

Cadres in the cities of Harbin, Kirin, and Antung, were also criticized for having fragmented urban political power by concentrating their main organizing and educational efforts at the street level.[132] Initially, cities in the liberated areas were governed by a three-tiered administrative structure at the municipal, district, and street levels. On June 22, 1949, this system was formally abolished in Tientsin and denounced as an erroneous method of municipal administration. A Hsinhua editorial condemned it as an attempt to transfer forms of rural political power—the *hsien, ch'ü,* and *ts'un* level governments—into the city. In the rural areas, the economy and population were decentralized and dispersed, not concentrated as in the cities. Urban factories, banks, schools, and other organizations could not be managed effectively by district and street governments. This fragmentation of political power was responsible for the "anarchical situation" in many cities, making it impossible for the municipal government's policies to be implemented. Henceforth, the editorial asserted, municipal decision-making powers should rest solely with the city government, and policies should be carried out directly by its various work departments.[133]

In Tientsin, the announcement abolishing the *ch'ü* and street level political units was made at a conference attended by 560 municipal, district, and street cadres. The secretary of the municipal government criticized them for their lack of discipline. He also deplored the redundancy in political work that had developed at the district and street levels. With the abolition of these political units, all of their work including education, propaganda, culture, organizing, public health, security, household registration, and the management of business, industry, and cooperatives, was centralized in the various bureaus of the municipal government.[134]

A second type of problem also became evident soon after the official change of emphasis from village to urban work had been announced. This announcement had apparently inspired the feeling among rural Party leaders and cadres—many of the latter, it must be added, were by this time intellectual youth

131. Tung-pei chih-kung tsung hui, "Kuan-yü kung-hui fei te chueh-i" [Resolution on union dues], Jan. 9, 1949, in Hua-pei tsung kung-hui ch'ou-pei wei-yuan-hui, ed., *Ti-liu tz'u ch'üan kuo lao ta chueh-i*, pp. 55-57. Members were to contribute 1 percent of total monthly income as dues.

132. *Ju-ho kuan-ch'e*, p. 2.

133. "Pa wo-men tsai ch'eng-shih chung te tsu-chih hsing-shih ho kung-tso fang-shih shih-ying ch'eng-shih te t'e-tien" [Make the form and manner of our organization and work in the cities conform to the characteristics of the cities], June 22, 1949, in Liu Shao-ch'i, ed., *Ch'eng-shih cheng-ts'e*, pp. 47-48.

134. Hsin hua she, "T'ien-chin shih jen-min cheng-fu hsuan-pu pien-keng ch'ü chieh tsu-chih hsing-shih" [The Tientsin Municipal People's Government announces a change in the form of district and street organization], June 22, 1949, in *ibid.*, pp. 49-50. A *ch'ü* office in each district, with a staff of seven or eight, was to assist in implementing the decisions of the city government, and report on local conditions. Branches of the municipal public security bureau in each district, and under them 272 precinct offices of the city police, were to maintain public order and carry out resident registration.

recruited from northern cities [135]—that there was no longer any need to do rural work. Suddenly everyone wanted to go to or remain in the towns and cities. In some cases, even when the town had little industry and was otherwise of minimal significance, large numbers of cadres congregated within it while the surrounding villages continued to suffer the depredations of bandits, landlord remnants, and other trouble-makers.

This problem had become an object of some concern by the time Lin Piao's armies reached central China. Local Party leaders there had to be reminded that the countryside must first be thoroughly reformed before the city could lead the villages. In the Northeast and in north China, land reform had already been accomplished and the people's government established throughout the rural areas creating the preconditions for the Party's shift to the cities. Elsewhere, these tasks had not yet been completed and in such places, local Party organs were not to turn their backs on the countryside. This was the argument Lin Piao used in his "Report on the Future Work of the Central China Bureau." He declared that the core of the Party's work in the region was still in the villages. "All of the Party's organization, propaganda, education, and government work must be centered around this core," he wrote. "The Party's intention is not to remain in the cities, but to face the villages resolutely."[136]

Nevertheless, by 1949, the Chinese Communists had begun moving successfully against some of China's most basic urban problems—despite the handicap of inexperience in the fields of urban administration and industrial management. Unlike the Nanking Government, the Communists were developing a reasonably effective strategy toward labor based in part on models provided by the Soviet Union. The strategy relied on social, normative, and material incentives to increase worker productivity. It included concrete measures designed to guarantee a basic level of economic security for the labor force but denied demands which would seriously interfere with production and economic growth. This labor policy was also an important feature of the campaign to dispel the reservations of private entrepreneurs, whose experience and capital the Chinese Communists also sought to utilize. This particular effort was never entirely successful. But by early 1950, Kao Kang could point with pride to the accomplishments of the Party during its first full year in Manchuria.

According to Kao Kang, plans for all publicly-managed enterprises had been drawn up. The plans for those designated as keypoints of industrial development had all been overfulfilled—although production in these industries was on the average still only about one-third what it had been under Japanese rule in 1943. These industries were iron, steel, copper, coal, electricity, and machine manufacturing. The plan for the development of railway transport had also been fulfilled, although those for agriculture and some light industries such as cotton spinning, weaving, and paper manufacture had not.

Private enterprises were also reviving. Kao claimed that in Shenyang between June and December, 1949, the number of private industrial establishments had

135. See Chapter Nine.
136. Quoted by Yang K'uei-chang, pp. 20-22 (see note 125 above).

increased by 23 percent and the number of workers employed by 18 percent. In 1948, prices in the Communist-held areas of the Northeast rose by eight times, but in 1949, the general price level rose only 80 percent. The real value of wages had risen due to the stabilization of prices and the institution of labor insurance and medical benefits for workers. The peasants' burdens were also lightened. In 1948, the Communist government had requisitioned 23 percent of the total agricultural output, but in 1949 the figure was down to 20 percent.

Kao summarized the significance of these achievements in the following terms:

> The past year has proven that our Party is not only good at activating the masses to carry out land reform and revolutionary war . . . but can also lead the people to construct a new China and to manage well the work of economic construction. This work has only just begun but it is a reality and this is a good start. This modernization and economic construction is for us a completely new and difficult thing. In the past year, the heart of our Party's work has shifted from war and land reform to economic construction; our Party has raised up and sent out thousands of cadres to participate directly in the work of economic construction. The cadres have book knowledge about the management of the economy and of cities and now they are learning directly. They are now at the first stage of understanding the things they did not understand before; and the things they could not do in the past they are now beginning to be able to do. Just as in the past we learned about land reform and fighting war, now in the same way the new work of economic construction can also be studied and learned.[137]

Many components of the Party's urban policy in 1949 would be abandoned or modified in the years that followed, as symbolized most strikingly by its break with the Soviet Union. But the fundamental concept of "the cities leading the countryside" would not be seriously challenged until the 1960s. During the Cultural Revolution, Liu Shao-ch'i would be accused, among other things, of having advocated a course that favored the cities and neglected the countryside. In the post-Cultural Revolution atmosphere of opposition to the "tyranny of the city," the Chinese have declared their aversion to the patterns of industrialization and urbanization characteristic of the West and the Soviet Union. One official even went so far as to tell a foreign visitor that "we are attempting to urbanize the countryside and ruralize our cities,"[138] a notion that Chinese Communists in 1949 had regarded as "charming but useless."

137. Kao Kang, *Chan tsai tung-pei ching-chi chien-she te tsui ch'ien-mien*, p. 6. This was Kao Kang's report to the First Northeast Party Congress.

138. Quoted in B. Michael Frolic, "A Visit to Peking University: What the Cultural Revolution Was All About," *New York Times Magazine*, Oct. 24, 1971, p. 122.

IX

A New Beginning: The Communist Take-over from the Kuomintang

This study began with the KMT take-over of urban China from the Japanese immediately following World War II. It is fitting therefore to end with an evaluation of the Communist take-over of the same cities from the KMT. However great the grievances of China's urban population, the cities were the Government's last bastion of support. They fell to the Communists not through any popular uprising from within, but were taken by the advancing Communist armies. Peasant soldiers provided most city folk with their first glimpse of the Chinese Communists about whom such wildly conflicting rumors had circulated during the past two decades.

Whether the reception they received would quickly turn to resentment, as had been the case with the returning KMT, depended on the performance of these peasant soldiers and the inexperienced cadre administrators who followed their advance. The comparison would not be lost on those groups whose help and support the Communists needed most as they took control, within just one year, of all the major urban centers on the Chinese mainland. Such hostility, should it occur, would carry far greater immediate dangers for the Communists than it had for the KMT regime four years previously, when it was recognized and welcomed as the legitimate government of China.

The issues that had aroused the greatest public criticism in 1945-46 were: the Government's reluctance to punish collaborators; the venality and undisciplined behavior of its military and civilian personnel; the failure to implement sound economic and financial measures for the immediate take-over period; and the generally condescending posture adopted by those returning from the interior toward their compatriots who had remained in Japanese-occupied territory.

By 1949, the Communists were fully aware not only of the strategic importance of urban China and the theoretical challenge it represented, but also of the major pitfalls that awaited them there. In each of the above aspects except the first (there was no comparable public demand to punish members of the defeated KMT regime), the Communists acted positively—if not always with complete success—to avoid the mistakes committed by the KMT Government in 1945. As with everything else they had done, however, this was not an achievement that came effortlessly.

LAW AND ORDER

That their cadres and soldiers were not immune to the same weaknesses that had plagued the KMT, was demonstrated by the Communist take-over of cities and towns in Manchuria during the first half of 1948. According to the Communists' own accounts, there had been considerable seizing of property by their troops particularly during the take-over of Szupingkai, Kirin, and Anshan. In addition, many of the personnel following the troops, personnel belonging to health, sanitation, supply, and communications units, took over commercial and industrial properties, dismantled factory equipment, carried off machinery and materials, and destroyed many installations. In some places, take-over personnel even tore up railway tracks, transforming the rails into scrap metal and the ties into firewood.[1]

All of this was done more or less in conformity with the time-honored guerrilla practice of removing in a "planned and organized manner" materiel from areas that could not be held permanently. The practice was intended to be applied to items of "military use" and to "enemy property." The persistence of this habit into 1948 meant that urban public enterprises owned or managed by central and local governments, and the major industries controlled by KMT bureaucratic capitalists, suffered the most serious destruction as "enemy property." Other targets were industrial and commercial enterprises owned by private persons known to have actively supported the KMT Government or to have maintained some relationship with it such as quartering troops, caring for the wounded, and the like.[2]

Many of the civilian organizations which moved in after the fighting ended concerned themselves only with the welfare of their own units and in the process disrupted business and prices. The urban poor took advantage of the fighting to steal and loot. Peasants entered the cities, seizing the urban holdings of village landlords. The take-over troops, instead of safeguarding property, allowed the people to do as they wished.[3] Such violations of official policy were reported from all but "a small number of cities" captured by Communist forces in the Northeast during the first half of 1948.[4]

According to the official appraisal, the combat troops were poorly disciplined. Neither they, nor their supporting units, nor the civilian personnel in their rear, had been sufficiently instructed concerning the party's policy of

---

1. "Pao-hu kuo-chia te ts'ai-ch'an" [Safeguard national property], *Tung-pei jih-pao,* editorial, reprinted in Hua-pei hsin hua shu-tien, ed., *Kuan-yü ch'eng-shih cheng-ts'e te chi-ko wen-hsien* (hereafter *Kuan-yü ch'eng-shih*), pp. 27-29.

2. "Kuan-yü pao-hu hsin shou-fu ch'eng-shih te chih-shih" [Directive on protecting newly captured cities], issued by the CCP Northeast Bureau on June 10, 1948, in *ibid.,* p. 2.

3. See the reference to the situation in Kirin in Chapter Eight, note 110.

4. Yingkow may have been one of these exceptions. One observer had nothing but praise for the Communist take-over in late February. He particularly noted the discipline of the troops: they invariably refused even the smallest gifts. Ming Lang, "Chi kung-chün k'ung-chih hsia te ying-k'ou" [A record of Yingkow under Communist army control], *STPP,* Aug. 15, 1948. Yingkow subsequently fell to Government forces, but was retaken by the Communists before the end of the year.

protecting the cities. Civilian and military personnel still looked upon the occupation of cities as a temporary affair. They had not yet understood that a new situation was emerging to give new functions and significance to the cities. The Northeast Party Bureau issued its June 10, 1948, directive with the intention of correcting this state of affairs. Similar instructions would be contained in the proclamations of every military commander whose troops moved into China's cities and towns during the year that followed.

MILITARY DISCIPLINE

The Northeast Party Bureau directed that authority be centralized, as it had not been during the take-over of Kirin and other cities that spring. The highest command of the troops attacking any city would henceforth be held directly responsible for the initial stages of the occupation, including the actions of all Party and government units and civilian cadres. The length of time the city remained under military rule would depend on the local situation as determined by the military commander. Once order had been reestablished, responsibility would be transferred from the military control committee to the city government and the municipal Party committee.

Before the battle for any city began, the combat troops, supply units, and all military and civilian cadres were to be instructed concerning the Party's policy and the discipline required during the occupation. The troops were authorized to confiscate only arms, ammunition, and other military items. These were all to be entrusted immediately to an officer and reported to the high command; individual soldiers were forbidden to keep such materials. The troops were specifically forbidden to confiscate other property, whether public or private, and were ordered to prevent anyone else from doing so. Supply and service units were also "absolutely forbidden" to take over any property.

The combat troops were authorized to take as prisoners armed enemy forces, other personnel only if armed and resisting, military spies, and major war criminals. All other law-abiding public servants including the local police were to be allowed to remain at their posts, and were ordered to carry on as usual. After the fighting, all troops with the exception of those necessary to maintain order were to be withdrawn outside the city. Party, government, and other organizations were instructed not to allow their members to buy or sell property or engage in any kind of commerce. Peasants were not to be allowed to enter cities and towns on their own for the purpose of seizing property or arresting suspected criminals.[5]

These instructions constituted the essence of the Party's occupation policy during the remainder of the Civil War. They were proclaimed by advancing Communist troops and broadcast over the radio prior to the take-over of every city; afterwards they appeared again on wall posters and in the newspapers. The policy was reiterated in the Seven Point Provisional Law promulgated by General Ch'en I prior to the take-over of Tsinan, and in the regulations announced by the Tsinan Military Control Committee the day Communist forces took the city,

5. See note 2 above.

September 25, 1948.[6] It was reiterated again in the Eight Point Provisional Law promulgated by Lin Piao prior to the surrender of Tientsin and Peiping,[7] and finally in the Eight Point Provisional Law of the People's Liberation Army General Command proclaimed on April 25, 1949, by Mao and Chu Teh as Communist armies advanced to the South and Northwest.[8]

In addition, the army's famous rules of discipline and points for attention were revised to guide the behavior of peasant soldiers as they entered China's major cities. The revised rules and points as issued by the Commanding Headquarters and Political Department of the Third Field Army on April 26, 1949, were as follows:[9]

The Three Main Laws

1. Observe all laws, ordinances, and stipulations proclaimed by the military control committees and the people's governments.

2. Observe city policy and protect municipal administration.

3. Maintain the frugal tradition of revolutionary soldiers.

The Ten Points for Attention

1. Do not shoot without permission.

2. Do not occupy civilian houses and commercial establishments. Do not disturb theaters and places of amusement.

3. Do not go out except on business, and ask for leave before doing so.

4. Do not drive carts and horses recklessly in the streets.

5. Do not eat in the streets. Do not walk arm-in-arm in the streets. Do not jostle in crowds.

6. Transact business fairly.

7. Keep your quarters clean. Urinate and defecate in latrines only.

8. Consultation with fortune tellers, gambling, and spending nights with prostitutes shall not be permitted.

9. Corrupt practices for selfish ends shall not be permitted.

10. Scribbling and drawing on walls shall not be permitted.

Had it enforced similar regulations in 1945, the KMT Government could have spared itself much of the criticism inspired by its take-over operation. Instead, the KMT moved back to Shanghai and then on to Peiping, Tientsin, and into Manchuria, without correcting even the most flagrant abuses being committed by its returning personnel. Their behavior was, if anything, more undisciplined in the cities of Manchuria than elsewhere. By contrast, the Communists, who initially seem to have been guilty of some of the same blunders as the returning KMT, acted to correct them before too much damage had been done. Thus by the time Communist forces emerged from the relative obscurity of Manchuria

6. *Kuan-yü ch'eng-shih,* pp. 6-9.

7. *Ibid.,* pp. 45-46.

8. Liu Shao-ch'i, ed., *Hsin min-chu-chu-i ch'eng-shih cheng-ts'e,* pp. 39-41.

9. U.S. Cons., Peiping, Hsinhua radio, Peiping, Apr. 26, 1949.

into the bright lights of Tientsin, Peiping, Nanking, and Shanghai, those cities witnessed the unprecedented spectacle of Chinese soldiers who refused even the gift of a cigarette from sympathetic passersby.

One not-so-sympathetic middle school teacher, who chose to leave Tsinan, acknowledged that discipline had been well maintained during and after the take-over of the city. The public was asked to report any transgressions to the authorities, and two soldiers were executed. Some looting by civilians occurred after the main body of the combat forces had been withdrawn from the city, but order was quickly restored.[10]

In Peiping, another none-too-sympathetic observer also remarked on the good behavior of the take-over personnel. He wrote that the majority of the political cadres conducted themselves in a "modest and unpretentious" manner. The armed forces were so well disciplined that they took nothing by force, nor did they fail to return what they borrowed. As a result, the people neither hated nor feared them.[11]

In Shanghai, even anti-Communist foreigners were impressed. There, as elsewhere, the soldiers refused gifts of food and other items. Service and supply corps personnel moved equipment into the city on their backs rather than requisition civilian vehicles for that purpose. The conservative American-owned *Shanghai Evening Post and Mercury* termed the conduct of the entering PLA forces "exemplary." The editor, Randall Gould, took note of their efforts to return to their owners vehicles requisitioned by retreating KMT personnel and then abandoned. These efforts called to mind, he wrote, the situation just four years previously when returning KMT officials had scrambled to take over Japanese automobiles which they kept for their own use.[12]

In another incident evoking memories of the recent past, a PLA truck hit and killed a Tungchi University student. The date was June 3, just a week after the liberation of Shanghai. As noted, such incidents, particularly those involving U.S. military vehicles, had aroused considerable public resentment. The new administration was anxious to avoid unflattering comparisons and the driver was sentenced to death. The sentence was later commuted in response to public sympathy for the man, who had only recently gone over to the PLA from the KMT army. But the case became the subject of intense study for all troops in the city. Drivers were reclassified and stricter standards established. Heavy vehicles were forbidden to enter the city except when absolutely necessary and all army vehicles were ordered not to exceed fifteen miles per hour.[13]

10. *Chung chien* [China reconstructs], Dec. 5, 1948, quoted in Derk Bodde, *Peking Diary*, p. 87. According to Anna Louise Strong, one reason for the smoothness of the take-over in Tsinan was the thoroughness of the preparations. For three months before the final assault, the city's future administrators were gathered in a nearby town studying the Party's city policy and organizing the municipal government. Departments were formed, regulations drawn up, staff assignments made, jobs discussed, and the layout of the city learned by those who had not lived there. Anna Louise Strong, *The Chinese Conquer China*, pp. 248-49.

11. *Hsin-wen pao*, Shanghai, Apr. 4, 1949 (*CPR*, Apr. 8).

12. Quoted in Lynn and Amos Landman, *Profile of Red China*, pp. 108-9.

13. *Chieh-fang jih-pao* (CFJP), Shanghai, June 6, 1949 (*CPR*, June 4-6).

Another event which marked the passing of the old order in Shanghai that summer was the effort to instill discipline into the police force. In keeping with Party policy, officers and constables who were not guilty of serious counter-revolutionary activities and wished to remain in the force were allowed to do so. Something nevertheless had to be done about habits carried over from the old regime. In August, members of several police precinct offices or public security stations met, sometimes with residents of the neighborhood, to deal with individual cases. Disciplinary action was taken, for example, against two members of the Chiangwan Station after they admitted at a neighborhood meeting on August 5 that they had accepted bribes from the owners of three unlicensed bicycles. More serious were the transgressions of Ch'en Peng-fei and Li Kuo-hua. At a meeting of officers and constables of the Lousa Station on August 18, the former admitted to keeping mistresses and protecting street walkers. The latter acknowledged that he had "dallied with womenfolk" while on duty. Ch'en was turned over to the court for trial, Li was dismissed from the force, and both were called upon to apologize to the public at a mass meeting.[14]

Contemplating such events, the initial reaction of the American community to the behavior of Communist take-over personnel was "distinctly favorable." [15] All things considered, the reactions of the Chinese public were probably much the same.

THE FACTORY PROTECTION MOVEMENT

Although the cities of China did not surrender to the Communists as a result of any uprising from within, underground Communist cadres were able to organize support for the take-over, particularly among workers and students. The immediate objective was to protect industry, communications, public utilities, and academic institutions from any disorder during the take-over period.

The sources of danger were manifold. They included, in addition to those just cited, destruction by the retreating KMT and looting by the workers themselves who had a tendency to regard such behavior as their rightful share in the spoils of a Communist victory. In Shenyang, Anshan, Fushun, and Penhsi, a "machine and materials surrendering campaign" had to be launched in January and February, 1949, among miners and industrial workers. Workers from the First Machine Factory in Shenyang were persuaded to hand over a thousand pieces of machinery and equipment which they had "hidden away." Employees of the Fushun Coal Mining Administration and the Shenyang Chemical Factory similarly participated in the campaign. Workers at Anshan turned over, during a three-week period, 210,000 items including component parts of the town's electrical generating equipment. The workers' "contribution" was said to have

14. *CFJP*, Shanghai, Aug. 22, 1949 (*CPR*, Aug. 24).
15. Landman, *Red China*, p. 109, quoting John Cabot, American Consul General in Shanghai.

shortened the period necessary for restoration of the electrical supply there by at least a month.[16]

The effort to safeguard China's urban economic infrastructure seems to have been a fairly universal feature of Communist take-over policy. Factory protection teams were organized in Kalgan in 1945. And even in Kirin where substantial disruption did occur, workers in at least two enterprises reportedly stood guard day and night to protect factory installations and supplies.[17] Preparations for the movement appeared to grow more systematic as the Communist armies moved south. This probably reflected both a more extensive Communist underground organization in Tientsin, Peiping, and Shanghai prior to liberation; and the bandwagon effect on popular support as the certainty of Communist victory grew more apparent.

In Tientsin, three hundred of the one thousand employees at the Hua I Paper Mill, the largest in North China, worked side by side with the PLA to protect the plant. While fighting raged nearby, the workers remained at the mill guarding the machinery, warehouses, and water supply. Workers at the Tientsin branches of the Central Machine Factory and the North China Iron and Steel Works, both affiliated with the KMT Government's National Resources Commission, organized themselves into teams and stood guard day and night over factory installations. Workers did the same at the Tientsin Motor Repair Works and in most of Tientsin's public utilities. This was said to be one reason why electricity, telephone, tram water, and postal services could all be resumed almost immediately after Communist forces entered the city.[18]

In Shanghai, plans for the factory protection movement were under way for almost a year prior to the liberation of the city in May, 1949. At the Sixth All-China Labor Conference in August, 1948, a representative from the Shanghai underground vowed that after liberation, all factories and warehouses in the city would be handed over to the people intact and public utilities would be resumed as soon as possible.[19] Preparations began in earnest after the Huai-Hai Campaign (November 5, 1948 to January 10, 1949).

In late January, the Communists began preparatory work for the take-over of the twenty-eight affiliated units of the National Resources Commission in Shanghai. Yeh Chu-pei, Chairman of the National Resources Commission in the liberated areas, broadcast instructions to his former colleagues. He advised them to remain at their posts and assured them that they would be able to retain their positions and salaries after liberation. He also warned that the destruction of the Commission's installations would not be tolerated and outlined plans for the take-over period. A Shanghai newspaper reported in early February that the local agencies and concerns of the Commission were following Yeh's instructions "to the letter." The employees were already stockpiling foodstuffs, preparing lists of staff members' names, clearing warehouses where employees might

16. U.S. Cons., Peiping, Hsinhua radio, North Shensi, Feb. 20 and 24, 1949.
17. U.S. Cons., Peiping, Hsinhua radio, North Shensi, Apr. 21, 1948.
18. U.S. Cons., Peiping, Hsinhua radio, North Shensi, Jan. 24, 25, 30 and Feb. 2, 1949.
19. U.S. Cons., Peiping, Hsinhua radio, North Shensi, Aug. 15, 1948.

deposit their belongings for safekeeping, and organizing factory protection teams.[20]

In April, the Party cell in the French Water and Power Company circulated a letter signed by Chu Chün-hsin, a labor leader in the Company who had fled to the liberated areas. Copies of the letter were distributed to the employees asking them to safeguard the Company's installations when the Communists took the city. The Party cell also organized a protection team which assumed responsibility for police work both inside and outside company installations on May 25, the day the PLA entered Shanghai in force.[21]

Similarly, the Party cell in the Shanghai Power Company, which supplied electricity to the city's industrial districts, organized protection and emergency repair teams. Members of the protection team dissuaded a KMT military unit from mounting its guns on the roof of a Power Company building, arguing that a direct hit to the building could cause a fire that would engulf the whole neighborhood in flames. With the arrival of the PLA, the protection team changed its designation to the People's Security Corps and took the surrender of the KMT troops stationed on the company premises. Workers remained at their posts around the clock and kept the generators and equipment running under the watchful eyes of the new security guards. Because of this effort, the supply of electricity was never shut off, nor did the Power Company suffer any damage until its installations were bombed by KMT planes on June 2.[22]

The Party branch in the Shanghai Customs began to prepare for liberation in mid-February. Committees were organized among upper and lower level employees, a general employee registration drive carried out, and relief supplies stockpiled. One hundred and twenty men were mobilized from among the harbor and customs police forces to serve as an armed protection team. Thirty harbor police under the direct leadership of Party members broke into the customs arsenal shortly before the PLA entered Shanghai and seized 583 rifles as well as ammunition and other weapons.[23]

Dock workers organized an underground United Shipworkers Union and set up their own protection teams, engaged in work slowdowns, adopted delaying tactics, hid cargo, and generally did what they could to obstruct the KMT's flight. In the Chiangnan Shipyards, then Shanghai's largest shipbuilding concern, several hundred workers allegedly thwarted an attempt to move equipment to Taiwan. First, the men announced that they were production, not transport, workers and refused to dismantle, crate, and load the machinery. KMT soldiers were called in to do the job but were inadequate for the task and the workers

20. *Lih pao*, Shanghai, Feb. 3, 1949 (*CPR*, Feb. 5-7). Yeh Chu-pei had been director of a NRC copper smelting plant in Chungking. Shortly after the Japanese surrender, he left for the liberated areas via London and Moscow.

21. See Chapter Four, note 58.

22. See Chapter Four, note 13.

23. See Chapter Four, note 51.

were compelled to take over the operation. They then adopted various delaying tactics, worked slowly, hid some of the most valuable pieces of machinery, and packed many crates with defective and non-essential equipment. Some engineers were also in on the plot, contributing to the success of the substitution effort. In the end, less than ten thousand tons of mostly inferior machinery and equipment was shipped to Taiwan. The retreating KMT was avenged several days later, however, when its bombers scored several direct hits on this shipyard inflicting considerable damage.[24]

At Chiaotung University, where the Communist Youth League was able to recruit about four hundred students between January and May, 1949, a similar order to prepare to evacuate was actively opposed by many professors and students. They formed a committee and passed a resolution declaring that "the school absolutely must not be moved." Classes continued and students remained on campus throughout the lunar New Year holiday to keep troops from occupying the school. As liberation approached, teachers and students formed a protection team to prevent removal of the library, laboratory equipment, and other movable items. The students also did what they could to collect information, which was passed on to the advance units of the PLA, about KMT defense installations in the vicinity of the university.[25]

Other concerns where similar preparations were reported to have been organized included the Lienchin Auto Works, Shanghai Chemicals, Yinglien Shipyards, Jihya Iron and Steel Works, Tungyung General Machine Manufacturing Company, the Shanghai plant of the China Agricultural Implements Company, Shanghai Electrical Machines Company, Shanghai Public Transportation Company, Chapei Water and Electric, and the Shanghai Post Office. Many workers' protection teams were transformed into units of the People's Security Corps immediately after liberation. They assumed responsibility for policing the industrial districts and in some cases, for disarming KMT troops in those areas.[26]

According to later claims, sixty thousand people were organized into protection teams prior to the liberation of Shanghai; as a result, the city's factories and public utilities suffered no significant damage or losses.[27] These claims are difficult to verify. Disruption of business and industry did occur. But as we shall see below, this does not seem to have been due to any physical destruction of the industrial plant during the initial take-over period. Moreover, one of the key goals of the protection movement—the maintenance of essential public services— was successfully achieved. The Communists prided themselves on the rapidity

24. Shang-hai tsung kung-hui mi-shu-ch'u, ed., *Chieh-fang hou shang-hai kung yun tzu-liao*, pp. 4-6.
    25. Hua-tung jen-min ch'u-pan-she, ed., *Tsai tou-cheng li chuang-ta*, pp. 86-100; and Chang Hui, ed., *Shang-hai chin pai nien ko-ming shih-hua*, pp. 211-13.
    26. Chang Hui, ed., *Shang-hai chin pai nien*, pp. 212-22; and *Chieh-fang hou shang-hai*, pp. 1-15 (see note 24 above).
    27. *Chieh-fang hou shang-hai*, p. 1.

with which they were able to restore electricity, water, telephone, postal service, and public transport in newly captured urban areas in 1949.

ECONOMICS AND FINANCE

One additional aspect of the Communists' preparatory work was the stockpiling of grain and other essential foodstuffs. These commodities were moved into the cities as soon as possible after the fighting ended in order to help stabilize prices, feed the population, and provide grain for relief purposes. The supplies were also used as a source of ready payment for civilians recruited to aid the army in clearing away the debris of war. Cities where this practice of moving in large quantities of grain and basic foodstuffs was reported to have been effectively accomplished included Shihchiachuang, Yingkow, Tsinan, Changchun, Peiping, Tientsin, and Shanghai.[28]

ANTI-INFLATIONARY MEASURES

The most serious urban problem the Communists inherited from the KMT was, of course, the inflation. In order to succeed, any effort to stabilize prices would require something more than an adequate supply of foodstuffs and an undamaged industrial plant, however important these basic preconditions might be.

The first order of business was the conversion of KMT currency, known after the August, 1948, reform as the gold *yuan* (GY), into people's notes or *jen-min-pi* (JMP). In 1945, it took the returning KMT Government several months to call in all of the puppet currency throughout the former Japanese-occupied territories. In 1949, Peiping surrendered on January 22, but was policed and administered by existing personnel until January 31, when the PLA entered the city in force. By February 3, the new currency exchange rates had been announced. Currency conversion was completed by February 23, and the gold *yuan* banned from circulation in Peiping as of that date. The exchange rate was fixed at 10 GY to 1 JMP. Workers, teachers, students, and the poor were allowed to exchange currency at a more favorable rate of 3 GY to 1 JMP—a concession that was abandoned by the time the Communists reached Shanghai, because of the opportunity it gave for speculation. In Tientsin, taken by the Communists on January 15, currency conversion was completed by the first week of February. In Shanghai, the exchange was completed and KMT currency banned within two weeks after the city was liberated.[29]

Yet there seemed to be little more public confidence in the new currency than there had been in the old. The market for silver, gold, and foreign

28. U.S. Cons., Peiping, Hsinhua radio, North Shensi, concerning: Shihchiachuang—Nov. 26, 1947; Tsinan—Oct. 14, 15, 16, 21 and Nov. 19, 1948; Changchun—Oct. 20, 22, 25, 1948; Peiping—Feb. 3, 4, 11, 1949; Tientsin—Feb. 8, 1949. Also, Ming Lang, p. 23 (see note 4 above). Strong, *The Chinese Conquer China*, pp. 249, 255; Landman, *Red China*, p. 60.

29. U.S. Cons., Peiping, Hsinhua radio, North Shensi, Jan. 26 and Feb. 19, 1949; Bodde, *Peking Diary*, p. 116; Landman, *Red China*, p. 53.

currencies continued to flourish. Prices and wages were often calculated in terms of the old Chinese silver dollar rather than the new JMP. Speculation mounted accordingly, in effect devaluing the JMP within days after its first appearance. In Shanghai during the first week of June, the price of one silver dollar rose from JMP 660 to JMP 1,800, and the price of gold per tael from JMP 39,000 to JMP 110,000. Commodity prices followed those of silver and gold.[30]

According to the manager of the People's Bank of China in Shanghai, the rate of increase of retail prices there during that one week equaled the rate of increase in the liberated areas during the entire preceding year.[31] The newly reorganized Shanghai Chamber of Commerce daily declared that such "intangible evils" as the lack of enthusiasm for saving, the habit of attaching greater value to commodities than to currency, the practice of devoting time and energy to speculation and profiteering, and the lack of interest in production, were all still "deeply rooted" among the people.[32]

After a short period during which they relied primarily but unsuccessfully on exhortation, the Military Control Committees in Peiping, Tientsin, Nanking, and Shanghai banned the circulation of, dealings in, and computation of prices in terms of, silver, gold, and all foreign currencies. Although transactions in them were forbidden, the people were allowed to hold gold, silver, and foreign currencies, on deposit in the People's Bank. Holdings could be withdrawn on demand in JMP at the official rate of exchange on the date of withdrawal.

One official noted that the public must have assumed the Communists' regulations and decrees, like those of the KMT, need not be taken seriously. In Peiping, the prohibition was announced on February 28. On March 2, the Military Control Committee began arresting money changers who had ignored what one radio broadcast discreetly termed the Committee's "advice." By March 4, some 116 dealers had been arrested. Most of them were soon released after being required to register and to agree that they would give up dealing in silver dollars.[33]

In Shanghai where the process of currency conversion had been carried out at an even faster pace than in the northern cities, the effort to make JMP the sole medium of exchange took a somewhat more dramatic turn. On the morning of June 10, PLA troops threw a cordon around the stock exchange building, known to be the center of gold and silver speculation in the city. They took into custody 2,113 persons. After being lectured, 1,863 of these were released within twenty-four hours. The remaining 250 were detained, their offenses having been judged more serious. Among this group were some of the most notorious speculators in Shanghai.[34]

30. *CFJP*, Shanghai, June 11, 1949 (*CPR*, June 11-13).
31. *CFJP*, Shanghai, June 10, 1949 *(CPR)*.
32. *Shang pao*, Shanghai, June 15, 1949 *(CPR)*.
33. U.S. Cons., Peiping, Hsinhua radio, North Shensi, Mar. 2 and 7, 1949.
34. *TKP*, Shanghai, June 12 and 13, 1949 (*CPR*, June 11-13).

At the same time, the new authorities also began mobilizing popular support behind its anti-silver campaign, asking workers, public enterprises, government organs, and schools to refuse to accept or use silver dollars. On June 9, the Shanghai Students Association called a mass meeting attended by 6,400 students from over one hundred colleges and middle schools, to mobilize student support for the campaign. Several hundred student publicity teams were soon on the streets lecturing businessmen and money changers, and advertising the new financial regulations to every passerby.[35]

Having applied both exhortation and coercion, the Communists rounded out their attack by adding an economic incentive in the form of the parity or commodity savings deposit unit. This was designed to protect savings from the worst effects of inflation and thus eliminate the primary motive for investing in silver or gold. Under the new system, savings deposited in JMP were converted on deposit into commodity units, each unit representing the sum of the current market prices of one pint of rice, one foot of cloth, one catty of coal, and one ounce of edible oil. When savings were withdrawn, payment would be made in terms of the prices of these commodities prevailing at the time of withdrawal, plus interest.[36] Eventually, loans from all government banks were also calculated in terms of the commodity units, as were also the wages of all public employees and many others.

Another device to encourage savings and absorb purchasing power was the sale of government bonds. The promotion campaign began in the Northeast and moved south thereafter. Having so recently witnessed the devaluation of KMT bond issues into worthless scraps of paper, the public was understandably chary of supporting this undertaking. Subscription committees were set up in every city, and an ambitious promotion campaign was aimed primarily at business and industrial circles. Unlike the last bond issue of the KMT Government, this first one of the new regime was ultimately fully subscribed.[37]

Within a few months after the take-over of each city, businessmen and industrialists, and particularly the former, also became the major targets of a fairly heavy graduated tax system. Loopholes were few and protestations many, but the Communists were adamant. They maintained that in the past the peasantry had borne the major cost of the war and that now the cities must contribute as well. The countryside continued to contribute its share, however, with tax rates set at about 13 percent of the crop in newly liberated areas and around 20 percent in the old.

Finally, in order to prevent the hoarding and price manipulation by merchants that had added to the plight of the urban consumer in the KMT

---

35. *CFJP*, Shanghai, June 10 and 14, 1949 (*CPR*, same dates).

36. The commodity savings unit was introduced in Tientsin in late February and in Peiping on April 1. In Peiping, the unit was based on the market prices of wheat flour, corn flour, and cotton cloth. U.S. Cons., Peiping, Hsinhua radio, North Shensi, Mar. 6, 1949, and Hsinhua radio, Peiping, Apr. 10, 1949; *Shang pao,* Shanghai, June 10, 1949 *(CPR);* Bodde, *Peking Diary,* p. 149.

37. U.S. Cons., Peiping, Hsinhua radio, Peiping, Apr. 10, 1949; Landman, *Red China,* pp. 58-59.

economy, the new authorities sought to ensure a steady supply of necessary commodities from government-controlled sources. In addition to rationing certain essential items, the new municipal governments also built up stocks of basic necessities such as rice, millet, salt, oil, and coal. These were put on the market to help stabilize prices when they showed signs of violent fluctuation.[38] This was done through the municipal trading companies which were part of larger area-wide networks of government trading organizations. They engaged also in regular retail sales, and were responsible for supplying stocks to the consumer cooperatives.

During the final week of February, the North China Trading Company, for example, began selling grain, coal, and cloth in Peiping at prices somewhat below the prevailing market rate. The Trading Company set up its own shops and also commissioned a number of private merchants to sell state-supplied commodities at fixed prices. The merchants were allowed to continue selling their own merchandise at market prices.[39] The private agent system proved unsatisfactory, however, and the state trading companies came to rely increasingly on the consumer cooperatives as the main outlet for government supplied commodities. Although their quality was often the subject of criticism in the press, the number of these cooperatives grew rapidly. They were organized—as they had been in the older liberated areas—among the employees of individual factories, plants, government offices, and the like, with membership closed to outsiders or members of the general public.[40]

Thus in the immediate post-liberation period, the Communists had done, or at least attempted to do, almost everything in the area of economic, financial, and monetary policy that the KMT had been criticized for neglecting during its take-over from the Japanese. The Communists' efforts to safeguard the urban economic infrastructure seem to have achieved the desired result by 1949. Essential services including transport and communications were resumed as rapidly as possible after the fighting ended. The process of currency conversion could not have been conducted with greater dispatch, and the new authorities immediately began to introduce controls on various sources of inflationary pressure. With the conversion to the new currency, all competing forms of exchange were banned. Black market dealings in silver, gold, and foreign currencies were brought under control by arresting the principal offenders, by fixing reasonably realistic exchange rates, and by providing an alternative form of investment for the public. In addition, the Communists began collecting

38. *TKP,* Shanghai, June 8, 13, and 14, 1949 (*CPR,* June 8, 11-13, and 14, 1949 respectively); U.S. Cons., Peiping, Hsinhua radio, Peiping, Apr. 2, 1949.

39. U.S. Cons., Peiping, Hsinhua radio, North Shensi, Mar. 15, 1949, and Hsinhua radio, Peiping, Apr. 10, 1949.

40. By the first week of April, thirty large concerns in Peiping had set up their own consumer cooperatives with a total membership of 68,300. A month later there were reported to be 71 such co-ops. A cooperative organizing campaign in Tientsin reported 224 co-ops by the end of April with membership of 356,000 (out of a city population of less than two million). U.S. Cons., Peiping, Hsinhua radio, Peiping, Apr. 8, 1949; Bodde, *Peking Diary,* p. 179.

taxes, instituted some rationing of essential commodities, and took steps to maintain a steady flow of such items into the cities where they were sold at controlled prices.

The economy responded at once to these efforts, but the response was slow and uneven. Throughout the first months of Communist rule, prices continued to climb, although at a lesser rate than had been the case during the last months of the KMT.[41] In Tientsin, the average weekly increase in wholesale prices between January 25 and August 23, 1949, was 11.38 percent, while the average weekly increase in the workers' cost of living was 9.51 percent. Comparable figures during the last months of KMT rule in Tientsin, August 24, 1948, to January 11, 1949, were 26.03 percent and 31.2 percent respectively.[42] In Shanghai as in Tientsin, however, food prices rose sharply within a month after liberation. The price of rice in Shanghai registered a six-fold increase and the value of one commodity savings unit rose from JMP 100 to JMP 894 on July 19, and up to JMP 967 on August 1.[43]

CONTINUING AGITATION ON THE LABOR FRONT

Despite the official emphasis on reviving industry and trade, the disruption that occurred tended to counteract other more immediately successful efforts to dampen inflationary pressures. Tientsin authorities claimed that by mid-February, 1949, approximately 90 percent of the city's enterprises had reopened their doors.[44] But subsequent reports indicated that it was difficult to keep them that way.

In addition to (and aggravated by) the continuing rise in production costs, the proliferation of labor disputes under the new Communist administration created a major problem for business and industry. These disputes followed the same pattern they had assumed in Kalgan in 1945, and subsequently in the cities of

41. One measure of inflation during the last eighteen months of KMT control is the local currency equivalent of US $1.00:

Jan. 1948	CNC $179,000
Aug. 1948	CNC $12,000,000
Aug. 1948	GY 4
May, 1949	GY 23,000,000

See Chang Kia-ngau, *The Inflationary Spiral: the Experience in China, 1939-1950*, pp. 314, 317, 319.

42. Bodde, *Peking Diary*, p. 276 (Appendix: Price Fluctuations in Tientsin). These figures were based on statistics of the Institute of Economic Research of Nankai University in Tientsin; see also *T'ien-chin kung-jen sheng-huo-fei chih-shu* [Tientsin worker's cost-of-living index] (Tientsin: Nan-k'ai ta-hsueh ching-chi yen-chiu-so, 1950). Prof. Bodde, living in Peiping, suggested that if comparable figures had been available for Peiping, they would probably be similar. The impact of the general upward trend was serious despite occasional respites, such as occurred in Tientsin during the last week of February. After a sharp rise in food prices during the first month after liberation, the Tientsin Military Control Committee put large quantities of grain onto the market for sale to the public at prices fixed somewhat below those current. Wheat flour fell temporarily from JMP 1,400 to 1,100 per bag; corn flour from JMP 12 to 9.50 per catty. U.S. Cons., Peiping, Hsinhua radio, North Shensi, Mar. 2 and 9, 1949.

43. *TKP*, Shanghai, Aug. 12, 1949 *(CPR)*.

44. U.S. Cons., Peiping, Hsinhua radio, North Shensi, Mar. 2, 1949.

Manchuria. The new authorities, either because they were unwilling or unable to do otherwise, allowed the workers' agitation for wage increases, cost of living allowances, increased severance pay, and better treatment, to continue for several months. This was the case in cities taken in the spring of 1949, one full year after Party leaders had first denounced as a "leftist error" this same sort of labor agitation.

The Tientsin office of the preparatory committee of the North China General Labor Federation set up a workers' information office soon after Communist forces entered the city. By early February, the office had replied to over two thousand inquiries, many concerning wage payments and the employer's rights in disputes with employees.[45] The exact nature of the answers given was not disclosed. But labor disputes mounted during the next two months over these and related issues. During the same week in March that the Hsinhua News Agency claimed increased productivity in six privately-owned Tientsin factories after the latter accepted their workers' demands for improved working conditions,[46] a local newspaper reported the closing of an increasing number of establishments due to labor disputes and rising labor costs.[47] The report was written by Ch'ien Chia-chü, economic advisor in the People's Bank of China. He later noted that some of Tientsin's entrepreneurs had resorted to the gradual liquidation of their industrial assets in order to meet the workers' demands for wage increases.[48]

In Peiping, the problem of labor unrest was such that the ten district governments in the city called together labor and management representatives from many different enterprises (including flour mills, iron works, match factories, barber shops, and pedicab and rickshaw firms) for a series of conferences. The representatives of the government announced that wage disputes had to be settled according to the principle of consideration for both capital and labor. The authorities also reiterated the Party's policy of protecting industrial and commercial establishments and reminded those present that liquidation struggles had no place in such a policy.[49]

According to a later report by Shanghai's new Mayor, General Ch'en I, some two thousand labor disputes had occurred during the month of July alone in that city.[50] The workers resorted to all the tactics they had relied on during the preceding four years of labor agitation under the KMT. They engaged in strikes, work slowdowns, sit-ins, and various forms of employer harassment. Randall

45. U.S. Cons., Peiping, Hsinhua radio, North Shensi, Feb. 28, 1949.

46. U.S. Cons., Peiping, Hsinhua radio, North Shensi, Mar. 8, 1949.

47. *Chin-pu jih-pao,* Tientsin, Mar. 13, 1949, cited in Kenneth Lieberthal, "Mao versus Liu? Policy Towards Industry and Commerce, 1946-49," *China Quarterly,* No. 47 (July-September 1971), p. 511. *Chin-pu jih-pao* [Progressive daily] was the name adopted by the Tientsin edition of the *Ta kung pao* when it was reorganized, as were all newspapers, immediately after liberation.

48. *Hsin-wen jih-pao,* Shanghai, Aug. 4, 1949 (*CPR,* Aug. 5).

49. U.S. Cons., Peiping, Hsinhua radio, North Shensi, Mar. 11, 1949.

50. Ch'en I, "Inaugural Address at the Opening Session of the Second Shanghai Conference of People's Representatives," Dec. 5, 1949, in all Shanghai newspapers Dec. 14 (*CPR,* Dec. 15).

Gould of the *Shanghai Evening Post and Mercury* was no longer quite so enthusiastic about the new Communist administration after being locked in his office by some of his employees until he agreed to meet their wage demands. From foreign and Chinese employers alike, Shanghai's workers demanded wage increases, loans, bonuses for the Dragon Boat Festival, and increases in severance pay. Rarely did the new authorities in Shanghai intervene, despite the new emphasis on benefiting capital as well as labor that had already been introduced in Peiping and Tientsin.

As noted in Chapter Four, labor unrest in the major cities, and particularly in Shanghai, was a common feature of economic life throughout much of the Civil War period. Although it is not entirely clear that this was one of their motives, the Communists may have consciously opted against the imposition of a tighter rein on labor's demands immediately after the liberation of each major city— rather than alienate a labor force which even the KMT had tried to placate. Indeed, the demands were the same that the Communists themselves, in their major policy statements on the labor movement in the KMT areas and through their underground organization there, had encouraged the workers to make. Without due preparation and explanation, it would have been awkward to announce at once that the workers must stop agitating for the very benefits that liberation was supposed to bring. The rhetoric of revolution clearly encouraged such a response from labor.

This situation was also related, of course, to the Communists' ability to impose a rein on labor's demands. Both the Kalgan experience and the anti-leftist campaign in Manchuria suggest that at least three conditions were essential for the successful accomplishment of this task: (1) the ability to provide a basic level of economic security in the form of guaranteed supplies of low cost essential commodities; (2) a cadre of activists willing and able to explain and implement the Party's policy; and (3) the extension of a Communist-dominated union organization among key elements of the labor force. In view of the economic disruption surrounding the take-over of most cities, the severe shortage of cadres at this time, the lack of discrimination applied in selecting new recruits, and the superficial training all newcomers were receiving, it seems unlikely that these conditions could have been very well developed anywhere in the immediate wake of the PLA's advance in 1949.

This highlights the basic difference between the anti-leftist campaign in the countryside and that in the cities. In the countryside, the land reform movement seems to have been purposely pushed to excess by the Party center in order to destroy the ruling elite and equalize land ownership. The anti-leftist campaign was not enforced until that objective had been achieved—thus representing the successful completion of a genuine mass movement. In the cities, on the other hand, the Party apparently had little choice but to tolerate a short period of "excessive" behavior on the part of the workers immediately after liberation. Given the relatively advanced development of the labor movement in China's major cities, and the relatively weak state of its own preparedness there, the

Party was in no position to enforce at once its policy of safeguarding capitalist production against the demands of the urban proletariat.

A CRISIS OF CONFIDENCE AND OTHER PROBLEMS

For several reasons, the economic dislocation of the take-over period was greater in Shanghai than elsewhere. As early as February, 1949, the *Ta kung pao* had reported that the greater part of the machine-making industry had shut down; that only about 10 percent of the city's flour mills were in operation, owing to the lack of wheat; and that the cotton mills, paper mills, and makers of various daily necessities were all selling their products at a loss, owing to rising labor, power, and other manufacturing costs.[51]

By the time Communist forces arrived in May, Shanghai's business and industry was at a virtual standstill. Unlike their colleagues in Tientsin, the new authorities in Shanghai could not claim within a month after liberation, that 90 percent of the city's enterprises had resumed operations. On June 21, the *Ta kung pao* reported that a little over half the factories and shops in Shanghai remained closed. The remainder were open for business, although most were operating only on a limited basis. Machine manufacturing was on the brink of collapse, and production costs in the textile industry were higher than selling prices. Customers were few, and soaring food prices were contributing to widespread labor agitation.

According to Ch'ien Chia-chü, the difficulties of Shanghai's industrialists were in many respects similar to those that had been experienced by their counterparts in Tientsin immediately after liberation. In both cases, the basic problems were a shortage of raw materials, rising labor costs, and marketing difficulties. The situation in Tientsin was somewhat less severe because the surrounding countryside had been liberated before the urban districts, land reform had been carried out, and the new currency had already replaced the old. Thus after Tientsin surrendered, its lines of communication with neighboring rural districts could be quickly reestablished in a manner that was not possible in the Shanghai area.[52]

Another reason for the seriousness of Shanghai's economic plight that summer was the air raids which began in June. KMT forces tried with some success to inflict the kind of damage that their hasty retreat the month before had precluded. Also in June, KMT forces began an effective naval blockade of the city. In July, flooding during one of the worst typhoons in Shanghai's history caused considerable economic losses. In addition, the Yangtze River rose to floodtide, as did the Yellow River to the north and many rivers in southern China as well, inundating large areas of its hinterland and contributing further to Shanghai's woes.

Yet not all the blame could be laid to "objective circumstances." Many problems derived specifically from the new economic and financial measures themselves and were not confined to the Shanghai area or even to east China.

51. *TKP,* Shanghai, Feb. 23, 1949 (*CPR,* Feb. 24).
52. See note 48 above.

The Communists freely admitted that they were learning and experimenting in many areas of urban administration. But the impression of moving in fits and starts, which their experimentation created, did little to bolster public confidence in the Communists' ability to cope with the situation they had inherited. For example, an income tax instituted in north China was soon rescinded. The use of two different exchange rates—one for the general public and the other for workers, students, and the poor—for conversion of gold *yuan* into people's notes soon had to be abandoned. Immediately after the Communists arrived in Peiping, the practice of paying wages in millet was adopted. But this, too, proved impractical and was soon abandoned. Merchants to whom the workers were obliged to exchange their wages for cash began manipulating the price of millet—as might have been anticipated.

The state trading companies ran into immediate difficulties with the attempt to use private agents, but the alternative consumer cooperatives had serious problems. A number of new tax regulations were found to be unreasonable and were rescinded, although this was done only on an *ad hoc* basis in response to businessmen's complaints. Similarly, the regulation requiring importers to arrange exports of equal value, which in effect meant conducting foreign trade by barter, proved unworkable and had to be dropped.

Experiences such as these, plus the continuing inflation, labor agitation, and the memory of the KMT's economic mismanagement, were obviously sufficient to undermine public confidence in the new currency and the competence of the new regime. There was no rush to take advantage of the new system of saving based on the commodity unit guarantees.[53] And the government's victory bonds were subscribed only after considerable "persuasion." Shanghai's Mayor, Ch'en I, later indicated the general feeling in the summer of 1949, when he acknowledged that "Pessimism prevailed among a portion of the public who considered the stabilization of commodity prices impossible and that there was no future for trade and industry with the blockade on and the outlet by sea closed."[54]

The Campaign of the Six Major Tasks

The Communists' response to this gloomy prognosis was predictable. They launched a campaign. In east China, it officially began with the First Conference of Representatives of the People of Shanghai, convened in early August for a "centralized discussion" of the problems facing the city. Liu Shao-ch'i's visit to Tientsin between April 18 and May 7 had marked the start of a similar phase in that city.[55] The significance of Liu's Tientsin visit was publicized in Shanghai by Ch'ien Chia-chü after his own arrival there. Ch'ien declared in an interview with Shanghai reporters that during Liu's stay in Tientsin the Party's policy of

53. *TKP,* Shanghai, June 14, 1949 *(CPR).*
54. See note 50 above.
55. Lieberthal, pp. 512-17 (see note 47 above). Two speeches by Liu Shao-ch'i from this period were published during the Cultural Revolution. See his *Wu-ko ts'ai-liao.* Since contemporary editions are not available, it remains impossible to verify the integrity of the Red Guard publication.

benefiting capital as well as labor had been clarified. Thereafter, a "radical change" occurred in the attitude of private industrialists, who abandoned their apathy and defeatism and adopted a more active enterprising spirit.[56]

The campaign in Shanghai took shape with the publication of a program known as "the six major tasks," submitted by the Shanghai committee of the CCP to the First Conference of People's Representatives and unanimously adopted by its 650 delegates. The six tasks were:

1. To actively support the PLA in liberating Fukien and Taiwan.

2. To disperse the population. The objective was to return to their native places the refugees who had crowded into Shanghai during the war so as to relieve the unemployment problem. The plan also called for the transfer of certain factories into the hinterland, closer to sources of fuel and raw materials cut off by the sea blockade.

3. To reorient the production goals of Shanghai's industries to conform to the most pressing needs of the economy and the lack of foreign raw materials; to protect the interests of labor and capital; and to unify the labor force through well-organized unions.

4. To mobilize large numbers of Party members, cadres, workers, and students to carry out typhoon relief in the Shanghai suburbs, emergency repairs on the sea dykes, and land reform, particularly in the rural districts of southern Kiangsu passed over quickly by the PLA on its march southward.

5. To develop communications between Shanghai and the hinterland, and encourage the flow of supplies and commodities between the urban and rural areas.

6. To promote thrift and reduce public expenditures. All Party, administrative, military, and civilian units were called upon to simplify their organization, carry out personnel retrenchment, and resist wasteful spending.[57]

Labor and Production

Although not immediately apparent from its formal outline, one of the key problems which the campaign of the six major tasks was intended to overcome was labor unrest.[58] The Shanghai Military Control Committee accordingly promulgated on August 19 two sets of regulations intended to eliminate labor problems as an obstacle to the development of industry and commerce. One set concerned the termination of operations, and the hiring and dismissal of workers. Management could petition the municipal government for permission to cease production (which had formerly been forbidden) and could hire or discharge employees in accordance with production needs, as well as discharge workers and employees found to be incompetent or unsatisfactory. Concerning its responsibilities, management was to resume operations as soon as possible; could not fire workers because of their participation in union or political

56. See note 48 above.
57. *CFJP*, Shanghai, July 27 and Aug. 7, 1949 (*CPR*, July 23-27, and Aug. 9).
58. *TKP*, Shanghai, Aug. 8, 1949 (*CPR*, Aug. 6-8).

activities; and was required to pay severance allowances of not less than one month's pay but not more than three months' pay to all discharged employees.

The second set of regulations dealt with procedures for settling labor disputes in private enterprises. If agreement could not be reached by the parties concerned, either party could request mediation by the Municipal Labor Bureau. While such mediation was in progress, management was forbidden to close the enterprise or reduce the pay or treatment of its employees. Similarly, strikes, work slowdowns, and all violations of labor discipline by workers were also forbidden. Should mediation fail, the Labor Bureau could set up an arbitration committee, which was to include representatives of management and labor. Finally, if arbitration also failed, labor disputes could be submitted to the People's Court, the decision of which would be binding.[59]

Capitalists were advised that they had nothing more to worry about with respect to labor disputes, and that it was time for them to get back to work both for their own personal profit and for the welfare of the nation. The workers were advised to accept "reasonable exploitation" by capital for the time being, since economic conditions precluded any immediate significant improvement in wages and benefits.

The new regulations, in combination with the expanding union organization, did eventually bring quiet to the Shanghai labor front. As the Party's organizational and educational efforts among the workers developed, it became easier to induce voluntary agreements such as that arranged at the Tatung Knitting and Dye Works. Employees receiving wages above a certain basic minimum agreed to accept a pay reduction to help tide the company over its difficulties.[60] By mid-September, many clerical employees and workers were said to be "spontaneously" asking for wage reductions to help their factories carry on production.[61] Three months later, municipal authorities were able to report that the number of labor disputes had "steadily decreased" since August. The workers, feeling their position more secure, were beginning to take the initiative in cooperating with management to develop production.[62]

One of the most novel means of introducing the Party's policies was inspired by a directive from the Headquarters of the Woosung-Shanghai Garrison in September to all army units under its command. The directive called on them to launch a campaign promoting mutual education between the army and the workers. According to one report, garrison troops of the PLA's Third Field Army had been assigned to guard duty in a number of factories in July. Considerable friction arose between the troops stationed in the factories and the workers. The troops did not understand how the workers could be called exploited, when they were clearly better dressed and provided for than many others in society. For their part, the workers found the peasant soldiers some-

59. *TKP,* Shanghai, Aug. 19, 1949 (*CPR,* Aug. 23).

60. *TKP,* Shanghai, Aug. 9, 1949 *(CPR).*

61. *CFJP,* Shanghai, Sept. 11, 1949 (*CPR,* Sept. 13).

62. Deputy Mayor P'an Han-nien, report to the Second Shanghai Conference of People's Representatives on Dec. 5, 1949, in *CFJP,* Shanghai, Dec. 15 (*CPR,* Dec. 16).

what rustic. They were also difficult to talk to, since most of them spoke dialects not commonly understood in Shanghai.

In accordance with the September directive, army-worker social gatherings and discussion meetings were held where the soldiers told war stories and the workers described KMT oppression. Army cadres visited factories in order to gain a clearer understanding of modern production methods, and to develop greater respect for the workers. The soldiers helped run classes for workers which were being formed in many Shanghai factories. The soldiers also helped organize patrol squads, teaching their worker-members how to fire weapons and perform guard duties. Finally, the Political Department of the Garrison Headquarters organized eleven work teams and assigned them to aid the existing labor unions in organizing and educating the workers. By the end of the year, these teams had reportedly helped to organize 11,900 new union members, recruit 4,462 men into patrol squads, and bring 831 young workers into the Communist Youth League.[63]

Having thus provided the basis for solving one of their chief difficulties, the Shanghai authorities turned their attention to production itself. The goals, as noted, were to reduce the dependence of local industry on foreign raw materials, and to meet basic demands for essential commodities at prices a majority of the population could afford to pay. Certain high quality products were to be reserved for export, in exchange for much-needed raw materials and machinery. The Shanghai Power Company converted entirely to coal because fuel oil was cut off by the blockade. By exploiting inland mines and restoring transport, the new administration was able to provide an adequate supply of coal to meet Shanghai's needs by the autumn of 1949.

The greatest difficulty for the textile industry, which accounted for over half of all Shanghai's industrial output, was the procurement of raw cotton. If production was to be restored at once, the Communists had no choice but to rely temporarily on foreign imports. During 1949, large quantities of cotton imports came from the U.S. and were transshipped in Tientsin and Hong Kong.[64] Meanwhile, the government bought up as much domestic cotton as possible and restored rail transport for its shipment to Shanghai.[65]

Refugees, Beggars, and Thieves

The announced objective of removing factories to the hinterland does not seem to have been seriously attempted during the take-over period. The dispersal of the refugee population was—but with little success. On August 5, the East China Bureau of the Party issued its "Directive on the Return of Refugees in Shanghai to Their Native Districts to Participate in Production." Although issued specifically for Shanghai, the directive called on all cities and congested areas in southern Kiangsu and Chekiang to follow the spirit of its instructions and draw up similar plans for the dispersal of their surplus populations.

63. *CFJP*, Shanghai, Jan. 31, 1950 *(CPR)*.
64. Landman, *Red China*, pp. 61-67.
65. See note 48 above.

As for Shanghai, the city was supposed to mobilize the refugees for their return and to arrange transportation. At the same time, local authorities in Shantung, northern Kiangsu and northern Anhwei were to assume responsibility for receiving the returnees, and arranging living accommodations and jobs for them. The governments and peasant associations of various *hsien* in these regions were to send representatives to Shanghai to aid in the mobilization campaign. This was to include propaganda and educational efforts intended to alleviate the anxieties of those, such as landlords and rich peasants, who had fled the rural areas in fear of land reform. The Party's attitude now was to "forget the past" and welcome back everyone. Relief allowances were to be reduced or withheld entirely for all those who refused to leave the city.[66]

The Shanghai Military Control Committee immediately set up a transit center to handle food and transport problems for departing refugees and for those returning home via Shanghai.[67] According to reports at this time, there were 100,000 landlord and rich peasant refugees in the city and some 170,000 "unemployed vagrants." Both groups were scheduled for the earliest possible departure. In addition, plans were also readied to return an estimated 650,000 "impoverished residents" to their native places.[68]

Investigations conducted by six work stations of the Shanghai Refugee Relief Association revealed, however, that there were still 454,147 refugees in Shanghai as of mid-September. It was also discovered that, beginning in early September, refugees had been entering the city, some for the second time, at a rate averaging one hundred per day. The new influx was blamed on the floods and the resulting poor harvests in northern Kiangsu, northern Anhwei, and parts of central Shantung. This was also probably one of the main reasons that Shanghai authorities had difficulty obtaining any cooperation from the local areas themselves for the return movement.[69]

Deputy Mayor P'an Han-nien later claimed that only 7,000 refugees had departed the city between September and November, and that 150,000 new refugees had arrived during that same time.[70] By mid-December, the refugee return movement was an acknowledged failure. The municipal government was concentrating simply on keeping the refugees alive, and even this was not a complete success. The *Ta kung pao* editorialized on the shame of still finding refugees dead in the streets, once a common occurrence on winter mornings in pre-liberation Shanghai. Recalling the slogan of the old liberated areas that, "not a single man should be allowed to freeze or starve to death," the paper declared that Shanghai's citizens should themselves assume responsibility for the success of the relief program and not leave everything to the government. The government was then in the process of setting up a number of relief centers around the

66. *CFJP*, Shanghai, Aug. 5, 1949 *(CPR)*.
67. *Hsin-wen jih-pao*, Shanghai, Aug. 18, 1949 *(CPR)*.
68. *Hsin-wen jih-pao*, Shanghai, Aug. 8 and 13, 1949 *(CPR*, Aug. 6-8 and 13-15); also Deputy Mayor's report, see note 62 above.
69. *TKP*, Shanghai, Sept. 19, 1949 *(CPR*, Sept. 20).
70. See note 62 above.

city.[71] An East China Committee for Production and Relief was also formed to try to cope with more fundamental problems. The function of this committee was to mobilize resources and support for the development of irrigation, production, and relief programs in the rural areas themselves.

Another aspect of the winter relief and refugee repatriation program, as outlined in the resolutions of the Second Shanghai Conference of People's Representatives in early December, was the reform of beggars, pickpockets, and thieves. In accordance with these resolutions, the Civil Affairs and Public Security Bureaus began rounding up such persons from the streets of Shanghai on the evening of December 12. Within a few days, over 5,000 including dependents were taken into custody and sent to the Children's Nursery, the Women's Training Center, and the Disabled Persons' Training Center. The 3,700 adults among them deemed fit for work were put at once into a reform and training program, essentially the same as that introduced in Kalgan as described in Chapter Eight.

Initially there was some unrest among the internees because of rumors that they were about to be sent to do forced labor in the Northeast and to fight in the Taiwan campaign. Order was restored once the officers in charge explained that experts and technicians were required for the reconstruction of the Northeast, not incompetents and vagabonds, and that the PLA was capable of liberating Taiwan without them. The program was expected to transform the beggars and pickpockets of Shanghai into honest workers, as it already had their counterparts in Manchuria and north China.[72]

Administrative Austerity

Another of the six tasks that ran into immediate difficulty was the drive to reduce public expenditure. In mid-August, the East China Bureau of the Party issued a five-point "Plan for Reorganization and Economy in All Public Organs and Military Units." The plan applied to the three cities of Nanking, Shanghai, and Hangchow, as well as to the provinces and districts in the region. All governmental and military units were directed to reduce financial expenditures; to keep clear accounts of all supplies and funds taken over from the KMT Government; to place public enterprises on a self-sufficient footing; and to promote "productive labor."

Reduction of financial expenditures would be achieved by economizing on the use of gasoline, water, and electricity; by opposition to all forms of self-indulgence, which was infecting some rural cadres after their move to the cities; by wage cuts for some employees; and by a reduction of two to four ounces in the rice ration for all public employees, in effect rescinding the increase in food allotments granted just prior to the crossing of the Yangtze.

In order to make public enterprises such as the postal service, telegraph, and the railways self-supporting, managers were directed to compile and publicize

71. *TKP*, Shanghai, Dec. 16, 1949 (*CPR*, Dec. 17).
72. *TKP*, Shanghai, Dec. 16 and 24, 1949 (*CPR*, same dates); *CFJP*, Shanghai, Jan. 5, 1950 (*CPR*).

clear accounts of profits and losses in order to prepare the public for price increases; to mobilize workers for a competitive movement to economize on supplies and increase efficiency; to work out a system whereby the profits of one unit could be used to make up the losses of another; and to learn to do business without having to rely on the Treasury or the banks for subsidies and loans.

The principal economy measure, however, was to have been the retrenchment of surplus personnel. In Nanking, Hangchow, and Shanghai, all unnecessary units and offices taken over from the KMT Government were to be abolished. All unnecessary personnel were to be transferred elsewhere if they possessed special technical skills, or discharged with one month's severance pay if they did not. "Absolutely useless" persons who had retained their positions through the influence of friends and relatives were ordered dismissed without severance pay. Some cadres from Communist military and political units that had moved into the cities would be sent to fill urgent personnel needs in the countryside. In the provinces and rural areas, all Party, government, and military units and civilian enterprises were instructed to abolish or amalgamate any redundant offices or units, and to retire or transfer all old, ailing, and unnecessary personnel.[73]

The number of people dismissed was not publicized. But on September 10, a member of the Shanghai Party Committee stated that in some administrative units and public industries the retrenchment campaign had been carried out "without due regard for the principles laid down by the Government." As a result, many former public employees now found themselves among the ranks of the unemployed. He therefore announced a new set of regulations stipulating that dismissed personnel who were unable to find other jobs would be reinstated. If no work could be found for them, as in the case of old people nearing retirement age, they were to be guaranteed a subsistence income.[74] The new regulations were implemented and the dismissed employees reinstated. So ended, in Shanghai at least, the new administration's first attempt to streamline the KMT bureaucracy it had inherited. The municipal government could claim only that its action in recalling the dismissed employees was a manifestation of its spirit of responsibility and concern for their welfare.[75]

THE PRINTING PRESS RESTORED

Reports had begun to indicate a levelling off of the price spiral during August and September.[76] Then on September 11, the People's Bank issued new currency notes in denominations of 500 and 1,000, the highest having previously been 100. According to Tseng Shan, one of Shanghai's Deputy Mayors, the primary reason for the new note issue was the rapid expansion of the new currency's circulating area. But there were other reasons. The autumn crops

73. *CFJP*, Shanghai, Aug. 17, 1949 (*CPR*, Aug. 18).
74. *Hsin-wen jih-pao,* Shanghai, Sept. 12, 1949 (*CPR,* Sept. 13).
75. *TKP*, Shanghai, Dec. 16, 1949 (*CPR*, Dec. 17); also Deputy Mayor's report, see note 62 above.
76. *TKP*, Shanghai, Aug. 12, 1949 *(CPR); CFJP*, Shanghai, Nov. 17 *(CPR).*

would soon reach the market and, because of the inflation, the amount of currency in circulation was insufficient to pay for them. The government needed large amounts of capital for the purchase of raw materials such as cotton and other commodities which it was trying to supply to urban markets, as well as for immediate investment in the reconstruction of transport facilities. Finally, the government had been obliged to rescind its order on personnel retrenchment and could not reduce its expenditures in that area as planned.[77]

By October, prices had resumed their upward course, the new note issue having aggravated, as it had so often during the KMT era, the public's loss of confidence in the government's ability to stabilize the currency. The new upward trend occurred not just in Shanghai but nationwide and continued throughout October and November. In Shanghai, a spokesman for the East China Finance and Economic Commission declared that the new wave of instability, despite its intensity, was only temporary. He blamed it on the increased volume of note issue and the conditions that made it necessary, including the far-flung military campaigns then in progress to complete the liberation of the country. He also cited raw material, power, and equipment shortages which were making it impossible for Shanghai's industries to meet the demands upon them. In addition, peasants in the surrounding newly liberated districts of east China were still wary of the new currency. As a consequence, it tended to circulate there only briefly and then to make its way back to the cities where it added to the accumulation of idle capital. And in the cities, the black market showed signs of revival, further aggravating the situation.[78]

The Second Shanghai Conference of People's Representatives was convened on December 5, in an attempt to bolster public confidence. Ch'en I, in his opening address, declared:

> The pity is that there are some people who not only fail to distinguish the differences between the price soaring situation in July and that in October, but who also refuse to distinguish between the People's Government and the former reactionary Kuomintang Government, refuse to distinguish between the temporary difficulties that must follow our victory and the insoluble difficulties that faced the Kuomintang on the eve of their extinction.

The speakers who addressed the Conference reviewed the accomplishments of the new regime since the First Conference in August, pointing out that commodity prices had responded favorably in August and September to the government's anti-inflationary efforts. The speakers emphasized the differences between the price rise that occurred in July and that of October and November. A new set of problems had replaced the first, and the second set would be overcome as the first had been. In July, the KMT blockade had just begun and the Government had not yet devised a plan to circumvent its most harmful

---

77. From a speech by Deputy Mayor Tseng to a Sept. 12 meeting of 2,000 "elite workers" called by the preparatory committee of the Shanghai General Labor Union to discuss the new note issue. *CFJP,* Shanghai, Sept. 13, 1949 *(CPR).*

78. *CFJP,* Shanghai, Nov. 17, 1949 *(CPR).*

effects. Communications had not been fully restored with the hinterland, stocks of essential commodities were low, and industry and commerce remained in a state of near collapse. Yet these problems had all been basically solved. The new ones reflected in the expanded note issue would be only temporary if the people cooperated with the Government to surmount them. The expansion of the liberated areas would soon be complete, and with the new revolutionary order would come increased revenues and financial resources. The new volume of currency had been invested in productive enterprises. The continuing development of transportation would ensure the exchange of supplies and commodities between urban and rural areas, and the development of Sino-Soviet trade would benefit the development of industry and the procurement of supplies.

In short, the new Government was in full command of the situation; there was no cause for anxiety or pessimism. Or, as Mao Tse-tung explained at the December 2 meeting of the Central People's Government Council: "We have financial difficulties, we shall tell the people where these difficulties are, we shall not hide our difficulties from the people, but we must at the same time assure the people that we know the way of surmounting the difficulties. Since we are able to surmount our difficulties, there is hope for us."[79]

THE VICTORS AND OTHERS: AN ALLIANCE
OF THE GREATEST POSSIBLE NUMBER

While overlooking the past of many known collaborators, the returning KMT Government adopted policies in 1945-46 which condemned the population in the former Japanese-occupied territories to the status of quislings and puppets. These policies fell most heavily on the intellectual community. But they were reinforced generally by the condescending attitude that officials and others returning from Free China adopted toward their countrymen who had remained in the Japanese controlled areas.

If KMT leaders thought at all about the political costs of such action, they probably dismissed the resentment it created as being of little consequence. The Communists could scarcely afford so cavalier an attitude and strove consciously to avoid it. Aware of the relative precariousness of their position within the cities, Communist leaders renewed their efforts to put together the broadest possible coalition of urban support. This resulted in perhaps the most successful political achievement of the immediate post-liberation period.

SOLDIERS AND BUREAUCRATS

By proclamation of the General Headquarters of the PLA, all KMT officers and government officials suspected of war crimes were to be arrested, thoroughly investigated, and strictly punished in accordance with the law. War crimes included murder and the forceful seizure or destruction of the people's property; killing or harming prisoners-of-war; the destruction of arms and ammunition; the

79. Quoted by Mayor Ch'en I in his inaugural address, see note 50 above.

destruction of communications equipment, documents, telegrams, files, et cetera; the destruction of grain supplies; and the destruction of public utilities, factory installations, banks, cultural relics, and all public property.[80]

With the exception of persons found guilty of these acts, everyone who so wished was welcomed into the service of the new regime. The Communists prescribed political reeducation for all such people, as the returning KMT had done for students and teachers in 1945-46. The Communists, however, attached no stigma to those who attended and completed the reform courses. Surrendering units of the KMT armies were integrated into the PLA, as they had been throughout the Civil War. Prisoners-of-war were given the choice of returning home or joining the Communist forces. Officers were generally given the same choice, after a period of reform and training. By October, 1948, some 800,000 soldiers from the KMT armies had joined the PLA in this manner.[81]

After Fu Tso-i surrendered Peiping to the Communists without fighting in January, 1949, the terms of the agreement were unusually generous and were widely publicized in the hope of inducing others to follow his example. But political cadres were assigned to all former KMT units to ensure that their reorganization was a genuine political renovation and not just a change of colors and insignias. Upon the cadres devolved the task of teaching both officers and men the political system of the PLA; of creating a new command relationship between the officers and their troops; and of developing a new awareness among both concerning their relationship to the people.

Officers who chose to return home rather than serve in the PLA were allowed to do so. They were issued three month's pay and given train fare home as well as free meals and lodging along the way while travelling in the liberated areas. Each man returning home was also issued a document acknowledging his "meritorious service" as a participant in the peaceful liberation of Peiping. Even these men were assured that should they change their minds and wish to serve in the PLA in the future, they would be welcome to do so.[82]

This same policy was applied to the members of the civilian bureaucracy, although the necessity of changing their work style was recognized as a major challenge. In March, 1949, Tung Pi-wu, Chairman of the North China government, identified it as one of the three main tasks after the conclusion of the war and the revival of production.[83] Hence everyone was required to participate in the political reform program. In Shanghai, this began for the personnel of the KMT municipal government on June 13. The course generally lasted one month. The trainees attended lectures which outlined the Party's main principles and policies. They were then divided into small groups for discussion and debate. By

---

80. "Ch'eng-ch'u chan-cheng tsui-fan ming-ling" [Order on the punishment of war criminals], in Hua-pei hsin hua shu-tien, ed., *Kuan-yü ch'eng-shih*, pp. 10-11.

81. Mao Tse-tung (Oct. 10, 1948), *Selected Works*, 4:271.

82. U.S. Cons., Peiping, Hsinhua radio, North Shensi, Feb. 20 and Mar. 1, 1949.

83. U.S. Cons., Peiping, Hsinhua radio, North Shensi, Mar. 6, 1949.

December, some fifty thousand of Shanghai's public employees had completed the training course.[84]

The key consideration at this time was the expertise of the individuals involved rather than their political inclinations. Everywhere, it was the skilled and the technically competent that the Party went out of its way to welcome. Typical was a directive of the Northeast Bureau of the Party on August 1, 1948, concerning the treatment of staff members in public enterprises taken over from the KMT. Technical personnel were to be retained even if they were "ideologically in disagreement with communism" so long as they performed their duties faithfully. The same applied to all high level administrators, except those who had in the past genuinely oppressed the workers. Recognizing that many staff members and workers in public enterprises had been forced to join the KMT or its Youth Corps to keep their jobs, the directive emphasized that employees were not to be discriminated against solely because of membership in these organizations.[85]

STUDENTS AND INTELLECTUALS

Nowhere was the success of this approach more apparent than in the Party's relationship with the student community. As a result, the Communists were able to tap a major source of energy and enthusiasm for reform among a group which had remained in the KMT-controlled cities throughout the Civil War—one which, if given the opportunity, would probably not have chosen a Communist government for China. That these students were not entirely to the Party's liking was demonstrated by its persistent efforts to discipline them after the tasks of the immediate post-liberation period had been accomplished. Even then, the new regime tried to avoid holding itself morally or ideologically above them. More significant, it welcomed their service and allotted them positions of relative prestige and importance as cadres responsible for the implementation of its policies.

This is not to claim that the Party did not make "mistakes" in its treatment of intellectuals both young and otherwise. As noted, the Communists themselves acknowledged that errors had been committed against teachers in the countryside and technical personnel in the cities. But the attack on left adventurism in the Party's dealings with intellectuals had been an integral part of the 1948 anti-leftist campaigns. By the time the PLA began taking China's largest cities, where the most active intellectual population was concentrated, any remaining adventurist tendencies had been left firmly behind.

The theoretical rationale for this policy of moderation has been outlined in Chapter Six. The more immediate practical considerations were explained in a

84. *TKP,* Shanghai, June 11 and 20, 1949 (*CPR,* June 11-13 and 18-20); and Deputy Mayor Pan's report, see note 62 above.

85. U.S. Cons., Peiping, Hsinhua radio, North Shensi, Aug. 17, 1948. The full text of the directive did state, however, that although KMT and Youth Corps members were to be given work, they were "for a short time" not to be given important responsibilities. See Chapt. Eight, note 61; see also, *Hsin kung-shang cheng-ts'e,* p. 179.

Hsinhua editorial in October, 1948. It noted that the military victories were creating new needs for large numbers of politically progressive people capable of supplementing the regular cadres. Hence the Party had decided to set up short-term schools and training classes on a large scale. These would take in intellectual youth and, after giving them the necessary political training, assign them to posts where they were most needed. It was anticipated, however, that such short-course schools would not be able to meet the needs of government and public enterprises. The Party therefore called upon the existing regular middle schools to try to prepare large numbers of students for these new tasks.[86]

Phase One: Joining the Revolution

At Yenching University just outside Peiping, 500 of the school's 950 students responded to the first call to participate in the liberation of the city. The vicinity of the university was occupied by Communist forces several weeks prior to the surrender of Peiping, and the students spent much of the interim preparing for their tasks. Altogether some 2,300 students from Tsinghua, Yenching, Peiping Normal, and Peking Universities were initially mobilized for this work. Organized into propaganda teams and literary and artistic groups, they explained to their juniors in middle schools the duties of young intellectuals in the new society and staged cultural performances for the entertainment of factory workers. On street corners, university student propaganda teams collaborated with those of the PLA in lecturing passersby concerning the programs and policies of the new administration.[87]

At the Fourteenth All-China Student Representatives Conference which met in Peiping from March 1 to 6, delegates were reminded of the concrete tasks their colleagues had performed in the service of the revolution, which they, too, could perform. Many thousands of students had left school to become backbone cadres during the Anti-Japanese War. In Yenan, middle school students and teachers had organized themselves into medical teams and followed the troops for thousands of miles. In the liberated areas of east China, students had been given responsibility for food transport, and in northern Kiangsu they had formed armed education brigades. In Harbin, Tsitsihar, and Chiamuszu, students had organized blood transfusion teams for the PLA; and in many industrial areas of the Northeast students had entered factories, organized the workers, and set up night schools for them.[88]

The opportunities to serve the revolution were seemingly unlimited and the students of Peiping responded accordingly. Several thousand of them appeared

86. "Hui-fu ho fa-chan chung-teng chiao-yü te chung-ta cheng-chih jen-wu" [The important political task of restoring and developing secondary education], Oct. 14, 1948, in *Chih-shih-fen-tzu yü chiao-yü wen-t'i,* p. 18.

87. U.S. Cons., Peiping, Hsinhua radio, North Shensi, Feb. 13, 1949; and Ralph and Nancy Lapwood, *Through the Chinese Revolution,* pp. 38-54.

88. "Chieh-fang-ch'ü hsueh yun pao-kao chi-yao" [Abstract of the report on the student movement in the liberated areas], in *Chung-kuo hsueh-sheng ta t'uan-chieh,* pp. 17-18. This report was made to the Fourteenth All-China Student Representative Conference by Li Hsiu-chen.

for the entrance examinations at the four newly established cadre training centers in the Peiping area. Of the four, the North China University, successor to the old Anti-Japanese University from Yenan days, maintained the strictest entrance requirements. It admitted recommended university and middle school graduates by examination for a five- to six-month training course. The North China Military and Political University also maintained fairly strict entrance requirements for its six-month training course. Only persons between the ages of eighteen and twenty-eight with at least a junior middle school education were eligible to take the entrance examination. This institution was run by the PLA, its purpose being to turn out cadres in a wide range of fields including politics, economics, and culture. The North China People's Revolutionary University also based admission on examination but admitted applicants with all levels of educational attainment including elementary school graduates.[89]

Finally, almost everyone who applied was admitted to the six-week training course of the PLA's Southward-bound Service Corps. So enthusiastic was the response that in the five days between February 26 and March 2, 2,500 students, technicians, and even some college professors enrolled to take the Service Corps examination.[90] By mid-March, over 3,000 persons, mostly local college and middle school students, had passed the examination. A solemn matriculation ceremony addressed by Lo Jung-huan, Political Director of the PLA on the Peiping-Tientsin Front, and T'ao Chu, Deputy Director of the Army's Political Department, was held on March 12 for the first group of students to begin training. This group was made up largely of students from the major Peiping universities.[91] A month later, 2,600 successful applicants were welcomed into the Service Corps at another matriculation ceremony in Chungshan Park addressed by Commander Lin Piao.[92] The Southward-bound Service Corps also set up a training camp in Tientsin which was apparently as successful as the Peiping unit in recruiting volunteers.[93]

The three universities had begun enrolling students in mid-February. Within a month, some 30,000 local students, government functionaries, shop clerks, and unemployed young people had taken the entrance examinations. Approximately half of the total were admitted. The first classes were roughly as follows: North China University, 5,500; North China Military and Political University, 1,700; and North China People's Revolutionary University, 8,300. About 60 percent of the successful applicants were students.[94] A branch of the North China People's Revolutionary University was also set up in Tientsin, as was a North China Workers' Cadre School, which planned to begin enrollment on April 1 and to admit about 2,000 students.[95]

89. U.S. Cons., Peiping, Hsinhua radio, North Shensi, Feb. 27, 1949; and *Hsin-wen pao*, Shanghai, Apr. 4, 1949 (*CPR*, Apr. 8).
90. U.S. Cons., Peiping, Hsinhua radio, North Shensi, Mar. 9, 1949.
91. U.S. Cons., Peiping, Hsinhua radio, North Shensi, Mar. 14, 1949.
92. U.S. Cons., Peiping, Hsinhua radio, North Shensi, Apr. 10, 1949.
93. U.S. Cons., Peiping, Hsinhua radio, North Shensi, Mar. 18 and 21, 1949.
94. U.S. Cons., Peiping, Hsinhua radio, North Shensi, Mar. 18, 1949.
95. U.S. Cons., Peiping, Hsinhua radio, North Shensi, Mar. 27, 1949.

These numbers are significant considering that the entire college-level student population of Peiping numbered only some 20,000 at this time. Many of Peiping's major colleges and universities had officially reopened by mid-March. But one observer reported that, with the possible exception of the engineering and science departments, classes could hardly be said to be proceeding normally, since so many students had joined the cadre training programs or were organizing and propagandizing in Peiping itself.[96]

As the Communist armies moved south, the cadre recruiting drive moved with them. In the Shanghai-Nanking area it was officially launched in mid-June. By that time, the East China Military and Political University had established two training centers, one in Nanking and the other in Soochow, and had begun enrolling students for the first course scheduled to commence in July.[97]

In Shanghai, the Students Association called together 1,000 student delegates, many of them members of the student self-governing associations, from every university, college, and middle school in the city. The meeting, held on June 16, called upon the delegates to begin, within the coming week, the mobilization of their classmates to serve the new People's Government. Chang Yu-min, Chairman of the Shanghai Students Association, announced the quotas to be filled: 6,000 to 8,000 students were needed for the PLA's Southward-bound Service Corps; 5,000 for the East China Military and Political University; 600 to serve as trade and labor union cadres; 400 for the Alien Affairs Service of the People's Government; and 100 for cultural work in Shanghai. He advised that recruiting be concentrated among those eighteen years old and above. He also advised students in engineering, medicine, agriculture, and the sciences to remain in school in order to complete their studies for future service to the nation.[98]

The next day, the Shanghai recruiting drive for the Service Corps was launched with a plea from Chang Ting-ch'eng, Director of the Corps and member of the CCP Central Committee, to the intellectual youth of the city. He urged them to join the "Southern Expedition" of the PLA and carry the revolution throughout the country. According to Chang, the tasks of the Corps were, first, to mobilize the masses to support the army through publicity and educational work; and second, to participate in take-over work following the completion of military operations.[99] Within a few days, over 1,000 students had volunteered for the Service Corps, including 400 from Futan University and 200 from Chinan University.[100]

The Shanghai Service Corps volunteers, like those in Peiping and Tientsin, received only the most rudimentary training. After five to six weeks devoted

96. *Hsin-wen pao,* Shanghai, Apr. 4, 1949. Derk Bodde (*Peking Diary,* p. 130) reported that only 1,804 out of 2,482 Tsinghua students were in attendance when classes resumed in early March. He assumed that most of the absentees had chosen to follow the PLA southward. On the number of college-level students in Peiping, see Chapter Three, note 22.

97. *CFJP,* Shanghai, June 13, 1949 (*CPR,* June 11-13).

98. *CFJP,* Shanghai, June 17, 1949 *(CPR).*

99. *TKP,* Shanghai, June 19, 1949 (*CPR,* June 18-20).

100. *TKP,* Shanghai, June 20, 1949 (*CPR,* June 18-20).

largely to studying the constitution of the New Democratic Youth League, the CCP's eight-point proclamation on conditions for peace with the KMT, the PLA's rules of discipline and points for attention for the urban areas, and Mao's "The Present Situation and Our Tasks," the trainees were sent south in coordination with the advancing units of the PLA.[101]   During September, more than 2,500 young intellectuals in the Service Corps arrived in Foochow from Shanghai. Some were sent on to work in other towns, but most remained in Foochow itself. They were assigned to work in the finance, economic, education, cultural, and public security agencies of the Fukien provincial government, as well as in the Youth League and the local People's Revolutionary University.[102]

A rural service corps was also formed. About 10,000 cadres, military workers, and "youthful members of the intelligentsia" were organized by PLA units and local authorities into the Chekiang Rural Service Corps under the provincial Party Committee. Commencing in early August, the Corps was to inaugurate social reforms, organize poor peasants and tenant farmers for land reform, and generally to eliminate counter-revolutionary influences in the countryside. A South Kiangsu Rural Service Corps, with training centers in Wusih and Soochow, was also organized about the same time.[103]

These hastily trained intellectual cadres, most of whom were known to be devoid of "strong ideological belief" in the Party's principles, were regarded with open suspicion by some Party members and older cadres. The Party tried to maintain a distinction at this time between the training programs for ordinary intellectuals and those for cadres.[104]   As regards the latter, the cadre work conferences, training programs, and rectification campaigns were all similar in method and approach, and have been described at length elsewhere.[105]   The initial education programs for ordinary intellectuals tended to eschew the intense criticism and personal introspection that cadres were required to undergo. The political courses concentrated on lectures and discussions about current events, basic questions of the Chinese revolution, and policies of the CCP. The six-week training courses of the Southward-bound Service Corps were generally of this type, although its young members regularly assumed cadre-like roles as part of their subsequent work.

To quiet the fears this aroused, Party leaders argued that participation in the Service Corps was itself a form of political training as was organizing the workers and other such tasks. "In this way," commented one editorial, "the defects of ideological ignorance and vacillation in action will be remedied. This gigantic

101. *CFJP,* Shanghai, July 19, 1949 *(CPR).*
102. *CFJP,* Shanghai, Oct. 25, 1949 *(CPR).*
103. *CFJP* and *TKP,* Shanghai, Aug. 16, 1949 *(CPR).*
104. See Chapter Six, notes 68, 69.
105. On rectification and the work conference, see William Hinton, *Fanshen,* pp. 319-416. On the cadre training course at North China University, see Robert J. Lifton, *Thought Reform and the Psychology of Totalism,* pp. 253-73.

revolutionary task will thus prove of far-reaching importance in the reformation of the members of the intelligentsia."[106]

Certainly, this was more effective than a reform program that openly discriminated against them as the unstable elements many held them to be. Nor did the editorial writers allow this point of comparison with the KMT to go unrecorded. In the past, they emphasized, many who sought careers in public service were forced to join the KMT or its Youth Corps. In 1949, the Communists could truthfully claim that no such obstacles were being placed in the way of university and middle school graduates who wished to serve the people. Finally, the Party could also take credit for having found a solution, albeit a partial and temporary one, for another problem of great concern to the intellectual community. As noted previously, unemployment was a major worfy for students during the Civil War years, aggravated of course by the war itself. The saying, *"pi-yeh chi shih-yeh"* (graduation equals unemployment) was a common one among college students at this time. Hence the significance of the claim that "This year in our newly liberated areas, things are entirely different. The new China's work of political, economic, military, and cultural construction is just developing and there is need of talent everywhere. Cadres are needed and our graduates have an opportunity to be of much service."[107]

Phase Two: Back to School

For those who did not choose to participate actively in the revolutionary enterprise, the Party called upon the municipal student associations and the New Democratic Youth League to sponsor summer school political study programs.[108] The target was primarily the ordinary student, rather than the activist. According to one writer, the past method in newly liberated areas had always been to concentrate first on the most progressive elements. Hence this early attempt at "mass" political education of intellectual youth was regarded as something of an experiment.[109]

In Peiping, some 12,000 students participated. About 10,000—mostly middle school students—attended the Young People's Summer School. Another 1,900 joined the University and Middle School Students Summer Study Corps. About

106. *TKP*, Shanghai, June 24, 1949 *(CPR)*.

107. "Pi-yeh i-hou" [After graduation], *Chung-kuo ch'ing-nien* [Chinese Youth], No. 9, reprinted in Ch'ing-nien ch'u-pan-she, ed., *Chung-kuo hsueh-sheng yun-tung te tang-ch'ien jen-wu* (hereafter *Hsueh-sheng yun-tung*), p. 52. In Tientsin, an estimated 1,000 young people, unemployed or unable to continue their studies, applied at the Tientsin office of the joint enrollment committee of North China University, North China Military and Political University, and North China People's Revolutionary University, to sit for the entrance examinations (U.S. Cons., Peiping, Hsinhua radio, North Shensi, Feb. 22, 1949).

108. "Shu-chia k'uai tao le" [Summer vacation will soon be here], *Chung-kuo ch'ing-nien*, no. 9, and "Kuan-yü shu-ch'i hsueh-hsi" [Concerning summer study], *ibid.*, no. 14, both reprinted in *Hsueh-sheng yun-tung*, pp. 54-57.

109. Hsu Li-ch'ün, "Pei-ching shih shu-ch'i te ch'ing-nien szu-hsiang chiao-yü kung-tso" [Peking's summer youth education work], in *Hsueh-sheng yun-tung*, p. 72.

half the participants in the latter were ordinary university and middle school students, while the other half were members of the New Democratic Youth League. The program was a combination Youth League training course and a mass training class.

The students' enthusiasm was said to be great. But because time was short and many of them had only the most superficial knowledge of the revolution, the work load was kept relatively light. It concentrated on providing only an introduction to the most important topics, such as dialectical materialism, the class struggle, the development of history, the relationship between education and political affairs, and Mao Tse-tung's "On the People's Democratic Dictatorship." In addition, many famous revolutionaries, including P'eng Chen, Po I-po, and Ai Szu-ch'i, came to lecture to the students. They avoided lengthy theoretical discussions in favor of revolutionary tales and war stories thought to be more suitable for a mass audience. Plays, films, sports, and excursions rounded out the summer school program in Peiping, which upon its conclusion was declared to have been a great success.[110]

A summer of well-meaning lectures and social activities was, of course, only the beginning. During the latter half of 1949 and early 1950, scores of articles and pamphlets were written to assist student association leaders and Youth League cadres in educating the student population. The study materials invariably began with the usual positive statements concerning the importance of intellectuals for the revolution, and the Party's need for their talent and support in building the new society. The intellectuals' weaknesses were primarily a legacy of the old society and could be overcome. Toward that end, they were enumerated and analyzed: fear of class struggle; lack of practical knowledge; the tradition of holding physical labor in low regard; the tendency to view education primarily as a means to achieve wealth; traits of individualism and liberalism; undisciplined behavior; inability to persevere under adverse circumstances; insufficient knowledge about the Party and its work; and lack of cohesion as a social group.

These general weaknesses were creating a number of problems for young intellectuals in the new society. For example, there were the conflicts between their loyalty to their landlord or rich peasant families and their desire to work with the Party for the construction of a new China. Some felt resentment towards the Party for the treatment their parents received; others felt themselves suspect in the eyes of the Party because of their class origins. Some felt both resentment and fear simultaneously. These conflicts were intensified when young people were not allowed to work in localities where there could be conflicts of interest arising from their family backgrounds. The Northeast regulation temporarily barring intellectual cadres from holding positions at the district and village levels had been a source of much uncertainty and unhappiness. There were other problems, such as having to discontinue studies because of financial difficulties or inadequate facilities; and the common phenomenon of unemployment following graduation. Certainly these were all carry-overs from

110. *Ibid.*, pp. 71-75.

the old society; despite the efforts of the new regime, they could not be solved everywhere immediately.[111]

Finally, there were many problems within the schools themselves which demanded attention. On the one hand, some teachers were too conservative and seemed to think that once the political revolution had been accomplished they could go back to teaching the same subjects in the same manner as before. Many thousands of teachers and professors had participated in summer study classes which introduced them to the basic elements of the New Democracy. Still, the reform of teaching methods, textbooks, and school curricula could not be carried out all at once, and this caused impatience and dissatisfaction among the more progressive students.

On the other hand, many of these same students lacked self-discipline. If the emphasis this particular problem received is any indication, it was a major one during the autumn term of 1949. The new academic administrators found themselves confronted, as their KMT counterparts had been, by a situation bordering on anarchy. The Communists' were partly to blame for this: the declarations they made immediately after liberation gave students and teachers "the right and the freedom to participate in revolutionary activities."[112] Nevertheless, the kind of "enthusiastic student movement" that had preceded and accompanied liberation, having served its purpose, could not be allowed to continue indefinitely.

In the early months immediately after liberation, noted one critic, the students had actively aided the new Government in its work. They had gone out on street corners propagandizing, they had attended cadre schools, and gone to work in newly liberated areas. They had listened to reports, held discussion meetings, studied revolutionary theory, and carried out thought reform. This student movement, in coordination with the final advance of the PLA, had roused the spirit of the entire country, aided the establishment of the new revolutionary order, and hastened the students' own development. This was necessary and correct. All newly liberated cities and towns had first gone through this stage of excitement and enthusiasm, and much had been achieved because of it. But once that stage was past, the students' main task was to return to their studies.[113]

111. See, for example: (a) Feng Wen-pin, "Yü kung nung ch'ün-chung chieh-ho wei kung nung ch'ün-chung fu-wu" [Unite with the worker-peasant masses to serve the worker-peasant masses], a report to the Fourteenth All-China Students Representative Conference on Mar. 2, 1949, reprinted in *Chung-kuo hsueh-sheng ta t'uan-chieh*, pp. 5-10; (b) Ch'eng Fang-wu, "Kuan-yü chih-shih yü chih-shih-fen-tzu wen-t'i" [On knowledge and the problem of the intellectuals], Hsin hua jih-pao tzu-liao shih, ed., *Lun chih-shih-fen-tzu: hsueh-hsi ts'ung-shu*, pp. 6-10; (c) Hsieh Mu-ch'iao, "Chih-shih-fen-tzu kai-tsao wen-t'i" [The problem of reforming intellectuals], *ibid.*, pp. 18-22; (d) Ch'en I, "Kuan-yü chih-shih-fen-tzu ts'an-chia chieh-fang-ch'ü hsueh-hsi yu kung-tso wen-t'i" [On the problems of intellectuals participating in study and work in the liberated areas], *ibid.*, pp. 28-32.

112. *TKP*, Shanghai, July 22, 1949 *(CPR)*.

113. Chiang Nan-hsiang, "Lun k'ai-chan hsueh-hsiao chung te hsin min-chu-chu-i hsueh-hsi" [On developing new democratic studies in the schools], in Ch'ing-nien ch'u-pan-she, ed., *Hsueh-sheng yun-tung*, p. 20.

Yet in almost every newly liberated city that autumn, there were students who refused to attend classes regularly, who refused to open a book, and who ignored their teachers.[114] In one Peking middle school, classes normally contained about sixty students, but often only twelve or thirteen showed up. At another middle school, students intentionally scheduled meetings during class time. Some students attended only the classes they thought important, such as political studies or their science courses, their attitude being that since they were now liberated they could manage their own education.[115] Nor did the youth work cadres always act to contain this anarchical behavior. On the contrary, the student cadres (members of the school's Youth League branch, the Party branch, and the officers of the student body association) were often so busy attending meetings that they had little time left for their own studies.[116]

At the other extreme, some students tried to reform study methods by launching study competition campaigns modeled on the labor emulation drives of factory workers. Educational authorities tried to discourage this. They pointed out that production and study were two different things, making it impossible to assume that the more and the faster students studied, the better they would learn.[117] But by this time the autumn term was nearing an end and they found themselves combating yet another problem: a groundswell of student opinion against taking examinations. This, too, was at least partly the fruit of the Communists' own past denunciations of the KMT educational system for making examinations and grades the sole ends of study. In January, 1950, therefore, school officials called upon the student associations and the Youth League to start a "review movement." Its purpose was to prepare students for exams and to explain the significance of these under the new democratic educational system.[118]

SUMMARY

The achievements of the CCP during its take-over from the KMT were neither unmixed nor did they come effortlessly. They were noteworthy only by comparison with a similar episode, still fresh in the public mind, which had marked the beginning of the end of urban support for the KMT.

114. "Tsai hsueh-hsiao k'ai hsueh ch'ien te chi chü hua" [A few words before school starts], *Chung-kuo ch'ing-nien,* no. 17, reprinted in Shang-hai shih hsueh-sheng lien-ho-hui, ed., *Chung-kuo hsueh-sheng yun-tung te tang-ch'ien jen-wu,* pp. 1-2.

115. "Ying chiu-cheng hsueh-hsi shang san-man hsien-hsiang" [Undisciplined manifestations in studies should be corrected], *Chung-kuo ch'ing-nien,* no. 8, in Ch'ing-nien ch'u-pan-she, ed., *Hsueh-sheng yun-tung,* pp. 44-45.

116. "K'ai-hui pu yao t'ai-to" [There should not be too many meetings], *Chung-kuo ch'ing nien,* no. 8, in Ch'ing-nien ch'u-pan-she, ed., *Hsueh-sheng yun-tung,* p. 46.

117. "Hsueh-hsi ching-sai pu i t'i-ch'ang" [It is not correct to advocate study competitions], *Chung-kuo ch'ing-nien,* no. 32, in Ch'ing-nien ch'u-pan-she, ed., *Hsueh-sheng yun-tung,* pp. 63-64.

118. Yao pu yao k'ao-shih" [Whether or not to hold examinations], *Chung-kuo ch'ing-nien,* no. 31, in Ch'ing-nien ch'u-pan-she, ed., *Hsueh-sheng yun-tung,* p. 48; and *CFJP,* Shanghai, Jan. 4 and 13, 1950 (*CPR,* same dates).

With respect to discipline and order, the behavior of Communist personnel both military and civilian was exemplary—or at least it had become so by the time they emerged from the relatively obscure cities of Manchuria. Initially, Communist forces seem to have been guilty of many of the same kinds of errors as the KMT. Unlike their counterparts, however, Communist leaders acted to correct the errors before too much damage had been done. Even those who otherwise had little sympathy with their cause had nothing but praise for the behavior of the soldiers and cadres who entered China's largest cities in 1949. This discipline, supplemented by the factory protection movement, seems also to have safeguarded China's urban economic infrastructure from many of the physical dangers of the take-over period.

Less easily solved were the economic problems the CCP inherited from the KMT. In the immediate post-liberation period, the Communists did, or tried to do, almost everything in the area of economic, financial, and monetary policy that the KMT had been criticized for neglecting during its take-over from the Japanese. But while the rate of inflation during the first year of Communist rule never reached the extremes experienced under the KMT, it was many months before the effort to stabilize the market began to show significant results. The Communist take-over was marked, as the KMT's had been four years previously, by enough economic dislocation and monetary instability to undermine public confidence in the new administration.

In the case of the KMT, its troubles arose in large measure from the folly of its own policies and actions compounded by the continuing economic misman-agement of the Civil War years. The difficulties of the CCP, on the other hand, were due in large measure to the enormity of the problems it had inherited, and only in lesser degree to its own actions and inexperience. But these were sufficient to arouse apprehension and uncertainty in business and industrial circles, as did the labor agitation which seemed to erupt everywhere during the first months after the Communist take-over.

Nevertheless, enforced austerity in food and clothing, made possible by increasingly effective government control over essential commodities, helped the cities through the lean winter of 1949-50. Thus the new administration was able to minimize the most harmful effects of inflation on the livelihood of the people, and by spring there began to be indications that the inflation would be broken. That the CCP possessed a formula for coping with China's economic problems, as well as the ability to implement it, became apparent by the slow but steady progress toward monetary stability and the revival of production during the Communists' first year in power.

Politically, the most successful achievement of the take-over period emerged from the efforts to put together the broadest possible coalition of urban support. These efforts extended to the officers and men of the KMT armies, to the members of its civilian bureaucracy, and to the intellectual community. In this way, the Communists gained positive assistance during the transition period from an unlikely source—groups that had remained with the KMT until the end. Far from denouncing them as opportunists, the Communists welcomed their collaboration to maintain the day-to-day administration of the country, restore its economy, and expand the ranks of the advancing PLA.

Within the student community, which had at least developed a vocal resistance to the KMT, the Party was able to tap a major source of energy and enthusiasm for reform. Temporarily overlooking their "weaknesses" and lack of commitment to communism, the Party gave them positions of relative prestige and importance as cadres responsible for the implementation of its policies. The Communists thus gained many thousands of urgently needed activists to supplement its regular work force. At the same time, the new recruits received in-service training which was for them as effective an introduction to the goals and mores of the new order as any political reeducation course.

In 1945, the KMT first managed to alienate a large segment of the intellectual community by officially assuming that it remained tainted by its exposure to the Japanese. Then, preoccupied with the war against the Communists to the exclusion of all else, KMT leaders adopted an all-or-nothing approach in their dealings with the intellectual community. In the process, they virtually threw away the residual support they retained within it. By contrast, the Communists were able to capitalize on their own share of goodwill by avoiding immediate demands of total commitment. As a result, they managed to enlist the intellectuals' active participation in an enterprise that most of them had not previously chosen to serve.

X
The Politics of Civil War

What conclusions can be drawn concerning the KMT's loss of support, and the shift of allegiance to the Chinese Communists? In terms of policy and performance, was the outcome a Communist victory? Or was it more accurately a KMT debacle, as was often suggested at the time? Did the Communists win a genuine mandate to rule? Or were they the accidental beneficiaries of the KMT's mistakes and Japan's excesses?

As the year 1948 drew to a close, there were few sectors of Chinese society that had not experienced the adverse effects of KMT rule. Popular resentment had been given overt expression in the form of labor disputes, peasant uprisings, rice riots, rebellion in Taiwan, student demonstrations, and a steady stream of criticism from the intellectual community. The Chinese people were demanding social justice; the elimination of corruption; economic security; less repressive government; a change in the form of government away from one-party KMT rule; and an end to the neglect and exploitation that characterized the KMT Government's relationship with the countryside. Everyone, including members of the KMT itself, seemed to know what was wrong; but the demands for change and reform did not influence the conduct of the Government in any substantial way.

THE CITIES

In the cities, the beginning of widespread disillusionment with the KMT Government came in 1945-46, during its return to the areas occupied by the Japanese. By the end of World War II, the words "incompetent" and "corrupt" had already become standard shorthand terms in Free China to summarize the weaknesses of KMT rule. After August, 1945, the meaning of those words was defined by firsthand experience for virtually everyone in the former Japanese-occupied cities of east, north, and northeast China. In these areas, the sense of public disillusionment was perhaps greater because the incompetence and corruption came from a government that had stood for eight years as the symbol of the nation's will to survive. The welcome for the returning KMT cooled within a matter of weeks.

The administrative structure set up to implement the take-over was chaotic and incapable of performing the tasks required of it. Lacking adequate institutional constraints, the men who staffed the structure could hardly be expected to rise above it. Corruption reached truly unprecedented proportions as the take-over officials, both military and civilian, scrambled to appropriate for their own use property owned or occupied by the Japanese and their collaborators. In addition, take-over policies were either ill-conceived or improperly implemented. Workers found themselves without adequate relief to tide them over months of unemployment caused by the suspension of industrial production in the recovered areas and the depression in the hinterland. Industrialists in the interior who had sustained the wartime production of Free China were brought to the verge of bankruptcy as anticipated compensation from the Government did not materialize. In the Kiangsu-Chekiang area, industrialists and businessmen were hurt by the depreciation of puppet currency formalized in the official exchange rate for its conversion into Government currency. Students and teachers were antagonized by the Government's reconversion policy in education, which reduced them to puppet status—while many who had actively collaborated with the Japanese-sponsored Wang Ching-wei regime were able to buy respectability from the take-over authorities.

Still the take-over period did not provide the basis for challenging the KMT's right to rule. There was no public demand for a change of government, but only for the reform of the one in power. Unfortunately for the KMT, most of the issues which aroused such widespread criticism during the take-over were never satisfactorily resolved. Thus what might have been dismissed as a temporary interlude of confusion and maladministration in the immediate wake of the Japanese surrender, developed with the passage of time into the beginning of popular urban disaffection with KMT rule.

The continuing mismanagement of the economy had even more serious consequences. The Government's policy of inflationary finance was only the most dramatic example of its failures in this area. Perhaps the most dangerous consequence of the reliance on printing press money was that it lulled the Government into believing there could be a relatively painless solution to its financial problems. The economy of Free China did manage to survive the Anti-Japanese War on this basis. But eventually, this solution proved more hazardous than what had initially seemed the more difficult course of austerity and self-reliance. Inflationary forces were set in motion that could not be halted without drastic and far-reaching revisions in the Government's extravagant life style. Without any past experience in implementing the hard decisions that such changes would have necessitated, Government leaders chose to finance their war against the Communists in the same manner as the one that had preceded it. The result was a political regime with neither the will nor the capacity to do anything but preside over the deterioration of the urban economy.

More specifically, the inflation provided a ready-made issue for a labor force suddenly freed at the end of World War II from the constraints of eight years of Japanese rule and ten years of KMT control before that. Within the context of rampant inflation, the Government could not reassert its pre-war hold over labor. During the first six months after the Japanese surrender, labor ignored with impunity officially established procedures for the resolution of labor-management disputes. As a result, the Government had no choice but to acquiesce to labor's demand for automatic wage adjustments corresponding to the rise in the cost of living.

This decision not only accelerated the upward wage-price spiral; it also compromised the KMT's long-standing alliance with business and industry. The Government was in effect obliged to trade a fitful peace on the labor front for the resentment of entrepreneurs, who argued that concessions to labor were contributing to soaring production costs. High wage payments were only part of the problem. But the Government seemingly could not win, since it was responsible, either because of the inflation itself or because of the inadequate attempts to minimize its consequences, for virtually all other components of the problem as well. The resentment culminated in the August, 1948, reforms which finally brought the Shanghai Chamber of Commerce and the Shanghai Industrial Association into open denunciation of the Government's policies.

Meanwhile, business, industry, and the public at large had for some time been demonstrating their lack of confidence in more concrete ways. Commercial and financial circles refused to respond positively when the Government floated a bond issue. The public demonstrated an understandable tendency to invest its savings elsewhere than in the bank. Merchants held back supplies for cities where prices were controlled during the emergency reform programs of 1947 and 1948. Entrepreneurs indulged in hoarding and speculation as these became more profitable than regular business and productive operations, and so added to the recession-unemployment cycle. The Government's mishandling of the economy thus produced a general erosion of public confidence in its ability to govern. This was fed by, and in turn contributed to, the inadequacy of most of the Government's efforts to reduce inflationary pressures. It was unable to induce— and unwilling to enforce—compliance with reform measures, even when these were identified as necessary components of the struggle against the Communists.

This erosion of public confidence was general and not confined, as was sometimes assumed, to the urban salaried middle class. It was often argued that the inflation cost the KMT regime at least the "support" of these middle income groups which had emerged from World War II as a new depressed class and remained in that state throughout the Civil War years. The main groups involved were professors and teachers, military officers, and civil servants, and they did bear the major personal burden of soaring prices and depreciating currency. Yet none of these groups as such actually abandoned the KMT until its defeat on the battlefield made indefinite exile the apparent condition for continued support.

The impoverishment of the academic community did, of course, inspire one of the major themes of the student anti-war movement. The professors themselves precipitated the Anti-Hunger Anti-Civil War demonstrations in 1947 with their demands for, among other things, an increase in basic salary and automatic wage adjustments geared to the rise in the cost of living. The economic depriva-tions caused by the Government's use of the printing press to finance the war provided one important issue for those who argued against the Civil War, and obviously helped to undermine support for it within the intellectual community. But unlike the labor movement, which fed directly on the economic chaos created by the inflation, the intellectuals' aversion to the Civil War was based on a more complex assessment of the nature of KMT rule and the sacrifices the nation as a whole should have to bear in order to preserve it. The intellectuals' own impoverishment was only one of the considerations apparent in their assessment. They opposed the Civil War because they reasoned it was too high a price to pay in order to keep in power the KMT regime as it was then constituted.

This reasoning was based on the view, widely held until about the middle of 1948, that the Civil War was likely to continue indefinitely because neither side had the capacity to defeat the other. As for the costs of the war, these were calculated in terms of both the inflation which had completely disrupted the urban economy, and the further impoverishment of the rural areas. The printing press may have been the Government's chief source of revenue, but the Govern-ment depended also on a land tax, on the compulsory purchase of grain at lower than market prices, and on the collection of grain on loan. These levies, together with the requisitions to support local needs, the abuses associated with conscrip-tion, and the disruptions caused by a poorly disciplined and underpaid army in the field, created insupportable burdens for the peasantry. Finally, an increas-ingly militaristic government, and increased political alienation among the public, were also condemned as direct results of the war. For all of these reasons, the Government's insistence on fighting it, while failing to implement any of the reforms that might have made it more acceptable, provided the strongest possible evidence to support the charge that the KMT Government did not exist "for" the people; that, to the contrary, it was willing to sacrifice the interests of the nation as a whole in pursuit of its own selfish aims; and that it was basically incapable of serving even that end effectively.

The KMT could nevertheless have saved itself in the eyes of most of its critics who were actually pleading with it to do so. However much they had been hurt by the Government's economic mismanagement, it was probably true that business and industrial circles feared the Communists would be worse. Despite the state of open confrontation that had developed between the Government and the student community in the course of its anti-war movement, a majority of the students, even at the end of 1948, were still willing to have the KMT participate in a coalition government. As for the older generation of intellec-tuals, their goals were explicitly stated. Their objective had never been to destroy the KMT but only to reform it, although here, too, the condition for reform was almost always stated in terms of a coalition government which would have included the Communists. As late as April, 1948, Ch'u An-p'ing was still pleading with the KMT to change its style of work and do something meaningful for the country. He and others did so because they calculated that the chances, however limited, of achieving the liberal democratic society they desired were greater under KMT rule than they would be under that of the CCP.

The intellectuals, then, did not abandon the KMT because of the damage that inflation wreaked upon their material wellbeing. But for a number of reasons, they did refuse to support the one objective the KMT deemed most necessary to its survival, namely, the military defeat of the Chinese Communists. The KMT was therefore trapped in a dilemma of its own making. The only way it could retain the residual support it still enjoyed was by heeding the demands for reform and/or by seeking a peaceful accommodation with the CCP. While various sectors of the public in effect made reform the condition for cooperating with the Government, the Government demanded unconditional support from them, offering little in return but lip service to principles that were never realized in practice. Hence the pronouncements and decrees of the Central Government and its local representatives were ignored, if not openly defied, by workers, students, teachers, businessmen, industrialists, and financiers. In so doing, each group, in its own way and for its own reasons, withheld support for and cooperation with the Government in its war against the Communists. This ultimately was the price that the KMT had to pay for its years of political recalcitrance and economic mismanagement, and its refusal to heed the demands for reform being made upon it.

In addition, the popular disillusionment with KMT rule contributed to the decision of so many to remain on the Mainland in 1949. Exile was too great a sacrifice for a Party that had dissipated its popular mandate as this one had. Those who chose to stay included most of China's best trained minds, virtually all of its student population, many of its businessmen and industrialists, more than enough of its civil servants, and hundreds of thousands of soldiers from the KMT armies. Also contributing to that decision, however, was their estimation of the Chinese Communists.

Many of those who stayed behind in 1949 obviously had their "doubts and fears and misgivings." This was so within the intellectual community, as well as in commercial and industrial circles. In the student polls which indicated a majority preference for a coalition government, even fewer favored national rule by the CCP alone than continued one-party KMT rule. Their elders shifted toward a position of qualified support for the CCP only after the path toward liberal reform as they knew it ceased to exist. However these liberal intellectuals may have rationalized their decision to accept Communist rule, there is no indication that they extended anything like unequivocal support to the new regime, or that the compromises they were willing to make were fundamental or permanent. They accepted most of the goals set forth in the CCP's New Democracy, but certainly not the ultimate Communist objectives of one-party rule and proletarian dictatorship.

Nevertheless, the reservations of the intellectuals about the CCP were only partial. They applied more to the forms of Communist rule than the substance of current Chinese Communist programs and policies, which were by and large admired. This ambivalence in the attitude of the liberal intellectual toward the Communists was a reflection of the Communist success in coping with the same types of problems that had undermined confidence in the KMT Government.

First, the Communists had built a record of credibility which served them well in 1949. The KMT had a habit of saying one thing and doing another, of promulgating reform measures and never implementing them. The Communists, by contrast, had a reputation for keeping their word, for actually implementing their policies, and for correcting their mistakes. The Communists said that their ultimate goal was the realization of communism in China. No one doubted that this was their goal. But the Communists also said that it would take many years to achieve it, and that in the meantime they planned to build a New Democratic society in which there would be a place and a need for everyone, bourgeois intellectual and national capitalist as well as worker and landowning peasant. Since the Communists said this, intellectuals and capitalists were inclined to believe it.

Second, in terms of administrative integrity, political competence, and ability to cope with the economic costs of the war, the Communist record of achievement by the end of 1949 was impressive. The Chinese Communists had begun moving successfully against some of China's most basic urban problems—despite the handicap of inexperience in the fields of urban administration and industrial management. In March, 1949, when Mao Tse-tung arrived in the city of Peiping, the CCP had behind it not quite four years of direct experience with urban management, limited primarily to Kalgan, Harbin, and a few other medium-sized cities in Manchuria. The experience had been put to good use, however. During that time, Chinese Communist thinking on urban problems had overcome many of the idealistic impulses characteristic of newly empowered leftist parties.

In the first flush of their enthusiasm to solve all the problems of urban China in accordance with the principles of the New Democracy, the Communists in Kalgan and elsewhere made commitments both to labor and to management that they soon found impossible to fulfill. The repudiation was formalized, toward the end of 1947, with the advent of the campaign against left adventurism. At this time, the Party's orientation toward business, industry, labor, and the intelligentsia shifted explicitly towards maximizing production and creating an alliance of the greatest possible number in the interests of achieving total victory. The new line stressed cooperation with private capital, the rationalization of management in public enterprise, and the necessity of winning over the intellectuals regardless of their ideological differences with communism. The practice of remunerating labor according to need or political criteria was officially cast aside in favor of wage differentials based on skill, seniority, and effort. The goal of resolving the material difficulties of the working class was not abandoned but deferred, being limited in the immediate present to certain basic guarantees and to minimizing the effects of inflation on the workers' living standards. Meanwhile, the promise of future gratification was symbolized by the experimental labor insurance program for public enterprise workers, introduced in Manchuria early in 1949.

The anti-leftist campaigns of 1948 provided the basis for the successful take-over of urban China in 1949. Compared with the performance of the KMT four years previously, when it had taken over many of the same cities from the Japanese, that of the victorious Communist forces was noteworthy. The behavior of Communist personnel, both military and civilian, was exemplary by the time they reached China's largest urban centers in 1949. Those cities were treated to the unprecedented spectacle of incorruptible officials and soldiers who acted on their own initiative to safeguard property whether public or private. Industrial and commercial establishments were protected and preserved intact and wherever possible in operation.

Politically, the most successful achievement of the take-over was the creation of a broad coalition of urban support. The effort extended to officers and men of the KMT armies, to the members of the civilian bureaucracy, and to the intellectual community. In this way, the Communists gained needed assistance during the transition period from groups that had remained with the KMT until the end. Far from denouncing them as opportunists, the Communists welcomed their collaboration to maintain the day-to-day administration of the country, restore its economy, and expand the ranks of the advancing PLA. Nowhere was this approach more apparent than in the Party's treatment of the student population in newly liberated cities. Temporarily overlooking their lack of commitment to communism, the Party was able to use large numbers of them in positions of relative prestige and importance as cadres responsible for the implementation of its policies.

Even at this level, however, the Communists' successes were not unmixed. In the immediate post-liberation period, they tried to do almost everything in the area of economic, financial, and monetary policy that the KMT had been criticized for neglecting during its take-over from the Japanese. But, while the rate of inflation during the first year of Communist rule did not reach the extremes experienced under the KMT, it was many months before the effort to stabilize the economy began to show significant results. This was due in large measure to the enormity of the problems it had inherited, but also to the new regime's own actions and inexperience. This period was therefore marked by enough economic dislocation and monetary instability in the cities to partially undermine public confidence in the new administration.

THE COUNTRYSIDE

By necessity rather than by choice, the Communists had concentrated their efforts in the countryside; and it was in the countryside that their political victory over the KMT was most decisive. Contemplating the disarray of the urban economy, Chiang Kai-shek was wont to stress the underlying stability and inertia characteristic of the economy as a whole because of its agrarian foundations.[1] The notion of stability and inertia was symbolic of the KMT's relationship with the countryside. The Central Government by its actions and inaction sought primarily to maintain the status quo in rural China until it was too late, that is, until after the flight to Taiwan.

The bankruptcy of this posture was apparent in those portions of the Communist Border Regions retaken by KMT forces in 1946-47. The KMT's natural allies there were dispossessed landlords and other "struggle objects" intent on resuming their former way of life. Local officials in alliance with returning landlords embarked upon a systematic campaign of extortion and revenge characterized by the "voluntary surrender and repentance" programs and the various activities of the return-to-the-village corps, the "administration promotion" associations, and the rent collection committees. The main forces of the Communist army, militia, and Party organization fled before the advance of the KMT armies, and unarmed peasants paid with their lives. Thousands were killed as landlords and others settled accounts of their own.

Reform measures for the pacification areas had been promulgated by the Central Government in Nanking, but there was no one in the countryside to implement them except the same individuals whose interests they were ostensibly intended to restrain. So long as it remained unchallenged, the inertia of the status quo in the countryside was indeed a source of strength for the KMT; but the inequities contained within it also provided the foundation upon which the dynamic of the Communist-led revolution was built.

The winning formula had emerged during the war with Japan. Having abandoned violent land confiscation in the interest of the anti-Japanese united front, the Communists were obliged to look for new ways of transferring wealth from those who had it to those who did not. This shift was particularly significant in north China, where tenancy was not the dominant problem and a majority of the peasants owned the land they tilled. As a result of their search, the Communists' rural land policy had expanded by 1945, through the "settling of old accounts" tactic, to encompass the full range of issues that would provide benefits for the "basic masses" of north China. In addition to the material incentives provided by the redistribution of wealth derived from the settling accounts struggles, the Communists could also offer a solution for what the peasantry as a whole perceived as its most immediate grievance: the corrupt and arbitrary use of political power and social position within the village community.

In exploiting these issues, together with all the others associated with the ownership and use of land, unpaid labor, and indebtedness, the CCP had discovered the formula for "mass activation through class struggle" even in areas where landlords were not a problem that concerned the village masses. In the process, the Chinese Communists had not only found the means of destroying the rural system of economic and political power; they had also discovered how to mobilize peasant support for the construction of a new one.

1. According to Ambassador J. Leighton Stuart, in U.S. Dept. of State, *Foreign Relations of the United States, 1947, the Far East, China*, p. 76.

The second lesson they had learned was how to make the struggle against the ruling class the "mother of all other work." At the start of the Anti-Japanese War, there had been little coordination or differentiation between primary and secondary tasks. Little was accomplished until the Party as a whole had learned to make mass activation through class struggle the starting point of all other village work, including Party building and military recruitment.

A third crucial lesson from the Anti-Japanese War years concerned the conditions necessary for the successful initiation of class struggle. Before the Party's land policy could be thoroughly implemented in any district, the enemy had to be expelled militarily, his political hold broken, and the nucleus of a new power structure created. All Party directives stressed the importance of minimizing class friction in districts immediately threatened by the enemy. The land policy and the intra-village conflict it generated could become the focal point of village work only after military and political preconditions had been met in the area as a whole. The anti-Japanese resistance had mobilized the manpower, and the CCP provided the leadership necessary to establish these preconditions on a significant scale across north China as the Japanese tide began to recede after 1943.

The land reform program was the Communists' key revolutionary effort of the subsequent Civil War period. The development of that program in north China, and the experience gained in the manner of and conditions for its implementation, must be counted among the most important experiences the Communists brought with them from the Anti-Japanese War. These lessons were formalized in the Party's directive of May 4, 1946, which marked the official shift from rent reduction to land reform. Land reform as outlined in the May Fourth Directive, however, was nothing more nor less than the multi-featured struggle movement that had been developing in practice throughout the Anti-Japanese War.

The relationship between land reform and the prerequisites for implementing it was one that was mutually sustaining. Land reform was significant as a means of mobilizing the peasants to participate in the struggle against Chiang Kai-shek. At the same time, the purpose of the armed struggle was to make possible the realization of land reform.[2] That the most basic condition for the successful implementation of land reform was the military capacity to protect it against its enemies was proven in the wake of the unanticipated advance of KMT forces into the liberated areas in 1946-47. This advance eliminated all the prerequisites for instigating intra-village class friction, as defined during the Anti-Japanese War. Communist forces could no longer operate freely, and the Central Government was rebuilding its own structure of political power in the rural areas with the support of the enemies the Communists had created during the struggle movement.

The dangers of trying to carry out land reform under such circumstances were acknowledged by the Party center in May, 1948, when it reestablished essen-

2. Mo Han, "Jen-min chieh-fang-chün yü t'u-ti kai-ko" [The People's Liberation Army and land reform], *Ch'ün-chung* [Masses], Hong Kong, no. 42, Nov. 13, 1947, p. 18.

tially the same prerequisites adopted during the Anti-Japanese War. Land reform was not to be carried out unless the area in question was militarily secure; unless a majority of the peasants demanded land division; and unless enough cadres were on hand to lead the work. These conditions did not generally obtain in areas liberated after the summer of 1947, the "new liberated areas." They were therefore directed to abandon land reform temporarily in favor of the more moderate policy of reducing rent and interest rates.

Where the conditions for its implementation permitted, however, land reform made possible the mobilization and organization of the "basic masses" into a new structure of rural political power led by the CCP. The standard explanation was that as soon as the peasants' lives had been improved through the redistribution of land and other property, their consciousness was raised, and they were willing to act in support of the CCP's armed struggle against the KMT. Certainly the Communists sought, and undoubtedly received, "support" in return for the benefits tangible and otherwise provided by property redistribution and the reform of the local administration. But the process was never so simple or straightforward. The peasant with a newly gained plot of land wanted to remain at home and till it. The traditional bias against joining the army was not so easily overcome. Intra-Party criticism suggests that the nascent class consciousness engendered by the struggle movement and redistribution of property did not, as was claimed, result directly in the specific kinds of support necessary to fight the war against the KMT.

The primary function of the land revolution in this regard was the overthrow of the existing rural elite, whether or not it was made up of landlords. Land reform destroyed the political and economic domination of the ruling class, an essential step in the creation of a new order. And the construction of that order marked the second key component of land reform as the starting point of all other work. Peasants who participated most actively in the multi-featured accusation movement provided new recruits for the CCP and new village leadership. Recipients of land and property added their numbers to the peasant associations and other village organizations. The Communists could then rely on this institutional structure, manned by the peasants themselves, to assume responsibility for collecting the grain tax, organizing military transport teams, and exerting social pressure on reluctant recruits.

Initially, the struggle movement cut across class lines, an inevitable consequence of the many objects it contained. Until 1945, this feature of the movement was also apparent in the distribution of the struggle fruits, despite the general emphasis on taking from the rich and giving to the poor. After 1945, class lines were drawn more sharply with the increasingly concerted movement to transfer property directly to poor and hired peasants who constituted at least a dominant minority if not an absolute majority in the villages of north China. This effort was formalized in the first edition of the Outline Agrarian Law of October, 1947, which called for the equalization of village land and property. Given the scarcity of wealth in north China and the large number of middle peasants, both new and old, this provision made it necessary to encroach upon them if property was to be absolutely equalized. The contradictions that had characterized the Party's treatment of middle peasants seemed finally to have been resolved with this implicit demand to include them in the levelling process.

That the issue had not been resolved became apparent in early 1948, with the abandoning of absolute equality in deference to the middle peasants who still made up 30 to 40 percent of the Communist armies. The attempt to eliminate poor peasants as a class was clearly too advanced an objective in 1947. But it was also too important a goal, within the context of the mass movement, to be abandoned outright despite the danger of alienating the middle peasants. The most serious efforts to conciliate middle peasants in the final formulation of the Party's Civil War land policy, were reserved for areas where land reform had already been thoroughly implemented.

Whatever contradictions they contained, these were the "roots" the CCP was putting down in the countryside as a result of land reform. When KMT forces invaded the Communist base areas in 1946-47, the most they could do was attempt to extract the roots and reestablish the old system of political power. Hence the growing sense of futility among liberal critics, aware of the source of the CCP's strength and of the KMT's inability to match it.

Politically, therefore, the CCP's victory was as genuine as the KMT's defeat. In the cities, both were tempered by fears among intellectuals and capitalists that the Communists would in certain respects be worse than the KMT. In the countryside, the alienation of the ruling class was more than balanced by the strength of the mass base mobilized and organized in the process. In terms of their ability to cope with the problems that had undermined public confidence in the KMT Government, the CCP's record was clearly positive. The Communists did not just happen to be in the right place at the right time to benefit from the KMT debacle. They did not win an unqualified mandate in 1949 to establish one-party Communist rule in Mainland China. But their achievements had been substantial enough to provide the basis for a transfer of popular allegiance to the new Communist-led Government.

The search for the key ingredient in the successful struggle of the Chinese Communists—whether in the form of the Japanese invasion, the strength of a Stalinist organization, socio-economic conditions, the weaknesses of the KMT, or the amount of foreign aid given and withheld—seems somewhat analogous to the quest of the proverbial blind men *vis-à-vis* the elephant. Each of these variables contributed to the political context within which the CCP found itself. Its own particular achievement lay more immediately in the flexibility and patience with which it adapted its struggle for power to that environment, step by step and directive by directive. These were capabilities learned the hard way, through trial and error and at great cost.

However great a contribution the Japanese invasion may have made to the success of the Communist movement in China, the Japanese presented both the CCP and the KMT with the same opportunity in 1937. The CCP was particularly well equipped to capitalize on it by reason of a decade of concentrated effort to develop guerrilla warfare and peasant revolution following the destruction of its urban base in 1927. The CCP thus exploited the opportunity presented by the Japanese, using it to build rural base areas, and emerging as the most dynamic political force in the country at the end of World War II.

The KMT Government, by contrast, did little to exploit the opportunity that the Japanese invasion similarly provided to it. The Government may have won national and international recognition as the symbol of Free China, but it had achieved little else in terms of domestic political strength or popular support by 1945. The KMT Government did sponsor guerrilla and underground operations in Japanese-occupied territory. But these were never expanded into a widespread resistance movement. Unlike the Communists, the KMT built no bases of military and political support behind the Japanese lines. The years of retreat in Chungking were used to no constructive purpose, and the weaknesses inherent in the KMT political system developed accordingly. This resulted in its unfortunate performance during the take-over of urban China following World War II, which marked the culmination of the KMT's failure to respond to the challenge of the Japanese invasion. To argue, as some have, that the Japanese invasion made possible the Communist victory by preventing Chiang Kai-shek's forces from administering the *coup de grace* to the defeated Communist army in 1936-37, is to admit the KMT's inability to compete with the Communists on a more equal footing during the years that followed.

Because they were Communists genuinely committed to revolutionary objectives, Party leaders continued to search during the Anti-Japanese War for new ways of transferring wealth from those who had it to those who did not, despite the official adherence to the united front land policy. The socio-economic realities of north China, far from discouraging their search, led them to expand the definition of exploitation in practice to include the range of issues that could make it meaningful for the peasants of the region.

Yet it was not just because they were Communists that CCP leaders had succeeded in transforming their party into a rural-based movement after its first defeat at the hands of the KMT in 1927; and succeeded also in launching an agrarian revolution in north China after the second defeat in Kiangsi in 1934. Examples of Communist parties that have not been able to adapt themselves so readily to their environment are numerous indeed. The clues to the success of the CCP in this respect can be found within the Party reform movement of 1942-44.

In 1937, when the full-scale Japanese invasion of China began, the Party's membership was forty thousand. By 1942, when the Party reform movement was launched, Party membership had grown to several hundred thousand. They were a diverse assortment of people drawn to the Party for a diversity of reasons. Their task was to transform the anti-Japanese resistance into a unified revolutionary movement in the isolated and far-flung base areas behind the Japanese lines. The purpose of the reform program was to inculcate standards of thought and action that would make this possible in the absence of more conventional methods of administrative coordination and control. Toward that end, the Party went to school. The subject matter centered around two major themes: the necessity of rectifying internal Party problems; and the necessity of rectifying problems in the Party's relationship with Chinese society. With respect to the first, the reform movement sought to strengthen intra-Party discipline and obedience—of the individual to the organization, and of the entire organization to the Central Committee.

Mao Tse-tung's chief preoccupation, however, seemed to be with the second set of problems, which dominated his two lectures inaugurating the reform movement in February, 1942. He stressed the importance of adapting Marxism-Leninism to the Chinese environment and of applying this principle at every level of the Party's work. He condemned the spirit of learning which mechanically absorbed the writings of Marx, Engels, Lenin, and Stalin, but failed to use their concepts and methods to analyze contemporary Chinese affairs. He condemned the dogmatism of those who treated Marxism-Leninism as a ready-made panacea. For him it was a theoretical tool, the utility of which could only be verified through practical research into the actual living conditions of the various social classes in China. He condemned the tendency within the Party to separate itself from the world outside. The achievement of the Party's revolutionary objectives would be "absolutely impossible" in the absence of a close alliance with people outside the Party. Finally, he condemned formalism in the spoken and written language, demanding that everyone from military commanders to Party propagandists learn to address themselves to the people in language the people understood.[3]

This preoccupation with the immediate context of the struggle for power lies at the heart of the Party's achievement. Marx, Lenin, and Stalin provided the analytical tools and organizational models. But it was the meticulous application of these at every level of thought and action, from the details of village work to the formulation of policy by the Central Committee, that produced during the 1940s a comprehensive program adapted to local conditions and local needs. By identifying its own interests with those of a substantial proportion of the Chinese population in this way, the CCP created a base of mass support capable of sustaining its demands for grain and manpower, and its struggle against the KMT.

3. Mao Tse-tung, "Reform in Learning, the Party, and Literature," and "In Opposition to Party Formalism," trans. by Boyd Compton in his *Mao's China: Party Reform Documents, 1942-44*, pp. 9-53.

Bibliographic Notes

THE *TA KUNG PAO* (1902-1948)

Although nominally independent, the *Ta kung pao*'s association with the Political Study Clique *(Cheng hsueh hsi)* of the KMT was well known. During the four or five months prior to the Communist take-over of Shanghai while the KMT administration there was disintegrating, a number of pamphlets and news sheets, many fairly leftist, appeared. Having little else to do, since most of the city's regular newspapers were by then either banned or severely reduced in content, the translators at the American Consulate included these publications in the *Chinese Press Review*. Their accuracy with respect to the *Ta kung pao* seems to be at least approximate despite their generally critical disposition. The following sketch of the paper's history has been gleaned from a comparative reading of these and other sources listed below.

The *Ta kung pao* was founded in 1902 by a Manchu, Ying Lien-chih, who built it into a respected journal which circulated in Peking and Tientsin. In those early years, the paper became known for its attacks on corruption in the Imperial Government. After the Revolution of 1911, Ying sold the paper to Wang Tsu-san. Tuan Ch'i-jui, head of the An-fu Clique and a dominant figure in the Peiyang militarist regimes in Peking between 1912 and 1926, was a principal backer of the *Ta kung pao* during those years. Sun Yat-sen is also said to have contributed some financial support to the paper, which often spoke up for him, as well as for the various militiarists who were from time to time allied with Tuan. At this time, however, the *Ta kung pao* reflected primarily the position of its chief backer and was not revolutionary in its orientation. Hu Lin (Hu Cheng-chih) was the chief editor of the paper from 1916 to 1925, as well as founder and publisher of *Kuo wen chou pao*, which was also apparently supported by Tuan and was affiliated with the *Ta kung pao*.

The origin of the Political Study Clique's association with the paper lay in its association with Tuan Ch'i-jui. As for the Political Study group itself, one source traces its origins back to the *Ou-shih t'ao-lun hui* (Society for the Discussion of European Affairs). This society was formed in the U.S. about 1915, by General

Huang Hsing and a group of KMT members who left China after Huang disagreed with Sun Yat-sen over policy toward Japan and its 21 Demands. When members of the group returned to south China, they changed the name of their organization to the Political Study Society *(Cheng hsueh hui)*. They involved themselves actively in the politics of Sun's Canton regime and the deliberations of the parliamentary sessions that were held there. According to Ch'ien Tuan-sheng, it was the activities of the Political Study group—whose members were at this time advocating a reunification with the warlord regime in Peking and who caused the suspension of many parliamentary sessions—which inspired in Sun a contempt for his old followers, for party politics, and even for parliamentary government itself.

In any case, the Political Study group was willing to cooperate with the warlords in the North, and in particular associated itself with Tuan Ch'i-jui and the An-fu Clique. This association placed the group on the extreme right of the various cliques within the KMT. But the decline of Tuan Ch'i-jui in the 1920s, resulted also in the temporary eclipse of the Political Study group. One of its leaders was Wu Ting-ch'ang, who had held a number of important economic and financial posts under various warlord regimes in Peking between 1912 and 1920. He was then eased out of office apparently as a result of Tuan's shifting fortunes. Wu became chairman of the board of the Yienyieh Bank and in 1923 also became head of the Joint Treasury of four leading north China banks: the Yienyieh Bank, the Kincheng Banking Corporation, the Continental Bank, and the China and South Seas Bank.

Wu Ting-ch'ang was credited with the idea of reviving the Political Study group's fortunes through the publication of a newspaper. He was able, with capital put up primarily by Chou Tso-min, founder, general manager, and chairman of the board of directors of the Kincheng Banking Corporation, to form a new holding company which purchased the Tuan Ch'i-jui backed *Ta kung pao* and the *Kuo wen* enterprises.

The reorganized *Ta kung pao* began publication in Tientsin on September 1, 1926. The paper was rapidly acknowledged a journalistic as well as a financial success. It had made a profit several times the original capital investment of its backers as early as 1932. In this new venture, which some called the cultural enterprise of the four northern banks, Chou Tso-min was the most important financier, Wu Ting-ch'ang the chairman of the board of directors, former editor Hu Lin became the business manager, and the editorial writer Chang Chi-luan (Chang Chih-chang) was made editor-in-chief. Wang Yun-sheng, well known as the editor of the *Ta kung pao* during the 1940s, was in 1926 a reporter for a minor Tientsin newspaper. He came to the attention of Chang Chi-luan through an argument which the two men carried on in a series of editorials. Wang impressed Chang, who brought the young journalist to work on the paper. Wang inherited the post of editor-in-chief when his mentor retired in the late 1930s.

During Chang Chi-luan's tenure as editor of the *Ta kung pao,* the paper gained a reputation as one of the most reliable forums for the expression of news and editorial comment in .the country. This did not mean, however, that the paper's declared non-partisanship—the official translation of the paper's name was "The Impartial"—remained always above suspicion. Immediately after its reorganization, the new *Ta kung pao* was often critical of Chiang Kai-shek. This gradually changed with his successful conclusion of the Northern Expedition and his equally successful attempt, or so it was said, to woo Chang Chi-luan.

When Japan invaded Manchuria in 1931, the paper won the enmity of those who wished to fight back at once, by supporting Chiang's position that China was not yet ready for a war with Japan. The *Ta kung pao* changed its stand only after Chiang Kai-shek abandoned his anti-Communist extermination campaigns and finally went to war with Japan in 1937. The paper then became a staunch supporter of the war effort, and moved with the KMT Government to Chungking. In 1941, the *Ta kung pao* gained international recognition when it received an award for distinguished service to journalism from the University of Missouri's School of Journalism.

During the Anti-Japanese War, the paper allegedly became a supporter not only of the resistance but also of the Generalissimo himself. This last was attributed in part to the chief editor's by then personal friendship with Chiang Kai-shek. But whatever the case, the *Ta kung pao*'s editorial policies seemed to reflect the interests of the bankers, businessmen, and politicians of the Political Study Clique. Thus, despite the paper's generally liberal stand and its frequent criticism of conditions in China, it avoided criticizing Chiang Kai-shek specifically. It also avoided naming names in corruption or other unflattering cases, especially when important members of the Political Study Clique were involved.

By the 1940s, the Political Study Clique had become the most liberal and the least influential of the three major groups vying for power within the KMT. The other two were the military Whampoa Clique and the CC (for Central Club or *Chung-yang chü-le-pu*) Clique of the Ch'en brothers, Li-fu and Kuo-fu. The CC Clique's power was based in its control of the KMT's Organization Department. The Political Study people, having little chance of gaining control within the central party organization, concentrated on building a foothold in provincial administrations, and on financial and business operations. Because most of them had been educated in the U.S. or Japan and understood the value of effective administration, the members of this group were regarded by foreign observers as being superior in ability and experience to those of the other two more traditional and conservative cliques. The Political Study Clique was thus characterized as being "pragmatic" and "somewhat more tolerant of the democratic spirit of the West" than its rivals. It also remained conservative in its economic views, reflecting the extensive business interests of its members.

During the late 1940s, the policy-making body of the *Ta kung pao* was its General Office with Hu Lin as general manager, Tsao Ku-pin and Chin Chen-fu as assistant general managers, Wang Yun-sheng as editor-in-chief, and Kung Chao-kai and Chang Chin-nan as assistant editors. Responsibility for making editorial policy was nevertheless popularly attributed to Wang Yun-sheng. The paper's board of directors was made up of its principal shareholders, who were Chou Tso-min, general manager of the Kincheng Bank; Wu Ting-ch'ang, secretary-general of the Office of the President in the KMT Government; Wu Yun-tsai; Hsu Kuo-mao, Shanghai manager of the Kincheng Bank; Wang I-lin, assistant manager of the Kincheng Bank and son-in-law of Hu Lin; and from the staff of the paper, Hu Lin, Wang Yun-sheng, Fei I-ming, Tsao Ku-pin, Chin Chen-fu, and Li Tze-kuan.

After Wang Yun-sheng took charge of the *Ta kung pao*'s editorial department, he reportedly asserted a greater degree of independence from the paper's political and financial backers than had his predecessor. Wang was said to be more "scholarly" than most of his colleagues on the board of directors and less wont to compromise when political interests demanded. Nevertheless, during the Civil War years, the paper voiced support for the Government's position on certain issues, which aroused the ire of the liberal community as its opposition to the Chiang Kai-shek Government hardened.

The differences among the members of the paper's editorial staff became fully apparent in 1947, when the assistant general manager, Tsao Ku-pin, temporarily took over the editorial department in Wang Yun-sheng's absence and wrote some indisputably "rightist" editorials, very much in line with the Government's position on the student movement. Nor were the three editions of the paper identical in their editorial policies. The Tientsin edition, for example, voiced outspoken support for the students' 1947 protest activities (see Chapter Three). The Hong Kong edition, which did not resume publication after World War II until 1948, was noticeably to the left of the other two.

The differences between the Government and a few key figures at the paper came to a head during the latter half of 1948. Wang Yun-sheng refused to heed repeated warnings from the Central Government to stop attacking its emergency economic reform program being supervised in Shanghai by the Generalissimo's son, Chiang Ching-kuo. Wang left Shanghai soon thereafter. He travelled to Hong Kong in December, and from there to the Communist areas in January. Wu Ting-ch'ang announced his resignation from the *Ta kung pao*'s board of directors, and from the post of secretary-general in the Office of the President, in late 1948. Fei I-ming is today ·the publisher of the one surviving edition of the *Ta kung pao* in Hong Kong, and has been a dominant figure at the paper since it officially came under Communist control in 1949.

SOURCES

Feng Ming-ting, "The *Ta kung pao* changes" *Current News Series* [pamphlet], Shanghai, no. 1, Dec. 4, 1948 (*CPR*, Dec. 16).

Chien-sien jih-pao, Shanghai, Dec. 28, 1948 (*CPR*, Dec. 31).

Revelation Monthly [liberal-leftist], Shanghai, no. 1, Jan. 1, 1949 (*CPR*, Jan. 7).

Newsweek [connected with elements in the KMT], Shanghai, no. 3, Jan. 7, 1949 (*CPR*, Jan. 8-10).

Chung Chia-chi, "A study of the *Ta kung pao*", *From All Angles* [independent], Shanghai, no. 5, Jan. 30, 1949 (*CPR*, Jan. 29-31).

Huang Pin, "Factional Strife in the KMT", *New Hope Weekly* [connected with the KMT military], Shanghai, no. 6, Mar. 21, 1949 (*CPR*, Mar. 25 and 26-28.

Ch'u An-p'ing, "Lun *Wen hui, Hsin min, Lien-ho wan-pao* pei-feng chi *Ta kung pao* tsai che tz'u hsueh ch'ao chung so piao-shih te t'ai-tu" (On the banning of the *Wen hui pao, Hsin min wan-pao,* and *Lien-ho wan-pao,* and the attitude of the *Ta kung pao* during this student tide), *KC,* May 31, 1947, pp. 5-7.

Wang Shui, "Pei-fang hsueh yun te yuan-yuan-pen-pen" (The origins of the student movement in the North), *KC,* June 21, 1947, p. 20.

Ch'ien Tuan-sheng, *The Government and Politics of China,* pp. 72, 85-86, 129-31.

Harrison Forman, *Changing China,* p. 291.

On a number of points of emphasis and interpretation, this outline of the *Ta kung pao*'s history differs from biographical sketches, particularly of Chang Chi-luan and Wu Ting-ch'ang, in Howard Boorman, ed., *Biographical Dictionary of Republican China.*

KUAN-CH'A SUBSCRIPTION STATISTICS

The record of *Kuan-ch'a*'s growth can be traced in the editor's periodic reports. The following figures on *Kuan-ch'a* subscribers, based on questionnaires sent out by the journal, are taken from these reports. No similar information exists for total circulation. Subscriptions reportedly fluctuated between 15 and 20 percent of total circulation.

Kuan-ch'a Subscribers by Occupation

	Vol. 1	*Vol. 2*	*Vol. 3*	*Vol. 4*
Total Subscriptions	2,709	4,973	6,732	16,086
Occupation		*Percentage*		
Students	23	19	23.4	26
Government Employees	22	21	16.9	13
Industry, Business, and Banking Circles	22	25	22.3	17
Military	6	3	4.6	4
Others (including lawyers doctors, teachers, etc.)	4	3	—	—
No Response	23	29	32.8	40

Approximate Geographic Breakdown of *Kuan-ch'a*'s Subscribers (percentage)

	Vol. 1	*Vol. 2*	*Vol. 3*	*Vol. 4*
Central China	18	18	18.8	18
North China	10.5	10	8.3	6
Northwest China	10	13	13.6	7

South China	5.5	8	13.4	13
Northeast China		Negligible		
Szechwan	17	12.5	12	11
Kiangsu-Chekiang	12	12	12.3	14
Yunnan-Kweichow	6	5	4.2	3
Shanghai	8.5	7.5	7.9	12
Nanking	7.5	6	5.5	9
Peiping-Tientsin	5	6	—	6

These figures are taken from the following issues of *Kuan-ch'a:* Vol. 1, No. 24, Feb. 8, 1947, pp. 3-9; Vol. 2, No. 1, Mar. 1, 1947, p. 27; Vol. 2, No. 24, Aug. 9, 1947, pp. 3-8; Vol. 3, No. 24, Feb. 7, 1948, pp. 3-8; Vol. 4, No. 1, Feb. 28, 1948, p. 23; Vol. 4, No. 23-4, Aug. 7, 1948, pp. 3-8.

A Note on the Revised Bibliography

If the 1945–1949 Chinese civil war does not inspire renewed interest among scholars in years to come, it will not be for want of research materials. This period, like many others, has benefited from the new "post-revolutionary" era that began with Mao Zedong's death in 1976. During the years since, a vast amount of primary and secondary source materials has been published in China on the late 1940s. Partly in response to this new output from their mainland People's Republic rivals, and partly as an independent trend dating from the mid-1970s, Republic of China archives in Taiwan are also serving as the basis for extensive new documentary collections and historical studies.

These still largely unmined sources on the 1945–1949 period are sufficient to keep scholars busy for years to come, even without direct access to unpublished archival holdings, which have become the new foundation for research on modern China, including both pre-1949 history and post-1949 work on everything else. This development follows from Beijing's policy of opening state archives for public use as formalized in the 1988 Archives Law. The law stipulates a 30-year cut-off date, meaning 30 years must pass before materials can be authorized for public use, which places all 1940s holdings well within the limits of permitted access. One can easily lapse into an old-timer's lament upon contemplating the younger generation, spoiled by its new embarrassment of riches and heedless of how its pioneering forebears spent years scouring the world for their precious scraps and fragments.

The bibliography that follows here has been amended to illustrate the new and old sources. Both have been joined in an expanded and updated English secondary publications list that includes not just work on the civil war period, but also selections from the much larger body of literature now available on China's pre-1949 revolutionary history and the origins of the Chinese communist movement. Chinese-language materials are separated, however, with the original bibliography followed by a new, "selected update" section. A comprehensive bibliography of Chinese-language materials on the 1945–1949 years could itself easily grow into a book-length project. The lists shown here are therefore designed to introduce only a representative sample of the goods now on offer, including both primary and secondary sources. The spartan style of bibliographic presentation *circa* 1980—when "selected" could be interpreted to mean only those works actually used or cited, and even some historians got away with less—makes the original bibliography appear positively skeletal by contrast with present norms.

For a full perspective on the new opportunities, one must now begin with the archives themselves, however, and the recently published guide prepared by Ye Wa and Joseph Esherick points the way (unless otherwise indicated, full citations for all works mentioned in this note are given in the appended reference list). They cite a figure of 3,522 archives of all kinds, including those at the central, provincial, local, and enterprise levels in China, as of 1990. More important is the basic information given on 597 of these archives at various levels within the state system, exclusive of enterprise and other separate work unit repositories. This guide contains data on the nature and extent of holdings plus other necessary information for potential users. Parallel to the Ye and Esherick volume are two Chinese publications: *Zhongguo dang'anguan minglu* (Directory of Chinese national archives) (1990) prepared by the Guojia dang'anju (State Archives Bureau), in Chinese and English; and a 1997 update, *Zhongguo dang'anguan jianming zhinan* (Concise guide to China's archives).

Most of the repositories listed contain materials of some sort on the 1945–1949 period, however, and the above three directories provide only general information on relevant holdings. Fortunately, detailed book-length guides are beginning to appear for individual provincial and city archives. Ye and Esherick include brief summaries from the few such volumes available in the early 1990s, for Sichuan, Shanghai, and Chongqing, as well as that for the Number Two Historical Archives in Nanjing. This latter is the main repository for national government documents and records from the entire republican era (1912–1949). Additional guidebooks for the Liaoning, Heilongjiang, Fujian, and Guangzhou archives have since been published and are included in the reference list below. Archive users may, of course, consult the specific catalogs and indexes that large repositories typically maintain. The Shanghai Municipal Archives, for example, publish and sell for a nominal sum lists of its files as these are selectively opened. The Shanghai catalog lists have been published regularly since 1987, with a brief hiatus during 1989 and 1990. Most file categories or record groups (*quanzong*) are from the 1940s and 1950s, but a few extend back to the last century, and many on the most recent (especially the 1997) lists contain material dated as late as 1966.

Access is not automatic, however, and to declare that 30-year-old documents can be opened is not to guarantee they will be. Experienced researchers routinely note the variable conditions associated with use by foreign as well as Chinese scholars. These conditions may be negotiable but they are also contingent on time, place, and topic, with the power to grant access ultimately held by the local archival authorities themselves. General principles also guide their decisions, however, and are of particular relevance for the late 1940s. These principles thus suggest reasons both general and specific as to why the period remains relatively under-researched.

Current scholarly interest in social history and economics is therefore fortuitous but also reinforced by the easier access being granted in those general areas for both pre- and post-1949 research topics. By contrast, the 1945 to 1949 years were dominated by all-out war and its political equivalents, two categories of China's experience for which the discretion of archival guardians is most strictly exercised and access most difficult to obtain. In this respect, local authorities only follow the lead of Beijing, where the two most important national political and military archives remain closed to foreign scholars and evidently to all but authorized Chinese personnel as well. These are the Central Archives (*Zhongyang dang'anguan*) and the People's Liberation Army Archives (*Zhongguo renmin jiefangjun dang'anguan*), which contain Chinese Communist Party (CCP), central government, and military holdings for both the pre-1949 past and post-1949 present.

As a result, researchers must either tailor their topics to the relatively less sensitive materials available at Nanjing's Number Two Historical Archives, where the right to access is often still conservatively interpreted, or work in provincial and local archives while continuing to probe the parameters of official tolerance. Except at the national level, pre-1949 government and "revolutionary history" (CCP-related) materials, as well as post-1949 records, are all housed in the same repositories. The CCP-led military and police or public security archival systems (for pre- and post-1949) remain separate and evidently inaccessible at all levels.

While waiting for access to archival precincts, however, scholars can busy themselves with the mountain of documentary collections, official biographies, battle histories, and other publications that have become the chief means whereby primary political and military sources enter the public domain. Such publications are in fact seen as one way of fulfilling the mandate to open archival holdings for both sensitive and more mundane materials. On the plus side, these publications have created a rich new resource base that will take years to mine and develop. The negatives concern matters of emphasis and interpretation by authorized compilers and editors, whose processing efforts inevitably transform such material into a kind of primary-source-once-removed. For example, serious (as opposed to polemical) biographies have not been authorized for important figures in pre-1949 history who fell from grace thereafter and have yet to be exonerated. Lin Biao is the most obvious such figure from the civil war period; Chen Boda and Kang Sheng are two others. Their absence from the official biography roster indicates the selective approach to compilation that remains an obvious handicap.

These bibliographic conventions and divisions of labor are well illustrated in a valuable new research guide, the *Zhongguo dang'an wenxian cidian* (Dictionary of Chinese archival materials). This 536-page dictionary is actually an annotated, selected bibliography of primary source materials focusing mainly on the last imperial dynasty and the pre-1949 Chinese Republic. Materials for the republican period are divided between two sections: one for sources and concerning matters associated with the Nationalist (Kuomintang or KMT) government; the other for "Chinese Communist Party revolutionary archival materials." This division represents standard archival and bibliographic practice, in conformity with the main national division between Nanjing's Number Two Historical Archives and the central political/military holdings in Beijing. Late 1940s sources from the Nationalist regime cited in the dictionary concentrate on economics, general public administration, provincial government gazettes, National Assembly resolutions, and consultative conference materials. Sources are cited mostly in their original state, and annotations for many items are especially helpful in identifying the repositories where they are currently housed. By contrast, virtually all revolutionary history materials from the 1945–1949 period have been recently published or are earlier publications recently reprinted. In this section, the archival repositories are also identified, but only as the sponsoring units for the books and periodicals cited.

The "selected update" for Chinese-language sources that follows here contains only a small and hopefully representative sample of these new publications. They include book-length works as well as the equally important materials now appearing in a multitude of new (post-1978) archival journals and serial publications. Contemporary (that is, post-1978) daily newspapers, general current events magazines, and university journals (*xuebao*) sometimes carry noteworthy articles on the civil war period. Most useful, however, are the specialized periodicals and serials. The new periodicals list below contains a selection of such titles, which are drawn primarily from the main or core national and provincial publications. Most of those listed can be found, together with their sponsoring units, in the *Dictionary of Chinese Archival Materials* annotations or in one of the three periodical guides cited on the reference list. Additional useful introductions to the contents of these new specialized periodicals can be found in the *Zhonggong dangshi wenzhai niankan* (Annual abstracts of Chinese Communist Party history), which was prepared each year in book-length volumes from 1982 through 1990, under the auspices of the Zhonggong zhongyang dangshi yanjiushi (CCP Central Committee's Party History Research Office). Citations are arranged in chronological order, and the 1945–1949 civil war is well represented in each annual volume.

The periodicals and serial publications are, however, variable in content and duration. They come and go or merge and change names with disarming frequency. Some disappeared after only a few years. Others have continued since the early 1980s, without serious interruption. An example in the latter category is *Zhonggong dangshi ziliao* (Chinese Communist Party history materials), also sponsored by the central Party History Research Office. This publication has averaged four issues per year since 1982, even while dropping its original *neibu* or "internal" restricted circulation status and permitting open sale of the back *neibu* issues. The transformation from internal to open, with retroactive effect, also represents a general trend, and so no attempt has been made to differentiate the new materials listed below by their circulation status.

One additional large body of publications represented in the bibliographic update is the historical literature (*wenshi*) compilations sponsored by the Chinese

People's Political Consultative Conference and its local committees throughout China. Memoirs and biographies of civil war participants, observers, and defectors constitute a major portion of these materials, for which a five-volume index was published in 1992: *Quanguo geji zhengxie wenshi ziliao pianmu suoyin* (Index list of historical literature from the Chinese People's Political Consultative Conference at various levels throughout the country). Relying on such sources can be problematic, but those who have begun to use them remind us of their value (Fogel, 1988a; Benton, 1992; Cochran, 1996). The memoir literature also reminds us, more urgently, that "live" interviews can be of even greater value in a research world now dominated by officially edited documentary sources including the often posthumously polished biographies and recollections. Interviews conducted long after the event may be equally problematic, but with handicaps thus equalized, the relative benefits of differing perspectives can justify the effort. Time passes swiftly, however, and the urgency for research on the pre-1949 period lies in conducting interviews and recording oral histories while events remain a living memory (Seybolt, 1989).

Still, the selected update below does not do justice to the full range of materials now available (as of early 1999), including complete runs of old newspapers, periodicals, and government gazettes (*gongbao*), as well as the newly compiled local gazetteers (*difangzhi*) and work unit histories such as those for universities, schools, and major enterprises. Joseph Yick's *Making Urban Revolution in China* is the first civil war period study to rely primarily on the new sources, and his bibliography represents a good cross section, with specific reference to Beijing and Tianjin.

China's civil war adversaries have, of course, always presided over separate sources of information concerning their common history. Nor is access to Chinese archives a totally new experience even for non-Chinese researchers. When the Nationalists retreated to Taiwan in 1949, they took a considerable portion of China's pre-1949 archival records with them, including those of the central government, its army, and the Kuomintang. Foreign scholars have long enjoyed limited access to these materials, and until the post-Mao era they, together with the Hoover Library at Stanford University, served as the foundation for everyone's research on pre-1949 CCP and KMT history.

Conditions with respect to the use of these materials were discreetly summarized by one Taiwan scholar, who wrote that "the first phase, lasting twenty-four years from 1949 to 1973, was a time when the Republic of China's government did not encourage historical research on the Republican period" (Chang Yu-fa, 1992, p. 177). By contrast, the second phase, comprising all the years since, has seen an upsurge of research and publications much like that in China itself, albeit less voluminous. Taiwan's experience in this respect has been well chronicled by the late Lloyd Eastman and others. A small selection of the new Taiwan publications is also included in the updated bibliography below.

As for the archival holdings themselves, Ye and Esherick list the main repositories in a separate chapter on Taiwan. These include the foreign affairs and economics archives at the Academia Sinica's Institute of Modern History (Zhongyang yanjiuyuan jindaishi yanjiusuo) and the Ye/Esherick reference list includes a good selection of its publications. The Academia Historica (Guoshiguan) serves as the main repository for pre-1949 government archives. But more important for civil war political research are the Presidential Archives of Chiang Kai-shek and the KMT archives now housed jointly and administered by the Kuomintang Historical Commission (Zhongguo guomindang zhongyang weiyuanhui dangshi weiyuanhui, or Dangshihui for short). The commission's predecessor was known as the Kuomintang Historical Documents Compilation Committee from its inception in 1930 until the early 1970s (Mast and Li, 1971; Ch'in Hsiao-yi, 1983; Chang Yu-fa, 1992). Equally important are the Justice Ministry's Bureau of Investigation (Diaochaju) archives and the Defense Ministry's Bureau of Intelligence (Qingbaoju) library.

Access for non-Chinese researchers may not be as routine as Ye and Esherick imply. But the number of sensitive subjects continues to diminish as political liberalization progresses overall, in a trend that parallels China's own receding sensitivities. Unfortunately, 1945–1949 civil war topics remain among the most difficult for Kuomintang authorities to confront, and that period is the least well-documented in the voluminous contents of Taiwan's recent archival/historical publications. For example, the Kuomintang Historical Commission's new series, *Zhonghua minguo zhongyao shiliao chubian* (Important historical materials on the Republic of China, preliminary compilation) (see updated bibliography for full citation), comprises 26 volumes to date, of which only the last four concern the post-1945 years. These four volumes also do not cover the civil war itself, but only the preliminaries or events immediately following Japan's surrender, including the takeover of Japanese occupied territory, the Soviet Union's occupation of northeast China, the abortive peace talks with the communists, and the American mediation effort. This new series supersedes the old but ongoing *Geming wenxian* (Documents of the revolution) (see updated bibliography), which began in 1953 and by 1989 had reached volume 117, covering selected subjects that had yet to include the 1945–1949 civil war. The Academia Historica's massive, ongoing *Zhonghua minguo shishi jiyao, chugao, 1894–1974* (Important historical records of the Republic of China, preliminary draft, 1894–1974) (see updated bibliography), initially contained major gaps for the 1945–1949 years. The "missing" volumes appear from time to time, but as of 1992, the record for those years was still not quite complete even though the series as a whole had already entered the 1970s. The Defense Ministry's Bureau of Historical Compilation also has yet to match its many volumes of recently published Sino-Japanese war histories with comparable output on the civil war battles.

As for paths not taken, Japanese sources do not in any case represent the cutting edge of Chinese civil war research, with all due respect otherwise to the intentions of one persistent critic (Fogel, 1988b). Once the time period is less narrowly drawn, however, pre-1945 roots and origins can hardly escape the Japanese record, as scholars have long demonstrated. Most recent among them are Taiwan's military historians with their multi-volume output on the 1937–1945 Sino-Japanese war years. This work must in turn become the basis for scholars continuing on to research late-1940s military questions. Of additional, albeit marginal, importance for the 1945–1949 period are "remnant" Japanese issues such as demobilization, those who "stayed on" for various reasons, the Japanese troops who joined anti-communist forces in Shanxi, the controversial Hainan investment plan, and so on.

In fact, there is a new frontier but it lies in the opposite geographic direction. One regret that has waxed and waned over the years, as questions came and went unanswered, is my long-ago decision to abandon "Sino-Soviet studies" for matters of more immediate political "relevance." The full cost of that youthful opportunism has now come due with the gradual opening of former Soviet bloc archives in Russia and eastern Europe (Westad, 1992; Kramer, 1993). All the same difficulties and drawbacks experienced by archive users in China seem to apply in Russia as well. But as in China, the new openness evidenced both in published Russian-language sources and in archival materials suggests unprecedented possibilities for research on the pre-1949 years and beyond. Some early results of these new opportunities were presented at the New Evidence on the Cold War in Asia conference held in Hong Kong in January 1996, sponsored jointly by Hong Kong University's history department and the Woodrow Wilson International Center for Scholars, Washington, D.C.

It is always a pleasure to acknowledge help received, and in this case several people came to the rescue with advice as well as information about specific publications. I would like to thank especially Amy Yeen-mei Wu, Nancy Hearst, Lau Yee-fui, Eddy U, Pierre Landry, Steve MacKinnon, Chalmers Johnson, and John P. Burns, with the largest debt being owed as usual to Jean Hung (Xiong Jingming) and other staff members at the Universities Service Centre, Chinese University of Hong Kong (CUHK). Despite the Centre's concentration on post-1949 acquisitions, its collection includes many valuable sources on the pre-1949 years, as does the CUHK main library, and the Fung Ping Shan Library, University of Hong Kong.

REFERENCE LIST: GUIDES, AIDS, AND BIBLIOGRAPHIC ESSAYS

Benton, Gregor. "Memoirs and How to Use Them," *Mountain Fires: The Red Army's Three-Year War in South China, 1934–1938.* Berkeley: University of California Press, 1992.

CCP Research Newsletter, nos. 1–10/11 (fall 1988–spring/fall 1992).

Chan, Ming K. *Historiography of the Chinese Labor Movement, 1895–1949: A Critical Survey and Bibliography.* Stanford, Calif.: Hoover Institution Press, Bibliographical Series, no. 60, Stanford University, 1981.

Chang, Julian. "Society and Government in China: A Twenty-Year Index of Soviet Sinology," *CCP Research Newsletter,* no. 3 (summer 1989), pp. 27–35.

Chang Yu-fa. "Republican China Historical Research in Taiwan," *Republican China,* vol. 18, no. 1 (November 1992), pp. 177–205.

Ch'in Hsiao-yi. "An Introduction to the Historical Commission of the Kuomintang," *Chinese Republican Studies Newsletter,* vol. 8, no. 2 (February 1983), pp. 16–22.

Cochran, Sherman. "A Guide to Memoirs in Chinese Periodical Literature: A Review of a New Bibliography," *Republican China,* vol. 21, no. 2 (April 1996), pp. 91–93.

Cold War International History Project Bulletin, Woodrow Wilson International Center for Scholars, Washington, D.C., 1991.

Donovan, Peter, Carl E. Dorris, and Lawrence R. Sullivan. *Chinese Communist Materials at the Bureau of Investigation Archives, Taiwan.* Ann Arbor: University of Michigan, Michigan Papers in Chinese Studies, no. 24, 1976.

Eastman, Lloyd. "The Burgeoning but Fragile State of Republican Studies in Taiwan," *Chinese Republican Studies Newsletter,* vol. 4, no. 1 (October 1978), pp. 7–14.

———. "Republican Studies in Taiwan, 1981," *Chinese Republican Studies Newsletter,* vol. 7, no. 2 (February 1982), pp. 16–19.

Far Eastern Affairs, Moscow (a bimonthly journal of social science and political analysis, published by the Russian Academy of Sciences Institute of Far Eastern Studies), esp. the periodic "archive" section.

Feuerwerker, Albert, and S. Cheng. *Chinese Communist Studies of Modern Chinese History.* Cambridge: East Asian Research Center, Harvard University, 1961.

Fogel, Joshua A. "Mendacity and Veracity in the Recent Chinese Communist Memoir Literature," *CCP Research Newsletter,* no. 1 (fall 1988a), pp. 31–34.

———"Review of *The Cambridge History of China,* vol. 13." *Journal of Asian Studies* (May 1988b).

———, ed. and trans. *Recent Japanese Studies of Modern Chinese History.* Armonk, N.Y.: M. E. Sharpe, 1984.

Fujiansheng dang'anguan zhinan [Guide to Fujian Provincial Archives]. Beijing: Zhongguo dang'an chubanshe, 1997.

Guangzhoushi dang'anguan zhinan [Guide to Guangzhou City Archives). Beijing: Zhongguo dang'an chubanshe, 1997.

Guojia dang'anju, ed. *Zhongguo dang'anguan minglu* [Directory of Chinese National Archives]. Beijing: Dang'an chubanshe, 1990.

Han Weizhi, Xu Xinping, and Lin Dehui, eds. *Shanghaishi dang'anguan jianming zhinan* [A brief guide to the Shanghai Municipal Archives]. Beijing: Dang'an chubanshe, 1991.

Hearst, Nancy, and Tony Saich. "Newly Available Sources on CCP History from the People's Republic of China," in *New Perspectives on State Socialism in China,* edited by Timothy Cheek and Tony Saich, pp. 323–338. Armonk, N.Y.: M. E. Sharpe, 1997.

Heilongjiangsheng dang'anguan zhinan [Guide to the Heilongjiang Provincial Archives]. Beijing: Zhongguo dang'an chubanshe, 1994.

Hsueh, Chun-tu. *The Chinese Communist Movement 1921–1937: An Annotated Bibliography of Selected Materials in the Chinese Collection of the Hoover Institution on War, Revolution and Peace.* Stanford, Calif.: The Hoover Insitution, Bibliographical Series, no. 8, 1960.

———. *The Chinese Communist Movement 1937–1949: An Annotated Bibliography of Selected Materials in the Chinese Collection of the Hoover Institution.* Stanford, Calif.: The Hoover Institution, Bibliographical Series, no. 11, 1962.

Hunt, Michael H., and Odd Arne Westad. "The Chinese Communist Party and International Affairs: A Field Report on New Historical Sources and Old Research Problems," *China Quarterly,* no. 122 (June 1990), pp. 258–272.

Kaple, Deborah A. "The China Scholar in Moscow," *CCP Research Newsletter,* no. 5 (spring 1990), pp. 36–43.

Kiely, Jan. "Third Force Periodicals in China, 1928–1949: Introduction and Annotated Bibliography," *Republican China,* vol. 21, no. 1 (November 1995), pp. 129–168.

Kokubun, Ryosei. "The Current State of Contemporary Chinese Studies in Japan," *China Quarterly,* no. 107 (September 1986), pp. 505–518.

Kramer, Mark. "Archival Research in Moscow: Progress and Pitfalls," *Cold War International History Project Bulletin,* Woodrow Wilson International Center for Scholars, Washington, D.C., fall 1993, pp. 1, 18–39.

Liaoningsheng dang'anguan zhinan [Guide to the Liaoning Provincial Archives]. Beijing: Zhongguo dang'an chubanshe, 1994.

Lu Dayue, ed. *Chongqingshi dang'anguan jianming zhinan* [A brief guide to the Chongqing Municipal Archives]. Chongqing: Keji chubanshe, 1990.

Mast, Herman, with Li Yun-han. "Changing Times at the Historical Archives Commission of the Kuomintang," *Journal of Asian Studies,* vol. 30, no. 2 (February 1971), pp. 413–418.

Moss, William W. "Dang'an: Contemporary Chinese Archives," *China Quarterly,* no. 145 (March 1996), pp. 112–129.

Quanguo geji zhengxie wenshi ziliao pianmu suoyin, 1960–1990 [Index list of historical literature from the Chinese People's Political Consultative Conference at various levels throughout the country, 1960–1990]. Beijing: Zhongguo wenshi chubanshe, 1992, 5 vols: vol. 1, politics, military, foreign affairs; vol. 2, economics, culture; vol. 3, society, geography; vol. 4, personnel; vol. 5, personnel, misc.

Republican China, 1983–April 1997; formerly (1975–1983) *Chinese Republican Studies Newsletter;* from November 1997, renamed *Twentieth-Century China.*

Rhoads, Edward J. M., Edward Friedman, Ellis Joffe, and Ralph L. Powell. *The Chinese Red Army, 1927–1963: An Annotated Bibliography.* Cambridge: Harvard University, East Asian Research Center, East Asia Monographs, no. 16, 1964.

Rinden, Robert, and Roxane Witke. *The Red Flag Waves: A Guide to the* Hung-ch'i p'iao-p'iao *Collection.* Berkeley: University of California, China Research Monographs, no. 3, 1968.

Seybolt, Peter J. "The Second Sino-Japanese War, 1937–1945: The Current Status of Research and Publication in the People's Republic of China," *Republican China,* vol. 14, no. 2 (April 1989), pp. 110–120.

Shanghaishi dang'anguan kaifang dang'an quanzong mulu [Catalog of open record groups in the Shanghai Municipal Archives], nos. 1–10, 1987–1997.

Shi Xuancen and Zhao Mingzhong, chief eds. *Zhongguo di'er lishi dang'anguan jianming zhinan* [Brief guide to the Number Two Historical Archives of China]. Beijing: Dang'an chubanshe, 1987.

Sichuansheng dang'anguan guancang dang'an gaishu [A general record of files held by the Sichuan Archives]. Chengdu: Sichuan shehui kexue yuan chubanshe, 1988.

"Soviet Studies: Chinese Communist Movement Bibliography," *CCP Research Newsletter,* no. 8 (spring 1991), pp. 47–57.

"Soviet Studies: Chinese Communist Movement Bibliography," *CCP Research Newsletter,* no. 9 (fall 1991), pp. 28–30.

Stranahan, Patricia. *Molding the Medium: The Chinese Communist Party and the* Liberation Daily. Armonk, N.Y.: M. E. Sharpe, 1990.

Thogersen, Stig, and Soren Clausen. "New Reflections in the Mirror: Local Chinese Gazetteers *(Difangzhi)* in the 1980s," *Australian Journal of Chinese Affairs,* no. 27 (January 1992), pp. 161–184.

Ting, Lee-hsia Hsu. *Government Control of the Press in Modern China, 1900–1949.* Cambridge: Harvard University, East Asia Research Center, 1974.

Wasserstrom, Jeffrey N. "Bibliographic Essay," in *Student Protests in Twentieth-Century China: The View from Shanghai.* Stanford: Stanford University Press, 1991.

Westad, Odd Arne. "Materials on CCP History in Russian Archives," *CCP Research Newsletter,* nos. 10/11 (spring/fall 1992), pp. 52–53.

Yamada, Tatsuo. "Recent Japanese Studies of Modern China's Political History," *Modern China,* vol. 6, no. 1 (January 1980), pp. 94–120.

Ye Wa and Joseph W. Esherick. *Chinese Archives: An Introductory Guide.* Berkeley: University of California, China Research Monograph, no. 45, 1996.

Yick, Joseph K. S. "Bibliography," in *Making Urban Revolution in China: The CCP-GMD Struggle for Beiping-Tianjin, 1945–1949.* Armonk, N.Y.: M. E. Sharpe, 1995.

Zhonggong zhongyang dangshi yanjiushi, Liao Gailong and Wang Hongmu, chief eds. *Zhonggong dangshi wenzhai niankan, 1982–1990* [Annual abstracts of Chinese Communist Party history, 1982–1990]. Beijing: Zhonggong dangshi ziliao chubanshe, 1982–1994, 9 vols.

Zhongguo dang'anguan jianming zhinan [Concise guide to China's archives]. Beijing: Zhongguo dang'an chubanshe, 1997.

Zhongguo dang'an wenxian cidian [Dictionary of Chinese archival materials], Zhu Jinfu, chief ed., with Ni Daoshan, Cao Xishen, and Yu Yuzhu. Beijing: Zhongguo renshi chubanshe, 1994.

Zhongwen hexin qikan yaomu zonglan [A guide to the core journals of China]. Beijing: Beijing daxue chubanshe, 1992.

Zhongwen hexin qikan yaomu zonglan, di'erban [A guide to the core journals of China, second edition]. Beijing: Beijing daxue chubanshe, 1996.

"Zhongyang dang'anguan jianjie" [Introduction to the Central Archives], Beijing, October 1989. Trans. in *CCP Research Newsletter,* no. 8 (spring 1991), pp. 29–45.

Zuixin Zhongguo qikan quanlan [Most recent Chinese periodicals]. Beijing: Xiandai chubanshe, 1989.

Selected Bibliography

I. NEWSPAPERS, PERIODICALS, RADIO BROADCASTS

Chieh-fang jih-pao, Yenan, 1945-1946.

Ch'ün-chung [*Masses*], Shanghai, March, 1946-March, 1947; Hong Kong, April, 1947-October, 1949.

Foreign Broadcast Information Branch, Far Eastern Section, *Daily Report*, February, 1947-December, 1949.

Kuan-ch'a [*The Observer*], Shanghai, September, 1946-December, 1948.

Peiping Chronicle, Peiping, 1946-1948.

The Shanghai Weekly Review, Shanghai, 1946-1948.

The Shanghai Weekly Review, Monthly Report, Shanghai, 1946-1947.

Shih-tai p'i-p'ing [*Modern Critique*], Hong Kong, June, 1947-December, 1948.

*U.S. Consulate General (and U.S. Information Service), Canton, China, *Chinese Press Review*, April 1, 1946-July 9, 1948.

U.S. Consulate General (and U.S. Office of War Information), Chungking, China, *Chinese Press Review*, January 3, 1945-October 21, 1946.

U.S. Consulate, Kunming, China, *Chinese Press Review*, September 14, 1945-July 18, 1948.

U.S. Consulate General, Mukden, China, *Chinese Press Review*, June 6, 1947-July 26, 1948.

U.S. Embassy, Nanking, China, *Chinese Press Review*, May 1, 1946-August 6, 1948.

U.S. Consulate (and U.S. Information Service), Peiping, China, *Chinese Press Review*, Peiping and Tientsin, January 2, 1946-July 27, 1948.

U.S. Consulate, Peiping, China, *Translations Radio Broadcasts of Communist Hsin Hua Station*, November 20, 1947-July 10, 1949.

U.S. Consulate General (and U.S. Information Service), Shanghai, China, *Chinese Press Review*, September 17, 1945-February 15/16, 1950.

U.S. Consulate General (and U.S. Information Service), Tientsin, China, *Tientsin Chinese Press Review*, November 8, 1945-July 19, 1948.

U.S. Information Service, Shanghai, China, *For Your Information: Yenan Broadcasts*, January 30, 1946-January 19, 1947.

*The United States Consular press translations are available on microfilm at the Library of Congress, Washington, D.C.

II. *BOOKS, PAMPHLETS, ARTICLES: CHINESE*

Items marked with an asterisk (*) are from the microfilm collection of The Hoover Library, Stanford University.

A Che. *Chung-kuo hsien-tai hsueh-sheng yun-tung chien shih* [A short history of the contemporary Chinese student movement]. Hong Kong: Ta sheng ch'u-pan-she, n.d.

Chang-chia-k'ou ch'üan shih kung-jen shou chieh tai-piao ta-hui [The first Kalgan all-city workers representative conference]. Kalgan: Chang shih kung-jen shou chieh tai-piao ta-hui, December 25, 1945.

Chang Hen-shui. *Wu tzu teng-k'o* [Five Graduates]. Hong Kong: Nan kuo ch'u-pan-she, 1958.

Chang Hui, *et al. Shang-hai chin pai nien ko-ming shih-hua* [History of the revolution in Shanghai during the past 100 years]. Shanghai: Jen-min ch'u-pan-she, 1963.

Chang Tzu-k'ai. "Sheng-li hou chieh-shou te ching-yen" [The take-over experience after victory], *Chuan-chi wen-hsueh* [Biographical literature], Taipei, March 1967, pp. 47-50.

Chang Yu-i, ed. *Chung-kuo chin-tai nung-yeh shih tzu-liao* [Historical materials on Chinese agriculture in modern times]. Vol. 3. Peking: San lien, 1957.

Ch'en Lei. *Hsiang p'ao-k'ou yao fan ch'ih* [Begging for food from the muzzles of guns]. Shanghai: Hu pin, 1947.

Ch'en Po-ta, *et al. Kuan-yü kung-shang-yeh te cheng-ts'e* [On industrial and commercial policy]. Hong Kong: Chung-kuo ch'u-pan-she, May, 1948.

———, *et al. Lun ch'ün-chung lu-hsien* [On the mass line]. Hong Kong: no pub., 1949.

Ch'en Shao-hsiao [Major Ch'en]. *Chin-ling ts'an-chao chi* [Sunset in Nanking]. Hong Kong: Chih ch'eng ch'u-pan-she, 1963-72, 5 vols.

Cheng pao ch'u-pan-she, ed. *Kuan-yü chih-shih-fen-tzu te kai-tsao* [On the reform of intellectuals]. Hong Kong: Cheng-pao ch'u-pan-she, December, 1948.

Chi-nan hsing-shu ti-i tz'u ts'ai lien hui pao-kao yü tsung-chieh [Report and summary of the first joint financial conference of the south Hopei administrative office]. n.p.: Chi-nan hsing-shu, January, 1946.

Chiang ko-ming chin-hsing tao-ti [Carry out the revolution to the end]. n.p.: Chi-tung hsin hua shu-tien, 1949.

Chieh-fang she, ed. *Chiang ko-ming chin-hsing tao-ti* [Carry out the revolution to the end]. Shanghai: Chieh-fang she, 1949.

*———, ed. *Lun hsin chieh-fang-ch'ü t'u-ti cheng-ts'e* [On land policy in newly liberated areas]. n.p.: Hsin hua shu-tien, 1949.

———, ed. *Mu-ch'ien hsing-shih ho wo-men te jen-wu* [The present situation and our tasks]. n.p.: Hsin hua shu-tien, 1949.

Chih-shih-fen-tzu yü chiao-yü wen-t'i [Problems of intellectuals and education]. Hong Kong: Hsin min-chu ch'u-pan-she, 1949.

Chin-ch'a-chi hsin hua shu-tien, ed. *T'u-ti kai-ko yü cheng tang* [Land reform and party rectification]. n.p.: Chin-ch'a-chi hsin hua shu-tien, 1948.

Chin-ch'a-chi jih-pao she, ed. *Ch'üan-t'i nung-min ch'i-lai p'ing fen t'u-ti* [All peasants arise to divide the land equally]. n.p.: Chin-ch'a-chi hsin hua shu-chü, January, 1948.

Chin-ch'a-chi pien-ch'ü hsing-cheng wei-yüan-hui. *Chin-ch'a-chi fa-ling hui-pien* [A collection of the laws of the Shansi-Chahar-Hopei Border Region]. n.p.: no pub., 1946.

Chin-ch'a-chi pien-ch'ü tsung kung-hui kung-jen pao she, ed. *Chin-ch'a-chi pien-ch'ü kung-jen wu-i chi-nien hua-ts'e* [Shansi-Chahar-Hopei Border Region workers May 1 commemorative pictorial]. Kalgan: Chin-ch'a-chi pien-ch'ü tsung kung-hui kung-jen pao she, April, 1946.

*Chin-chi-lu-yü pien-ch'ü cheng-fu, chi-lu-yü hsing-shu, ed. *Chien-i ho-li fu-tan che-hsing pan-fa* [Provisional regulations for simple and fair taxes]. n.p.: Chin-chi-lu-yü pien-ch'ü, chi-lu-yü ti-shih hsing-cheng tu-ch'a chuan-yuan kung-shu, 1945.

Chin-chi-lu-yü pien-ch'ü cheng-fu, ti-i t'ing, ed. *Chien tsu chien hsi i-wen chieh-ta* [Questions and answers about the reduction of rent and interest]. n.p.: Hua-pei hsin hua shu-tien, n.d.

Chin-chi-lu-yü yuan-ch'ü tzu-chüeh t'uan-chieh yun tung te ching-yen [The experience of Yuan-ch'ü, Shansi-Hopei-Shantung-Honan, in the self-conscious unification movement]. n.p.: no pub., 1947?.

Chin I-hung. *Chung-kung t'u kai yü Chung-kuo t'u-ti wen-t'i* [Chinese Communist land reform and China's land problems]. Hong Kong: Tzu-yu ch'u-pan-she, October, 1950.

Chin-sui pien-ch'ü sheng-ch'an wei-yuan-hui, ed. *Hsin chieh-fang-ch'ü te ch'ün-chung sheng-ch'an* [The production of the masses in the new liberated areas]. n.p.: Chin-sui pien-ch'ü sheng-ch'an wei-yuan-hui, February, 1946.

Ch'ing-nien ch'u-pan-she, ed. *Chung-kuo hsueh-sheng yun-tung te tang-ch'ien jen-wu* [The present tasks of the Chinese student movement]. Peking: Ch'ing-nien ch'u-pan-she, February, 1950.

Ch'ing-nien sheng-huo [Youth Life]. Liaoning, December, 1948.

Chu Tzu-chia. *Wang cheng-ch'üan te k'ai-ch'ang yü shou-ch'ang* [The rise and fall of the Wang Ching-wei regime]. Hong Kong: Ch'un-ch'iu tsa-chih she, 1959-64. 5 vols.

Ch'ün yun chih-shih hui-pien [A compilation of mass movement directives]. n.p.: Chung-kung chi-lu-yü pien-ch'ü tang-wei, September, 1945.

Chung-hua ch'üan kuo hsueh-sheng lien-ho-hui, ed. *Chung-kuo hsueh-sheng te kuang-jung ch'uan-t'ung* [The glorious tradition of China's students]. Peking: Chung-kuo ch'ing-nien ch'u-pan-she, 1956.

Chung-kung chung-yang wei-yuan-hui. *Chung-kuo t'u-ti fa ta-kang* [The outline agrarian law of China]. n.p.: Hua-pei hsin hua shu-tien, February, 1949.

Chung-kung jen-ming-lu pien-hsiu wei-yuan-hui, ed. *Chung-kung jen-ming-lu* [Chinese Communist biographies]. Taipei: Chung-hua-min-kuo kuo-chi kuan-hsi yen-chiu-so, 1967.

Chung-kuo hsueh-sheng ta t'uan-chieh [The great unification of China's students]. Hong Kong: Hsin min-chu ch'u-pan-she, June, 1949.

Chung-kuo kung-ch'an-tang yü t'u-ti ko-ming [The Chinese Communist Party and the land revolution]. Hong Kong: Cheng pao she t'u-shu-pu, n.d.

Chung-kuo lao-kung yun-tung shih pien-tsuan wei-yuan-hui, ed., Ma Ch'ao-chün, chief ed. *Chung-kuo lao-kung yun-tung shih* [History of the Chinese labor movement]. Taipei: Chung-kuo lao-kung fu-li ch'u-pan-she, 1959. 5 vols.

Fang Le-t'ien. *Tung-pei wen-t'i* [The Northeast question]. Shanghai: Shang-wu yin-shu kuan, 1933.

Fei-ch'ing chuan-t'i yen-chiu ts'ung-shu: kung-fei t'u-ti cheng-ts'e chih yen-chiu [Chinese bandit problems research series: research on the land policy of the communist bandits]. Taiwan: Yang ming shan, October, 1957.

Ha-erh-pin Chung Su yu-hao hsieh-hui, ed. *Chih-kung ts'an-k'ao wen-hsien* [Reference documents on labor]. Harbin: Ha-erh-pin Chung Su yu-hao hsieh-hui, 1948.

Hsin hua jih-pao kuan, ed. *Tung-pei wen-t'i* [Manchurian problems]. n.p.: Hsin hua jih-pao kuan, December, 1946.

Hsin hua jih-pao tzu-liao shih, ed. *Lun chih-shih-fen-tzu: hsueh-hsi ts'ung-shu* [On intellectuals: a study series]. Wusih: Su-nan hsin hua shu-tien, December, 1949.

Hsin hua she, ed. *Jen-min chieh-fang chan-cheng liang chou-nien tsung-chieh ho ti-san nien te jen-wu* [Summary of two years of the people's war of liberation and the tasks of the third year]. Hong Kong: Cheng pao she t'u-shu-pu, August, 1948.

Hsin kung-shang cheng-ts'e [New industrial and commercial policies]. Hong Kong: Hung mien ch'u-pan-she, March, 1949.

Hsin min-chu-chu-i kuo-chia te chih-kung-hui [Labor unions in the new democratic nations]. Translated by Yang Hui-lin. n.p.: Chih-shih shu-tien, August, 1949.

Hsu Ti-hsin. *Chung-kuo ching-chi te tao-lu* [The path of China's economy]. Hong Kong: Hsin chung-kuo shu-chü, 1949.

Hu En-tse, ed. *Hui-i ti-san tz'u kuo-nei ko-ming chan-cheng shih-ch'i te Shang-hai hsueh-sheng yun-tung* [Recollections of the Shanghai student movement during the third revolutionary civil war]. Shanghai: Jen-min ch'u-pan-she, 1958.

Hu Hua, *et al. Chung-kuo hsin min-chu-chu-i ko-ming shih ts'an-k'ao tzu-liao* [Reference materials on the history of the new democratic revolution in China]. Shanghai: Shang-wu yin-shu kuan, 1951.

Hu Lin. *I-erh-i te hui-i* [Recollections of December first]. Hong Kong: Hai hung, 1949.

Hua-pei hsin hua shu-tien, ed. *Kuan-yü ch'eng-shih cheng-ts'e te chi-ko wen-hsien* [Some documents on city policy]. n.p.: Hua-pei hsin hua shu-tien, 1949.

Hua-pei hsueh-sheng yun-tung hsiao shih pien-chi wei-yuan-hui, ed. *Hua-pei hsueh-sheng yun-tung hsiao shih* [A short history of the student movement in North China]. n.p.: no pub., 1948.

Hua-pei tsung kung-hui ch'ou-pei wei-yuan-hui, ed. *Ti-liu tz'u ch'üan kuo lao ta chüeh-i* [Resolutions of the Sixth All-China Labor Congress]. n.p.: Chung-yuan hsin hua shu-tien, June, 1949.

Hua shang pao tzu-liao shih, ed. *Chieh-fang-ch'ü mao-i hsü chih* [Necessary information about trade in the liberated areas]. Hong Kong: Hua shang pao she, March, 1949.

Hua-tung jen-min ch'u-pan-she, ed. Tsai tou-cheng li chuang-ta [Growing up in the struggle]. Shanghai: Hua-tung jen-min ch'u-pan-she, August, 1951.

Hua-tung jen-min ch'u pan-she, ed. *Tung-pei chien-li hsuan-ch'uan kang te ching-yen* [The experience of the Northeast in establishing a propaganda network]. Shanghai: Hua-tung jen-min ch'u-pan-she, 1951.

Huang Chen-hsia, ed. *Chung-kung chün-jen chih* [Mao's Generals]. Hong Kong: Tang-tai li-shih yen-chiu-so, 1968.

*_I-chiu-szu-ch'i-nien shang-pan-nien lai ch'ü tang wei kuan-yü t'u kai yun-tung te chung-yao wen-chien_ [Important documents on the land reform movement during the first half of 1947 from the (Hopei-Shantung-Honan) regional party committee]. n.p.: Chi-lu-yü ch'ü tang wei, June, 1947.

I-chiu-szu-ch'i-nien shou-ts'e [1947 handbook]. Hong Kong: Hua shang pao she, January, 1947.

I-chiu-szu-pa-nien shou-ts'e [1948 handbook]. Hong Kong: Hua shang pao she, January, 1948.

I-chiu-szu-chiu-nien shou-ts'e [1949 handbook]. Hong Kong: Hua shang pao she, January, 1949.

I-chiu-wu-ling jen-min nien-chien [1950 people's yearbook]. Hong Kong: Ta kung shu-chü, January, 1950.

Ju-ho kuan-ch'e tung-pei ch'üan tang te chuan-pien? [How to change thoroughly the entire party in the Northeast?]. Dairen: Ta-lien tung-pei shu-tien, June, 1949.

Kao Kang. _Chan tsai tung-pei ching-chi chien-she te tsui ch'ien-mien_ [Standing at the very forefront of economic construction in the Northeast]. Peking: Hsin hua shih-shih ts'ung-k'an she, March, 1950.

K'o Lan and Chao Tzu. _Pu szu te Wang Hsiao-ho_ [The immortal Wang Hsiao-ho]. Peking: Kung-jen ch'u-pan-she, 1955.

*_Kuan-yü ch'üeh-ting chieh-chi ch'eng-fen ch'u-shen wen-t'i_ [On resolving problems of class composition and origin]. n.p.: Chiao-tung chün-ch'ü cheng-chih-pu tsu-chih-pu, August, 1946.

Kung-fei t'u-ti cheng-ts'e chung-yao wen-chien ts'ung-pien [A collection of important land policy documents of the communist bandits]. n.p.: no pub., n.d.

Kung-jen shou-ts'e [Workers handbook]. Hong Kong: Ta kung shu-chü, 1950.

Kung-jen te hsin t'ien-ti [The workers' new world]. Hong Kong: Kung-jen wen-hua she, July, 1948.

*_Kung-tso t'ung-hsun, 24_ [Work correspondence, no. 24]. n.p.: Chung-kung po-hai-ch'ü tang wei, July, 1947.

*_Kung-tso t'ung-hsün, 32: yu-chi chan-cheng chuan-hao_ [Work correspondence, no. 32: special issue on guerrilla warfare]. n.p.: Chi-lu-yü ch'ü tang wei min-yun-pu, June, 1947.

* "Lai-tung hsien cheng-fu: i-chiu-szu-liu-nien shang-pan-nien min cheng kung-tso tsung-chieh" [Lai-tung hsien government: a summary of the work of the democratic government during the first half of 1946]. Unpublished report, 1946.

Li Hsien-liang. _K'ang-chan hui-i-lu_ [Recollections of the anti-Japanese war]. Tsingtao: Kan k'un ch'u-pan-she, 1948.

Li Keng. _Chieh-fang-ch'ü te sheng-ch'an yun-tung_ [The production movement in the liberated areas]. Hong Kong: Chung-kuo ch'u-pan-she, July, 1947.

———, ed. _Chieh-fang-ch'ü te t'u-ti cheng-ts'e yü shih-shih_ [Land policy and implementation in the liberated areas]. Hong Kong: Chung-kuo ch'u-pan-she, February, 1947.

Li T'ien-min. _Chung-kung yü nung-min_ [The Chinese Communists and the peasantry]. Hong Kong: Yu-lien ch'u-pan-she, 1958.

Li Tu and Wang Li, _et al. Tung-pei te hei-an yü kuang-ming_ [Darkness and light in the Northeast]. n.p.: Li-shih tzu-liao kung-ying she, n.d.

Li Wen erh lieh-shih chi-nien wei-yuan-hui, ed. *Jen-min ying-lieh* [The people's heroic martyrs]. n.p.: Li Wen erh lieh-shih chi-nien wei-yuan-hui, 1946.

* Li Yü. *Lun ch'ün-chung lu-hsien yü shan-tung ch'ün-chung yun-tung* [On the mass line and the mass movement in Shantung]. n.p.: Chung-kung chiao-tung-ch'ü tang-wei, February, 1946.

Liang Shu-ming and Chou Hsin-min. *Li Wen an tiao-ch'a pao-kao-shu* [Report on the investigation of the Li-Wen case]. Nanking: Chung-kuo min-chu t'ung-meng tsung-pu, 1946.

Liu Ch'ang-sheng, *et al. Chung-kuo kung-ch'an-tang yü Shang-hai kung-jen: Shang-hai kung-jen yun-tung li-shih yen-chiu tzu-liao chih erh* [The Chinese Communist Party and the Shanghai workers: Shanghai labor movement historical research materials, no. two].. Shanghai: Lao-tung ch'u-pan-she, August, 1951.

Liu Shao-ch'i, ed. *Hsin min-chu-chu-i ch'eng-shih cheng-ts'e* [New democratic city policy]. Hong Kong: Hsin min-chu ch'u-pan-she, August, 1949.

———, *et al. T'u kai cheng tang tien-hsing ching-yen* [Model experiences in land reform and party rectification]. Hong Kong: Chung-kuo ch'u-pan-she, April, 1948.

———. *Wu-ko ts'ai-liao* [Five statements by Liu Shao-ch'i]. Red Guard publication, 1967.

* *Lu-chung-ch'ü k'ang-jih min-chü cheng-ch'üan chien-she ch'i nien lai te chi-pen tsung-chieh chi chin-hou chi-pen jen-wu* [A basic summary of the construction of anti-Japanese political power in Central Shantung District during the past seven years and the basic tasks for the future]. n.p.: Lu-chung hsing-cheng kung-shu, July, 1945.

Lu Feng. *Kang-t'ieh te tui-wu: Su-pei chieh-fang-ch'ü shih-lu chih i* [The iron and steel corps: an account of the north Kiangsu liberated area, no. one]. Hong Kong: Yang-tzu ch'u-pan-she, 1947.

Lun hsin chieh-fang-ch'ü t'u-ti cheng-ts'e [On the land policy of the new liberated areas]. n.p.: Hsin min-chu ch'u-pan-she, 1949.

Mao Tse-tung. *Ching-chi wen-t'i yü ts'ai-cheng wen-t'i* [Economic and financial problems], 1942. Hong Kong: Hsin min-chu ch'u-pan-she, 1949.

———, *et al. Hsin min-chu-chu-i kung-shang cheng-ts'e* [The new democratic industrial and commercial policy]. Hong Kong: Hsin min-chu ch'u-pan-she, 1949.

Nei-cheng-pu tiao-ch'a-chü. *Chien-fei hsien-chuang hui-pien: t'u kai* [A compilation on current traitor bandit affairs: land reform]. Taipei: Nei-cheng-pu tiao-ch'a-chü, 1950.

Pa tsu-kuo t'ui-hsiang tu-li tzu-yu chieh-fang [Push the fatherland toward independence, freedom, and liberation]. Shanghai: St. John's University, 1948.

Shang-hai shih hsüeh-sheng lien-ho-hui, ed. *Chung-kuo hsüeh-sheng yun-tung te tang-ch'ien jen-wu* [The present tasks of the Chinese student movement]. Shanghai: Hsin hua shu-tien, 1949.

Shang-hai tsung kung-hui mi-shu-ch'u, ed. *Chieh-fang hou Shang-hai kung yun tzu-liao* [Materials on the Shanghai labor movement after liberation]. Shanghai: Lao-tung ch'u-pan-she, 1950.

* *Shan-tung sheng cheng-fu chi Shan-tung chün-ch'ü kung-pu chih ko-chung t'iao-li kang-yao pan-fa hui-pien* [A compilation of various regulations, programs,

and methods issued by the Shantung provincial government and the Shantung military region]. n.p.: Chiao-tung ch'ü hsing-cheng kung-shu, 1945.

* Shan-tung sheng Chiao-tung-ch'ü cheng-li t'u-ti teng-chi ch'en-pao teng-chi che-hsing pan-fa [Provisional methods of grading, reporting, and registering for land adjustments in Chiaotung district, Shantung province]. n.p.: no pub., 1946.

* Shan-tung sheng Chiao-tung ch'ü san-shih-wu nien-tu cheng-liang pan-fa [Methods for requisitioning grain for the year 1946 in Chiaotung district Shantung province]. n.p.: no pub., 1946?.

Shen Chih-yuan, *et al. Chung-kuo t'u-ti wen-t'i yü t'u-ti kai-ko* [China's land problems and land reform]. Hong Kong: Hsin chung ch'u-pan-she, March, 1948.

* Sung Jen-ch'iung t'ung-chih liu-yueh shih-wu-jih tsai chung-yang-chü tang hsiao kuan-yü cheng-chih kung-tso te pao-kao [Comrade Sung Jen-ch'iung's report on political work at the central Party school on June 15]. n.p.: Chin-chi-lu-yü chün-ch'ü cheng-chih-pu, December, 1947.

Szu-fa hsing-cheng-pu tiao-ch'a-chü, ed. *Kung-fei hsueh yun kung-tso te p'ou-shih* [Disclosures of Communist bandit work in the student movement]. Taiwan: Szu-fa hsing-cheng-pu tiao-ch'a-chü, 1961.

Ta ko-ming i-lai Shang-hai kung-jen chieh-chi wei cheng-ch'ü t'ung-i t'uan-chieh erh tou-cheng [The struggle of the Shanghai working class for unity since the great revolution]. Shanghai: Lao-tung ch'u-pan-she, July, 1951.

* Ta-tien ch'a chien tou-cheng tsung-chieh [A summary of the struggles to investigate reductions in Ta-tien]. n.p.: Chung-kung Shan-tung fen-chü, October, 1944.

T'ang Jen. *Chin-ling ch'un meng* [Dreams of spring in Nanking]. Hong Kong: Wen tsung ch'u-pan-she, 1955. 4 vols.

* T'u-ti cheng-ts'e chung-yao wen-chien hui-chi [A collection of important documents on land policy]. n.p.: Chung-kung Chin-ch'a-chi chung-yang-chü hsuan-chuan-pu, 1946.

T'u-ti kai-ko chung te chi-ko wen-t'i ho san-ko tien-hsing ching-yen [Some land reform problems and three model experiences]. Tsitsihar: Tung-pei shu-tien, April, 1948.

* T'u-ti kai-ko yü cheng tang [Land reform and party rectification]. n.p.: Chin-ch'a-chi hsin hua shu-tien, 1948.

* T'u-ti tsung-chieh pao-kao (ts'ao-an) [Land summary report (draft)]. n.p.: no pub., 1944?.

Tung-pei shu-tien, ed. *Chih-kung yun-tung ts'an-k'ao tzu-liao* [Reference materials on the labor movement]. Harbin: Tung-pei shu-tien, August, 1948.

———, ed. *Chih-kung yun-tung wen-hsien* [Documents on the labor movement]. Vol. 1. Harbin: Tung-pei shu-tien, n.d.

———, ed. *Chih-kung yun-tung wen-hsien* [Documents on the labor movement]. Vols. 3, 4. Harbin: Tung-pei shu-tien, 1949.

———, ed. *Hsin te jen-wu yü hsin te li-liang* [New tasks and new strength]. n.p.: Tung-pei shu-tien, 1948.

T'ung-i ch'u-pan-she, ed. *Jih-pen t'ou-hsiang hou te chung-kuo kung-ch'an-tang* [The Chinese Communist Party after the Japanese surrender]. n.p.: T'ung-i ch'u-pan-she, December, 1947.

Wang Chien-min. *Chung-kuo kung-ch'an-tang shih-kao* [Draft history of the Chinese Communist Party]. Taipei: Wang Chien-min, 1965. 3 vols.

Wang Hao. "Chung-kuo chih hsing te chi-tien kuan-kan" [A few impressions from travelling in China], *Ch'i-shih nien-tai* [The seventies], Hong Kong, January, 1973, pp. 54-59.

Wang Nien-k'un. *Hsueh-sheng yun-tung shih-yao chiang-hua* [A historical outline on the student movement]. Shanghai: Shang tsa ch'u-pan-she, 1951.

Wei shun-chieh tang te tsu-chih erh tou-cheng [Struggle to purify the Party's organization]. Hong Kong: Cheng pao she, 1948.

Yang Hsieh, ed. *Chung-kuo hsueh-sheng yun-tung te ku-shih* [The story of the Chinese student movement]. Nanking: Chiang-su jen-min ch'u-pan-she, 1957.

Yang K'uei-chang. *Ch'eng hsiang kuan-hsi wen-t'i* [Problems in urban-rural relations]. Hong Kong: Chung-yuan ch'u-pan-she, 1949.

Yang Ping-an, ed. *Chung-kuo jen-min chieh-fang chan-cheng* [The Chinese people's war of liberation]. Shanghai: Hsin chih-shih ch'u-pan-she, March, 1955.

Yü Tsai hsien-sheng chi-nien wei-yuan-hui, ed. *I-erh-i min-chu yun-tung chi-nien chi* [Commemorative writings on the democratic December first movement]. Shanghai: Chen hua, 1946.

III. *SELECTED UPDATE: CHINESE*

A. *Current (post-1978) Archival and Historical Journals, Serial Publications, and the Sponsoring Units*

Anhui dangshi yanjiu [Anhui party history research], Hefei, Zhonggong Anhui shengwei dangshi gongzuo weiyuanhui

Beijing dang'an [Beijing archives], Beijingshi dang'anguan

Beijing dang'an shiliao [Beijing archival materials], Beijingshi dang'anguan

Beijing dangshi tongxun [Beijing party history bulletin]

Beijing dangshi yanjiu [Research on Beijing party history], Zhonggong Beijing shiwei dangshi yanjiushi

Dalian dangshi ziliao tongxun [Dalian bulletin on party history materials]

Dang de wenxian [Party documents], Beijing, Zhonggong zhongyang wenxian yanjiushi, Zhongyang dang'anguan

Dang'an [Archive], Lanzhou, Gansusheng dang'anju, Gansusheng dang'an xuehui

Dang'an shiliao yu yanjiu [Archival materials and research], Harbin, Heilongjiang dang'-anguan

Dang'an yu lishi [Archives and history], Shanghai, Shanghaishi dang'anguan; post-1990, changed to *Shanghai dang'an gongzuo* [Shanghai archival work]

Dangdai Zhongguo yanjiu [Research on contemporary China], Beijing, Dangdai Zhong-guo yanjiusuo

Dangshi wenhui [Party history collection], Taiyuan, Zhonggong Shanxi shengwei dangshi yanjiushi

Dangshi yanjiu yu jiaoxue [Research and teaching on party history], Fuzhou

Dangshi yanjiu ziliao [Party history research materials], Beijing, Zhongguo geming bo-wuguan dangshi yanjiushi

Dangshi ziliao tongxun [Party history materials bulletin], Beijing, Zhongyang dangxiao

Dangshi zongheng [All about party history], Shenyang, Zhonggong Liaoning shengwei dangshi yanjiushi

Difang gemingshi yanjiu [Local revolutionary history research], Wuhan, Zhonggong Hubei shengwei dangshi ziliao zhengji bianyan weiyuanhui, E-Yu bianqu gemingshi bianji weiyuanhui

Dongbei difangshi yanjiu [Northeast local history research], Shenyang, Liaoning shehui kexue yuan, lishi yanjiusuo

Geming huiyilu [Revolutionary memoirs]

Geming yinglie [Revolutionary heroes], Xi'an, Zhonggong Shaanxi shengwei dangshi ziliao zhengji yanjiu weiyuanhui

Gemingshi ziliao [Materials on revolutionary history], Shanghai, Shanghai renmin chubanshe

Guizhou dang'an shiliao [Guizhou historical archive materials], Guizhousheng dang'anguan

Henan dangshi yanjiu [Henan party history research], Zhengzhou, Zhonggong Henan shengwei dangshi gongzuo weiyuanhui

Henan wenshi ziliao [Henan historical literature], Zhengzhou, Zhongguo renmin zhengzhi xieshang huiyi Henansheng weiyuanhui wenshi ziliao yanjiu weiyuanhui

Hubei dang'an shiliao [Hubei historical archive materials], Hubeisheng dang'anguan

Hubei wenshi ziliao [Hubei historical literature], Wuhan, Zhongguo renmin zhengzhi xieshang huiyi Hubeisheng weiyuanhui wenshi ziliao yanjiu weiyuanhui

Hunan dangshi yuekan [Hunan party history monthly], formerly (1982–1987) *Hunan dangshi tongxun* [Hunan party history bulletin], Changsha, Zhonggong Hunan shengwei dangshi ziliao zhengji yanjiu weiyuanhui

Jiangsu dangshi ziliao [Jiangsu party history materials], Jiangsusheng dang'anguan, Zhonggong Jiangsu shengwei dangshi gongzuo weiyuanhui

Jilin wenshi ziliao [Jilin historical literature], Changchun, Zhongguo renmin zhengzhi xieshang huiyi Jilinsheng weiyuanhui

Jindaishi yanjiu [Studies in modern history], Beijing, Zhongguo shehui kexue yuan jindaishi yanjiusuo

Jindaishi ziliao [Modern history materials], Beijing, Zhongguo shehui kexue yuan jindaishi yanjiusuo

Junshi lishi [Military history], Beijing, Junshi kexueyuan junshi lishi yanjiusuo

Junshi shilin [Military affairs history collection], Beijing, Zhongguo renmin geming junshi bowuguan

Junshi ziliao [Military history materials], Beijing, Zhongguo renmin jiefangjun dangshi ziliao zhengji weiyuanhui

Kang Ri zhanzheng yanjiu [Research on the war of resistance against Japan], Beijing

Liaoning dangshi tongxun [Liaoning party history bulletin]

Longjiang dangshi [Longjiang party history], Harbin, Zhonggong Heilongjiang shengwei dangshi gongzuo weiyuanhui

Mao Zedong sixiang yanjiu [Studies in Mao Zedong thought], ˙Chengdu, Sichuansheng shehui kexue yuan, Zhonggong Sichuan shengwei dangshi gongzuo weiyuanhui, et al.

Meiguo yanjiu cankao ziliao [American research reference materials], Beijing, Zhongguo shehui kexue yuan Meiguo yanjiusuo

Minguo chunqiu [Republic of China annals], Nanjing, Jiangsu guji chubanshe

Minguo dang'an [Republic of China archives], Nanjing, Zhongguo di'er lishi dang'anguan

Minguo yanjiu [Republic of China research], Nanjing, Nanjing daxue chubanshe

Neimenggu dang'an [Inner Mongolia archives], Neimenggu zızhiqu dang'anju, Dang'an xuehui

Qingnian yundong xuekan [Youth movement studies periodical]

Qingyunshi yanjiu [Research on youth movement history], Beijing, Zhongyang tuanxiao qingyunshi yanjiushi

Renwu [Personalities], Beijing, Renmin chubanshe

Shandong dang'an [Shandong archives], Shandongsheng dang'anguan

Shandong dangshi ziliao [Shandong party history materials], Zhonggong Shandong shengwei dangshi ziliao zhengji yanjiu weiyuanhui

Shanghai dang'an gongzuo [Shanghai archival work], Shanghaishi dang'anguan; formerly (pre-1990) *Dang'an yu lishi*

Shanghai dangshi ziliao tongxun [Shanghai party history materials bulletin], Zhonggong Shanghai shihwei dangshi ziliao zhengji weiyuanhui

Shanghai gong yun shiliao [Historical materials on the Shanghai labor movement]

Shanghai wenshi ziliao xuanji [Selected materials from Shanghai historical literature], Shanghaishi zhengxie wenshi ziliao gongzuo weiyuanhui

Shanxi geming genjudi [Shanxi revolutionary base area], Taiyuan, Shanxisheng dang'anju

Shanxi wenshi ziliao [Shanxi historical literature], Taiyuan, Zhongguo renmin zhengzhi xieshang huiyi Shanxisheng weiyuanhui wenshi ziliao yanjiu weiyuanhui

Shixue yuekan [Historiography monthly], Kaifeng, Henansheng lishi xuehui, Henan daxue

Sichaun dang'an shiliao [Historical materials from Sichuan archives], Sichuansheng dang'anguan

Sichuan dangshi yuekan [Sichuan party history monthly], Chengdu, Zhonggong Sichuan shengwei dangshi gongzuo weiyuanhui

Tianjin lishi ziliao [Tianjin historical materials]

Tianjin wenshi ziliao xuanji [Materials selected from Tianjin historical literature]

Tongyi zhanxian [United front], Wuhan, Zhonggong Hubei shengwei tongzhanbu, Hubeisheng tongzhan lilun yanjiuhui

Tongzhan lilun yanjiu [Research in united front theory], Harbin, Zhonggong Heilongjiang shengwei tongzhanbu

Wenxian he yanjiu [Documents and research], Zhonggong zhongyang wenxian yanjiushi

Wuhan wenshi ziliao [Wuhan historical literature], Zhengxie Wuhanshi weiyuanhui wenshi ziliao yanjiu weiyuanhui

Yunnan dang'an shiliao [Yunnan archival materials], Kunming, Yunnansheng dang'anguan

Zhonggong dangshi tongxun [Chinese Communist Party history bulletin], Beijing, Zhongguo Zhonggong dangshi xuehui, Zhongyang dangxiao; see introduction in *CCP Research Newsletter*, nos. 6/7 (summer/fall 1990), pp. 32–35.

Zhonggong dangshi yanjiu [Research on Chinese Communist Party history], Beijing, Zhonggong zhongyang dangshi yanjiushi

Zhonggong dangshi ziliao [Chinese Communist Party history materials], Beijing, Zhonggong zhongyang dangshi yanjiushi, Zhongyang dang'anguan

Zhongyang dang'anguan congkan [A series from the Central Archives], Beijing, Zhongyang dang'anguan

B. *Archival Compilations, Biographies, Chronologies, Histories, Memoirs*

Beijingshi dang'anguan. *Beiping heping jiefang qianhou* [The peaceful liberation of Beiping from beginning to end]. Beijing: Beijing chubanshe, 1989.

————. *Jiefang zhanzheng shiqi Beiping xuesheng yundong* [The Beiping student movement during the liberation war period]. Beijing: Guangming ribao chubanshe, 1991.

"Beiping fan ji'e fanneizhan da youxing jishi" [A record of the great Beiping anti-hunger anti-civil war demonstration], *Beijing dang'an shiliao*, no. 2 (1986).

"Beiping heping jiefang gaibian Guomindang jundui guochengzhong fasheng de wenti" [Problems occurring in the changeover of Guomindang troops during the peaceful liberation of Beiping], *Beijing dan'an shiliao*, no. 4 (1988).

Bo Yibo wenxuan [Selected works of Bo Yibo]. Beijing: Renmin chubanshe, 1992.

Cai Dejin. *Zhao Qin mu Chu de Zhou Fohai* [Zhou Fohai, the man who served Qin in the morning and Chu in the evening]. N.p.: Henan renmin chubanshe, 1992.

Cai Huilin and Sun Weihou, eds. *Guangrong de jueze: yuan Guomindang zhun qiyi jiangling huiyilu* [A glorious choice: the recollections of former insurrectionary Guomindang officers]. Beijing: Zhongguo renmin jiefangjun guofang daxue chubanshe, 1986–1987. 2 vols.

Cao Hong and Li Li. *Disan yezhanjun* [The Third Field Army]. N.p.: Guofang daxue chubanshe, 1998.

Chen Boda. *Renmin gongdi Jiang Jieshi* [The people's public enemy Chiang Kai-shek]. Beijing: Xinhua shuju, 1954.

Chen Fangming, ed. *Er'erba shijian xueshu lunwenji* [Academic papers on the February 28 incident]. Taibei (?): Qianwei chubanshe, 1989.

Chen Jimin. *Minguo guanfu* [Government officials in Republican China]. N.p.: Jinling chubanshe, 1992.

Chen Lian. *Juezhan licheng* [The course of the decisive war]. Hefei (?): Anhui renmin chubanshe, 1991.

Chen Mushan. *Er'erba zhenxiang tantao* [Searching for the truth about February 28]. Taibei (?): Boyuan chubanshe, 1990.

Chen Shaochou. *Liu Shaoqi zai baiqu* [Liu Shaoqi in the white areas]. Beijing: Zhonggong dangshi chubanshe, 1992.

Chen Shaochou, Teng Wenzao, and Lin Jianbo, eds. *Baiqu douzheng jishi* [A factual account of the struggle in the white areas]. Beijing: Beijing shifan xueyuan chubanshe, 1990.

"Chen Yi tongzhi guanyu rucheng jilu de baogao" [Comrade Chen Yi's report on discipline for entering the cities], *Dang'an yu lishi*, no. 2 (1989).

Chen Yi zhuan [Biography of Chen Yi] Beijing: Dangdai Zhongguo chubanshe, 1991.

Chen Yongfa. *Yan'an de yinying* [Yan'an's Shadow]. Taibei: Academia Sinica, 1990.

Chen Yun wenxuan, 1926–1985 [Selected works of Chen Yun, 1926–1985]. Beijing: Renmin chubanshe, 1984–1986. 3 vols.

Chen Zhili, ed. *Zhongguo gongchandang jianshe shi* [A history of CCP building]. Shanghai: Renmin chubanshe, 1991.

Chongqing tanpan ziliao [Materials on the Chongqing negotiations]. Chengdu: Sichuan renmin chubanshe, 1982.

Chongqingshi zhengxie wenshi ziliao yanjiu weiyuanhui, et al., eds. *Guomin canzhenghui jishi: 1938–1948, Wuhan, Chongqing, Nanjing* [Record of the People's Political Council: 1938–1948, in Wuhan, Chongqing, and Nanjing]. Chongqing: Chongqing chubanshe, 1985. 2 vols.

Cong er'erba dao wuling niandai baise kongbu [The white terror from February 28 to 1950]. Taibei: Shibao wenhua gongsi, 1992.

Dai Changle and Liu Lianhua, eds. *Disi yezhanjun* [The Fourth Field Army]. N.p.: Guofang daxue chubanshe, 1998.

Deng Xiaoping. *Lun Xianggang wenti* [On Hong Kong questions]. Hong Kong: Sanlian, 1993.

Deng Xiaoping wenxuan, 1938–1992 [Selected works of Deng Xiaoping, 1938–1992]. Beijing: Renmin chubanshe, 1983–1993. 3 vols.

Deng Yuanzhong. *Sanminzhuyi lixingshe shi* [History of the Three People's Principles Vigorous Promotion Society]. Taibei: Shijian chubanshe, 1984.

Disanci guonei geming zhanzheng dashi yuebiao: 1945 nian 7 yue zhi 1949 nian 10 yue [A monthly record of events during the Third Revolutionary Civil War: July 1945 to October 1949]. Rev. ed. Beijing: Renmin chubanshe, 1983.

Disanci guonei geming zhanzheng gaikuang [An overview of the Third Revolutionary Civil War)]. Rev. ed. Beijing: Renmin chubanshe, 1983.

Dong Biwu xuanji [Selected works of Dong Biwu]. Beijing: Renmin chubanshe, 1985.

Dong Shigui and Zhang Yanzhi. *Beiping hetan jishi* [An account of the Beiping peace talks]. Beijing: Wenhua yishu chubanshe, 1991.

Dong Weikang, et al. *Jiang Jingguo zai dalu* (Jiang Jingguo on the mainland). Beijing: Zhigong jiaoyu, 1988.

Dongbei jiefangjun zhanzheng dashiji [The PLA's war record in the Northeast]. Beijing: Zhonggong dangshi ziliao chubanshe, 1987.

Dongbei renwu da cidian [A grand biographical dictionary of the Northeast]. N.p.: Liaoning renmin chubanshe, 1992.

Dou Aizhi. *Zhongguo minzhu dangpai shi* [A history of China's democratic parties]. Tianjin: Nankai daxue chubanshe, 1992.

Du Yuming. *Guo-Gong neizhan milu: yuan Guomindang jiangling de huiyi* [A secret record of the GMD-CCP civil war: memoirs of a former Guomindang general]. Taibei: Babilun chubanshe, n.d.

Gan Guoxun, et al. *Lanyishe, fuxingshe, lixingshe* [The Blue Shirt, Rejuvenation, and Vigorous Promotion Societies]. Taibei: Zhuanji wenxue chubanshe, 1984.

Geming wenxian [Documents of the revolution]. Taibei: Originally, Zhongguo guomindang zhongyang weiyuanhui dangshi shiliao bianzuan weiyuanhui; now, Dangshi weiyuanhui, 1953–1989. 117 vols.

Gongqingtuan Beijing shiwei qingnian yundongshi yanjiushi. *Beijing qingnian yundongshi, 1919–1949* [A history of the Beijing student movement, 1919–1949]. Beijing: Beijing chubanshe, 1989.

Gongqingtuan zhongyang qingyunshi yanjiushi. *Zhongguo qingnian yundongshi* [A history of the Chinese youth movement]. Beijing: Zhongguo qingnian chubanshe, 1984.

Gongqingtuan zhongyang qingyunshi yanjiushi, et al. *Jiefang zhanzheng shiqi xuesheng yundong lunwenji* [A collection of essays on the student movement during the liberation war]. Shanghai: Tongji daxue chubanshe, 1988

Guan Dongguo, et al. *Du Yuming jiangjun* [General Du Yuming]. Beijing: Zhongguo wenshi chubanshe, 1986.

"Guanyu Liao Shen zhanyi de wenxian" [Documents on the Liaoxi-Shenyang campaign], *Dang de wenxian,* no. 5 (1989).

"Guanyu nongye hezuohua wenti de wenxian" [Documents on questions concerning agricultural cooperativization], *Dang de wenxian,* no. 1 (1989).

Guo Qingshu, chief ed. *Zhongguo renmin jiefangjun lishi jianbian* [A concise history of the Chinese People's Liberation Army]. Shenyang: Liaoning daxue chubanshe, 1985.

Guofangbu shizhengju, ed. *Kanluan zhanshi congshu: Song-Hu baoweizhan* [Bandit suppression histories: the defense of Woosung-Shanghai]. Taibei (?): Guofangbu shizhengju, 1961.

Guomin dahui mishuchu, ed. *Guomin dahui daibiao tian* [Representatives' proposals at the National Assembly]. N.p.: Guomin dahui mishuchu, n.d., 17 vols; each volume can also be found in bibliographies cited separately under the title *Diyijie guomin dahui diyici huiyi tian yuanwen* [Original proposals at the first meeting of the first National Assembly].

Guomindangjun daoge neimu [Story behind the Nationalist Army's transfer of allegiance]. N.p.: Huayi chubanshe and Jiangxisheng xinhua shudian, 1990. 2 vols.

He Dong and Chen Mingxian. *Beiping heping jiefang shimo* [The peaceful liberation of Beiping from beginning to end]. Beijing: Jiefangjun chubanshe, 1985.

He Long zhuan [Biography of He Long]. Beijing: Dangdai Zhongguo chubanshe, 1993.

Hebeisheng dang'anguan, ed. *Hebei tudi gaige dang'an shiliao xuanbian* [A selection of historical archival materials on land reform in Hebei]. N.p.: Hebei renmin chubanshe, 1990.

Heilongjiang lishi dashiji, 1945–1949 [A chronicle of events in Heilongjiang history, 1945–1949]. Harbin: Heilongjiang renmin chubanshe, 1985.

Hongqi piaopiao [Red flag waving]. Beijing: Zhongguo qingnian chubanshe, 1957–1961, vols. 1–16; 1979–1993, vols. 17–32.

Hu Hua. *Zhongguo gemingshi jiangyi* [Lectures on China's revolutionary history]. Rev. ed. Beijing: Zhongguo renmin daxue chubanshe, 1979. 2 vols.

Hu Qiaomu. *Zhongguo gongchandang de sanshinian* [Thirty years of the Chinese Communist Party]. Beijing: Renmin chubanshe, 1951.

Hu Sushan (Suzanne Pepper). *Zhongguo de neizhan: 1945–1949 nian de zhengzhi douzheng* (Civil War in China: the political struggle, 1945–1949). Trans. Wang Hailiang, et al., ed. Jin Guangyao. Beijing: Zhongguo qingnian chubanshe, 1997.

Hu Zhixin, ed. *Zhongguo gongchandang tongyi zhanxian shi* [A history of the Chinese Communist Party's united front]. Beijing: Huaxia chubanshe, 1988.

Hua Yingshen. *Zhongguo gongchandang lieshi zhuan* [Biographies of Chinese communist martyrs]. Beijing: Qingnian chubanshe, 1951.

Huabei renmin zhengfu yinianlai gedi gongzuo baogao huibian [A collection of North China People's Government reports on work in various places during the past year]. N.p.: Huabei renmin zhengfu mishuting, 1949.

"Huadongju guanyu Jiangnan xinqu gongzuo sange zhongyao zhishi" [Three important directives from the East China Bureau on work in the new districts of southern Jiangsu], *Dang'an yu lishi,* no. 3 (1989).

Huai-Hai zhanyi [The Huai-Hai campaign]. Beijing: Zhonggong dangshi ziliao chubanshe, 1988.

Huang Youlan. *Zhongguo renmin jiefang zhanzheng shi* [History of the Chinese people's liberation war]. N.p.: Dang'an chubanshe, 1992.

Huashidai de huiyi: Zhengzhi xieshang huiyi [A landmark meeting: the Political Consultative Conference]. N.p.: Xinshidai yinshua, 1946.

Hubeisheng E-Yu bianqu gemingshi bianjibu, et al., eds. *Zhongyuan tuwei shi* [A history on breaking out of the encirclement on the central plains]. Beijing: Junshi kexue chubanshe, 1996.

Jiang Jieshi (Chiang Kai-shek). *Xian zongtong Jiang gong sixiang yanlun zongji* [Collected thoughts and speeches of the late President Chiang]. Taibei: Zhongguo guomindang zhongyang weiyuanhui dangshi weiyuanhui, 1984. 40 vols.

Jiang Jingguo. *Jiang zongtong Jingguo xiansheng yanlun zhushu huibian* [The collected speeches and writings of Mr. President Jiang Jingguo]. Taibei: Liming wenhua shiye, 1981–1982. 12 vols.

Jiang Shen. *Huai-Hai zhi zhan* [The Huai-Hai Campaign]. Beijing: Jiefangjun chubanshe, 1989.

Jiang Shuchen. *Fu Zuoyi zhuanlue* [A concise biography of Fu Zuoyi]. Beijing: Zhongguo qingnian chubanshe, 1990.

Jiangsusheng dang'anguan, Anhuisheng dang'anguan, eds. *Dujiang zhanyi* [Fighting across the Yangzi River]. N.p.: Dang'an chubanshe, 1989.

"Jianguo chu jiaofei zuozhan wendian xuan zai" [Selected documents and cables on fighting to suppress rebels in the early period of the People's Republic], *Dang de wenxian,* no. 6 (1990).

"Jianguo chuqi zhenya fangeming wendian" [Documents and cables on suppressing counter-revolutionaries in the early days of the People's Republic], *Dang de wenxian,* no. 2 (1988).

Jie Lifu. *Jiefang zhanzheng shilu—liangzhong mingyun de juezhan* [An account of the liberation war—battles that decided two destinies]. Shijiazhuang: Hebei renmin chubanshe, 1990. 2 vols.

"Jiefang Taiyuan zhan di tongxun zhuanji" [A collection of communications on the campaign to liberate Taiyuan], *Shanxi geming genjudi* [Shanxi revolutionary base area], no. 2 (1989).

Jiefang zhanzheng jishi [A record of the liberation war]. Beijing: Jiefangjun chubanshe, 1987.

Junshi kexueyuan junshi lishi yanjiubu. *Zhongguo renmin jiefangjun qishinian* [Seventy years of the Chinese People's Liberation Army]. Beijing: Junshi kexue chubanshe, 1997.

"Kangzhan hou Shanghai zijin liuxiang Xianggang shiliao" [Historical materials on Shanghai funds moving to Hong Kong after World War II], *Dang'an yu lishi,* no. 4 (1988).

Kanluan zhanshi [A military history of rebellion suppression]. Taibei: Guofangbu shizheng bianyiju, 1980–1981. 4 vols.

Kong Zhaokai. *Jiu Dagongbao zuoke ji* [An account of working at the old *Dagongbao*]. N.p.: Zhongguo wenhua lishi chubanshe, 1992.

Li Bingnan [Lee Ben-nan]. *Zhengzhi xieshang huiyi yu Guo-Gong tanpan* [The Political Consultative Conference and the GMD-CCP negotiations]. Taibei: Yongye chubanshe, 1993.

Li Hua, ed. *Zhengzhi xieshang huiyi wenxian* [Documents from the Political Consultative Conference]. N.p.: Zhongwai chubanshe, 1946.

Li Jianbai. *Dongbei kangRi jiuwang renwu zhuan* [Biographies of anti-Japanese national salvation personages in the Northeast]. N.p.: Dabaike chubanshe, 1992.

Li Shaoyu, chief ed. *Zhongyuan tuwei jishi* [Breaking out of the encirclement on the central Plains]. N.p.: Jiefangjun chubanshe, 1992.

Li Xin, chief ed. *Zhongguo xin minzhuzhuyi geming shiqi tongshi* [A comprehensive history of China's new democratic revolutionary period]. Beijing: Renmin chubanshe, 1961–1962. Reprints 1980–1981. 4 vols.

Li Xu, ed. *Zhengzhi xieshang huiyi zhi jiantao* [An examination of the Political Consultative Conference]. N.p.: Qingnian chubanshe, 1946.

Li Yong and Zhang Zongtian, eds. *Jiefang zhanzheng shiqi tongyi zhanxian dashiji* [A record of major united front events during the liberation war]. Beijing: Zhongguo jingji chubanshe, 1988.

Li Zongren with Tang Degang. *Li Zongren huiyilu* [The memoirs of Li Zongren]. Hong Kong: Nanyue chubanshe, 1986; also published in 2 vols. by Guangxi renmin chubanshe, 1980.

Liangge Zhongguo mingyun di juezhan [Decisive battles in the fate of two Chinese destinies]. Beijing: Changcheng chubanshe, 1987.

Liao Gailong. *Quanguo jiefang zhanzheng jianshi* [A short history of the national liberation war]. Shanghai: Renmin chubanshe, 1984.

Liao Gailong, Zhao Baoxu, and Du Qingliu, chief eds. *Dangdai Zhongguo zhengzhi dashidian* [Dictionary of major political events in modern China]. Changchun: Jilin wenshi chubanshe, 1991.

Liu Baiyu. *Shidai de yinxiang* [Impressions of the time]. Harbin: Guanghua shudian, 1948.

Liu Bocheng zhuan [Biography of Liu Bocheng]. Beijing: Dangdai Zhongguo chubanshe, 1992.

Liu Han, et al. *Luo Ronghuan yuanshi* [Marshal Luo Ronghuan]. Beijing: Jiefangjun chubanshe, 1987.

Liu Jianqing, Wang Jiadian, and Xu Liangbo, eds. *Zhongguo guomindang shi* [A history of China's Nationalist Party]. Nanjing (?): Guji chubanshe, 1992.

Liu Jizeng. *Zhongguo guomindang mingrenlu* [Who's who in China's Nationalist Party]. N.p.: Hubei renmin chubanshe, 1992.

Liu Shaoqi xuanji [Selected works of Liu Shaoqi]. Beijing: Renmin chubanshe, 1981–1985. 2 vols.

Liu Yonglu, et al. *Zhang Xuesi jiangjun* [General Zhang Xuesi]. Beijing: Jiefangjun chubanshe, 1985.

Liu Yunjiu. *Guomindang tongzhiqu de minzhu yundong* [The democratic movement in the areas controlled by the Nationalist Party]. Harbin: Heilongjiang renmin chubanshe, 1986.

Lu Xiuyi. *Riju shidai Taiwan gongchandang shi* [A history of the Taiwan Communist Party during the Japanese occupation]. N.p.: Qianwei chubanshe, 1990.

Luo Ronghuan zhuan [Biography of Luo Ronghuan]. Beijing: Dangdai Zhongguo chubanshe, 1991.

Luo Ronghuan zhuan bianxiezu, ed. *Huiyi Luo Ronghuan* [Remembering Luo Ronghuan]. Beijing: Jiefangjun chubanshe, 1987.

Ma Hongwu, Wang Debao, and Sun Qiming, chief eds. *Zhongguo gemingshi cidian* [Dictionary of China's revolutionary history]. Beijing: Dang'an chubanshe, 1987.

Ma Shitu. *Zai dixia—baiqu dixiadang gongzuo jingyan chubu zongjie* [Underground—a preliminary summation of the underground party's work experience in the white areas]. Chengdu: Sichuan daxue chubanshe, 1987.

Mao Zedong. *Mao Zedong ji* [Collected works of Mao Zedong]. Hong Kong; Jindai shiliao gongyingshe, 1975. 10 vols.

Mao Zedong. *Mao Zedong sixiang wansui* [Long live the thought of Mao Zedong]. N.p.: no pub., 1967, 1969. 2 vols.

Mao Zedong. *Mao Zedong xuanji* [Selected works of Mao Zedong]. Beijing: Renmin chubanshe, 1952–1977. 5 vols.

Meng Xianzhang. *Meiguo fu Jiang qin Hua zuixing shi* [An account of America's criminal acts in supporting Jiang Kai-shek and invading China]. Shanghai: Zhonghua shuju, 1951.

Min Xie. *Zhonggong qunyun yu qingyun pouxi* [An analysis of the Chinese communist mass and youth movements]. Taibei: Liming wenhua shiyu gongsi, 1980.

Minguo congshu [Collected works reprinted from the republican period], series one. Shanghai: Shanghai shudian, 1989. 100 vols.

Minguo congshu [Collected works reprinted from the republican period], series two. Shanghai: Shanghai shudian, 1990. 100 vols.

Minguo congshu [Collected works reprinted from the republican period], series three. Shanghai: Shanghai shudian, 1991. 100 vols.

Mu Xin. *Nanxian xunhui* [Touring the southern front]. Beijing: Renmin chubanshe, 1951.

Nanjingshi dang'anguan, ed. *Nanjing jiefang* [The liberation of Nanjing]. Nanjing (?): Jiangsu guji chubanshe, 1990.

Nie Rongzhen huiyilu [The memoirs of Nie Rongzhen]. Beijing: Jiefangjun chubanshe, 1984. 3 vols.

Niu Jun. *Cong Hu'erli dao Maxie'er: Meiguo tiaochu Guo-Gong maodun shimo* [From Hurley to Marshall: a full account of the American mediation of the contradictions between the Nationalist and Communist Parties]. Fuzhou: Fujian renmin chubanshe, 1988.

Peng Dehuai zhuan [Biography of Peng Dehuai]. Beijing: Dangdai Zhongguo chubanshe, 1993.

Peng Qingxia and Liu Weishu, eds. *Zhongguo minzhu dangpai lishi renwu* [Historical figures in China's democratic parties]. Beijing: Yanshan chubanshe, 1992.

Pu Yuhuo and Xu Shuangmi. *Dang de baiqu douzheng shihua* [A historical account of the party's struggle in the white areas]. Beijing: Zhonggong dangshi chubanshe, 1991.

Qi Mingfu and Zhai Taifeng, eds. *Zhongguo gongchandang jianshe dacidian, 1921–1991* [A grand dictionary on the building of the CCP, 1921–1991]. Chengdu: Sichuan renmin chubanshe, 1991.

Qian Duansheng, Sa Shijiong, et al. *Minguo zhengzhi shi* [A history of government in the Republic of China]. Rev. ed. Shanghai: Shangwu, 1946; reprinted in *Minguo congshu*, series one, vol. 24.

Qiao Jiacai. *Dai Li he ta di tongzhi* [Dai Li and his comrades]. Taibei: Zhongwai tushu chubanshe, 1985.

Qiao Xizhang. *Yan Xishan* [Yan Xishan]. Beijing: Huayi chubanshe, 1992.

Qin Qianmu, et al. *Zhongguo zhengdang shi* [A history of China's political parties]. Taiyuan: Shanxi renmin chubanshe, 1991.

Quan Weitian. *Cong jiu Zhongguo dao xin Zhongguo—disanci guonei geming zhanzheng shiqi jingji shilue* [From old to new China—a brief economic history of the Third Revolutionary Civil War period]. Shanghai: Xin zhishi chubanshe, 1957.

Renmin zhengxie wenxian, 1949 [Documents of the People's Political Consultative Conference, 1949]. N.p.: Jingji kuaibao she, n.d.

Shaan-Gan-Ning bianqu canyihui wenxian huiji [A compilation of documents on the Shaanxi-Gansu-Ningxia Border Region people's council]. Beijing: Kexue chubanshe, 1958.

Shaanxisheng zhengfu mishuchu, ed. *Shaan zheng sinian jilue, 1944–1948* [A four-year compilation of the Shaanxi government, 1944–1948]. N.p.: no pub., 1948.

Shandong geming lishi dang'an ziliao xuanbian [A selection of archival materials on Shandong's revolutionary history]. N.p.: Shandong renmin chubanshe, 1984–1987. 23 vols.

Shandongsheng dang'anguan, ed. "Shandong tudi gaige zhuanti dang'an shiliao" [Historical archival materials on special topics about land reform in Shandong], *Shandong dangshi ziliao*, nos. 2–4 (1988) and nos. 1–3 (1989).

Shandongsheng Linyi diqu dang'anguan, ed. *Binhai diqu tudi gaige shiliao xuanbian* [A selection of historical materials on land reform in Binhai district]. N.p.: Linyi diqu chuban bangongshi, 1990.

Shanghai xuesheng yundongshi [A history of the student movement in Shanghai]. Shanghai: Renmin chubanshe, 1983.

Shanghaishi dang'anguan, ed. *Shanghai jiefang* [The liberation of Shanghai]. Shanghai: Dang'an chubanshe, 1989.

Shangyebu shangye zhengce yanjiuhui, ed. *Jianguo qianhou shangye gongzuo shilu* [A factual account of commercial work during the establishment of the People's Republic]. Beijing: Zhongguo shangye chubanshe, 1988.

Shanxisheng Yanbei diqu dang'anju, et al., eds. *Renmin fudan diaocha dang'an huibian* [Compilation of investigation records on the people's burdens]. N.p.: Shanxisheng Hunyuanxian yinshuachang, 1986.

Shen Si. "Shenru pipan Lin Biao de 'liuge zhanshu yuanze' " [Deeply criticizing Lin Biao's 'six tactical principles'], *Hongqi* [Red Flag], no. 8 (1974), pp. 49–56.

Shen Xiaoyun. *Li Zongren de yisheng* [The life of Li Zongren]. N.p.: Henan renmin chubanshe, 1992.

Shen Ximeng. *Nan zheng bei zhan* [Fighting south and north]. Shanghai: Zhonghua shuzhu, 1952.

Shen Zui and Wen Qiang. *Dai Li qi ren* [Dai Li the man]. Beijing: Wenshi ziliao chubanshe, 1980.

Shi Weiqun. *Zhongguo xuesheng yundongshi, 1945–1949* [A history of the Chinese student movement, 1945–1949]. Shanghai: Renmin chubanshe, 1992.

Su Yu. *Su Yu junshi wenji* [Su Yu's collected writings on military affairs]. Beijing: Jiefangjun chubanshe, 1989.

Taihang geming genjudi shigao [Outline history of the Taihang revolutionary base area]. Taiyuan: Shanxi renmin chubanshe, 1987.

Taihang geming genjudi shiliao congshu [A series of historical materials on the Taihang revolutionary base area]. Taiyuan: Shanxi renmin chubanshe, 1987–1991. 9 vols.

Tang Liangxiung. *Dai Li zhuan* [A biography of Dai Li]. Taibei: Zhuanji wenxue, 1982.

Tang Ren (Yan Qingshu). *Shinian neizhan* [Ten years of civil war]. Xianggang: Yangyong, 1975.

Tian Ming and Xu Jianchuan, eds. *Gonghui dacidian* [Expanded labor union dictionary]. Beijing: Jingji guanli chubanshe, 1989.

Wang Gong'an and Mao Lei, eds. *Guo-Gong liangdang guanxi tongshi* [A general history of the relationship between the Nationalist and Communist Parties]. Wuhan: Wuhan chubanshe, 1991.

Wang Jianchu and Sun Maosheng. *Zhongguo gongren yundong shi* [A history of the Chinese labor movement]. Shenyang: Renmin chubanshe, 1987.

Wang Jianying. *Hongjun renwuzhi* [Red Army personnel records]. Beijing: Jiefangjun chubanshe, 1988.

Wang Qingkui. *Zhongguo renmin jiefangjun zhanyi ji* [A record of the campaigns of the Chinese People's Liberation Army]. Beijing: Jiefangjun chubanshe, 1987.

Wang Shoudao huiyilu [The memoirs of Wang Shoudao]. Beijing: Jiefangjun chubanshe, 1987.

Wang Xiaoting and Wang Wenyi, eds. *Zhandou zai Beida de gongchandang ren, 1920.10– 1949.2, Beida dixia dang gaikuang* [The Communist Party members who fought at Beijing University: a survey of the underground party at the university from October 1920 to February 1949]. Beijing: Beijing daxue chubanshe, 1991.

Wang Xinsheng. *Zhongguo junfa shi cidian* [Historical dictionary of China's warlords]. N.p.: Guofang daxue chubanshe, 1992.

Wang Zhongxing and Liu Liqin. *Di'er yezhanjun* [The Second Field Army]. N.p.: Guofang daxue chubanshe, 1998.

Wang Zuanzhong, chief ed. *Liu-Deng dajun qiangdu Huanghe ziliao xuan* [A selection of materials on the great army of Liu Bocheng and Deng Xiaoping fighting across the Yellow River]. N.p.: Shandong daxue chubanshe, 1987.

Wei Chunjiang. *Ye Ting* [Ye Ting]. N.p.: Zhongguo qingnian chubanshe, 1992.

Wu Wenwei. *Taiyuan baoweizhan* [The defense of Taiyuan]. Taizhong, Taiwan: Wu Wenwei, 1979.

Wu Yitang. *Zhongguo gupiao nianjian* [Yearbook of Chinese stocks]. N.p.: Taipingyang yinshua gongsi, 1947.

Wuhanshi dang'anguan, ed. *Zhonggong Wuhan shiwei wenjian xuanbian, 1949–1951* [A selection of documents from the Wuhan City Communist Party Committee, 1949–1951]. 1989.

Xi'anshi dang'anju, et al., eds. *Xi'an jiefang dang'an shiliao xuanji* [A selection of historical archival materials on the liberation of Xi'an]. N.p.: Shaanxi renmin chubanshe, 1989.

Xianxing faling huibian [Compilation of current laws]. N.p.: Guomin zhengfu, 1948. 6 vols.

Xiao Chaoran, chief ed. *Beijing daxue xiaoshi, 1898–1949* [A history of Beijing University, 1898–1949]. Rev. ed. Beijing: Beijing daxue chubanshe, 1988.

Xiao Chaoran, Liang Zhu, and Wang Qilai, chief eds. *Zhonggong dangshi jianming cidian* [A concise dictionary of the Chinese Communist Party's history]. Beijing: Jiefangjun chubanshe, 1986–1987. 2 vols.

Xinan fuwutuan bangongshi, ed. *Nanjingshi junguanhui renmin zhengfu zhengce faling huibian* [Collection of policy decrees by the Nanjing City Military Administration Commission and People's Government]. N.p.: Xinhua ribao de'erchang, 1949.

Xinghuo liaoyuan [A single spark can start a prairie fire]. Beijing: Renmin wenxue chubanshe, 1958–1963, 10 vols. Reprint, Beijing: Zhongguo renmin jiefangjun zhanshi chubanshe, 1977–1982.

Xiong Xianghui, et al. *Zhonggong dixia dang xianxingji* [An account of the true nature of the underground Chinese Communist Party]. Taibei: Zhuanji wenxue chubanshe, 1991. 2 vols.

Xu Xiangqian zhuan [Biography of Xu Xiangqian]. Beijing: Dangdai Zhongguo chubanshe, 1991.

Xu Zhucheng. *Du Yuesheng zhenzhuan* [A true biography of Du Yuesheng]. Hangzhou: Zhejiang renmin chubanshe, 1982.

Xuechao yu zhanhou Zhongguo zhengzhi, 1945–1949 [The student tide and Chinese politics after the war, 1945–1949]. Taibei: Dongda faxing, 1994.

Yan Qi, et al. *Zhongguo guomindang shigau* [An outline history of China's Nationalist Party]. Harbin: Heilongjiang renmin chubanshe, 1991.

Yang Bichuan. *Riju Taiwanren fankang* shi [A history of Taiwanese resistance during the Japanese occupation]. Taibei (?): Daoxiang chubanshe, 1988.

Yang Guiqing. *Luo Ronghuan zai Dongbei jiefang zhanzheng zhong* [Luo Ronghuan during the war of liberation in the Northeast]. Beijing: Jiefangjun chubanshe, 1986.

Yang Guoyu and Chen Feiqin. *Di'er yezhanjun jishi* [A history of the Second Field Army]. Shanghai: Shanghai wenyi chubanshe, 1988.

Yang Guoyu, Chen Feiqin, and Wang Wei, eds. *Liu-Deng dajun zhengzhan ji* [Record of the Liu-Deng army's campaigns]. Kunming: Yunnan renmin chubanshe, 1984. 3 vols.

"Yang Lianggong, He Hanwen guanyu Taiwan 'er'erba' shibian diaocha baogao" [The report of Yang Lianggong and He Hanwen on the investigation of the February 28 incident in Taiwan]. *Minguo dang'an,* no. 4 (1988).

Yao Fu, chief ed. *Jiefang zhanzheng jishi* [A record of events during the liberation war]. Beijing: Jiefangjun chubanshe, 1987.

Yao Longjing, chief ed. *Zhongguo gongchandang tongyi zhanxian shi, xin minzhuzhuyi geming shiqi* [A history of the Chinese Communist Party's united front in the new democratic period]. Taiyuan: Shanxi renmin chubanshe, 1991.

Yige geming genjudi de chengzhang: kangRi zhanzheng he jiefang zhanzheng shiqi de Jin-Ji-Lu-Yu bianqu gaikuang [Growth of a revolutionary base area: the Shanxi-Hebei-Shandong-Henan border region during the anti-Japanese and liberation wars]. Beijing: Renmin chubanshe, 1958.

"1947–1948 nian you guan Jiulongcheng shijian de Zhong-Ying jiaoshe shiliao" [Historical materials on the Sino-British negotiations concerning the 1947–1948 Kowloon City incident], *Minguo dang'an,* no. 3 (1990).

Yu Gan. *Zhongguo ge minzhu dangpai* [The various Chinese democratic parties]. Beijing: Zhongguo wenshi chubanshe, 1987.

Yu Hui, chief ed. *Guomindang jun daoge neimu* [The story behind the Nationalist army's change of allegiance]. N.p.: Huayi chubanshe, 1990. 2 vols.

Yuan Lunqu. *Zhongguo laodong jingjishi* [An economic history of Chinese labor]. Beijing: Beijing jingji xueyuan chubanshe, 1990.

Yuan Wei, ed. *Zhongguo renmin jiefangjun wuda yezhan budui fazhan shilue* [An outline history of the development of the People's Liberation Army's five great field armies]. Beijing: Jiefangjun chubanshe, 1987.

Yuan Zhanxian and Liu Dongyuan. *Guandong chunxiao: Dongbei da jiaofei* [Spring dawn east of Shanhaiguan: bandit suppression in the Northeast]. Beijing: Jiefangjun chubanshe, 1998.

Zhang Bingjun. *Zhongguo xiandai lizi zhongyao zhanyi zhi yanjiu: kanluan zhanyi shuping, Dongbei zhanchang Xibei zhanchang* [Research on important battles in contemporary China: a review of the rebellion suppression campaigns on the Northeast and Northwest battle fronts]. Taibei(?): Guofangbu qingbao canmou zizhang yinzhichang, 1986.

Zhang Pengzhou. *Jin wushinian Zhongguo yu Riben, 1932–1982* [China and Japan during the last 50 years, 1932–1982]. Chengdu: Sichuan renmin chubanshe, 1985.

Zhang Qingtai, ed. *Yi Lin Feng* [Remembering Lin Feng]. Shenyang: Liaoning renmin chubanshe, 1987.

Zhang Shun, Jing Rao, Sun Weihou, and Cai Huilin, eds. *Baiwan guomindang jun qiyi toucheng jishi* [Record of the revolt and surrender of a million Nationalist soldiers]. Beijing: Zhongguo wensh chubanshe, 1991. 2 vols.

Zhang Wei. *Zhongguo guomindang shigang* [An outline history of China's Nationalist Party]. Shenyang: Liaoning daxue chubanshe, 1992.

Zhang Wentian. *Zhang Wentian xuanji* [Selected works of Zhang Wentian]. Beijing: Renmin chubanshe, 1985.

Zhang Zhenbang, et al. *Guo-Gong guanxi jianshi* [A short history of Nationalist-Communist Relations]. Taibei: Guoli zhengzhi daxue guoji guanxi yanjiu zhongxin, 1983.

Zhang Zhenglong. *Xuebai xuehong: guogong dongbei dajue zhanshi zhenxiang* [Snow white, blood red: the truth about the decisive war between the KMT and the CCP in the Northeast]. Xianggang: Dadi chubanshe, 1991.

Zhang Zhuhong. *Zhongguo xiandai gemingshi shiliaoxue* [A study of materials on China's contemporary revolutionary history]. Beijing: Zhonggong dangshi ziliao, 1987.

Zhao Shenghui. *Zhongguo gongchandang zuzhishi gangyao* [An outline of the organizational history of the Chinese Communist Party]. Wuhu: Anhui renmin chubanshe, 1987.

Zhao Sufen. *Zhou Baozhong jiangjun zhuan* [A biography of General Zhou Baozhong]. Beijing: Jiefangjun chubanshe, 1988.

Zhao Xihua. *Minmeng shihua 1941–1949* [A historical account of the Democratic League, 1941–1949]. Beijing, 1992.

Zhejiangsheng dang'anguan, Zhejiangsheng dangshi ziliao zhengji yanjiu weiyuanhui, eds. *Zhonggong Zhejiang shengwei wenjian xuanbian* [Selected documents of the Zhejiang Provincial Committee of the Chinese Communist Party]. N.p.: no pub., 1988–1991. 5 vols.

Zheng Deyong and Zhu Yang, eds. *Zhongguo gemingshi changbian* [An extended compilation of China's revolutionary history]. Changchun: Jilin renmin chubanshe, 1991. 2 vols.

Zheng Guang and Lou Chengquan, eds. *Zhongguo qingnian yundong liushi nian, 1919–1979* [Sixty years of the Chinese youth movement, 1919–1979]. Beijing: Zhongguo qingnian chubanshe, 1990.

Zheng Lei. "Ping 'Dongbei jiefang zhanzheng shiqi de Lin Biao'" [Criticizing Lin Biao in the Northeast during the liberation war period], *Hongqi* [Red flag], no. 4 (1974), pp. 23–28.

Zhengxie xianshi weiyuanhui wenshi ziliao weiyuanhui, Xi'anshi dang'anguan, eds. *Xi'an jiefang - Xi'an wenshi ziliao, di 15 ji* [The liberation of Xian - Xian historical materials, no. 15 compilation]. Xi'an: Shaanxi renmin chubanshe, 1989.

Zhengzhou zhanyi ziliao xuanbian [A selection of materials on the battle of Zhengzhou]. Zhengzhou: Henan renmin chubanshe, 1985.

Zhong Lin, Lin Feng, Zhang Gaoling, eds. *Di'yi yezhanjun* [The First Field Army]. N.p.: Guofang daxue chubanshe, 1998.

Zhonggong Beijing shiwei dangshi yanjiushi. *Beijing dangshi yanjiu wenji* [A research collection on the history of the Communist Party in Beijing]. Beijing: Beijing chubanshe, 1989.

Zhonggong Beijing shiwei dangshi yanjiushi, ed. *Fan ji'e fan neizhan yundong ziliao huibian* [A collection of materials on the anti-hunger anti-civil war movement]. Beijing: Beijing daxue chubanshe, 1992.

Zhonggong daibiaotuan Meiyuan xincun jinianguan, ed. *Guo-Gong tanpan wenxian ziliao xuanji, 1945.8 - 1947.3* [Selected documentary materials on the Nationalist-Communist negotiations, August 1945–March 1947]. Rev. ed. N.p.: Jiangsu renmin chubanshe, 1980.

Zhonggong Dalian shiwei dangshi ziliao zhengbian weiyuanhui, ed. *Dalian dixia dang shiliao xuanbian* [Selected historical materials on the underground Communist Party in Dalian]. Dalian: Dalian dangshi ziliao congshu, 1986.

Zhonggong dangshi renwuzhuan [Biographies from Chinese Communist Party history]. Xi'an: Shaanxi renmin chubanshe, 1980-ongoing; multi-volume series originally under the editorial direction of the late Hu Hua.

Zhonggong dangshi shijian renwulu [A record of events and people in Chinese Communist Party History]. Shanghai: Renmin chubanshe, 1983.

Zhonggong Hebei shengwei dangshi yanjiushi, ed. *Yiqie weile qianxian: Ping-Jin zhanyi zhiqian ziliao huibian* [All for the front: a collection of materials on supporting the front in the Beijing-Tianjin campaign]. N.p.: Zhongyang dangshi chubanshe, 1992.

Zhonggong Henan shengwei dangshi gongzuo weiyuanhui, Henansheng dang'anguan, eds. *Meiyou qiangsheng de zhandou* [A battle without gunfire]. N.p.: Henan renmin chubanshe, 1990.

Zhonggong Shandong shengwei dangshi ziliao zhengji yanjiu weiyuanhui, et al., eds. *Jinan zhanyi* [The Jinan campaign]. N.p.: Shandong renmin chubanshe, 1988.

———. *Laiwu zhanyi* [The Laiwu campaign]. N.p.: Shandong renmin chubanshe, 1986.

———. *Luxinan zhanyi* [The battle for southwest Shandong]. N.p.: Shandong renmin chubanshe, 1989.

———. *Mengliangqu zhanyi* [The battle of Mengliangqu]. N.p.: Shandong renmin chubanshe, 1987.

Zhonggong Shanghai shiwei dangshi ziliao zhengji weiyuanhui. *Jiefang zhanzheng shiqi de Zhonggong zhongyang Shanghaiju* [The Shanghai bureau of the Central Committee of the Chinese Communist Party during the liberation war]. Shanghai: Xuelin chubanshe, 1989.

Zhonggong zhongyang dangshi yanjiushi. *Zhongguo gongchandang lishi* [History of the Chinese Communist Party]. Beijing: Renmin chubanshe, 1991.

Zhonggong zhongyang dangshi ziliao zhengji weiyuanhui, ed. *Huai-Hai zhanyi* [The Huai-Hai campaign]. Beijing: Zhonggong dangshi ziliao chubanshe, 1988. 3 vols.

———. *Liao-Shen juezhan* [The decisive Liaoxi-Shenyang campaign]. Beijing: Renmin chubanshe, 1988. 2 vols.

"Zhonggong zhongyang guanyu tingjin zhongyuan de zhanlue fangzhen de yizu dianbao" [A group of telegrams from the Central Committee of the Chinese Communist Party on battle strategy for driving forward on the central plains], *Dang de wenxian*, no. 3 (1989).

Zhonggong zhongyang shujichu. *Liuda yilai: dangnei mimi wenjian* [Since the Sixth Congress: the Communist Party's secret internal documents]. Beijing: Renmin chubanshe, 1980–1981. 2 vols.

Zhonggong zhongyang wenxian yanjiushi and Jin Chongji, eds. *Zhou Enlai zhuan, 1898–1949* [A biography of Zhou Enlai, 1898–1949]. Beijing: Renmin chubanshe, Zhonggong zhongyang wenxian chubanshe, 1989.

Zhongguo di'er lishi dang'anguan, ed. *Feng Yuxiang riji* [The diaries of Feng Yuxiang]. N.p.: Jiangsu guji chubanshe, 1992. 5 vols.

———. *Jiang Jieshi nianpu chugao* [First draft of a chronicle on Chiang Kai-shek's life]. N.p.: Dang'anguan chubanshe, 1992.

———. *Taiwan guangfu he guangfu hou wunian shengqing* [The recovery of Taiwan and the five years thereafter]. Nanjing: Nanjing chubanshe, 1989. 2 vols.

———. *Zhonghua minguo shi dang'an ziliao huibian (1911–1949)* [Compilation of archival materials on Chinese republican history (1911–1949)]. N.p.: Jiangsu renmin chubanshe, Jiangsu guji chubanshe, 1979–1994 (multi-volume, comprehensive series, with 40+ volumes published for the years 1911 through the mid-1930s, and continuing).

Zhongguo ge minzhu dangpai shi renwu zhuan [Biographies from China's various democratic parties]. Beijing: Huaxia chubanshe, 1991–1995.

Zhongguo gongchandang dangshi jingjian [The reflective mirror of the Chinese Communist Party's History]. Beijing: Hongqi chubanshe, 1997. 5 vols (1945–1949 period, vol. 2).

Zhongguo gongchandang jianshe quanshu, 1921–1991 [Complete work on Chinese Communist Party construction, 1921–1991]. N.p.: Shanxi renmin chubanshe, 1991. 9 vols.

Zhongguo gongchandang lici zhongyao huiyiji [A record of successive important meetings of the Chinese Communist Party]. Shanghai: Shanghai renmin chubanshe, 1982. 2 vols.

Zhongguo gongchandang tongzhi [Encyclopedia of the Chinese Communist Party]. Beijing: Zhongyang wenxian chubanshe, 1997. 3 vols.

Zhongguo junshi bowuguan, ed. Yuan Wei, chief ed. *Zhongguo zhan dian* [A dictionary of Chinese battles]. Beijing: Jiefangjun chubanshe, 1994. 2 vols.

Zhongguo minzhu tongmeng zhongyang wenshi ziliao weiyuanhui, ed. *Zhongguo minzhu tongmeng lishi wenxian, 1941–1949* [Historical documents of the Chinese Democratic League, 1941–1949]. N.p.: Wenshi ziliao chubanshe, 1983.

Zhongguo renmin jiefangjun diyi yeshanjun zhanshi [The history of the First Field Army of the People's Liberation Army]. Beijing: Jiefangjun chubanshe, 1995.

Zhongguo renmin jiefangjun guofang daxue dangshi dangjian zhenggong jiaoyanshi, ed. *Zhonggong dangshi jiaoxue cankao ziliao* [Education reference materials on Chinese Communist Party history]. Beijing: Guofang daxue, 1979–1988, 27 vols. to date, 32 vols. planned; vol. 18 concerns the 1945–1949 civil war period; collection reviewed by Warren Sun in *CCP Research Newsletter*, nos. 10/11 (spring/fall 1992), pp. 16–20.

Zhongguo renmin jiefangjun lishi ziliao congshu bianshen weiyuanhui. *Liao-Shen zhanyi* [Liaoxi-Shenyang campaign]. Beijing: Jiefangjun chubanshe, 1993.

――― . *Ping-Jin zhanyi* [The Beiping-Tianjin campaign]. Beijing: Jiefangjun chubanshe, 1991.

――― . *Xin sijun* [The New Fourth Army]. Beijing: Jiefangjun chubanshe, 1993.

Zhongguo renmin jiefangjun tongjian, 1927–1996 [An appraisal of the Chinese People's Liberation Army, 1927–1996]. Lanzhou: Gansu renmin chubanshe, 1997). 3 vols.

Zhongguo renmin jiefangjun wu da yezhan budui fazhan shilue [An outline history of the development of the five great field armies of the Chinese People's Liberation Army]. Beijing: Jiefangjun chubanshe, 1987.

Zhongguo renmin jiefangjun zhanshi [Battle history of the Chinese People's Liberation Army]. Beijing: Jiefangjun junshi kexueyuan, 1987.

Zhongguo renmin jiefangjun zongbu, ed. *Zhongguo renmin jiefang zhanzheng junshi wenji* [A collection of military documents on the Chinese people's liberation war]. N.p.: no pub., 1951. 6 vols.

Zhongguo renmin zhengzhi xieshang huiyi Beijingshi weiyuanhui wenshi ziliao yanjiu weiyuanhui. *Beiping dixia dang douzheng shiliao* [Historical materials on the struggle of the Beiping underground Communist Party]. Beijing: Beijing chubanshe, 1988.

Zhongguo renmin zhengzhi xieshang huiyi quanguo weiyuanhui wenshi ziliao yanjiu wei-yuanhui. *Fu Zuoyi shengping* [The life of Fu Zuoyi]. Beijing: Wenshi ziliao chubanshe, 1985.

――― . *Huai-Hai zhanyi qinliji, yuan Guomindang jiangling de huiyi* (Personal histories of the Huai-Hai campaign: recollections of former Guomindang officers). Beijing: Wenshi ziliao chubanshe, 1983.

――― . *Liao-Shen zhanyi qinliji, yuan Guomindang jiangling de huiyi* [Personal histories of the Liaoxi-Shenyang campaign: recollections of former Guomindang officers]. Beijing: Zhongguo wenshi chubanshe, 1985.

――― . *Ping-Jin zhanyi qinliji, yuan Guomindang jiangling de huiyi* [Personal histories of the Beiping-Tianjin campaign: recollections of former Guomindang officers]. Beijing: Zhongguo wenshi chubanshe, 1989.

Zhongguo renming da cidian [An expanded biographical dictionary of China]. Shanghai: Shanghai cishu chubanshe, 1989–1992. 3 vols.

Zhongguo shehui kexue yuan, zhongyang dang'anguan, eds. *Jiben jianshe touzi he jian-*

zhuye juan [A volume on basic construction investment and the building industry]. N.p.: Zhongguo chengshi jingji shehui chubanshe, 1989.

————. *Zhonghua renmin gongheguo jingji dang'an ziliao xuanbian* [Selections from archival materials on the economy of the People's Republic of China]. N.p.: Zhongguo chengshi jingji shehui chubanshe, 1990.

Zhongguo tudi gaige shi, 1921–1949 [A history of China's land reform, 1921–1949]. Beijing; Renmin chubanshe, 1990.

Zhonghua minguo jingji fazhanshi [The History of Economic Development in the Republic of China]. Taibei: Jindai Zhongguo chubanshe, 1983. 3 vols.

Zhonghua minguo mingrenzhuan [Eminent persons of the Republic of China]. Taibei: Jindai Zhongguo chubanshe, 1984–1992. 12 vols.

Zhonghua minguo shishi jiyao, chugao, 1894–1974 [Important historical records of the Republic of China, preliminary draft, 1894–1974]. Taibei: Zhonghua minguo shiliao yanjiu zhongxin, Guoshiguan, 1971–1992. 88 vols. covering 1894–1949 (as of the mid-1990s).

Zhonghua minguo zhongyao shiliao chubian—dui Ri kangzhan shiqi [Important historical materials on the Republic of China, preliminary compilation—the period of the resistance war against Japan]. Taibei: Zhongguo guomindang zhongyang weiyuanhui dangshi weiyuanhui, 1981, 3 vols. This is a 26-volume series, all published under the same general title in 1981, in seven parts: *Di'er bian, zuozhan jingguo* [Part two, the war in progress], 4 vols. *Disan bian, zhanshi waijiao* [Part three, wartime foreign relations], 3 vols. *Disibian, zhanshi jianshe* [Part four, wartime construction], 4 vols. *Diwubian, Zhonggong huodong zhenxiang* [Part five, truth about Chinese Communist activities], 4 vols. *Diliubian, kuilei zuzhi* [Part six, puppet organizations], 4 vols. *Diqibian, zhanhou Zhongguo* [Part seven, China after the war], 4 vols.

Zhonghua renmin gongheguo kaiguo wenxian [Documents on the founding of the Chinese People's Republic]. Hong Kong: Xin minzhu chubanshe, 1949.

Zhongyang dang'anguan, ed. *Jiefang zhanzheng shiqi tudi gaige wenjian xuanbian* (Selected documents on land reform during the war of liberation). N.p.: Zhonggong zhongyang dangxiao chubanshe, 1981.

————. *Zhonggong zhongyang wenjian xuanji* [Selected documents of the Chinese Communist Party Central Committee]. Beijing: Zhonggong zhongyang dangxiao chubanshe, 1989–1992, 18 vols.; reissue of the original 14-volume *neibu* (internal, restricted access) compilation, published between 1982 and 1987; reviewed by the New China News Agency (see *Foreign Broadcast Information Service,* FBIS-CHI-92–236, 8 December 1992).

Zhongyang tongzhanbu, zhongyang dang'anguan, eds. *Zhonggong zhongyang jiefang zhanzheng shiji tongyi zhanxian wenjian huibian* [A collection of Chinese Communist Party Central Committee documents on the united front during the liberation war period]. Beijing: Dang'an chubanshe, 1988.

Zhou Enlai tongyi zhanxian wenxuan [Selected works by Zhou Enlai on the united front]. Beijing: Renmin chubanshe, 1984.

Zhou Enlai xuanji [Selected works of Zhou Enlai]. Beijing: Renmin chubanshe, 1980–1984. 2 vols.

Zhou Erfu. *Songhuajiang shang de fengyun* [Storms across the Sungari River]. Hong Kong: Zhongguo chubanshe, 1947.

Zhou Fohai riji [The diary of Zhou Fohai]. Ed. Cai Dejin. Beijing: Zhongguo shehui kexue chubanshe, 1986. 2 vols.

Zhu De xuanji [Selected works of Zhu De]. Beijing: Renmin chubanshe, 1983.

Zuijin caijing gaige jiyao [A summary of the most recent financial and economic reforms]. Chongqing: Lianhe zhengxin suo yinshuachang, 1949.

IV. *BOOKS, PAMPHLETS, ARTICLES: ENGLISH (revised)*

Acheson, Dean. *Present at the Creation: My Years in the State Department.* New York: W. W. Norton, 1969.

Agrarian China: Selected Source Materials from Chinese Authors. London: George Allen and Unwin, 1939.

Alitto, Guy S. *The Last Confucian: Liang Shu-ming and the Chinese Dilemma of Modernity.* Berkeley: University of California Press, 1979.

Amerasia Papers: A Clue to the Catastrophe of China. Prepared by the Committee on the Judiciary, United States Senate. Washington, D. C.: Government Printing Office, 1970.

The American Assembly. *The United States and Japan.* Englewood Cliffs, N.J.: Prentice-Hall, 1966.

Arendt, Hannah. *On Revolution.* New York: Viking, 1965.

Armstrong, J. D. *Revolutionary Diplomacy: Chinese Foreign Policy and the United Front Doctrine.* Berkeley: University of California Press, 1977.

Averill, Stephen C. "More States of the Field, Part Two: The Communist-Led Revolutionary Movement," *Republican China,* vol. 18, no. 1 (November 1992), pp. 225–255.

———. "The New Life in Action: The Nationalist Government in South Jiangxi, 1934–37," *China Quarterly,* no. 88 (December 1981), pp. 594–628.

———. "Party, Society, and Local Elite in the Jiangxi Communist Movement," *Journal of Asian Studies,* vol. 46, no. 2 (May 1987), pp. 279–303.

Bachrack, Stanley D. *The Committee of One Million: "China Lobby" Politics, 1953–1971.* New York: Columbia University Press, 1976.

Bagby, Wesley M. *The Eagle-Dragon Alliance: America's Relations with China in World War II.* Newark, N. J.: Associated University Presses, 1992.

Band, Claire and William. *Two Years with the Chinese Communists.* New Haven: Yale University Press, 1948.

Barnett, A. Doak. *China on the Eve of Communist Takeover.* New York: Praeger, 1963.

———. *China's Far West: Four Decades of Change.* Boulder: Westview, 1993.

Barrett, David D. *Dixie Mission: The United States Army Observer Group in Yenan, 1944.* Berkeley: University of California, China Research Monograph, no. 6, 1970.

Beal, John Robinson. *Marshall in China.* New York: Doubleday, 1970.

Bedeski, Robert E. *State-Building in Modern China: The Kuomintang in the Prewar Period.* Berkeley: University of California, China Research Monograph, no. 18, 1981.

Belden, Jack. *China Shakes the World.* New York: Harper, 1949.

Beloff, Max. *Soviet Policy in the Far East, 1944–1951.* London: Oxford University Press, 1953.

Benton, Gregor. *China's Urban Revolutionaries: Explorations in the History of Chinese Trotskyism, 1921–1952.* Atlantic Highlands, N. J.: Humanities Press International, 1996.

———. *Mountain Fires: The Red Army's Three-Year War in South China, 1934–1938.* Berkeley: University of California Press, 1992.

Bergere, Marie-Claire. "Civil Society and Urban Change in Republican China," *China Quarterly,* no. 150 (June 1997), pp. 309–328.

———. *The Golden Age of the Chinese Bourgeoisie, 1911–1937.* Translated by Janet Lloyd. New York: Cambridge University Press, 1989.

Bernal, Martin. *Chinese Socialism to 1907.* Ithaca, N.Y.: Cornell University Press, 1976.

Bernhardt, Kathryn. *Rents, Taxes, and Peasant Resistance: The Lower Yangzi Region, 1840–1950.* Stanford: Stanford University Press, 1992.

Bernstein, Thomas Paul. "Leadership and Mobilization in the Collectivization of Agriculture in China and Russia: A Comparison." Ph.D. dissertation, Department of Political Science, Columbia University, New York, 1970.

Bertram, James M. *Crisis in China: The Story of the Sian Mutiny.* London: Macmillan, 1937.

——— . *Unconquered: Journal of a Year's Adventures among the Fighting Peasants of North China.* New York: John Day, 1939.

Bianco, Lucien. *Origins of the Chinese Revolution, 1915–1949.* Translated by Muriel Bell. Stanford: Stanford University Press, 1971.

——— . "Peasant Responses to CCP Mobilization Policies, 1937–1945," *New Perspectives on the Chinese Communist Revolution.* Ed. Tony Saich and Hans van de Ven, pp. 175–187. Armonk, N. Y.: M. E. Sharpe, 1998.

Bisson, T. A. *Yenan in June 1937: Talks with the Communist Leaders.* Berkeley: University of California, China Research Monograph, no. 11, 1973.

Bodde, Derk. *Peking Diary: 1948–1949, A Year of Revolution.* Greenwich, Conn.: Fawcett, 1967.

Bondurant, Joan V. *Conquest of Violence: The Gandhian Philosophy of Conflict.* Berkeley: University of California Press, 1965.

Boorman, Howard L., ed. *Biographical Dictionary of Republican China.* New York: Columbia University Press, 1967–1979. 5 vols.

Borg, Dorothy, and Waldo Heinrichs, eds. *Uncertain Years: Sino-American Relations, 1947–1950.* New York: Columbia University Press, 1980.

Borisov, Oleg, and B. T. Koloskov, eds. *Soviet Chinese Relations, 1945–1970.* Bloomington: Indiana University Press, 1975.

Boyle, John H. *China and Japan at War, 1937–1945: The Politics of Collaboration.* Stanford: Stanford University Press, 1972.

Brandt, Conrad. *Stalin's Failure in China, 1924–1927.* Cambridge: Harvard University Press, 1958.

Brandt, Conrad, Benjamin Schwartz, and John K. Fairbank. *A Documentary History of Chinese Communism.* Cambridge: Harvard University Press, 1952.

Braun, Otto. *A Comintern Agent in China, 1932–1939.* Translated by Jeanne Moore. Stanford: Stanford University Press, 1982.

Brugger, William. *Democracy and Organization in the Chinese Industrial Enterprise, 1948–1953.* Cambridge: Cambridge University Press, 1976.

Buck, David D. *Urban Change in China: Politics and Development in Tsinan, Shantung, 1890–1949.* Madison: University of Wisconsin Press, 1978.

Buck, John L. *Land Utilization in China.* Shanghai: Commercial Press, 1937.

Buhite, Russell D. *Patrick J. Hurley and American Relations in China.* Ithaca, N.Y.: Cornell University Press, 1973.

Bush, Richard Clarence. *The Politics of Cotton Textiles in Kuomintang China, 1927–1937.* New York: Garland, 1982.

Byron, John, and Robert Pack. *The Claws of the Dragon: Kang Sheng—The Evil Genius behind Mao.* New York: Simon and Schuster, 1992.

Carlson, Evans Fordyce. *The Chinese Army: Its Organization and Military Efficiency.* New York: Institute of Pacific Relations, 1940.

——— . *Twin Stars of China.* New York: Dodd, Mead, 1940.

Chan, F. Gilbert, ed. *China at the Crossroads: Nationalists and Communists, 1927–1949*. Boulder, Colo.: Westview, 1980.

Chang, Carsun. *The Third Force in China*. New York: Bookman, 1952.

Chang Chung-li. *The Chinese Gentry: Studies on Their Role in Nineteenth Century Chinese Society*. Seattle: University of Washington Press, 1955.

Chang, Gordon H. *Friends and Enemies: The United States, China, and the Soviet Union, 1948–1972*. Stanford: Stanford University Press, 1990.

Chang Kia-ngau. *The Inflationary Spiral: The Experience in China, 1939–1950*. Cambridge: Massachusetts Institute of Technology Press, 1958.

————. *Last Chance in Manchuria: The Diary of Chang Kia-ngau*. Edited by Donald G. Gillin and Ramon H. Myers. Translated by Dolores Zen. Stanford: Hoover Institution Press, 1989.

Chang, Maria Hsia. *The Chinese Blue Shirt Society: Fascism and Developmental Nationalism*. Berkeley: University of California, China Research Monograph, no. 30, 1985.

————. "Fascism and Modern China," *China Quarterly*, no. 79 (September 1979), pp. 553–567.

Chao Kuo-chun. *Agrarian Policy of the Chinese Communist Party, 1921–1959*. Bombay: Asia Publishing House, 1960.

Chassin, Lionel Max. *The Communist Conquest of China: A History of the Civil War, 1945–1949*. Translated by Timothy Osato and Louis Gelas. Cambridge: Harvard University Press, 1965.

Cheek, Timothy, and Tony Saich, eds. *New Perspectives on State Socialism in China*. Armonk, N. Y.: M. E. Sharpe, 1997.

Ch'en Han-seng. "Agrarian Reform in China," *Far Eastern Survey*, February 25, 1948, pp. 41–43.

Ch'en, Jerome. *The Highlanders of Central China: A History, 1895–1937*. Armonk, N. Y.: M. E. Sharpe, 1992.

————. *Mao and the Chinese Revolution*. London: Oxford University Press, 1965.

Ch'en Li-fu. *The Storm Clouds Clear over China: The Memoir of Ch'en Li-fu, 1900–1993*. Edited by Sidney H. Chang and Ramon H. Myers. Stanford: Hoover Institution Press, 1994.

Chen, Percy. *China Called Me: My Life Inside the Chinese Revolution*. Boston: Little, Brown, 1979.

Ch'en Po-ta [Boda]. *Critique of "China's Destiny."* Bombay: People's Publishing House, 1944.

————. *A Study of Land Rent in Pre-liberation China*. Peking: Foreign Languages Press, 1966.

Chen Yung-fa. *Making Revolution: The Communist Movement in Eastern and Central China, 1937–1945*. Berkeley: University of California Press, 1986.

Chern, Kenneth C. *Dilemma in China: America's Policy Debate, 1945*. Hamden, Conn.: Anchor, 1980.

Chesneaux, Jean. *The Chinese Labor Movement, 1919–1927*. Translated by H. M. Wright. Stanford: Stanford University Press, 1968.

————. *Peasant Revolts in China, 1840–1949*. Translated by C. A. Curwen. London: Thames and Hudson, 1973.

Chesneaux, Jean, Francoise Le Barbier, and Marie-Claire Bergere. *China from the 1911 Revolution to Liberation*. Translated by Paul Auster, Lydia Davis, and Anne Destenay. Hassocks, England: Harvester, 1977.

Ch'i Hsi-sheng. *Nationalist China at War: Military Defeats and Political Collapse, 1937–1945.* Ann Arbor: University of Michigan Press, 1982.

———. *Warlord Politics in China, 1916–1928.* Stanford: Stanford University Press, 1976.

Chi Wen-shun. "Liang Shu-ming and Chinese Communism," *China Quarterly*, no. 41 (January-March 1970), pp. 64–82.

Chiang Chung-cheng [Chiang Kai-shek]. *Soviet Russia in China: A Summing-Up at Seventy.* New York: Farrar, Straus and Cudahy, 1958. Rev. ed.

Chiang Kai-shek. *China's Destiny and Chinese Economic Theory,* with notes and commentary by Philip Jaffe. New York: Roy Publishers, 1947.

Chiang Monlin. *Tides from the West.* New Haven: Yale University Press, 1947.

Ch'ien Tuan-sheng. *The Government and Politics of China.* Cambridge: Harvard University Press, 1950.

The China Handbook, 1937–1945. Revised with 1946 supplement. Compiled by the Chinese Ministry of Information. New York: Macmillan, 1947.

The China White Paper (originally issued as *U.S. Relations with China with Special Reference to the Period, 1944–1949*). Stanford: Stanford University Press, 1967. 2 vols.

The Chinese Communist Movement: A Report of the U.S. War Department, July 1945. Stanford: Stanford University Press, 1968.

Chiu Hungdah and Leng Shao-chuan, eds. *China: Seventy Years after the 1911 Hsin-hai Revolution.* Charlottesville: University Press of Virginia, 1984.

Chiu, S. M., ed. *Chinese Communist Revolutionary Strategy, 1945–1949.* Princeton, N. J.: Center for International Studies, 1961.

Chou, Eric. *A Man Must Choose.* New York: Alfred A. Knopf, 1963.

Chou Li-po. *The Hurricane.* Peking: Foreign Languages Press, 1955.

Chou Shun-hsin. *The Chinese Inflation: 1937–1949.* New York: Columbia University Press, 1963.

Civil War in China. Vol. 2, 1945–1950. Special monograph, prepared at the field level; issued by Chief of Military History Office, Department of the Army, Republic of China.

Clubb, O. Edmund. *Communism in China: As Reported from Hankow in 1932.* New York: Columbia University Press, 1968.

———. *Twentieth Century China.* New York: Columbia University Press, 1964.

Coble, Parks M., Jr. *Facing Japan: Chinese Politics and Japanese Imperialism, 1931–1937.* Cambridge: Harvard University Press, 1991.

———. *The Shanghai Capitalists and the Nationalist Government, 1927–1937.* Cambridge: Harvard University Press, 1980.

Cochran, Sherman. *Big Business in China: Sino-Foreign Rivalry in the Cigarette Industry, 1890–1930.* Cambridge: Harvard University Press, 1980.

Cohen, Paul A. *Discovering History in China: American Historical Writing on the Recent Chinese Past.* New York: Columbia University Press, 1984.

Cohen, Warren I. *The Chinese Connection: Roger Greene, Thomas Lamont, George Sokolsky, and American-East Asian Relations.* New York: Columbia University Press, 1978.

———, ed. *New Frontiers in American-East Asian Relations: Essays Presented to Dorothy Borg.* New York: Columbia University Press, 1983.

Colling, John. *The Spirit of Yenan: A Wartime Chapter of Sino-American Friendship.* Hong Kong: API Press, 1991.

Compton, Boyd. *Mao's China: Party Reform Documents, 1942–1944*. Seattle: University of Washington Press, 1966.

Crook, Isabel and David. *Revolution in a Chinese Village: Ten Mile Inn*. London: Routledge and Kegal Paul, 1959.

Dai Qing. *Wang Shiwei and "Wild Lilies": Rectification and Purges in the Chinese Communist Party, 1942–1944*. Edited by David Apter and Timothy Cheek. Translated by Nancy Liu and Lawrence Sullivan. Armonk, N. Y.: M. E. Sharpe, 1994.

Dickson, Bruce J. "The Lessons of Defeat: The Reorganization of the Kuomintang on Taiwan, 1950–1952," *China Quarterly*, no. 133 (March 1993), pp. 56–84.

Dirlik, Arif. *Anarchism in the Chinese Revolution*. Berkeley: University of California Press, 1991.

———. *The Origins of Chinese Communism*. Oxford: Oxford University Press, 1989.

Dittmer, Lowell. *Sino-Soviet Normalization and Its International Implications, 1945–1990*. Seattle: University of Washington Press, 1992.

Donnithorne, Audrey. *China's Economic System*. London: George Allen and Unwin, 1967.

Dorris, Carl E. "Peasant Mobilization in North China and the Origins of Yenan Communism," *China Quarterly*, no. 68 (December 1976), pp. 697–719.

Dreyer, Edward. *China at War, 1901–1949*. London: Longmans, 1995.

Du Pengcheng. *Defend Yanan*. Translated by Sidney Shapiro. Beijing: Foreign Languages Press, 1983.

Duara, Prasenjit. *Culture, Power and the State: Rural North China, 1900–1942*. Stanford: Stanford University Press, 1988.

Dulles, Foster Rhea. *American Policy Toward Communist China, the Historical Record: 1949–1969*. New York: Thomas Y. Crowell, 1972.

Dupuy, Trevor Nevitt. *The Military History of the Chinese Civil War*. New York: Franklin Watts, 1969.

Eastman, Lloyd E. *The Abortive Revolution: China under Nationalist Rule, 1927–1937*. Cambridge: Harvard University Press, 1974.

———. "China's Democratic Parties and the Temptations of Political Power, 1946–1947," *Republican China*, vol. 17, no. 1 (November 1991), pp. 117–132.

———. "Fascism and Modern China: A Rejoinder," *China Quarterly*, no. 80 (December 1979), pp. 838–842.

———. "New Insights into the Nature of the Nationalist Regime," *Republican China*, vol. 9, no. 2 (February 1984), pp. 8–18.

———. "The Rise and Fall of the 'Blue Shirts'," *Republican China*, vol. 13, no. 1 (November, 1987), pp. 25–48.

———. *Seeds of Destruction: Nationalist China in War and Revolution, 1937–1949*. Stanford: Stanford University Press, 1983.

———. "Who Lost China? Chiang Kai-shek Testifies," *China Quarterly*, no. 88 (December 1981), pp. 658–668.

Eastman, Lloyd E., Jerome Ch'en, Suzanne Pepper, Lyman P. van Slyke. *The Nationalist Era in China, 1927–1949*. Cambridge: Cambridge University Press, 1991.

Eckstein, Harry. *Division and Cohesion in Democracy*. Princeton, N. J.: Princeton University Press, 1966.

Epstein, Israel. *Notes on Labor Problems in Nationalist China*. New York: Institute of Pacific Relations, 1949.

———. *The People's War*. London: Victor Gollancz, 1939.

———. *The Unfinished Revolution in China*. Boston: Little, Brown, 1947.

Esherick, Joseph W. "Deconstructing the Construction of the Party-State: Gulin County in the Shaan-Gan-Ning Border Region," *China Quarterly*, no. 140 (December 1994), pp. 1052–1079.

Esherick, Joseph, and Mary Rankin, eds. *Chinese Local Elites and Patterns of Dominance.* Berkeley: University of California Press, 1990.

Evans, Paul M. *John Fairbank and the American Understanding of Modern China.* New York: Basil Blackwell, 1988.

Fairbank, John K. *The United States and China.* Cambridge: Harvard University Press, 1979. 4th ed.

Fairbank, John K., and Albert Feuerwerker, eds. *The Cambridge History of China: Vol. 13, Republican China, 1912–1949.* Cambridge: Cambridge University Press, 1986.

Fang Fu-an. *Chinese Labour: An Economic and Statistical Survey of the Labour Conditions and Labour Movements in China.* Shanghai: Kelly and Walsh, 1931.

Fei Hsiao-t'ung. *China's Gentry: Essays on Rural-Urban Relations.* Chicago: University of Chicago Press, 1968.

———. *Peasant Life in China: A Field Study of Country Life in the Yangtze Valley.* London: Routledge and Kegan Paul, 1939.

Fei Hsiao-t'ung and Chang Chih-i. *Earthbound China: A Study of Rural Economy in Yunnan.* London: Routledge and Kegan Paul, 1948.

Feis, Herbert. *The China Tangle.* New York: Atheneum, 1965.

Feuerwerker, Albert. *The Chinese Economy 1912–1949.* Ann Arbor: University of Michigan, Michigan Papers in Chinese Studies, no. l, 1968.

Fewsmith, Joseph. *Party, State, and Local Elites in Republican China: Merchant Organizations and Politics in Shanghai, 1890–1930.* Honolulu: University of Hawaii Press, 1985.

Fishel, Wesley R. *The End of Extraterritoriality in China.* Berkeley: University of California Press, 1974.

Fitzgerald, John. *Awakening China: Politics, Culture, and Class in the Nationalist Revolution.* Stanford: Stanford University Press, 1996.

Forman, Harrison. *Blunder in Asia.* New York: Didier, 1950.

———. *Changing China.* New York: Crown, 1948.

———. *Report from Red China.* New York: Henry Holt, 1945.

Freyn, Hubert. *Prelude to War: The Chinese Student Rebellion of 1935–1936.* Shanghai: China Journal Publishing Company, 1939.

Fried, Morton H. *Fabric of Chinese Society: A Study of the Social Life of a Chinese County Seat.* New York: Octagon, 1974.

Friedman, Edward. *Backward Toward Revolution: The Chinese Revolutionary Party.* Berkeley: University of California Press, 1974.

Friedman, Edward and Mark Selden. *America's Asia: Dissenting Essays on Asian-American Relations.* New York: Vintage, 1971.

Furuya, Keiji. *Chiang Kai-shek: His Life and Times.* Translated by Chang Chun-ming. New York: St. John's University Press, 1981.

Galbiati, Fernando. *P'eng P'ai and the Hai-Lu-Feng Soviet.* Stanford: Stanford University Press, 1985.

Gallicchio, Marc S. *The Cold War Begins in Asia.* New York: Columbia University Press, 1988.

Gamble, Sidney D. *North China Villages: Social, Political, and Economic Activities Before 1933.* Berkeley: University of California Press, 1963.

————. *Ting Hsien: A North China Rural Community.* New York: Institute of Pacific Relations, 1954.

Garver, John W. *Chinese-Soviet Relations, 1937–1945: The Diplomacy of Chinese Nationalism.* New York: Oxford University Press, 1988.

Geisert, Bradley K. *Power and Society: The Kuomintang and Local Elites in Kiangsu Province, China, 1924–1937.* Ph.D. dissertation, University of Virginia, Charlottesville, 1979.

George, Alexander L. *The Chinese Communist Army in Action: The Korean War and Its Aftermath.* New York: Columbia University Press, 1967.

Gillin, Donald G. "Problems of Centralization in Republican China: The Case of Ch'en Ch'eng and the Kuomintang," *Journal of Asian Studies,* vol. 29, no. 4 (August 1970), pp. 835–850.

————. "Review Article: 'Peasant Nationalism' in the History of Chinese Communism," *Journal of Asian Studies,* vol. 23, no. 2 (February 1964), pp. 269–289.

————. *Warlord: Yen Hsi-shan in Shansi Province, 1911–1949.* Princeton, N.J.: Princeton University Press, 1967.

Gillin, Donald G., and Charles Etter. "Staying on: Japanese Soldiers and Civilians in China, 1945–1949," *Journal of Asian Studies,* vol. 42, no. 3 (May 1983), pp. 497–518.

Gittings, John. *The Role of the Chinese Army.* New York: Oxford University Press, 1967.

Goldman, Merle. *Literary Dissent in Communist China.* Cambridge: Harvard University Press, 1967.

Goldstein, Steven M. "The Chinese Revolution and the Colonial Areas: The View from Yenan, 1937–41," *China Quarterly,* no. 75 (September 1978), pp. 594–622.

Gray, Jack. *Rebellions and Revolutions: China from the 1800s to the 1980s.* Oxford: Oxford University Press, 1990.

————, ed. *Modern China's Search for a Political Form.* London: Oxford University Press, 1969.

Greene, Ruth Altman. *Hsiang-Ya Journal.* Hamden, Conn.: Anchor, 1977.

Grieder, Jerome B. *Hu Shih and the Chinese Renaissance: Liberalism in the Chinese Revolution, 1917–1939.* Cambridge: Harvard University Press, 1970.

Griffin, Patricia E. *The Chinese Communist Treatment of Counter-Revolutionaries, 1924–1949.* Princeton, N. J.: Princeton University Press, 1976.

Griffith, Samuel B., II. *The Chinese People's Liberation Army.* New York: McGraw-Hill, 1967.

Griggs, Thurston. *Americans in China: Some Chinese Views.* Washington, D.C.: Foundation for Foreign Affairs, 1948.

Griswold, A. Whitney. *The Far Eastern Policy of the United States.* New Haven: Yale University Press, 1962.

Guillermaz, Jacques. *The Chinese Communist Party in Power, 1949–1976.* Translated by Anne Destenay. Boulder, Colo.: Westview, 1972.

Han Suyin. *Birdless Summer.* New York: G. P. Putnam and Sons, 1968.

Harding, Harry, and Yuan Ming, eds. *Sino-American Relations, 1945–1955: A Joint Reassessment of a Critical Decade.* Wilmington, Del.: Scholarly Resources, 1989.

Harrison, James Pinckney. *The Long March to Power: A History of the Chinese Communist Party, 1921–1972.* New York: Praeger, 1972.

Hartford, Kathleen. "Step by Step: Reform, Resistance, and Revolution in the Chin-Ch'a-Chi Border Region, 1937–1945," Ph.D. dissertation, Stanford University, Stanford, California, 1980.

Hartford, Kathleen, and Steven M. Goldstein, eds. *Single Sparks: China's Rural Revolutions.* Armonk, N. Y.: M. E. Sharpe, 1989.

Head, William P. *America's China Sojourn: America's Foreign Policy and Its Effects on Sino-American Relations, 1942–1948.* Lanham, Md.: University Press of America, 1983.

Hershatter, Gail. *The Workers of Tianjin, 1900–1949.* Stanford: Stanford University Press, 1986.

Hinton, Harold. *China's Turbulent Quest: An Analysis of China's Foreign Relations Since 1945.* New York: Macmillan, 1970.

Hinton, William. *Fanshen: A Documentary of Revolution in a Chinese Village.* New York: Random House, 1968.

Ho Kan-chih. *A History of the Modern Chinese Reovlution.* Peking: Foreign Languages Press, 1960.

Ho Ping-ti and Tsou Tang, eds. *China in Crisis: China's Heritage and the Communist Political System.* Chicago: University of Chicago Press, 1968. 2 vols.

Hofheinz, Roy. *The Broken Wave: The Chinese Communist Peasant Movement, 1922–1928.* Cambridge: Harvard University Press, 1977.

Hooton, E. R. *The Greatest Tumult: The Chinese Civil War, 1936–1949.* London: Brassey's, 1991.

Howe, Christopher. *Wage Patterns and Wage Policy in Modern China, 1919–1972.* Cambridge: Cambridge University Press, 1973.

Hsiao Kung-chuan. *Rural China: Imperial Control in the Nineteenth Century.* Seattle: University of Washington Press, 1960.

Hsiao Tso-liang. *The Land Revolution in China, 1930–1934: A Study of Documents.* Seattle: University of Washington Press, 1969.

Hsiung, James C., and Steven I. Levine, eds. *China's Bitter Victory: The War with Japan, 1937–1945.* Armonk, N. Y.: M. E. Sharpe, 1992.

Hsu, Francis L. K. *Americans and Chinese: Passage to Differences.* Honolulu: University of Hawaii Press, 1981. 3rd ed.

Hsu Long-hsuen and Chang Ming-kai. *History of the Sino-Japanese War (1937–1945).* Translated by Wen Ha-hsiung. Taipei: Chung Wu Publishing, 1971.

Hsueh Chun-tu, ed. *Dimensions of Chinese Foreign Policy.* New York: Praeger, 1977.

———. *Revolutionary Leaders of Modern China.* New York: Oxford University Press, 1971.

Hu Kuo-tai. "The Struggle Between the Kuomintang and the Chinese Communist Party on Campus During the War of Resistance, 1937–1945," *China Quarterly,* no. 118 (June 1989), pp. 300–323.

Hu Sheng. *Imperialism and Chinese Politics.* Peking: Foreign Languages Press, 1955.

Huang, Philip C. C. *The Peasant Economy and Social Change in North China.* Stanford: Stanford University Press, 1985.

———. *The Peasant Family and Rural Development in the Yangzi Delta, 1350–1988.* Stanford: Stanford University Press, 1990.

Huebner, Jon W. "Chinese Anti-Americanism, 1946–1948," *Australian Journal of Chinese Affairs,* no. 17 (1987), pp. 115–126.

Hughes, T. J., and D. E. T. Luard. *The Economic Developent of Communist China, 1949–1960.* London: Oxford University Press, 1961.

Hunt, Michael H. *The Genesis of Chinese Communist Foreign Policy.* New York: Columbia University Press, 1996.

Hutchings, Graham. "A Province at War: Guangxi During the Sino-Japanese Conflict, 1937–45," *China Quarterly,* no. 108 (December 1986), pp. 652–679.

Ilchman, Warren F., and Norman Thomas Uphoff. *The Political Economy of Change.* Berkeley: University of California Press, 1969.

Iriye, Akira. *China and Japan in the Global Setting: Power, Culture, Economics.* Cambridge: Harvard University Press, 1993.

———, ed. *The Chinese and the Japanese: Essays in Political and Cultural Interactions.* Princeton, N. J.: Princeton University Press, 1980.

Isaacs, Harold Robert. *The Tragedy of the Chinese Revolution.* Stanford: Stanford University Press, 1962.

——— ed. *New Cycle in Asia: Selected Documents on Major International Developments in the Far East, 1943–1947.* New York: Macmillan, 1947.

Israel, John. *Lianda: A Chinese University in War and Revolution.* Stanford: Stanford University Press, 1998.

———. *Student Nationalism in China: 1927–1937.* Stanford: Stanford University Press, 1966.

Israel, John, and Donald W. Klein. *Rebels and Bureaucrats: China's December 9ers.* Berkeley: University of California Press, 1976.

Ito, Takeo. *Life Along the South Manchurian Railway: The Memoirs of Ito Takeo.* Translated by Joshua Fogel. Armonk, N. Y.: M. E. Sharpe, 1988.

The Japan-Manchoukuo Year Book, 1940. Tokyo: no pub., 1940.

Jeans, Roger B. *Democracy and Socialism in Republican China: The Politcs of Zhang Junmai (Carsun Chang), 1906–1941.* Lanham, Md.: Rowman and Littlefield, 1997.

———, ed. *Roads Not Taken: The Struggle of Opposition Parties in Twentieth-Century China.* Boulder, Colo.: Westview, 1992.

Jespersen, Christopher. *American Images of China, 1931–1949.* Stanford: Stanford University Press, 1996.

Johnson, Chalmers A. "An Intellectual Weed in the Socialist Garden: The Case of Ch'ien Tuan-sheng," *China Quarterly,* no. 6 (April–June 1961), pp. 29–52.

———. *Autopsy on People's War.* Berkeley: University of California Press, 1973.

———. *Peasant Nationalism and Communist Power: The Emergence of Revolutionary China, 1937–1945.* Stanford: Stanford University Press, 1962.

———. "Peasant Nationalism Revisited: The Biography of a Book," *China Quarterly,* no. 72 (December 1977), pp. 766–785.

Johnston Committee. "The Report Prepared by the Johnston Committee and Submitted to the U.S. Secretary of the Army Kenneth Royal, May 19, 1948—Text of the 'Summary of the Report,' " *Contemporary Japan: A Review of East Asiatic Affairs,* no. 17 (April–June, 1948), pp. 211–214.

Jones, F. C. *Manchuria since 1931.* London: Royal Institute of International Affairs, 1949.

Jordan, Donald A. *The Northern Expedition: China's National Revolution of 1926–1928.* Honolulu: University of Hawaii Press, 1976.

Kahn, E. J., Jr. *The China Hands: America's Foreign Service Officers and What Befell Them.* New York: Viking, 1975.

Kalyagin, Aleksandr Ya. *Along Alien Roads.* Translated by Steven I. Levine. New York: Occasional Papers of the East Asian Institute, Columbia University Press, 1983.

Kapp, Robert A. *Szechwan and the Chinese Republic: Provincial Militarism and Central Power, 1911–1938.* New Haven: Yale University Press, 1973.

Kataoka, Tetsuya. "Communist Power in a War of National Liberation: The Case of China," *World Politics,* April 1972, pp. 410–427.

————. *Resistance and Revolution in China: The Communists and the Second United Front.* Berkeley: University of California Press, 1974.

Kerr, George H. *Formosa Betrayed.* London: Eyre and Spottiswoode, 1966.

————. *Formosa: Licensed Revolution and the Home Rule Movement, 1895–1945.* Honolulu: University Press of Hawaii, 1974.

Kessler, Lawrence D. *The Jiangyin Mission Station: An American Missionary Community in China, 1895–1951.* Chapel Hill: University of North Carolina Press, 1996.

Kidd, David. *Peking Story: The Last Days of Old China.* New York: Griffin Paperback, 1988.

Kim, Ilpyong J. *The Politics of Chinese Communism: Kiangsi under the Soviets.* Berkeley: University of California Press, 1973.

King, Frank H. H. *A Concise Economic History of Modern China.* New York: Praeger, 1968.

Kirby, E. Stuart. *Russian Studies of China: Progress and Problems of Soviet Sinology.* London: Macmillan, 1975.

Kirby, William C. *Germany and Republican China.* Stanford: Stanford University Press, 1984.

————. "More States of the Field," *Republican China,* vol. 18, no. 1 (November 1992), pp. 206–224.

Klein, Donald W., and Anne B. Clark. *Biographic Dictionary of Chinese Communism, 1921–1965.* Cambridge: Harvard University Press, 1971.

Klein, Sidney. *The Pattern of Land Tenure Reform in East Asia after World War II.* New York: Bookman, 1958.

Koen, Ross Y. *The China Lobby in American Politics.* New York: Harper and Row, 1974.

Kuhn, Philip A. *Rebellion and Its Enemies in Late Imperial China: Militarization and the Social Structure, 1796–1864.* Cambridge: Harvard University Press, 1970.

Kuo, Warren. *Analytical History of the Chinese Communist Party.* Taipei: Institute of International Relations, 1968–1971. 4 vols.

Lai Tse-han, Ramon H. Myers, and Wei Wou. *A Tragic Beginning: The Taiwan Uprising of February 28, 1947.* Stanford: Stanford University Press, 1991.

Landman, Lynn and Amos. *Profile of Red China.* New York: Simon and Schuster, 1951.

Lang, Olga. *Pa Chin and His Writings.* Cambridge: Harvard University Press, 1967.

Lapwood, Ralph and Nancy. *Through the Chinese Revolution.* London: Spalding and Levy, 1954.

Lary, Diana. *Region and Nation: The Kwangsi Clique in Chinese Politics, 1925–1937.* London: Cambridge University Press, 1974.

————. *Warlord Soldiers: Chinese Common Soldiers, 1911–1937.* Cambridge: Cambridge University Press, 1985.

Lattimore, Eleanor H. *Labor Unions in the Far East.* New York: American Council, Institute of Pacific Relations, 1945.

Lattimore, Owen. *China Memoirs: Chiang Kai-shek and the War Against Japan.* Tokyo: University of Tokyo Press, 1991.

————. *Manchuria, Cradle of Conflict.* New York: Macmillan, 1932.

Ledovsky, Andrei. *The USSR, the USA, and the People's Revolution in China.* Moscow: Progress Publishers, 1982.

Lee Chong-sik. *Revolutionary Struggle in Manchuria: Chinese Communism and Soviet Interest, 1922–1945.* Berkeley: University of California Press, 1983.

Lee, Frank C. "Land Redistribution in Communist China," *Pacific Affairs,* no. 21 (March 1948), pp. 20–32.

Lee, Lai To. *Trade Unions in China, 1949 to the Present.* Singapore: Singapore University Press, 1986.

Levich, Eugene William. *The Kwangsi Way in Kuomintang China, 1931–1939.* Armonk, N. Y.: M. E. Sharpe, 1993.

Levine, Steven I. *Anvil of Victory: The Communist Revolution in Manchuria, 1945–1948.* New York: Columbia University Press, 1987.

Lewis, John Wilson, ed. *Peasant Rebellion and Communist Revolution in Asia.* Stanford: Stanford University Press, 1974.

Li, Lincoln. *The Japanese Army in North China, 1937–1941: Problems of Political and Economic Control.* London: Oxford University Press, 1975.

———. *Student Nationalism in China, 1924–1949.* Albany: State University of New York Press, 1994.

Li Tsung-jen, with Te-kong Tong. *The Memoirs of Li Tsung-jen.* Boulder, Colo.: Westview, 1979.

Liang Chin-tung. *General Stilwell in China, 1942–1944: The Full Story.* N.p.: St. John's University Press, 1972.

Liang Hsi-huey. *The Sino-German Connection: Alexander von Falkenhausen Between China and Germany, 1900–1941.* Amsterdam: Van Gorcum, 1978.

Liao Kai-lung [Gailong]. *From Yenan to Peking: The Chinese People's War of Liberation.* Peking: Foreign Languages Press, 1954.

Lieberthal, Kenneth. *Revolution and Tradition in Tientsin, 1949–1952.* Stanford: Stanford University Press, 1980.

Lieu, D. K. *China's Economic Stabilization and Reconstruction.* New Brunswick, N. J.: Rutgers University Press, 1948.

Lifton, Robert Jay. *Thought Reform and the Psychology of Totalism.* New York: W. W. Norton, 1963.

Lin Piao [Biao]. *Long Live the Victory of People's War!* Peking: Foreign Languages Press, 1965.

———. *Selected Works of Lin Piao.* Edited by China Problems Research Center. Hong Kong: Chih Luen Press, 1970.

Lindsay, Michael. *China and the Cold War.* Melbourne: Melbourne University Press, 1955.

———. *The Unknown War: North China, 1937–1945.* London: Bergstrom and Boyle, 1975.

Liu, F. F. *A Military History of Modern China, 1924–1949.* Princeton, N. J.: Princeton University Press, 1956.

Liu Shaoqi. *Collected Works of Liu Shao-ch'i.* Hong Kong: Union Research Institute, 1968–1969. 3 vols.

———. *Selected Works of Liu Shaoqi.* Beijing: Foreign Languages Press, 1984.

Loh, Pichon P. Y., ed. *The Kuomintang Debacle of 1949: Conquest or Collapse?* Boston: D. C. Heath, 1965.

Loh, Robert. *Businessmen in China.* Hong Kong: China Viewpoints, 1960.

Loh, Robert, as told to Humphrey Evans. *Escape from Red China.* New York: Coward-McCann, 1962.

Lowi, Theodore J. *The End of Liberalism: Ideology, Policy, and the Crisis of Public Authority.* New York: W. W. Norton, 1969.

Lutz, Jessie Gregory. *China and the Christian Colleges, 1850–1950.* Ithaca, N.Y.: Cornell University Press, 1971.

MacFarquhar, Roderick, Timothy Cheek, and Eugene Wu, eds. *The Secret Speeches of Chairman Mao.* Cambridge: Harvard University Press, 1989.

MacKinnon, Janice and Stephen. *Agnes Smedley: The Life and Times of an American Radical.* Berkeley: University of California Press, 1988.

MacKinnon, Stephen, and Oris Friesen. *China Reporting: An Oral History of American Journalism in the 1930s and 1940s.* Berkeley: University of California Press, 1987.

Madsen, Richard. *China and the American Dream: A Moral Inquiry.* Berkeley: University of California Press, 1995.

Mann, Susan. *Local Merchants and the Chinese Bureaucracy, 1750–1950.* Stanford: Stanford University Press, 1987.

Mao Tse-tung [Zedong]. *Selected Works.* Peking: Foreign Languages Press, 1961–1965. 4 vols.

Mao Zedong. *Report from Xunwu.* Translated by Roger R. Thompson. Stanford: Stanford University Press, 1990.

Mao's Road to Power: Revolutionary Writings, 1912–1949. Vol. 4, The Rise and Fall of the Chinese Soviet Republic, 1931–1934. Edited by Stuart Schram, Nancy Hodes, and Stephen Averill. Armonk, N. Y.: M. E. Sharpe, 1997.

Marks, Robert B. *Rural Revolution in South China: Peasants and the Making of History in Haifeng County, 1570–1930.* Madison: University of Wisconsin Press, 1984.

Marshall, George C. *Marshall's Mission to China, December 1945–January 1947: The Report and Appended Documents.* Introduction by Lyman P. van Slyke. Arlington, Va.: University Publications of America, 1976.

Martin, Brian G. *The Shanghai Green Gang: Politics and Organized Crime, 1919–1937.* Berkeley: University of California Press, 1996.

Martin, Edwin W. "The Chou Demarche," *Foreign Service Journal,* November 1981, pp. 13–16.

———. *Divided Counsel: The Anglo-American Response to Communist Victory in China.* Lexington: University Press of Kentucky, 1986.

May, Gary. *China Scapegoat: The Diplomatic Ordeal of John Carter Vincent.* Washington, D.C.: New Republic Books, 1979.

Mazur, Mary G. "Intellectual Activism in China During the 1940s: Wu Han in the United Front and the Democratic League," *China Quarterly,* no. 133 (March 1993), pp. 27–55.

McCormack, Gavan. *Chang Tso-lin in Northeast China, 1911–1928: China, Japan, and the Manchurian Idea.* Stanford: Stanford University Press, 1977.

McDonald, Angus W., Jr. *The Urban Origins of Rural Revolution: Elites and the Masses in Hunan Province, China, 1911–1927.* Berkeley: University of California Press, 1978.

McLane, Charles B. *Soviet Policy and the Chinese Communists, 1931–1946.* New York: Columbia University Press, 1958.

Meisner, Maurice. *Li Ta-chao and the Origins of Chinese Marxism.* Cambridge: Harvard University Press, 1967.

———. *Marxism, Maoism and Utopianism: Eight Essays.* Madison: University of Wisconsin Press, 1982.

Melby, John F. *The Mandate of Heaven.* Toronto: University of Toronto Press, 1968.

Mendel, Douglas. *The Politics of Formosan Nationalism.* Berkeley: University of California Press, 1970.

Mi Zanchen. *The Life of General Yang Hucheng.* Translated by Wang Zhao. Hong Kong: Joint Publishing, 1981.

Miles, Milton E. *A Different Kind of War.* Garden City, N. Y.: Doubleday, 1967.

Millis, Walter, ed. *The Forrestal Diaries.* New York: Viking, 1951.

Moorad, George. *Lost Peace in China.* New York: E. P. Dutton, 1949.

Moore, Barrington, Jr. *Social Origins of Dictatorship and Democracy: Lord and Peasant in the Making of the Modern World.* London: Allen Lane, 1967.

Myers, Ramon H. *The Chinese Peasant Economy: Agricultural Development in Hopei and Shantung, 1890–1949.* Cambridge: Harvard University Press, 1970.

Nagai, Yonosuke, and Iriye Akira, eds. *The Origins of the Cold War in Asia.* New York: Columbia University Press, 1977.

Nathan, Andrew J. "Some Trends in the Historiography of Republican China," *Republican China,* vol. 17, no. 1 (November 1991), pp. 117–131.

Neils, Patricia, ed. *United States Attitudes and Policies Toward China: The Impact of American Missionaries.* Armonk, N. Y.: M. E. Sharpe, 1990.

Newman, Robert P. *Owen Lattimore and the Loss of China.* Berkeley: University of California Press, 1992.

Nie Rongzhen. *Inside the Red Star: The Memoirs of Marshal Nie Rongzhen.* Translated by Zhong Renyi. Beijing: New World Press, 1988.

North, Robert C. *Kuomintang and Chinese Communist Elites.* Stanford: Stanford University Press, 1952.

———. *Moscow and the Chinese Communists.* Stanford: Stanford University Press, 1963.

Ojha, Ellen F. "Fluctuations in Chinese Communist Agrarian Policy, 1946–1950," Harvard Papers on China, December 1969, pp. 20–48.

The Orient Year Book, 1942. Tokyo: The Asia Statistics Company, 1942.

Parsons, James Bunyan. *The Peasant Rebellions of the Late Ming Dynasty.* Tuscon: University of Arizona Press, 1970.

Paulson, David Mark. "War and Revolution in North China: The Shandong Base Area, 1937–1945." Ph.D. dissertation, Stanford University, Stanford, California, 1982.

Payne, Robert. *China Awake.* New York: Dodd, Mead, 1947.

———. *Chungking Diary.* London: William Heinemann, 1945.

Peck, Graham. *Two Kinds of Time.* Boston: Houghton Mifflin, 1950.

Peng Dehuai. *Memoirs of a Chinese Marshal—The Autobiographical Notes of Peng Dehuai, 1898–1974.* Translated by Zheng Longpu. Beijing: Foreign Languages Press, 1984.

Peng Ming-min. *A Taste of Freedom: Memoirs of a Formosan Independence Leader.* New York: Holt, Rinehart and Winston, 1972.

Pepper, Suzanne. "Hong Kong Joins the National People's Congress: A First Test for One Country with Two Political Systems," *Journal of Contemporary China,* March 1999.

———. "The KMT-CCP Conflict, 1945–1949." In *The Cambridge History of China,* edited by John K. Fairbank and Albert Feuerwerker, vol. 13, pp. 723–788. Cambridge: Cambridge University Press, 1986.

Perkins, Dwight H. *Agricultural Development in China, 1368–1968.* Cambridge: Harvard University Press, 1970.

———. *Market Control and Planning in Communist China.* Cambridge: Harvard University Press, 1966.

Perry, Elizabeth J. *Rebels and Revolutionaries in North China, 1845–1945.* Stanford: Stanford University Press, 1980.

———. *Shanghai on Strike: The Politics of Chinese Labor.* Stanford: Stanford University Press, 1993.

Popkin, Samuel L. *The Rational Peasant: The Political Economy of Rural Society in Vietnam.* Berkeley: University of California Press, 1979.

Powell, John B. *My Twenty-five Years in China.* New York: Macmillan, 1945.

Price, Jane L. *Cadres, Commanders, and Commissars: The Training of the Chinese Communist Leadership, 1920–1945.* Boulder, Colo.: Westview, 1976.

———. "Chinese Communist Land Reform and Peasant Mobilization, 1947–1948." Master's essay. Columbia University, New York, 1970.

Pulleyblank, Edwin G. *The Background of the Rebellion of An Lu-shan.* New York: Oxford University Press, 1955.

"Reappraising Republican China," special issue, *China Quarterly,* no. 150 (June 1997), *passim.*

Reardon-Anderson, James. *Yenan and the Great Powers: The Origins of Chinese Communist Foreign Policy, 1944–1946.* New York: Columbia University Press, 1980.

Rickett, Allyn and Adele. *Prisoners of Liberation.* New York: Anchor, 1973.

Ronning, Chester. *A Memoir of China in Revolution.* New York: Pantheon, 1974.

Rosinger, Lawrence K. *China's Wartime Politics, 1937–1944.* Princeton, N. J.: Princeton University Press, 1944.

Saich, Tony, with Benjamin Yang. *The Rise to Power of the Chinese Communist Party: Documents and Analysis.* Armonk, N. Y.: M. E. Sharpe, 1996.

Saich, Tony, and Hans van de Ven, eds. *New Perspectives on the Chinese Communist Revolution.* Armonk, N. Y.: M. E. Sharpe, 1995.

Salisbury, Harrison. *The Long March: The Untold Story.* New York: Harper and Row, 1985.

Scalapino, Robert A., ed. *The Communist Revolution in Asia: Tactics, Goals, and Achievements.* Englewood Cliffs, N. J.: Prentice-Hall, 1965.

———. *Elites in the People's Republic of China.* Seattle: University of Washington Press, 1972.

Schaller, Michael. *The U.S. Crusade in China, 1938–1945.* New York: Columbia University Press, 1979.

Schiffrin, Harold Z. *Sun Yat-sen and the Origins of the Chinese Revolution.* Berkeley: University of California Press, 1968.

Schram, Stuart. *Mao Tse-tung.* Harmondsworth, England: Penguin, 1966.

———. *The Thought of Mao Tse-tung.* Cambridge: Cambridge University Press, 1989.

Schran, Peter. *Guerrilla Economy: The Development of the Shensi-Kansu-Ninghsia Border Region, 1937–1945.* Albany: State University of New York Press, 1976.

Schrecker, John E. *Imperialism and Chinese Nationalism: Germany in Shantung.* Cambridge: Harvard University Press, 1971.

Schuman, Julian. *Assignment China.* New York: Whittier Books, 1956.

Schurmann, Franz. *Ideology and Organization in Communist China.* Berkeley: University of California Press, 1968.

Schwartz, Benjamin I. *Chinese Communism and the Rise of Mao.* Cambridge: Harvard University Press, 1958.

Scott, James C. *The Moral Economy of the Peasant: Rebellion and Subsistence in Southeast Asia.* New Haven: Yale University Press, 1976.

———. *Weapons of the Weak: Everyday Forms of Peasant Resistance.* New Haven: Yale University Press, 1985.

Selden, Mark. *China in Revolution: The Yenan Way Revisited.* Armonk, N. Y.: M. E. Sharpe, 1995.

———. *The Yenan Way in Revolutionary China.* Cambridge: Harvard University Press, 1971.

Selznick, Philip. *The Organizational Weapon: A Study of Bolshevik Strategy and Tactics.* Glencoe, Ill.: The Free Press, 1960.

Service, John S. *The Amerasia Papers: Some Problems in the History of U.S.-China Relations.* Berkeley: University of California, China Research Monograph, no. 7, 1971.

―――. *Lost Chance in China: The World War II Despatches of John S. Service.* Edited by Joseph Esherick. New York: Vintage, 1975.

Seybolt, Peter J. "Terror and Conformity, Counter-Espionage Compaigns, Rectification, and Mass Movements, 1942–1943," *Modern China,* vol. 12, no. 1 (1986), pp. 39–73.

Seymour, James D. *China's Satellite Parties.* Armonk, N. Y.: M. E. Sharpe, 1987.

Shanghai Evening Post and Mercury Correspondents. *Through Four Provinces.* Shanghai, 1937.

Shapiro, Sidney. *An American in China: Thirty Years in the People's Republic.* Peking: New World Press, 1979.

Shaw Yu-ming. *An American Missionary in China: John Leighton Stuart and Chinese-American Relations.* Cambridge: Harvard University Press, 1992.

Shen, T. H. *Agricultural Resources of China.* Ithaca, N. Y.: Cornell University Press, 1951.

―――. *The Sino-American Joint Commission on Rural Reconstruction: Twenty Years of Cooperation for Agricultural Development.* Ithaca, N. Y.: Cornell University Press, 1970.

Shen Zui. *A KMT War Criminal in New China.* Translated by Liang Xintu and Sun Binghe. Peking: Foreign Languages Press, 1986.

Sheridan, James E. *China in Disintegration: The Republican Era in Chinese History, 1912–1949.* New York: The Free Press, 1975.

―――. *Chinese Warlord: The Career of Feng Yu-hsiang.* Stanford: Stanford University Press, 1966.

Shewmaker, Kenneth E. *Americans and Chinese Communists, 1927–1945: A Persuading Encounter.* Ithaca, N. Y.: Cornell University Press, 1971.

Shieh, Milton J. T., ed. *The Kuomintang: Selected Historical Documents, 1894–1969.* New York: St. John's University Press, 1970.

Shum Kui-kwong. *The Chinese Communists' Road to Power: The Anti-Japanese United Front (1935–1945).* Hong Kong: Oxford University Press, 1988.

Sih, Paul K. T., ed. *Nationalist China During the Sino-Japanese War, 1937–1945.* Hicksville, N. Y.: Exposition Press, 1977.

―――. *The Sino-Soviet Treaty of Friendship and Alliance of 1945: The Inside Story.* Hicksville, N. Y.: Exposition Press, 1977.

―――. *The Strenuous Decade: China's Nation-Building Efforts, 1927–1937.* New York: St. John's University Press, 1970.

Skocpol, Theda. *States and Social Relations: A Comparative Analysis of France, Russia and China.* Cambridge: Cambridge University Press, 1979.

Smedley, Agnes. *Battle Hymn of China.* New York: Alfred A. Knopf, 1943.

―――. *China Fights Back.* New York: Vanguard, 1938.

―――. *The Great Road: The Life and Times of Chu Teh.* London: John Calder, 1958.

Snow, Edgar. "A Conversation with Mao Tse-tung," *Life Magazine,* April 30, 1971.

―――. *The Long Revolution.* New York: Vintage, 1973.

―――. *The Other Side of the River: Red China Today.* New York: Random House, 1962.

―――. *Red Star over China.* New York: Modern Library, 1938.

So Wai-chor. *The Kuomintang Left in the National Revolution, 1924–1931: The Leftist Alternative in Republican China.* Hong Kong: Oxford University Press, 1991.

Spence, Jonathan. *The China Helpers: Western Advisers in China, 1620–1960.* London: Bodley Head, 1969.

Stein, Gunther. *The Challenge of Red China.* London: Pilot Press, 1945.

Stilwell, Joseph W. *The Stilwell Papers.* Edited by Theodore White. New York: Sloane, 1948.

Stranahan, Patricia. *Molding the Medium: The Chinese Communist Party and the* Liberation Daily. Armonk, N. Y.: M. E. Sharpe, 1990.

———. *Underground: The Shanghai Communist Party and the Politics of Survival, 1927–1937.* Lanham: Rowman and Littlefield, 1998.

Strauss, Julia C. "The Evolution of Republican Government," *China Quarterly,* no. 150 (June 1997), pp. 329–351.

Strong, Anna Louise. *The Chinese Conquer China.* New York: Doubleday, 1949.

———. *Tomorrow's China.* New York: Committee for a Democratic Far Eastern Policy, 1948.

Stuart, John Leighton. *50 Years in China: The Memoirs of John Leighton Stuart.* New York: Random House, 1954.

Stueck, William. *The Wedemeyer Mission.* Athens, Ga.: University of Georgia Press, 1984.

Sun, Kungtu C. *The Economic Development of Manchuria in the First Half of the Twentieth Century.* Cambridge: Harvard University, East Asian Monographs, 1969.

Swarup, Shanti. *A Study of the Chinese Communist Movement, 1927–1934.* Oxford: Clarendon, 1966.

Tai Hsuan-chih. *The Red Spears, 1916–1949.* Translated by Ronald Suleski. Ann Arbor: University of Michigan, Monographs in Chinese Studies, no. 54, 1985.

Tanaka, Kyoko. "Mao and Liu in the 1947 Land Reform: Allies or Disputants?" *China Quarterly,* no. 75 (September 1978), pp. 566–593.

Tawney, R. H. *Land and Labour in China.* Boston: Beacon, 1966.

Taylor, George E. *The Struggle for North China.* New York: Institute of Pacific Relations, 1940.

Teiwes, Frederick C. *Politics and Purges in China.* Armonk, N. Y.: M. E. Sharpe, 1993, 2nd ed.

——— , with Warren Sun. *The Formation of the Maoist Leadership, from the Return of Wang Ming to the Seventh Party Congress.* London: Contemporary China Institute, School of Oriental and African Studies, Research Notes and Studies, no. 10, 1994.

Thaxton, Ralph A., Jr. *Salt of the Earth: The Political Origins of Peasant Protest and Communist Revolution in China.* Berkeley: Univeristy of California Press, 1997.

Thomas, S. Bernard. *Labor and the Chinese Revolution: Class Strategies and Contradictions of Chinese Communism, 1928–1948.* Ann Arbor: University of Michigan, Monographs in Chinese Studies, no. 49, 1983.

Thomson, James C., Jr. *While China Faced West: American Reformers in Nationalist China, 1928–1937.* Cambridge: Harvard University Press, 1969.

Tien Hung-mao. *Government and Politics in Kuomintang China, 1927–1937.* Stanford: Stanford University Press, 1972.

Ting, Lee-hsia Hsu. *Government Control of the Press in Modern China, 1900–1949.* Cambridge: Harvard University, East Asia Research Center, 1974.

Ting Ling. *The Sun Shines over the Sangkan River.* Peking: Foreign Languages Press, 1954.

The Tokyo War Crimes Trial: The Complete Transcripts of the Proceedings of the International Military Tribunal for the Far East. 20 vols. New York: Garland, 1981.

Tong, Hollington K., ed. *China after Seven Years of War.* New York: Macmillan, 1945.

Topping, Seymour. *Journey between Two Chinas.* New York: Harper and Row, 1972.

Townsend, James R. *Political Participation in Communist China.* Berkeley: University of California Press, 1967.

Trotsky, Leon. *Problems of the Chinese Revolution.* New York· Paragon, 1966.

Tsou Tang. *America's Failure in China, 1941–1950.* Chicago: University of Chicago Press, 1963.

Tuchman, Barbara. *Stilwell and the American Experience in China, 1911–1945.* New York: Macmillan, 1970.

Tucker, Nancy Bernkopf. *Patterns in the Dust: Chinese-American Relations and the Recognition Controversy, 1949–1950.* New York: Columbia University Press, 1983.

United States Department of State. *Foreign Relations of the United States, the Far East, China, 1945–1949.* Washington, D.C.: U.S. Government Printing Office, 1969–1978. 9 vols.

van Aduard, E. J. Lewe. *Japan: from Surrender to Peace.* The Hague: Martinus Nijholt, 1953.

van de Ven, Hans J. *From Friend to Comrade: The Founding of the Chinese Communist Party, 1920–1927.* Berkeley: University of California Press, 1992.

———. "The Military in the Republic," *China Quarterly,* no. 150 (June 1997), pp. 352–374.

van Slyke, Lyman P. *Enemies and Friends: The United Front in Chinese Communist History.* Stanford: Stanford University Press, 1967.

Vincent, John Carter. *The Extraterritorial System in China: Final Phase.* Cambridge: Harvard University Press, 1970.

Vladimirov, P. *The Vladimirov Diaries: Yenan, China, 1942–1945.* New York: Doubleday, 1975.

Wakeman, Frederic, Jr. *Policing Shanghai, 1927–1937.* Berkeley: University of California Press, 1995.

———. "A Revisionist View of the Nanjing Decade: Confucian Fascism," *China Quarterly,* no. 150 (June 1997), pp. 395–432.

Wales, Nym [Helen Foster Snow]. *The Chinese Labor Movement.* Freeport, N. Y.: Books for Libraries Press, 1970.

———. *Notes on the Chinese Student Movement, 1935–1936.* Stanford: Hoover Institution Press, 1959.

———. *Red Dust, Autobiographies of Chinese Communists.* Stanford: Stanford University Press, 1952.

Wang Ching-wei. *China's Problems and Their Solution.* Shanghai: China United Press, 1934.

Wang Ming. *Mao's Betrayal.* Moscow: Progress Publishers, 1979.

Wang, Y. C. *Chinese Intellectuals and the West, 1872–1949.* Chapel Hill: University of North Carolina Press, 1966.

———. "Tu Yueh-sheng; A Tentative Political Biography," *Journal of Asian Studies,* vol. 26, no. 3 (May 1967), pp. 433–455.

Wasserstrom, Jeffrey N. *Student Protests in Twentieth-Century China: The View from Shanghai.* Stanford: Stanford University Press, 1991.

Wasserstrom, Jeffrey N., and Elizabeth J. Perry, eds. *Popular Protest and Political Culture in Modern China.* Boulder, Colo.: Westview, 1994, 2nd ed.

Watson, Andrew, ed. *Mao Zedong and the Political Economy of the Border Region: A*

Translation of Mao's Economic and Financial Problems. Cambridge: Cambridge University Press, 1980.

Wedemeyer, Albert C. *Wedemeyer Reports!* New York: Holt, 1958.

Wei, William. *Counter-Revolution in China: The Nationalists in Jiangxi during the Soviet Period.* Ann Arbor: University of Michigan Press, 1985.

West, Philip. *Yenching University and Sino-Western Relations, 1916–1952.* Cambridge: Harvard University Press, 1976.

Westad, Odd Arne. *Cold War and Revolution: Soviet-American Rivalry and the Origins of the Chinese Civil War, 1944–1946.* New York: Columbia University Press, 1993.

White, Theodore H., and Annalee Jacoby. *Thunder Out of China.* New York: William Sloane, 1961.

Whiting, Allen S. *Soviet Policies in China, 1917–1924.* Stanford: Stanford University Press, 1953.

Whitson, William, with Huang Chen-hsia. *The Chinese High Command: A History of Communist Military Politics, 1927–1971.* New York: Praeger, 1973.

Witke, Roxane. *Comrade Chiang Ch'ing.* Boston: Little, Brown, 1977.

Wong, John. *Land Reform in the People's Republic of China: Institutional Transformation in Agriculture.* New York: Praeger, 1973.

Wong Young-tsu. "The Fate of Liberalism in Revolutionary China: Chu Anping and His Circle, 1946–1950," *Modern China*, vol. 19, no. 4 (1993), pp. 457–490.

Wou, Odoric Y. K. *Militarism in Modern China: The Career of Wu P'ei-fu, 1916–1939.* Canberra: Australian National University Press, 1978.

―――. *Mobilizing the Masses: Building Revolution in Henan.* Stanford: Stanford University Press, 1994.

Wu Tien-wei. *The Sian Incident: A Pivotal Point in Modern Chinese History.* Ann Arbor: University of Michigan, Michigan Papers in Chinese Studies, no. 26, 1976.

Wylie, Raymond F. *The Emergence of Maoism: Mao Tse-tung, Ch'en Po-ta, and the Search for Chinese Theory, 1935–1945.* Stanford: Stanford University Press, 1980.

Yang, Benjamin. *From Revolution to Politics: Chinese Communists on the Long March.* Boulder, Colo.: Westview, 1990.

Yang, C. K. *A Chinese Village under Early Communist Transition.* Cambridge: Massachusetts Institute of Technology Press, 1959.

Yang, Martin C. *A Chinese Village: Taitou, Shantung Province.* New York: Columbia University Press, 1945.

Yang Shang-kuei. *The Red Kiangsi-Kwangtung Border Region.* Peking: Foreign Languages Press, 1961.

Yeh Wen-hsin. *The Alienated Academy: Culture and Politics in Republican China, 1919–1937.* Cambridge: Harvard University Press, 1990.

Yick, Joseph K. S. *Making Urban Revolution in China: The CCP-GMD Struggle for Beiping-Tianjin, 1945–1949.* Armonk, N. Y.: M. E. Sharpe, 1995.

Young, Arthur N. *China and the Helping Hand, 1937–1945.* Cambridge: Harvard University Press, 1963.

―――. *China's Wartime Finance and Inflation: 1937–1945.* Cambridge: Harvard University Press, 1965.

Yu, George T. *Party Politics in Republican China: The Kuomintang, 1912–1924.* Berkeley: University of California Press, 1966.

Zheng Chaolin. *An Oppositionist for Life: Memoirs of the Chinese Revolutionary Zheng Chaolin.* Translated by Gregor Benton. Atlantic Highlands, N. J.: Humanities Press, 1997.

Zhou Enlai. *Selected Works of Zhou Enlai.* Beijing: Foreign Languages Press, 1981.

Index

Acheson, Dean, 72
Agrarian problem, 229-232 *passim*
Agrarian revolution, 7, 233, 274-277 *passim*, 289, 311, 378, 432-434
Agriculture. *See* Production and production plans (CCP)
Agriculture, Ministry of, 19
Ai Szu-ch'i, 418
All-China General Labor Union, 361
All-China Students Association, 58, 66-67, 70n, 81
An-fu Clique, 436, 437
Anhwei, 11, 150, 166, 167, 406
Anshan, 25; CCP take-over of, 386, 390-391
Anti-American protests, 52-58, 72-78, 115-116
Anti-Civil War Association, 45
Anti-Hunger Anti-Civil War Movement, 58-70, 111, 129
Anti-Japanese University, 414
Anti-Japanese War (1937-1945): KMT during, 7-9, 95, 130, 260, 433-434; CCP growth during, 7, 202, 259, 434; military hostilities during, 7, 249, 250, 255, 260-261, 262, 299; intellectuals during, 36-38 *passim*, 45, 59, 87; inflation during, 95, 130, 253; CCP land policies during, 231, 241n, 245, 248-277, 278, 280, 281, 283, 296, 298, 307, 309; lessons of for CCP, 253, 274-277, 309, 327-329, 430-434. *See also* Japan; United front
Anti-leftist campaigns (CCP), 376-378; intellectuals, 222-224, 412; land reform,

316-327; labor, 351-366, 402-405; commerce and industry, 368-373, 402-405
Anti-Oppression Anti-Hunger Movement, 71-72
Anti-war movement, Chapter 3 *passim*; intelligentsia's support for, 158-160, 188-189
Antung city, 223, 332, 357, 370, 382
Antung province, 180n
Anyang *hsien*, Honan, 302-303, 308
Armies. *See* Military forces (CCP); Military forces (KMT)
Aurora University, Shanghai, 214

Barnett, Doak, 89n, 75n, 127n
Beggars, 209, 333, 407
Belden, Jack, 227, 302-303, 308
Black land, 231, 255-258 *passim*, 270, 277
Black market, 34, 110, 120, 124, 125, 207, 397, 409
Blockades, 117n, 345, 401, 402, 405
Bodde, Derk, 174, 398n, 415n
Border Regions. *See* Individual regions by name
Brazil, 32
Broken shoes, 263, 267, 270
Buck, John Lossing, 234
Bullitt, William, 172
Bureau of Investigation and Statistics, 47n, 63n
Bureaucracy and bureaucrats: work style of, 28, 206; salaries of, 128, 155-157, 312; bureaucratization, 157-158, 206; CCP